CCIE Professional Development
Large-Scale IP Network Solutions

Khalid Raza, CCIE
Mark Turner

Cisco Press
201 West 103rd Street
Indianapolis, IN 46290 USA

Large-Scale IP Network Solutions

Khalid Raza, CCIE
Mark Turner

Copyright © 2000 Cisco Press

Cisco Press logo is a trademark of Cisco Systems, Inc.

Published by:
Cisco Press
201 West 103rd Street
Indianapolis, IN 46290 USA

Printed in the United States of America 1 2 3 4 5 6 7 8 9 0

Library of Congress Cataloging-in-Publication Number: 98-86516

ISBN: 1-57870-084-1

Warning and Disclaimer

This book is designed to provide information about IP networks. Every effort has been made to make this book as complete and as accurate as possible, but no warranty or fitness is implied.

The information is provided on an "as is" basis. The authors, Cisco Press, and Cisco Systems, Inc. shall have neither liability nor responsibility to any person or entity with respect to any loss or damages arising from the information contained in this book or from the use of the discs or programs that may accompany it.

The opinions expressed in this book belong to the authors and are not necessarily those of Cisco Systems, Inc.

Trademark Acknowledgments

All terms mentioned in this book that are known to be trademarks or service marks have been appropriately capitalized. Cisco Press or Cisco Systems, Inc. cannot attest to the accuracy of this information. Use of a term in this book should not be regarded as affecting the validity of any trademark or service mark.

Feedback Information

At Cisco Press, our goal is to create in-depth technical books of the highest quality and value. Each book is crafted with care and precision, undergoing rigorous development that involves the unique expertise of members from the professional technical community.

Readers' feedback is a natural continuation of this process. If you have any comments regarding how we could improve the quality of this book, or otherwise alter it to better suit your needs, you can contact us through e-mail at ciscopress@mcp.com. Please make sure to include the book title and ISBN in your message.

We greatly appreciate your assistance.

Publisher	John Wait
Executive Editor	John Kane
Cisco Systems Program Manager	Jim LeValley
Managing Editor	Patrick Kanouse
Senior Acquisitions Editor	Brett Bartow
Development Editors	Kezia Endsley
	Kimberly Wright
Project Editor	Theresa Wehrle
Technical Reviewers	Johnson Liu
	Thomas Kramer
Reviewers	Alexander Marhold
	Mark J. Newcomb
Team Coordinator	Amy Lewis
Book Designer	Regina Rexrode
Cover Designer	Karen Ruggles
Production	Argosy
Indexer	Kevin Fulcher
Proofreaders	Debra Neel
	Debbie Williams

CISCO SYSTEMS

Corporate Headquarters
Cisco Systems, Inc.
170 West Tasman Drive
San Jose, CA 95134-1706
USA
http://www.cisco.com
Tel: 408 526-4000
       800 553-NETS (6387)
Fax: 408 526-4100

European Headquarters
Cisco Systems Europe s.a.r.l.
Parc Evolic, Batiment L1/L2
16 Avenue du Quebec
Villebon, BP 706
91961 Courtaboeuf Cedex
France
http://www-europe.cisco.com
Tel: 33 1 69 18 61 00
Fax: 33 1 69 28 83 26

Americas Headquarters
Cisco Systems, Inc.
170 West Tasman Drive
San Jose, CA 95134-1706
USA
http://www.cisco.com
Tel: 408 526-7660
Fax: 408 527-0883

Asia Headquarters
Nihon Cisco Systems K.K.
Fuji Building, 9th Floor
3-2-3 Marunouchi
Chiyoda-ku, Tokyo 100
Japan
http://www.cisco.com
Tel: 81 3 5219 6250
Fax: 81 3 5219 6001

Cisco Systems has more than 200 offices in the following countries. Addresses, phone numbers, and fax numbers are listed on the Cisco Connection Online Web site at http://www.cisco.com/offices.

Argentina • Australia • Austria • Belgium • Brazil • Canada • Chile • China • Colombia • Costa Rica • Croatia • Czech Republic • Denmark • Dubai, UAE Finland • France • Germany • Greece • Hong Kong • Hungary • India • Indonesia • Ireland • Israel • Italy • Japan • Korea • Luxembourg • Malaysia Mexico • The Netherlands • New Zealand • Norway • Peru • Philippines • Poland • Portugal • Puerto Rico • Romania • Russia • Saudi Arabia • Singapore Slovakia • Slovenia • South Africa • Spain • Sweden • Switzerland • Taiwan • Thailand • Turkey • Ukraine • United Kingdom • United States • Venezuela

About the Authors

Khalid Raza, CCIE #1192, has been involved with the design of large networks for Cisco Systems, Inc. for longer than five years. He holds a master's degree in engineering management, and a bachelor's degree in electrical engineering. Khalid's contributions to the CCIE program include helping to write the lab portion of the exam and the new IP-ISP test for CCIE re-certification. Khalid's specialization is in routing protocols, and he has given presentations at various conferences on designing scalable IP networks.

Mark Turner is a development manager for large-scale switching and routing at Cisco Systems, Inc. He has been involved with the design of large-scale IP networks since the early 1990s, when he contributed to the maintenance and expansion of the Australian Academic and Research Network. Since then, he has worked in an engineering and network management capacity on several large corporate intranets, most recently for the NASA Science Internet. Mark's contributions to major projects over the years have included the complete design of secure and open networks, as well as incremental upgrades to physical and logical routing infrastructures of existing large networks.

Dedications

I dedicate this book with my deepest love and affection to my wife Nabeela Sajjad Raza, and my parents Sajid and Musarat Raza. Their love, wisdom, and strength have inspired me to write this book.

—Khalid Raza

I dedicate this to my Father for encouraging me to gain knowledge to solve some problems, and for showing me great courage in overcoming others.

—Mark Turner

Acknowledgments

I would like to thank Cisco Press and Cisco Systems, Inc. for allowing me to contribute to this book, as well as our technical editors. I would also like to thank Atif Khan, Henk Smit, and Mossadiq Turabi for their tips during hallway discussions. My sincere appreciation should also be extended to Mark Johnson and Ray Rios for their help during my early days at Cisco. Finally, I am grateful to Mike Quinn and Joe Pinto for their flexibility during this book project.

—Khalid Raza

I would like to thank many friends and colleagues at Cisco Systems, Inc. who shared ideas that I have included in this book. These include Srihari Ramachandra, and Ravi Chandra, for BGP; Enke Chen on ideas for scaling BGP; John Meylor, Dave Meyer, and John Zwiebel for multicast; Dave Rowell for expertise in switching, and coffee; and my co-author Khalid for many interesting discussions on routing.

I also would like to thank Jim McCabe for his insight into network design. A special thank-you goes to: My friends who understood why I was so busy at night and on weekends for many months, Charles Goldberg for encouraging me to enjoy life, Angelo for making sure I exercised as well as wrote, Jude for battle strategy, and Em for just about everything else.

—Mark Turner

Contents at a Glance

Table of Contents

Introduction

Today's networks are involved in almost every kind of business and social interaction, from ordering a pizza to marketing products. Millions of people are making the transition to a wired world—and while they were initially satisfied with simple text or message transfers, they now want sound and graphics—and they want it quickly. Rapid growth in the number of users and their expectations makes scalability a crucial part of any network design. Chances are, even if your network is small today, it will be large within a few short years. Networks that cannot scale suffer a long and costly death. If your network is critical to your business—and most are—you will find this book an invaluable aid for design and maintenance.

This book summarizes the techniques that have led to the successful deployment and maintenance of many large networks. It draws on the experience of the authors, gained in both the enterprise and service provider environments, and presents the ideas in a "cookbook" fashion—it provides "recipes" for success in almost any network conditions. Unlike other networking texts that focus on describing the technology in abstract terms, this book highlights scalability features and emphasizes deployment issues.

Who Should Read This Book

This book is designed for network engineers, administrators, or architects involved in the design, deployment, and maintenance of IP networks. The focus remains on designing for scalability, and the approach involves hands-on application using real configurations derived from real networks. Although the configuration examples are based on Cisco IOS, many of the ideas are generally applicable to any routing platform.

This book is primarily aimed at the intermediate to expert networking professional. Readers are expected to have a basic understanding of TCP/IP, Cisco IOS, IP routing, and networking devices such as hubs, switches, and routers. Those without this understanding can refer to the several fine texts already available in the Cisco Press series.

What Is Covered in This Book

The material in this book is separated into two parts:

- Part I—Chapters 1 through 5—covers general aspects of network design, WAN, LAN, and router technologies.
- Part II—Chapters 6 through 16—discusses the deployment of routing protocols, QoS issues, and network management.

Chapter 1, "Evolution of Data Networks," describes the evolution of the world's largest IP network: the Internet. You will discover what lessons have been learned in scaling the Internet from just a few users to hundreds of millions. You will also see some of the reasons for the demise of other network protocols.

Chapter 2, "IP Fundamentals," reviews the basics of IP.

Chapter 3, "Network Technologies," provides an overview of the current network link technologies. You will learn about the basic concepts of switching techniques used in today's communications networks.

Chapter 4, "Network Topology and Design," examines constraints in modern network design and explores the various tools and techniques that can be used to produce a scalable network architecture. A hierarchical network design is presented.

Chapter 5, "Routers," traces the evolution of router architectures to the present day. The operation and use of today's scalable distributed switching paradigms are described. A case study also looks at the interaction among routing, fast switching, and express forwarding tables.

Chapter 6, "Routing Information Protocol," explains the operation of distance vector algorithms and delves into the details of RIP itself. After describing the basic use of RIP, the chapter goes on to look at complications introduced in classless environments. The limitations of RIP and possible workarounds are discussed as well.

Chapter 7, "Routing Information Protocol Version 2," details the enhancements to RIP to support classless routing. On-demand and snapshot routing are explained, and the use of distances and offset-lists to provide optimal and backup routing is demonstrated. Finally, route authentication and enforcing routing policy are addressed.

Chapter 8, "Enhanced Interior Gateway Routing Protocol," describes the operation of Enhanced IGRP. The DUAL algorithm, Enhanced IGRP message, metrics, and topology table are discussed. The chapter illustrates the use of Enhanced IGRP in low-bandwidth environments, mechanisms for route summarization, and ways to implement routing policy.

Chapter 9, "Open Shortest Path First," provides a general introduction to link-state protocols. This is followed by an overview of OSPF operation and then a packet-level description of the protocol. Next, the concept of OSPF area types is discussed. Configurations of Regular, Stub, Totally Stubby, and Not So Stubby areas are described, and point-to-point, broadcast multi-access, and non-broadcast multi-access media are included in the configuration examples.

Chapter 10, "Intermediate System-to-Intermediate System," addresses the second of the popular link-state protocols (with OSPF being the other). The chapter begins with an overview of the operation of IS-IS. Concepts discussed include IS-IS addressing and its relationship with IS-IS areas and hierarchy; the function of pseudonodes in LAN operations; and the difference between level 1 and level 2 routing. Next, the chapter describes operation of IS-IS at the packet level. Scalability issues such as flooding of updates and route summarization are addressed as well. Finally, the use of IS-IS metrics and default routes are explored.

Chapter 11, "Border Gateway Protocol," describes the protocol and its use for both interdomain and intradomain routing. Next, BGP's attributes and finite state machine are detailed. Finally, the chapter covers scalability features, such as route reflection and peer groups, and their application in large networks.

Chapter 12, "Migration Techniques," draws upon material presented in earlier chapters and highlights the issues in migrating between routing protocols. Reasons for migrating are listed, and the following cases are examined: migration from classful to classless protocols (including IGRP to Enhanced IGRP, and RIP to Enhanced IGRP); migration from IGP to IBGP for scalability.

Chapter 13, "Protocol Independent Multicast," provides an overview of the operation of the Internet Group Management Protocol and Protocol Independent Multicast. This is followed by a packet-level description of the protocols. Finally, the multicast scalability features are described, and deployment issues are addressed.

Chapter 14, "Quality of Service Features," describes congestion-management and congestion-avoidance algorithms. Congestion management via first-in, first-out queuing; priority queuing; custom queuing; weighted fair queuing; and selective packet discard are compared and contrasted. Congestion avoidance through the use of weighted random early detection, committed access rate, BGP QoS policy propagation, and the Resource Reservation Protocol is described, and a blueprint for scalable deployment of QoS technologies is developed.

Chapter 15, "Network Operations and Management," breaks the network management task into five functional areas: fault, configuration, security, accounting, and performance. The use of the Simple Network Management Protocol, Cisco's AAA model, and Netflow to meet these five functional tasks is described. The chapter goes on to discuss logging of network status, deployment of the Network Time Protocol, router configuration revision control, rollout of new software revisions, securing both routing protocols and configuration control of routers, capacity planning, and traffic engineering. This chapter concludes with a network management checklist, which you can use to develop or audit your own network management practices.

Chapter 16, "Design and Configuration Case Studies," details three large-scale network case studies. The first demonstrates, using actual router configurations, hierarchical and regionalized routing within a large enterprise network. The second case study examines the hub-and-spoke architecture common to many large enterprises with highly centralized facilities. The third case study examines the overall architecture of a large ISP network. The final case study looks at unicast and multicast routing for both the intradomain and interdomain levels. Router configuration for operations and network management purposes are summarized, and a model for providing differentiated services is developed.

Conventions Used in This Book

Most chapters conclude with a case study, a set of review questions, and a selection of material for further reading. The case studies reinforce the major ideas in the chapter; the review questions test your understanding and, in some cases, set the stage for further reading.

A number of Cisco IOS configuration commands are discussed, but only the command options relevant to the discussion are described. Hence, the command options are usually a subset of those described in the Cisco IOS Command Reference. The same conventions as the Command Reference are used:

- Vertical bars (|) separate alternative, mutually exclusive, elements.
- Square brackets ([]) indicate optional elements.
- Braces ({ }) indicate a required choice.
- Braces within square brackets ([{ }]) indicate a required choice within an optional element.
- **Boldface** indicates commands and keywords that are entered literally as shown.
- *Italics* indicate arguments for which you supply values.

Cisco configuration code fragments are used throughout the book. These are presented in a distinctive typeface (mono-type) for easy identification.

Other elements used in the text are:

- Notes are sidebar comments related to the discussion at hand but that can be skipped without loss of understanding or ambiguity.
- Tips are sidebar comments that describe an efficient shortcut or optimal way of using the technology.

PART

The Internet

This chapter provides a gentle introduction before you embark on the more technical material in the rest of the book. The following issues are covered in this chapter:

Overview of communications history   This section briefly traces the evolution of communications infrastructure from its earliest times until the present day.

Evolution of the Internet   This section takes an in-depth look at the development of the Internet. It focuses mainly on the technical details, but it discusses some political, social, and economical issues as well. As the story of the Internet unfolds, you will begin to understand the critical issues in scaling large IP networks. Issues such as network topology, routing, network management, and the support of distributed and multimedia applications are discussed.

The Internet today   Having learned from the lessons of the past, you will read about the modern Internet architecture. This section describes key research initiatives, Internet NAPs, routing policy, and network address registration. It concludes with an overview of today's Internet topology.

Evolution and demise of proprietary and OSI networking   This section glimpses the rapidly dwindling world of non-IP networking protocols. It describes both the positive and negative aspects, and it explains why these technologies are becoming less critical for the future.

Future of the Internet   In this section, you will look into the future to discover the possible direction of the Internet and large-scale networks.

## CHAPTER 1

Evolution of Data Networks

The historical perspective in this chapter will help you understand where and why improvements were made as data networks have evolved and scaled. This chapter also illustrates a more salient point: The use of ideas in development is often cyclic. This cyclical nature of development places a whole new meaning on the so-called "wheel of invention."

Improvements in technology enable you to renew your outlook on solutions that were previously dismissed as technically or economically unfeasible. An extreme example is the use of optical communications. Although successful many years ago in the form of torches and flares, in the last century, optical communication was disbanded because it was much easier to guide lower-frequency electromagnetic radiation using simple copper cable. With the advent of optical fiber, however, this is no longer true.

The switching of data packets also has historically been accomplished in the electrical domain for similar reasons. However, recent innovations in wave division multiplexing and optical networks soon may obviate the need for electronic switching in many high-bandwidth communication infrastructures.

Overview of Communications History

Networks are now a core component of our business and personal lives. Today, businesses that may hobble along with the loss of telephone service can be rendered nonfunctional by the loss of their data network infrastructure. Understandably, corporations spend a great deal of time and money nursing this critical resource.

How and why did this dependency occur? Simply because networks provide a means to amplify all the historical communication mechanisms. Nearly 50,000 years of speech, at least 3500 years of written communication, and many thousands of years of creating images all can be captured and communicated through a network to anywhere on the planet.

In the 1980s, fiber optics improved the distance, cost, and reliability issues; CB radio taught us about peer-to-peer communication and self-regulation without a centralized communications infrastructure provider. The needs of the military led to the development of network technologies that were resilient to attack, which also meant that they were resilient to other types of failure. Today's optical switching and multiplexing again demonstrate that to take the next leap in capability, scalability, and reliability, businesses and individuals cannot afford to cling to tried-and-true techniques.

Data communications grew from the need to connect islands of users on LANs to mainframes (IBM's Systems Network Architecture [SNA] and Digital's DECnet) and then to each other. As time passed, these services were required over wide geographical areas. Then came the need for administrative control, as well as media and protocol conversion. Routers began to become key components of a network in the 1980s, which was within the same time that Asynchronous Transfer Mode (ATM) cell switching was being developed as the technology for the deployment of worldwide networks supporting multimedia communications.

The designers of ATM were constrained by the need to support the traditional voice network. This is not surprising, however, for at that time voice revenues exceeded other forms of communications infrastructures. If new applications were to develop, many people thought they were likely to take the form of video, either for communication or entertainment.

Very few people predicted the coming of the Internet. After all, it was not real-time voice or video that stole the show, but the ubiquity of home personal computers coupled with a few applications. These included the simple one-to-one or one-to-many communication applications, such as e-mail and chat groups, and the powerful Web browsers and Internet search engines that turned the Internet into a virtual world in which people could journey, learn, teach, and share. Users did not need megabits per second to enter this world: 32 Kbps was happiness, 64 Kbps was bliss, and 128 Kbps was heaven.

The increases in desktop computing power and in peer-to-peer applications had a fundamental impact on network architectures. Modern network architectures expect intelligence and self-regulation at the user workstation, and they provide a network infrastructure that maintains only the intelligence sufficient to support packet forwarding. This contrasts significantly with the approach of connecting simple terminal devices to intelligent mainframes using a complex networking device that is used by many proprietary solutions, notably IBM's SNA.

NOTE   Some schools of thought suggest that networks will become more intelligent—and the user stations less so. They believe bandwidth will be cheaper than local storage or CPUs, so computational resources are better kept in a central shared facility. Web-TV and voice-messaging services are examples of this philosophy at work.

The impact of technological development, and the changing needs of businesses, consumers, and society in general, is clear. Data networking is growing at 25 percent per year, traditional voice is increasing by only 6 percent, and the Internet is doubling every few months. (The term *traditional voice* is used because the Internet now carries voice, and in the last year or so several providers have announced their intent to supply voice over IP services.)

The revenue to be gained from carrying data packets is close to, or perhaps even exceeds, that of carrying traditional telephone voice circuits. Voice is rapidly becoming just another variation on the data-networking theme—just packets for another application.

Ultimately, competition drives design and development, whether it be the telegraph versus the telephone, or traditional telephony versus Internet telephony. Providers attempt to gain a commercial advantage over their competitors by adopting new technologies that will provide a service that is either cheaper, better, or more flexible. Naturally, a network that is well designed, planned, and implemented will be in a position to take on new technologies.

Evolution of the Internet

Socially, economically, culturally, and technologically, for many of us the Internet already has changed our lives dramatically. For many more of us, it soon will. Along with telephones, televisions, and automobiles, Internet connectivity is rapidly becoming a commodity in every home. Yet, as dramatic as the changes have been, it is worth remembering that—initially, at least—the Internet grew at a considerably slower pace than the telephone network (although some would argue that this is merely because the former is dependent on the latter).

In the 1960s, the idea of a ubiquitous communication network was not new, but the angle of using the network for more than just personal communications—and, in particular, for the exchange of computer programs and other forms of arbitrary data—was fairly radical. For one thing, communications technology at the time was not flexible enough to allow it to happen. Then, ARPANET entered the picture.

ARPANET

Technology researchers working independently at MIT, RAND, and NPL from 1961 through 1967 conducted a number of experiments in what was later termed *packet networking*. One of the papers about those experiments, published in 1967, was a design for an experimental wide-area packet-switched network, called the ARPANET.

This was the technological turning point. It would have a profound impact on the capability of networks to grow and evolve to meet the changing needs of their users—and, in particular, to support the world of peer-to-peer networking and multimedia communications. While replacing the traditional time-division multiplexing in the LAN environment, ARPANET provided the capability, through layering, of exploiting the benefits of TDM systems in a wide area, and seamlessly interconnecting the two.

In 1969, after several years of observing this technology in the lab, the U.S. Department of Defense commissioned ARPANET, connecting four nodes from SDS, IBM, and DEC at 50 Kbps rather than the originally planned 2.4 Kbps. The Information Message Processors (IMPs) used in the network were Honeywell 516 minicomputers, with a whopping 24 KB of memory, with code supplied by BBN Inc. These were followed by BBN C-30s and C-300s, and subsequently were renamed Packet Switch Nodes in 1984. Aside from its historical significance, the ARPANET was characterized by two traits that remain true of the Internet to this day: The end hosts came from different manufacturers, and the initial bandwidth proposed was far less than necessary.

One of the end nodes was at the Stanford Research Institute (SRI), which provided the first Network Information Center and RFC repository. This open repository of design and discussion documents related to network engineering, and provided an astoundingly successful forum for publishing and critiquing ideas. Ironically, the easy availability of Internet standards, as opposed to those prepared by Open Systems Interconnect (OSI) forums, was one major contributor to the eventual demise of the OSI suite.

In 1970, the details of the Network Control Protocol (NCP) were fleshed out, and the ARPANET hosts began using that protocol for communication. At that point, application designers could begin work. Electronic mail was introduced in 1972 and remained a dominant application, second only to FTP in terms of traffic levels until the World Wide Web surpassed even FTP in March, 1995.

NCP's limitations soon became apparent: scalability and address-ability limitations and the reliance on the network for reliable data transfer were major issues.

TCP/IP was proposed for end systems and it addressed issues fundamental to the operation of the Internet today. The design allowed networks to be autonomously owned and managed, with address allocation the only significant issue requiring Internetwork coordination. Further considerations (and thus attributes of TCP/IP) included the following:

- Assumes best-effort delivery by the network
- Maintains no per-traffic flow state in packet switches
- Provides a way to detect and discard looping packets
- Provides multiple in-transit packets and routing
- Includes efficient implementation, but not at the expense of other properties
- Supports packet fragmentation and reassembly
- Provides a method for detecting packet duplication and to correct errors
- Includes operating system independence
- Provides flow and congestion control
- Offers operating system independence
- Supports extensible design

UDP was later added when it became obvious that some error-correction decisions, such as those for real-time data, are best left to the application. For example, in a real-time audio application, there is little worthiness in correcting a corrupted segment of sound if the time to play that sound has already passed.

Independent implementations of the protocol were originally commissioned by DARPA contracts, but as time passed, commercial vendors began implementing the protocol for many operating systems and platforms, including the IBM PC.

An unfortunate choice at the time was to use a 32-bit address space, the first eight bits of which designated the network ID, and the remaining 24 of which designated the host ID. The initial protocol specification was released before the introduction of LANs, only one year after the original idea of Ethernet was suggested, and at least 15 years before the PC became a desktop commodity.

With the introduction of LAN technology in the late 1970s, it soon became apparent that the 8/24-bit network/host address allocation scheme was not going to work. Many small network operators who wanted to join the experiment required far fewer than 24 bits of host address space. The classful address allocation scheme now known as Classes A, B, and C was introduced. This was another unfortunate decision, as it turned out, because it soon became apparent that the Class A address space was too large an allocation block. With CIDR and classless routing introduced in the 1990s, the classful behavior of routers led to confusing and conflicting router behavior in the presence of subnet routes—or, more accurately, the lack thereof.

NOTE	*Classless routing* allows the network and host portions of the IP address space to be allocated freely rather than in accordance with predefined Classes A, B, and C boundaries.

January 1983 was the flag month for the transition from NCP to TCP/IP. With only a few hundred hosts at the time, this transition was feasible and was executed surprisingly smoothly. Within the Internet today, however—and even on modest corporate networks—smooth migration plans are an essential part of any new technology-replacement program.

Also in 1983, aided by the transition to TCP/IP, the ARPANET was effectively split. One half, still called ARPANET, was dedicated to research, and MILNET was created for unclassified military activities. MILNET was subsequently integrated with the Defense Data Network.

By 1984, the number of hosts exceeded 1000. At this point, relating machine addresses to functions or location became nearly impossible, so the Domain Name System (DNS) was invented. The DNS supported hierarchical allocation and resolution of network node names (mapping from name to IP address). As time continued to pass, however, DNS became much more than a way to map names to IP addresses: its capability of supporting various resource records, coupled with its scalability and widespread deployment, meant that it could be used for all manner of resource-locating functions.

During the early 1980s, a number of commercial alternatives to ARPANET (many featuring e-mail as the primary application) began to emerge. Over time, these were connected to the ARPANET, or the Internet proper, usually through message gateways. However, such gateways were not consistent with one of the major design strengths of the Internet protocols suite: its capability of providing seamless connection of autonomously operated networks. Ultimately, seamless TCP/IP won, and the other networks either disappeared or evolved into academic or commercial Internet service providers (ISPs).

Another interesting trend began to take place in the early 1980s: LANs became widespread. Individual ARPANET sites wanted to connect not just one computer to the network, but many computers. The Internet began to look like a collection of LANs connected to the ARPANET core by a router and a wide-area network connection (see Figure 1-1). In 1982, the Exterior Gateway Protocol (EGP) was specified in RFC 827, and the first signs of the modern large-scale IP network hierarchy began to emerge.

Figure 1-1   *ARPANET Network Hierarchy: The Prelude to the Modern Internet Architecture*

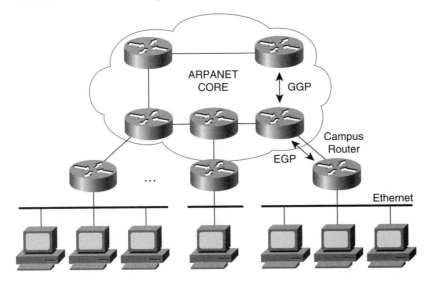

The ARPANET backbone consisted of a small number of core routers, operated by a single administrative body (the Internet Network Operations Center). A much larger number of non-core routers connected ARPANET customers to the backbone and were operated by the customers themselves. These non-core routers generally pointed a default route at one of the core routers, which were themselves defaultless. In other words, the core routers contained a routing entry for every network in the Internet.

NOTE   A *defaultless* (or *default-free*) router must contain an explicit route for every network it needs to reach.

The routing protocol used within the core was the distance-vector Gateway-to-Gateway Protocol (GGP). GGP is a distance-vector routing protocol with capabilities to ensure the reliable transfer of routing updates between adjacent nodes. GGP suffered from the usual poor convergence characteristics of early distance-vector protocols, but by 1988 the ARPANET core routers had been upgraded to the BBN Butterfly, running an early link-state routing protocol called SPREAD.

SPREAD was particularly interesting in its use of network delay, which was determined by examining the transmit queue on a link interface, as a route metric. This provided the capability to route around congested links—those with excessive delay. Steps must be taken to avoid route oscillation when dynamically routing around congested links. The problem is not simple to solve as networks become increasingly complicated, and it is significant that neither of the two major link-state IP routing protocols in use today—IS-IS and OSPF—dynamically route around congestion.

At one point, a vulnerability of the SPREAD routing protocol corrupted link-state advertisements (SPREAD used a circular sequence number space for LSAs). The "Which is most recent?" issue, which occurs when sequence numbers have wrapped around, was avoided by limiting both the generation rate of LSAs and their lifetime. Unfortunately, the designers did not account for hardware problems that created the issue through sequence number corruption. This resulted in a network meltdown due to LSA storming, which shut down the entire ARPANET and reinforced the critical nature of implementation, configuration, and algorithm of link-state routing protocols.

The ARPANET was decommissioned in 1990, at which point the NSFNET and other federal networks formed the Internet core.

NSFNET

In 1984, designers announced plans for JANET, a network to connect academic and research communities in the United Kingdom. The National Science Foundation announced similar plans for the United States in 1985, as did a number of other countries in subsequent years. The NSFNET design was three-tiered, consisting of a national backbone that formed a single default-free (or defaultless) core, a set of mid-level networks for regional distribution, and a larger number of campus access networks. The NSFNET was a major component of the Internet core until its privatization in 1995.

56 Kbps and Fuzzball Routers

One of the early purposes of the NSFNET was to provide researchers and scientists with access to NSF supercomputers. The initial core consisted of 56 Kbps links connecting six major U.S. supercomputer centers. Each supercomputer center was equipped with an LSI-11 microcomputer, which ran the affectionately named "fuzzball" router code and the HELLO routing protocol.

This distance-vector protocol was also notable in its use of packet delay rather than the traditional hop count as the routing metric.

The UNIX routing software (gated) was used for mutual redistribution, including metric translation between the HELLO protocol used on the NSFNET backbone and the IGP (usually RIP) of each of the regionals. The routing redistributions were often filtered according to pre-arranged policy to maintain network stability in the event of misconfiguration.

Carnegie Melon University maintained both an NSFNET fuzzball and an ARPANET PSN. In effect, CMU became the first Internet exchange, a connection point for peer networks.

The network architecture shown in Figure 1-2 has all the same elements of the modern Internet architecture—core, distribution, and access networks of ISPs—with each ISP (in this case ARPANET and NSFNET) meeting at the early equivalent of an Internet NAP (CMU, Pittsburgh).

Figure 1-2 *Original NSFNET, Just Prior to the 1998 Upgrade (for Simplicity, Only Three Out of Seven Regionals Are Shown)*

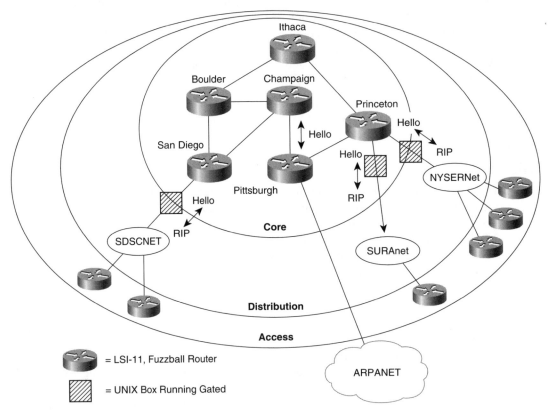

T1 and NSS Routers

A victim of its own success, the original network backbone was soon saturated, in typical Internet fashion. A Request For Proposals was quickly issued for a second NSFNET backbone, and the accepted proposal evolved into a partnership of Merit Inc. (a regional network operated at the University of Michigan), IBM, and MCI.

Although all members of the partnership worked in close collaboration, it is clear that an obvious representation of expertise arose in network operations, computer network equipment development, and long-distance communications services.

The second NSFNET backbone upgraded the fuzzball routers of the original backbone with 13 nodal switching subsystems (NSSs). Each NSS contained up to 14 IBM RTs, connected by dual Token Rings that acted as an internal bus for inter-processor communication (see Figure 1-3):

- One RT was the routing and control processor. As its name suggests, this processor performed routing algorithm calculations, created the IP routing table, and was responsible for the overall control of the box.
- Five RTs were packet-switch processors.
- Four contained a line card for WAN connectivity (448 Kbps initially, and T1 later).
- One—the external PSP—contained an Ethernet card for LAN connectivity. The PSPs were responsible for packet forwarding between line interfaces, and the design accommodated parallel switching between PSPs.
- The remaining three RTs served as backup systems.

Each NSS also contained two IBM PS/2 model 80s. One was used as the internal Token Ring bridge manager; the second ran NetView and LAN Manager, and was responsible for network-monitoring functions.

An IBM implementation of the OSI IS-IS link-state routing protocol modified for IP (see Chapter 10, "Intermediate System-to-Intermediate System") ran on the NSS routers forming the new NSFNET backbone. Routing exchange between the core and the regionals was accomplished using interior-mode EGP. EGP is a reachability protocol rather than a routing protocol: It does not interpret the distance metrics for networks in an EGP update to make routing decisions. Therefore, EGP restricted the topology of the Internet to a tree, with NSFNET at the core. Route dampening—a method of reducing router processor usage during periods of high network instability—was discussed but not implemented at the time (see Figure 1-4).

Figure 1-3   *NSS Router*

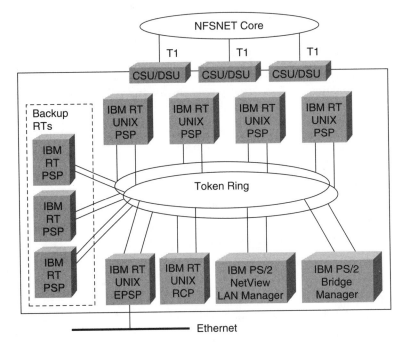

Supporting the NSFNET backbone routers was an evolutionary exercise, requiring close collaboration between the network operators and the code developers. This proved to be one of the great strengths of the team from Merit, IBM, and MCI, as they provided ongoing engineering to support a network that grew by as much as 500 percent per year.

The rapid growth of the NSFNET, coupled with a requirement that the regional networks directly connect to each other rather than relying on the NSFNET backbone, led the NSFNET operators to introduce a rudimentary policy-routing system.

Among other points, the policy-routing system involved filtering all networks advertised to the NSFNET from the regionals based on both network prefix (at this point, it was actually network number because Internet routing was still classful) and autonomous system number. The policy-routing system also set the metric of all accepted routes. These functions were performed in consultation with a distributed policy routing database (PRDB).

Figure 1-4   *The T1 NSFNET Backbone 1990 (Regionals Added after 1990 Are Shaded)*

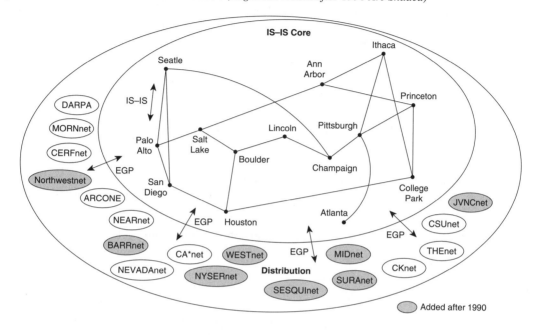

NOTE   A similar policy was prescribed for routing between NSFNET and the ARPANET and MILNET (collectively referred to as the Defense Data Network [DDN]).

The limitations of EGP were well recognized during this period, and design work began on a replacement interdomain routing protocol, the Border Gateway Protocol (BGP), to address these limitations. BGP was deployed on the NSFNET, and version 4 of BGP still forms the core of the Internet.

In 1990, the new NSS node Atlanta was added to the NSFNET core, bringing the total to 14 routers. In addition, Merit, IBM, and MCI formed a new nonprofit company: Advanced Network and Services. This company would continue running the NSFNET as a standalone entity. In 1991, ANS CO+RE Systems was spun off as a for-profit enterprise.

Management and Interoperability Issues of the Internet

By the end of 1989, the Internet consisted of more than 300,000 hosts and more than 2000 networks. Not surprisingly, users began to focus on network-management techniques; and the Simple Network Management Protocol (SNMP) was developed as an extensible way to query and control not only routers, but also any network-connected entity. SNMP was considered by some people as a stepping stone to the OSI Common Management Information Protocol. As it turned out, SNMP is now ubiquitous, whereas CMIP has experienced the same fate as the typewriter.

Interoperability issues also became a focus of attention—September, 1988 saw the inaugural *Interop*, a technical trade show at which vendors demonstrate the capabilities and interoperability of their networking products. This show also became a forum for the exchange of ideas, partly because vendor competition was tolerated slightly more than at the IETF standards meetings. The show now runs annually in the United States, and sister shows have emerged in Europe and Australia.

SNMP made its debut at the Interop trade show in 1990 on a unique platform: the Internet toaster.

NSFNET-T3 and ENSS Routers

By the end of 1993, traffic on the NSFNET backbone had increased to the point of requiring 45 MB (T3) connections. Although the ARPANET had been decommissioned for three years by then, increased NSFNET connectivity more than compensated for this fact, through growth in the regionals and by the peer networks operated by the remainder of the "Big Four": the Department of Energy, the Department of Defense, and NASA. NSFNET also encouraged academic and research usage through its "Connections" program (see Figure 1-5).

The NSFNET NSS routers also were redesigned to cater to the massive increase in packet-switching requirements. The new routers consisted of a single IBM RS/6000 workstation equipped with T3 line cards. Each line card ran a reduced UNIX kernel and IP Protocol stack, and the overall system was capable of switching more than 100,000 packets per second. Two types of routers were produced:

- Core Nodal Switching Systems (CNSS) were optimized for use at either end of the MCI T3 backbone trunks.

- Exterior Nodal Switching Systems were optimized for connecting each regional to the backbone.

A parallel T3 NFSNET backbone was established in 1990. After significant testing and refinement, several of the T1 backbone sites cut over to T3 for production traffic. The network was very well-engineered, and overall reliability increased significantly after the upgrade.

Figure 1-5   *Big Four Federal Network and Exchanges, Prior to Privatization*

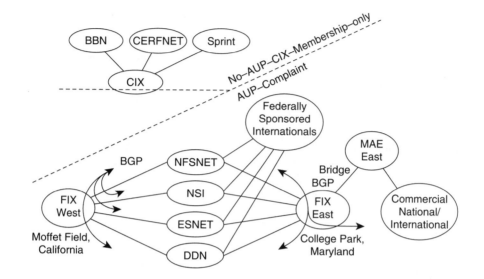

In addition to providing comprehensive national connectivity, each of the Big Four provided fairly extensive—and usually mutually convenient—international connectivity. Federal Internet exchanges were established at NASA Ames (FIX-West) in California, and in College Park, Maryland (FIX-East) to connect the Big Four. These exchanges were to become the model upon which later commercial NAPs were based. Indeed, MAE-East was soon established and bridged into the FIX-East facility. The Commercial Internet exchange was also established by providers who wanted freedom from AUP restrictions. As an organization, the CIX still exists today, although exchange operations have since been moved to the Palo Alto Internet exchange (PAIX), operated by Digital.

The federal networks also ran commercial routers—NSI, originally a Proteon-based network, migrated to Cisco. The AGS router, loaded with 64 MB of memory, became a common feature at both FIXs, and BGP4 began to emerge as core Inter-provider routing protocol.

The World Wide Web

In 1991, WAIS, Gopher, and the World Wide Web were released as a means to seek out and follow information on the Internet in a far more intuitive and accessible way than the previous directory search "Archie" tools. The evolution of the World Wide Web and the emergence of the Web browser as the dominant Internet application increased the overall attraction and accessibility of the Internet to the public. In addition, it induced rapid growth in traffic levels that continue to be a challenge to network operations engineers and router vendors alike.

The MBONE

In 1992, a fascinating experiment on the Internet began: the efficient transmission of audio and video. The real step forward was the efficient delivery mechanism: multicast.

If two people want to communicate over the Internet using audio or video today, they can do so relatively easily, if not with a great deal of quality. A camera, a microphone, a PC at each end, some software, and a UDP session is essentially all that are required.

What if, instead of a two-user session, we have one source and many recipients. Sending a separate copy of the data to each recipient is a highly inefficient use of network bandwidth and switching capacity, not to mention computer resources used for packet replication at the source. This is a fundamental problem that multicast network technology attempts to solve. Multicasting saves bandwidth by sending only one copy of a packet over each link in the network. The packet replication load is spread over routers in the network. (Moving the packet replication function onto network routers is arguably not a good thing, but it is necessary to make switching and bandwidth savings.)

The MBONE, the virtual multicast backbone on the Internet, was initially created using the *mrouted* (multicast routing daemon) program that initially ran on UNIX workstations with modified kernels. The mrouted program is an implementation of the Distance-Vector Multicast Routing Protocol (DVMRP, RFC-1075), which essentially describes a RIP-like way to advertise source networks, and provides a technique for forwarding multicast packets so that a *spanning tree* (a loop-free subset of a network topology) from the source is created.

Initially, mrouters used the truncated reverse path broadcast algorithm to construct the spanning tree. This meant that for the first MBONE demonstrations, everyone received all traffic on the MBONE up to their "leaf" network (usually the local LAN). At that point, traffic was either multicast or not multicast onto the LAN, depending on user subscription communication to the local router via the Internet Group Management Protocol (IGMP). Unfortunately, this usually meant that WAN links carried all MBONE traffic. Figure 1-6 shows the MBONE topology in 1995.

The mrouted program was quickly revised to include a pruning mechanism. Internet links carried only multicast traffic for a particular group, if users dependent on those links had joined (via IGMP) the multicast group in question. Periodically, however, multicast routers would send out traffic for all groups over all links. This was necessary so that downstream routers could determine which groups to prune and when to create a prune state. Ultimately, this periodic "leaking" presents a scalability problem for the Internet. You will learn about solutions to this issue in Chapter 13, "Protocol Independent Multicast."

Initially, the MBONE multicast packets were sent from mrouter to mrouter using the loose-source-route IP packet option. This was a painful experience and showed that most commercial routers had a processor-intensive switching path for optioned packets. These packets were later changed to use IP-in-IP encapsulation.

Figure 1-6   *MBONE Topology in 1995*

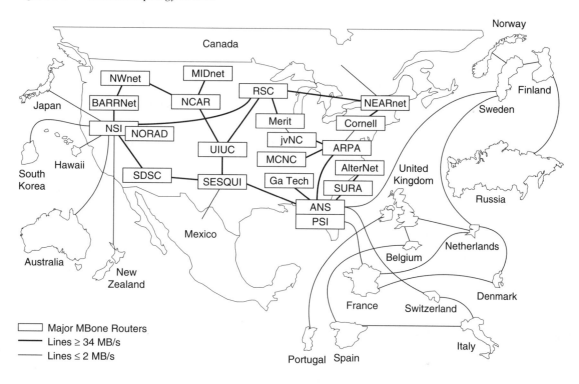

In 1992, the initial MBONE infrastructure was established. Although the MBONE topology consists of meshed interprovider connectivity and tree-like distribution and access infrastructure, the DVMRP itself does not support any routing hierarchy. Moreover, no concept of interior and exterior routing exists. As the number of MBONE routes has grown from 40 in 1992 to more than 5500 today, the scalability limitations of the DVMRP-based MBONE infrastructure are becoming more apparent.

As you will see in Chapter 13, "Protocol Independent Multicast," the solutions are still in the early deployment phase and are the subject of ongoing research and IETF activity.

Privatization of the Internet

Although commercial traffic was encouraged on the regional level, any traffic passing over the NSFNET backbone had to comply with the Acceptable Usage Policy (AUP). This included all connectivity obtained through any of the Big Four. The aim of this policy was to encourage the development of a national commercial Internet infrastructure, and it succeeded, with companies such as UUNET, PSI, and ANS providing commercial Internet services. As mentioned previously, in 1991 the Commercial Internet exchange (CIX) was established for the exchange of Internet traffic among commercial providers.

Recognizing that the policy was not entirely successful and was certainly impossible to police, the NSF made a final solicitation for privatization of the entire NSFNET infrastructure in May, 1993. This final solicitation required solutions to five major needs:

- Selection of a routing arbiter

- Creation of a geographically dispersed set of network access points for commercial national provider peering

- Movement of the NSFNET regional distribution (mid-level) networks onto one of the previously mentioned commercial providers

- Selection of a network information services manager

- Selection of a provider for operation of a very-high-speed Backbone Network Service (vBNS) to carry government and research traffic

These actions built the framework from which the Internet architecture of today has evolved. The extremely aggressive transition schedule required the decommissioning of NSFNET. Clearly, the challenges went far beyond the technical considerations. Not surprisingly, many delays arose as a result.

The Internet Today

From July 1988 until NSFNET was officially shut down in April 1995, the network grew from 217 networks to more 50,000 networks, and truly established itself as the Internet core. So many users existed at this point—many of them pursuing commercial interests over the Internet—that privatization was inevitable.

The Very High Speed Backbone Network

However, the NSF believed that certain functions could not be fulfilled by a commercial Internet. Infrastructure was one—in particular, the stringent requirements of the supercomputer centers and their associated research community. NSF awarded MCI a $50 million contract to design, operate, and maintain a backbone network connecting the same supercomputer centers as the original NSFNET backbone (refer to Figure 1-4). The backbone was activated for testing in late 1994 and was officially launched in April, 1995. Unlike its predecessor, the vBNS has not become a significant part of the Internet routing core. It peers with other providers and bodies of interest at the four NAPs awarded by the NSF, at various private interconnect points, and at MAE-East. The initial backbone was OC3 (150 Mbps) and combined FORE ASX-1000 ATM switches, Cisco 7507s, and Ascend Gigarouters. The Cisco routers were chosen because they were well-established in the market and were tested in production environments. The Ascend Gigarouter was selected because it supported the HIPPI interface, it was important for the supercomputer environment, it offered intended support for OC12 interface cards, and it provided the capability of adding custom features to the routing code (the code was derived from the public-domain gated software).

All sites connected to the vBNS are equipped with IP—some also have raw ATM-level connectivity. The ATM infrastructure was built on top of MCI's new commercial ATM offering, which effectively made vBNS the first "customer" of the new service. OSPF is used for internal routing, with each backbone core router configured as one hop away from any other. Alternate IP-level routing, through another backbone router, occurs in the event of ATM link or node failure.

BGP4 is used, where appropriate, for peering with external organizations. Full Internet connectivity is provided by peering with InternetMCI at each of the NAPs. As with its commercial sister, InternetMCI, vBNS makes extensive use of BGP communities. In the case of vBNS, two communities were established—primary and secondary communities—and each vBNS "customer" was allocated into one of the two communities: vBNS-approved institutions (VAIs) or vBNS partner institutions (VPIs). Route announcement is configured so that VAI routes are announced to all sites and VPI routes are announced only to VAIs. As a result, VAIs can communicate among themselves and with the VPIs, but VPI sites cannot communicate with each other, and instead must use the Internet or some other private infrastructure. This technique is explored in Chapter 11, "Border Gateway Protocol."

The vBNS network has been very progressive in pursuit of its "new technologies" charter—specifically, the deployment and analysis of intra- and interprovider IP multicast, IP only and IP-to-ATM quality of service, network statistics collection using the "OC3MON" IP over ATM packet-sniffing tool, and IP at OC12 speeds.

NOTE   Recently, vBNS has been considered for involvement in the Internet II (I2) initiative, specifically as a backbone service provider. I2 is a consortium of universities and their government and industry partners who believe that the current commercial Internet environment is not conducive to the development of new broadband networking applications (such as distance learning) and other research activities. To resolve this situation, I2 plans to create a leading-edge networking service. Any R&D conducted using the new networks will satisfy the immediate needs of the I2 community and will be rapidly disseminated to the wider networking and Internet community.

Movement of Regionals onto Commercial Providers

The NSFNET regional and mid-level networks that previously provided the distribution layer of the network needed a new core. However, more than one core existed in the new architecture, and these commercial core providers were connected to the four Internet NAPs. Each regional network then had two connection choices:

- Connect directly to a NAP, establish peering relationships with other regionals, and establish a customer relationship with one or more of the commercial core providers
- Connect directly to a core commercial provider through a private infrastructure

Each of the regionals also was required to provide ongoing support for network registration, management, and policy in relation to the activities of the InterNIC, Routing Arbiter, vBNS, and NAPs. In return, the NSF financial support would decrease and cease within four years.

Commercial core providers, often referred to as national service providers (NSPs), became InternetMCI, Sprintlink, and ANS networks. The routing significance of the NSPs is their defaultless environment. In other words, somewhere within the routing hierarchy of each NSP, there is a router that can reach every destination on the Internet. During this time, this consisted of more than 50,000 networks.

The Internet NAPs

The network access points (NAPs) were intended as the key peering points for NSPs that provided core routing services for the NFSNET's regional distribution networks. The NAPs were modeled on the FIXs, which were used to connect the Big Four during the operation of the NSFNET backbone. Traffic within the NAPs, however, was supposed to operate freely of the acceptable usage policy (AUP).

Although the NSF NAP Manager solicitation had some admirable goals in statistics collection and support for end-to-end service monitoring, today's NAP operator essentially provides a physically secure, conditioned collocation facility that guards against power failure, has a well-connected communications infrastructure, and is geographically significant.

Within the facility (which is monitored 24 hours a day, 365 days a year), there exists a Layer 2 link infrastructure, such as FDDI, to which all customers can connect. This infrastructure usually supports the cabling for private interconnects between customer routers.

The four initial NAPs were

- MFS "MAE-East" (Washington, D.C.)
- Sprint NAP (Pennsauken, NJ)
- Ameritech NAP (Chicago, IL)
- PACBell NAP (San Francisco, CA)

The MAE-East (Metropolitan Area Ethernet) facility had been operating since 1992. As its name suggests, MAE-East initially served as an Ethernet, and in 1994 was upgraded to FDDI. The FIX-East facility was bridged to MAE-East to enable the Federal networks to establish peering relationships with the NSPs.

On the west coast, PACBell ran into some early problems with the ATM infrastructure in the San Francisco NAP (similar problems appeared at the Ameritech NAP in Chicago—both were due to insufficient buffer sizes in the switches, and both NAPs deployed FDDI as an interim measure). This, along with the locality of FIX-West and Silicon Valley, created the market for a MAE-West facility, spread between NASA Ames and an MFS exchange in San Jose. As of this writing, MAE-West remains one of the most critical NAPs in the Internet. Like its counterpart in Washington, MAE-West provides a switched FDDI environment, based on DEC GIGASwitches. The GIGASwitch arrays in San Jose are bridged to those at Ames via load-sharing OC3 ATM circuits.

Figure 1-7 shows the typical NAP topology. Even the GIGASwitches were not problem-free. As traffic levels increased, it soon was soon clear that their switching architecture was vulnerable to head of line (HOL) blocking.

This problem occurs when multiple packets contend for the same output interface. In Figure 1-7, three input interfaces exist, all with packets contending for the output interface connected to R4. These contending packets block packets behind them in the input interface buffers, even though those packets may be destined for uncongested output interfaces.

This was particularly annoying to the competitive ISPs because an ISP that operated links congesting the NAP could cause packet loss between operators, even though they had gone to the effort of ensuring that their own links were uncongested.

Unless they were customers of another NSP at the NAP, routers collocated at the major NAP ran default-free routing tables. Today, thanks to CIDR, this is still maintained (as of this writing) at about 50,000 routes. However, NAPs do not need to be default-free. Rather than operating at the core level, NAPs can operate within the distribution network to better regionalize traffic.

It is beneficial to retain localization of traffic. First of all, it minimizes the delays associated with interprovider traffic. Secondly, it decreases the effective cost to carry the traffic. Finally, it minimizes the workload. A smaller workload also decreases potential congestion on the links and on the switching infrastructure within the NAP itself.

Because this is the case, you might ask: Can hundreds of NAPs exist? Certainly, there are many more than the original four. MFS (now WorldCom), in particular, is establishing more MAE facilities, both with the United States and internationally. Connecting to NAPs at the distribution network can make routing more complicated, however. You will learn in Chapter 11 how to simplify this process as much as possible.

Figure 1-7   *Typical NAP Topology and the HOL Problem*

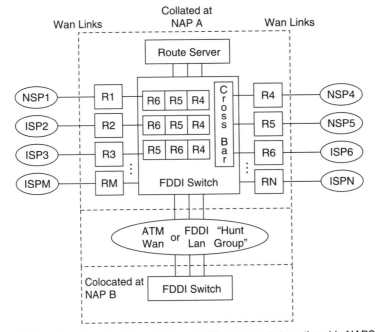

NSP = National Servicer Provider – Nationwide Wan connects to nationwide NAPS
ISP = Internet Server Provider – Regional Wan connects to regional NAPS

Large NSPs also treat the NAPs with some suspicion. For one thing, it is possible to abuse NAP connectivity by pointing a default route at another router in the NAP, and then allow that router to peer for you. Another difficulty is that, essentially, NAP switching capacity is removed from the hands of its customers. These customers must rely on the NAP operator to do a good job, which can be difficult in the massive growth and "problem of the week" environment of the Internet. For these and other reasons, many of the large NSPs prefer private interconnects.

A likely future model is one in which regional providers exchange traffic at regional NAPs, reserving their out-of-region traffic for links to an NSP. The major NSPs will continue to invest in a private regional interconnect infrastructure.

Routing Policy and the Routing Arbiter Service

Remember that NSFNET has been using a Policy Routing DataBase (PRDB) since 1989, both to prevent routing loops when EGP was used between the backbone and the regionals, and to ensure that each regional announced correct routing information. (Incorrect information could be announced simply due to configuration errors in the regional networks.)

When it was introduced, BGP made loop detection easy by virtue of its path attribute. If an AS appears in the path twice, the route is a loop and can therefore be ignored. The need to ensure correct route announcements from each of the regionals remained, as did the need for a PRDB.

With the establishment of new NAPs and the introduction of new providers in the ISP market, the community grew concerned about the explosion of peering sessions at the NAPs. A full mesh of neighbor peering sessions is required by the BGP protocol, which is configured on a neighbor-by-neighbor basis. Consequent bandwidth consumption also would affect the NAP switches—and, worse, router CPU utilization would become an issue because all routers at the NAP had to independently enforce routing policy.

To alleviate these problems, the NSF solicited for a Routing Arbiter Service. Its role included peering with all routers at the NAP, and applying policy to incoming and outgoing routes in accordance with information in the distributed Internet Routing Registry (IRR).

The IRR represented a collaboration of the information in the NSFNET PRDB and the registries of the RIPE NCC in Europe, MCI, ANS, and CA*net. The format of the database was in accordance with RFC 1786, which was based on RIPE-181, the pioneering work of the European Routing Registry. A significant, tireless, and highly commendable effort on Merit's part converted the entire PRDB to RIPE-181 format.

It is important to understand that the Route Server does not pass data traffic. When re-announcing BGP routing updates that comply with the policy, the Route Server leaves the BGP next-hop attribute untouched, allowing data traffic to flow directly between the peering routers. The Route Server itself is, therefore, not really a significant packet-forwarding device. In fact, SPARCstation 20s were used to perform the functionality at each NAP.

By applying a centralized intelligence to route-exchange at each of the NAPs, it was also possible to collect statistics related to route-exchange that previously had been maintained by the NSFNET. Statistics included route-flaps, the number of networks announced, and the number of routed ASs.

Unfortunately, this centralized approach also posed a problem for the Route Server model. Even though two SPARCstations were deployed for redundancy reasons, certain NSPs (particularly the large ones) were reluctant to put their critical peering capability into someone else's hands—no matter how historically competent that person might be. That remained a factor, even if they could reduce the number of peering sessions from 50 or more to two, one for each Route Server. Ultimately, the Routing Arbiter service at the NAP was relegated to the roles of database collation and statistics collection.

Not surprisingly, NSF selected a partnership that included Merit Inc. to provide the Routing Arbiter Service.

Network Information Services, the InterNIC, and ARIN

These network information services represented a collection of functions previously undertaken by various organizations with strong NSFNET ties, or by other organizations to further the success of the Internet. The NSF was concerned that these should continue, and issued a solicitation and subsequent award to a joint team from AT&T, General Atomics, and Network Solutions Inc. This resulted in the establishment of the InterNIC, whose purpose was threefold:

- AT&T provided the database services. These included repository and lookup mechanisms for WHOIS and RFCs.

- General Atomics provided information services. Funding to GA was discontinued in February 1995 as the result of a performance review, which discovered that the agreed level of service was not being provided. NSI subsequently took on the role, which essentially involves fostering a relationship with users of the InterNIC and related services to gain feedback on their use.

- Finally, NSI was given the unenviable job of registration services. These included the allocation of Internet domains, addresses, and AS numbers. Policy on domain and address allocation has been an area of hot debate among the Internet community, so the services of NSI often receive extreme scrutiny.

IP address allocation policy has a significant impact on global Internet routing. When the NSFNET backbone was decommissioned, the global routing table contained almost 50,000 routes. As of this writing, almost the same number still exists, despite the enormous growth in the Internet since 1995. This has been achieved through two mechanisms:

- The first mechanism is a policy of allocating classless address space on a per-provider or geographical NIC basis. Large providers are allocated address blocks on non-natural net boundaries (Classes A, B, or C; from largest to smallest), which they then re-allocate to their own customers. In addition, international NICs (such as RIPE in Europe or the Asian Pacific NIC) are allocated very large address blocks for suballocation to providers in respective coverage regions.

- To be useful for keeping routing tables small, this new allocation policy is coupled with a second mechanism: classless interdomain routing (CIDR). Rather than utilizing routing tables containing natural nets and their subnets, the Internet router became classless. In other words, the routing tables were upgraded to support network entries with arbitrary masks. (Of course, this was not completely arbitrary—contiguous masks were always standard practice for global Internet routing and address allocation policy.)

NOTE   *Classless interdomain routing (CIDR)* circumvents the old Classes A, B, and C network boundaries by combining arbitrary networks and masks to form a prefix that is used for routing.

The BGP routing protocol was updated to version 4, primarily to allow *prefixes* (the combination of the network and the mask), rather than announcing classful networks to peers. Therefore, large providers could announce both supernets and subnets to their peers, significantly reducing the prefix count in core Internet routing tables. Indeed, based on their knowledge of address allocation history, many large providers began to actively filter incoming route announcements, ignoring those that did not meet their minimum size policy.

NSI also managed the allocation of domain names within the United States. Not surprisingly, the biggest area of contention was the .com domain because various companies disputed the allocation of particular domain names based on their registered names. Several court battles ensued, some inevitably involving NSI in one role or another. For the most part, NSI merely abided by the rulings of the courts.

NSI maintained the databases of the so-called *root nameservers,* which contain the zone files for all top-level domains. Although NSI operated root nameservers, there were many others around the world. Some operated on a voluntary or government-funded basis, and some operated to provide commercial service. NSI makes the root zone files available to operators of the root nameservers through methods other than DNS, such as FTP. All nameservers connected to the Internet are primed with the addresses of the root nameservers as a point of origin for the demand-based creation of a DNS cache.

The NSF funding of NSI served as an interim measure that enabled the Internet community to establish policies and procedures for governing the functions, and eventually to become self-sufficient. As a result of heavy consultation with IANA, the IETF, RIPE, the APNIC, and the NSF (among others), the American Registry for Internet Numbers (ARIN) became operational on December 22, 1997. IANA then transferred the role of assigning Internet addresses from NSI to ARIN.

ARIN, a not-for-profit body, operates under a self-funding procedure achieved through registration charges for new IP address allocations. The charge is levied annually and is proportional to the size of the address allocation. The funding model is based on experience reported by the APNIC and RIPE, and recognizes that the per-address price of allocations decreases with the size of the allocation. For example, an allocation of 8192 hosts (32 Class Cs) costs 30 U.S. cents per address per year. These charges are not applied to preARIN allocations.

Modern Internet Architecture

For some time, the FCC has been encouraging the telephony industry, through legislation, to allow competition in both the long-distance and local-area markets. The Internet is already there without legislation, but certainly has used the help of government policy through the NSF. From a technological viewpoint, the peer-to-peer model of IP has contributed greatly to the ease with which competition has been introduced.

Today, a number of national service providers operate peer networks, and compete for the same market segment in the same geographical area (see Figure 1-8). Similar arrangements exist abroad. In the final year or so of the twentieth century, there has been a consolidation of players through mergers or buyouts—at least five major NSPs exist within the United States. Some smaller commercial and larger federal networks still maintain peer status with the Big Five NSPs, although this is likely to change in time.

Figure 1-8 *Modern U.S. Internet Architecture*

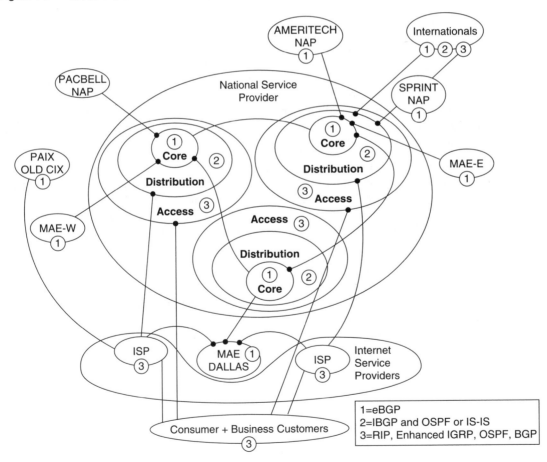

Within the United States, major NSPs peer at both public and private NAPS, with most tending toward the latter. The NAPs in San Jose, Washington, Pensauken, and Chicago are still important exchange points for the major NSPs—particularly for the middle-size NSPs and large federal networks. Peering always takes place via BGP.

Usually, the networks fall into the three-layer hierarchical model, consisting of a core, a distribution, and an access network:

- Peers usually connect their core routers via high-speed links and use BGP for route exchange. Core network links generally range between DS3 and OC12 speeds, traditionally using IP over HSSI, then ATM, and more recently directly over Sonet at OC12 and OC48.

  Core routing is usually achieved via internal BGP and either IS-IS or OSPF. Many of the larger providers prefer IS-IS, simply because of its demonstrated stability. Most large networks minimize the number of routes carried in the link-state backbone: In many cases, only the routes for links between routers themselves are necessary. This is sufficient to enable internal BGP as the workhorse that carries the bulk of the routes injected from the access layer (customers).

- Within the distribution layer, geographical regions may be divided into OSPF areas or IS-IS level 1 domains. Again, internal BGP is pervasive through the distribution layer. Due to its ease of administration and its capability of filtering routes, smaller networks may use RIP within the distribution layer, with subsequent redistribution into the link-state core. Wide-area technologies typically include ATM, Frame Relay, and T1.

- At the access level, several routing protocols may be found. In most cases, these are distance-vector protocols, such as BGP, RIP, IGRP, or even static routes because they can be readily filtered. Here, the widest range of Layer 2 technologies can be found, including Frame Relay, ATM, T1, SMDS, ISDN, ASDL, and, of course, POTS.

The Internet has come a long way since its four hosts in 1969. Figure 1-9 shows the astronomical growth of the network's hosts, networks, and domains.

Figure 1-9   *The Impressive Growth of the Network in Terms of Hosts, Networks, and Domains*

Date	Hosts	Date	Hosts	Networks	Domains
1969	4	07/89	130,000	650	3,900
04/71	23	10/89	159,000	837	
06/74	62	10/90	313,000	2,063	9,300
03/77	111	01/91	376,000	2,338	
08/81	213	07/91	535,000	3,086	16,000
05/82	235	10/91	617,000	3,556	18,000
08/83	562	01/92	727,000	4,526	
10/84	1,024	04/92	890,000	5,291	20,000
10/85	1,961	07/92	992,000	6,569	16,300
02/86	2,308	10/92	1,136,000	7,505	18,100
11/86	5,089	01/93	1,313,000	8,258	21,000
12/87	28,174	04/93	1,486,000	9,722	22,000
07/88	33,000	07/93	1,776,000	13,767	26,000
10/88	56,000	10/93	2,056,000	16,533	28,000
01/89	80,000	01/94	2,217,000	20,539	30,000
		07/94	3,212,000	25,210	46,000
		10/94	3,864,000	37,022	56,000
		01/95	4,852,000	39,410	71,000
		07/95	6,642,000	61,538	120,000
		01/96	9,472,000	93,671	240,000
		07/96	12,881,000	134,365	488,000
		01/97	16,146,000		828,000
		07/97	19,540,000		1,301,000

Evolution and Demise of Enterprise and Open Networks

This section discusses proprietary protocols and OSI protocols. The aim is not to explore every detail, which would take volumes, but rather to examine each protocol at a high-level. This discussion provides an account of the successes and failures of each protocol suite.

Systems Network Architecture

Released in 1973, SNA was IBM's blueprint for computer communications. SNA featured multiple domains in a strictly arranged hierarchy, which was ideal for the mainframe/terminal operational model. In addition, this represented a vast improvement over the single mainframe port-per-terminal approach that had been used previously. In many ways, SNA was a great contribution to networking because it operated predictably and reliably.

The original SNA hierarchy consisted of 3270 terminals connected to cluster controllers (CCs), which connected to local or remote front-end processors (FEPs), and then connected to the mainframe. Later enhancements provided for the PC terminal emulation software to connect to a CC via a Token Ring network (see Figure 1-10).

Figure 1-10 *The SNA Hierarchy and Comparison with the OSI Model*

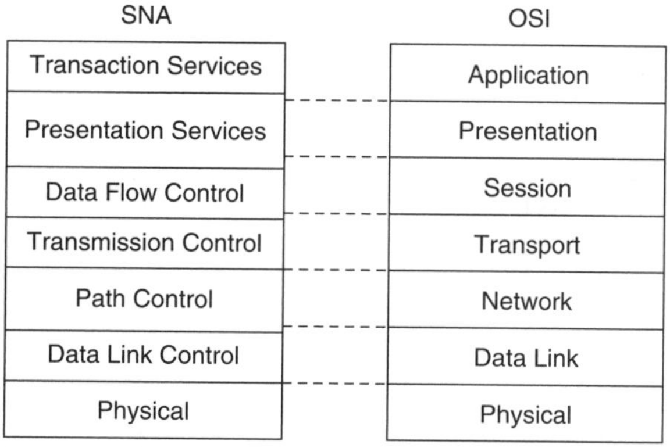

SNA	OSI
Transaction Services	Application
Presentation Services	Presentation
Data Flow Control	Session
Transmission Control	Transport
Path Control	Network
Data Link Control	Data Link
Physical	Physical

With only a limited scope for multiplexing, scalability proved to be more of a mainframe CPU issue than a problem of network or protocol design. SNA's demise was as much a result of its incapability of supporting peer-to-peer networking as its proprietary nature.

Although IBM introduced its advanced peer-to-peer networking, which improved on the mediocre routing functions of standard SNA, this only eased the support issues for legacy systems, and opened the doors for router vendors rather than creating new opportunities for IBM and SNA. Nevertheless, by the end of the 1980s, more than 20,000 licensed SNA sites existed. Support of SNA continues to be an important market. Connecting SNA islands is now accomplished with the support of IP tunneling techniques.

AppleTalk

The AppleTalk protocol was introduced in 1985, with further refinements in scalability and media support in 1989. Following the plug-and-play ideal of the Apple Macintosh computer, small AppleTalk networks required literally no configuration to share resources such as printers and disks.

AppleTalk maps fairly well to the OSI model of network protocol layering (see Figure 1-11). In addition to offering support for multiple physical media and link-level protocols, AppleTalk contained a datagram delivery protocol that was very similar to IP and offered equivalents of ARP, ping, and DNS.

One useful feature of AppleTalk, for small networks at least, is its capability of grouping users and resources into networking communities via the Zone Information Protocol (ZIP). No real notion of this feature exists in the TCP/IP suite: the function is left to higher-level applications.

Figure 1-11   *Comparison of AppleTalk and the OSI Model*

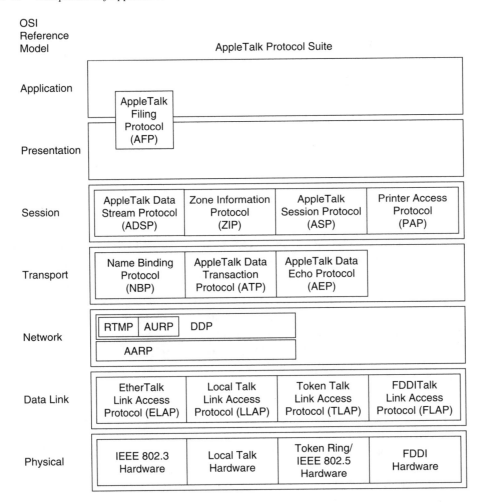

In terms of routing, AppleTalk included the Routing Table Maintenance Protocol, which is a RIP-derived, distance-vector protocol. In addition, the AppleTalk Update Routing Protocol (AURP) provided another set of scalability features, including tunneling over an IP WAN, route filtering for security purposes, hop count reduction to overcome the RTMP 16-hop limit, and additional routing metrics to provide more flexible use of alternate routes within the network.

AppleTalk supports a similar range of physical and data-link protocols to IP. The address structure is 24 bits, with 16 bits for the network identifier and an 8-bit node address. A physical LAN could support more than one network assigned in a similar manner as IP secondary addresses.

The plug-and-play characteristics of AppleTalk were no mean feat, but scalable self-configuration proved to be an incredible challenge. As AppleTalk networks became larger, more manual configuration became necessary to present the saturation of links with periodic topology and service information. Ultimately, AppleTalk was always associated with one vendor and, despite its strengths as a protocol suite, it suffered as Macintosh did as it lost its grip on market share.

Novell NetWare

It is debatable whether OSI or IPX represented the most serious contender to TCP/IP as the ubiquitous networking technology of the future. At one time, IPX enjoyed an installed base that far exceeded IP, and numerous plans arose to build the IPX equivalent of the Internet.

Novell NetWare (see Figure 1-12) is based upon a client-server paradigm, with the initial intent of sharing large disk volumes among a set of relatively meagerly equipped clients. As with AppleTalk, Novell NetWare employs a broadcast approach to network service advertisement, which presents significant issues when deployed on a large scale. IPX WANs often required the manual configuration of SAP filtering.

Figure 1-12 *Comparison of IPX and OSI Model*

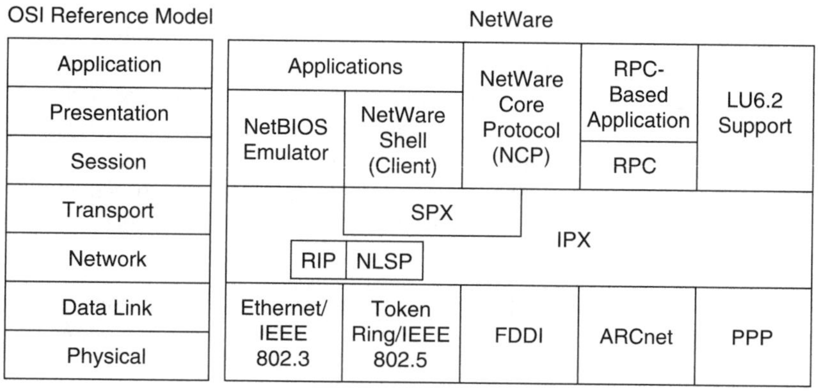

OSI Reference Model / NetWare

OSI Reference Model	NetWare				
Application	Applications		NetWare Core Protocol (NCP)	RPC-Based Application	LU6.2 Support
Presentation	NetBIOS Emulator	NetWare Shell (Client)			
Session				RPC	
Transport		SPX		IPX	
Network		RIP	NLSP		
Data Link	Ethernet/ IEEE 802.3	Token Ring/IEEE 802.5	FDDI	ARCnet	PPP
Physical					

IPX supports a similar range of physical and data-link protocols to IP. The real difference occurs at the network layer, where the Internetwork Packet Exchange Layer protocol (a derivative of the Xerox Network System [XNS] network layer) provides a connections-datagram delivery service. The IPX addressing structure differs from IP in the subnetwork, and MAC addresses are included in Layer 3. The full IPX addresses consist of a 16-bit socket number, a 32-bit subnetwork address, and a (typically) 48-bit node address corresponding to the data-link/MAC address of the node.

The Service Advertising Protocol (SAP) is the aforementioned broadcast service mechanism in IPX. Again, no real equivalent exists in IP, in which these services are left to the higher layers.

The NetWare Core Protocol (NCP) provides session control, including request differentiation, error-checking, and sequencing for communication between clients and servers. It includes a sequence, connection, and task number combination that performs a similar role to the source address/port, destination address/port, and socket ID 5-tuple used in TCP/UDP-based socket communication.

IPX routing also increased in sophistication, evolving from a distance-vector IPX Routing Information Protocol (RIP) protocol to the very sophisticated Network Link Service Protocol, based on the ISO IS-IS link-state protocol. NLSP works in conjunction with Novell's IPX WAN version 2 (IW2) specification to improve the behavior of IPX over WANs.

Ultimately, the depth of sophistication of the IP routing protocols, developed through years of refinement on the ARPANET and NSFNET, and the ease with which autonomously operated networks could be connected with IP, are leading to a slow decline of IPX in the wide-area networking environment. With the help of the Internet phenomenon, TCP/IP has now obtained critical mass, relegating IPX to a dwindling share in the local-area market.

DECNET

DEC's proprietary networking solution was introduced in 1976. It enjoyed fairly widespread deployment and underwent three revisions, which added scalability and host support as well as SNA gatewaying. This culminated in the release of DEC Network Architecture Phase IV (DNA IV) in 1982. DNA IV features a well-organized network-addressing hierarchy and a peer-to-peer networking philosophy similar in many ways to IP. Indeed, many of the large U.S. federal networks (notably ESNet and NSI) ran parallel DECNet and IP national and international infrastructures using early multiprotocol routers for many years. Some are still in use for specific applications.

Layers 1 and 2 of DNA are similar to the IP Protocol suite, with the sometimes annoying exception that DNA nodes modify their MAC-layer address based on a translation from the Layer 3 address (see Figure 1-13).

Therefore, there is no need for an equivalent of ARP in the DNA IV.

The network-layer address is 16 bits, with the first six bits used to identify an area and the remaining 10 bits used as a node address. Addresses are usually written in the form *area.node*, where area is 1–, and node is 1–1023. This area/node distinction enables DNA IV to perform hierarchical routing. Level 1 routing is used between nodes in the same area, and Level 2 routing is used between areas.

Figure 1-13   *Comparison of DNA IV and the OSI Model*

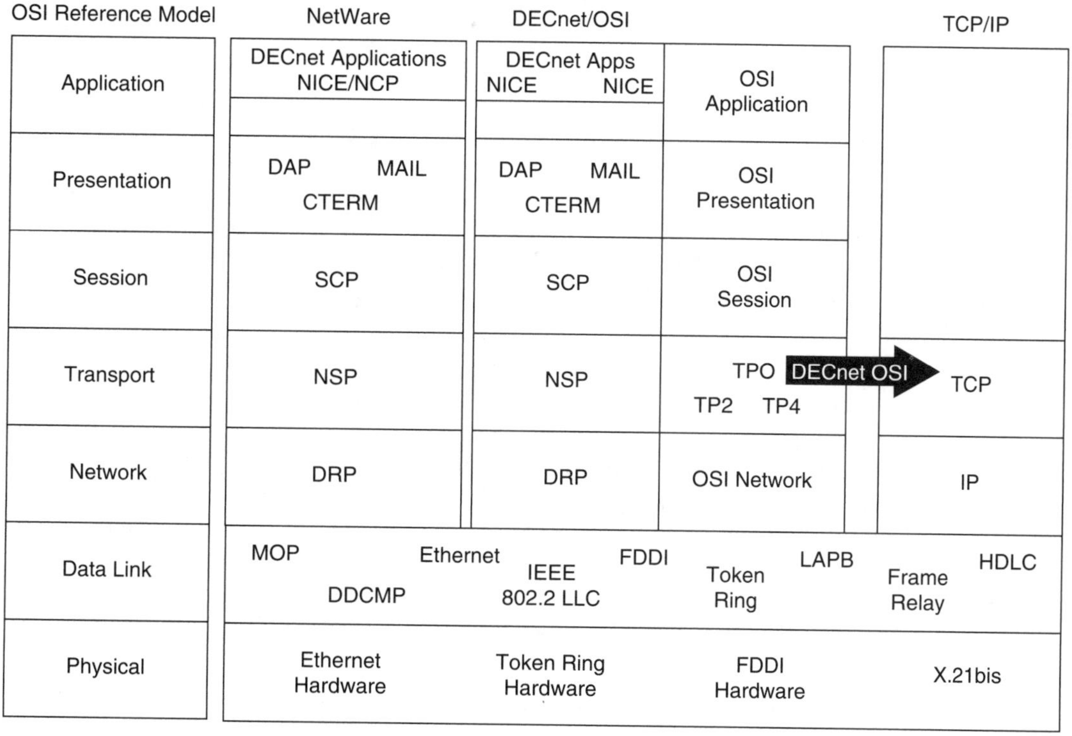

OSI Reference Model	NetWare	DECnet/OSI		TCP/IP
Application	DECnet Applications NICE/NCP	DECnet Apps NICE NICE	OSI Application	
Presentation	DAP MAIL CTERM	DAP MAIL CTERM	OSI Presentation	
Session	SCP	SCP	OSI Session	
Transport	NSP	NSP	TP0 DECnet OSI ▶ TP2 TP4	TCP
Network	DRP	DRP	OSI Network	IP
Data Link	MOP Ethernet FDDI DDCMP IEEE 802.2 LLC		Token LAPB Ring	Frame HDLC Relay
Physical	Ethernet Hardware	Token Ring Hardware	FDDI Hardware	X.21bis

This arrangement enforces a network design that provides for efficient route computation. A similar effect can be achieved in IP networks using hierarchical address allocation and summarization. As with IP secondary networks, nodes in different areas commonly share the same physical media.

The DECNET Routing Protocol (DRP) is a distance-vector protocol. Instead of using hop counts, however, it relies on path costs assigned to each link by the network manager. Of course, if the path costs in the network are all 1, the DRP looks very similar to RIP. DRP advertises nodes in the case of Level 1 routing, and advertises areas in the case of Level 2. As with modern RIP implementation, DRP updates are triggered by network events and are backed up by periodic retransmission.

Many of the ideas and experience gained with DECNET have been used to refine the Internet Protocol suite. As with the other proprietary protocols, DECNET was mainly limited to DEC hardware platforms, and this limited its deployment to some extent. In recognition of this, DEC undertook the development of DNA V on the basis of the OSI protocol suite.

Open Systems Interconnect

No discussion of the evolution of data networking would be complete without some commentary on OSI.

Benefits of OSI

By the early 1980s, the networking community was tired of being tied to proprietary networking solutions. To promote a smoother system with more support, both hosts and networking infrastructure had to come from the same vendor. Admittedly, development according to standards could squash creativity, but from a customer perspective, this was an acceptable price to pay for establishing the data networking arena as one in which multiple vendors could play.

The problem, then, was deemed a lack of standards. In the mid-1970s, a group of technical staff at Honeywell working on distributed database design saw the need for a standardized, layered communications architecture. The group surveyed a number of proprietary protocols and examined the ARPANET experiment. The researchers came to the conclusion that layering was indeed a key need in any standardization effort. In 1977, they invented a seven-layer model—about the same time as the British Standards Institute was convincing the ISO of the need for a standardized communication mechanism. After the Honeywell group proposed the seven-layer model, ANSI submitted it as the United States' contribution to the ISO standardization efforts. In March, 1978, the ISO reached consensus that the model met most foreseeable needs.

Figure 1-14 shows a comparison of the OSI model, OSI, and the IP suite.

The OSI protocol was designed by committee. This approach differed from, say, the IETF design process, in which a model had to be implemented and proven to work before it could be approved as a standard. One commentator likened the OSI design effort to creating a time machine—the focus was to design the protocols to be capable of all foreseeable necessary functions.

This proposed layering model was not new, but it enabled each OSI subcommittee to conduct its design efforts relatively independently. The subcommittee incorporated at least some well-established standards into the framework, especially those in the lower layers, such as ISDN, X25, and the IEEE LANs. The groups also spent considerable time refining and developing new ideas related to routing protocols, such as IS-IS, hierarchy in network design and end-station addressing, error-correction and flow control in transport protocols, session protocols, and network management, to provide the impetus to SNMP. The subcommittees also pioneered work in presentation-layer protocols and network protocol conformance testing.

Figure 1-14   *Comparison of OSI model, OSI, and IP Protocol*

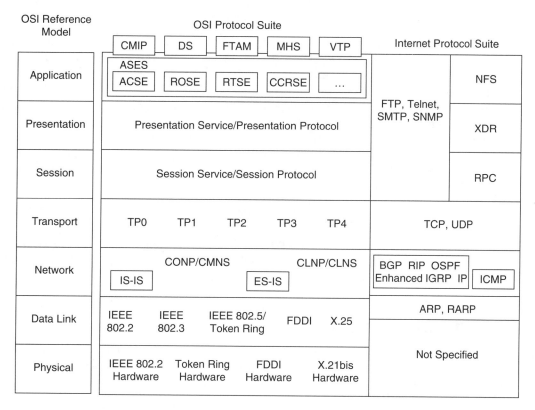

Drawbacks of OSI

OSI standards tended to be overly rigid, however, with respect to layering. In addition, they were cumbersome and slow because of the need to support all contingencies, and the standards were developed slowly because consensus was hard to reach. The success of OSI played upon customer and government fears of depending on a single vendor, yet, with a few exceptions, failed to encourage useful implementations.

The standards were written in the style of legalese, which made them difficult to read and understand. They were even more difficult to obtain. To make matters worse, vendors began nit-picking on the basis of a standard's wording (unfortunately, this is an increasing trend with respect to Internet RFCs).

OSI took the attitude that the industry must conform. Unfortunately, only the larger vendors—notably DEC—could afford to do so, for all the previously mentioned reasons. Users themselves, with the exception of the government, did not want to pay for or understand the complexity. Thus, it became cheaper and necessary to run multiprotocol networks. This provided an opportunity for smaller vendors to develop simpler robust protocols, based on the evolution of operational technology.

OSI ultimately was unsuccessful because it was fundamentally over-engineered. The "rough consensus and running code" approach of the IETF and the resulting growth of the Internet infrastructure created an installed base with which neither OSI nor any of the proprietary protocols could compete. In many respects, this was unfortunate because OSI offered solutions to many of the problems that plagued the IP suites. Nevertheless, as with many other product development endeavors, the process turned into a game of numbers, in which time-to-market and installed base were critical. The foresight of the original designers of IP was probably only extended 20 years or so, but it is unlikely that OSI would have been an improvement. Had they limited their scope to only the most pressing issues of the designs, many more protocols may have been deployed and used today.

In the beginning of this chapter, you read that development is cyclical. Ideas that were once too cumbersome to implement may become possible, even easy, as technology develops. Many people in the industry believe that OSI offers only historical significance. However, remember that what lies in history is often the key to the future, and the OSI documents contain many good ideas yet to be implemented.

The Future of the Internet

The world of IP networking certainly has a rosy future. The industry anticipates a general convergence of voice and data networks. Gateways between traditional voice networks and IP networks are already commercially available, and many multimedia applications now support operation over an IP network.

As the installed base of fiber increases, you can expect IP routers to interface directly to fiber via Packet Over Sonet (POS) at extremely high speeds. Each fiber interface may support thousands of aggregated customer connections.

Router technology will, therefore, need both speed enhancements and feature enhancements to provide gateway capabilities for today's legacy voice networks. Massive increases in the number of users could also place extreme demands on the routing protocols underlying the Internet infrastructure, unless a more scalable method than simple globally-unique IP addresses is used to identify network users.

Does this mean that the future of communications needs will be met by a single IP network infrastructure that directly reaches the desktop or CATV outlet? It is likely that such a convergence will occur, although it will be a few years before full convergence is available in pilot areas—and many years before this technology propagates throughout the world.

However, the single home communications and entertainment interface is not far off—and whatever physical form it takes, it is a good bet that the network protocol will be IP.

Summary

This chapter provided a fairly detailed history of the development of the Internet. From the early ARPANET experiment, through the NSFNET, to the commercialization of the Internet infrastructure, you have seen that simplicity, scalability, and the willingness of its developers to start small and think big were critical to the success of the Internet. In particular, the following high-level issues were discussed:

- The motivation behind the design of IP
- The importance of hierarchy in network design, and how it improved scaling from the experimental ARPANET to the commercial Internet of today
- How a router's architecture affects IP switching performance
- The role of interior routing protocols, and the application of interior protocols within the ARPANET
- The need for exterior routing protocols, and how they aided the segmentation of the Internet into the NSFNET backbone and the regional networks
- The importance of network operations, management, and standards, as well as the roles played by the IETF, Interop, the InterNIC, and Merit
- The convergence of application technology onto IP networks, including multimedia Web content and the MBONE
- Why OSI and proprietary protocols met their demise, despite being technically superior to IP in many ways

The remainder of this book examines these concepts in more detail.

Review Questions

1 What is the difference between the core and backbone layers of a network?

2 Who owns the Internet?

3 Who manages the Internet?

4 What is the difference between an ISP and an NSP?

5 Are the NSFNET, ARPANET, and the Big Four still in existence?

6 Were the NSFNET routers ever sold commercially?

Answers:

1 No difference exists between the core and backbone layers of a network—they are one and the same. Similarly, "distribution" and "regional" networks are used interchangeably, as are "access," "perimeter," and "edge" networks.

2 No single organization owns the Internet. As with the telephone network, portions of it are owned by large national and international companies, and even, in the case of the infrastructure in your home, by individuals.

3 The Internet is managed collaboratively by Internet service providers throughout the world. There is no central management authority, but there is a spirit of cooperation spurred by the business needs of the providers.

4 NSPs were originally used to describe the small number of providers who ran a national network and carried the full Internet routing table. ISPs were customers of NSPs. More recently, the term "Tier 1" ISPs is being used in place of NSPs. In the generic sense, an ISP is anyone who maintains an infrastructure that provides Internet connectivity to customers.

5 In one form or another, these "Big Four" still exist. Some of the Big Four networks have effectively become government intranets. NSFNET is still heavily involved in vBNS, and DARPA still runs an IP network for research purposes.

6 The NSFNET routers were never sold as a large-scale commercial venture. However, many of the ideas (and people) involved in the NSFNET moved on to contribute to products developed by commercial vendors or to ISP engineering.

For Further Reading . . .

Black, Uyless. *ISDN and SS7*. Upper Saddle River, NJ: Prentice Hall, 1997.

Comer, Douglas. *Internetworking with TCP/IP, Volume 1*. Upper Saddle River, NJ: Prentice Hall, 1991.

Dickie, Mark. *Routing in Today's Internetworks*. New York, NY: John Wiley & Sons, 1994.

Ford, Merilee (Editor), H. Kim Lew, Steve Spanier, and Tim Stevenson. *Internetworking Technologies Handbook*. Indianapolis, IN: Cisco Press, 1997.

Halabi, Bassam. *Internet Routing Architectures*. Indianapolis, IN: Cisco Press, 1997.

ITU-TU. *Recommendation Q.708*.

Keshav, Srinivasan. *An Engineering Approach to Computer Networking*. Reading, MA: Addison-Wesley, 1997.

Krol, Ed. *The Whole Internet: User's Guide and Catalog*. Cambridge, MA: O'Reilly & Associates, 1995.

Kumar, Vinay. *MBONE: Interactive Multimedia on the Internet*. Indianapolis, IN: New Riders, 1996.

Leiner, *et al.* "A Brief History of the Internet: Part 1." *On the Internet Magazine*. The Internet Society, 1997.

Perlman, Radia. *Interconnections: Bridges and Routers.* Reading, MA: Addison-Wesley, 1992.

RFC 823. *The DARPA Internet Gateway.*

RFC 891. *DCN Local Network Protocols.*

RFC 1009. *Requirements for Internet Gateways.*

RFC 1222. *Advancing the NSFNET Routing Architecture.*

RFC 1133. *Routing Between the NSFNET and the DDN.*

RFC 1787. *Routing in a Multi-provider Internet.*

Russell, Travis. *Signaling System #7.* New York, NY: McGraw-Hill, 1995.

This chapter provides an overview of the IP routing fundamentals, including the following issues:

Basic IP concepts   The Internet Protocol provides service between hosts, and transfers information in the form of packets, with the assumption that the underlying networks consists of different media and technologies.

Variable-length subnet masking   When an IP address is assigned to an organization, the network portion of the address is fixed, and the host portion is given to the organization to assign internal addresses. Organizations can further divide the network into smaller segments called subnets. In this section, we discuss variable-length subnet masking within this context.

Classless interdomain routing (CIDR)   The growth of the Internet caused the networking industry to seriously consider the growth of routing tables for Internet routers. As smaller companies began to advertise their services to the rest of the Internet, the routing table began to grow exponentially. To curb the growth of routing tables on the Internet, CIDR was introduced. With CIDR, groups of contiguous class C and class B networks can be advertised as one route.

IP routing   All traffic sent from a source to a destination must be routed if the source and destination are not directly connected. A router that connects to the source looks at the destination inside the IP packet, and routes the packet toward the destination based on its routing table. If the router does not have a route to the destination, the packet is silently dropped.

## CHAPTER 2

IP Fundamentals

Basic IP Concepts

Internet Protocol (IP) routing is the heart of the Internet today. It is the only protocol that carries information between different domains. All other protocols (for example, Novell and AppleTalk) work locally within their own domains.

Because IP is designed to send information packets from source to destination without understanding the underlying technologies, it does not guarantee delivery of the packet. It simply puts forth its best effort to send the packet to its destination. IP packets that are sent using the best-effort delivery are sometimes called datagram services. Because IP is also connectionless, there is no guarantee that all the data packets from the same connection will follow the same path or be delivered in order.

IP can communicate across any set of interconnected networks. It is as well suited for a local-area network (LAN) as a wide-area network (WAN), largely because of bandwidth economy. The protocol will pass datagrams, which are blocks of data packages of bits, regardless of the underlying media.

The creation and documentation of IP is similar to an academic research project. Protocols are specified in documents called Requests for Comments (RFCs), which are official standards in the Internet community. Just as in academic research, RFCs are generated after discussions take place between people of various backgrounds, such as industry and academia. Usually, an RFC is the work of several people with experience in networking.

IP is a Layer 3 protocol in the Open Systems Interconnect (OSI) model. The OSI model is divided into seven layers, as shown in Figure 2-1. Protocols working in each layer perform a specific function and service only the protocols in the adjacent layers.

IP services the data link and transport protocols. The network layer protocol's function is to provide path selection between different systems, such as routing, translation between different media types, and subnet flow control. Thus, the protocol forms a virtual connection between endpoints. In addition to Internet routing, IP provides fragmentation and reassembly of datagrams, and error reporting.

The mode of operation for IP is to transmit datagrams from one application to another on a different machine. IP modules attach the datagram header, and then attach the data to it. The IP model determines the local address of the machine, and then attaches this Internet address for identification by the local machine.

Packet size is limited because the packet traverses multiple transmission units. Therefore, it is necessary for IP to provide fragmentation. The identification field aids in identifying the fragments for reassembly.

Reassembly occurs at the receiving machine. In this process, the receiver of the fragment uses the identification field to ensure that fragments of different datagrams are not mixed.

NOTE   In error-reporting, IP is not a reliable datagram service; it is a best-effort delivery. A separate protocol called Internet Control Message Protocol (ICMP) provides basic support for IP as if it were a higher-layer protocol. ICMP should be an integral part of IP.

Figure 2-1   *Seven-Layer OSI Model*

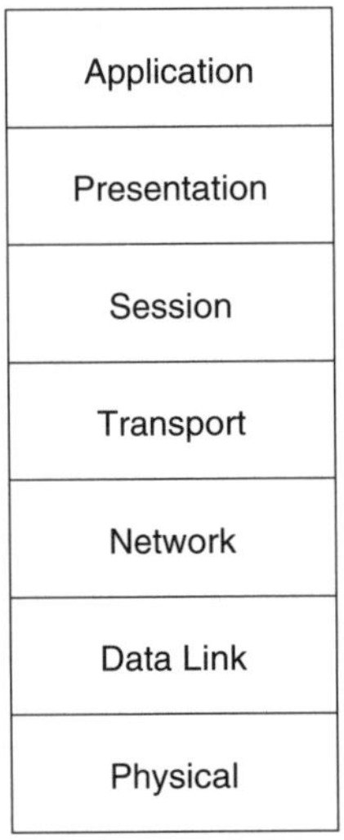

| Application |
| Presentation |
| Session |
| Transport |
| Network |
| Data Link |
| Physical |

IP Parameters

IP is responsible for transmitting a datagram from an application program on one machine to another machine. The sending application prepares the data and passes it to its local IP module. The IP module prepares a datagram header and attaches the application data to it (see Figure 2-2). IP then passes the packet to the local network interface for transmission.

Figure 2-2   *The IP Module*

Version	IHL	Type of Service	Total Length
Identification		Flags	Fragment Offset
Time to Live	Protocol Header		Checksum
Source Address			
Destination Address			
Options			Padding

Information contained in the IP header is used to send the packet toward the destination. The following parameters define the IP packet:

- *IP Header*   The IP header is 20 bytes long, unless options are present. Options may or may not appear in the datagram. All IP modules (host or routers) must implement options.

- *Options*   This field varies in length, and may contain zero or more options. There are two cases for the format of option:

    Case 1: A single octet of option-type
    Case 2: An option-type octet, an option-length octet, and the actual option data octet

    Currently, these Internet options are defined: security, loose source routing, strict source routing, record route, and time stamp.

- *Version*   The IP header begins with the version number. The current version running on the Internet is four, so IP is sometimes referred to as IPv4.

- *IP Header Length (IHL)*   This field indicates header length in 32-bit words. A four-bit field limits the header length to 60 bytes.

- *Type of Service (TOS)*   This parameter indicates how the upper-layer protocols would like to manage the current datagram. TOS bits are used for delay, reliability, throughput, and cost. Only one of the values can be used at one time. If the values are set to 0, the current datagram is sent with normal service.

- *Total Length*   This parameter indicates the total length (in bytes) of the packet, including the data and the header.

- *Identification*   This field contains an integer that identifies the current datagram, and is used to piece the fragments together. The identification is set by the sender of the packet to aid in assembling the fragments of the datagram.

- *Flags*   Three bits are used to indicate fragmentation. One bit indicates whether the packet is fragmented. The last bit indicates whether the packet is the last packet in the fragment series.

  Bit 0: This bit must be 0.
  Bit 1: If set to 1, the packet will not be fragmented. If set to 0, it may be fragmented.
  Bit 2: If set to 0, this is the last fragment. If set to 1, more fragments will follow.

- *Time To Live (TTL)*   This parameter maintains a counter that gradually decrements to zero, at which point the datagram is discarded. This allows the packet an escape from routing loops.

- *Protocol*   This indicates the upper-layer protocol that will receive the packet after the IP processing is complete. The values of various protocols are specified in the assigned RFCs.

- *Header Checksum*   Used to check the IP header, the IP checksum affects only the IP header, not the data. Some fields in the IP header (TTL) are variable, so the checksum is recomputed and verified at each point the header passes.

- *Source Address*   This field specifies the source address of the datagram and points to the sending node. When a host sends an IP packet, this field puts the address in the packet to identify the originator of the datagram.

- *Destination Address*   This field specifies the destination of the datagram and points to the receiving node.

IP Addressing

Routing of IP datagrams is clearly dependent on the IP addressing scheme. An IP address is 32 bits, divided into two parts by default and sometimes into three parts through *subnetting*, which is explained later in this chapter. The first part is the network address; the second part is the host address. Subnet addresses are present only if the administrator decides to use subnets. IP addresses are represented in dotted decimal format. After an organization is assigned an IP address, the network portion of the address cannot be changed by the network administrator. However, the network administrator does have the authority to change the host portion of the network. All networks are not designed around one wire; most networks have multiple segments, as shown in Figure 2-3.

IP addressing supports five network classes. The first three left-most bits in the first octet indicate the network class. In the case of class D, the fourth bit is also included (see Figure 2-4).

Figure 2-3   *Subnetting Shown for Network 131.108.0.0/16*

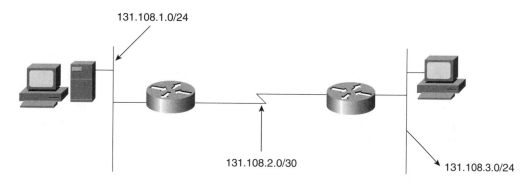

131.108.1.0/24

131.108.2.0/30

131.108.3.0/24

Major net 131.108.0.0/16
Divide the network into subnets
131.108.1.0/24
131.108.2.0/30
131.108.3.0.24

Figure 2-4   *IP Addressing Supports Five Network Classes*

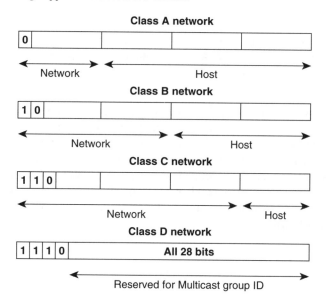

- *Class A*   Currently used by very few large networks, this class provides only seven bits for the network field and 24 bits for the host portion. It ranges from one to 127 network numbers.

- *Class B*   In this class, 14 bits are allocated for the network portion and 16 bits are used for the host portion, which provides an even balance between network and host portions. Class B networks range from 128 to 191 decimal values in the first octet.

- *Class C*   This class allocates 22 bits for the network portion and eight bits for the host portion. Within class C, hosts per network is a limiting factor. The range of class C addresses is from 192 to 223 decimal values in the first octet. In class C networks, only 255 hosts could be assigned per network.

- *Class D*   Reserved for multicast groups, this class consists of a range of addresses from 224 to 239 decimal values in the first octet.

- *Class E*   This class is reserved for future use. (Not shown in diagram.)

Subnetting

Subnetworks, or subnets, provide flexibility to a network by dividing a large network into smaller units. This is useful when a multi-level, hierarchical routing structure is needed. Subnets are arbitrary divisions created by the network administrator to protect a large network from the addressing complexity of attached networks. In IP, subnets share a particular subnet address.

Subnets may be used, for example, in a large network that extends to several parts of the world. In the absence of a hierarchy created by subnetting, we would not have the capability of extending the network in size. For example, a non-hierarchical, or flat, network, such as an Ethernet, would not be able to extend the network or connect the hosts from the United States to Japan.

Subnetting is carried out using the host address portion of the network address and the subnet mask, which is explained in the following section. In a class A network, the first seven bits are the network address and the last 24 bits are used for the host portion. The entire host portion theoretically can share the same network, but it is impractical to configure such a large number of hosts on the same physical network. Host bits could be used to further divide the network, rather than changing the network number. Similarly, in a class B network, the first 14 bits are the network address and the last 16 bits are the host address. Classes of networks will be discussed further in later sections.

Subnet Masking

Before fully explaining how subnetting is performed, it is necessary to define subnet masking. Recall that the network portion of the address cannot be changed. For a router to decide what part of the address is the network and what part is the host, a 32-bit number is used to mask out each portion.

This mask performs a logical AND operation with the IP address. Wherever the mask is binary one, it is considered the network portion; when the mask is zero, it is considered the host. A zero in the network portion tells the router not to consider this part of the network during routing decisions (see Figure 2-5).

Figure 2-5   *Subnetting Using the Logical AND Operation*

```
Decimal                         Binary
Address 131.108.0.0             1000 0011.0110 1100.0000 0000.0000 0000
Mask 255.255.0.0                1111 1111.1111 1111.0000 0000.0000 0000
```

If you want to do subnetting, you can mask the host portion for the router. If you want to use eight bits from the host portion of the address, then this is 8-bit masking—at this point, we will have 254 subnets for the class B network.

```
Decimal                         Binary
Address 131.108.0.0             1000 0011.0110 1100.0000 0000.0000 0000
Mask 255.255.255.0              1111 1111.1111 1111.1111 1111.0000 0000
```

Subnetting is performed by borrowing bits from the host portion of the address, and then using them to indicate different segments on the network. A network administrator can borrow any number of bits from the host portion, as long as a few bits are left available to assign host addresses.

NOTE   *Subnetting* extends the network portion of the assigned address to accommodate all physical segments of a network.

Subnetting Example

In network 131.108.0.0, suppose that you want to perform eight-bit masking of the class B network. Recall that the first two bytes cannot be altered in a class B network. Therefore, to perform subnet masking, you must borrow bits from the third byte and use it completely.

As mentioned earlier, subnet masking is performed by borrowing bits from the host portion of the assigned network address, which assigns more routable network addresses within the assigned network address. For subnet masking, you would perform a logical AND operation between the network number and the mask assigned, as shown here:

> 1 ANDed with 1 = 1
> 1 ANDed with 0 = 0

For eight-bit masking, you can further divide the network into smaller segments to produce the following:

```
    ^8
2 - 2 =  256 - 2 = 254 subnets
```

All zeros and all ones signify the broadcast address so that they usually cannot be assigned as the subnet, but Cisco Systems does allow subnet zero to be used as a subnet address. To enable the subnet zero as an IP subnet, you must use the **ip subnet zero** command:

```
ip subnet zero
```

This should be done carefully to ensure that there are no old hosts that do not understand subnet zero as the broadcast address. Cisco leaves the choice to the network administrator. If the administrator is sure that all hosts in the network do not treat subnet zero as the broadcast address, this additional subnet can be used on the network.

Subnetting is completed between the network number and the subnet mask by a logical AND operation:

```
131.108.0.0
255.255.255.0
```

When a logical AND is performed between the network numbers, the third byte is advertised as the network portion. Recall that anything ANDed with one yields the same number. If you assign an IP address of 131.108.1.1 to an interface, the result, after performing the logical AND with the mask, is 131.108.1.0—anything ANDed with zero yields zero.

Subnetting is performed to assign addresses to different segments of networks, as well as to isolate the broadcast domains. It also provides more flexibility to a network.

On the host portion of each subnet, there is a maximum of 254 hosts. Remember, however, that there are eight bits left for the host portion because the network was subnetted after borrowing eight bits from the assigned class B network address. Because eight bits are left for the host portion, there are 256–2 addresses left for each host per subnet. You cannot use all zeros and all ones in an address, which disqualifies two addresses out of the 256 host addresses.

Variable-Length Subnet Masking

With eight-bit masking, there are 254 subnets and 254 hosts per subnet. This model works well on transit broadcast networks, in which a large number of hosts share a common media. As shown in Figure 2-6, the serial line needs only two addresses to assign an address with a subnet mask of /24. Therefore, leaving space for 254 hosts is a waste of address space.

Address waste is a serious problem in today's networks. Obtaining an IP address is difficult because of constant growth and increasing numbers of users. Aggressive effort is required to spare address space from being used inappropriately. This issue will be discussed further in the next section, "Classless Interdomain Routing."

For this reason, you should perform variable-length subnet masking (VLSM) with point-to-point networks. VLSM grants transit broadcast networks a large number of bits for the host portion, and only allows the point-to-point network to use two bits for the host portion.

NOTE	Using a different mask for several types of media within the same major network is called variable-length subnet masking.

You can subnet further for the serial link so that each link has only two addresses to assign to it—one for each end of the link's connection. For example, suppose you wanted to further subnet the 131.108.10.0 subnet. You know that the original subnet mask was the eighth bit in the third octet. For the serial point-to-point connection, you can perform additional masking in the fourth octet, to essentially create a subnet of a subnet.

As shown in Figure 2-7 depicting serial links, you can use the same third octet value of two and further subnet the fourth octet. Figure 2-7 shows the new subnets. The original subnet of 131.108.2.0/24 is now further divided into additional subnets of 131.108.2.0/30–131.108.2.252/30.

If you borrow six bits from the fourth octet and leave two bits for the host portion, the result is as follows:

$$2^6 - 2 = 64$$

In this case, the serial line addresses are 131.108.2.0 and 255.255.255.252, and the host addresses are 131.108.2.1 and 131.108.2.2. You cannot assign addresses of 131.108.2.0 and 131.108.2.3 as the host address because they become the broadcast address for this subnet. This way, you then can reach 131.108.2.252.255.255.255.0 with the host addresses of 131.108.2.253 and 131.108.2.254. Similarly, you cannot assign host addresses of 131.108.2.252 and 131.108.2.255 because they are the broadcast address for this subnet.

Figure 2-6 *VLSM for Point-to-Point Links*

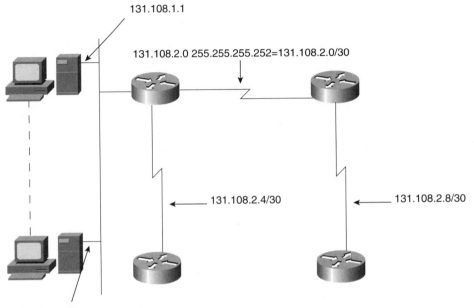

Classless Interdomain Routing

As the popularity of the Internet has grown, it has become the global media for the transfer of information.

However, as popularity increased, new problems continued to appear. Small organizations applied for IP addresses, but providing them all with a class A or class B address was not feasible. Instead, these organizations were assigned class C addresses, or, in a large number of cases, multiple class Cs. With such a large distribution of IP addresses, the routing table on the Internet began to grow exponentially. This is the reason CIDR entered the arena.

The following issues led to CIDR:

- Lack of midsize address space and exhaustion of the class B network address space. Class C is quite small (with 254 hosts), and class B is relatively large (with 65,534 addresses).

- Growth of Internet routing tables.

- Eventual exhaustion of the 32-bit IP address space.

It became evident that the first two problems needed to be addressed immediately. This led to the proposal of RFC 1519, which prompted slower growth of the Internet routing table by condensing groups of network addresses that fell within close range (called *route aggregation*).

Route aggregation is performed similar to masking, which led to its other name, *supernetting*. With CIDR, the masks in the assigned address are grouped into one update. If an ISP holds an address range for several class C networks, it does not need to advertise all the specific networks. The ISP simply can send one update by supernetting them.

NOTE   *Route aggregation* is the grouping of contiguous class C or class B networks into one update.

As an example of route aggregation, assume that ISP A owns class C networks from 201.1.0.0 to 201.1.127.0. Instead of the ISP advertising all the class C networks, it can group them into one update and advertise a single supernet network. Supernetting helped significantly slow the growth of routing tables on the Internet routers.

As shown in Figure 2-8, ISP A does not need to advertise all the specific routes from its customer to the neighboring ISP B. Instead, ISP A can send only a single route to all its neighboring ISPs because it can target specific customers. The neighboring ISPs only need to forward traffic to ISP A for the range of networks.

Figure 2-7   *Introduction of CIDR and Route Aggregation*

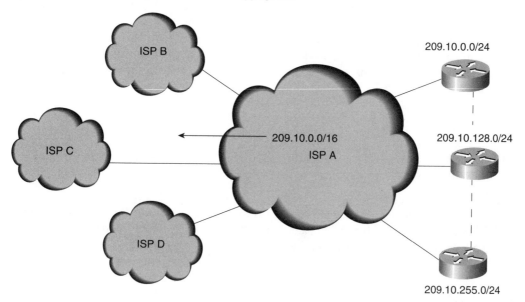

IP Routing

In the section on subnetting, you learned how a network is divided into smaller groups known as subnets. Each subnet is given an individual identity. All subnets need to be advertised by an algorithm within the autonomous system, and the network as a whole must be advertised outside the system.

To propagate the network within the autonomous system and beyond, *routing protocols* are used. Routing protocols are divided into two types: First, *Interior Gateway Protocols (IGPs)* are used to propagate routing information within an autonomous system. Second, *Exterior Gateway Protocols (EGPs)* are used to pass routing information between autonomous systems.

Routing protocols running on the Internet include Routing Information Protocol (RIP), Open Shortest Path First (OSPF), and Intermediate System-to-Intermediate System (IS-IS). All these protocols are standards-based. In addition, both the Interior Gateway Routing Protocol (IGRP) and the Enhanced IGRP are Cisco-proprietary protocols. The only EGP presently on the Internet is BGP, and the current version is four. Each of these protocols is briefly introduced in the following sections.

RIP

RIP is a distance-vector protocol that uses the Balman Ford algorithm to compute the shortest route to the destination. It is based on hop count, and does not have the capability to detect real-time parameters for making proper decisions to reach a destination. This protocol also has a hard limit of 15 hops, which a network cannot exceed. For more information about RIP, see Chapter 6, "Routing Information Protocol," and Chapter 7, "Routing Information Protocol Version 2."

IGRP

IGRP is also based on distance-vector routing. Cisco developed this protocol in response to RIP's shortcomings—for example, routers ignore a better bandwidth route in favor of a shorter hop path.

IGRP has more intelligence to make routing decisions than RIP. It relies on composite metrics of load, reliability, delay, bandwidth, and MTU. It does not have the 15-hop limit—an IGRP network can use up to 254 hops, thereby increasing the dimension of the network.

Enhanced IGRP

Enhanced IGRP is an advanced distance vector. Unlike RIP and IGRP, this protocol ensures that updates are not propagated beyond the affected nodes, ensuring that the entire network is unaffected. This protocol uses diffuse update algorithm (DUAL) to achieve rapid, loop-free convergence. Every router maintains a neighbor table, as well as the relevant information received from the neighbor. For more information on Enhanced IGRP, see Chapter 8, "Enhanced Interior Gateway Routing Protocol."

OSPF and IS-IS

OSPF and IS-IS are both link-state protocols; each router within an area maintains an identical database. Every router advertises all its connected functional links after the information is received in the database. Then, the SPF algorithm is executed to find the shortest path to the destination.

BGP

BGP exchanges routing information between autonomous systems. It is called a path-vector protocol because it carries path information from the source, and attaches all the systems that the route has traversed. This path information is used to detect routing loops. As networks grow and large organizations merge, BGP is increasingly moving into enterprise backbones because of its scalability. BGP was designed to handle routing updates and route processing for the dynamic Internet environment.

Summary

In this chapter, you learned the fundamentals of IP and its addressing structure. IP can communicate across any set of interconnected networks, but is not a reliable datagram service; it is a best-effort delivery. An IP address is 32 bits, which includes a network address and a host address.

You also learned about subnets, subnet masking, variable-length masking, and why they are necessary. Subnets provide flexibility to a network by dividing a large network into smaller units, so that the entire network is not restricted by one network address. Subnet masking is performed by borrowing bits from the host portion of the assigned network address, so that more routable network addresses may be assigned within the network address. Variable-length masking is crucial for preserving valuable address space and to allow continued growth of a network.

Another area covered in this chapter is Classless Interdomain Routing. CIDR controls the size of Internet routing tables. It assists the ISP environment by limiting the number of routes advertised, which is done by condensing the number of contiguous prefixes that ISP must advertise.

Finally, you were introduced to the two types of major routing processes currently used on the Internet: Interior Gateway Protocols and Exterior Gateway Protocols. IGPs include RIP, OSPF, IS-IS and EIGRP; EGPs include only BGP. You will read about each of these in more depth in the following chapters.

Review Questions

1 How long is an IP address?

2 When is the best time to perform subnet masking? When is not good practice to use it?

3 What is route aggregation? When should it be utilized?

Answers:

1 An IP address is 32 bits long and is divided into four octets. Each octet is separated by a dotted decimal, as in 131.108.1.1.

2 Subnet masking is necessary for any IP network, even when you have a single interface and cannot attach thousands of hosts. If you have a large number of hosts in your network, you should subnet to separate broadcast domains.

3 Route aggregation deals with groupings of contiguous addresses. You should perform it as a regular practice whenever you have a contiguous block of addresses, or major nets that are all behind a certain router. You should remove unnecessary routing information, so that it is not sent where it is not required.

For Further Reading . . .

RFC 791

Stevens, W. Richard. *TCP/IP Illustrated, Volume 1*. Reading, MA: Addison-Wesley, 1994.

This chapter provides an overview of current local-area network (LAN), wide-area network (WAN), and metropolitan-area network (MAN) technologies, emphasizing their use in deploying IP networks. In particular, you will learn about the following:

Packet, circuit, and message switching   This section introduces these three switching paradigms and discusses how they relate to IP networks.

Local-area networks and technologies   You will read about the difference between token passing and collision-detection technologies. Then, we describe why Ethernet has become a ubiquitous form of LAN technology. Finally, we introduce the basic operation of IP over Ethernet.

Wide-area networks and technologies   This section contrasts serial Time Division Multiplexing (TDM) for leased lines, Frame Relay, ATM, and Packet over SONET. We describe the main benefits and drawbacks of these technologies, as well as their interaction with the Internet Protocol.

Metropolitan-area networks and technologies   In this section, we briefly introduce various MAN technologies, along with our thoughts on the future direction of MANs.

## CHAPTER 3

Network Technologies

Packet, Circuit, and Message Switching

The three switching paradigms that you are likely to encounter with IP networks (packet switching, circuit switching, and message switching) each have their own characteristics and requirements that you should consider before deciding which one best suits your network. The sections that follow define these switching paradigm characteristics and requirements.

Packet-Switched Networks

The Internet, and IP networks in general, are *packet-switching networks*. This means that all data is segmented into variable-length IP packets, which are then routed across the network as discrete entities, as shown in Figure 3-1. Each IP packet contains a source and a destination, as well as mechanisms to detect packet corruption. Routing in IP networks is usually based on an IP destination address.

Figure 3-1 *Packet Switching*

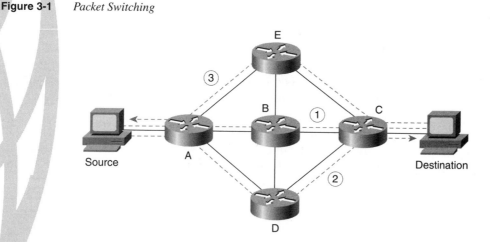

Packet routers in IP networks are able to detect IP packet errors, but they do not perform error correction or provide substantial congestion control (Internet Control Message Protocol [ICMP] source-quench messages are typically ignored by routers and host). These functions are left to the Transport Control Protocol (TCP) stack that is implemented on the hosts that connect to the network. While certain WAN technologies may implement error correction and congestion control in Layer 2, this process is transparent to the IP router. Many experts argue that performing such functions in Layer 2 can interfere with the performance of TCP, which causes TCP to degrade. For large IP networks, therefore, it is not advisable to configure any Layer 2 error correction or congestion control algorithms.

Sequential IP packets do not necessarily follow the same path through the network, although in stable routed environments they generally should. For example, the situation depicted in Figure 3-1, in which IP packets 1, 2, and 3, take different routes over the network is undesirable. This is important because performance of the TCP error correction/congestion control is degraded by the rapid changes in round trip times when packets take multiple routes—it will look like congestion. Note that load sharing traffic over multiple parallel WAN links is usually not problematic, if the propagation delay over each link is similar.

IP packets may be fragmented by IP routers to fit inside the maximum transmission unit (MTU) associated with particular Layer 2 technologies. The packets are re-assembled by the IP host that ultimately receives packets, rather than being re-assembled by routers. Fragmentation normally reduces the efficiency of routers and IP hosts alike. For this reason, it is important to avoid fragmentation within your network in most cases. Note that most modern TCP applications also set the Don't Fragment-Bit in the header and are using the Path-MTU-Discovery mechanism (described in RFC 1191) to automatically detect the maximum possible path MTU size.

Because most host IP implementations usually source IP packets that require routing with a length of 512 bytes, fragmentation is generally not an issue in networks employing common WAN or LAN technologies that support much larger frame sizes. It is worth noting that the ATM Adaptation Layer 5, usually via hardware assisted code, segments the IP packets into cells. It then re-assembles them in the full IP packet prior to routing to other media. Therefore, IP fragmentation is not an issue in ATM networks, providing the reassembly buffer at the remote end of the ATM cloud matches (or is at least smaller than) the MTU sizes used by other WAN or LAN technologies in the network. Packet over SONET technologies are even more desirable, because the segmentation function and associated cell tax is completely avoided.

NOTE   *Cell tax* refers to the relatively low ratio of data payload (48 bytes) to header size (5 bytes) in an ATM cell. Compare this with Ethernet frames, in which the ratio can be as high as 1500:26. While cell tax may not be in issue for applications that generated data in small discrete quantities, for applications involving bulk data transfer (such as downloading images), cell tax leads to a significant decrease in useful data throughput compared with other technologies operating at the same wire speed.

A packet-switched IP network, in conjunction with careful provisioning and congestion control techniques that are cognizant of TCP, offers extremely scalable technology for supporting a wide range of both non-real and real-time applications. This scalability and flexibility is causing the communications world to focus on the use of IP networks to provide the traditional "Internet" applications, as well as applications that were traditionally carried by circuit-switched telephone networks. IP packet switching is necessary for many large corporations and progressive carriers as the underlying technology for large networks of the future.

Circuit-Switched Networks

Packet-switched networks fundamentally differ from circuit-switched networks. As shown in Figure 3-2, a connection must first be established between two end hosts in order for them to communicate in a circuit-switched network. This can be achieved by in-band signaling (call_setup) within a circuit—in other words, the end host transmits a set of signals that allows the circuit to be extended, hop-by-hop, through the network. Alternatively, as in the case of the Integrated Services Digital Network (ISDN), the circuits can be established with the assistance of a second "control-plane" network, which is usually a lower-bandwidth, packet-switched network, and carries only the call setup packets. This requirement for a pre-established circuit prior to communication is in contrast to IP's "connectionless" paradigm, in which a host can begin transmitting to any other host on the network at any time.

Figure 3-2   *Circuit Switching*

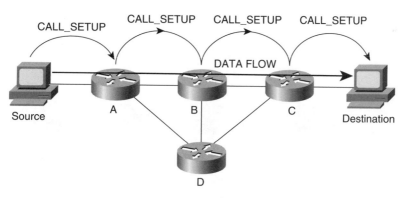

Also, unlike packet-switched networks, once the circuit is established, all data flows over the same path through the network. In Figure 3-1, all data associated with the call passes through nodes A, B, and C; and follows the symetrical return path. Therefore, the parameters of the session, such as delay and bandwidth, are fixed—this is both an advantage and a limitation to end-user applications. The advantage of fixed delay for real-time applications is guaranteed delivery at regular intervals. For example, in telephone calls, this is important for smooth reproduction of conversations. The limitation, in terms of bandwidth, is that some applications may use all of the available bandwidth within their circuit, whereas others may use much less. The application that consumes more bandwidth cannot contribute its spare bandwidth to the application that requires less bandwidth. The result of this limitation is poor performance in environments where bandwidth requirements change over time. For example, when you are downloading or reading Internet Web pages, the process becomes frustratingly slow. However, given their predictable delay and bandwidth characteristics, circuit-switched networks are a convenient choice for fixed-bandwidth, real-time applications such as telephone services.

Message-Switched Networks

Message switching is a technology that overlays packet- or circuit-switched networks. The routing paradigm is one of "store-and-forward." For example, suppose that, as shown in Figure 3-3, host X (Source) wants to send a message to host Y (Destination). Assume that host X cannot send the message directly to host Y because of network congestion, security limitations such as a firewall, or an outage. Instead, host X will pass the message to another node, C, that is closer to the ultimate destination, host Y. Node C will then store, and, at some later time, forward the message to host Y. Node C may perform some error-checking or other functions on the message prior to forwarding it to host Y.

Figure 3-3   *Message Switching*

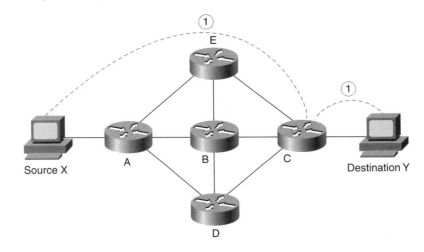

Routing e-mail over an IP packet network is an example of message switching. If one host needs to send an e-mail message to another host that is unreachable, it can use the Domain Name System (DNS) to find alternative mail-exchangers for the unreachable host. Such hosts will accept and store the message until the ultimate destination is again on-line. Clearly, message switching is unsuitable for time-sensitive or real-time applications.

Local-Area Networks and Technologies

Local-area network (LAN) technologies, as the name suggests, are extremely localized, covering a small geographic area up to only a few thousand meters. For example, they can connect computers within or between buildings, or within a particular department, such as Accounting or Marketing. Whenever there is a situation in which you are able to install your own physical media to connect peripherals, workstations, and terminals, you would employ LAN technologies. Because of their limited range, LANs will not perform well where there is a large distance between sites.

LAN technologies usually operate with the assumption of a single physical media shared among many computers. However, the sharing algorithms are divided into two categories: those sharing algorithms that use collision detection, such as Ethernet; and those sharing algorithms that employ a token to arbitrate access to the LAN media, such as Token Ring and Fiber Distributed Data Interface (FDDI). Most technologies employ error detection; however, the most commonly used technologies do not provide error correction. The error rate on LANs, compared to WANs, is low in the "normal" operating environments of offices and other similar environments.

LANs: The Heart of the Internet

It is a little-recognized fact that LAN technologies, because of their low price/speed ratio, still form the "heart" of the Internet—the place in which large numbers of major providers meet to exchange traffic with other providers. The original MAE-East and Federal Exchange points were based on Ethernet until they were later upgraded to FDDI and then switched FDDI, using Gigaswitches from Digital.

ATM was used at one or two public exchange points. However, more recently, Gigabit Ethernet switches are looking to be a promising technology. Providers establishing private peering at a co-location facility may use LAN technologies to connect their routers, rather than using ATM or Packet over SONET interfaces, which are more expensive in terms of price as well as router slot space.

Ethernet

Although Ethernet was invented in the 1970s, a commercially available product did not become widely used until the early to mid-1980s. From that point on, however, Ethernet technology experienced explosive growth, which continues today.

The operation of Ethernet is relatively simple. A broadcast medium, such as coaxial cable or an interconnected twisted pair, connects all hosts. A host or a router on an Ethernet LAN may begin transmitting only if no other messages are currently being transmitted on the media. There is a period called the *collision window,* related to the length of the Ethernet media, in which two hosts may both begin transmitting without hearing each other. Eventually, however, the signals will collide. Because of signal corruption during reading, both hosts will recognize that a collision has occurred. Both stations then will execute a back-off algorithm, causing them to reattempt their transmissions randomly at a later time. All being well, further collisions will be avoided.

Although coaxial cable was Ethernet's original chief support, this has more recently become optical fiber for links between buildings, and Category 5 unshielded twisted-pair (UTP) within buildings. As shown in Figure 3-4, a typical installation may consist of a hierarchy of hubs and switches, with a router at the highest level providing WAN connectivity or LAN segmentation.

Figure 3-4 *10BaseT/100BaseT Ethernet Topology*

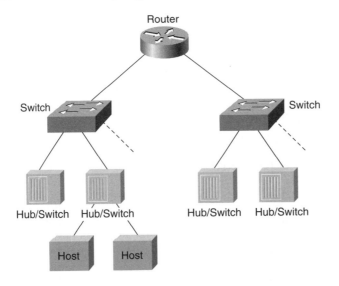

The theoretical data transmission rate of Ethernet is 10 Mbps. In practice, the data rates observed could vary widely with the number of computers on the LAN, their distribution and length of the LAN media, and the nature of the data flows. Excessive collision can slow the usable data rate to a crawl. This has led many users to embrace the 100 Mbps token passing technology of FDDI. However, with the introduction of Fast Ethernet technologies (100 Mbps) and Gigabit Ethernet technologies (1000 Mbps), the LAN market has settled on these as the end-user technologies. In some cases, Asynchronous Transfer Mode (ATM) switches are used to connect large Ethernet switching hubs.

The interaction between Ethernet and IP is relatively simple. All Ethernet interfaces, which may be on computers or routers, are assigned a unique six-octet Media Access Control (MAC) address. When one IP host needs to send an IP packet to another host on a LAN, the ARP protocol requests the MAC address that corresponds to a particular host. As a result of standardization, two encapsulations of IP in Ethernet frames are currently being used:

- **Ethernet II**—Specified in RFC 984
- **IEEE 802.3**—Specified in RFC 1042

Usually, only routers listen to and convert between the two types. Modern Ethernet cards and Fast Ethernet components use only the latter.

Token Passing Technologies, which we'll discuss next, also employ ARP to resolve IP addresses into MAC addresses.

Token Passing Technologies

The advantage of token passing technologies is predictable degradation as utilization increases. A *token* is a small frame containing control information, and is passed from one computer to another. It allows a network device to transmit data onto the network. Each computer may absorb the token for a certain maximum period of time, during which it may transmit any packets it may have. The data packets propagate around a ring until they are read by the destination. Then, they continue cycling the ring until they are removed from the ring by the original source of the packet.

Figure 3-5 illustrates a typical Token Ring topology. One or more Multistation Access Units (MAUs) are connected in a ring configuration. Each MAU adds one or more hosts or routers into the ring. The MAU may detect host failure and remove it from the ring.

Figure 3-5   *Token Ring Topology*

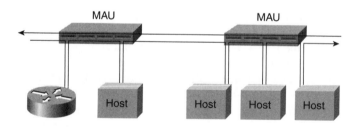

FDDI, a LAN standard defined by the American National Standards Institute (ANSI) in X3T9.5, uses dual-ring architecture to provide redundancy. FDDI allows multiple packets plus a token on the ring at any one time, whereas Token Ring (without the Early-Token Release Feature) allows only one packet—each station holds the token until it removes any packets it has transmitted from the ring. By adjusting the token holding time on a per-host basis, it is possible to share bandwidth fairly equally between all computers, and to intentionally allocate certain hosts more bandwidth than others. In addition, by using dual physical rings, hosts can "wrap around" physical breaks in the ring. A host may connect to one (Single Attach Station) or both (Dual Attach Station), according to reliability requirements. FDDI and variants on FDDI were also proposed as the basis for MAN technologies.

Figure 3-6 illustrates a typical FDDI topology. The left configuration demonstrates a number of DASs and a router connected in a physical ring. The right configuration shows a number of SASs (including a router) connecting to a central switch (or hub).

Figure 3-6   *FDDI Topology*

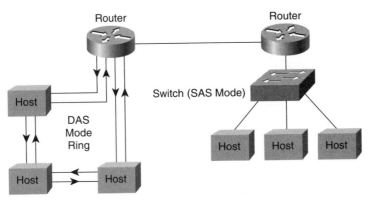

Ethernet versus Token Passing Technologies

Token Ring, which is a token-passing LAN developed and supported by IBM, enjoyed enormous popularity during the days of IBM's Systems Network Architecture (SNA) networks, which developed in the 1970s. FDDI, a 100 Mbps optical fiber-based system, also was briefly popular due to its substantial speed advantage over the contemporary 10 Mbps Ethernet and its immunity to electrical interference. FDDI's largest drawback was the high cost of optical components. However, the lower cost and "plug-and-play" nature of 10 Mbps Ethernet over UTP (10BaseT) led to a massive foothold in the market, despite its speed limitation. This allowed higher speed implementations of the Ethernet link layer protocol, and large-scale deployment of "switched" LAN segments. It became more expedient to connect 10 Mbps and 100 Mbps "Fast Ethernet" LANs using switches. If UTP was used as the media, both speeds could run on the same media, and a single switch supported hosts of different speeds through an auto-negotiation process between switch and host.

Wide-Area Networks and Technologies

Wide-area network (WAN) technologies are characterized as networks covering a broad geographical area. These technologies use common carrier facilities. On a seven-layer model, they operate on the physical, data link layer. WANs are divided into three types of links:

- **Point-to-point (leased line)**—There are several common protocols used in these links—the most common are Point-to Point Protocol (PPP), Synchronous Data Link Control (SDLC), and High-Level Data Link Control (HDLC). Because point-to-point links and their protocols are the most widely used, we discuss them in more detail in the sections that follow.

- **Packet-switching**—The packet-switching protocol finds the most efficient paths for routing packets, and multiple connections are allowed to share a communications channel. It uses statistical multiplexing, ATM, Frame Relay, X.25, and Switched Multimegabit Data Service (SMDS). Later in this chapter, we will discuss the two most commonly used packet switched technologies—ATM and Frame Relay.

- **Circuit-switching**—Circuit-switching protocols are used most often in the telephone industry, in which a dedicated physical circuit path between sender and receiver is necessary. ISDN is a commonly used circuit-switching protocol.

Point-to-Point Links

Point-to-point links, as the name indicates, provide a pre-established path between two points. Connection is established through a carrier network, which is a permanently defined circuit between two points on the customer network. These circuits are dedicated solely for the private use of the customer. As mentioned in the preceding list, the most commonly employed protocols by point-to-point links include SDLC, HDLC, and PPP, as discussed in the sections that follow.

SDLC/HDLC

Other than PPP, there are two types of commonly used protocols for point-to-point links—SDLC and HDLC. These are synchronous, bit-oriented, full-duplex protocols. HDLC, a derivative of SDLC, was developed by IBM in the mid-1970s for use in SNA networks. By default, Cisco employs HDLC framing for synchronous data transfer on point-to-point links.

SDLC supports many link types, and it can be applied in both point-to-point and multipoint technologies. Two types of nodes are defined—primary and secondary. The primary node controls the operation of the secondary node, and it polls the secondary nodes with a defined method. The secondary node can transmit data during this polling process if it has data to be sent. Figure 3-7 shows the frame format for SDLC.

Figure 3-7 *SDLC Frame*

Flag	Address	Control	Data	FCS	Flag

Information Frame Format

Receive Sequence Number	Poll Final	Send Sequence Number	0

Supervisory Frame Format

Receive Sequence Number	Poll Final	Function Code	0	1

Unnumbered Frame Format

Function Code	Poll Final	Function Code	0	1

The frame is bounded by a Flag pattern. The Address field is used for indicating the secondary node involved for communication. Because primary is always either the source or the destination of the communication, that is why it is not in the SDLC frame. All the secondaries already know the primary's address. The Control field in the frame is altered according to the type of SDLC frame used, as explained in the list that follows.

- **Information (I) frames**—Carry upper-layer information and some control information. Send and receive numbers and poll final (P/F) also does error correction. Send and receive sequences are used to indicate the frame number being sent and received. The primary node uses the P/F bit to indicate to the secondary node that it needs immediate response. The secondary node uses these bits to indicate whether this is the last frame in the response.

- **Supervisory (S) frames**—Used to request and suspend the transmission, report on status, and acknowledge the receipt of I frames. Supervisory frames do not have any data.

- **Unnumbered(U) frames**—Used for control purposes (that is, to initialize the secondary node, and so forth). Unnumbered frames are not sequenced.

Because HDLC is a derivative of SDLC, they share the same frame format. HDLC has a few capabilities that are additional to those in SDLC. For example, SDLC supports only one transfer mode, whereas HDLC supports three:

- **Normal Response Mode (NRM)**—Both HDLC and SDLC use this mode. In this mode of operation, the primary node cannot communicate unless permitted by the secondary node.

- **Asynchronous Response Mode (ARM)**—Unique to HDLC, in this mode, the secondary node can initiate communication without the permission from the primary node.

- **Asynchronous Balanced Mode (ABM)**—Unique to HDLC, in this combined mode, either the primary or the secondary node can initiate communication without the permission from the other.

Point-to-Point Protocol

Point-to-point links are also connected by using the Point-to-Point Protocol (PPP). Invented in the 1980s, PPP filled the industry's demand for a connection between LAN and WAN. PPP provides a standard-based protocol to connect point-to-point IP links.

As the name suggests, PPP is used for data transfer across point-to-point serial links. The protocol has three main components:

- It uses HDLC for the encapsulating datagrams over serial point-to-point links.

- It has an extensible link control protocol to establish, test, and data-link connections.

- It uses several network control protocols for establishing different network layer protocols.

For the operation of PPP connections, the sending station sends Link Control Protocol (LCP) frames for testing. This configures the data link. After the data link has been established, the originating station sends Network Control Protocol (NCP) frames for the selection of the network protocol. After the selected network protocol has been established, packets for the network protocol can be sent across the link. The link remains active for the protocol unless explicit messages are sent signaling that the link should be closed.

Packet-Switching Links: Frame Relay

Frame Relay was initially developed by the American National Standards Institute (ANSI) in 1984. Cisco Systems undertook major redevelopment of Frame Relay in 1990. StrataCom (now part of Cisco Systems), Northern Telecom, and Digital Equipment Corporation formed a consortium to focus on the development of Frame Relay technology. This consortium developed some additional features for the internetworking environment.

Frame Relay is a packet-switching technology that provides a connection between a router and a packet switch device. A Frame Rely network that provides connection can be either a public network or a privately owned network. To connect a network with a user interface, Frame Relay creates virtual circuits, which are created by statistically multiplexing many logical connections over single physical links. Statistical multiplexing provides a more efficient way of using the available bandwidth.

Frame Relay is capable of managing multiple virtual circuits using HDLC encapsulation between connected devices. One of the biggest advantages of Frame Relay is its efficient digital design, unlike its predecessors, such as X.25 (that it essentially replaces), which were developed when analog technology was used and circuits were unreliable. Instead of having to perform error corrections, Frame Relay includes the cyclic redundancy check (CRC) called frame check sequence (FCS), which informs network devices of data corruption so that bad data can be discarded. This technology leaves error-correction algorithms for the upper-layer protocols.

Because upper-layer protocols are capable of performing explicit flow control per virtual circuit, this function is not included in Frame Relay. Instead, Frame Relay provides a very simple notification procedure that signals the user devices when network resources are close to congestion. This also signals upper-layer protocols to activate the flow control feature when a link is congested.

Frame Relay provides connection-oriented, data link layer communication. This service is implemented by using virtual circuits, which are logical, bidirectional connections between the two end-node devices across the packet-switched network. These virtual circuits are uniquely identified by a Data Link Connection Identifier (DLCI). A virtual circuit can pass through any number of switches in a Frame Relay network, as illustrated in Figure 3-8.

Figure 3-8 *Frame Relay Connections via Switches*

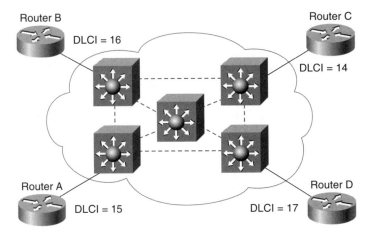

In addition to simplifying the protocol, the consortium specification includes Local Management Interface (LMI) extensions, which simplified the Frame Relay implementation over large networks. These extensions deal with number of Frame Relay switches located within a Frame Relay network. These virtual circuits can be switched virtual circuits (SVCs) or a permanent virtual circuit (PVC). The LMI extension includes virtual circuit message status, global addressing, multicasting, and flow control.

Packet-Switching Links: ATM

ATM adopts a strategy of segmenting all IP packets into small, 53-byte cells carrying a 48-byte data payload. The motivation for small cells is based on minimizing packetization delay, which makes the technology suitable for time-sensitive applications. The motivation for fixed cells is to allow the switching to occur in hardware, because hardware switching of variably sized frames is more complex. The choice of small cell size has been a source of debate. Nevertheless, in local area environments, the low cost/speed ratio of ATM switches makes them attractive. Prior to Gigabit Ethernet, ATM switches were the only options for LAN operation at hundreds of megabits per second.

ATM promises scalable bandwidth and quality of service guarantees with minimal cost. It is a cell-based technology that facilitates development at hardware-level, high-performance switches. An ATM network consists of ATM switches connected via point-to-point links. ATM supports two types of interfaces: the User-Network Interface (UNI) and the Network-Node Interface (NNI). The UNI interface connects the ATM switch with the end system, such as the router or host. The NNI interface interconnects two ATM switches. Figure 3-9 illustrates a typical ATM network setup.

Figure 3-9   *ATM Network Setup via Switches*

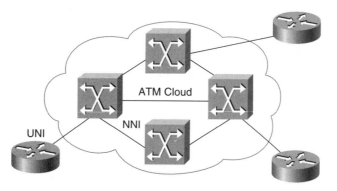

By nature, ATM networks are connection-oriented, which means that a virtual circuit needs to be established prior to data transfer. ATM has two basic types of circuit indicators that are used for setting up the virtual circuit: Virtual Path Identifier (VPI) and Virtual Channel Identifier. Both VPI and VCI have only local significance across a particular link. ATM operates as follows:

Step 1   The ATM network receives a cell across a particular link on a known VCI or VPI.

Step 2   Switch looks up the connection in the local translation table to determine the outgoing port and the VCI/VPI value of the connection.

Step 3   Switch sends the cell on the outgoing links.

The ATM switch is also relatively simple, due to an external method of organizing the local table for data transfer. There are two fundamental types of tables: Permanent virtual circuits and switched virtual circuits.

In WAN environments, in which the "cell tax" is very significant, there is increasing importance placed on IP Packet Over SONET (POS) solutions.

Circuit-Switching Links: ISDN

Integrated Services Digital Network (ISDN) is used by telephone companies to carry digitized voice and data over the existing telephone system. ISDN has emerged as one of the leading technologies for telecommuting and remote office connection into the corporate headquarters.

On the seven layer model, ISDN operates at the physical, data link, and network layers. ISDN basic rate interface (BRI) provides two barrier channels (commonly referred as B channels). Each of these B channels carries data at 64 kbps. The D channel coexists along with B channels. The D channel operates at 16 kbps and is usually used for carrying control information.

The ISDN primary rate interface (PRI) service delivers 23 B channels and one 64-kbps D channel in the US and Japan with a total bit rate of 1.544 Mbps. In other parts of the world, the PRI service provides 30 B channels for a total bit rate of 2.048 Mbps.

ISDN consists of three network components: ISDN terminal equipment, termination devices, and reference points. ISDN terminal equipment has two basic terminal equipment types:

- **TE1**—A specialized ISDN terminal that includes computers equipment and phones.
- **TE2**—DTE equipment that connects to the ISDN line through a terminal adapter (TA).

ISDN Network Termination Devices are called network termination (NT) devices. There are three supported NT types:

- **NT1**—Treated as a customer premises equipment in North America, elsewhere it is provided by carrier.
- **NT2**—Found in PBXs, this device type provides Layer 2 and Layer 3 functions and concentration services.
- **NT1/2**—Combines the functions of both NT1 and NT2 and is compatible with both NT1 and NT2 devices.

ISDN reference points are used for logical interface. Four reference points are defined:

- **R reference point**—Defines the logical interface between no-ISDN equipment and TA.
- **S reference point**—Defines the reference point user terminal and NT2.
- **T reference point**—Located between NT1 and NT2 devices.
- **U reference point**—Located between NT1 and line-termination equipment in a carrier network.

Circuit-Switching Links: Synchronous Optical Network

Synchronous Optical Network (SONET) was defined in the 1980s as a standard by which carriers could build multivendor transport infrastructure. SONET is divided into three areas: Physical, Payload, and DCC.

SONET uses a frame structure that repeats itself every 125 ms, enables providers to set up a hub topology rather than just point-to-point connections, and supports a fiber optic ring, which is created by fiber optics. In case of a failure, a bidirectional ring can be used, which is capable of rerouting traffic from the affected nodes within a millisecond. This protects providers from service outages. SONET uses Add-Drop Multiplexers (ADM) to create network protection architectures, known as Unidirectional Path Switched Rings (UPSR). ADM provides UPSR protection by multiplexing a tributary onto the two outgoing channels, diversely routed over different fiber paths to an end node. The UPSR protection system allows multiple elements to be located within a ring. The UPSR add-and-drop mechanism permits many customers to share traffic across a local-area network. Many nodes could be added to a UPSR to provide a high level of fiber utilization. Each remote location can be added or dropped along the path as the ring traverses customer locations.

Metropolitan-Area Networks and Technologies

Around the same time that the IEEE was developing LAN standards and IEEE 802.3, a new consortium was formed to study metropolitan-area networks (MANs). The consortium's original intent was to bridge the gap between WAN technologies such as ATM or ISDN, and LAN technologies such as Ethernet or local ATM. The original design goals were to provide a shared, fairly high-speed fiber optic network that was optimized to operate over distances from several city blocks to approximately 30 miles, about the size of large city.

Distributed Queue Dual Bus

The standard resulting from this IEEE study is numbered 802.6, and named Distributed Queue Dual Bus (DQDB), which essentially describes both the topology used by the technology, and the media access mechanism.

In this technology, illustrated by Figure 3-10, two optical fiber buses carry communications between all stations. The buses are unidirectional, and a DQDB station needs to attach to both, either through a passive or active fiber tap. One bus communicates with upstream stations, and the other communicates with downstream stations. Therefore, over time, the stations must learn which stations are upstream or downstream. Otherwise, data must be transmitted on both buses until the necessary upsteam/downstream intelligence is gained. Although the intent of DQDB was to operate on high-speed optical fiber such as OC3, it is capable of operating on T1 or DS3 cable infrastructure. In fact, because of its popularity in the US during DQDB development, a detailed standard for DQDB over DS3 has been established.

Figure 3-10   *DQDB Topology*

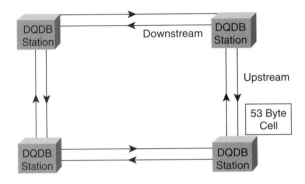

The Distributed Queue access protocol arbitrates access to the Dual Bus media. The protocol allows each station to reserve time slots, and supports three levels of priority. A station must honor the reservations of downstream stations. Therefore, the majority of the Distributed Queue protocol is concerned with communicating reservations from downstream stations to upstream stations.

DQDB uses the same fixed 53-octet cell size used by ATM. Physical switching between ATM and DQDB is therefore relatively simple. In addition, DQDB recognizes both 60-bit ISDN and 48-bit LAN addressing, enabling the technology to carry both local and wide-area data traffic. In the latter case, ATM-like segmentation and reassembly of LAN frames is necessary.

Limitations of DQDB

The 802.6 DQDB standard never became popular as a means to interconnect LAN or digital telephony systems. Within the US, DQDB made a brief appearance as a commercial service in the form of the Switched Multimegabit Data Service (SMDS). However, in terms of tariff or capabilities, it never held any real advantage over Frame Relay, and had only marginal advantage over T1. Moreover, in many ways MANs are based upon the assumption that customers want to connect LANs at Layer 2. As the communications world began converging on IP, and as routers became an inexpensive data communications commodity, this assumption became less valid. Designers of IP networks preferred the simplicity of dedicated, point-to-point, Layer 2 services, because this allowed the IP engineer to determine traffic patterns and fail-over mechanisms via IP routing protocols. The "shared" nature of SMDS translated to "unpredictable" in the IP engineer's mind. Although there is nothing to stop SMDS from connecting two routers, in the absence of a highly differentiated cost (over, say, a T1), there was little to recommend the MAN technology over traditional TDM services. Today, it is common to see Frame Relay, T1, or even dark fiber filling the application space originally intended for MANs.

Summary

This chapter provided a brief introduction to the switching network paradigms; and LAN, WAN, and MAN technologies. IP is a connectionless, packet-switching technology, which allows highly efficient use of network resources for all users. In LANs, Ethernets at 10, 100, and 1000 Mbps have become the technology of choice. To a lesser extent, ATM is also used, whereas use of token-passing technologies such as Token Ring and FDDI is rapidly declining.

In WANs, traditional Time Division Multiplexing (TDM) "leased-line" technologies, such as T1, are still widely deployed. At speeds in the low Mbps and below, Frame Relay is also widely being deployed. At higher speeds, Packet over SONET is gaining popularity in the US, and ATM is widely used in other areas of the world.

Finally, in MANs, DQDB was used briefly as the SMDS service. SMDS offered very little advantage over the available WAN, or the more-recent, dark-fiber services for the connection of LANs over distances of less than 30 miles.

This chapter merely introduces these networking technologies to provide the reader with basic contextual knowledge of data link and physical layer services. Unlike large-scale IP routing, the published literature on LAN and WAN technologies is vast—for additional information on these areas, there are many excellent references, which are listed at the end of this chapter.

Review Questions

1 If a router needs to forward a packet to an IP destination on a LAN, how does it discover the Layer 2 (MAC) address of the destination?

2 Do you need a router to connect 10 Mbps Ethernet to higher-speed Ethernet LANs?

3 What are the two modes used by HDLC that are additional to the mode used by SDLC?

4 What is the cell size of ATM?

Answers:

1 The Address Resolution Protocol (ARP) is used to broadcast a request for the Layer 2 address associated with a particular Layer 3 address.

2 A router can be used and may be desirable to provide a "safety barrier" between two LANs. This can help LANs to scale. However, the benefit of the various Ethernet technologies is that they may be connected by simple inexpensive switches. A single switch may support multiple Ethernet speeds.

3 Asynchronous Response Mode (ARM) and Asynchronous Balance Mode (ABM).

4 53 bytes.

For Further Reading . . .

Alles, Anthony. *ATM Internetworking.* San Jose, CA: Cisco Systems Inc., 1995.

Alles, Anthony, and Minoli, Dan. *LAN, ATM, and LAN Emulation Technologies.* Norwood, MA: Artech House, 1997.

Black, Ulysses. *ATM: Foundations for Broadband Networks.* Englewood Cliffs, NJ: Prentice-Hall, 1995.

Black, Ulysses, and Waters, Shareen. *SONET T1: Architectures for Digital Transport Networks.* Upper Saddle River, NJ: Prentice-Hall, 1997.

Black, Ulysses. *Data Link Protocols.* Upper Saddle River, NJ: Prentice-Hall, 1993.

Black, Ulysses. *Physical Layer Interfaces and Protocols, Second Edition.* Los Alamitos, CA: IEEE Computer Society Press, 1996.

Cisco Systems, Inc. *Introduction to WAN.* San Jose, CA: Cisco Systems Inc., June 17, 1999.

Cisco Systems, Inc. *The Cisco ISR 3303 Integrated SONET Router.* San Jose, CA: Cisco Systems Inc., 1999.

Dorling, Brian et al. *Internetworking over ATM—An Introduction.* Upper Saddle River, NJ: Prentice-Hall, 1996.

Kercheval, Berry. *TCP/IP over ATM: A No-Nonsense Internetworking Guide.* Upper Saddle River, NJ: Prentice-Hall, 1998.

Kyas, Othmar. *ATM Networks.* Second Edition. Boston, MA: International Thomson Computer Press, 1997.

Ginsburg, David. *ATM: Solutions for Enterprise Internetworking.* Harlow, UK: Addison Wesley Longman, 1996.

Golway, Thomas, and Minoli, Dan. *Planning and Managing ATM Networks.* Greenwich, CT: Manning Publications, 1997.

Goralski, Walter J. *SONET: A Guide to Synchronous Optical Networks.* New York, NY: McGraw Hill, 1997.

IEEE. IEEE Std 802.5-1989. *Token Ring Access Method.* New York, NY: IEEE Inc, 1989.

Johnson, Howard W. *Fast Ethernet: Dawn of a New Age.* Upper Saddle River, NJ: Prentice-Hall, 1996.

Stallings, William. *Data and Computer Communications.* New York, NY: Macmillan Publishing Company, 1989.

Stallings, William. *Networking Standards: A Guide to OSI, ISDN, LAN, and MAN Standards.* Reading, MA: Addison-Wesley, 1993.

This chapter explores design issues related to overall network topology. The following sections discuss the traditional issues of bandwidth, delay, and reliability; as well as the often overlooked issues of operational simplicity and scalability, particularly as they pertain to routing. Specifically, the following issues are discussed:

Requirements and constraints of the network   This section examines the requirements of a network and the importance of scalability and extensibility. You will also read about constraints on the design effort, including labor, economic, social, time, and space issues; as well as the need to support legacy technologies.

Tools and techniques   You will explore some of the tools for building large networks. Modularization, layering, multiplexing, and caching are discussed in the context of the overall design. This section briefly examines the use of soft-state mechanisms, hysterisis, and dampening in routing protocols; and finally discusses network failure modes.

Issues of hierarchy   This section demonstrates that hierarchy and redundancy must be carefully balanced to craft a network that can grow to meet future needs without becoming an operational nightmare. Experience gained from the Internet is also discussed. (For additional information on this topic, see Chapter 1, "Evolution of Data Networks.") Finally, this section examines the principles of layering and regionalization of a large network into core, distribution, and access networks.

Backbone network design, as well as distribution, regional network design, and access design   In these three sections, you will examine the details of designing core, distribution, and access networks. The role of each is discussed, and the pros and cons of various approaches are described.

## CHAPTER 4

Network Topology and Design

Requirements and Constraints

Before delving into the typical topologies, it is wise to understand the overall network design process. As with any systems design effort, network design is an exercise in meeting new and old requirements while working within certain constraints. These constraints include money, labor, technology, space, and time. In addition, there may be social or political constraints, such as the mandated use of certain standards or vendors.

Economic constraints play a major role in any network design. Unless you are very fortunate, you often must compromise in the capacity of WAN links, the switching capabilities of routers, the type of interfaces used, and the level of redundancy achieved. Achieving the "best possible service at the lowest possible cost" was a design paradigm invented—tongue-in-cheek, to some extent—by one network manager to satisfy both management and network users. This paradigm fails to explain how this task is achieved, other than through a carefully considered compromise, but neither does it say anything that is incorrect.

Labor effort should be of paramount concern in any network design. In this case, the first area of concern is the amount of effort and level of skill necessary to connect a new customer to the network or to expand the capacity of the network infrastructure. As a general rule, the more often a task must be executed, the more the design should focus on making that task simple and efficient—in other words, the goal involves optimizing the common case. In addition to prudent network design, labor costs can also be reduced through investment in network management tools. It is noteworthy that for many networks, the capital cost is dwarfed by the ongoing charges for highly skilled support personnel.

Processor speed doubles every 18 months. Nevertheless, as you have already seen in Chapter 1, Internet traffic levels can increase at a far more rapid rate. Thus, computation is still a constraint of network design, particularly in the case of routers. Typical computational limitations that apply to network design are associated with processing of routing updates, accounting, security filtering and encryption, address translation, and even packet forwarding.

Space issues include the physically obvious, such as the cost of expensive air-conditioned points of presence (POPs) or co-location facilities. Space also includes subtler, but nonetheless important resources, such as the buffer capacity in a router or the bandwidth of a WAN link.

One time constraint that affects the success of a design is the time-to-market. It is useless to design an extremely sophisticated network if the customers have gone elsewhere by the time it is operational. Time constraints also include packet forwarding and propagation delays, which have a fundamental impact on bandwidth (in a TCP/IP environment) and response time.

Social constraints include those that may not seem sensible to achieve the major requirements of the network. These could include a mandated use of standards that are difficult to obtain, to use, or to understand. Thankfully, this has been less common since the demise of OSI. (At one time in the industry, a play on the OSI reference model included a "political" layer above the application layer—the so-called "eighth layer of networking.") Alternatively, you may be constrained to using a certain vendor's equipment because of a prearranged partnership agreement.

The need to support legacy applications is usually expressed as a requirement, but it generally manifests itself as a serious constraint. Building networks that are backward-compatible with legacy applications—such as the need to support protocols such as SNA and DECNET—can be extremely demanding.

Scalability and extensibility are the hallmarks of a good network design. They will haunt or compliment you long after the economic pain is forgotten. This is why network routing is so critical to the design process. Switching and physical-layer technologies may come and go, but the network control plane (of which routing is a major part) must survive many generations of underlying technology.

The control plane is much more difficult to upgrade incrementally than the technologies of the underlying layers, so careful planning pays dividends. In the networking world, those dividends can return in months rather than years.

Many writings on network design emphasize the importance of requirement analysis. Indeed, in terms of the initial delivery of a *turnkey*, or productized network service, requirement analysis is very important. However, in our experience, nowhere in the industry does the initial-requirements definition document age more quickly than in large-scale networking—particularly where the Internet is involved.

Too many network designs never leave the ground because of an overly zealous requirements-definition phase. This is an unfortunate side effect of vendors providing "shrink-wrapped" networks to customers.

Valuable engineering cycles spent on extremely detailed requirements or network flow analysis would be better spent ensuring an extensible and scalable network infrastructure, and explaining contingency plans to the customer, if the actual requirements exceed those projected. Unfortunately, stringent requirement analysis seems to be a contractual necessity, so this situation is unlikely to change.

Tools and Techniques

Network design is both an art and a science. The *science* involves exploiting various methodologies to meet all the requirements within the given constraints. Each of these methods trades one constrained resource for another. The *art* involves choosing the best balance between constrained resources, resulting in a network that is *future-proof*—one that will grow to meet increased, or even radically new, requirements.

Modularization and Layering

Two of the most common design and implementation methodologies are those of *modularization* and *layering*. Both enable the network problem to be broken down into something more manageable, and both involve the definition of interfaces that enable one module or layer to be modified without affecting others. These benefits usually compensate for inefficiency, due to hidden information between layers or modules. Nevertheless, when designing the interfaces between modules or layers, it is good practice to optimize the common case. For example, if there is a large flow of traffic between two distribution networks, perhaps this flow should be optimized by introducing a new dedicated link into the core network.

Layering typically implies a hierarchical relationship. This is a fundamental technique in network protocol design, as exemplified by the ubiquitous OSI reference model. Modularization typically implies a peer relationship, although a hierarchy certainly can exist between modules. In an upcoming section, "Hierarchy Issues," as well as in many of the remaining chapters in this book, the text continues to emphasize and develop the practice of hierarchy and modularization in network design.

Layering the network control plan above a redundant physical infrastructure is a vital part of resilient network design. Critical control information, such as network management or routing updates, should be exchanged using IP addresses of a virtual interface on the router rather than one associated with a physical interface. In Cisco routers, this can be achieved using *loopback interfaces*—virtual interfaces that are always active, independent of the state of any physical interfaces.

Another common approach used when a physical address must be used for routing is to permit two or more routers to own the same IP address, but not concurrently. A control protocol, such as Cisco's Hot Standby Router Protocol (HSRP), arbitrates the use of the IP address for routing purposes.

Network Design Elements

Multiplexing is a fundamental element of network design. Indeed, you could argue that a network is typically one huge multiplexing system. More specifically, however, multiplexing is a tool that provides *economies of scale*—multiple users share one large resource rather than a number of individual resources.

NOTE   *Multiplexing* is the aggregation of multiple independent traffic flows into one large traffic flow. A useful analogy is the freeway system, which multiplexes traffic from many smaller roads into one large flow. At any time, traffic on the freeway may exit onto smaller roads (and thus be de-multiplexed) when it approaches its final destination.

As an added benefit, if the multiplexing is statistical in nature, one user may consume the unused resources of someone else. During periods of congestion, however, this statistical sharing of the resource might need to be predictable to ensure that basic requirements are met. In IP networks, bandwidth is the resource, and routers provide the multiplexing.

Traditionally, multiplexing has been a best-effort process. However, increasingly deterministic behavior is required—you can read about such techniques in Chapter 14, "Quality of Service Features." For now, it suffices to say that multiplexing saves money and can provide performance improvements while guaranteeing a minimum level of service.

Randomization is the process of applying random behavior to an otherwise predictable mechanism. This is an important approach to avoid the synchronization of network data or control traffic that can lead to cyclic congestion or instability. Although critical to the design of routing protocols, congestion control, and multiplexing algorithms, randomization is not currently a major factor in network topology design. However, this may change if load sharing of IP traffic through random path selection is ever shown to be a practical routing algorithm.

Soft state is the control of network functions through the use of control messages that are periodically refreshed. If the soft state is not refreshed, it is removed (or timed out). Soft state is also extremely important to routing functions. When routers crash, it becomes difficult to advise other routers that the associated routing information is invalidated. Nearly all routing information is kept as soft-state—if it is not refreshed, or at the very least reconfirmed in some way, it is eventually removed.

Soft state can be obviated by the use of static or "hard-coded" routes that are never invalidated. Static routes should therefore be used with extreme caution.

Some level of *hysterisis* or *dampening* is useful whenever there is the possibility of unbounded oscillation. These techniques are often used for processing routing updates in Interior Gateway Protocols (IGPs). If a route is withdrawn, a router may "hold down" that route for several minutes, even if the route is subsequently re-advertised by the IGP. This prevents an unstable route from rapidly oscillating between the used and unused states because the route can change its state only once per hold-down period.

Similarly, the external routing Border Gateway Protocol (BGP) applies dampening to external routes. This prevents CPU saturation that can occur when repeatedly calculating new routes, if large numbers of routes are involved.

Stabilizing routes in this manner also can improve network throughput because the congestion control mechanisms of TCP do not favor environments with oscillating or rapidly changing values of round-trip time or throughput on the network.

Localization and *caching* represent a variation on the earlier technique of optimizing the common case. Even in today's peer-to-peer networking model, many extremely popular data repositories (such as major Web farms) still exist. By *caching* commonly accessed Web data (in other words, making a localized copy of this data) it is possible to save long-distance network traffic and improve performance. Such caches can form a natural part of the network hierarchy.

Finally, any network topology should be carefully analyzed during failure of the design's various components. These are usually known as *failure modes.* The topology should be engineered for graceful degradation. In particular, the failure of links constitutes the most common failure mode, followed by the failure of critical routing nodes.

Topologies

There are essentially four topological building blocks: rings, buses, stars, and meshes. (See Figure 4-1.) A large, well-designed network normally will exploit the benefits of each building block—either alone or combined—at various points within its architecture.

Although initially attractive due to minimal dependence on complex electronics, the use of bus media, such as repeated Ethernet segments, is decreasing. For the most part, this is due to an increase in the reliability and flexibility of the technology that is implementing rings, stars, and meshes. In particular, bus LAN topologies are typically converted into stars using a LAN switch. This offers increased aggregate bandwidth and superior diagnostic capabilities.

Operational experience has also shown that a passive shared broadcast medium does not necessarily create a more reliable environment because a single misbehaving Ethernet card can render a bus LAN useless for communication purposes.

Figure 4-1 *Mesh, Star, Ring, and Bus Topologies (from top)*

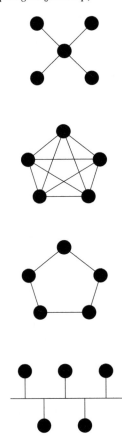

Hierarchy Issues

Just as the Internet hierarchy had to adapt to accommodate an increase in players, so has the enterprise network. Early data networks facilitated the basic requirement of communication between terminals and a central mainframe. The need for a simple hierarchy, from terminal to IBM cluster controllers to front-end processors, was readily apparent from this basic requirement. In today's world of peer-to-peer networking, however, the reasons for network hierarchy and its inner workings are subtler, yet just as important for successful network design.

Figure 4-2 presents the high-level network architecture developed in Chapter 1. Notice that the *network backbone* (also called the *network core*—the terms *core* and *backbone* are equivalent) consists of mesh-connected backbone routers that reside at distribution centers (DCs) within each service region.

Each DC, which may house a LAN topology that is resilient to single node failure, forms the hub of a star distribution network for that region. Finally, the access network consists of both provider and customer premise equipment, which is typically homed to one or more access POPs.

Figure 4-2   *Modularization of a Large Network*

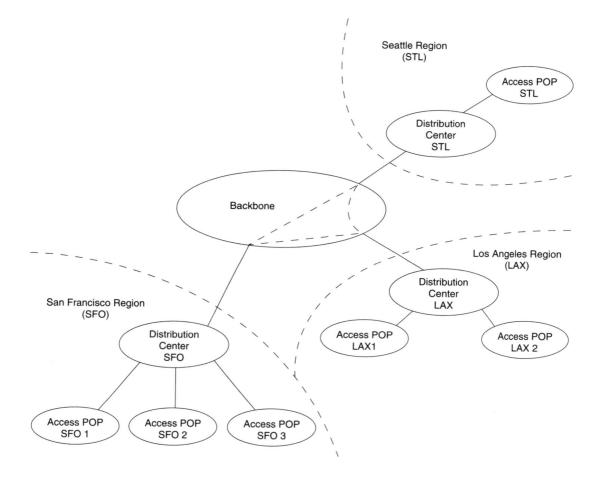

In the example in Figure 4-2, only three regions/DCs and, at most, three POPs in a region are shown. However, the hierarchical model will scale much more than this using current commercial routers.

A typical large IP network, whether an ISP or a large corporate intranet, will consist of routers performing a number of different roles. It is convenient to define three major roles corresponding to each layer in the hierarchy: backbone, distribution, and access.

As shown in Figure 4-3, which illustrates the arrangement in a typical high-resilience DC, these roles possess a specific hierarchical relationship. Backbone routers are at the top, distribution routers are in the middle, and access routers are at the bottom.

Figure 4-3 *Distribution Center Architecture*

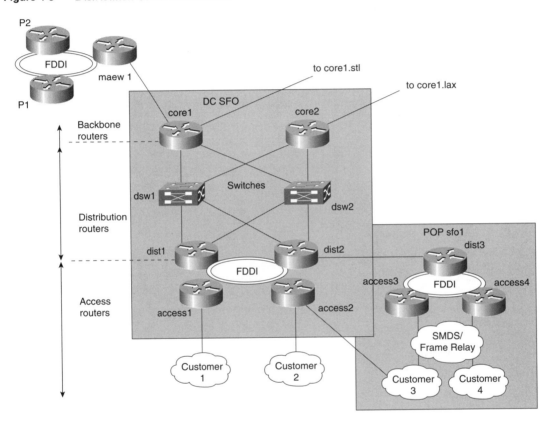

Backbone Routers

The backbone routers core1.sfo and core2.sfo reside in the San Francisco DC and are responsible for connecting the regional network to the backbone. These routers forward packets to and from the region. They also advertise reachability for that region, either to the core routers of other regions (in other major cities), or to external peer networks (other ISPs).

Backbone routers are also peers in terms of the useful reachability information they possess. This does not imply that router core1.sfo has the same detailed topological information about Los Angeles as, say, router core1.lax, but it does indicate that core1.sfo understands that core1.lax and core2.lax, rather than core1.stl, are the gateways to all destinations in the Los Angeles region.

Backbone routers contain reachability intelligence for all destinations within the network. They possess the capability to distinguish between the gateway information and the information that explains how to reach the outside world, which is through other peer networks or the Internet.

Distribution Routers

Distribution routers consolidate connections from access routers. They are often arranged in a configuration that is resilient to failure of a single core router. Distribution routers usually contain topological information about their own region, but they forward packets to a backbone router for inter-region routing.

NOTE   In smaller regions, distribution and backbone routers may be one and the same. In larger regions, distribution routers themselves may form a hierarchy.

High-performance customers on permanent WAN links often may connect directly to distribution routers, whereas dial-on-demand customers typically do not because this would impose the need to run dial-authentication software images of distribution routers.

Access Routers

Access routers connect the customer or enterprise site to the distribution network. In the ISP case, the router at the remote end of an access link is typically the customer premises equipment, and may be owned and operated by the customer.

For large enterprise networks, in which the LANs and WANs are managed by different divisions or contractors, the access router typically is managed by either the WAN or the LAN operator—usually this is the latter if the LAN is very large.

You now may wonder: Why is it important to distinguish between the backbone, access, and distribution routers? The reason is that they are increasingly becoming very distinct hardware/software combinations. In access routers, for example, you already have seen the need for support of dial-on-demand and authentication, as well as route filtering and packet filtering and classification.

In distribution routers, the emphasis is on economical aggregation of traffic and the support of varied media WAN types and protocols. In backbone routers, the emphasis is on supporting extremely high speeds, and aggregation of a very limited set of media types and routing protocols. These differences are summarized in Table 4-1.

Table 4-1 *Characteristics of Backbone, Distribution, and Access Routers*

Router Type	Characteristics
Backbone router	Scalable: packet forwarding, WAN links, QoS, routing Expensive Redundant WAN links National infrastructure
Distribution router	Scalable: WAN aggregation, LAN speeds Redundant LAN links Less expensive
Access router	Scalable: WAN aggregation Cheap Complex routing/QoS policy setting, access security, and monitoring capabilities

This discussion focused attention on the WAN environment and has avoided any issues of LAN design, other than the use of specific LAN technology within the distribution or access networks. In particular, at the individual user or network host level, access technologies include ATM, FDDI, Token Ring, or the ubiquitous Ethernet; rather than such technologies as Frame Relay, T1, SMDS, and SONET.

Scaling LANs through the use of hierarchy is itself the subject of much literature. To study this area further, interested readers should refer to the references listed at the end of this chapter.

The origins of the three-tiered, backbone-distribution-access hierarchy can be traced to the evolution of the Internet (refer to Chapter 1). However, hierarchical design is certainly nothing new and has been used in telephone networks and other systems for many years. In the case of IP data networking, there are several reasons for adding hierarchy.

Not only does hierarchy allow the various elements of routing, QoS, accounting, and packet switching to scale; but it also presents the opportunity for operational segmentation of the network, simpler troubleshooting, less complicated individual router configurations, and a logical basis for distance-based packet accounting.

These issues are examined in great depth in Part II of this book, "Core and Distributing Networks." For the moment, we will examine the topologies used within the backbone, distribution, and access layers of the network architecture.

Backbone Core Network Design

In early data networking, the topology for the network backbone was relatively simple: Operations were centralized, so a star topology made the most sense—and, in some cases, this was the only topology the technology would support. This did cause the center of the star to become a single point of failure, but because no real traffic flows existed between spokes on the star, this was not a major cause for concern. With the move toward multiple client-server and peer-to-peer relationships, the choice of core network topology is not as clear.

The purpose of the backbone is to connect regional distribution networks and, in some instances, to provide connectivity to other peer networks. A national infrastructure usually forms a significant part of the operational cost of the network. Given its position at the top of the network hierarchy, two requirements of the backbone topology are clear: it must be reliable and it must scale.

Making the Backbone Reliable

Reliability can be acquired by employing two methods. First, you can create more reliable routers through the use of "carrier-class" characteristics, such as multiple CPUs, power supplies, and generators; and even redundant routers. Ultimately, however, any backbone will include WAN links that rely on a great deal of equipment and environmental stability for their operation, which represents a real risk of ultimate failure. If the carrier's up-time guarantees are not sufficient, you have no choice but to design a backbone that is resilient to link failure.

The second option is to simply connect all distribution networks with a full mesh. However, in terms of minimizing hop count within the network, the full mesh approach has several drawbacks:

- First, given N regional distribution networks, you must have N(N-1)/2 backbone links in the core. This creates expense in WAN circuitry, as well as in router and WAN switch hardware (channelized or ATM technology can reduce these issues).

- Moreover, PVC sizing requires that the traffic levels between any two distribution networks should be well understood, or that the network has the capability to circumvent congestion. Although traffic engineering calculations and circumventing congestion are common in the telephone network, common IP networks and their associated routing protocols do not provide this capability as readily. One good reason is that the resources required by any TCP/IP session are not known *a priori*, and IP networks are traditionally engineered as best-effort. Chapter 14 explores how to bypass best-effort by providing differentiated service in IP networks.

- A full PVC mesh can also obviate one of the benefits of multiplexing, or *trunking,* in a best-effort network. Round-trip time and TCP window size permitting, any user can burst traffic up to the full line rate of the trunk. Furthermore, the routing complexity in a full mesh can consume bandwidth, computational, and operational management resources.

Most backbone topologies are, therefore, initially designed based on financial constraints, such as user population density, or application requirements; and WAN service availability. This initial design can be subsequently refined quite effectively by statistical analysis of traffic levels after the backbone is operational, and the availability of new WAN technologies is known. Data network requirements analysis is a relatively new art. See [McCabe, 1998] for thorough coverage of this area.

Building the Backbone Topology

Because you have a basic need for resilience in the backbone, a good starting point for the backbone topology is a ring connecting all distribution networks. This ring could represent the minimum cost of WAN circuits, compromised by an initial estimate of major traffic flows, and possibly some very particular delay requirements (although this is rare, with notable exceptions being high-performance networks).

Next, existing links can be fattened, or direct connections between backbone routers can be added as required or as is cost-effective. This incremental approach should be considered when selecting WAN technologies, routing nodes, and interface types.

Backbone routing protocols, such as IBGP, properly coupled with OSPF, IS-IS, and Enhanced IGRP, can rapidly circumvent failures by simple link-costing mechanisms. However, the bandwidth allocations with the core topology should consider failure modes. What happens when the ring is broken due to WAN or node failure? Is the re-routed path sufficient to carry the additional traffic load? Although TCP performs extremely well in congested environments compared with other protocols, it is still possible to render the network useless for most practical applications.

Analysis of historical traffic levels, captured by SNMP, for example, provides for a relatively accurate estimation of the consolidated load on the remaining links during various failure modes.

Traditionally, the use of a ring topology made it difficult to estimate the traffic levels between individual distribution networks. SNMP statistics, for example, provided only input and output byte counts for WAN interfaces, making it difficult to determine the appropriate sizing for new direct links between distribution networks.

Typically, this had to be accomplished using a cumbersome approach, such as "sniffers" on WAN links, or through accounting capabilities within routers that scaled rather poorly. However, IP accounting facilities, such as Netflow, now provide a scalable way for network managers to collect and analyze traffic flows, based on source and destination addresses, as well as many other flow parameters. This significantly eases traffic engineering and accounting activities. It is now possible to permanently collect and archive flow data for network design or billing purposes.

NOTE   Netflow is a high-performance switching algorithm that collects comprehensive IP accounting information and exports it to a collection agent.

Load sharing is possible on the backbone network. With Cisco routers, this can be either on a per-packet or a per-flow basis. The latter usually is recommended because it avoids possible packet re-ordering, is efficiently implemented, and avoids the potential for widely varying round-trip times, which interfere with the operation of TCP. This is not a problem for per-packet load sharing over parallel WAN circuits, but it can be a problem when each alternate path is one or more routed hops.

It is possible to connect regional networks directly, avoiding the backbone altogether and possibly providing more optimal routing. For example, in Figure 4-2, the DCs in SFO and LAX could be connected by a direct link. Traffic between the SFO and LAX regional networks could then travel over this link rather than over the backbone.

However, this exercise should be viewed as the effective consolidation of two regional distribution networks, and the overall routing architecture for the newly combined regions should be re-engineered to reflect this.

On an operational note, the backbone network and routers may be under different operational management teams to the regional networks. One historical example is the arrangement between the NSFNET backbone and the regional networks described in Chapter 1. Today, many smaller ISPs use the NSPs for WAN connectivity.

In this situation, the routing relationship between the backbone and the distribution networks is likely to be slightly different because an Exterior Gateway Protocol such as BGP will be used. In this book, the operators of the backbone and regional networks are generally considered to be the same, which makes it possible for the two to share a hierarchical IGP. In Chapter 16, "Design and Configuration Case Studies," you will examine a case study for scaling very large enterprise networks in which this is not the case.

Distribution/Regional Network Design

The role of the regional network is to route intra- and inter-regional traffic. The regional network generally is comprised of a DC as the hub and a number of access POPs as the spokes. Usually, two redundant routers in each regional network will connect to the backbone.

DCs may also provide services such as Web-caching, DNS, network management, and e-mail hosting. In some cases, the latter functionality may be extended into major POPs.

Placement of DCs is generally an economical choice based on the geographical proximity to a number of access sites. However, this does not mean that an access POP cannot be a mini-distribution center or transit for another access POP, but this is the exception rather than the rule.

When an access POP site provides such transit, and when that transit is the responsibility of the service provider, it should be considered part of the distribution network functionality.

Although the DC may be the center of a star topology from a network or IP perspective, this does not limit the choice of data-link or WAN connectivity to point-to-point links. Frame Relay or other cloud technologies can be—and often are—used to provide the connectivity from the customers, or from other distribution and access sites to the DC. Even within the DC, a provider may utilize Layer 2 aggregation equipment, such as a Frame Relay or ATM switch, or even an add/drop multiplexor.

A major DC typically consists of many routers, carrying either intra-regional or backbone-transit traffic. As more customers receive service from the DC, the higher the stakes become. Therefore, the backbone and intra-distribution network infrastructure must become more reliable.

A common option at major DCs is to provide dual aggregation LANs, dual backbone routers, and dual backbone WAN connections, as shown in Figure 4-3. This approach also can provide an element of load sharing between backbone routers. Of course, a single aggregation LAN and single backbone router will also serve this purpose. It is important to weigh the cost-versus-reliability issues, and bear in mind that most simple MTBF calculations consider hardware, but often ignore both software bugs and human error.

FDDI rings are a logical choice for the aggregation LAN because of their inherent fail-over mechanisms. However, with the development of low-cost/high-reliability LAN switches based on FDDI, Ethernet, or ATM technology—not to mention the ever-increasing intra-DC traffic levels—it is not uncommon to implement the dual aggregation LANs using switched media. IP routing circumvents LAN failure at either the single line card or the single switch level, as discussed in upcoming chapters.

Of course, many other critical reliability issues have not yet been considered. These include facilities, such as power supply and the choice of router and switching equipment.

NOTE   The distribution network is hierarchical. Router dist3 is located as an access POP, which services fewer customers, and therefore is not a resilient design.

The backbone/distribution/access hierarchy can be bypassed to achieve lower delays at the expense of reliability. Customer 4 may connect directly to router core2.sfo. However, if core2.sfo fails—albeit a rare event—customer 4 is effectively cut off from the network. Alternatively, customer 4 may have a backup connection via dist3.sfo.

This arrangement is satisfactory, provided that it does not confuse the role of each router. For example, directly connecting customer routers to the core router indicates that they may have to perform dial-up authentication, packet and router filtering, and packet classification. Not only will this occupy precious switching cycles on the core router, but it also could mean running a larger and possibly less reliable software image.

Other possible failure modes include the following:

- *Core1* All intra-network traffic is routed through core2. All traffic to other ISPs is also routed through core2, presumably to another NAP connected to a backbone router elsewhere in the network.
- *Ds1* Traffic destined for a remote distribution network is switched through ds2, as is traffic destined for other locations in the local distribution network.
- *Dist1* Customer 2 is re-routed through Dist2.
- *Dist3* Customer 3 is cut off.

It is worth noting that any resilience at Layer 3 results in routing complexity. This is examined in detail in Part II. As a matter of policy, the network service provider may choose not to allow customers to connect to core routers or even to dual distribution routers.

However, in the enterprise environment, reliability affects user satisfaction. In the commercial environment, this may affect their choice of provider. Policy that simplifies engineering must be carefully balanced against customer requirements.

Policy also must be balanced against the risk of human error. A resilient routing environment might be more reliable in theory, but in practice it might have a greater risk of human configuration error, and possibly algorithmic or vendor implementation flaws.

Access Design

In most cases, an access router serves a large number of customers. With modern access technology, this number can reach the thousands. As a result, resilient connectivity to the distribution routers is recommended. This may be accomplished using a self-healing LAN technology, such as FDDI. Alternatively, as with the connectivity between distribution and backbone routes, this may involve the use of redundant LAN switches. If the access router is the only node in a small POP, redundant WAN connections to the nearest DC are an option.

The design of the access topology is generally a choice of WAN technology between the CPE and the access router. For redundancy or load-sharing purposes, two or more links may be homed into the same access router or possibly onto different access routers. This is an issue of provider policy and capabilities.

Although the topology of the access network is relatively simple, it is here that the "policing" of customer connections, in terms of traffic rates and accounting, QoS, and routing policy, occurs. The configuration and maintenance must be executed carefully. The consequences of a router misconfiguration can be severe.

Summary

Network design involves the art and science of meeting requirements while dealing with economic, technological, physical, and political constraints. Scalability and extensibility are the hallmarks of a successful large-scale network design, and are encouraged through layering, modularization, and hierarchy. Randomization, soft state, dampening, separation of the control plane, regionalization, and optimizing the common case are also important considerations for routing protocols and the overall routing topology.

Although requirement analysis is an important aspect of design, it should be viewed as an ongoing task and should be ratified by the collection of traffic statistics that describe actual network usage.

By categorizing routers into the roles of backbone, distribution, and access, you will simplify the hardware/software combinations and configuration complexity required for any particular router. This consequently simplifies the operational support of the network.

Within the various tiers of the hierarchy, the topologies of ring, star, bus, and mesh may be employed. The choice depends on reliability, traffic, and delay requirements. In the case of WAN topologies, carrier service pricing also could be a determining factor.

Review Questions

1 If you need to support protocols other than IP in a large network, what would you do?

2 When would you consider breaking the hierarchy of a network design by linking distribution networks directly?

3 ATM is an ideal technology to grow a ring backbone to a partial mesh, and then to a full mesh. Does this make it a better choice for a backbone technology than point-to-point links? Why or why not?

4 Could you use different routers in your access, distribution, and core networks?

Answers:

1 If at all possible, try to tunnel the protocol in IP. The current trend among vendors of routers for large networks is to support only IP. At some point, native support of other protocols simply may not be an option.

2 Break network hierarchy only when you have a very solid business case for doing so. You should consider the expense of the additional operational complexity in adding the link. In most cases, you may find that the same result can be achieved by adding more backbone capacity.

3 It all comes down to cost, and this varies greatly from country to country. Determine the cost of the two approaches over 1, 3, 5, and 10 years; and compare. Of course, you can only estimate your future backbone requirements, which means that any approach will be a carefully calculated risk.

4 If you are using standardized protocols, yes. However, a multi-vendor environment increases operational complexity and vulnerability to interoperability issues. Certainly, within the access network, you could run a mix of routers. As you go up the hierarchy into the distribution and core networks, mixing products from different vendors becomes more risky.

For Further Reading . . .

The available literature on network design (other than an abstract mathematical treatment) is surprisingly small. If you have well-known requirements, McCabe's book is unique in its treatment of network design through requirements and flow analysis.

Bennett, G. *Designing TCP/IP Internetworks*. New York, NY: John Wiley & Sons, 1997.

Galvin, P. B. and A. Silberschatz. *Operating System Concepts*. Reading, MA: Addison-Wesley, 1997.

Keshav, S. *An Engineering Approach to Computer Networking*. Reading, MA: Addison-Wesley, 1997.

McCabe, J. *Practical Computer Network Analysis and Design*. San Francisco, CA: Morgan Kaufmann Publishers, 1998.

Pressman, R. *Software Engineering: A Practitioners Approach,* Fourth Edition. New York, NY: McGraw-Hill, 1996.

The fundamental role of the router is route computation, packet scheduling, and forwarding. This role has become confused as vendors bundle more functionality into operating systems and platforms that traditionally focused on simple routing and packet forwarding.

Accounting, security filtering, encapsulation, tunneling, address translation, packet classification, and proxying are just a few of the capabilities being squeezed into what is more accurately termed a general-purpose network *appliance*. Routing is merely a subset of this appliance's capabilities.

This chapter provides an overview of modern IP routers. We focus on router functionality that is central to building a large-scale network. Specifically, the following issues are covered:

Router architecture   Router hardware architectures have undergone three generations of development. This section traces that development, summarizing the improvements that occurred within each generation.

The evolution of switching paradigms   Packet-switching algorithms also have evolved with each generation of router architecture. The evolution of the Cisco product line from process switching to Cisco Express Forwarding is described.

Routing and forwarding   The functions of routing and forwarding are often confused. Routing protocols and route-computation are contrasted with forwarding algorithms and route-lookup.

Switching with QoS and Policy   A router's job is complicated by the need to provide differentiated service. This section summarizes queuing algorithms and introduces the role of a packet scheduler.

## CHAPTER 5

Routers

Router Architecture

In Chapter 1, "Evolution of Data Networks," you learned about the evolution of router technology within the early Internet. Essentially two approaches were presented:

- A single computer/central-processor approach, such as the original NSFNET "fuzzball" routers
- The parallel switching/multi-processor nodal switching subsystems (the successor)

Each approach is discussed in more detail in the following sections.

NOTE   A *router* isolates the link-layer broadcast domains of subnetworks, forwards IP packets between the domains, decrements the TTL, and sometimes performs media translation and fragmentation. To make a forwarding decision, the router exchanges topological information about the network with other routers.

Single CPU Designs

The first approach utilizes a single CPU-controlled shared bus that connects a number of slave interface cards. This arrangement can be based on a general-purpose computer, such as a PC running UNIX or Windows NT. Various bus communication strategies (such as shared memory, DMA, and bus mastering), together with high-performance RISC CPUs, can result in a router of significant forwarding capabilities.

A large number of dedicated-purpose centralized CPU router platforms also are available on the low-end market, such as the ubiquitous Cisco 2500 series. Over time, the forwarding performance and cost of such architectures have improved through the introduction of ASICs.

The advantage of the single CPU approach is the simplicity of software: The majority of the packet-switching intelligence, and certainly all of the route calculation intelligence, is in the single CPU. Little danger exists of synchronization problems, such as inconsistent forwarding behavior between line cards.

In addition, if the CPU is a general-purpose computer, the interaction between the CPU motherboard and the line cards usually conforms to an open bus/operating-system standard, enabling the administrator to choose among multiple vendors for both the line cards and the CPU. Single CPU designs also can be very cost-effective because the majority of the complex hardware is focused on the CPU itself.

The clear disadvantage of single CPU designs, however, is scalability and reliability. Involving a single CPU and shared bus in all forwarding decisions is problematic when the number of interfaces or the traffic level becomes very high. Moreover, even if using shared memory for packet storage minimizes bus transactions, shared memory access times can become a limiting factor.

Parallel Switching Designs

An obvious improvement to the single CPU design is the introduction of more independent processing power. One way to achieve this is to connect clusters of routers by using conventional LAN technology and routing protocols. Each router in the cluster is required to perform only switching and route-calculations within the bounds of a single-CPU router design.

This approach is similar to that used in parallel processing supercomputers. Unfortunately, even with modern routing protocols, RISC processors, and high-speed LANs, the use of generic networking components to connect routers does not provide the level of integration needed by most network managers. Administrational overhead of such router clusters is high, and the protocols used for general-purpose network connectivity are inefficient and inflexible.

The necessary refinement may involve a generic high-speed switching fabric, connecting line cards with peer computational capabilities. However, such multiprocessor designs are inherently complex to design and debug, as well as expensive to build. It has taken some time for vendors to develop such packet switches, and it has taken time for network providers to accumulate the traffic levels that require these sophisticated systems.

Three Generations of Routers

The development of routers can be characterized through three generations. The first generation consists of a single CPU controlling relatively unsophisticated line cards through a general-purpose shared I/O bus. Packet queues between line cards are maintained in central or shared memory by the CPU, which coordinates all packet forwarding. In the worst case, packets may traverse the I/O bus twice to complete the forwarding process.

A second-generation switch supplements central switching functions with forwarding intelligence on the line cards. The CPU usually places this forwarding information in the line card upon reception of the first packet in a flow. Line cards communicate with the CPU and forward packets between one another using a *passive shared bus* (a bus with no electronics that provides switching intelligence).

Third-generation switches replace the shared bus with an active switching fabric, containing specialized packet-switching electronics, which supports the simultaneous transfer of multiple packets. This simultaneous transfer of packets circumvents the electrical problems inherent in extremely high-speed shared buses. Both the switching fabric and the line cards are controlled by a central processor. Figure 5-1 shows the first-, second-, and third-generation packet switches.

Routers may be input-queued, or both input- and output-queued. If the switching fabric is slower than the sum of the interface card speeds, both input and output queuing can occur. Otherwise, queuing tends to occur at the outputs only, due to contention for the output interface. Queues traditionally were first-in, first-out; with the introduction of service differentiation, however, *per class-of-service queuing* is increasingly common. In other words, routers may have to maintain queues for packets, depending on information in the packet header that describes the priority of the packet, its source or destination, or the user application generating the packet.

Evolution of the Cisco Switching Algorithms

The Cisco core product line has evolved through the generations, from the AGS of 1986 to the GSR of 1997. The next sections examine this evolution in more detail.

Process Switching

The original Cisco AGS was a central CPU packet switch that was similar to host-based routers, except that the range of protocols and interfaces supported was greater, and the operating system was optimized for packet-forwarding functions. Interface cards were connected to the CPU motherboard through the Motorola 16 Mbps Multibus, and interface cards maintained the simple packet buffers necessary when there was contention on the internal bus and external media (see Figure 5-2).

All packets were passed over the multibus to the CPU, which performed a routing table lookup, recalculated CRCs, and passed the packet again over the multibus to the appropriate line card. Processing switching performance of 2000+ packets per second (pps) was possible with 68000-based CPUs.

Figure 5-1   *First-, Second-, and Third-Generation Packet Switches*

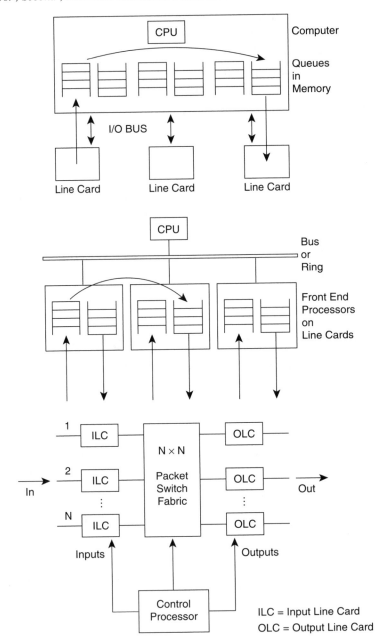

Figure 5-2   *Cisco AGS Architecture*

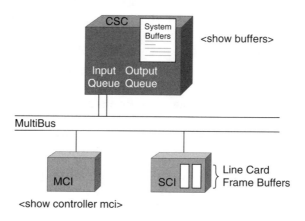

Fast Switching

Route lookup is an expensive computation; in Cisco routers, a hash-table mechanism is used. A more efficient mechanism, called a *trie,* has since become the method of choice.

NOTE	A *trie* is simply a method of arranging IP addresses that assists in locating a route with a minimal number of steps.

Because IP network transactions usually result in a stream of packets, it is a reasonable assumption that after a packet to a particular destination has been switched, another is likely to arrive in the near future.

By building a cache of recently switched destinations, there are considerable savings in full route table lookups for subsequent packets to the same destinations. Moreover, other information that is required for the MAC header rewrite can be stored in the cache, rather than being recalculated. This arrangement is called *fast switching;* it is the default switching mechanism on all Cisco router platforms. Fast switching reduced the CPU utilization associated with packet switching and boosted the performance of the AGS to 20,000 pps.

NOTE	*Fast switching* uses a cache prepopulated by the process switch engine, and operates at the CPU interrupt level.

Naturally, entries in the fast-switching route cache must be periodically timed-out; otherwise, the cache will grow boundlessly. In addition, changes to the IP routing table must invalidate the cache. Unfortunately, in an environment with high route churn, such as the Internet, the benefits of route caches are fairly limited. This problem spurred the development of Cisco Express Forwarding (see the section, "Cisco Express Forwarding," later in this chapter).

NOTE   *Cisco Express Forwarding* (CEF) combines the benefits of caching MAC rewrite information and trie lookup algorithms.

Fast switching represents an ideal cost/performance compromise for low-end Cisco router architectures, such as those illustrated in Figure 5-3. Both the CPU and the line cards share memory for packet queuing and switching functions, whereas the CPU has dedicated memory for generic processing purposes. Fast switching performance of low-end platforms was typically 6,000 pps (2500), 14,000 pps (4000), and 45,000 pps (4700).

Figure 5-3   *Cisco Low-End Router Architecture*

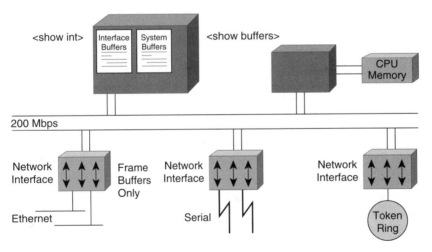

TIP   Note that security features are not bypassed by fast switching, or by using any of the autonomous or distributed schemes that follow. If traffic is administratively forbidden, the fast-switching cache does not become populated. This can entail a performance hit for complicated access lists, such as those involving TCP-level conditions. However, Netflow switching (covered later in this chapter) addresses these issues.

Autonomous Switching

One advantage of the single CPU architecture is that performance improvements could be obtained merely by increasing the speed of the CPU (which occurred through the CSC and CSC3 motherboards, respectively). However, as the demand for greater throughput increased, it became necessary to increase the bus speed and offload some of the switching from the CPU. A new series of bit-slice-processor interface cards, coupled with a 533 Mbps cbus and associated controller, did just that.

In effect, the route-cache functionality was moved from the CPU to an auxiliary switching processor, so the CPU is interrupted only when a route-cache lookup fails (see Figure 5-4).

Figure 5-4   *Cisco AGS+ Architecture*

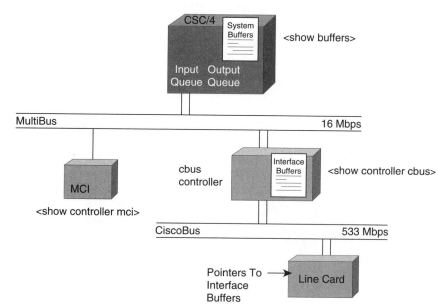

Upon receiving a packet, cbus interface cards query the cbus controller for the destination line card. The cbus controller performs a local route-cache lookup for the destination—if this is the first packet to the destination, the cache lookup fails and the cbus controller sends a query to the CSC card for a route-table lookup.

The CSC returns the result to the cbus controller, which caches the result and responds to the query from the original line card. The receiving line card forwards the packet over the cbus to the appropriate destination line card, and subsequent packets to the same destination can now be autonomously switched over the cbus without the intervention of the centralized CPU. This boosted the performance of the AGS+ platform to 80,000 pps.

Within the AGS+ architecture, interface buffers were maintained on the cbus controller and system buffers on the CSC/4 CPU card.

Only four of the AGS+ chassis slots could be used for cbus interface cards. With the introduction of the 7000 and 7010 series, Cisco maintained the same auxiliary-switching processor design paradigm, but introduced a new range of processor cards. The extended Cisco bus included connectivity to every slot—five slots, in the case of the 7000; three slots, in the case of the 7010.

The switch processor performed an identical role as the cbus controller: to offload fast-cache lookup from the CPU so that packets that had a cache hit could be forwarded autonomously; and to perform the MAC layer-rewrite, writing the new MAC header to the packet.

Recognizing that the CPU was now predominantly used for route calculations, Cisco renamed it the route processor, and the auxiliary switching engine was renamed the switch processor. An all-time high of 200,000 pps was achieved on the 7000 router performing autonomous switching (see Figure 5-5).

One additional refinement took place on the 7000 series. The *silicon switch processor* (also known as the silicon switch engine, or SSE) is a hardware-accelerated alternative to the standard switch processor. An SSE cache was precomputed on the route processor card and regularly was dumped into the SSP. The result was more than 270,000 pps.

Figure 5-5   *Cisco 7000 Architecture*

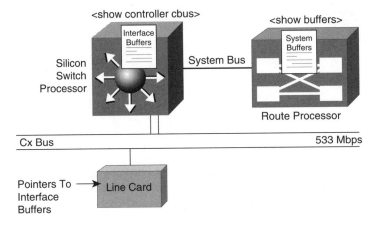

Optimum Switching

In 1995, Cisco introduced the 7500 series. Refinements relevant to switching included the combination of both the route and the switch processors on a single card, and a new CyBus of 1.077 Gbit/s capacity that was backward-compatible with the cbus interface processors of the 7000 series.

A new route-cache mechanism, based on an *m-trie* lookup algorithm, provided switching capacity similar to the 7000 series with SSP—around 270,000 pps. Operationally, however, it performed the same role as autonomous switching: offloading switching functions from the Route Switch Processor (RSP). Optimum switching is the default on the 7500 series interfaces.

Distributed Switching

With the introduction of the Versatile Interface Processor (VIP) cards, Cisco made the ultimate step toward a peer multiprocessor architecture. Each VIP card contains its own MIPS r4600 RISC processor, runs a mini-IOS kernel, and has configurable levels of SRAM and DRAM. Although the VIP1 was available for a short time, most of the installed base consists of VIP2s. The distributed features are targeted at the 7500 series (see Figure 5-6), but a VIP1 without distributed features is supported in a 7000 platform equipped with an RSP7000 (combined RP/SP).

Each VIP card participates in an interprocess communication system with the RSP over the CyBus. IPC maintains an up-to-date copy of the RSP's fast switching cache on each VIP card, enabling each to perform switching independent of the RSP, with the exception of the use of packet memory.

Hence, within the constraints of the system bus, packet throughput is increased linearly with the number of VIP cards installed in the router. Switching local to a VIP is performed at more than 120,000 pps, and between VIPs at more than 70,000 pps.

Netflow Switching

As discussed in Chapter 4, "Network Topology and Design," accounting of data traffic is not only important for customer billing, but is a crucial part of traffic engineering. For example, knowing the relative size of flows between routers in the network core can help you calculate the most cost-effective topology and circuit size of the core network.

In terms of operation, Netflow switching is similar to the fast-switching cache: The first packet of any flow is process switched and involves a routing table lookup by the CPU/Route Processor (RP). Subsequent packets in the flow can be switched using a fast-cache lookup rather than an expensive routing table traverse. In addition, on platforms capable of autonomous or optimum switching, Netflow cache lookup and packet forwarding can occur without interrupting the RP.

The differences between Netflow and the fast-cache–based switching paradigms is the information maintained in the cache, as well as the fact that, in Netflow switching, this information can be periodically exported to collector hosts for further post-processing and analysis.

Figure 5-6 *Cisco 7500 Architecture*

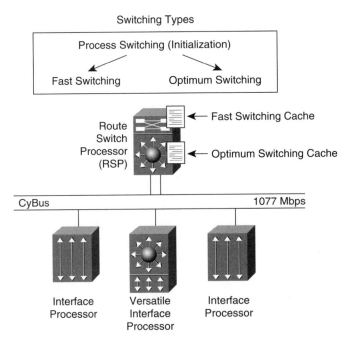

Per-flow information that is maintained by the Netflow cache includes the following:

- IP source and destination address
- Next-hop router address
- Input and output physical interfaces
- Packet and byte counts
- Start-of-flow and end-of-flow timestamps
- TCP/UDP source and destination application port numbers
- IP protocol (such as TCP, UDP, and so on)
- Type of service (indicates packet priority in multi-class service)
- TCP flags
- Source and destination autonomous system numbers
- Source and destination subnet masks

Other than the obvious accounting capabilities, Netflow switching improves performance in the presence of complicated administrative filtering features, such as access lists. As with fast switching, Netflow can operate in centralized or distributed switching mode. Distributed mode supports the maintenance and exportation of the cache from individual VIPs.

Cisco Express Forwarding

Operational experience proves that the demand-cache mechanisms described previously did not scale well in highly dynamic routing environments such as the Internet. Fast-switching caches must generally be invalidated when there is a change in the routing table. Although route holddown can prevent cyclic churn, rebuilding the cache is computationally expensive because packets that initiate cache entries must be process-switched.

CEF resolves this problem by building and maintaining a forwarding information base (FIB) with entries that include a one-to-one correspondence with entries in the IP routing table. Each entry in the FIB points to an IP next-hop that exists in an adjacency table. The adjacency table contains the information necessary for MAC-layer rewrites (see Figure 5-7).

Figure 5-7   *Routing, FIB, and Adjacency Table Entries*

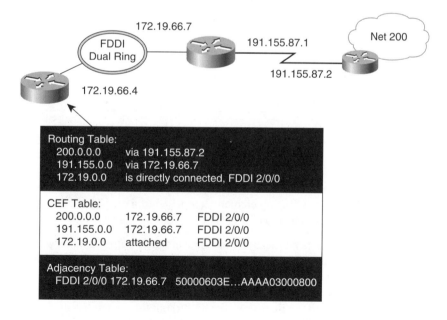

NOTE   Adjacency information is the MAC-layer header to which a router must forward IP packets to another device on the interface.

Unlike fast-cache entries, which are comprised of host routes only, CEF entries can include hosts, subnets, or even supernets. In core-routing environments, the FIB table, therefore, may actually be smaller than a demand-built fast-cache. The FIB is created immediately after router boot-up.

CEF is able to run in centralized or distributed mode (see Figure 5-8). In distributed mode (see Figure 5-9), a FIB and an adjacency database are maintained on each VIP card. As with DFS, interprocess communication over the cybus is used to coordinate the distribution of the FIB table.

Figure 5-8   *CEF Operation*

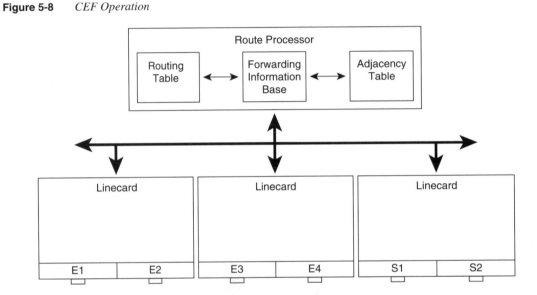

With the introduction of the Gigabit Switch Router platform family, Cisco replaced the traditional passive backplane used in earlier core products, such as the 7000 and 7500. An active and extensible bit-slicing switching element comprised of a crossbar and associated control ASICs is used to connect line cards for packet-forwarding purposes.

A central route processor performs systems management, routing, and forwarding table calculations; and is responsible for distributing the CEF table to individual line cards. A separate maintenance bus exists between line cards and the RP for bootstrapping and other diagnostic and maintenance operations. However, large data transfers, such as CEF table downloads from the RP to the line cards, occur through the switch fabric. Although the GSR operates with distributed CEF tables, recursion is carried out at the RP rather than at individual line cards.

Figure 5-9   *dCEF Operation*

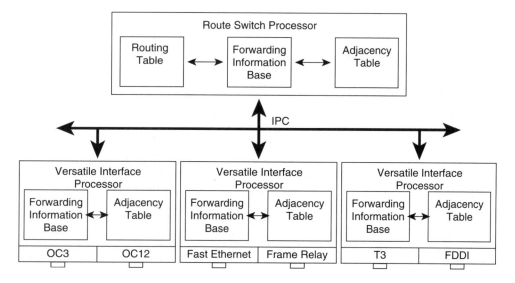

CEF has special handling of access lists and other per-interface intricate features that are comparable, in performance terms, to optimum or autonomous switching. However, Netflow can offer superior performance over CEF in the presence of complex access lists and other policy-configuration features. In terms of accounting, CEF maintains basic per-prefix and adjacency packet/byte counts. It also can be used with Netflow to provide more comprehensive accounting functions and accelerated performance in the presence of access lists.

CEF also performs efficient per-packet or per-destination load sharing. Prior to CEF, per-packet load sharing was always process-switched.

CEF is activated globally on routers, but both CEF and fast switching modes can be run concurrently by disabling CEF on a per-interface/VIP basis. Concurrent operation is not recommended, however, because this consumes resources for maintenance of both the FIB and the fast switching cache.

Tag Switching

Tag switching aims to solve many of the problems facing large-scale networks. Among these are the ever-increasing performance and scalability requirements; along with the need for service differentiation, virtual private networks, and the means to easily control the path of traffic through the network backbone. Tag switches—which may be dedicated tag-switching devices or IP routers—forward packets based on a *shim*, which is an extra field on which to base a switching decision. The shim is inserted between the Layer 2 and Layer 3 packet headers. In the case of ATM, the shim may be the combination of the VPI and VCI.

A Tag Distribution Protocol (TDP) is used with standard IP routing protocols to distribute tag information between switches within the network. Switching based on tags is extremely efficient and is more readily implemented in hardware than the longest match lookups necessary for forwarding based on IP destination addresses.

Tag switching is similar to CEF: A forwarding table is created, based on the contents of the IP routing table. This Tag Information Base (TIB) is keyed based on incoming tags, and contains entries of the form of outgoing tags, outgoing MAC-layer rewrites, and outgoing interfaces. As with CEF, the TIB is prepopulated, based on the IP routing table rather than being built on a packet-forwarding process on demand. Therefore, it scales well in dynamic routing environments. Cisco's implementation of tag switching works efficiently with CEF because they share common data structures and maintenance mechanisms.

Packets that arrive without a tag may be CEF or fast-switched, depending on the specific router configuration. As with CEF, tag switching can operate in centralized or distributed mode on VIP-capable platforms; it is enabled globally, but may be disabled on a per-interface/VIP basis (see Figure 5-10).

Figure 5-10 *Tag Switching*

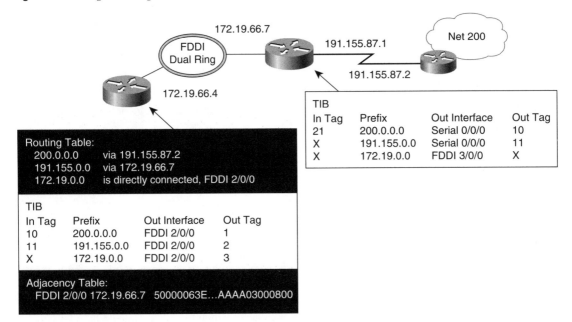

Routing and Forwarding

IP routers are typically capable of multiple routing processes, each of which maintains its own RIB. These are either link-state protocols, such as IS-IS or OSPF; or distance-vector protocols, such as RIP, IGRP, and BGP.

Each routing protocol may have multiple routes to the same destination, and the selection of the best route by each protocol is normally determined on the basis of longest match, followed by other routing protocol metrics. The per-protocol decision algorithm can be quite complex and can depend on many locally configured variables that control routing policy.

Distance-vector routing protocols also may have incoming or outgoing policy filters—that is, they may choose to ignore certain prefixes. Link-state protocols, however, do not generally have this capability because they must flood consistent topological information. Some filtering is possible, but if this is not part of the protocol itself (such as filtering between levels in IS-IS), it must be used with extreme caution.

Populating the FIBs

IP prefixes from each routing process are inserted in the central forwarding information base (FIB). This is the routing table used for actual packet forwarding. When there are two equal-length prefixes from the different RIBs or different routing processes or protocols, an *administrative distance* is applied to break the tie. This distance typically is applied to the whole routing process—with the notable exception being BGP, which has different administrative distances for external, internal, and locally generated routes.

Routes in the central FIB (which are only those actually chosen as the best routes for packet-forwarding purposes) may be redistributed between routing protocols. This redistribution also may be subject to local policy filters. Within a Cisco router, this central FIB is used for process switching.

Improving FIBs: Fast IP Route-Lookup

With the staggering growth of the Internet and consequent demands on core Internet routers, the field of fast IP route-lookup has been the subject of intense interest. Although route churn in the Internet is relatively high, packet forwarding, rather than route-computation, is proving to be the critical area requiring optimization. This signifies that lookup time is optimized at the expense of routing table update time.

Route-lookup is the process of finding the best match between the destination IP address of a packet and entries in the routing table. This may not be an exact match, but it is the most specific supernet containing the destination IP address. This rule does not guarantee a unique choice if non-contiguous subnet masks are used, which is one of many reasons their use is deprecated. Most modern lookup techniques assume contiguous masking to achieve efficiency. In some cases, the best route actually may be the default route.

Traditional approaches to route-lookup, such as those implemented in the BSD UNIX operating system, employed tree structures. More recently, however, attention has been focused in three areas: hardware-assisted lookups, using content addressable memories or caches; compression techniques, allowing the routing table to fit in the high-speed cache of off-the-shelf processors; and sophisticated hashing techniques. Cisco routers use a combination of these techniques, depending on the switching mode employed.

As you read earlier in this chapter, the evolution of route-lookup and the resultant availability of many lookup techniques means that modern routers may have a number of switching paths. Each switching path maintains its own FIB, which is optimized for a certain type of forwarding/switching paradigm, such as demand-built fast route-cache, or a special-purpose, possibly hardware-assisted lookup mechanism.

Within a Cisco router, such as the c7500, these FIBs are used in a hierarchical manner. CEF is an exception: A lookup failure in the CEF FIB results in a packet discard. When a lookup fails in the lowest-level FIB, which is usually the fastest, switching of the packet is transferred to a higher-level FIB, which is generally slower. Use of a particular FIB often can be configured on a per-interface basis.

Switching with QoS

Traditionally, queuing of packets within IP routers has been first-in, first-out (FIFO). More recently, Layer 3 quality of service features have been introduced to enable large-scale IP networks to effectively handle a mix of best-effort, and mission-critical or time-sensitive applications. This is typically achieved through congestion management and control algorithms implemented in a packet scheduler associated with the outgoing interface.

The scheduler may perform a number of functions:

- Classifying packets assigns them particular priorities based on protocol type, and then sends the packets in priority order. There is no minimum service level in priority queuing, so lower-priority traffic can be locked out by higher-priority traffic.

- Custom queuing to ensure that packets match certain criteria (such as source address, destination port, or IP precedence) is provided with a minimum service level. This is also referred to as *class-based queuing*. Note that packets in the same class are still treated as FIFO.

- Weighted fair queuing, which attempts to bound traffic latency, provides priority for interactive traffic flows, and provides equitable treatment for large-volume (such as FTP) flows. WFQ is supported in all switching modes, and can be used either with a default set or a customer-supplied set of weights. Distributed WFQ requires CEF switching.

- Traffic shaping of outgoing packet streams occurs to meet agreed sustained and burst rates. Traffic shaping can be applied, based on most fields in the IP header.

- Random Early Detection (RED) monitors the outgoing packet queue, and randomly discards packets when user-configurable thresholds have been reached. When used with TCP traffic, RED preempts congestion by backing off selected flows individually over a period of time. This is preferable to a simple queue tail-drop, which results in multiple TCP backoffs, and can induce cyclic congestion and "wave-like" link utilizations. Distributed RED is possible with the distributed CEF switching mode.

- Committed Access Rate allows the maximum rate of traffic input or output on an interface to be controlled. All packets are classified, based on conformity to or exceeding of configured CAR; as a result, the packet can be dropped, or it can have its IP precedence field adjusted. CAR requires CEF switching and may be run in distributed mode. Unlike the other features described here, use of input CAR requires an input scheduler.

It is also possible to base routing decisions on fields other than the destination IP address. This may be necessary due to QoS, security, or other policies. This cannot be accomplished through an output scheduler, however, because the decision must be made prior to switching. An output scheduler feasibly could route packets onto logical subinterfaces of a single physical interface.

Caching Technique Case Study

In previous sections about Cisco switching techniques, we discussed how fast switching is performed, how cache is created from the routing table, and what information is kept in cache. You might be wondering how the cache is populated. During the case study, the text discusses what happens when a packet that must be fast-switched reaches the router.

The cache is built from the routing table. In the scheme prior to CEF, the routing table is built when the routing protocol injects routes. Before a packet is forwarded, a process performs a lookup in the routing table and decides how the packet should be forwarded. Each entry in the routing table for the network is considered. An example of entries in the routing table is shown here:

```
Show ip route

150.150.6.0/24 [20/30] via 150.150.5.31, 00:00:23, Fddi2/0
150.150.0.0/16 [20/10] via 150.150.5.31, 00:20:23, Fddi2/0
171.68.0.0/16 [20/40] via 131.108.5.31, 01:50:2, Serial 0/0
171.68.0.0/16 [20/40] via 131.108.5.10, 01:05:2, Serial 0/1
10.10.10.1/32 [110/1572] via 131.108.5.10, 01:5:23, Serial 0/1
10.0.0.0/8 [20/10] via 131.1.1.1, 01:5:11, Ethernet 3/1
204.10.0.0/16 [20/40] via 150.150.5.31, 00:20:23, Fddi2/0
204.10.10.1/32 [20/30] via 150.150.5.31, 01:20:23, Fddi2/0
0.0.0.0/0 [20/20] via 150.150.5.31, 00:20:23, Fddi2/0
```

In the **show ip route** output shown above, the router has nine routing entries in the routing table. The first two routing entries correspond with network 150.150.0.0. The first of the two is a subnet entry 150.150.6.0/24, and the second correlates to the major network 150.150.0.0/16. The next two entries correspond to major network 171.68.0.0/16. Following that, there are two entries for the 10.0.0.0 network; the first is a host route to 10.10.10.1/32, and the second is an entry corresponding to major network 10.0.0.0/8.

Next, there is a single entry for a CIDR block for 204.10.0.0/16. A host route to 204.10.10.1/32, which is a network out of the CIDR block range, follows. The final entry corresponds to the default route 0.0.0.0/0.

This example of an ip route explains how a Cisco router creates fast-switching cache entries, which is shown in a **show ip cache**. We will begin by looking at the entries for network 150.150.0.0. The router has two entries in the routing table—one for the major network of 150.150.0.0/16 and one for the subnet of 150.150.6.0/24. Because the longest prefix mask for this major net is /24 in the routing table, cache entries for any destination in 150.150.0.0 are created as /24. If you send a packet to a destination of 150.150.8.1, the entry will be cached as 150.150.8.0/24, even though the major network of 150.150.0.0/16 covers the route for this destination.

Now, consider the second case for the network 171.68.0.0/16. In this case, you have two equal cost paths to the network. In this instance, /32 host entries are cache.

There is a misconception that load sharing is performed per session. In actuality, load sharing is performed per destination. As an illustration, assume that a user wants to Telnet to 171.68.1.1. The router will cache 171.68.1.1/32 via one of the interfaces. All future packets to this destination will use this cache entry, so it will always be sent out the same interface. The host sending a packet through the router will make a connection to 171.68.1.1 TCP port number 23. If another user FTPs to the same host, 171.68.1.1, via this router, the router will use the newly created cache entry.

Although both users are connecting to the same destination, each session is different, but all packets take the same path that was created originally in the cache entry. This is the reason that load sharing is per-destination and not per-session in fast switching. Now assume that another user wants to connect to a different host on the same destination subnet. For example, if a third user wants to connect to 171.68.1.2, this will cause a second cache entry to be created through the second path, which is also a /32 entry. For this reason, cache entries during load sharing can become very large.

The third entry in the routing table corresponds to network 10.0.0.0/8.The router has a /8 entry and a /32 entry in the routing table. Each entry in the routing table would be cached for network 10.0.0.0/32, although there are only two entries in the routing table for the network 10.0.0.0/8. All the entries for this network are created as /32. Remember from previous discussions that caching is always done on the longest prefix in the routing table for the same major network.

TIP   A good practice for ISPs is to avoid receiving a /32 route from the Internet. ISPs should use an access list to avoid routes with longer prefixes from being received from other ISPs or customers. The only /32 routes an ISP should have in its routing table are routes from its own autonomous system.

Note that Cisco routers still cache a *classful entry* for a CIDR route unless you are using CEF.

The routing table shown in the previous example has an entry of 204.10.0.0/16 and 204.10.10.1/32—in this case, the caching for all the CIDR networks would be performed as a classful entry. If the router wanted to send a packet to the network 204.10.1.0/24, it would not cache this route as a /16 because no explicit entry exists for network 204.10.1.0/24, and because it is covered by 204.10.0.0/16.

The router also would not cache the route as a /32. Only entries for network 204.10.10.0 would be cached as /32 because a host route of 204.10.10.1/32 exists in the routing table. No other entry in the CIDR block of 204.10.0.0/16 would be cached as a /32.

Finally, the routes not found in the routing table will take the default route 0.0.0.0. All the entries would be cached as a *classful mask*. If, for example, the router needs to send a packet to the destination of 161.10.1.1, a cache entry would be created for network 161.10.0.0/16, not for 0.0.0.0/0.

Cache and Recursive Lookup

You can see from the previous discussion that, although this technique is efficient, it has drawbacks, such as scalability problems. These problems do not affect the enterprise customer because the networks are not changed rapidly and frequently, and because they do not carry very large routing tables. Demand caching is a scalable method for the enterprise environment because packet flow is not very dynamic. Cache deletion frees space in the memory as well.

ISPs, on the other hand, see the effect of caching on their networks because ISPs carry routes from other networks, and they do not have control over the flapping. Therefore, routes appear and disappear due to changes in another user's network. In addition, most of the routes in the ISP environment are BGP-derived, so the next hops are not directly connected. For a router to resolve the non-connected next hop, it must resolve this recursive lookup during the cache-creation or during process switching. This can overload the router.

Cache entries also are aged from the cache table periodically (every minute), which contributes to cache trashing.

For example, the next hop is not directly connected in the following routing entry for BGP. This configuration shows the IP route for an IBGP-learned route:

```
    Routing entry for 200.200.200.0/24
Known via "bgp 2", distance 200, metric 0
Tag 1, type internal
Last update from 171.68.181.1 00:45:07 ago
Routing Descriptor Blocks:
* 171.68.181.1, from 150.150.3.11, 00:45:07 ago
    Route metric is 0, traffic share count is 1
    AS Hops 1
```

The next hop in this case is 171.68.181.1, which is not a connected route. The router before it forwards the packet to destination 200.200.200.0/24 and must resolve the next hop. The router first must search the routing table for network 200.200.200.0/24, and then must perform a lookup for the next hop: in this case, 171.68.181.1. Then, the router must find the connected interface that will be used to forward the traffic toward the next hop and, ultimately, to the destination. This is apparent in the **show ip route** output for the next hop:

```
C7000-2B#sh ip ro 171.68.181.1
Routing entry for 171.68.181.0/24
  Known via "eigrp 200", distance 90, metric 284160, type internal
  Redistributing via rip, eigrp 200
  Last update from 171.68.173.13 on Ethernet0/0, 00:16:59 ago
  Routing Descriptor Blocks:
  * 171.68.173.13, from 171.68.173.13, 00:16:59 ago, via Ethernet0/0
    Route metric is 284160, traffic share count is 1
    Total delay is 1100 microseconds, minimum bandwidth is 10000 Kbit
    Reliability 255/255, minimum MTU 1500 bytes
    Loading 1/255, Hops 1
```

After the router has discovered the connected interface toward the next hop, the router creates the cache entry, as seen in the following entry:

```
Prefix/Length        Age       Interface     Next Hop
200.200.200.0/24     00:06:43  Ethernet0/0   171.68.173.13
```

Since this type of recursive lookup during major churns is not successful in the ISP environment, Cisco created Express Forwarding for ISPs.

Populating Cisco Express Forwarding

CEF has two major components: the forwarding information base (FIB) and the adjacency database. The FIB is the lookup table that the router uses to make destination base-switching decisions during CEF operation. This table is almost an exact copy of the routing table. (The FIB/CEF table does not carry administrative distances and metrics). When the routing table topology is changed in the network, the routing table is updated and the changes are immediately reflected in the CEF table.

Consider the same entries discussed in the last section. The routing table router contains the following entries:

```
150.150.6.0/24 [20/1] via 150.150.5.31, 00:00:23, Fddi2/0
150.150.0.0/16 [20/10] via 150.150.5.31, 00:20:23, Fddi2/0
171.68.0.0/16 [20/0] via 131.108.5.31, 01:50:2, Serial 0/0
171.68.0.0/16 [20/0] via 131.108.5.10, 01:05:2, Serial 0/1
10.10.10.1/32 [110/1572] via 131.108.5.10 01:5:23 Serial 0/1
10.0.0.0/8 [20/10] via 131.1.1.1 01:5:11 Ethernet 3/1
204.10.0.0/16 [20/0] via 150.150.5.31, 00:20:23, Fddi2/0
204.10.10.1/32 [20/0] via 150.150.5.31, 01:20:23, Fddi2/0
0.0.0.0/0 [20/0] via 150.150.5.31, 00:20:23, Fddi2/0
```

Unlike the demand cache, in which the router created the cache entry on the longest prefix for the network, CEF copies the complete routing table in the cache.

Consider the case of the routing entries for network 150.150.0.0. In this case, the router has two entries for network 150.150.0.0/16 and 150.10.6.24. Unlike in the demand cache, if the router wants to send a packet to subnet 150.150.8.0/24, it will not create an entry based on the longest prefix. Instead, it will use the 150.150.0.0/16 entry.

Next, consider the case of network 171.68.0.0/16, in which the router has two equal-cost paths. Prior to CEF, the router had to maintain the /32 cache for per-destination load balancing. With CEF, the load sharing is now performed on the pair of source and destination caches. In our example, when the router wanted to do a per-packet load, it had to process-switch the packets because fast switching did not support per-packet load sharing.

With CEF, you can achieve per-packet load sharing, but the default is per-destination load sharing. Per-destination uses both source and destination for load sharing. Per-packet is more useful when the bulk of the traffic is destined for one host, such as a Web server. To balance the traffic from multiple users to the same destination with per–packet load sharing, the router sends packets to the same destination on different paths, as shown here:

Prefix	Next Hop	Interface
0.0.0.0/0	150.150.5.31	FDDI2/0
150.150.0.0/16	150.150.5.31	FDDI2/0
150.150.6.0/24	150.150.5.31	FDDI2/0
171.68.0.0/16	131.108.5.31	Serial 0/0
171.68.0.0/16	131.108.5.10	Serial 0/1
10.10.10.1/32	131.108.5.10	Serial 0/1
10.0.0.0/8	131.1.1.1	Ethernet 3/1
204.10.0.0/16	150.150.5.31	FDDI2/0
204.10.10.1/32	150.150.5.31	FDDI2/0

Again, in the case of network 10.0.0.0, the router has two entries: one for network 10.10.1.1/32 and another for network 10.0.0.0/8. Unlike the demand cache, no additional entries are created on the longest prefix.

Previously, classful entries were created for the CIDR route, and /32 entries were created for network 204.10.10.0. This is a marked reduction of the number of entries created for the CIDR route. Rather than creating 254 entries for the CIDR route plus 254 entries for the major net route, the router now needs to create only two entries.

In the demand-caching model, the router creates entries for all the networks to which it is sending packets on the classful mask for the default route, as discussed earlier. With CEF, an entry is created for the default network.

The next component of FIB is the MAC-layer rewrite, which is completed via the adjacency table. Network nodes are considered adjacent if they can be reached directly. CEF creates an adjacency table for Layer 2 information.

The adjacency table maintains Layer 2 next hop addresses for all the FIB entries. It is populated as the adjacencies are discovered; each time the adjacency entry is created, a link-layer header for that adjacency node is precomputed and stored in the adjacency table. After the route is determined, it points to a next hop and to the corresponding adjacency. This route is subsequently used for encapsulation during the CEF switching of packets.

Adjacency resolution is useful for load sharing. When a router is configured for load sharing, a pointer is added for the adjacency corresponding to the next hop interface for each resolved path.

Recursive Lookup and CEF

In recursive lookup, the next hop for IBGP routes is not directly connected. This problem must be resolved, as shown in the following output of **show ip route** for an IBGP-learned route:

```
Routing entry for 200.200.200.0/24
Known via "bgp 2", distance 200, metric 0
Tag 1, type internal
Last update from 171.68.181.1 00:45:07 ago
Routing Descriptor Blocks:
* 171.68.181.1, from 150.150.3.11, 00:45:07 ago
    Route metric is 0, traffic share count is 1
    AS Hops 1
```

In this case, the next hop, which is 171.68.181.1, is not directly connected, so this route must be learned via IGP. As shown, this route is learned via Enhanced IGRP:

```
Routing entry for 171.68.181.0/24
Known via "eigrp 200", distance 90, metric 284160, type internal
  Redistributing via rip, eigrp 200
  Last update from 171.68.173.13 on Ethernet0/0, 00:16:59 ago
  Routing Descriptor Blocks:
  * 171.68.173.13, from 171.68.173.13, 00:16:59 ago, via Ethernet0/0
      Route metric is 284160, traffic share count is 1
      Total delay is 1100 microseconds, minimum bandwidth is 10000 Kbit
      Reliability 255/255, minimum MTU 1500 bytes
      Loading 1/255, Hops 1
```

Notice the BGP entry for network 200.200.200.0. The next hop is not directly connected; so to reach the next hop, the router must find the connected interface used to reach 171.68.181.1. By reading the **show ip route** for 171.68.181.1, it has learned Enhanced IGRP on Ethernet 0/0. The connected next hop to reach 171.68.181.1 is 171.68.173.13, which is the directly connected next hop. CEF resolves this issue by attaching the BGP route to the immediately connected next hop. In this case, it will create the following CEF entries:

Prefix	Next Hop	Interface
171.68.181.0/24	171.68.173.13	Ethernet0/0
171.68.173.0/24	Attached	Ethernet0/0
200.200.200.0/24	171.68.173.13	Ethernet0/0

Different Types of Adjacencies

There are several types of adjacencies:

- *Null adjacency*   Packets destined for null-interface are dropped. This is used for dropping packets to unknown destinations. It can be used as an effective form of access filtering.

- *Glean adjacency*   When a router is connected to a subnet, the FIB table maintains a prefix for the subnet rather than for each individual host. This subnet prefix points to a glean adjacency. When a packet must be forwarded to a specific host, the adjacency database is gleaned for the specific prefix.

Output of **show ip cef glean** appears as follows:

Prefix	Next Hop	Interface
216.179.253.128/25	Attached	FastEthernet8/0
219.1.169.220/30	Attached	FastEthernet9/0
219.18.9.124/30	Attached	FastEthernet2/0
219.18.9.136/30	Attached	FastEthernet2/0
219.18.84.128/26	Attached	FastEthernet5/0

- *Punt adjacency*   Features that require special handling or are not yet supported with CEF are forwarded to the next switching layer for handling.
- *Drop adjacency*   Packets are dropped, but the prefix is checked.

These two examples provide you an opportunity to see how the cache is populated by demand cache, which is used for fast switching, as well as how CEF populates the cache.

Summary

The fundamental roles of routers are route-computation, packet scheduling, and forwarding. Router architecture has evolved through three generations, from a shared bus central CPU, to multiple peer-line cards connected by an intelligent switching fabric. With this evolution, the Cisco core product line has evolved from central CPU-orientated process switching through the use of a fast switching cache, to distributed CEF.

Routers may compute multiple RIBs, each associated with a particular routing protocol (OSPF, Enhanced IGRP, RIP, BGP, or IS-IS) or process. Similarly, routers also may contain multiple FIBs, each associated with a particular switching path (process, fast, CEF, or TAG). Improvement in route-lookup methodology, together with the cheaper availability of low-cost memory, has played a major part in increased packet throughput. These concepts are summarized in Figure 5-11.

Increasingly, network operators are calling for sophisticated, yet scalable accounting, security, packet scheduling, and traffic-engineering features. New switching techniques, such as CEF, TAG, and Netflow, address these needs. The choice of switching mechanisms depends on the placement of the router within the network architecture: The accounting and security features of Netflow and CEF are generally performed at the perimeter, whereas the performance of CEF, and the traffic engineering and performance of TAG are aimed at the core.

Scalable congestion control and management algorithms, such as RED, CAR, and WFQ, will be critical components of modern high-performance routers. Again, the roles of routers vary, depending upon their position within the network architecture. Classification of packets will be a function of the routers on the perimeter of the network, and the core routers will focus on highly scalable packet scheduling.

Figure 5-11   *Router Routing, Switching, and Scheduling Overview*

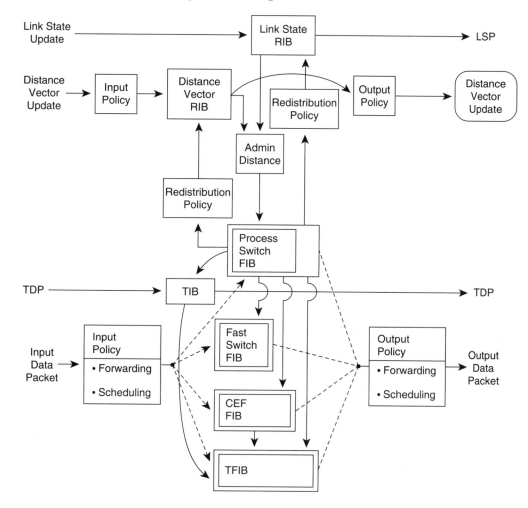

Review Questions

  1 When you see a cache ager running on a network, should you be alarmed?

  2 Why do you see so many /32 entries on a network, and what can you do to prevent these?

  3 Do you cache a CIDR route?

  4 How do you enable optimum switching?

  5 In what situation is it wise to disable fast switching?

6 What is CEF?

7 Will cache ager run with FIB?

8 If CEF does not process-switch, how does it receive the MAC-layer information?

9 What are adjacencies?

10 Does FIB support load sharing?

11 Does CEF support access lists?

Answers:

1 No. This is normal behavior for demand caching. Unused entries are aged out every minute.

2 Block /32 routes in your routing table from other autonomous systems. You might also perform load sharing.

3 No. Cache at the longest prefix or the classful network boundary for demand cache, if there is a CIDR or a default route.

4 It is the default on RSP processors. Disable it with **no ip route-cache optimum** because it is an interface subcommand.

5 Disable fast switching when you have a high-speed interface feeding a slower link and enough CPU power is available. This can be successful for enterprise environments, but not for an ISP.

6 CEF assists in making forwarding decisions; it is an exact copy of the routing table and performs well for large routing-table environments.

7 No. CEF does not create entries on demand; it copies the routing table.

8 CEF receives its MAC-layer information via adjacencies.

9 Two nodes are considered adjacent if they can reach each other via a single hop across a link. The adjacency database is a table of connected nodes, each with information about the L2 MAC rewrite.

10 Yes. It supports load sharing, based on both per-packet and per-destination.

11 Yes. Both inbound and outbound access lists are supported.

For Further Reading . . .

Bennett, G. *Designing TCP/IP Internetworks*. New York, NY: John Wiley and Sons, 1997.

Degermark, Brodnik, Carlsson, and Pink. *Small Forwarding Tables for Fast Routing Lookups*. France, Proc ACM SIGCOMM 97, September 1997.

Keshav, S. *An Engineering Approach to Computer Networking*. Reading, MA: Addison-Wesley, 1997.

Keshav and Sharma. "Issues and Trends in Router Design." *IEEE Communications Magazine*, (May 1998).

Kumar, Lakshman, and Stiliadis. "Beyond Best Effort: Router Architectures for the Differentiated Services of Tomorrow's Internet." *IEEE Communications Magazine*, (May 1998).

Core and Distribution Networks

This chapter provides an overview of the Routing Information Protocol (RIP), including the following topics:

Overview of RIP   This section discusses RIP's basic functions, its limitations, and the algorithm it uses.

Introduction to the distance vector protocol   In this section, we explain the algorithm based on Bellman Ford, and explore how the algorithm is executed, and how information is passed along the path.

Fundamentals of RIP operation   This section explains the basics of RIP, how routes are calculated, and how information is propagated.

Discontiguous networks   In this section, we discuss disconnected networks and how RIP behaves when parts of a major network are disconnected, and we offer suggestions on how to employ them.

## CHAPTER 6

Routing Information Protocol

Overview of RIP

RIP is a distance vector protocol that uses the Bellman Ford algorithm to compute the shortest route to the destination. RIP was originally designed for Xerox PARC and was used in Xerox Network Systems (XNS). It then became associated with TCP/IP and the UNIX system. The protocol is one of the first dynamic routing protocols used in the Internet. It was developed as a method of passing reachability information between routers and hosts.

Each entry in a RIP table contains a variety of information, including the ultimate destination, the next hop toward the destination, and the metric to reach the destination. The *metric* indicates the distance in number of hops to the destination. RIP maintains the best route to the destination, so when new information provides a better route, this information replaces the previous route in the table.

Although RIP is still a widely used protocol, it has several restrictions, including a 15-hop maximum. (The sixteenth hop has a special meaning in RIP, as you will discover in Chapter 7.) RIP also lacks support for variable-length subnet masking or supernetting. Currently, the Internet uses addresses that appear to be part of the class A network. RIP Version 1 will be incapable of utilizing these addresses because of its classful behavior. For these reasons, RIP has been declared a historic document in RFC 1923.

RIP is greatly hindered by its inability to consider real-time parameters, such as bandwidth, delay, or load. Consider the network in Figure 6-1. Here, router R1 learns about network 131.108.10.0 from two routers: R2 and R3. The route is advertised by R3 to network 131.108.10.0 with one hop, and router R2 advertises it with two hops. Because RIP is not concerned with the speed of the links between the routers, it chooses R3 to reach the destination, even though the link speed via R2 is approximately 30 times faster. Naturally, this decision is extremely undesirable.

With a hop-count limit of 15, any destination greater than 15 hops is considered unreachable. The RIP hop count greatly restricts its use in a large network. However, the restriction does prevent a count to infinity problem from causing endless routing loops.

Figure 6-1 *Suboptimal Path Taken by RIP on Number of Hops*

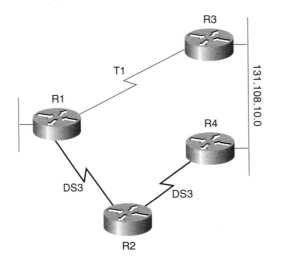

The count to infinity problem is shown in Figure 6-2. Here, router R1 can reach network A with a hop count of 1, and it advertises this route to router R2. Realizing that it can reach network A with a hop count of 2, R2 then sends this information back to R1. Now, R1 loses its connection to network A, and sees that it can reach network A via R2. As R2 is advertising network A with two hops, router R1 says that it can reach network A with three hops. Because R2's next hop to destination A was R1, R2 sees that R1 can reach destination A with three hops. R2 then changes its hop count to four. This problem continues indefinitely, unless some external boundary condition is imposed. This boundary condition is RIP's maximum hop count of infinity, which is the sixteenth hop.

Figure 6-2 *Count to Infinity*

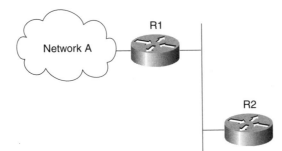

Three additional issues with regard to RIP also must be addressed: holddown, split horizon, and poison reverse:

- Holddowns prevent regular update messages from inappropriately installing a route that has become defective. When a route is defective, neighboring routers detect it, and then calculate new routes. The routers send out routing update messages to inform their neighbors of the route changes. This update might not arrive to all the routers at the correct time, however, which causes some routers to choose an incorrect path. A holddown tells routers to suppress any changes that might affect recently removed routes for some period of time. This period is greater than the time it takes to update the entire network with a routing change.

- A split horizon is derived from the fact that it is never useful to send information about a route back to the direction from which it came. For example, revisit Figure 6-2. Router R1 advertises routes from network A to router R2. Thus, it is unecessary for router R2 to include this route in its update back to R1 because R2 learned this route from R1 and because R1 is closer to the destination. The split horizon rule states that R2 should strike this route from any update sent to R1. Split horizon prevents looping problems between nodes.

- Poison reverse updates the sending neighbor about the route it has sent with an infinity metric. For example, in Figure 6-2, router R2 sends the route back to R1 with an infinity metric. Poison reverse updates also help prevent routing loops.

One of RIP's many drawbacks is that it does not support variable-length subnet masking. Classful in nature, version 1 packets do not carry mask information. If an update is received about a subnet of the connected network, this version infers that the mask is the same as that of connected interfaces on that network. The router will always summarize when crossing a network bound at a natural classful mask.

Consider the network shown in Figure 6-3. When router R1 sends updates about network 140.10.10.0/24 out of serial interface, it sends updates at a classful mask of 14.10.0.0/16 because the updates travel across a different major network. When R2 receives this update, it ignores this route because one of its interfaces is connected to the same major network.

With current Internet class A addresses being distributed to multiple companies, RIP will not be capable of routing packets if the network belongs to this class A network. If you want to advertise CIDR routes into RIP, all must be unsummarized at a natural network mask of classes A, B, and C; then they must be advertised into RIP.

Figure 6-3   *RIP and Discontiguous Networks*

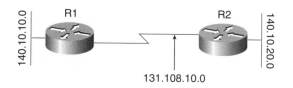

140.10.10.0 — R1 — 131.108.10.0 — R2 — 140.10.20.0

Introduction to the Distance-Vector Protocol

In a distance-vector protocol, each router or host that participates in the routing protocol maintains information about all other destinations within the autonomous system. This does not indicate that each router knows which router originated the information, as in link state, but each router is aware of the neighbor that will be used to reach that destination. Each entry in the routing table includes the next hop, to which the datagram should be sent on its route to the destination.

Each router along the path passes its distance (metric) to reach the destination; this distance is a generalized concept that may cover the time delay in sending the messages to the final destination. The distance vector protocol derives its name from its capability to compute the optimal route to a destination when the only information exchanged is the list of distances. The information exchanged between the routers takes place on a common segment to which they are adjacent.

Another class of protocols, called *link-state protocols*, instruct each router within their area to maintain identical databases. Each router within the network has full visibility of the network, and the link-state update informs all other routers about their neighbors. Link-state information is flooded within the area (see Chapter 9, "Open Shortest Path First," and Chapter 10, "Intermediate System-to-Intermediate System"), so every router has the same view.

The major difference between the link-state and the distance-vector protocols involves information propagation. Link-state protocols inform all routers only about its neighbors and its connected links. On the other hand, distance-vector protocols inform its neighbors about all the routing information in its routing table. A link-state router always knows the identity of the router originating the link-state. A distance-vector router, however, recognizes only the next hop router and its distance to reach the destination. In this case, the routers do not know the origin of the route.

In the distance-vector algorithm, every router is identified as a different address, and then a distance is assigned to each router. Each router also assigns itself a distance of zero, then every other destination is assigned a distance of infinity. Every router advertises its own distance vector to its neighbor. Usually, these advertisements are sent on a periodic basis. Each router receives the distance vector of its adjacent node and stores this information. Next, each router computes its least cost by comparing the received costs from all its neighbors, and then adds its own cost before installing the least-cost path. After the least-cost path is installed, the route is re-advertised to the router's neighbors (see Figure 6-4).

From Figure 6-4 with respect to R1, the first iteration is as shown by Figure 6-5.

In Figure 6-5, you can see that the origin (router R1) in its first iteration sets all destinations to infinity and lists only itself as having a distance of zero.

In the second iteration, router R1 has seen its neighbors R2 and R3, and includes their distances in its table. These distances are shown in Table 2 of Figure 6-5.

Figure 6-4   *Network Setup Calculates Distances for Each Destination*

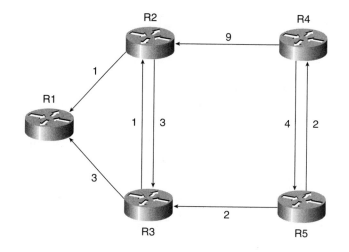

Figure 6-5   *Calculation for Distances for Each Destination with Respect to R1*

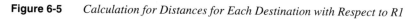

I#	R1	R2	R3	R4	R5
0	0	∞	∞	∞	∞

Table 1

I#	R1	R2	R3	R4	R5
3	0	1	2	10	4

Table 4

I#	R1	R2	R3	R4	R5
1	0	1	3	∞	∞

Table 2

I#	R1	R2	R3	R4	R5
4	0	1	2	8	5

Table 5

I#	R1	R2	R3	R4	R5
2	0	1	2	10	5

Table 3

In the third iteration, the router has installed the distances it has received from its two neighbors, R2 and R3, about R4 and R5. R2 has informed R1 about R4, and has updated R1 with its cost of reaching R4, which is nine. R1 then adds its cost of reaching R2 to the advertised cost of R2, and sets the cost of reaching R4 at 10. Similarly, R3 has a distance of two to reach R5. R1 already has a distance of three to reach R3, so it adds the distance and sets R5 at a distance of five.

Now, R2 also sends an update to R1 about R3 at a distance of one. When the distance of one is added with the cost of reaching R2, the total distance for reaching R3 is two via R2 and three via direct connection to R3. In version 3, this new shorter path is set in place to reach R3.

In the fourth iteration, the new distance is installed to reach R3, the distance to R5 is also changed to four because the distance to R3 is now two, and the distance from R3 to R5 is also two.

In the fifth iteration, the new distance is calculated to reach R4 via R3 because R3 advertises R4 via R5 at a distance of six. By adding R1's distance of reaching R3 (which is two), the new distance to reach R4 is eight, which is less than the distance for reaching R4 via R2.

In RIP, the concept changes because real-time parameters are not considered; instead, every router is one hop from its neighbor. As you can see, even if the cost of reaching routers is less through a greater number of hops, we cannot use RIP because of suboptimal path selection.

Fundamentals of RIP Operation

RIP is a hop-count, metric-based routing protocol. Each router contains routing information about every possible destination in the autonomous system. Information maintained in the routing table includes the destination network or, in some cases, the host, the next hop along the path to the destination, the physical interface used to reach the next hop, and the metric.

In Example 6-1, router R1 has received a route to destination 131.108.20.0/24 from 131.108.30.9. In this case, 131.108.30.9 is the next hop toward the destination. The bracketed information in the example depicts that 120 is the administrative distance assigned by Cisco routers to routing protocols. In RIP, the administrative distance is 120. After the administrative distance is metric, which is the RIP metric (hop count). The destination of 131.108.20.0 is one hop away from the local router and has a connected interface of serial 2/0 with the remote router from which the update has been received.

Example 6-1

```
R 131.108.20.0/24 [120/1]via 131.108.30.9,00:00:02,Serial2/0
C 131.108.10.0/24 is directly connected, Ethernet3/0
C 131.108.30.0/24 is directly connected, Serial2/0
```

The *metric* is the distance of the advertising router to the destination. In RIP, the metric is its hop count. Each router advertises a directly-connected interface with a hop count of one. When this information is passed to adjacent routers, the hop count is incremented by one, by every subsequent router. The maximum hop of a route is 15. As mentioned previously, the total length of the network cannot exceed 15 hops from the source, which is the originating router. This is the main reason that RIP's usefulness is limited.

Information about each destination is sent to all the routers within an autonomous system (AS). If the same destination is advertised by multiple routers, the route with the shortest hop count is selected as the preferred path.

RIP does support equal-cost load balancing. If a route is received from two separate next-hop routers with equal hop count, then the route is considered equal cost, as shown in Figure 6-6. Here, both R3 and R4 advertise network 131.108.10.0 as one hop away for router R1. Thus, both routes are equally attractive and are of equal cost. If the same destination is advertised by multiple routers with the same metric, the paths also are considered as equal cost, and both the routes are included in the routing table. In the Cisco environment, four equal-cost paths to a destination are maintained in the routing table, by default, which can be incremented to six by the **max-path** command.

Figure 6-6   *Load Balancing with Respect to R1*

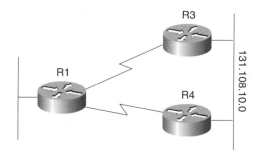

Therefore, if a router receives six routes to a destination that are equal in their number of hops, using the **max-path 6** command allows the router to install all six of them.

NOTE   RIP does not consider the connected link speed in calculating its metric to the destination. This can cause a lower-speed link to be preferred over a high-speed link if the lower-speed link has fewer hops to the destination.

In the example shown in Figure 6-7, router R1 can reach network N2 via R3 and R4. R3 connects to R5 directly through a 56K link. On the other hand, R4 connects to R5 via R6. Although both the links between R4 and R6 and between R6 and R5 are T3 speeds, RIP still chooses the slower link, because it involves fewer hops to the destination.

Figure 6-7 *RIP Does Not Always Take the Optimal Path*

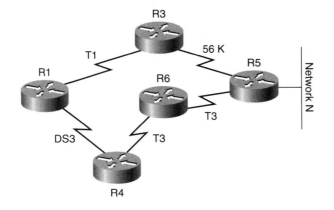

As mentioned, RIP's hop-count limitation poses a problem, which is described further in Chapter 7. Each new network destination must be less than 15 hops away, or it is declared unreachable. The sixteenth hop in RIP indicates that no route to the destination is present.

RIP Packet Format

RIP operates on top of UDP port 520. The packet format for RIP is shown in Figure 6-8. UDP can send datagrams with a minimum of protocol mechanism. The protocol avoids overhead because it provides no reliability—it simply sends the datagram that is encapsulated in the IP packet. Each host that runs RIP sends and receives datagrams on UDP port 520. All routing messages are sent from UDP 520, and a response to a request is sent to the port from which the request came. UDP is used in this manner because it offers a procedure for application programs to send messages to other programs, with a minimum of protocol mechanism.

The Command field is contained in every RIP datagram. This field indicates whether the datagram is a request or a response:

- *Request*   A request asks the neighbor to send its updates. A request is sent, asking the RIP responding system to send all or part of its routing table.

- *Response*   A response may be sent in response to a request or as a part of a regular update. The request message may contain some or all of the complete routing table. Depending on the request packet, the response is sent with all or part of the routing table.

Figure 6-8   *RIP Packet Format*

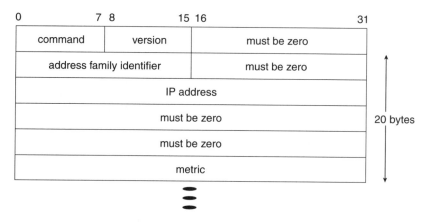

Version 1 is addressed for this discussion. Version 2 is addressed in Chapter 7, "Routing Information Protocol Version 2." (See also RFC 1723.) The address family identifier is currently only for IP, and the value of IP is two. None of the known IP implementation identifies any other address family. The IP address in the header is four octets in the network order. The metric field must contain values between one and 15, and this specifies the routers' current metric to reach the destination or determines that the value of 16 is unreachable. The maximum possible datagram should be 512 bytes, so by calculation, there could be 20×25 (number of routes) + 4 bytes for a common portion. This limits the update packet to fewer than 512 bytes.

To explain further: The first four bytes of the RIP header are common to every routing entry in a RIP packet. First, there is the command and version, and then the 20 bytes must change according to the route. There are two reasons for this: First, with every routing entry, a different IP address is advertised. Second, each IP address has a different metric.

Therefore, the equation becomes the following:

4 (common part) + [20 (bytes header changes with each entry)×25 (routes)] > 512 bytes

RIP and VLSM

RIP does not support VLSM (variable-length subnet mask). This causes a lack of address space because, for serial lines that have point-to-point connections, smaller masks can cause address waste. Therefore, it is important to understand how to utilize RIP in a VLSM environment. For a description of subnetting, refer to Chapter 2, "IP Fundamentals." If you recall from basic VLSM, when a major network has different masks for different types of networks, perhaps to accommodate the number of host addresses, you can use a different subnet mask for broadcast networks and a different subnet mask for point-to-point networks. RIP does not support VLSM. However, to utilize RIP in a VLSM environment, consider the following courses of action.

Assume, for example, that a network is migrating from RIP to OSPF. On the OSPF routers, VLSM has been configured. To propagate these routes into RIP, its mask must be matched (see Figure 6-8). As mentioned previously, RIP does not propagate route information about a destination whose mask does not match that of its outgoing interface. For example, in Figure 6-8, router R1's serial link is connected to network 131.108.0.0, and the subnet mask of the interface subnet is 255.255.255.252. R1 also has an Ethernet connection to the same major network 131.108.0.0, and the subnet mask of Ethernet is 255.255.255.0. Because R1 is running OSPF on the serial line and still has legacy RIPV1, RIP must receive route information about the serial interface. By default, RIP will not work with VLSM behind the Ethernet of R1. When R1 attempts to send routing information about its serial interface from the Ethernet, it cannot do so because of the unmatched masks. Any subnetwork that does not have the same mask as that on the Ethernet will have connectivity difficulties. Therefore, those subnetworks will not be propagated in RIP domain.

As shown in Figure 6-8, R1 is the redistributing router used to propagate subnet 131.108.10.0 into the RIP domain. The mask of the subnet should match that of the outgoing interface of RIP. In this case, the Ethernet mask is (255.255.255.0) 24-bit, and the serial is (255.255.255.252) 30-bit. You can create a route to subnet 131.108.10.0 that matches the RIP mask, and then redistribute that route into RIP. In this case, all the routers behind the Ethernet of R1 receive the route to destination 131.108.10.0 255.255.255.0. By default, RIP checks the interface mask on which it sends routing updates before actually sending these messages. When a route is informed about a destination that belongs to the same major network as the one on which updates are being sent, its mask is verified. If the mask of the connected interface is the same as that of the route being advertised for the same major network, then that route is advertised. Otherwise, the update for that subnet is dropped.

Then R1 would have two routes to 131.108.10.0—the first is the serial interface address of 131.108.10.0 255.255.255.252 (/30 mask); the other is 131.108.10.0 255.255.255.0 (/24 mask). When a packet is received that must be routed (such as 131.108.10.1, which is the IP address of the other end of the serial link), R1 compares its two routes. The first is /30 mask route and the second is the /24 mask route. The longest prefix mask wins—in this case, it is /30, and the routing continues, uninterrupted. The router, in this case, would select a 30-bit mask. When the router recognizes that a packet has been sent to a destination, the mask closest to the destination address packet is routed toward that address. For example, when router R1 in Figure 6-9 has a packet to send to 131.108.10.1/32, it has two choices: One is to send it to 131.108.10.0/30, and the other is to send it to 131.108.10.0/24. The longer the prefix mask, the more specific it is, making it more acceptable to the router. .

Figure 6-9   *Redistributing a VLSM OSPF Route into RIP*

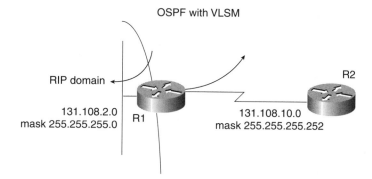

For example:

```
router rip
network 131.108.0.0
redistribute static
redistribute ospf 1
default-metric 1
ip route 131.108.10.0 255.255.255.0 null0
```

Now that you have a route with the same mask as that of the Ethernet of R1, this static route is redistributed into RIPV1 across the Ethernet of R1. R1 advertises this route, and all the routers behind the Ethernet of R1 in the RIP domain will have connectivity to all the VLSM destinations behind the R1-OSPF domain. This is not a solution to VLSM for RIP, however; it is merely one way to make RIP operable in a VLSM environment during migrations. (For further information on network migrations, see Chapter 12, "Migration Techniques.")

Now, we will discuss the configuration. The first command controls the RIP process; the second command tells RIP to run on all the connected interfaces of the local router that belong to network 131.108.0.0. The **redistribute static** command is used to send the static null route to accommodate the VLSM into the RIP domain. Next is the **redistribute OSPF** command, which redistributes the OSPF learned route with the same mask as the RIP route and routes from other major networks learned via OSPF. Finally, the **default metric** command is used for metric conversion between protocols because OSPF uses interface cost as its metric to a destination. Naturally, the destinations advertised by OSPF have a much higher metric than 15, so all the routes redistributed into RIP from OSPF will be considered infinity. To translate between metrics, you would use **default metric** command, which tells the RIP process that any routes redistributed into RIP via this router (R1, in this case) will have a hop count of one.

RIP and Discontiguous Networks

Recall that discontiguous networks have subnets of the same major network, separated by a different major network.

RIP does not carry a prefix mask, and it summarizes at the natural classful length mask. This raises another issue: How can you support discontiguous networks? This type of network must communicate exact addresses across the entire network. Referring again to Figure 6-3, when the router must send updates about subnet 140.10.20.0 to router R1, it summarizes the update at the natural network boundary across the serial line because the interface is configured with a different major network. As mentioned earlier, when an update is sent across a network boundary with RIPV1, it is summarized at the natural class A, B, C mask. This is done because a RIP update does not carry a mask, so network boundaries should be defined. When R1 receives this update, it drops an update about network 140.10.0.0/16 because one of its own interfaces is connected to one of the subnets of network 140.10.0.0/16. In this case, the subnet is 140.10.10.0. The RIPV1 router will not accept an update about a route to which its own interface is connected because all subnets of its connected major network should fall behind a classful boundary. Therefore, from Figure 6-3, R1 expects all the subnets of 140.10.0.0/16 to stay behind the Ethernet of R1. This is because the serial interface is a different major network, so no part of network 140.10.0.0 should exist behind the serial interface.

When R1 sends updates about subnet 140.10.2.0 through the serial interface, it sends a 140.10.0.0/16 classful mask, because it is sending the update across a different major network. When R2 receives this update, it drops it because it has a direct connection to one of the subnets of the same major network.

Therefore, RIPV1 is able to support discontiguous networks. You can make this topology work, as shown in Figure 6-10, using a Cisco router. One method to accomplish this is to configure a secondary address, as shown in Figure 6-10. In this case, you must ensure that the secondary address belongs to the same major network to which you are trying to connect, and that the subnet mask is consistent. As Figure 6-10 illustrates, the secondary address of the serial link is the same as that of the two Ethernets of R1 and R2. Now, the network is no longer discontiguous because the secondary address matches the major network.

Figure 6-10   *Secondary Address to Support Discontiguous Networks*

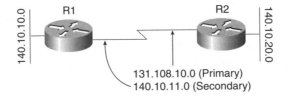

Consider the configuration of the serial interface of R1:

```
# interface serial 0
# ip address 140.10.11.1 255.255.255.0 secondary
```

The second method of dealing with the RIP topology is not as simple as the first. However, it will be successful when you do not have address space left to assign a secondary address for the network that you are making contiguous. As an example, this method would be helpful if there were no available space within network 140.10.0.0 to be assigned for the secondary address on the serial link. In that case, you could configure static routes on both routers for the destinations across the other end of the links.

For example, observe Figure 6-11. If the major network static is configured, then it must be configured on all the routers. So, for Figure 6-11, all routers should have a static route to 140.10.0.0. Obviously, this does not scale if there are multiple routers across both ends of the serial link of a discontiguous network. The most effective method to accomplish this is to create a static route that advertises the exact routes with the correct mask, instead of creating a major net route. In referring to Figure 6-11, a static route would be needed on R1 and R2.

Figure 6-11   *Static Routes to Support Discontiguous Networks*

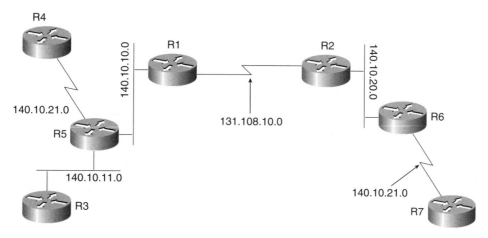

Router R1

```
R1# config t
ip route 140.10.20.0 255.255.255.0 serial 0 ip route 140.10.21.0 255.255.255.0
serial 0
 ip route 140.10.21.0 255.255.255.0 serial 0
 router rip
 network 140.10.0.0
 network 131.108.0.0
 redistribute static
 default-metric 2
```

The exact same configuration is required on router R2 for the links behind R1:

```
ip route 140.10.20.0 255.255.255.0 serial 0
ip route 140.10.21.0 255.255.255.0 serial 0
ip route 140.10.11.0 255.255.255.0 serial 0
ip route 140.10.12.0 255.255.255.0 serial 0
ip route 140.10.10.0 255.255.255.0 serial 0
router rip
network 140.10.0.0
network 131.108.0.0
redistribute static
default-metric 2
```

The solutions for the RIP and discontiguous networks explained here are not long-term, however. As a network administrator, you should use these as a workaround strategy and begin planning your network migration to scalable classless protocols such as OSPF, IS-IS, and Enhanced IGRP, which are discussed in Chapter 12.

RIP and Classful Masks

RIP does not carry masks with the prefix information in its update. For all the network prefixes, RIPV1 assumes a natural classful mask. Therefore, RIP cannot support *supernets*. Supernetting, as mentioned in Chapter 2, was introduced much later, and RIP existed before classless interdomain routing (CIDR). As a protocol, RIP was designed to have natural classful masks, so RIP does not understand routes that do not have natural class masks, such as eight-bit for class A, 16-bit for class B, and 24-bit for class C networks.

For a CIDR block to be propagated into RIP, it must be broken into each individual network entry. Because the Internet soon will use some class A addresses, RIP will not be capable of routing packets to some sites.

For further explanation, consider the case of CIDR blocks first, and then study RIP in the context of class A networks distributed to multiple companies. First, observe the network in Figure 6-12. Here, ISP Alpha.net is advertising routes to the enterprise Beta.com. When they own a large address block of the class C network, instead of advertising all individual class C networks, they advertise a single route that covers all the individual class C networks. For example, in Figure 6-12, ISP Alpha.net will not advertise all the class C components of 206.10.0.0/16; for example, it will not advertise 206.10.10.0/24.

When the CIDR block route of 206.10.0.0/16 is received by router R1, this route typically is received via the Border Gateway Protocol (BGP) because ISPs run BGP with their customers to advertise routes. However, you cannot advertise this CIDR block in the RIPV1 network, because RIPV1 is a classful protocol and does not understand any route that does not have a regular class A, B, or C mask. To advertise this CIDR block into RIPV1, you must divide this network into all the class C mask networks. This does not scale if you are receiving many CIDR routes.

Figure 6-12   *Supernet and Discontiguous Network Support Via the Internet*

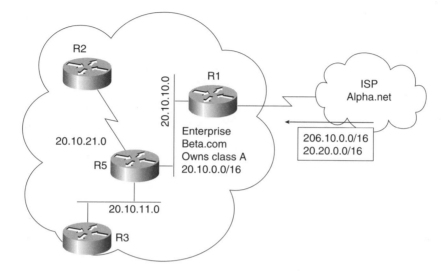

The next problem involves subnet routes for a class A network. As you can see in Figure 6-12, the enterprise Beta.com owns part of a class A network, while some parts of this class A network also are given to other organizations. When the ISP advertises other parts of the class A network, Beta.com will be ineffective because this class A network is discontiguous. In this case, the previously mentioned techniques for creating a discontiguous network do not scale here for two reasons. First, you cannot configure the entire Internet with the class A network as secondary. Second, you would have to configure static routes for all the organizations that own part of the class A network with the mask of the network, so that you could redistribute all the subnets of network 20.0.0.0. Then, you would have to redistribute those static routes if you received a /16, as shown in Figure 6-11. This /16 would have to be made into /24 masks for all destinations, and then would have to be redistributed because the mask in the AS is /24 for this class A network.

RIP Timers

One of the most important responsibilities of any routing protocol is to respond to the changes in its topologies. This is because you can have alternate routes to the destination; redundancy is provided because of the critical nature of business. Convergence should be achieved within a limited amount of time so that the application using this network does not time out.

To respond to the changes in topologies, all distance-vector protocols should have a technique for aging routes. RIPV1 updates are sent every 30 seconds by every participating router to all of that router's neighbors.

If the router does not hear from its neighbor for 180 seconds, the router assumes that the neighbor is down or that the link connecting the two neighbors is down. At this point, the route is marked as invalid. An invalid timer is used to determine that no fresh information is received about this route. This timer is set to 180 seconds for RIP. Upon expiration of the invalid timer, hold-down time begins. During the hold-down period, the route is marked as possibly down and the metric is set to infinity. In addition, the route is advertised to the router's neighbors with an infinity metric. When the hold-down timer expires, a request is sent to query neighbors for an alternate route to the destination. If a new route was received during the invalid or hold-down period, the router begins advertising this new route.

The last item is the flush timer, which begins immediately after the invalid timer expires, and lasts 60 seconds after the hold-down expires. Upon the expiration of the flush timer (240 seconds), the route is deleted if no replacement route is received. The advantage of these timers is that you can determine whether the route was not received because of some transient condition, or that the route has actually been removed. This ensures that if an interface has flapped, you can still converge to accommodate the flap. The disadvantage, however, is slow convergence. As routers and links are becoming faster, network administrators want faster convergence, rather than waiting for a protocol to install an alternate path after a long period of time.

Limitations of RIPV1

Because RIPV1 has been given historic status, it always should be used with simple topologies that have simple reachability. The protocol should be operated in a network that has fixed subnetting and only default routes to connect to the Internet. RIP does not support CIDR, and it does not include any security functions.

In today's complex networking environment, almost no network could be successful, given the limitations mentioned here. Therefore, RIP cannot scale to today's dynamic, fast-converging, fast-paced environment.

RIPV1 limitations include the following issues:

- *Classfulness: RIPV1*   With the current routing structure of the Internet, classless routing protocols would not be capable of propagating a route without a regular class A, B, or C mask. In addition, parts of a class A network that are now distributed between different organizations would not be capable of connecting with each other.

- *No support for VLSM*   RIPV1 does not support VLSM, which means that, as the network grows, the address waste within a network cannot be controlled. A network administrator cannot change his mask on point-to-point links. In the discussion of VLSM in Chapter 2, we noted that on serial links in which only two routers connect, it is possible to set a longer subnet mask; for LAN media to which many other machines (hosts or routers) are connected, it is possible to set a shorter subnet mask. The address we have saved by setting longer masks on point-to-point links could be used for other point-to-point links.

- *No support for discontiguous networks*   As mentioned in the discussion of RIP's classfulness, some class A networks are being divided among different organizations. If these parts of a class A network want to connect to each other, they have to do so via the

Internet. This creates a situation in which a major network is separated by the Internet. With a classful protocol such as the IGP, connections would not take place between these sites.

RIPV1 Configuration Examples

Enabling RIPV1 on a network is relatively simple. You only need to list the connected networks under the router RIPV1 statement for which you want to enable RIPV1 (see Figure 6-13).

Figure 6-13   *Enabling RIPV1 on Different Networks*

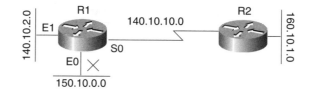

The configuration for R1 in Figure 6-13 is as follows:

```
router rip
network 140.10.0.0
```

Notice that network 150.10.0.0 is not listed; R1 will not send out RIPV1 broadcasts via Ethernet 0, and it will not include this network in its updates. Notice also that R1 does not need to list network 160.10.0.0 under its router RIPV1 statement; you only need to list the directly connected networks in the router RIPV1 statement.

You can filter RIPV1 updates for the complete RIPV1 process, or you can filter on a per-interface basis.

To stop accepting RIPV1 updates for certain networks only, or to stop advertising certain networks through the RIPV1 process, you can use the **distribute-list** command with the complete RIPV1 process. This is useful for avoiding routing loops that are caused during redistribution. For example, suppose that RIP originated a route into the routing domain and that the route was redistributed into IGRP. IGRP has a lower administrative distance then RIP, and it can overwrite the original RIP route with a physical loop, which causes a routing loop. For example, to block RIPV1 updates for network 150.10.0.0 from entering your RIPV1 process, you would use the following configuration:

```
Router rip
network 140.10.0.0
```

```
distribute-list 1 in
access-list 1 deny 150.10.0.0 0.0.255.255
access-list 1 permit 0.0.0.0 255.255.255.255
```

To block the updates for network 150.0.0.0 from entering serial 0, but still allow these updates from other interfaces, you would use the following configuration:

```
network 140.10.0.0
distribute-list 1 in serial 0
```

When redistributing RIPV1 into any routing protocol, be aware of metric conversion and administrative distances. Different routing protocols have different administrative distances, as shown in the following table:

Protocol	Administrative Distance
RIP	120
OSPF	110
Enhanced IGRP	90/170
IGRP	100
IS-IS	115
BGP	20/200
ODR	160

Figure 6-14 shows a sample RIP to IGRP redistribution setup.

Figure 6-14 *Routing Loop Created Due to Physical Loop in RIP to IGRP Redistribution*

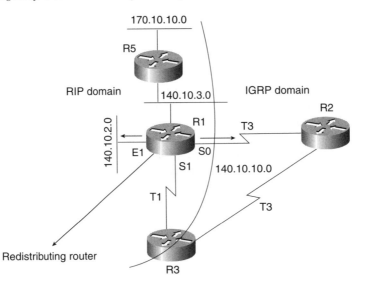

As demonstrated in Figure 6-14, if R5 advertises network 170.10.0.0, and R1 is running both RIP and IGRP, then R1 is responsible for redistribution. R1 will redistribute 170.10.0.0 into IGRP and will advertise 170.10.0.0 to its IGRP neighbors, which are R2 and R3. Both R2 and R3 will advertise their best metric to each other about 170.10.0.0. R2 learns the route to 170.10.0.0 from R1, and the link speed between R1 and R2 is T3. R3 learns this route from R1, and the link speed between R1 and R3 is T1. R2 will advertise the route to network 170.10.0.0 to R3. Looking at the link speed, which is T3, between R2 and R3, the metric to reach network 170.10.0.0 for R3 is more viable through R2 rather than R1. R3 will install an IGRP route to 170.10.0.0 via R2, and R3 will advertise this route to R1 via IGRP. Now, R1 has learned the route to network 170.10.0.0 via RIP from R5, and R1 learned the route from R3 via IGRP. R1 now compares the administrative distance between IGRP and the original RIP route. IGRP has a lower administrative distance than RIP, which will cause R1 to remove the original RIP route learned from R5 from the routing table, causing a routing loop. To avoid any possibility of routing loops, use the **distribute-list** command to block any routing loops:

```
Config on R1
router rip
network 140.10.0.0
network 150.10.0.0
redistribute igrp 109
default-metric 1


router igrp 109
network 140.10.0.0
network 150.10.0.0
redistribute rip
default-metric 1 1 1 1 1
distribute-list 1 in

access-list 1 deny 170.10.0.0 0.0.255.255
access-list 1 permit 0.0.0.0 255.255.255.255
```

Notice the **default metric** command under both RIP and IGRP. This command converts different types of metrics used by different routing protocols to the metric format of the redistributing routing protocol. RIP uses the hop count as a metric. The IGRP metric, on the other hand, is a combination of bandwidth, load, reliability, MTU, and delay; so it is always much greater than 15. Because RIP considers any value greater than 15 unreachable, it will drop an update with a metric higher than 15. The **default metric** command converts the IGRP route into RIP with the correct metric value that is not unreachable for RIP. If the **default metric** command is not used, then redistribution will be unsuccessful. Both IGRP and RIP will consider the metric values to be bogus, and will not redistribute the routes.

Summary

RIP is designed for small homogeneous networks, and could not be adopted as a core routing protocol in today's complex classless networks. Considering the rapid growth of the Internet, many destinations would not be routable for RIP.

RIP's inability to support VLSM causes significant address waste, merely to accommodate the protocol limitations. Point-to-point networks that need only two host IDs must have the same mask as the other multipoint interfaces in a network, which results in an enormous waste of valuable address space.

RIP is also less viable as a core routing protocol because it offers no support for discontiguous networks. With part of a class A network distributed between different organizations, that part becomes unroutable with RIP.

The inability of RIP to consider real-time parameters; as well as its reliance on number of hops without considering parameters such as bandwidth, load, and delay; deems RIP inoperable in large networks.

Legacy networks still running RIP are in the process of migrating to protocols that will be more successful in today's complex networking environment. You will learn more about network migration techniques in Chapter 12.

Review Questions

1 What is the maximum number of hops of a RIP network?

2 What is a split horizon?

3 What is the default update timer for RIP?

4 If your OSPF mask for subnetwork 140.10.1.0 is 255.255.255.0, and if your RIP mask is 255.255.255.192, how would you create a static route to accommodate VLSM?

Answers:

1 The maximum number of hops is 15.

2 The route could not be readvertised on the interface on which it was originally received.

3 The default update timer for RIP is 30 seconds.

4 The following static route should be created on R1. The interface that connects to R1 and R2 is serial 0:

```
ip route 131.108.15.0 255.255.255.192 serial 0
router rip
redistribute static
default-metric 2
```

For Further Reading . . .

Cisco IOS Manual Version 11.2

Hartinger, Jake. "RIP Version I, Private Communication." 1998–1999.

RFC 1058

RFC 1923

Stevens, W. Richard. *TCP/IP Illustrated, Volume 1*. Reading, MA: Addison-Wesley, 1994.

This chapter introduces the fundamental concepts of RIPV2 and explains the changes to version 2 from version 1. We will discuss solutions for discontiguous networks by using version 2, and we will explore today's classless environment and VLSM support. A brief discussion on RIP and demand routing is also provided.

The chapter also covers some configuration parameters in RIP and explains how and where they can be used. Specifically, the following issues are covered:

Fundamentals of RIP operation   This section includes the basic functions of RIP, with new additions to accommodate today's environments.

RIP over demand circuit routing   This section discusses the behavior for backup solutions that accommodate on-demand circuits. These circuits are not connected constantly, so they should be implemented so that they cannot be triggered by periodic behavior of protocols.

Cisco's RIP implementation   Cisco RIPV2 support includes VLSM support, authentication, discontiguous network, multicasting, and next hop address support.

## CHAPTER 7

Routing Information Protocol Version 2

Introduction to RIP Operation

RIP version 1 is not operable in today's classless environment. Because of its many limitations, it should be used only in moderately sized, fairly homogenous networks.

With the advent of Classless Interdomain Routing (CIDR), protocols must implement classless behavior. As companies grow, so does the consumption of address space. Two issues have become clear to most organizations: first, that serial point-to-point links do not require eight bits (254 hosts) for the host portion of the IP address; second, that the same subnet can be used by other serial links.

RIP's limitations introduced the need for different subnet masks for LAN and WAN interfaces. It was necessary for RIP to support VLSM, but RIPV1 is incapable of providing this support. In addition, there are no IGP/EGP interactions because the protocol does not understand autonomous systems, nor does it allow any authentication. RIP's incapability to carry subnet masks also limits it from supporting discontiguous networks. The lack of all these features led to an expansion of the protocol.

The current RIP message contains minimal information, which is used to route packets to the destination. The RIP header also has a large amount of unused fields, which it owes to its origin. The RIPV2 protocol is designed to accommodate changes in the current Internet environment, and extensions have been added to the protocol. As described in Chapter 6, "Routing Information Protocol," all the fields in RIP version 1 are still maintained. The changes to the protocol are shown in Figure 7-1.

The extension added in version 2 does not change the protocol, but the added extensions to version 1's message format grant the protocol the capability of accommodating today's networking needs. Recall that the first four octets in the RIP packet contain the header. The new RIP message format, shown in Figure 7-1, displays the command, version, IP address, metric, and address family identifier, all of which have the same meaning as in version 1.

The Version field is set to 2 for this message. Authentication is performed per message, and the Address Family Identifier field is used. If the address family identifier is 0xFFFF, the remainder of the message is used for authentication. The Route Tag field is added to the header and is used for separating the internal routes from the external routes.

Figure 7-1   *RIP Header for Version 2*

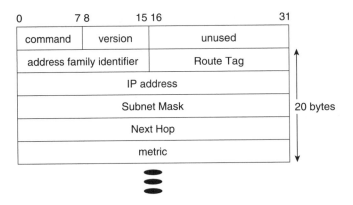

Route tagging should be preserved and readvertised with a route because it keeps track of internal RIP routes versus external RIP routes. External RIP routes can be imported from other routing protocols, whereas internal RIP routes are originated by the RIP routing processes.

In version 1, eight bytes were set to 0 for future use. In version 2, these eight bytes are now used to carry subnet mask and next hop information. The first four bytes are set for subnet masks, and the next four bytes are for the next hop. The following sections describe the new fields introduced in RIPV2.

Subnet Mask Support

The Subnet Mask Support field indicates the mask of the route. If this field is 0, the subnet mask is not included for that routing entry. The Subnet Mask field in RIPV2 assists VLSM because every route that is advertised by the RIPV2 routing process carries the actual mask of the route being advertised. This is unlike version 1, in which the router assumes that all the routes with knowledge of the connected network have the same masks as the connected network. RIPV1 does not have any subnet mask information, so it cannot support VLSM, CIDR, or discontiguous networks.

Next Hop

The immediate next hop to which packets are sent is specified by this route entry. When this field is set to 0.0.0.0, the packet should be forwarded to that advertising router. An address other than 0.0.0.0 specified as next hop must be directly connected on the logical subnet over which the advertisement is made.

Next hop is useful in an environment in which you need to avoid extra hops, as shown in Figure 7-2.

Figure 7-2   *RIPV2 and Next Hop*

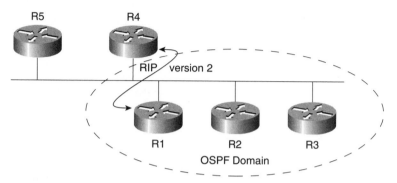

Routers R1 and R4, shown in Figure 7-2, are running RIP between them; R1 is running OSPF with R2 and R3. R1 learns a route from R2 or R3, instead of advertising itself to R4 as the next hop. R1 will advertise R2 or R3 as the next hop to R4 for the destinations that it has learned from those routers. R4 will then send traffic directly to R2 or R3, therefore avoiding extra hops. Because R1 can inform R4 directly to send traffic, it is unnecessary for R4 to send packets to R1, so that R1 can forward to R3 and R2.

Multicast Updates

Instead of using broadcast updates, RIP now sends multicast packets to a multicast address of 224.0.0.9. All routers listening to this group will receive the routing update. In version 1, updates are sent to the broadcast address 255.255.255.255. Even if the router is not running RIP it will still receive broadcast RIP packets. With multicasting, however, only the routers that are configured with RIP will process the RIPV2 updates.

CIDR Support

RIPV2 is able to support classless interdomain routes. It can propagate a classless route through redistribution. If the route were passed to RIPV1, on the other hand, the updates would be ignored.

Larger Infinity

Most network architects are hindered by RIP's 15-hop limit. Version 2 still does not introduce an infinity larger than 16 because of backward-compatibility. If a larger infinity was introduced, routers running version 1 would be confused—the routers would not be capable of processing routes with a metric larger than 16 because a 16th hop would indicate that no route to the destination exists.

RIP Over Demand Circuits

RIP version 2 has been modified without drastically changing the protocol. This section discusses a few of the enhancements to RIP provided for demand circuits, such as an ISDN or async connection.

NOTE   A *demand circuit* is a connection that is not in use for normal packet forwarding. It provides redundancy and cost savings. This is essentially a backup connection that is used only in the case of primary link failure.

In today's internetworking environment, networks are using ISDN to support the primary sites or to provide connections to a large number of remote sites. Such connections may be passing either very little or no data traffic during normal operation.

The periodic behavior of RIP can cause problems on such circuits. RIP has difficulty with periodic updates on point-to-point interfaces with low bandwidth because updates sent every 30 seconds with large routing tables use a large amount of bandwidth. This affects the data traffic: When data is sent on this slow-speed link, it competes with the routing updates. If you increase the update timer to a larger value, the convergence becomes slower.

There are two methods for resolving this problem:

- Snapshot routing
- Triggered RIP

Snapshot Routing

Snapshot routing is a time-triggered routing update facility that enables a remote "slave" router to learn dynamic routing and service information from a central "master" router during a short active period.

This learned information is then stored for a user-configurable period of inactivity (T2) until the next active period. If no routing updates are exchanged during the active period (because a DDR phone number or interface is unavailable), a user-configurable retry period (T3) is activated to ensure that a full inactive period does not pass before an attempt is made to exchange routing information again. Snapshot routing updates support IP (RIP and IGRP).

Snapshot routing enables routers at remote sites to collect and retain up-to-date network connectivity information. Snapshot routing is especially useful for ISDN environments, in which it provides a solution to the problem of implementing and maintaining static routes in large DDR networks.

Triggered RIP

Triggered RIP is designed for routers that exchange all routing information from their neighbors. If the router is changed in any way, only the changes are propagated to the neighbor. The receiving router should apply the changes immediately. Changes can be caused by events such as link flaps, next hop changes, or subnet mask changes.

Triggered RIP updates are sent only when these criteria are met:

- When a request for a routing update is received
- When new information is received
- When the destination changes from a circuit down to a circuit up
- When the network is first powered up

Cisco will support this feature as of the IOS 12.0 software release.

Cisco's RIP Implementation

Cisco's RIPV2 supports authentication, key management, route-summarization, CIDR, VLSM, and discontiguous networks. This section describes the Cisco implementation of RIPV2, and explains how to enable and run it.

Enabling and Running Cisco's RIPV2

By default, the Cisco router will send and receive both version 1 and version 2 RIP packets, depending upon the neighboring router. To configure the router to process a specific version, you must use the following command:

```
router rip
version {1 / 2}
```

At some point, parts of a network may be running legacy RIP version 1 while in the process of migrating to RIP version 2. You can configure certain interfaces to send and receive version 1 routes, and configure other interfaces to receive version 2 routes. This is illustrated in Figure 7-3.

As shown in Figure 7-3, router R1 is running RIP and wants to exchange version 1 updates on the Frame Relay cloud. It exchanges version 2 updates on FDDI, and exchanges both version 1 and 2 updates on the Ethernet. You can configure the router to send and receive only version 1 updates. It is possible to send only version 2 updates or both versions.

Figure 7-3   *A RIP Version 1 and 2 Mixed Environment*

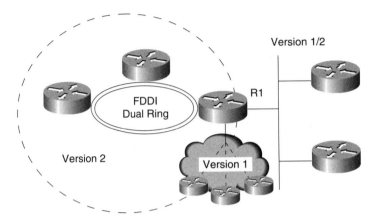

The configuration for R1 is as follows:

```
router rip
network 131.108.0.0
interface serial 0
ip rip send version 1
ip rip receive version 1
interface fddi 1
ip rip send version 2
ip rip receive version 2
interface ethernet 1
ip rip send version 1 2
ip rip receive version 1 2
```

RIPV2 and Authentication

RIPV2 supports authentication, and Cisco supports two types of authentication on an interface: MD5 and plain-text authentication (the default). MD5 is a block-chain hashing authentication algorithm, used for security. The algorithm operates over the entire data packet, including the header, and is used to secure the routing updates. If the key matches, the route is accepted; otherwise, it is not. A simple key is not as secure as MD5 because it is plain-text authentication.

RIPV2 and Discontiguous Networks

By default in Cisco, RIP version 2 supports automatic route summarization. This causes the route to be summarized as a classful boundary when crossing a major network. This affects discontiguous networks, as shown in Figure 7-4.

Figure 7-4   *RIPV2 and Discontiguous Networks*

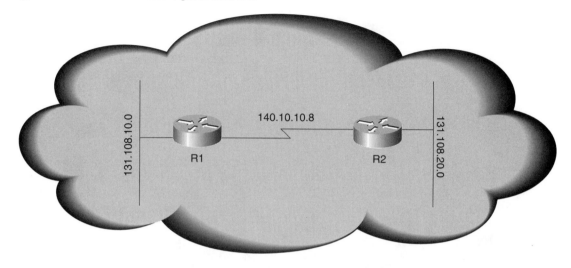

In Figure 7-4, R1 and R2 have their Ethernet interfaces connected to Network 131.108.0.0. The serial interface between the two routers is a different major network—in this case, 140.10.0.0. This setup is ineffective in RIPV1 because, as soon as a router crosses a major network, the updates of the connected network will be ignored. In this case, the update of 131.108.0.0/16 will be advertised through the Network 140.10.10.8/30 subnet. R1 is connected to Network 131.108.0.0, and it therefore will ignore the update.

RIPV2 will process this appropriately, as shown in Figure 7.4, because version 2 carries a subnet mask in the update and because 131.108.10.0/24 is a different route than 131.108.0.0/16. Now if you want to route a packet from R1 to the Ethernet of R2, you should use the 131.108.0.0/16 route. The routing table for R1 would be as follows:

```
131.108.0.0/16 is variably subnetted, 2 subnets, 2 masks
R       131.108.0.0/16 [120/1] via 140.10.10.9, 00:00:02, Serial 2/0
C       131.108.10.0/24 is directly connected, Ethernet3/0
C       140.10.10.8/30 is directly connected, Serial 2/0
```

As you can see from the routing table, RIPV2 supports disconnected subnets. Now, consider the situation in Figure 7-5. R1 does not know what part on 131.108.0.0 is behind R2 and what part of 131.108.0.0 is behind R3. If the Cisco router is process-switching, 50 percent of the packets would be lost. If the Cisco router is fast-switching, 100 percent of the packets could be lost.

Figure 7-5   *Discontiguous Networks Across Multiple Interfaces*

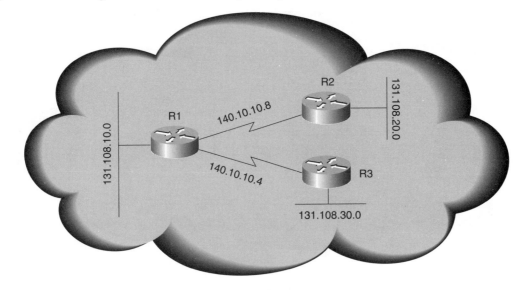

The routing table for R1 in Figure 7-5 would be as follows:

```
131.108.0.0/16 is variably subnetted, 2 subnets, 2 masks
R       131.108.0.0/16 [120/1] via 140.10.10.9, 00:00:24, Serial 2/0
R       131.108.0.0/16 [120/1] via 140.10.10.5, 00:00:02, Serial 3/0
C       131.108.10.0/24 is directly connected, Ethernet3/0
C       140.10.10.8/30 is directly connected, Serial 2/0
C       140.10.10.4/30 is directly connected, Serial 3/0.
```

To solve the problem shown in Figure 7-5, you must disable **auto-summary**. This command, which tells the router to stop creating summarized routes when crossing a major net route, must be entered on all the routers. (In Figure 7-5, this command must be entered on R2 and R3.)

The configuration for R1 is as follows:

```
router rip
network 131.108.0.0
network 140.10.0.0
no auto-summary

Configuration for R2
router rip
network 131.108.0.0
network 140.10.0.0
no auto-summary
```

The configuration for R3 would be as follows:

```
router rip
network 131.108.0.0
140.10.0.0
no auto-summary
Routing table for R1 then changes to:
131.108.0.0/24 is  subnetted, 3 subnets
R        131.108.20.0/24 [120/1] via 140.10.10.9, 00:00:24, Serial 2/0
R        131.108.30.0/24 [120/1] via 140.10.10.5, 00:00:02, Serial 3/0
C        131.108.10.0/24 is directly connected, Ethernet3/0
C        140.10.10.8/30 is directly connected, Serial 2/0
C        140.10.10.4/30 is directly connected, Serial 3/0.
```

With **auto-summary** disabled, R1 has the correct next-hop field for each destination.

RIPV2 and Unicast Updates

By default, RIPV1 is a broadcast routing protocol. Alternatively, RIPV2 is a multicast routing protocol. To disable the multicast routing protocol behavior, you can configure RIP in unicast mode, which is achieved by enabling the **neighbor** command.

To exchange updates with only a few neighbors, you would configure the **neighbor** command on broadcast media.

Figure 7-6 shows that R1 only wants to exchange updates with R2. The R1 interface must be made passive. Then, the **neighbor** command should be defined for the IP address of R2. All other routers on this segment will exchange RIP updates with each other. Even R1 will receive routing updates from all other routers, but will not send updates to any of them except R2.

Figure 7-6   *RIP in Unicase Mode*

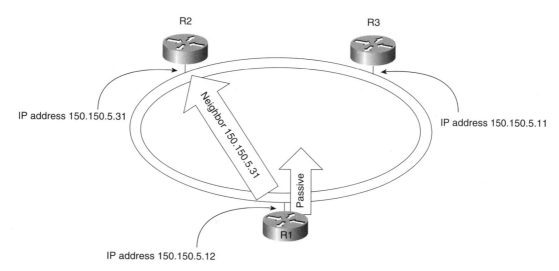

NOTE	*Passive interface* is used when the network administrator wants to block routing protocol packets from being sent. With RIP, the router that is in passive mode hears routing updates from other routers running RIP, but does not send any RIP packets on the passive interface.

The configuration for R1 is as follows:

```
router rip
  passive-interface Fddi3/0
 network 150.150.0.0
 network 10.0.0.0
 neighbor 150.150.5.31
Configuration of R2
router rip
network 150.150.0.0
```

The configuration for R3 is as follows:

```
router rip
network 150.150.0.0
```

Notice in the configuration for R2 and R3 that no passive neighbor is defined. In this case, R1 is in listening mode with R3, but is in both sending and listening mode with R2. This can be seen using the **show IP route** command on R1:

```
Show IP route on R1.
150.150.0.0/16 is variably subnetted, 10 subnets, 2 masks
R        150.150.1.0/24 [120/1] via 150.150.5.11, 00:00:18, Fddi3/0
R        150.150.2.0/24 [120/1] via 150.150.5.11, 00:00:18, Fddi3/0
R        150.150.6.0/24 [120/1] via 150.150.5.31, 00:00:17, Fddi3/0
R        150.150.11.0/24 [120/1] via 150.150.5.11, 00:00:18, Fddi3/0
R        150.150.15.1/32 [120/1] via 150.150.5.11, 00:00:18, Fddi3/0
R        150.150.15.0/24 [120/1] via 150.150.5.31, 00:00:17, Fddi3/0
```

As you can see from R1's **show IP route** command, R1 receives RIP updates from both R2 and R3. The passive interface feature blocks only updates from exiting, not from entering.

```
Show IP route on R2
150.150.0.0 is variably subnetted, 10 subnets, 2 masks
R        150.150.1.0/24 [120/1] via 150.150.5.11, 00:00:18, Fddi3/0
R        150.150.2.0/24 [120/1] via 150.150.5.11, 00:00:18, Fddi3/0
R        150.150.11.0/24 [120/1] via 150.150.5.11, 00:00:18, Fddi3/0
R        150.150.15.1/32 [120/1] via 150.150.5.11, 00:00:18, Fddi3/0
R        150.150.8.0 255.255.255.0 [120/1] via 150.150.5.12, 00:00:21, Fddi3/0
R     10.0.0.0 [120/1] via 150.150.5.12, 00:00:04, Fddi3/0
          You can see that R2 has routing updates from both router R1 and router
R3 because of the neighbor statement in R1:

Show IP route at R3
150.150.0.0/16 is variably subnetted, 10 subnets, 2 masks
R        150.150.6.0/24 [120/1] via 150.150.5.31, 00:00:23, Fddi2/0
R        150.150.15.0/24 [120/1] via 150.150.5.31, 00:00:23, Fddi2/0
```

R3 does not have any routes from R1 because of the passive interface setting. After the interface becomes passive, R1 does not send any RIP broadcast or multicast updates to the passive interface.

RIPV2 and the Distance Command

The **distance** command is used to change the administrative distance of the routing protocol and to sort the information received from different routing protocols. The default behavior of a Cisco router maintains RIP as the least believable protocol among all the interior gateway routing protocols.

Protocol	Distance Internal	Distance External
Enhanced IGRP	90	170
IGRP	100	
OSPF	110	
IS-IS	115	
RIP	120	
BGP	200	20

Now, consider the situation in Figure 7-7. As discussed in Chapter 6, RIP does not consider real-time parameters, which can cause suboptimal routing. R1 reaches the network 10.10.1.0 via R3 because of smaller hop count, but the link speed is faster via R2. Therefore, RIP considers the route via R3 because it has fewer hops.

The problem illustrated in Figure 7-7 can be solved in two ways:

- Using the **distance** command
- Using an offset list

These solutions are discussed in the following sections.

Figure 7-7   *RIP and Suboptimal Routing Because of Hop Count*

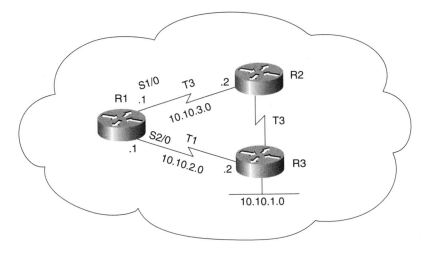

Using the Distance Command

In Figure 7-7, R1 learns routes to subnet 10.10.1.0 via R2 and R3. The route via R2 is two hops away, and the route via R3 is one hop away. Because RIP does not consider real-time parameters such as bandwidth, it will install the route via R3 because it has fewer hops. To use the path through R2 instead of R3, you would use the **distance** command. The configuration of R1 is as follows:

```
router rip
network 10.0.0.0
distance 100  10.10.3.2 0.0.0.0
```

The **distance** command tells the local router that all the routes learned from R2 have a lower administrative distance than the routes learned from R3. In this case, when a route is learned from R3 with one hop, R1 still installs the route from R2, even though it has two hops, because it now has a lower administrative distance value. Administrative distance in Cisco routers is the most believable parameter for route selection.

Using an Offset List

The offset list is the second option for solving the problem shown in Figure 7-7. In this case, you can increase the number of hops for the routes that are received. This command could be performed on both an inbound and an outbound basis. In Figure 7-7, either R3 can increase the metric on outbound routers, or R1 can increase it for inbound routers.

The inbound configuration for router R1 is as follows:

```
router rip
network 10.0.0.0
offset-list 1 in 3 serial 2/0
access-list 1 permit 10.10.1.0 0.0.0.255
```

This increases the number of hops for the networks that pass access list 1. In this case, subnet 10.10.1.0 is the only subnet that passes the access list; all other subnets are unaffected. When the update is received on serial 2/0, the updates about 10.10.1.0 are offset. Without the offset list, the route would appear in the routing table as the following:

```
R        10.10.1.0/24 [120/1] via 10.10.2.2, 00:00:10, Serial2/0
```

With the offset list configured, however, the RIP route via Serial 2/0 becomes four hops—one originally, plus the three added with the offset list. Therefore, the new route would be installed via serial 1/0 because the route advertised by R2 via serial 1/0 is two hops, and is shorter than the route received via R3.

Using Distribute List in RIPV2

The distribute list feature is very important for controlling routing information. In some situations, certain routes may be undesirable in the routing table. For example, you may want to send a default route only on certain interfaces. In addition, you may want to block certain routes when redistributing between routing protocols.

The distribute list is very useful, especially when you have performed redistribution in the network. Observe the network shown in Figure 7-8. Sometimes, the physical topology can create problems in a network with multiple routing protocols.

Figure 7-8   *Route Redistribution Loop*

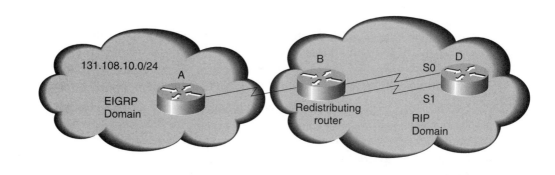

In Figure 7-8, Router A is connected to an Enhanced IGRP domain and a RIP domain. Router A learns 131.108.10.0/24 via an Enhanced IGRP external route, so the administrative distance in this case is 170. Then, router A advertises this route via Enhanced IGRP to router B. Router B is running RIP on its serial 0 and serial 1 interface. Router B sends this external route into RIP domain from the Enhanced IGRP domain. The external route is redistributed from Enhanced IGRP to RIP and is sent to router D on both interfaces.

Router D learns two equal-cost routes from B on two interfaces. The route it has learned on serial 0 is advertised on serial 1, and similarly the route learned on serial 1 is advertised on serial 0.

Router B has learned the route via RIP from D, which has a lower administrative distance. Therefore, Router B would install the RIP-learned route pointing to Router D, although the original source of the route for Router D was Router B. Instead of Router D receiving the correct route from Router B, Router B now points to Router D.

To ensure that the route does not come back to the redistributing router, you must configure the **distribute-list** command on the inbound interfaces. In Figure 7-8, for example, you would configure a **distribute-list** on the serial 0 and serial 1 interfaces of router B.

The configuration in this case would be as follows:

```
Router B
router rip
network 131.108.0.0
redistribute eigrp 100
default-network 1
distribute-list 1 in serial 0
distribute-list 1 in serial 1
access-list 1 deny 131.108.10.0 0.0.0.255
access-list 1 permit any
```

This configuration will not accept RIP routes for network 131.108.10.0 via the serial 0 and serial 1 on router B.

TIP   Another method to accomplish the above-mentioned task is to use the **distance** command for RIP so that its administrative distance is greater than the Enhanced IGRP external route.

Distribute list has an added feature for specifying which routes should be advertised for routes that will be redistributed between different routing protocols. For example, suppose you are learning networks 131.108.7.0 through 131.108.15.0 from Enhanced IGRP, and you do not want to advertise network 131.108.9.0 into the RIP domain. You can specify that the distribute list should not advertise network 131.108.9.0 into RIP.

The configuration for router RIP is as follows:

```
router rip
network 131.108.0.0
redistribute eigrp 100
distribute-list 1 out eigrp
default-metric 2

access-list  1 deny 131.108.9.0 0.0.0.255
access-list 1 permit any
```

Notice the use of the **default-metric** command in the previous configuration. When a route is redistributed into RIP from any other routing protocol, the metric is not properly understood because of differences in metric values. For example, if Enhanced IGRP uses bandwidth and delay to calculate the route metric, and that metric value is always greater than 16, the metric will be interpreted as infinity. The route will be dropped when the Enhanced IGRP route is redistributed into RIP.

To ensure that the routes redistributed between routing protocols are properly understood, you must configure the **default-metric** command. The metric value always should be less than 15 when redistributing a route into RIP. It then assigns the defined default metric value to the redistributed route.

RIP and Default Routes

The only route RIP understands as the default route is 0.0.0.0. It carries this route by default, which means that you do not have to specify it. For RIP to advertise a default route, it must find a route to the 0.0.0.0 network in its routing table. In the 11.3 software, a new feature exists, with which you can specify the router to send the default route on some interfaces, even if the router does not have a default route.

This command is as follows:

```
router rip
default-information originate route-map advertise.
route-map advertise
set interface serial 0.
```

This command sends a default route on serial 0, even when the local router does not have a default route in its routing table.

Summary

Although RIPV1 has limited capabilities, it is not yet obsolete. A large number of networks still run legacy RIP on their networks because, for one reason, migrating to another protocol would be a major effort for the network administrator. Another of RIP's limitations is its infinity of 16 hops. This means that the dimension of the network cannot exceed 15 hops.

When you are designing a large network, RIP should never be the core routing protocol, unless the network has a large hub and spoke setup that is capable of accepting it.

There are currently many other interior gateway protocols, including OSPF, IS-IS, and Enhanced IGRP. These protocols, as you will learn in other chapters, all scale to a much larger extent than RIP, so they are more appropriate in large networks.

Review Questions

1 Does RIPV2 have a larger infinity value than RIPV1?

2 By default, how frequently does a RIP router send updates?

3 How does RIPV2 broadcast its updates?

4 Does RIP understand any network as the default other than 0.0.0.0?

5 How many routing updates can you carry in a single RIP packet?

Answers:

1 No. RIPV2 still has the maximum hop count of 16.

2 A RIP router sends updates every 30 seconds.

3 RIPV2 uses multicast updates, which are sent every 30 seconds.

4 No. The only network RIP understands as the default is 0.0.0.0.

5 You can carry 25 routing updates per RIP packet.

For Further Reading . . .

RFC 1721

RFC 1722

RFC 1723

This chapter discusses the Enhanced Interior Gateway Routing Protocol (Enhanced IGRP), including the following topics:

Fundamentals and operation of Enhanced IGRP   This section describes Enhanced IGRP, which is an advanced distance-vector protocol, based on the concept that each router does not need to know all the router/link relationships for the entire network.

The DUAL algorithm   This section discusses the Distributed Update Algorithm (DUAL), which is the algorithm used to obtain loop-freedom at every instant throughout a route computation.

How the Enhanced IGRP topology table is built   Here, we explain how the topology table contains destinations advertised by neighboring routers. Associated with each entry is the destination address and a list of neighbors that have advertised the destination.

Enhanced IGRP configuration commands   In this section, we introduce the Enhanced IGRP configuration commands, which enable Enhanced IGRP.

Enhanced IGRP and bandwidth control   This section discusses Enhanced IGRP's bandwidth use. Because Enhanced IGRP is non-periodic, it consumes bandwidth only during an event.

## CHAPTER 8

Enhanced Interior Gateway Routing Protocol

Fundamentals and Operation

Enhanced IGRP is an interior gateway routing protocol designed for various networks and media. Enhanced IGRP is an advanced distance-vector protocol. The underlying concepts are the same as those of distance-vector protocols, except that Enhanced IGRP is a non-periodic incremental protocol. This differs from traditional distance-vector protocols, in which complete routing updates are sent periodically, using unnecessary bandwidth and CPU resources.

Improvements to Enhanced IGRP have achieved faster convergence as well, which is reliant upon Diffused Update Algorithm (DUAL) to achieve rapid, loop-free convergence. DUAL, in turn, enables synchronization of all devices involved in a topology change. Systems that are unaffected by topology changes are not involved in recompilations. The convergence time of DUAL rivals that of any other existing routing protocol. Enhanced IGRP is supported on IP, Novell IPX, and AppleTalk.

NOTE   Networks are becoming considerably more complex. The advent of classless routing, along with phenomenal network expansion, deems IGRP incapable of handling the growing complexity of today's networks. Enhancement was necessary to make IGRP more robust, scalable, and classless, as well as rapidly convergeable. *Enhanced IGRP* is based on the same basic principle as IGRP, except for the convergence algorithm. For this reason, the original version of IGRP is not discussed in this book.

The Distributed Update Algorithm

Distributed Update Algorithm (DUAL) is used by Enhanced IGRP to achieve fast, loop-free convergence with little impact on CPU cost and overhead. DUAL involves only the nodes affected by topology change and takes corrective action, such as sending queries about the lost route across only the affected nodes.

Nodes that are unaffected simply reply that they have an alternate path. DUAL works well when more than one change occurs simultaneously because only the affected nodes are responsible for processing information. Therefore, if multiple changes occur within the network, the entire network is not involved in recomputation.

Route States

Routes in Enhanced IGRP can exist in one of only two states: passive or active. A route is in the passive state when it is not performing a route recomputation. The route is in an active state when it is undergoing a route recomputation.

When the route is in a passive state, it can make forwarding decisions. The next hop used to forward packets is the shortest path to the destination. When the route is in active state, the router is in the process of finding an alternate path to the destination. When the route is in active state with an infinite metric set, it is unreachable.

The route state changes, depending on the topology of the network. A change in topology could be caused by link failure, node failure, or a metric change. When a router notices a topology change, it maintains the route in passive state if a feasible successor exists. If the router is informed of a metric change during an active state, it records that change, but does not make any routing decisions until it returns to a passive state. A route moves from an active to a passive state when a route is received from all its neighbors.

TIP

The *feasibility condition,* which occurs when a neighbor's advertised cost is less than or equal to the cost of the route used by the current successor, is one of the most important parts of DUAL: It ensures faster convergence. The feasibility condition enables DUAL to terminate as quickly as possible: Unaffected nodes simply reply to the queries from their neighbors, and remain in a passive state for that destination.

The following definitions are important to understand before continuing this discussion:

- *Successor*   This is the next hop router used to forward data traffic to the destination. Typically, the successor is the lowest-cost metric to the destination, as shown in Figure 8-1. The link speed between router A and router B is 45 Mb, and the link speed between router A and router C is T1. The composite metric is the shortest metric to the destination, so B is the successor.

- *Feasible successor*   This is a neighbor that meets the feasibility condition, which is a downstream neighbor to the destination, but not the least-cost path. The feasible successor is not used to forward data traffic to the destination.

  Figure 8-2 shows the route to network 140.10.1.0/24, which is advertised to router A by both router C and router B. The link speed between router A and router B is 45 Mb, and link speed between router A and router C is 1.544 Mb. Now, B is the shortest path to the destination and becomes the successor. If CD < AD, then the feasibility condition is met and C becomes the feasible successor.

- *Feasibility condition*   This condition is met when a neighbor's advertised cost is less than or equal to the cost of the route used from the current successor. A neighbor that advertises a route with a cost that does not meet the feasibility condition is not considered for the topology table.

Figure 8-1   *Successor for a Route in Enhanced IGRP*

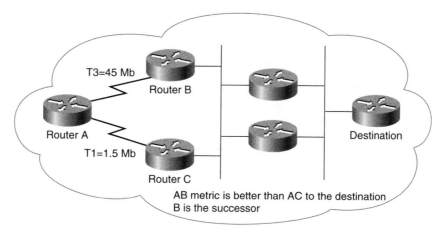

Figure 8-2   *Feasible Successor and Feasibility Condition*

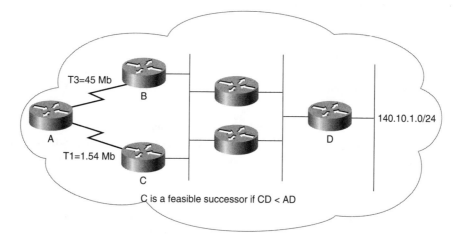

DUAL Message Types

DUAL messages are sent in one of three message types: queries, updates, and replies. Queries are sent when a destination becomes unreachable. Updates are sent to indicate a change of metric to advertise a new destination. Replies are sent in response to the queries from a neighbor.

If a query is received when no feasible successor is found, the query is propagated. If a feasible successor is found, the query is not propagated, and a reply is sent to the neighbor. Conditions for sending queries are as follows:

- When a direct connect interface is down
- When a query has been received
- When the metric has changed
- When an update has been received

Conditions for sending replies are as follows:

- When a feasible successor is present
- When a query is received from an active route
- When the route state changes from active to passive

Conditions for sending updates are as follows:

- When a new link is added
- When the metric has changed

Topology Changes with Feasible Successor

In Figure 8-3, router 4 wants to reach network N. Router 4 has two choices: either through router 2 or through router 1. Each interface has a pretend metric (45 and 55, respectively) as an example.

The metric from router 3 to its destination is 40, and this metric is less than router 4's current metric (45) via router 2 to reach network N. Therefore, the feasibility condition is satisfied. In this case, router 2 is the successor for router 4 to reach network N, and router 3 is the feasible successor.

Now, assume that the link between router 4 and router 2 fails. Router 4 will not enter an active state. In the same manner, assume that the link between router 2 and router 1 fails, which means that router 2 will enter the active state from destination N. Router 2 will send queries to all its neighbors. Router 4 determines that it has a feasible successor, and replies immediately with a metric of 55.

Figure 8-3   *Convergence Due to Feasible Successor*

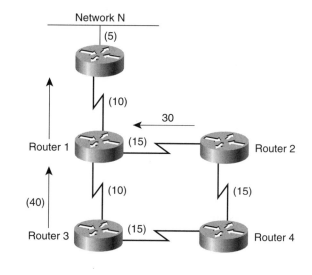

Now, router 4 will change its successor from router 2 to router 3; the router 4 for its destination N is in a passive state. Router 2 will receive the reply, and can transition from active to passive state because it has received a reply for its queries from router 4. In this case, router 4 was the only neighbor, so queries from router 2 have been answered by router 4. The other neighbor, router 1, is down. Note that router 1 and router 3 were not involved in the recomputation because they were not affected by the change.

Topology Changes without Feasible Successor

Figure 8-4 shows a case in which there is no feasible successor.

If the link between router 2 and router 4 fails in Figure 8-4, router 4 will become active for destination N because it has no feasible successors.

Router 4 will send a query to router 3 and router 5. Both of these routers have no feasible successors, so they become active for destination N. Because router 3 and router 5 do not have neighbors, they will send an unreachable message back to router 4. At this point, router 4 can enter a passive unreachable state for network N. The route to network N is then deleted from router 4's routing table.

Figure 8-4   *Convergence without a Feasible Successor*

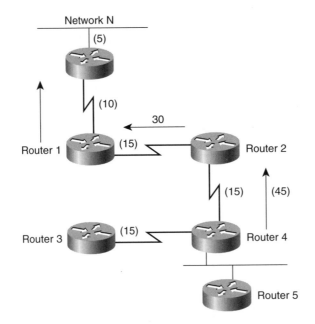

Enhanced IGRP Packets

Enhanced IGRP uses three packets for network discovery and convergence:

- *Query*   The query packet is sent by a router when it is in an active state. When a query packet is received, each destination triggers a DUAL event, and the state machine runs for each individual route.

- *Reply*   The reply packet is sent in response to the query. If the receiving router has an alternate path to the destination, the router responds with its own metric to the destination. Reply packets are sent after all the query packets are processed.

- *Request*   The request packet is sent for specific routes or entire routing tables from the neighbor. If a request packet is sent without a TLV, complete routing information is requested.

NOTE   The TLV (type length value) is used to request information by indicating the values in each category. These values then indicate the requested information.

Reliable Delivery

Enhanced IGRP demands reliability of the messages sent. For that reason, it has a reliable transport for ordered delivery and acknowledgments. Information such as sequence number and acknowledgment number are maintained on a per-neighbor basis.

When a router transmits a packet, it increments its sequence number and places the packet on a transmission queue for all the neighbors on the interface for which the packet is sent. A receiver must acknowledge each packet individually and will drop packets out of order. Duplicate packets are also discarded.

A reliable transport protocol behaves differently on various types of media. On point-to-point links, three potential situations exist: update-initiated packet exchange, query-initiated packet exchange, and request-initiated packet exchange. These are further discussed in the following sections.

Update Packets

Update packets must be exchanged reliably. Each update packet contains a sequence number that must be acknowledged upon receipt via the acknowledgment packet. If the update packet or the acknowledgment packet is lost on the network, the update packet is retransmitted. The update packet is sent to a multicast address of 224.0.0.10. The router that receives the update packet sends an acknowledgment to the sender. This acknowledgment packet is *unicast*.

Query Packets

Depending on the state of the destination, query packets are acknowledged either via the reply packet or via another query packet. The router responds with a reply packet under two conditions: the query is received for a destination that is in a passive state, and the receiving router has a feasible successor for the destination; or the receiving router is in active state for a destination, and the querying router is the successor.

If the destination is in a passive state with no feasible successor, the router responds to the query packet with another query packet.

Request Packets

Request packets can be sent multicast or unicast. The router receiving the request packet sends a unicast update. When a request packet is not given a reply or an acknowledgment, it is always retransmitted to guarantee the delivery of the packet.

Neighbor Discovery

Enhanced IGRP is not a periodic routing protocol, so it does not rely on periodic updates to distribute routing information. Because it only sends changes, it is a non-periodic incremental protocol. For this reason, it is very important for Enhanced IGRP to maintain a neighbor relationship and to reliably propagate routing changes throughout the network. Two routers become neighbors when they acknowledge each other's hello packets on a common network.

Hello Packets

When Enhanced IGRP is enabled on an interface, the router begins sending hellos to a multicast address of 224.0.0.10. That hello packet includes the configured Enhanced IGRP metric K values. The two routers become adjacent if their K values match. (See Figure 8-5.)

Figure 8-5   *Hello Packets Sent to a Multicast Address for a Neighbor Relationship*

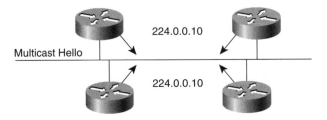

Hello packets are sent every five seconds on high-bandwidth links, such as Ethernet, Token Ring, and FDDI; as well as on serial point-to-point links. The hello packets are sent every 60 seconds on low-bandwidth multipoint links, for example Frame Relay links. Every neighbor must send periodic hello packets. By default, if three consecutive hello packets are not received from the neighbor, the hold time expires and the neighbor is declared dead. Unlike OSPF, hello and hold time do not have to match. Both hello and hold time are configurable parameters.

When a router detects a new neighbor through a hello packet, it sends a unicast update packet to the neighbor. In this update packet, the router will send information on all the routes that this router contains in its routing table. The advertised destination includes the following information: next hop, delay, bandwidth, MTU, hop count, reliability, load, subnet mask bit count, and the destination. An Enhanced IGRP route resembles the following:

```
Routing entry for 10.111.251.0/24
  Known via "Enhanced eigrp1", distance 90, metric 307200, type internal
  Redistributing via Enhanced eigrp 1
  Last update from 172.16.69.137 on Ethernet0/0, 00:41:12 ago
  Routing Descriptor Blocks:
  * 172.16.69.137, from 172.16.69.137, 00:41:12 ago, via Ethernet0/0
      Route metric is 307200, traffic share count is 1
      Total delay is 2000 microseconds, minimum bandwidth is 10000 Kbit
      Reliability 255/255, minimum MTU 1500 bytes
      Loading 1/255, Hops 1
```

The first update packet will include INIT-flag set, which indicates that the packet contains the complete routing table.

The Enhanced IGRP Topology Table

The first step toward building a routing table involves building the topology table. Unlike traditional distance-vector protocols, Enhanced IGRP does not rely on a forwarding table to hold all the routing information. Instead, it builds a separate table, known as a *topology table,* from which it constructs the routing table. The topology table contains information about the feasible successor, the next hop, and the metric (feasible distance) that is needed to reach the destination.

The topology table is built using information received from the neighbor network. This information indicates the distance that the neighbor needs to reach the destination.

Enhanced IGRP Metrics

Enhanced IGRP uses five metrics to determine the best path to a destination: lowest bandwidth, total delay, reliability, load, and MTU:

- *Lowest bandwidth* is calculated based on the minimum bandwidth to the destination network.

- *Total delay* is the sum of all the delays to the destination network.

- *Reliability* refers to how much the information can be trusted or how reliable the path is. This is not activated, by default.

- *Load* refers to how congested the outgoing link is; fully loaded is considered congested. This value is not a default.

- *MTU* is the maximum transmission unit of the exiting interface. By default, this is not used to calculate the metric.

By default, Enhanced IGRP uses only the composite delay and the minimum bandwidth to compute routing metrics. Both bandwidth and delay are determined by the values on the routers' interfaces.

The Enhanced IGRP metric formula is as follows:

Metric = [K1× bandwidth + (K2× bandwidth) / (256–load) + K3× delay]× [K5 / (reliability + K4)]

All K values, with the exception of K3 and K1, are set to zero. If zero is used instead of the other three K values in the Enhanced IGRP metric formula, the result would resemble this:

Metric = [K1× bandwidth + K3× delay]

After combining the scaling factor, the formula is as follows:

Metric = $[(10^7 \text{ / min bandwidth}) + \text{sum of delay}] \times 256$

NOTE   Configured interface delay is always divided by 10; bandwidth is always expressed in kilobits per second.

The output of the **show interface** Ethernet 0/0 command is as follows:

```
Ethernet0/0 is up, line protocol is up
    Hardware is cxBus Ethernet, address is 0010.2fac.7000 (bia 0010.2fac.7000)
    Internet address is 172.16.69.139/27
    MTU 1500 bytes, BW 10000 Kbit, DLY 1000 usec, rely 255/255, load 1/255
```

Figure 8-6 shows the values of the bandwidth and delays along the paths. In the present example, if you show the interface on the Ethernet of DC1 connected to the router, you see that the bandwidth is expressed in kilobits per second. This value is used as it is for the metric calculation. Delay is 1000 usec and is divided by 10 for the metric calculation.

Figure 8-6   *Metric Calculation for Enhanced IGRP Using Total Delay and Minimum Bandwidth*

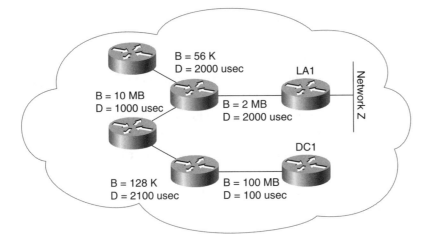

Consider a sample network, and study the metric calculation for Enhanced IGRP. In the example shown in Figure 8-6, the value of delay is already divided by 10.

In the following example, router DC1 wants to reach network Z:

```
Minimum bandwidth = 128 K
Composite Delay =    100 + 2100+ 1000 + 2000 =   5200

Metric =  [(10000000 / 128 )  + 5200] x 256 =   21331200
```

Stuck in Active

In some situations, it might take a very long time for a query to be answered. This can cause *Stuck in Active (SIA)* because the router becomes stuck in active mode. If this period of time is longer than the router issuing the query is willing to wait, the inquiring router will give up and clear its connection with the neighbor that has not responded to the query.

Queries are sent to all neighbors, in case a route is lost. The active timer responds to this query. When a query is received for a route from the neighbor, it sends the query to all its neighbors, and the process of passing the queries continues. Therefore, if the network does not have a solid addressing structure, and it has a flat architecture, it may require a long period of time to process the queries. The most common reasons for SIA include the following:

- The router is too busy. The router could be busy for a variety of reasons, including processing routing protocol packets or pushing traffic across.

- There is a bad connection because many packets have been dropped or because the link is not staying up for a long enough period of time. Another possibility is that the link could be staying up long enough to keep the neighbor up, but not all the queries are being processed.

- A slower link exists between the neighbors.

TIP   On slower links, you should increase the bandwidth usage on the link for Enhanced IGRP. In case of such an event, Enhanced IGRP will utilize most of the bandwidth to ensure that its packets are processed over limited link speed. The command used to change the active timers is **timer *active-time*,** in which time is reported in minutes.

Enhanced IGRP Configuration Commands

The following Enhanced IGRP configuration commands are covered in this section:

- Enable Enhanced IGRP
- Bandwidth control
- Summarization
- Passive interface
- Distribute-list

Enable Enhanced IGRP

Enhanced IGRP is enabled on a per-network basis. Eventually, it will be enabled on a per-subnet basis. Enhanced IGRP begins sending hello on all the interfaces in the specified networks. If a network is not specified under the Enhanced IGRP process, Enhanced IGRP will not send packets, nor will it include that network in Enhanced IGRP updates.

In Figure 8-7, to enable Enhanced IGRP for network 10.0.0.0 but not for 131.108.0.0, the configuration would be as follows:

```
router eigrp 1
network 10.0.0.0
```

Figure 8-7 *Enable Enhanced IGRP on a Router for Network 10.0.0.0*

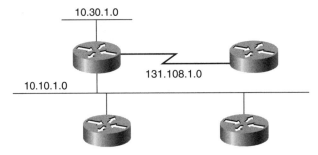

To enable Enhanced IGRP for network 131.108.0.0, you would add this network under EIGRP process. Enhanced IGRP then would begin sending packets on the serial line, and would include this network in its updates.

Enhanced IGRP and Bandwidth Control

Before continuing with Enhanced IGRP and bandwidth-related commands, you should understand bandwidth control. By default, Enhanced IGRP limits itself to 50 percent of the configured bandwidth. A benefit of controlling Enhanced IGRP usage is that it limits the Enhanced IGRP traffic in case of failure. This makes the rest of the bandwidth available for data traffic. Another advantage is that you avoid losing Enhanced IGRP packets, which could occur when Enhanced IGRP generates packets faster than the line rate.

The amount of bandwidth consumed by Enhanced IGRP depends on two commands. An interface command is used to specify the bandwidth:

```
bandwidth <nnn>
```

Because bandwidth is used for router metric calculations, the network administrator could deliberately set the bandwidth to a very low value, and then set Enhanced IGRP to use more than 100 percent of the configured bandwidth for Enhanced IGRP traffic:

```
config command
    ip bandwidth-percent eigrp <as-number> <value>
```

When bandwidth is set to a low value relative to actual link speed, Enhanced IGRP might converge at a slower rate. With a large routing table and slower convergence, you can trigger SIA. If the router is SIA, it displays the following message:

```
%DUAL-3-SIA:  Route XXX stuck-in-active state in IP-EIGRP AA. Cleaning up
```

If you receive many of these messages, there are two choices to solve this problem. First, you can change the active timers, which is achieved with this router command:

```
router eigrp 2
timers active-time <value>
```

The second—and more successful—way of solving this problem is to redesign the network to control the query range, so that queries are not sent from one end of the network to the other on a large network.

The default timer value is three minutes. Figure 8-8 shows illustrates this point.

Figure 8-8   *Enhanced IGRP SIA and Query Propagation*

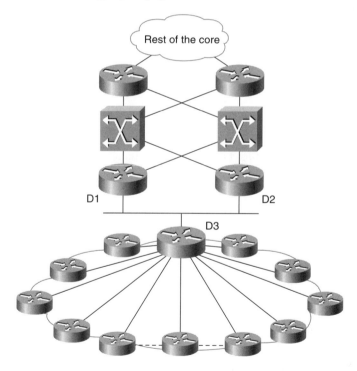

Figure 8-8 illustrates a Frame Relay cloud with several point-to-point or multipoint interfaces, each with a different committed information rate (CIR). The central router must wait for each neighbor to respond to its query, and then it must respond to the core routers. If all the remote

Frame Relay routers have contiguous address blocks, router D3 needs to summarize all the remote routers in one update.

For example, in Figure 8-8, when one of the remote Frame Relay neighbors fails, D3 queries all its neighbors, including D1 and D2. Because D3 is sending a single summary route to D1 and D2, both D1 and D2 immediately send unreachable messages to D3. In this situation, you do not need to increase the active timers; you need only to change the query range on the network. This way, the query range is not too large, and the network will not notice an SIA. The only router that might notice the SIA is router D3.

This bulleted list covers Enhanced IGRP bandwidth and behavior on different media:

- *Local-area network (LAN) interfaces*   For LAN interfaces, the bandwidth is set to the actual value. It is recommended that a fixed bandwidth be maintained, rather than changing it to a lower value.

- *Point-to-point*   For point-to-point serial interfaces, the default value is always taken as T1. If the actual line speed is different, it should be set to the actual bandwidth by using the **bandwidth** command.

- *NBMA interface*   It is critical to configure bandwidth properly for nonbroadcast, multiaccess (NBMA) networks; otherwise, you may experience Enhanced IGRP packet loss on the switched network.

There are three basic rules for configuring Enhanced IGRP over NBMA networks:

1 Enhanced IGRP traffic should not exceed the capacity of the virtual circuit.

2 Total Enhanced IGRP traffic for all the virtual circuits cannot exceed the actual line speed.

3 Bandwidth configured for Enhanced IGRP should be the same on both ends of the link.

With these rules in mind, consider some possible situations involving NBMA networks. The three possible forms of NBMA networks are:

- Pure multipoint
- Pure point-to-point
- Hybrid

Each of these scenarios is discussed in the following sections.

Pure Multipoint NBMA Networks

Pure multipoint Enhanced IGRP divides the configured bandwidth evenly across each virtual circuit. However, you must ensure that this does not overload each virtual circuit. The formula for multipoint is as follows:

Bandwidth × number of VC (virtual circuits)

For example, if you have an access line speed of T1 and there are four virtual circuits, each with 56 Kbps CIR, the bandwidth should be set to 4 × 56 Kbps = 224 Kbps. This will ensure that packets are not dropped. If the virtual circuits have different speeds, the bandwidth should be set to accommodate the lowest-capacity virtual circuit.

NOTE   A *virtual circuit (VC)* is not a physical connection between two endpoints; it is a connection across a switched network.

Figure 8-9 shows an example of three 256 Kbps VCs and one 56 Kbps VC. This indicates that the bandwidth should be set to 4 × 56 Kbps = 224 Kbps; otherwise, Enhanced IGRP packets can overrun the 56 Kbps pipe.

TIP   With VCs of different capacities, it is strongly recommended that the low-bandwidth VC is used as the point-to-point link.

Figure 8-9   *Multipoint Interface with Different VC Capacities*

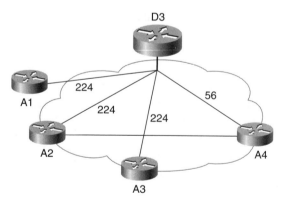

The configuration of a multipoint interface, will resemble this:

```
interface serial 0
ip address 131.108.1.1 255.255.255.0
bandwidth 224
```

If you change the setup so that the 56 Kbps virtual circuit is a separate point-to-point interface, the configuration would be as follows:

```
interface serial 0.1 multi-point
ip address 131.108.1.1 255.255.255.0
bandwidth 768

interface serial 0.2 point-to-point
ip address 131.108.2.1 255.255.255.0
bandwidth 56
```

With the second type of configuration, the slower link does not affect the convergence of the higher-speed links. Recall that Enhanced IGRP uses 50 percent of the configured bandwidth of the interface. By separating the high-bandwidth interface as a multipoint and a low-speed link as point-to-point Enhanced IGRP, you can make effective use of the available bandwidth during convergence.

Pure Point-to-Point NBMA Networks

The pure point-to-point network is the simplest of all the setups, and it allows maximum control over the network. Each point-to-point subinterface can be configured to maintain a separate bandwidth, if each VC has a separate capacity. Again, recall the three basic rules:

- Enhanced IGRP traffic should not exceed the capacity of the virtual circuit.
- Total Enhanced IGRP traffic for all the virtual circuits cannot exceed the actual line speed.
- Bandwidth configured for Enhanced IGRP should be the same on both ends of the link.

Consider, for example, oversubscribed hub and spoke. This is one of the most common configurations, and usually involves minimal transaction traffic between the hub and spoke, on which the access line to the hub is oversubscribed. If you have 10 VCs, with 56 Kbps access lines to each of the 10 spoke sites, there would be a total line speed of 256 Kbps to the hub.

Again, with the three basic rules in mind, the following considerations apply: If you perform the configuration for Figure 8-10, the line speed at the hub has a total bandwidth of $56 \times 10 = 560$ Kbps, which is greater than the actual link speed. In this case, divide the actual line speed at the hub by the number of virtual circuits. Any individual PVC should not be allowed to handle more than (256/10) 25 Kbps.

The spoke site has a speed of 56 Kbps and is configured at 25 Kbps to accommodate the second Enhanced IGRP rule. This would affect the convergence of Enhanced IGRP because the data traffic is fairly low. This means that you can allow Enhanced IGRP to use 90 percent of the configured bandwidth. Figure 8-10 shows that the hub site has 256 Kbps, and each of the 10 remote VCs has an actual bandwidth of 56 Kbps. Therefore, adding all the VCs shows that more bandwidth exists at the remote VCs than at the hub.

Figure 8-10   *Oversubscribed Hub and Spoke*

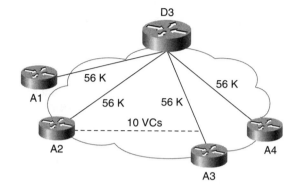

Configuration at the hub router for this example would be as follows:

```
interface serial 0
encapsulation frame-relay

interface s 0.1 point-to-point
bandwidth 25
ip bandwidth-percent eigrp 110 90


.........


interface s 0.10 point-to-point
bandwidth 25
ip bandwidth-percent eigrp 110 90


configuration at the spoke router

interface serial 3
encapsulation frame-relay
bandwidth 25
ip bandwidth-percent eigrp 110 90
```

Each spoke should have the same configuration to limit the Enhanced IGRP traffic to the same rate as the hub—remember, this is the third rule.

Note that Enhanced IGRP will not use more than 22.5 Kbps (90 percent of 25 Kbps) on each interface. This configuration will not affect the data traffic because each VC has a capacity of up to 56 Kbps.

Enhanced IGRP Classless Summarization

By default, Enhanced IGRP advertises at the natural classful network boundary for all the Enhanced IGRP internal routes. All external routes are not summarized when advertised across a major network. Before continuing with this discussion, you should understand the difference between internal and external routes in Enhanced IGRP.

Internal routes are routes that are learned from the same autonomous number running on the local router. *External routes* are routes that are learned from other routing protocols, from IGRP, or from another Enhanced IGRP autonomous system number.

As mentioned earlier, Enhanced IGRP summarizes internal routes at the natural network mask when propagated across a different major network. External routes are advertised as unchanged, even across different major networks. To change the default behavior of internal routes, you must disable auto-summarization, which is accomplished with the **router** subcommand:

```
router eigrp 109
no auto-summary
```

In Figure 8-11, for example, if router D1 wants to advertise subnets across the major network, you would need to disable the auto-summary.

Figure 8-11   *Enhanced IGRP and Auto-Summary*

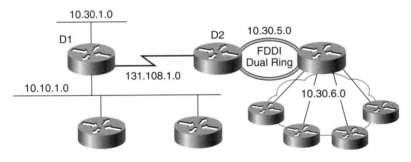

To disable the auto-summary, enter the following configuration on router D1:

```
Router D1
router eigrp 1
network 10.0.0.0
network 131.108.0.0
no auto-summary
```

Enter the following configuration for router D2:

```
Router D2
router eigrp 1
network 10.0.0.0
network 131.108.0.0
no auto-summary
```

If you leave the default behavior on router D1 and D2 as it is, maintaining the auto-summary on D1's routing table, you would have the following configuration:

```
Router D1# show ip route

10.0.0.0/24 is subnetted, 2 subnets
C       10.30.1.0 is directly connected, Ethernet0/3
D     10.0.0.0/8 [90/284160] via 131.108.1.1, 00:00:10,  Serial 1/2
      172.16.0.0/27 is subnetted, 1 subnets
C       10.10.1.0 is directly connected, Ethernet0/0
C       131.108.1.0/24 is directly connected, Serial 1/2
C       131.108.2.2/32 is directly connected, Loopback1
```

Now, if you disable auto-summary, the routing table would read:

```
10.0.0.0/8 is variably subnetted, 6 subnets, 2 masks
D       10.30.5.0/24 [90/2195456] via 131.108.1.1, 00:00:16, Serial 1/2
D       10.30.6.0/24 [90/2195456] via 131.108.1.1, 00:00:16, Serial 1/2
D       10.0.0.0/8 is a summary, 00:00:16, Null0
D       10.1.27.0/24 [90/284160] via 131.108.1.1, 00:00:16, Ethernet0/3
```

TIP

All Enhanced IGRP internal routes have an administrative distance of 90, and place D in front of them to indicate that they are Enhanced IGRP internal routes.

IGRP routes with the same autonomous system number as Enhanced IGRP are automatically redistributed into Enhanced IGRP. For the Enhanced IGRP routing process, IGRP routes are treated as external. When IGRP routes are propagated into Enhanced IGRP, the metric value of IGRP is multiplied by 256. This automatic redistribution does not cause a routing loop, although IGRP has an administrative distance of 100, and external Enhanced IGRP has an administrative distance of 170.

Before the routes are installed into the routing table, the metric of the routes is compared and the metric conversion is performed by multiplying with 256. The lower of the two metrics is selected and installed into the routing table.

NOTE

The Enhanced IGRP route is installed in the routing table when a route is learned from external Enhanced IGRP and the same route is learned from IGRP, and when these two routes have equal metric values. This holds true even though the administrative distance of IGRP is lower than that of Enhanced IGRP.

External routes in Enhanced IGRP are indicated with D EX. Routes that are redistributed from other routing protocols are also treated as external for Enhanced IGRP.

Summarizing External Routes

Now, the question remains: How do you summarize external routes in Enhanced IGRP across network boundaries? As mentioned earlier, external Enhanced IGRP routes are not summarized across a major network boundary.

Consider, for example, the network in Figure 8-12. One side of the network runs OSPF, and the other side runs Enhanced IGRP. Assume that you want to redistribute Enhanced OSPF into Enhanced IGRP and that you want to summarize over the serial interface S0 across the major network boundary.

Router D1 in Figure 8-12 would redistribute the routes. Notice that the interface between D1 and D2 has an IP address of 10.10.1.0. This indicates that if you had the same Enhanced IGRP process running across the entire network, with the default behavior of auto-summary activated, all the subnets of the 131.108.0.0 network would have been advertised as 131.108.0.0/16 routing entry, which is the major network class B.

Figure 8-12   *Summarization of External Enhanced IGRP Routes Across a Major Network Boundary*

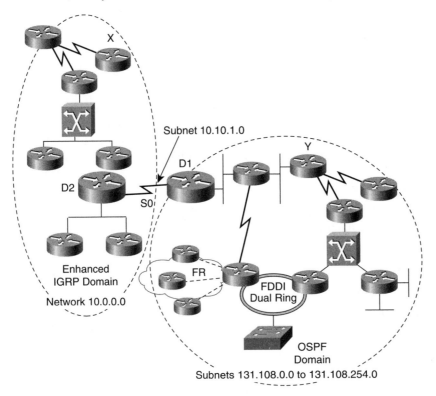

Now, assume that in the network shown in Figure 8-12, there are different routing protocols and you must redistribute OSPF into Enhanced IGRP. The configuration for D1 would be as follows:

```
router eigrp 1
network 10.0.0.0
redistribute ospf 1
default-metric 100000 1 1 1 1

 Show ip route at D2 for network 131.108.0.0:

D EX    131.10.1.0 [170/409600] via 10.10.1.1, 00:29:21, Serial0/3
D EX    131.10.2.0 [170/409600] via 10.10.1.1, 00:29:22, Serial0/3
D EX    131.10.30.0 [170/409600] via 10.10.1.1, 00:29:22, Serial0/3

.................................................. . .
D EX    131.10.252.0 [170/409600] via 10.10.1.1, 00:29:22, Serial0/3
D EX    131.10.253.0 [170/409600] via 10.10.1.1, 00:29:22, Serial0/3
D EX    131.10.254.0 [170/409600] via 10.10.1.1, 00:29:22, Serial0/3
```

Because these are all external routes into Enhanced IGRP, they are not summarized. To summarize all of them into one update across the serial line on router D1, there are two options: You could list this network under the Enhanced IGRP process, or you could use the **ip summary-address** command.

For the first option, the configuration commands on D1 would be as follows:

```
router eigrp 1
network 10.0.0.0
network 131.10.0.0
redistribute ospf 1
default-metric 100000 1 1 1 1
```

For the second option, the configuration commands on D1 would be as follows:

```
interface serial 0
ip address 10.10.1.1 255.255.255.0
ip summary-address eigrp 1 131.108.0.0 255.255.0.0
```

Now, when you perform a **show ip route** on D2, you will find a single route to network 131.108.0.0:

```
D   131.10.0.0/16 [90/409600] via 10.10.1.1, 00:29:22, Serial0/3
```

Whenever you use the **summary-address** command in Enhanced IGRP, the protocol follows two courses of action:

1 Creates a null route that matches the summary-address network and mask entry.

2 Limits the query propagation.

If the summary null route was not created by router D1 in its routing table, and router X in Figure 8-12 wants to send traffic to subnet 131.108.17.0/24, which does not exist, it would check its routing table and find a summary route via Enhanced IGRP to network 131.108.0.0/16.

This is the longest prefix the router has in its routing table. Router X would forward the packet to router D2, which would check its routing table and find a route to network 131.108.0.0/16 via D1. D2 would then forward the packet to D1. D1 does not have a subnet 131.108.0.0/17 in its routing table at this point, so D1 checks for the next closest prefix and finds 0.0.0.0/0 in its routing table via D2. Next, D1 forwards the packet back to D2. This ping-pong effect will continue until the TTL expires. With the null route in D1's routing table, a packet forwarded to D1 will be dropped by D1, and the router will send an ICMP unreachable message back to the source.

On the local router in which you configured the **summary-address** command (D1, in this case), Enhanced IGRP creates a matching masked route with the **summary-address** command to the null 0 interface. This action avoids routing loops. If you perform a **show ip route** on D1, the following route will appear:

```
D   131.10.0.0/16 is a summary, 00:29:22,  Null0
```

You may wonder: What are the advantages of the null 0 route, and how does it prevent routing loops? Using the example network shown in Figure 8-12 again, this time assume that router D2 is the Internet connection and that you are sending a default route from D2. When you perform a **show ip route** on D1, you will see the following entry in the routing table:

```
Gateway of last resort is 10.10.1.2 to network 0.0.0.0
```

This indicates that if the router does not have a specific route to a destination, it will use the default route or it will use the router that is the *gateway of last resort* to reach that particular destination. Recall that the *gateway of last resort* is based on the concept that if the router does not have a specific routing entry to a destination, it uses the default route of 0.0.0.0 as the last resort to reach that destination.

For example, if a router is trying to reach a destination of 140.10.10.0/24 and does not find a route to this destination, it will determine whether it has a shorter prefix to the major network 140.10.0.0/16. If the major network is not there, then the router looks for a CIDR route of 140.0.0.0/8. If it does not find any entry that covers the destination it is trying to reach, the router will use the default route as its last resort.

Auto-Summary: Enhanced IGRP Summarization and Query Scoping

Query propagation occurs when an Enhanced IGRP router loses a route to a destination, and therefore goes into an active state. During this process, the router queries all its neighbors for the lost destination. Query propagation stops one hop from the point of summarization and auto-summary.

This is a definite advantage—if all the routes were sent across to all the routers in the network, a remote node in one part of the network would send a query for a lost route to the other end of the network. Then, it would have to wait for a response from all the neighbors. Preventing queries from reaching end-to-end allows the network to converge more rapidly.

As an example, consider router D1 in Figure 8-13.

Figure 8-13   *Enhanced IGRP and Query Scoping*

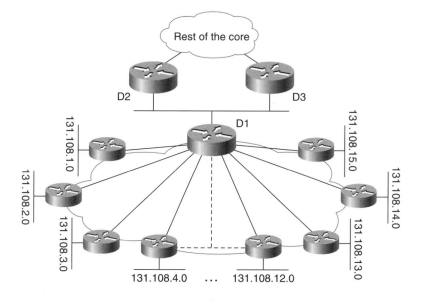

Router D1 has 16 remote sites connected to it via Frame Relay; each remote router advertises subnets from 131.108.1.0/24 to 131.108.15.0/24. D1 has all the specific routes in its routing table and can easily summarize all the subnets toward D2 and D3. If Ethernet 0 is the interface that connects D1 to D2 and D3, the interface configuration for Ethernet 0 on D1 would be as follows:

```
interface e 0
ip address 131.108.22.1 255.255.255.0
ip summary-address eigrp 1 131.108.0.0 255.255.240.0

router eigrp 1
network 131.108.0.0
```

With this configuration, whenever one of the remote subnets flaps, D1 will send queries to all its connected neighbors. Upon receiving the query, D2 and D3 will not propagate the query any further because they do not have specific routes in their tables—they have only a single summary via D1. Upon receiving the query, D2 and D3 will send an unreachable message back to D1.

Enhanced IGRP and Passive Interface

If you do not want to enable Enhanced IGRP on an interface, you must set it in passive mode. This prevents Enhanced IGRP from sending multicast hellos to an interface. The question then becomes: When would you want to set a passive interface?

There are situations in which you should set Enhanced IGRP in passive mode. First, you would use the passive mode when a router is connected to a large number of customer sites and you do not want to run Enhanced IGRP on those links. If you are an Internet Service Provider (ISP), your external peering router interface is the next hop for EBGP routes, and it must be advertised into your IGP. In this case, simply make the interface passive so that you do not send Enhanced IGRP hellos to an external neighbor.

This way, you will continue to advertise the interface into your IGP for the next hop of an EBGP route, and you will not form an Enhanced IGRP neighbor relationship. When an interface is passive for Enhanced IGRP, nothing is sent from it from a protocol standpoint.

NOTE   A *passive interface* prevents protocol packets from being sent on the interface. In Enhanced IGRP, OSPF passive interface stops the hello packets from being sent to the neighbor. When the hello packets are not sent on an interface, no neighbor relationships are formed, which means that routing will not occur between those routers.

The proper configuration for router D1 would be as follows:

```
router eigrp 1
network 131.108.0.0
passive-interface e 0
```

In Figure 8-14, for example, D1 will stop sending hellos on Ethernet, but will continue to send Enhanced IGRP hellos on the serial interface. If the other two routers on the Ethernet are running Enhanced IGRP for network 131.108.0.0, they will remain as neighbors, but will not receive any updates from D1 and will not form a neighbor relationship with D1.

Enhanced IGRP and Distribute-List

A *distribution list* is used to block routing information from being sent or received. This list can be applied on a per-routing protocol basis or a per-interface basis.

Figure 8-14   *Enhanced IGRP and Passive Interface*

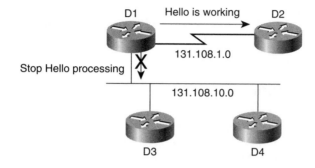

When applied on a per-routing protocol basis, the distribution list will block all routing updates that are exiting or entering the protocol that do not pass the access-list. For example, consider this code:

```
router eigrp 1
network 10.0.0.0
distribute-list 1 in

access-list 1 deny 10.10.10.0 0.0.0.255
access-list 1 permit any
```

In this example, updates to network 10.10.10.0/24 would not be accepted by the Enhanced IGRP process 1. Similarly, a **distribute-list out** command will prevent updates from being sent to neighbor networks that are not permitted by the list.

When applied on a per-interface basis, this list prevents the routes from entering that specific interface. For example, consider the same access-list and apply it to an interface, as shown here:

```
router eigrp 1
network 10.0.0.0
distribute-list 1 in Ethernet 3/0

access-list 1 deny 10.10.10.0 0.0.0.255
access-list 1 permit any
```

This would block updates about subnet 10.10.10.0/24 from being learned on interface Ethernet 3/0.

With Enhanced IGRP, the distribution list does not just block the routing updates distribution list—it also affects the queries. Instead of blocking the queries, the list will delineate any query reply as unreachable. Consider Figure 8-15, for example. Routers D1, D2, and D4 are connected to each other. Router D2 has a distribution list applied against its serial interface, which denies network 10.1.4.0 from being advertised to its neighbors.

Router D2 is using router D4 as its successor for network 10.1.4.0. If router D4's physical interface to network goes down, router D4 would send a query to router D2 for network 10.1.4.0. If router D2 has router D1 as its feasible successor, router D2 will send an unreachable message back to router D4. The unreachable message would be sent because of the distribution list, even though router D2 has a valid route to network 10.1.4.0.

Enhanced IGRP and Variance

Enhanced IGRP can simultaneously use unequal cost paths to the same destination, which indicates that traffic can be distributed among multiple (up to four, by default) unequal cost paths to provide greater overall throughput and reliability. An alternate path is used if the *variance* condition is met. The variance condition depends on two factors:

- The local metric must be greater than the metric of the next router, so the next hop router must be closer to the destination than the local best metric.

- The local best metric is multiplied by the variance number. The multiplier (variance) times the local best number must be greater than or equal to the metric through the next router.

If these conditions are met, the alternate route is considered feasible and is added to the routing table. This feature helps you balance traffic across all feasible paths and allows the router to immediately converge to a new path if one of the other paths fails. Although this feature does not provide much benefit for Enhanced IGRP during convergence, it does assist in performing unequal cost load balancing.

Consider the example in Figure 8-15.

Figure 8-15 *Enhanced IGRP and Variance*

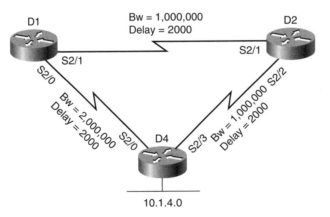

In Figure 8-15, router D2 is learning a route to destination 10.1.4.0 via D4 and also via D1. The metric for destination 10.1.4.0 via D4 is 53,760, and the metric via D1 is 104,960.

To determine whether D1 meets the condition for variance, follow these steps:

1 In this case, D1 is the alternate path: Its metric (104,960) should be more viable than the local best metric (in this case, the metric via D4 is 53,760). Variance can be used only if both of the conditions are met. In this case, we have seen that 104,960 >53,760, which meets the first condition.

2 In this case, you have configured a variance of two. The local best metric times variance (53,760 × 2) must be greater than or equal to the metric via the alternate path (the path via D1, which is 104,960). As shown here, the local best metric is greater than the metric via the alternate path, so this condition is met as well:

> Local best metric × variance multiplier = 53,760 × 2 = 107,520
> Metric through the next router = 104,960

The configuration for D2 is as follows:

```
hostname D2
!
enable password cisco
!
interface Ethernet0/0
ip address 171.68.173.12 255.255.255.192

interface Serial2/1
ip address 10.1.2.2 255.255.255.0
bandwidth 2000000
clockrate 2000000

interface Serial2/2
ip address 10.1.3.1 255.255.255.0
bandwidth 1000000

router eigrp 1
variance 2
network 10.0.0.0
```

This variance would enable router D2 to perform unequal cost load balancing.

Routing descriptor blocks are listed as the following:

```
* 10.1.3.2, from 10.1.3.2, 01:38:21 ago, via Serial2/2
    Route metric is 1,792,000, traffic share count is 1
    Total delay is 2000 microseconds, minimum bandwidth is 1000 Kbit
    Reliability 255/255, minimum MTU 1500 bytes
    Loading 1/255, Hops 1
  10.1.2.1, from 10.1.2.1, 01:38:21 ago, via Serial2/1
    Route metric is 3,584,000, traffic share count is 1
    Total delay is 4000 microseconds, minimum bandwidth is 2000 Kbit
    Reliability 255/255, minimum MTU 1500 bytes
    Loading 1/255, Hops 2
```

The * (asterisk) before the first entry indicates that this route will be used the next time a packet is sent to 10.1.4.0. *Traffic share count* refers to the router's load balancing across equal or unequal cost path links. Therefore, the router will perform a 1:1 time packet to the destination 10.1.4.0. This way, load balancing would be achieved across both links. The method by which the load is balanced depends on the switching mode used during process switching. The router will perform per-packet load sharing, so one packet will be sent via 10.1.3.2, and the next packet will be sent via 10.1.2.1 next hop. For fast switching, the router performs a per-destination load sharing.

By default, Cisco routers distribute traffic across the unequal cost paths if you configure variance. If you do not want to use this feature, but still want faster convergence to an alternate path, you can use the **traffic-share {balance / min}** command. With Enhanced IGRP, this is not very helpful because the router already has a feasible successor in its topology table for faster convergence. If **traffic-share min** is used, it installs the route in the routing table, but stops traffic through inferior links, as shown here:

```
Command
router eigrp 1
traffic-share min
```

This also would be reflected in the **sh ip** route:

```
10.1.2.1, from 10.1.2.1, 01:38:21 ago, via Serial2/1
    Route metric is 1153280, traffic share count is 0
    Total delay is 45000 microseconds, minimum bandwidth is 2000000 Kbit
    Reliability 255/255, minimum MTU 1500 bytes
    Loading 1/255, Hops 2
```

When the traffic share is set to minimum, traffic share count is set to zero.

Note that variance can be used only for a feasible successor because the variance condition is the same as a feasibility condition. The variance and feasibility condition has the same requirement. The local metric must be greater than the metric of the next router, so the next hop router must be closer to the destination than the local best metric.

Adjusting Enhanced IGRP Parameters

Enhanced IGRP sends periodic hellos to detect its neighbors. By default, a hello packet is sent every five seconds on all LAN and point-to-point interfaces and sent every 60 seconds on non-broadcast multiaccess media. Slower links are considered T1 or lower. To change this default, the command is as follows:

```
int serial 0
ip hello-interval eigrp 1 15
```

One is the autonomous-system number, and 15 seconds is the hello time.

Holdtime is advertised in the hello packet to inform the neighbor of the amount of time it should consider a route valid from a specific sender. The default behavior for holdtime is three times the hello, so if a router does not receive three hellos from the neighbor, the message is placed in holddown. This could be changed by using the following command:

```
interface serial 0
ip hold-time eigrp 1 45
```

Here, 1 is the autonomous system number and 45 is the holdtime.

Split Horizon and Enhanced IGRP

Recall that a split horizon occurs when a router will not advertise a route on the same interface from which it learned the route. In Figure 8-16, router D1 will advertise network 10.1.4.0 to D2 on serial 2/1, but D1 will not send it back to D4 on serial 2/0 because D1 learned this route from D4 on serial 2/0.

Figure 8-16 shows that the D1 router does not readvertise the route to itself, which assists in preventing routing loops.

Figure 8-16   *Split Horizon*

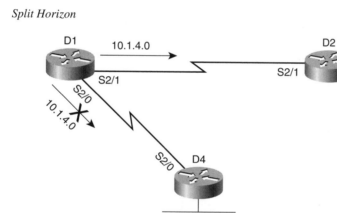

By default, split horizon is enabled on all LAN and point-to-point interfaces, but it is disabled on all NBMA networks for all distance-vector protocols, including Enhanced IGRP. In certain non-meshed NBMA networks, it becomes necessary to deactivate split horizon because in hub-and spoke-type setups, the hub router receives a route from all remote routers.

It will not send the route that it has learned from one remote route back to other remote routers because all the remote routers are connected by the same interface. (See Figure 8-17.)

Figure 8-17   *Hub and Spoke Connection and Split Horizon*

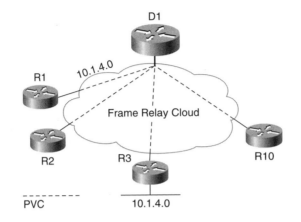

Take the case of Figure 8-17, for example, in which PVCs do not exist between R1 through R10, and all have a connection to the central router D1. A better solution is to configure point-to-point subinterfaces. If, for some reason, you want to keep all the remote sites on a common subnet and do not want to use point-to-point subinterfaces, you would need to disable split horizon to propagate routes from one remote site to another.

The configuration to disable split horizon is as follows:

```
interface serial s/2
no ip split-horizon eigrp 1
```

Summary

EIGRP is an advanced distance-vector classless protocol that employs DUAL for faster convergence. It is based on a neighbor relationship, so it selects the best route to the destination based on real-time parameters, such as delay and bandwidth.

There are three types of DUAL messages: queries, updates, and replies. Queries are sent to all neighbors, in case a route is lost. In some networks it may take a long time for a query to be answered, which causes the router to be Stuck in Active (SIA). If this period becomes too long, the inquiring router will give up and clear its connection with the neighbor that did not reply. Preventing queries from reaching end-to-end helps the network to converge more rapidly.

Enhanced IGRP is an interior gateway protocol and is non-periodic. Improvements on this protocol have achieved faster convergence, relying on DUAL to converge loop-free.

Finally, this chapter covered various configuration commands for EIGRP, and discussed several examples of how these would be practically applied in real-life networks.

Review Questions

1 What is the amount of bandwidth that Enhanced IGRP uses during failure?

2 What is SIA?

3 What is auto-summary, and what does it do?

Answers:

1 By default, Enhanced IGRP uses 50 percent of bandwidth during failure.

2 SIA stands for "Stuck in Active," which indicates the expiration of an active timer. This occurs when the router has not received a reply from all the neighbors about a route it queried during the active timer.

3 Auto-summary is the summarization of internal Enhanced IGRP routes to a classful network boundary when a router sends an update on an interface that belongs to a different major network from the subnet about which the update is sent.

For Further Reading . . .

Cisco IOS Manual.

Faranacci, Dino. "Introduction to EIGRP."

This chapter discusses the Open Shortest Path First (OSPF) protocol, including the following issues:

Fundamentals and operation of OSPF   OSPF is a link-state protocol used as an Interior Gateway Protocol (IGP). This section discusses how OSPF builds a database and how to build routing tables from that database.

Introduction to link-state protocols   Link-state protocols are like a jigsaw puzzle. Each router within an area maintains information about all the links and routers in its area. This section explains the fundamentals of link-state protocols and how to take advantage of them.

OSPF packet format   OSPF has five different packet types: hello, database description, update, request, and acknowledgment. Each is discussed in detail in corresponding sections.

Types of link-state   This section discusses the five main link states of OSPF: router, network, summary type 3, summary type 4, and external. The text also explains how each contributes to the database and routing tables.

Use of areas in OSPF   There are four types of areas in OSPF: regular, stub, totally stub, and not so stubby area. This section also details how these areas operate within the network, and covers what link states can be sent to these areas.

OSPF is discussed in detail in this chapter because it is one of most popular IGPs on the Internet today. As networks continue to expand, administrators are moving toward scalable IGPs. With the introduction of class routing, OSPF is becoming the preferred protocol as an IGP for many large organizations and ISPs.

## CHAPTER 9

Open Shortest Path First

Fundamentals of OSPF

OSPF is an Interior Gateway Protocol (IGP), whereby each router belonging to a single area maintains an identical database. The routing table is constructed from the information in this database by running a Shortest Path First algorithm. The route is installed in the table by first resolving the least-cost route to the destination. OSPF routes packets are based solely on the IP destination, so there is no room for source-based routing. OSPF also uses IP multicast for updates, but does not perform fragmentation. Instead, it relies on IP for fragmentation and reassembly.

OSPF has one very significant feature: It forces hierarchy into the network by introducing *areas*. Creating areas reduces the size of the database information that a router must maintain. All routers within their area maintain complete information about their area in the database. Areas assist in creating smaller, more manageable subdomains within a network. Every area must be connected to the backbone area. To implement OSPF in a network, the network must include hierarchy.

OSPF supports equal-cost paths to the same destination. Recall that, in Cisco routers, there are four equal-cost paths, by default. The equal-cost path values can be raised to six using the **max-path** command. OSPF does not have periodic updates like RIP; only changes are propagated.

OSPF update packets are sent to multicast addresses on all broadcast and non-broadcast multiaccess media (NBMA). This reduces traffic when other routers are present on the wire because they will not listen to OSPF updates. For each operational interface in OSPF, a cost is calculated based on a certain formula. OSPF uses this interface cost to select the best path to the destination; the optimal path is determined by the sum of interface costs.

NOTE   *Discontiguous networks* occur when subnets of the same major network are separated by a different major network in the middle.

OSPF offers full-featured support for IP subnetting. OSPF carries the network number and the mask pair in its updates, and it provides support for variable-length subnet masking (VLSM), supernets and subnets, and discontiguous networks. It is important that you become familiar with the concept of *discontiguous networks*. When subnets of the same major networks are separated by a different major network, the network is considered discontiguous.

Introduction to Link-State Protocols

In the field of networking, we compare link-state protocols to jigsaw puzzles—each router is one piece of the puzzle. When the routers are joined, they form the complete picture. Every router within an area holds a piece of the puzzle. All routers within the same area have identical information about all the links and routers. Therefore, all the routers in the same area know the identity of the router that originated the information about its link and its neighbors.

Every router advertises the costs and states of its links in the form of a link-state advertisement. This state information is then propagated one hop away. This propagation of information results in all routers having identical databases. Every router is identified by its unique ID, so a loop is avoided.

To reach a destination, all the costs of the links within the destination route are summed. After the router has received information about all the other routers and their links, each router runs the Shortest Path First algorithm to calculate the optimal path to each known destination.

OSPF Packet Format

OSPF is a routing protocol designed specifically for the TCP/IP environment, and it runs directly on top of IP protocol 89. Another noteworthy point about OSPF is that it does not perform fragmentation and reassembly; these functions are performed at the IP layer.

Every OSPF packet shares a common 24-byte protocol header, as shown in Figure 9-1. Routing protocol packets are sent with a type of service of zero.

Figure 9-1 *The 24-byte Common OSPF Header Shared by All Protocol Packets*

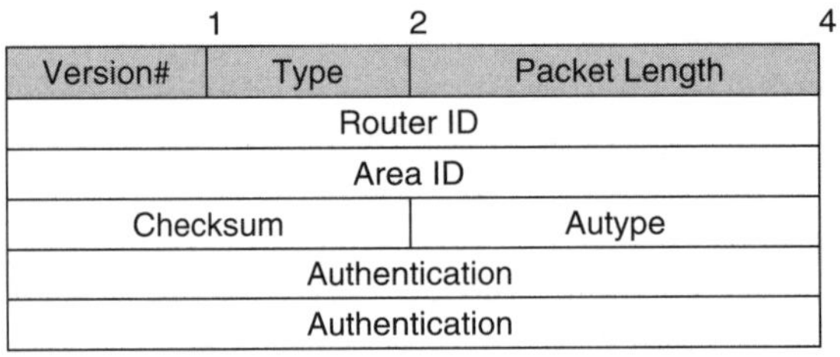

1	2	4
Version#	Type	Packet Length
Router ID		
Area ID		
Checksum		Autype
Authentication		
Authentication		

OSPF has five types of routing protocol packets; the Type field in the protocol header identifies each one as follows:

- *Version*   This is one byte; the current version of OSPF is two.
- *Type*   This is used to identify the OSPF packet. Five types of OSPF packets exist:

Type	Description
1	Hello
2	Database description packet
3	Link-state request
4	Link-state update
5	Link-state acknowledgment

Each of the packet types is discussed in detail later in this chapter.

- *Router ID*   This four-byte field is used to identify the router originating the OSPF packet.
- *Area ID*   This four-byte field is used to identify the area to which the packet belongs. All OSPF packets are sent one hop, except on virtual links. In virtual links, which are used to patch the backbone area, this field is set to 0.0.0.0.
- *Checksum*   OSPF uses regular IP checksum, which covers the complete packet except for the eight bytes of authentication.
- *Authentication*   This eight-byte field is used for authentication of the process used.

OSPF Packet Types

As mentioned previously, OSPF has five kinds of routing protocol packets, and each is identified by the Type field in the protocol header. Now, we will discuss those packet types in more detail.

The Hello Packet

OSPF Packet type 1, as shown in Figure 9-2, is the hello packet.

Hello packets are sent periodically to all functional OSPF interfaces, and are used to detect neighbors. OSPF packets are sent to the multicast address 224.0.0.5.

The basic function of the hello packet is to establish a neighbor relationship, to elect the designated router, and to negotiate optional capabilities. These optional capabilities include negotiating the E bit setting to determine whether the attached area is a stub, the DC bit to indicate demand circuit, the N/P bit indicating whether the router supports NSSA, and EA external attributes.

Figure 9-2 *OSPF Hello Packet*

Network Mask		
Hello Interval	Options	Rtr Pri
Router Dead Interval		
Designated Router		
Backup Designated Router		
Neighbor		

All routers connected to a common network must agree on all the parameters to form an adjacency. An *adjacency* is formed between two routers when complete database information is received and acknowledged. At this point, the adjacent routers agree that both of them have identical information in their databases.

Figure 9-3 shows the frequency with which hello packets are sent on different types of links. On broadcast and point-to-point links, hello packets are sent every 10 seconds, by default. On NBMA networks, hello packets are sent every 30 seconds, by default.

Figure 9-3 *Frequency of Hello Packets on Various Links*

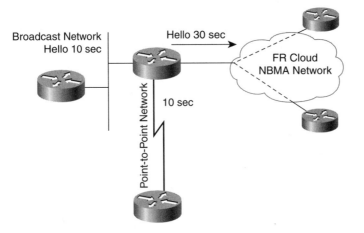

The following list describes the parameters upon which routers must agree to form an adjacency:

- *Network mask* This indicates the network and mask of the attached interface of the router. All routers sharing a common network interface must agree on this value. For example, if you have two routers connected on the same Ethernet, and one router has a subnet mask of 255.255.255.0, the other router that is sharing the same Ethernet should have the same subnet mask.

- *Hello interval*   This refers to the number of seconds between two consecutive hello packets. All routers attached to a common interface should have the same value.

- *Dead interval*   This interval is the amount of time before a neighbor is declared dead when a valid hello is not received from that neighbor. The default time for a dead timer is four times the hello interval.

- *Neighbor*   This is a list of all attached routers from which a valid OSPF hello packet has been received recently. Each neighbor is identified by its router ID. Valid packets from the neighbor should be received within the dead interval of the router.

TIP   Recall that the hello packet informs all other routers about the identity of the DR. If the DR field is 0.0.0.0, this means that no DR currently exists for this network.

The Designated Router and Backup Designated Router

A *designated router* is the central point for generating link-state algorithms (LSAs) about broadcast and non-broadcast multiaccess networks (NBMA). It is responsible for synchronizing the database with all the other routers on the wire.

The hello packet informs all other routers about the identity of the DR. If the DR is already elected, all routers must accept the router as the DR. If the DR field is 0.0.0.0, this means that no DR currently exists for this network.

The DR is elected based on the following information:

- Highest priority
- Highest router ID among all routers sharing the same network

The DR is generally responsible for advertising the broadcast/NBMA network via the network LSA, which means that every time the DR goes down, another router must be elected as the DR. This new DR then must synchronize the database with all the routers and reflood the new LSA.

During this synchronization and flooding, no data traffic passes through the transit network in question, and this delay causes scaling problems. To ensure smoother transition from a DR to a new DR during failure, the *backup designated router (BDR)* is used. Because all the routers on the local network already know the BDR, they do not need to synchronize the database with the BDR. Instead, the new DR simply must flood the new LSA. This provides a smoother transition and has less impact on the transit traffic.

How Hello Packets Are Sent

Hello packets are sent across each medium in a slightly different manner. On broadcast media, each router advertises itself by periodically multicasting hello packets. The hello packet contains the router's view of the DR/BDR and the list of neighbors whose hello has been received within the last dead interval.

Hello packets behave differently on NBMA networks, in which they first require manual configuration (the neighbors must be specifically listed), and then each router with the potential of becoming a DR has a list of all the attached routers on the network. These routers send hello packets to all the other routers with DR potential, in order to locate the existing DR on the network. When the DR is found or elected through the election process, it sends messages to all other routers on the network.

On point-to-multipoint networks, hello packets are sent directly to the neighbors to which the router can communicate.

The Database Description Packet

The database description (DBD) packet, which is OSPF packet type 2, is sent after routers have listed each other in their hello packets, and after two-way communication has been established. This is the initialization of adjacency.

DBD packets describe the contents of link-state databases; describing the entire database requires that multiple packets be sent. During the database-exchange process, one router is elected as master and the other as slave. The master is responsible for sending the DBD packets when either of the following is true:

- When the slave acknowledges the previous DBD packet by echoing the DD sequence number
- When a set number of seconds (configured by the retransmit interval) elapses without an acknowledgment, in which case the previous DBD packet is retransmitted

The slave is not allowed to form the DBD packet. DBD packets are sent in response only to DBD packets received from the master. If the DBD packet received from the master is new, a new packet is sent; otherwise, the previous DBD packet is re-sent.

If a situation arises when the master has finished sending the DBD packet, and the slave still has packets to send, the master sends an empty DBD packet with the M (more) bit set. The M bit is used to indicate that there are still more packets to send. At this point, the master sends an empty DBD packet with the M bit set.

Note that when a router receives a DBD packet that contains an MTU field larger than the largest IP datagram, the router will reject the packet. Figure 9-4 shows a DBD packet and all the fields in the packet.

Figure 9-4   *A DBD Packet*

Interface MTU	Options	0	0	0	0	0	1	M	MS
DD Sequence Number									
LSA Header									

The following list describes the fields in a DBD packet:

- *Interface MTU*   This is the largest IP datagram that can be sent across the interface without fragmentation.

- *I bit*   When set to 1, this bit indicates the first packet in the sequence of DBD packets.

- *M bit*   When set to 1, this bit indicates that more DBD packets are to follow.

- *MS bit*   This bit indicates the status of the router. When set to 1, the router is the master. When set to 0, the router is the slave.

- *DBD sequence number*   This indicates the sequence of DBD packets. The initial value should be unique, and the value must be incremented until the complete database has been sent.

- *LSA header*   As the name indicates, this field consists of the header of each LSA and describes pieces of the database. If the database is large, the entire LSA header cannot fit into a single DBD packet, so a single DBD packet will have a partial database. The LSA header contains all the relevant information required to uniquely identify both the LSA and the LSA's current instance.

The Link-State Request Packet

The link-state request packet, OSPF packet type 3, is sent in response to a router during the database exchange process. This request is sent when a router detects that it is missing parts of the database or when the router has a copy of LSA older than the one it received during the database exchange process. Figure 9-5 shows fields in the link-state request packet. The request packet contains each LSA specified by its LS type, link-state ID, and advertising router. This uniquely identifies the LSA.

Figure 9-5   *Link-State Request Packet*

LS Type
Link-State ID
Advertising Router

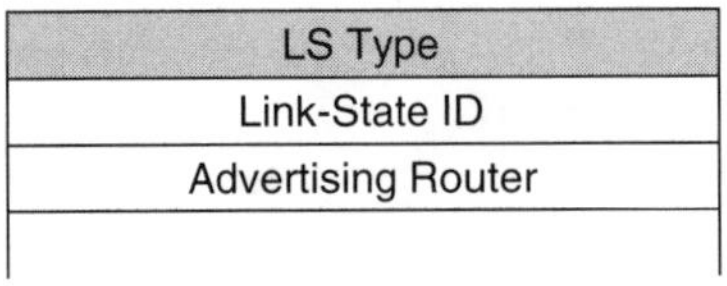

When the router detects a missing piece of the database, it will send the database request packet. In this request, the router indicates to the LSA what it hopes to find. The LSA is indicated by link type, link ID, and advertising router. When the router receives a response, it truncates the LSA from the request and then sends another request for the unsatisfied LSAs. This retransmission of unsatisfied LSAs occurs during every retransmission interval. The retransmission interval is a configurable constant; the default value is 5 seconds but can be modified according to the needs of an individual setup.

The Link-State Update Packet

The link-state update packet, OSPF packet type 4, is sent in response to the link-state request packet and implements the flooding of LSAs. The link-state update packet carries a collection of LSAs one hop from its origin. Several LSAs can be included in a single update.

Each LSA must be acknowledged. In response to the link-state update, a link-state acknowledgment packet is sent to multicast addresses on the networks that support multicast. If retransmission of certain LSAs is necessary, the retransmitted LSAs are always sent directly to the neighbor.

Figure 9-6 shows the link-state update packet, which contains the number of LSAs included in this update; the body of the link-state update packet consists of a list of LSAs. Each LSA begins with a common 20-byte header.

Figure 9-6   *Link-State Update Packet: #1 SAs and LSAs*

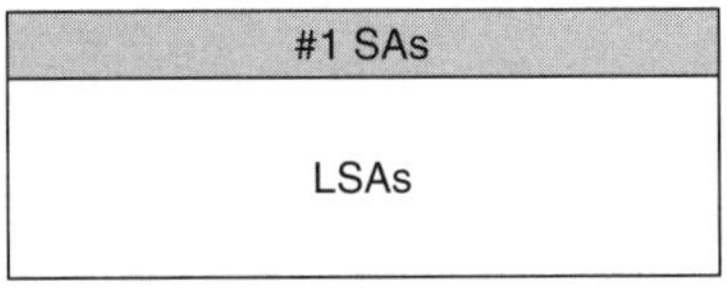

#1 SAs
LSAs

The Link-State Acknowledgment Packet

The link-state acknowledgment packet, OSPF packet type 5, is sent in response to the link-state update packet. An acknowledgment can be implicitly achieved by sending the link-state update packet. Acknowledgment packets are sent to make the flooding of LSAs reliable: Flooded LSAs are explicitly acknowledged. Multiple LSAs can be acknowledged in a single link-state acknowledgment packet, and this acknowledgment can be delayed.

Depending on the state of the sending interface and the sender of the corresponding link-state update packet, a link-state acknowledgment packet is sent either to the multicast address "AllSPFRouters," to the multicast address "AllDRouters," or as a unicast.

The advantages to delaying the link-state acknowledgment are:

- Packing of multiple LSAs. In this way, each LSA can be acknowledged one by one, so the router does not have to create many small acknowledgment (ack) packets.
- Several neighbor LSAs can be acknowledged at once by multicasting the acknowledgment.
- Randomizing the acknowledgment of different routers on the same segment. This is beneficial because all routers are not sending ack packets simultaneously, which could cause a bottleneck.

Categories of LSAs

In the discussion of link-state protocols, you read that every router advertises its active OSPF links to all its neighbors; you also learned about the five categories of links that the router advertises in OSPF. Recall that the five link states are:

Type	Description
1	Router link state
2	Network link state
3	Summary link state (type 3)
4	Summary link state (type 4)
5	External link state

All link states share a common LSA header because every link state must advertise some common information. Figure 9-7 shows the common 20-byte LSA header that is shared by all types of LSAs.

Figure 9-7   *Common 20-Byte LSA Header*

LS Age		Options	LS Type
Link-State ID			
Advertising Router			
LS Sequence Number			
LS Checksum		Length	

The common LSA header contains the following information:

- *LS age*   This is the time in seconds since the LSA was originated. This value is incremented with the passage of time, and the LSA age is always set to zero at the time of origin. LSA age is one of the parameters used to detect a newer instance of the same LSA.

- *LS type*   This describes the type of LSA being advertised. The value should be one of the five types of link states.

- *Link-state ID*   This field describes the portion of network being advertised. This value changes with each type of LSA. For router LSAs, this field is set to the router ID of the advertising router. For network LSAs, it is set to the IP address of the DR. For summary type 3, it is set to the IP network number of the network being advertised. For summary type 4, this field is set to the router ID of the autonomous system border router (ASBR). For external LSAs, it is set to the IP network number of the external destination being advertised.

- *Advertising router*   This field is set to the router ID of the router originating the LSA. For summary types 3 and 4, it is set to the IP address of the area border router (ABR).

- *Link-state sequence number*   This value describes the sequence number of the LSA; it must be set to a unique number, and successive instances must be given successive number values. This field is used to detect old or duplicate LSAs.

The Router LSA (Link-State Type 1)

Every OSPF router sends this LSA, which defines the state and cost of the routers' links to the area. All the routers linked to a single area must be described in a single LSA; the router LSA is flooded throughout only a single area. Examine the sample network shown in Figure 9-8.

R1 and R2 are area routers connected to a single area only. They have connections to the stub network (do not confuse a stub network with stub area) on Ethernet 0. Although Ethernet is a broadcast network, it is treated as a stub network because it has no OSPF neighbor.

Therefore, no network LSA is originated for Ethernet, so R1 and R2 are connected to a stub network. A broadcast network on the second Ethernet interface that connects all four routers (R1 through R4) is not treated as stub because all the routers have adjacencies on them; therefore, a network LSA would be generated for this interface. R4 and R3 are area border routers connected to area 1 and area 0. Both R3 and R4 will originate two router LSAs: one for area 1 and one for area 0.

Figure 9-9 shows the area setup for R3 in more detail. R3 will originate two separate router LSAs: one for area 0 and one for area 1. R3 has three active interfaces connected to it: two Ethernet interfaces in area 1 and the point-to-point serial interface in area 0.

Figure 9-8   *Sample Network Used to Explain Different LSA Types*

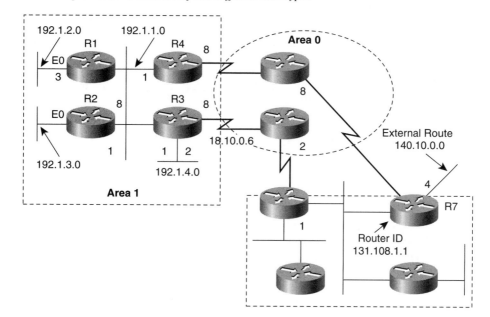

Figure 9-9   *Area Setup for Router R3*

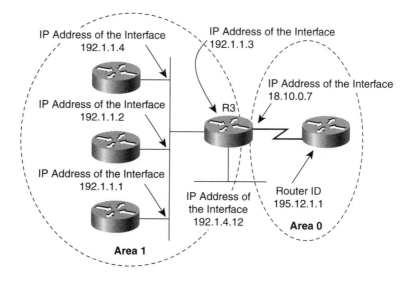

Figure 9-10 shows the router LSA on R3 in area 1. This is the output of **show ip ospf data router 192.1.1.3** (router ID of R3).

Figure 9-10 *Router LSA for R3 in Area 1*

```
LS age = 0                           Always 0 at origination
Options = (E-bit)
LS type = 1                          This is a router LSA
Link State ID = 192.1.1.3           Router ID of R3
Advertising Router = 192.1.1.3      Router ID of R3
bit E = 0                            Not an ASBR
bit = 1                              This is an ABR
# links = 2
    Link ID = 192.1.1.4             IP address of the DR
    Link Data = 192.1.1.3           Interface address of this router
    Type = 2                         This is a transit network
    # TOS metrics = 0
    metric = 1                       Cost to reach the interface
    Link ID = 192.1.4.0             IP network number
    Link Data = 255.255.255.0       Subnet mask of the interface
    Type = 3                         Stub network
    # TOS metrics = 0
    metric = 2
```

Figure 9-11 shows the router LSA for R3 in area 0.

Figure 9-11 *Router LSA for R3 in Area 0*

```
LS age = 0
Options = (E-bit)
LS type = 1
Link State ID = 192.1.1.3
Advertising Router = 192.1.1.3
bit E = 0
bit = 1
# links = 2
    Link ID = 192.12.1.1            Router ID of the neighbor
    Link Data = 18.10.0.7           IP interface address of the router
    Type = 1                         This is a point-to-point link
    #TOS metrics = 0
    metric = 8
```

The following fields appear in the router LSA:

- *Bit E* This bit indicates the status of the router in the OSPF network. When set to 1, it indicates that the router is an ASBR. When set to 0, the router is not an ASBR. In Figure 9-10, for example, notice that bit E is 0, which means that this router is not an ASBR.

- *Bit B*   This bit is used to indicate whether the router is an area border router. When the bit is set to 1, the router is an ABR. When the bit is set to 0, the router is an area router. In Figure 9-10, bit B is set to 1, which indicates that R3 is an ABR.

- *Number of links*   This field indicates the number of active OSPF links that the router has in a given area. If the router is an ABR, it will have separate values for each area. R3 has three active OSPF links, but two of these links are in area 1 and one is in area 0. Notice in Figure 9-10 that the number of links is 2; whereas in Figure 9-11, the number of links is 1.

- *Link ID*   This value changes according to the type of network. If the connected network is a point-to-point network, this field is set to the router ID of the neighbor. For a transit (broadcast) network, this field is set to the IP interface address of the designated router. For a stub network, this value is set to the IP network number. For a virtual link, it is set to the router ID of the neighbor.

  In Figure 9-10 and Figure 9-11, all types of links exist in the router LSA of R3. For area 1, R3 is connected to a stub network and a transit network. Therefore, the stub network link ID is set to 192.1.4.0 (IP subnet address). The transit network link ID is set to 192.1.1.4 (IP interface address of the DR). R3 also has a connection to area 0 and originates a router link state for area 0 as well. In area 0, R3 has a point-to-point connection, so the link ID is set to 192.12.1.1 (the router ID of the neighbor).

- *Link data*   This value changes according to the type of network. For point-to-point and transit networks, this value is set to the router's interface address on the link. For a stub network, the link data is set to the subnet mask of the interface. As Figure 9-10 and Figure 9-11 show, the stub network link data is set to 255.255.255.0, the IP subnet mask of the interface. The transit network link data is set to 192.1.1.3, the IP interface address on R3 on the transit network. The point-to-point link data is set to 18.10.0.7, the IP interface address of R3 on this link.

- *Link type*   This field describes the type of link in question. A router can connect to four types of links, as follows:

Type	Description
1	Point-to-point
2	Transit
3	Stub
4	Endpoint of a virtual link

The Network LSA (Link-State Type 2)

The network LSA is generated for all broadcast and NBMA networks, and it describes all the routers that attach to the transit network. The network LSA is originated by the designated router and is identified by the IP interface address of the designated router. During a designated router failure, a new LSA must be generated for the network. The network LSA is flooded throughout a single area and no further.

If the designated router were to go down, the backup designated router would take over. The network LSA originated by the designated router (the old DR now) also would be flushed and a new network LSA would be originated by the BDR (the new DR).

The BDR changes the link-state ID to its own IP interface address on the transit network. Figure 9-12 shows the connected routers that are neighbors on the transit network. This figure indicates the interface addresses and the router ID of the DR.

Figure 9-12   *Address of the Routers in the Transit Network for which the Network LSA Is Generated*

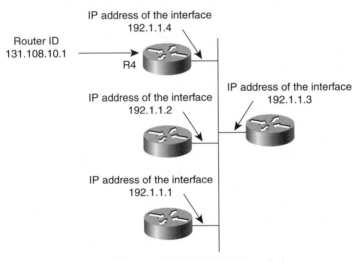

IP address of the interface
192.1.1.4

Router ID
131.108.10.1

R4

IP address of the interface
192.1.1.3

IP address of the interface
192.1.1.2

IP address of the interface
192.1.1.1

Network LSA originated by DR (R4)

Figure 9-13 shows the network LSA that was originated by the DR (R4, in this case). This output can be viewed by using the **show ip ospf data network 192.1.1.4** command (interface address of DR).

The following fields appear in the network LSA:

- *Network mask* Describes the IP subnet mask of the network for which the LSA is generated. All routers attached to this network should have the same IP subnet mask to become adjacent. In Figure 9-13, for example, the subnet mask for network 192.1.1.0 is 255.255.255.0.

- *Attached router*   Contains a list of routers attached to this transit network. All attached routers are identified by their router ID. In Figure 9-12, for example, R4 attaches to four routers on Ethernet, all three of which are its OSPF neighbors. Figure 9-13 shows that all four routers are attached routers, including router R4.

Figure 9-13   *Network LSA for Transit Network of 192.1.1.0*

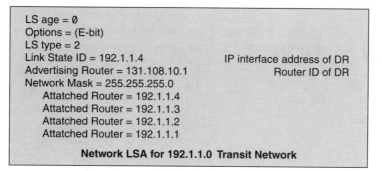

```
LS age = 0
Options = (E-bit)
LS type = 2
Link State ID = 192.1.1.4              IP interface address of DR
Advertising Router = 131.108.10.1            Router ID of DR
Network Mask = 255.255.255.0
    Attatched Router = 192.1.1.4
    Attatched Router = 192.1.1.3
    Attatched Router = 192.1.1.2
    Attatched Router = 192.1.1.1
    Network LSA for 192.1.1.0 Transit Network
```

Summary Link-State Types 3 and 4

Summary type 3 propagates information about a network outside its own area. Many network administrators assume that summary LSA generates information outside the area by summarizing routes at the natural network boundary, although this has been proven untrue. For example, a summary LSA will not summarize all subnets of a major network 131.108.0.0 in a /16 route.

Summary in OSPF does not mean that summarize occurs at the classful network boundary. In this case, summary means that the topology of the area is hidden from other areas to reduce routing protocol traffic. For summary type 3, the ABR condenses the information for other areas and takes responsibility for all the destinations within its connected areas.

For summary type 4, the ABR sends out information about the location of the autonomous system border router.

An ABR is used to connect any area with a backbone area. It could be connected to any number of areas only if one of them is a backbone area. An autonomous system border router (ASBR) is the endpoint of OSPF domain. It has an external connection from OSPF domain.

Figure 9-14 shows the area setup location of ABRs and the location of ASBR with the router ID ASBR.

Figure 9-15 shows the output of **show ip ospf data summary** on router R4.

Figure 9-14 *Location of ABR and ASBR for Summary Link States*

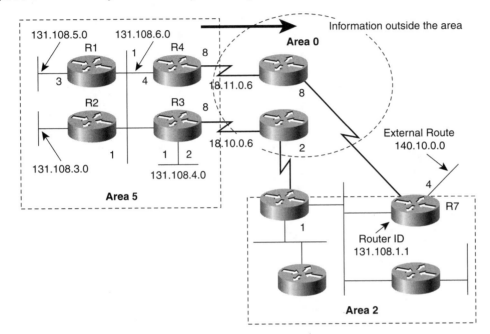

Figure 9-15 *Summary LSA Originated by ABR*

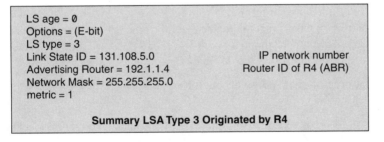

LS age = 0
Options = (E-bit)
LS type = 3
Link State ID = 131.108.5.0   IP network number
Advertising Router = 192.1.1.4   Router ID of R4 (ABR)
Network Mask = 255.255.255.0
metric = 1

Summary LSA Type 3 Originated by R4

TIP	Remember that summary in OSPF does not mean summarizing at the natural network boundary. In this case, summary means that you hide the topology of the area from other areas to reduce routing protocol traffic.

Notice in Figure 9-14 that router R4 is sending an update to area 0 and is crossing the major network 18.0.0.0. The summary output in Figure 9-15 shows that it does not send 131.108.0.0/16 out on serial interface. As shown in Figure 9-15, R4 hides the topology of area 1 from area 0, and takes responsibility for all the networks in area 1 by announcing itself as the advertising router.

The default route is always sent as an external LSA. For a stub area, where an external LSA is not allowed, the ABR sends a default route through summary LSA to describe all the external destinations.

External link states are flooded throughout the OSPF domain, except for the stub area. Summary LSA hides the topology between areas, and therefore advertises the location of the ASBRs to all the routers within the OSPF domain that are not in the same area as the ASBR.

The ABR sends a summary link-state type 4 by setting itself as the advertising router. As shown in Figure 9-14, R7 is the ASBR. R3 and R4 advertise summary type 4 link states, which set the link state ID to R7's router ID and set their route ID as the advertising router.

Router R4 advertises the location of the ASBR (R7) in area 1 and changes the advertising router field to its own router ID (see Figure 9-16). Router R4 also does not change the link-state ID field because it needs to inform all the routers within area 1 that although it (R4) is not the ASBR, it knows how to reach the ASBR.

Figure 9-16   *Summary Type 4 Advertised by ABR*

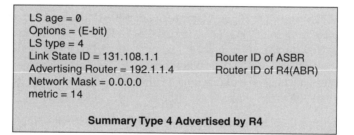

```
LS age = 0
Options = (E-bit)
LS type = 4
Link State ID = 131.108.1.1          Router ID of ASBR
Advertising Router = 192.1.1.4       Router ID of R4(ABR)
Network Mask = 0.0.0.0
metric = 14
```

Summary Type 4 Advertised by R4

External LSA (Link-State Type 5)

External LSA describes destinations outside the OSPF domain. A route received via another routing protocol and redistributed into OSPF is considered external to OSPF. Any destination that is not originated by the local OSPF process is also considered external.

Refer to Figure 9-14. Router R7 redistributes 140.10.0.0 into OSPF; 140.10.0.0 was not originated by the local OSPF process. In Figure 9-17, R7's link-state ID field is set to the external destination advertised (140.10.0.0), and the advertising router is set to the router ID of router R7 (131.108.1.1). This LSA is flooded throughout the network unaltered.

Bit E is also used for external LSA, and indicates the metric type being used. If this bit is set to 1, the router is advertising the external destination as metric type 2. If it's set to 0, the router is advertising the external destination as type 1. Cisco defaults to external type 2. Figure 9-17 shows the output of external LSA originated by the ASBR (R7).

Figure 9-17 *External LSA Originated by R7*

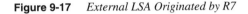

```
LS age = 0
Options = (E-bit)
LS type = 5
Link State ID = 140.10.0.0                    IP network number
Advertising Router = 131.108.1.1              Router ID of R7
Network Mask = 255.255.0.0
bit E = 1;                        Type 2 metric
metric = 4
Forwarding address = 0.0.0.0

          External LSA Originated by R7
```

External LSA can be propagated in two ways:

- *External type 1*   This is the total cost of sending the router to the external destination, and it includes the internal costs of the links.

  The network shown in Figure 9-18, network 140.10.0.0, is advertised by router R1 as well as by router R2. The external cost of R1 is 1, and the external cost of R2 is 2. Now, assume that router R3 wants to send a packet to network 140.10.0.0. R3 has two choices: via R1 or via R2. For external type 1, R3 selects R2 because the total cost of reaching destination 140.10.0.0 is 10 (8 + 2, internal + external) and the cost of reaching the network via R1 is 11.

- *External type 2*   This considers only the cost of the ASBR's link to the external destination. The idea behind external type 2 is that it is more expensive to leave the autonomous system than to pass traffic within the autonomous system.

  R3 has two ways to reach network 140.10.0.0: via R1 or R2. For external type 2, R3 selects R1 because the external cost of reaching network 140.10.0.0 is advertised lower via R1. External type 2 ignores the internal cost.

Another important aspect of external LSA is the *forwarding address*. This is the address to which data traffic to the external destination should be forwarded. If the external destination is learned on a network, the forwarding address is advertised by the ASBR, in case OSPF is enabled on the transit network. If OSPF is not enabled on the transit network, the ASBR becomes responsible for forwarding the traffic. The forwarding address is set to 0.0.0.0.

Figure 9-18   *Route-Selection Process Using External Type 1 and External Type 2*

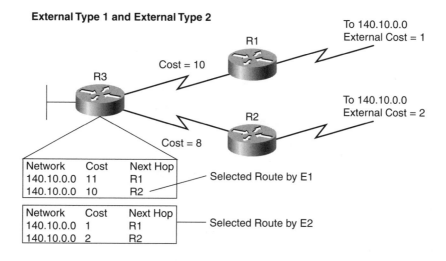

In Figure 9-19, R1 and R3 are running BGP. R1 is redistributing BGP routes into OSPF and learns 140.10.0.0 from R3 via BGP before redistributing the BGP route into OSPF.

OSPF sets 131.108.10.1 (IP interface address of R3) as the forwarding address if R1 has OSPF on its Ethernet interface. This is done to inform other OSPF routers in the network that if they have any other shorter path to reach 131.108.10.1, they can forward traffic through that path instead of forwarding traffic to R1. If OSPF is disabled on the Ethernet, the forwarding address is set to 0.0.0.0, and all traffic is forwarded to R1.

Forwarding addresses on all routers should be OSPF inter-area or intra-area routes within the routing table. Otherwise, the external route will exist in the database but not in the routing table. In the configuration section, we explain how the forwarding address can be set to a non-OSPF inter-area or intra-area route.

Figure 9-19 shows the network topology in which R1 and R3 are running BGP, R1 is redistributing BGP routes into OSPF, and the forwarding address is set to 131.108.10.1. All routers within this OSPF domain should have an intra- or inter-area route to 131.108.10.1 in their routing table. Otherwise, the route to 140.10.0.0 will not be installed in the routing table.

Figure 9-19   *Forwarding Address Concept for External LSA*

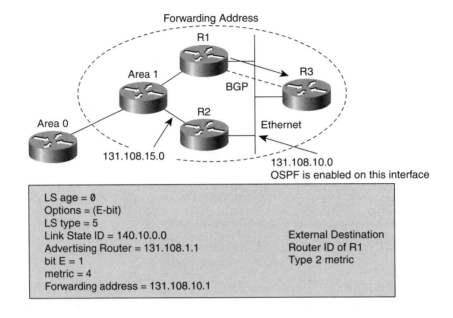

The OSPF Area Concept

One of the most important concepts in OSPF is the existence of hierarchy and areas. OSPF allows collections of contiguous networks to be grouped together. Such a group, together with the routers maintaining interfaces to any of the included networks, is called an *area*. Each area runs a separate copy of the basic link-state routing algorithm.

Rather than treating the entire autonomous system as a single link-state domain, the topology of an area can be hidden. It is then invisible from the outside of the area. Similarly, routers in other areas know nothing of the topology outside their own area, which markedly reduces routing traffic.

Now that multiple areas are created in the network, there is no need for all the routers in the autonomous system to hold the entire link-state database. Only routers in the same area should have identical databases.

With the creation of areas, routing in the autonomous system takes place at two levels: *intraarea* (connecting to destinations within the area) and *interarea* (connecting to destinations outside the local area).

By design, the OSPF protocol forces hierarchy in the network. For OSPF to be implemented on any network, hierarchical structure must exist or must be created. The concept of area forces the administrator to create the hierarchy in the network.

With the introduction of interarea routing comes the concept of the *backbone area*. All traffic that must flow between areas has to go through the backbone area. The OSPF backbone is the special OSPF area 0. The OSPF backbone always contains all ABRs and is responsible for distributing routing information between non-backbone areas. The backbone must be contiguous with other areas. If it is not, virtual links must be created to make the backbone contiguous so that the flow of traffic is uninterrupted.

Traffic cannot flow without the backbone's presence. However, if the entire network is only a single area, area ID is unimportant because it does not need to be the backbone area. If a single area is set up as a non-backbone and a second area is introduced, the second area should be established as the backbone because all interarea traffic must pass through it.

The main advantage to the OSPF hierarchy is that it hides the topology of other areas, which results in a marked reduction in routing protocol traffic. An area can be one or more networks, one or more subnets, and any combination of networks and subnets. If further reduction of routing updates is required, networks or subnets can be summarized. A contiguous address block is used for summarization.

Other than area 0, OSPF uses several types of areas. The Cisco environment uses four areas:

- Regular area
- Stub area
- Totally stubby area
- Not so stubby area (NSSA)

Each of these area types is discussed in more detail in the following sections. For information on configuring these areas, see the section entitled "Configuring Areas in OSPF," later in this chapter.

Regular Area

All types of LSAs are permitted in the regular area. All specific information from other areas is sent as a summary LSA, whereas redistributed information is sent as an external LSA.

In a regular area, all routers contain all the routing information and will have the optimal path to the destination. A drawback of regular areas is that flaps caused by link failure outside the area will force partial SPF calculations. Route flapping can have a serious impact on the network. With a strong addressing structure, an OSPF network will scale to a much higher dimension, and will support summarization of interarea routes.

The flapping of external routes is a serious difficulty with regular areas. For example, assume that an autonomous system was sending 100 routes via BGP, and you then redistributed those routes into OSPF. A problem with your neighbor's AS could adversely affect your network. Therefore, it is good practice to aggregate all contiguous external routes.

TIP	Unless optimal routing is very critical, avoid redistributing routes learned from other autonomous systems. Instead, let OSPF generate a default route.

Stub Area

As mentioned in the previous section, instability in neighboring ASs can cause scaling problems in a network. However, most administrators have a critical need for intelligent routing in the core or distribution sites. Usually, the core sites are high-CPU boxes and can handle flaps much more gracefully than remote locating low-end routers.

The administrator needs full routing information in certain parts of the network, but you cannot allow routing information into other areas. OSPF's solution is the *stub area*. No external information is permitted, so no external LSA is injected into the stub area. Interarea traffic is still injected into a stub area, so flaps from other areas still affect the local area.

For external destinations, the ABR propagates a summary default route. All routers in a stub area must agree on the stub area because if the E bit in the Optional field does not match on all the routers, they will not form adjacency. If any router in a stub area has a mismatched E bit, all other routers will dissolve their adjacency with the router.

Totally Stubby Area

For very large networks, it is quite common to have a large number of areas. It also is not uncommon to have low-end routers in these areas. Therefore, receiving a large amount of summary LSA data is a cause for concern. As a solution, OSPF created the totally stubby area.

As with a stub area, external LSAs are not advertised in a totally stubby area; unlike a stub area, however, a totally stubby area does not pass interarea traffic. Now, even summary link states are not propagated into this area. This assists routers that are ABRs for multiple areas because the router will not have to process the summary LSAs, and will not have to run SPF for interarea routes.

This saves memory as well—now the ABR does not have to create a summary link state for every area to which it is connected; it creates only a summary link state for area 0.

NSSA

NSSA is similar to the OSPF stub area, but it has the capability to import AS external routes in a limited capacity within the NSSA area. NSSA allows importing type 7 LSAs within the NSSA area by redistribution and then converts them into type 5 at the ABR. This enables the administrator to summarize and filter data at both ASBR and ABR levels.

Enabling and Configuring OSPF

The first step toward running any routing protocol on a network is enabling the routing protocol. OSPF requires a process-ID, which uniquely identifies the OSPF process for the router. A single router can use multiple OSPF processes. The concept of process-ID is different in OSPF than the concept of the autonomous system in Enhanced IGRP or BGP. In OSPF, the process-ID is local to the box and is not carried in routing protocol packets.

To enable OSPF in the global configuration mode, you must define the networks on which OSPF will be enabled. Finally, you must assign those networks to their specific areas. A single interface can belong to a single area only; if the interface is configured with a secondary address, both the primary and secondary addresses should belong to the same area.

The initial OSPF configuration is as follows:

```
router ospf  process id
network  address wild-card mask area area-id
```

Figure 9-20 shows a sample network, in which you want to run an OSPF router. R1 has multiple interfaces connected to it. You will bring one Ethernet (network 192.1.1.0) into area 0 and the other two interfaces into area 1.

Figure 9-20   *Sample Network to Enable OSPF in Multiple Areas*

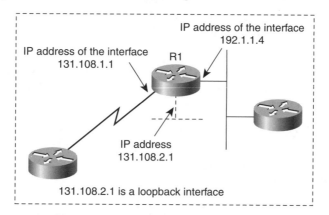

Configuration for Figure 9-20 is as follows:

```
router ospf 1
network 192.1.1.0 0.0.0.255 area 0
network 131.108.1.0 0.0.0.255 area 1
network 131.108.2.1 0.0.0.255 area 1

int serial 0
ip address 131.108.1.1 255.255.255.0
int ethernet 0
ip address 192.1.1.4 255.255.255.0

interface loopback 0
ip address 131.108.2.1 255.255.255.255
```

The router performs a logical OR operation between the address given and the wildcard mask given on the network statement. The router then performs a logical OR with the IP address assigned to the interface.

The first logical OR is between the network statement and the wildcard mask:

```
                    Decimal              Binary

Network             192.1.1.0            11000000.00000001.00000001.00000000

Wildcard Mask       0.0.0.255            00000000.00000000.00000000.11111111

Result              192.1.1.255          11000000.00000001.00000001.11111111
```

Next, you take the IP interface address and perform the logical OR operation with the wildcard mask. If the result matches the network statement, OSPF is enabled properly on the interface:

```
                        Decimal          Binary

Interface address       192.1.1.1        11000000.00000001.00000001.00000001

Wildcard Mask           0.0.0.255        00000000.00000000.00000000.11111111

Result                  192.1.1.255      11000000.00000001.00000001.11111111
```

Notice one point in Figure 9-20: There is a loopback on router R1. This loopback is for the Router ID; in the Cisco implementation, Router ID is the loopback address on the router. If the loopback interface is not configured, the highest IP interface address on the router becomes the Router ID.

By defining the loopback as the Router, you avoid unnecessary changes in the router ID if the physical interface were to fail. The loopback is a virtual interface in Cisco that never fails, as long as the router is running.

After configuring OSPF on the router, ensure that OSPF is enabled by using the **show ip ospf interface** command:

```
Serial4/0.1 is up, line protocol is up
  Internet Address 10.1.1.2/30, Area 1
  Process ID 1, Router ID 131.108.1.1, Network Type POINT_TO_POINT, Cost: 64
  Transmit Delay is 1 sec, State POINT_TO_POINT,
  Timer intervals configured, Hello 10, Dead 40, Wait 40, Retransmit 5
    Hello due in 00:00:05
  Neighbor Count is 1, Adjacent neighbor count is 1
    Adjacent with neighbor 10.1.23.1
  Suppress hello for 0 neighbor(s)
```

The next section discusses some of the uncommon interface parameters and explains instances in which they become necessary.

OSPF Interface Configuration Constants

OSPF has two types of constants:

- *Fixed constants*   These values have fixed architectural values and are not configurable. They include Link State Refresh Time, Min Link State Interval, Max Age, Link State Infinity, Default Destination, Initial Sequence Number, and Max Sequence Number.

- *Configurable constants*   These values can be changed according to the requirements. Configurable constants include Interface Output Cost, Retransmit Interval (RxmtInterval), Interface Transmit Delay, Hello, Dead Interval, and Router Priority.

Both of these constant types are discussed in more detail in the following sections.

Fixed Constants

The OSPF fixed constants are defined as follows:

- *Link State Refresh*   This is the maximum amount of time between distinct origination of the same LSA. When the LSA age reaches this interval, the router must originate a new instance of the same LSA, keeping everything the same. The value of this constant is 30 minutes.

- *Min Link State Interval*   The router must wait a minimum amount of time before it can reoriginate the same LSA. This waiting period is set to five seconds.

- *Max Age*   This is the maximum amount of time that the LSA can remain in the database when a refresh is not received. When the LSA age field reaches the maximum age, the LSA should be reflooded for the purpose of removing it from the database and the routing table. The value of MaxAge is one hour.

- *LSInfinity*   MaxAge indicates that the destination described in the LSA is unreachable. LSInfinty is an alternative to premature max aging used for summary and external LSAs. Instead of the router sending a MaxAge route, it can send the route with LSInfinity to indicate that the destination is unreachable. The value is 0xffffff.

- *Default Destination*   This is always set to 0.0.0.0 and should be advertised as the external LSA in a regular area, or as summary type 3 in a stub area. For NSSA, it is advertised as the type 7 link state. The network mask associated with this LSA should always be 0.0.0.0 as well.

- *Initial and Max Sequence Number*   This is the value of initial sequence of LSAs and should always be 0x80000001. The max sequence indicates the last instance of a sequence number and is always set to 0x7fffffff.

Configurable Constants

The OSPF configurable constants are defined as follows:

- *Interface Output Cost* This is the cost of sending a packet on the interface, and is expressed as the link-state metric. The cost must never be zero. In Cisco implementation, cost is determined by dividing 100 Mb by the actual bandwidth of the interface.

For serial, it is always $10^8/T1 = 64$, by default. For Ethernet, it is 10; for FDDI, it is 1. If higher bandwidth is introduced, the cost per interface must be modified by using the **ip ospf cost** command. To avoid this interface costing, Cisco has introduced a new command for router OSPF configuration:

```
router ospf 1
 ospf auto-cost reference-bandwidth <1-4294967> in terms of Mbits/sec.
```

This command enables the router to divide the reference bandwidth with the bandwidth on the interface. That way, it becomes unnecessary to change the cost per interface. By default, the router still uses 10^8 as the reference bandwidth for backward-compatibility purposes.

Typically, the **ip ospf cost** command is very useful in Frame Relay topology. In Figure 9-21, for example, the hub router has different sizes of PVC for different routers. In situations like this, it is always best to configure a point-to-point subinterface, so that each one will have a different cost according to the PVC.

Figure 9-21 *Frame Relay Setup with Different PVC Values*

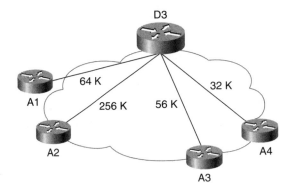

On router D3, a point-to-point subinterface is configured so that the cost is set according to the PVC:

```
interface Serial4/1
 no ip address
 encapsulation frame-relay
 cdp enable
!
interface Serial4/1.1 point-to-point
 ip address 10.1.3.126 255.255.255.252
 ip ospf cost 390 (for 256K PVC)
 frame-relay interface-dlci 199
!
interface Serial4/1.2 point-to-point
 ip address 10.1.3.130 255.255.255.252
ip ospf cost 1785 (56k PVC)
 frame-relay interface-dlci 198
!
interface Serial4/1.3 point-to-point
 ip address 10.1.3.134 255.255.255.252
ip ospf cost 1562 (64K PVC)
 frame-relay interface-dlci 197
!
interface Serial4/1.4 point-to-point
 ip address 10.1.3.138 255.255.255.252
 ip ospf cost 3125 (32K PVC)
 frame-relay interface-dlci 196
```

- *Retransmit Interval*   This is the amount of time between LSA retransmission for the adjacency on the interface, and it also can be used with DBD and LS request packets. This is useful when either the link or the remote router is slow, which causes the local router to retransmit packets repeatedly. The command to change the retransmission timer in Cisco is as follows:

  ip ospf retransmit-interval seconds

The default value is five seconds. This value also appears in the output of **show ip ospf interface** command, as shown here:

```
Serial4/0.1 is up, line protocol is up
  Internet Address 10.1.1.2/30, Area 1
  Process ID 1, Router ID 131.108.1.1, Network Type POINT_TO_POINT, Cost: 64
  Transmit Delay is 1 sec, State POINT_TO_POINT,
  Timer intervals configured, Hello 10, Dead 40, Wait 40, Retransmit 5
    Hello due in 00:00:05
  Neighbor Count is 1, Adjacent neighbor count is 1
    Adjacent with neighbor 10.1.23.1
  Suppress hello for 0 neighbor(s)
```

- *Transmit-Delay* This is the estimated amount of time to transmit an LSA out of this interface. The LSA in the update packet must be aged by this amount of time before transmission. This value must be greater than 0. In Cisco, this value is set to one second, by default. The command to change the interface transmit-delay is as follows:

  ip ospf transmit-delay seconds

- *Router ID* Router ID is used to identify a router; in Cisco implementation, it is the loopback interface address on the router. If the loopback is not configured, the highest IP address on the router is used.

- *Area ID* This defines the area to which the router belongs and is defined along with the **network** command. Area characteristics are defined with the **area** command. The command is as follows:

  ```
  router ospf 1
  network 131.108.1.0 0.0.0.0 area 1
  area 1 stub
  ```

  For the previous configuration, area 1 is defined as a stub. For regular areas, only the **network** statement with an area is required.

- *Hello/Dead Interval* Hello is used to discover OSPF neighbors; Cisco defaults to 10 seconds on broadcast and point-to-point networks, and 30 seconds on non-broadcast multiaccess networks.

  The *dead interval* is the amount of time a router waits for a hello packet before declaring the neighbor dead. Cisco defaults to 40 seconds on point-to-point and broadcast networks, and defaults to 120 seconds on NBMA networks.

  Hello/Dead timers should match on all the routers that connect to a common subnet. Cisco has enhanced its implementation so that, by default, if a router misses four hello packets, the neighbor is declared dead. This can be a problem over slow links. OSPF sends periodic database updates, and this flooding of packets may cause the routers to miss hellos, causing loss of adjacency. The new enhancement causes the dead timer to reset every time the router receives a packet from the neighbor.

- *OSPF priority*   This is used to decide the designated router on the transit network. The router with the highest priority becomes the designated router, by default. When a router is elected as the designated router and a new router appears on the segment with a higher priority, the new router cannot force election and must accept the designated router.

  To force the election of a new designated router, you must remove the existing designated and backup designated routers from the segment. A router with zero priority can never be elected as the designated router. The OSPF priority command is as follows:

  ip ospf priority value

OSPF Over Different Physical Media

Classically, networks can be divided into three types: broadcast (Ethernet, Token Ring, and FDDI), point-to-point (HDLC and PPP), and non-broadcast multiaccess (Frame Relay, SMDS, and X.25). Behavior of OSPF over broadcast and point-to-point networks is uncomplicated, but the behavior of OSPF over non-broadcast multiaccess networks (NBMA) requires further explanation.

When configuring OSPF over NBMA networks, you can configure the router to behave in four ways:

- Broadcast
- Non-broadcast
- Point-to-point
- Point-to-multipoint

Each of these methods is discussed in the following sections.

The Broadcast Model

The Cisco router can be configured to behave like a broadcast medium over NBMA networks. OSPF sends a multicast hello and elects both the designated router and the backup designated router. The designated router provides protection from flooding. All changes are sent via the designated router. By increasing its priority, you can force your most reliable router to become the designated router. This model has a fundamental problem, however, in that it requires constant full mesh. Therefore, losing a PVC detaches the router from the rest of the network.

Consider the network in Figure 9-22. Router R1 loses the PVC between itself and DR, and now has a problem with database sync. R1 will switch over to BDR, but the BDR still sends its hello packet to R1, declaring the identity of the original DR. Although R1 has other PVCs, it cannot synchronize with the DR and will not install routes in the routing table. This creates a *black hole*.

Figure 9-22 *OSPF Broadcast Model for NBMA Networks*

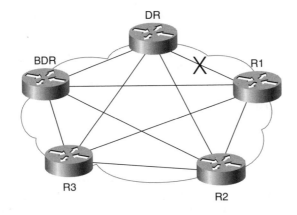

The second problem with the broadcast model is virtual circuit (VC) costing. VC costing cannot be performed on virtual circuits with different bandwidths. Therefore, even if a higher bandwidth value is available, you would have to treat all of them equally when calculating the OSPF metric. For the broadcast model, the DR can be forced. If you do not want to force DR to allow any router in the network to become the DR, you can leave the interface with a default priority:

```
interface serial 4/0
ip address 131.108.1.1 255.255.255.0
encapsulation frame-relay
ip ospf  priority 2
ip ospf network broadcast
```

This second configuration sets up a non-DR router. By setting the priority of R1 to 0, it ensures that R1 never becomes a DR:

```
Configuration of non DR (R1)
interface serial 0
ip address 131.108.1.2 255.255.255.0
encapsulation frame-relay
ip ospf network broadcast
ip ospf priority 0
```

The Non-Broadcast Model

When OSPF is first enabled on the NBMA network, OSPF defaults to the non-broadcast model. Hello packets and dead intervals are 30 and 120 seconds, and the non-broadcast model requires that neighbors be configured. The router then sends packets to configured neighbors to find the identity of the DR.

This is very similar to the broadcast model, except that the router sends unicast hellos to configured neighbors. The non-broadcast model also has slower convergence, and the problem of full meshing still exists. In the following configuration, all routers that can become the DR should be configured with a list of neighbors, as shown here:

```
Configuration of DR
Int s 0
Ip address 131.108.1.1
Encapsulation frame-relay
Ip ospf priority 0

Router ospf 1
network 131.108.1.0 0.0.0.255 area 0
neighbor 131.108.1.2
...........
neighbor 131.108.1.5
```

The Point-to-Point Model

The point-to-point model is the most robust of the four models—each PVC is treated as a point-to-point subinterface. Therefore, losing a single PVC does not cause loss of connectivity. Instead, each point-to-point subinterface is a separate subnet. Each PVC can have different costs, according to the CIR.

Point-to-point has faster convergence than any other model and allows for partial mesh. The point-to-point model has a serious problem with flooding, however. In a full mesh point-to-point model, a single LSA flap can become flooded $(n-1)^2$ times.

Figure 9-23 shows an instance in which the Ethernet attached to R1 goes down, so R1 sends a link-state update on the full meshed Frame Relay cloud. R2 receives the update and sends the update to all the neighbors except R1. Similarly, R3 sends the same update to all the neighbors except R1.

All the routers in the cloud do the same thing; a single LSA is sent to the network $(n-1)^2$ times. This flooding causes unnecessary traffic. Imagine a network with 100 routers in a mesh—one LSA will flood the cloud 9,801 times!

TIP

Cisco is introducing a new concept for OSPF in 12.0 IOS, already available for IS-IS, called *interface blocking*. Interface blocking is a command that prevents a flood storm on a cloud. With this command, you can selectively block interfaces from sending updates. Therefore, normal interfaces perform the usual flooding, and blocked interfaces never send updates. This reduces replication of the same update.

Figure 9-23 *OSPF Flooding Issue with Point-to-Point Model*

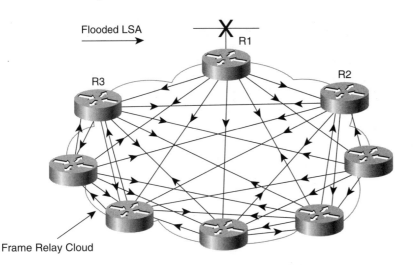

The configuration of R1 shown in Figure 9-23 is as follows:

```
Interface serial 0
No ip address
Encapsulation frame-relay

interface serial 0.1 point-to-point
ip address 131.108.1.1 255.255.255.252
ip ospf network point-to-point
ip ospf cost 390
frame-relay interface-dlci 197

interface serial 0.2 point-to-point
ip address 131.108.1.5 255.255.255.252
ip ospf network point-to-point
ip ospf cost 1785
frame-relay interface-dlci 198

interface serial 0.3 point-to-point
ip address 131.108.1.9 255.255.255.252
ip ospf network point-to-point
ip ospf cost 1562
frame-relay interface-dlci 199
```

The Point-to-Multipoint Model

The point-to-multipoint model is very similar to the point-to-point model. It provides one subnet for an entire cloud, and it maintains host routes to all the routers within the cloud. This also allows the use of non-meshed routers.

TIP   A new command was recently introduced to overcome the problem of sending multicast OSPF packets on the media that form dynamic connections, such as ATM SVC. By default, OSPF sends multicast packets to discover neighbors. With the new command **ip ospf network point-to-multipoint non-broadcast**, the router is configured to send unicast packets to neighbors. This command requires neighbors to be defined. It also enables the configuration of cost as per PVC.

Configuration for any router in the cloud is the same for all members of the cloud:

```
interface serial 0
ip address 131.108.1.1 255.255.255.0
ip ospf network point-to-multipoint non-broadcast

router ospf 1
neighbor 131.108.1.2 cost 15              /* Per VC costing*/
```

Configuring the Areas in OSPF

Recall that OSPF has four types of areas in the Cisco environment, which were defined in the earlier section "The OSPF Area Concepts":

- Regular area
- Stub area
- Totally stubby area
- NSSA

Configuring the Regular Area

Recall that in a regular area, every link state is flooded. Configuration for regular area is simple:

```
Configuration
router ospf 1
network 131.108.0.0 0.0.255.255 area 1
```

Configuring the Stub Area

External link states are not flooded in the stub area. All routers in that area need to be defined as stub. If any router within the area is not defined as stub, an adjacency is not formed.

The stub area configuration is as follows:

```
router ospf 1
network 131.108.0.0 0.0.255.255 area 1
area 1 stub
```

Configuring the Totally Stubby Area

External link states and summary link states are not permitted in the totally stubby area. Only the local area routes are included in the database, and the routing table for destinations outside the area. All routers default to the closest ABR. The configuration for the totally stubby area is as follows:

```
router ospf 1
network 131.108.0.0 0.0.255.255 area 1
area 1 stub no-summary
```

Configuring the NSSA

NSSA permits redistribution within this area. External type 5 routes are still not permitted into this area, but type 7 routes are generated. The configuration for the NSSA is as follows:

```
router ospf 1
network 131.108.0.0 0.0.255.255 area 1
area 1 nssa
```

NSSA also can be configured without a summary; this command prevents even interarea routes from entering the NSSA area. As mentioned previously, summarization can be done at the ASBR or at the ABR.

Consider the setup in Figure 9-24. Router R1 is an ABR, R2 and R3 have static routes configured toward a customer network, and R2 is redistributing routes into OSPF. All the routes redistributed into OSPF from R2 will be propagated as type 7 routes. These routes could be summarized either at R2 (the ASBR) or at R1 (the ABR). The advantage of NSSA is that you can propagate all the specific routes within NSSA and then summarize them at the ABR.

Figure 9-24   *OSPF NSSA Area Setup with Summarization*

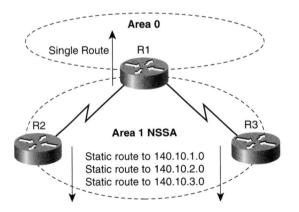

To summarize at ASBR (R2, in this example), you would use the following configuration:

```
Router ospf 1
Network 131.108.1.0 area 1
Area 1 nssa
Redistribute static subnets
Summary-address 140.10.0.0 255.255.252.0
```

Before we continue with this discussion, it is important that you understand the **summary-address** command. This command is used to summarize redistributed routes into OSPF. For redistribution in regular areas, this command is used at the ASBR only. After the external link state is originated in a link-state protocol, it cannot be filtered or summarized. NSSA is more robust because there are two points of origination: one at the NSSA ASBR, and the other at the ABR that translates type 5 to type 7.

Notice also the **redistribute static subnets** command in the previous configuration. Without the keyword **subnets**, OSPF redistributes the major net route only if the major net route is in the routing table. When only subnet routes are in the routing table without the keyword **subnets**, no routes are redistributed. Similarly, if there is a supernet route and a major net route, OSPF requires the keyword **subnets** again. The previous configuration will send a single NSSA route for all the static routes shown in Figure 9-24.

Recall that in NSSA you also can summarize at the ABR, so the configuration in this case at R2 would be the following:

```
router ospf 1
network 131.108.1.0 0.0.0.255 area 1
area 1 nssa
redistribute static subnet
```

The configuration for R1 would be the following:

```
router ospf 1
network 141.108.0.0 0.0.255.255 area 0
network 131.108.0.0 0.0.255.255 area 1
area 1 nssa
summary-address 140.10.0.0 255.255.252.0

Ship route on R1
140.10.0.0/16 is variably subnetted, 5 subnets, 2 masks
O N2    140.10.2.0/24 [110/20] via 10.1.1.1, 1d08h, Serial4/0.1
O N2    140.10.3.0/24 [110/20] via 10.1.1.1, 1d08h, Serial4/0.1
O       140.10.0.0/22 is a summary, 1d08h, Null0
O N2    140.10.1.0/24 [110/20] via 10.1.1.1, 1d08h, Serial4/0.1
```

NSSA routes are shown as O N2. With the **summary-address** command, the router creates an OSPF to a null interface.

Summary

This chapter discussed OSPF, which is a link-state protocol used as an IGP. There are five types of OSPF packets: hello, Database Description (DBD), request, update, and acknowledgment (ack). OSPF divides a large network into smaller subdomains, called areas. An area is a group of network segments and their interfaces. They are usually connected to each other by routers, creating a single autonomous system. There are four common types of areas in OSPF: regular, stub, totally stubby, and not so stubby (NSSA).

To enable OSPF in the global configuration mode, first define the network, and then assign those networks to specific areas. OSPF uses two types of configuration constants: fixed and configurable. There are four ways to configure OSPF over NBMA networks: broadcast, non-broadcast, point-to-point, and point-to-multipoint.

Review Questions

1 List the five types of link states.

2 What is a stub area?

3 Can you filter an LSA in OSPF?

4 Can you have a DR on point-to-point links as well?

Answers:

1 Router LSA, network LSA, summary LSA (type 3), summary LSA (type 4), and external LSA are the five types of link states.

2 A stub area is an area in which external LSA is not permitted.

3 Filtering of LSAs can occur at the point of redistribution.

4 DRs are only for transit networks, in which a network LSA is created.

For Further Reading . . .

RFC 2178

Intermediate System-to-Intermediate System (IS-IS) is a routing protocol that is based on an OSI intradomain routing protocol, and is designed for use with the ISO protocol for the Complete Sequence Number Protocol (CSNP) data unit. IS-IS may be used as the Interior Gateway Protocol (IGP) to support TCP/IP, as well as the OSI. IS-IS also can be used to support pure IP environments, pure OSI environments, and multiprotocol environments.

Because it supports both IP and OSI traffic, IS-IS can support traffic to IP hosts, OSI hosts, and multiprotocol end systems. This chapter discusses the following topics related to IS-IS:

Fundamentals and operation of IS-IS   IS-IS is a link-state protocol; therefore, it is based on the SPF algorithm, which finds the optimal path to the destination.

Addressing with IS-IS   Addressing in IS-IS for each node is identified by Network Service Access Points (NSAPs) and is based on the structure that allows multilevel hierarchy.

IS-IS area concepts   Areas are used in IS-IS to divide the network into smaller subdomains. An area number uniquely identifies each area. This helps maintain a manageable size for the link-state database within each area.

Understanding backbone and link-state concepts   IS-IS is a two-level hierarchy: Level 2 is considered the backbone, and all level 1 traffic must traverse through level 2 routers to pass traffic between multiple level 1 areas.

Using IS-IS pseudonode/non-pseudonode   These are the main components for building link-state databases. Pseudonode is formed for each broadcast network, and non-pseudonode is formed by each router for its links.

Understanding flooding   Flooding is the process in which the protocol sends topology changes within the network and refreshes at a periodic interval to maintain a consistent database through the network.

## CHAPTER 10

Intermediate System-to-Intermediate System

Introduction to IS-IS

IS-IS is based on link-state technology, which has two levels of hierarchy. Networks can be divided into manageable-sized subdomains called *areas*. An area's topology information is held within that area. This containment of information is known as level 1. Level 2 connects multiple level 1 areas, which is how level 2 became known as the *backbone area*.

IS-IS forwards both OSI and IP packets unaltered; packets are transmitted directly over the underlying link-layer protocols without the need for mutual encapsulation. IS-IS uses the Dijkstra algorithm to find the shortest path to the destination.

Fundamentals and Operation of IS-IS

As with any other link-state protocol, IS-IS also relies on neighbor information. Each router within an area maintains information about its connected network. This information is flooded to all the connected neighbors, and then the neighbors further flood the information.

During this flooding process, information about the origin of the routing information is preserved. This way, every router in the link-state database knows which router originated specific information within its area.

This is how all the routers within the IS-IS area receive complete information. When all the information is received, each router performs a Shortest Path First algorithm to find the best path to any destination. Every time a new link-state packet (LSP) is created or received, the router reruns the Dijkstra (SPF) algorithm and calculates new routes.

Each routing node in IS-IS is called an *intermediate system (IS),* so a router essentially is the intermediate system. Each intermediate system forms an adjacency with the connected intermediate systems by sending IS-IS hellos (IIHs).

As you may have noticed, IS-IS includes an abundance of terminology. The following list defines the important IS-IS terms:

- *Intermediate system (IS)* A router or a routing node.
- *Designated intermediate system (DIS)* A router on a LAN responsible for flooding information about the broadcast network.
- *End system (ES)* A host.

- *Network service access point (NSAP)*   An address to identify an intermediate system.
- *Network entity title (NET)*   An NSAP address with the last byte set to zero, which means that it does not have a transport user. Information is only for routing use.
- *Protocol data unit (PDU)*   Protocol packets.
- *Partial Sequence Number Protocol (PSNP) and Complete Sequence Number Protocol (CSNP)*   Used for synchronization of a database on different types of media.
- *Intermediate system-to-intermediate system hello (IIH)*   Used by intermediate systems to discover other intermediate systems.

Addressing with IS-IS

In IS-IS, each network node is identified by its NSAP address. This addressing scheme provides multilevel, hierarchical address assignments. These addresses provide the flexibility to answer two critical questions:

- How do you administer a worldwide address space?
- How do you assign addresses in a manner that makes routing feasible in a worldwide Internet?

An NSAP address consists of two parts: the initial domain part and the domain-specific part. For administrative purposes, the ISO addresses are also subdivided into the Initial Domain Part (IDP) and the Domain-Specific Part (DSP). IDP is standardized by ISO, and specifies the format and the authority responsible for assigning the rest of the address. The DSP is assigned by the addressing authority specified in the IDP.

The IDP and DSP divisions are not important other than for administrative purposes. For the purpose of routing IS-IS for IP, the NSAP address is divided into three parts:

- *Area address*   This field is of variable length. The area address identifies the routing domain length of the area field and should be fixed within a routing domain.
- *System-ID*   This is six octets long and should be set to a unique value within an area for level 1. This should be unique within all level 2 routers.
- *N selector*   This is always one octet long and specifies the upper-layer protocol. When an N selector is set to zero, it is called NET. A NET means that the routing layer for NSAP has no transport-layer information.

Cisco routers deal with NETs. To run IS-IS on Cisco routers, it is necessary to configure one NET per box, not per interface. You can configure multiple NETs on Cisco routers, but they merely act as secondary addresses.

Consider this code, for example:

```
48.0001.0000.0000.0001.00
Area Address          48.0001
System id:            0000.0000.0001
Nsel:                 00
```

Cisco requires at least eight octets for the address: one octet for the area address, six octets for the system ID, and one octet for the N selector. Figure 10-1 shows an NSAP address and how each field is divided. The first through 13th octets are used for the area number, six bytes are for system ID, and one octet is for the N selector.

Figure 10-1   *NSAP Address for IS-IS*

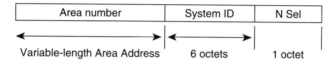

Area number	System ID	N Sel
Variable-length Area Address	6 octets	1 octet

Understanding the IS-IS Area Concepts

Routers with common area IDs belong to the same area. By the nature of its addressing system, IS-IS forces this hierarchy. IS-IS has two layers of hierarchy: level 1 and level 2 (backbone). The backbone must be contiguous. In IS-IS, the area border is on the links instead of the router. Routers that connect multiple areas maintain two separate link-state databases: one for level 1 areas, and the other for level 2 areas. The routers also run two separate SPF algorithms.

Directly connected routers in two separate areas cannot form level 1 adjacency with each other; they have to form level 2 adjacency. All routers within an area maintain the complete topology and know how to reach every other router within the area. All level 1 areas are stub, so in a level 1 area, no information about the networks in other areas is passed. The only way for the level 1 router to reach a network outside its area is to send traffic to the closest level 2 router.

Usually, all the routers within an area have the same area address. However, sometimes an area might have multiple area addresses. Multiple area addresses are common in the following scenarios:

- You want to change the area address on an already existing IS-IS area. This is best accomplished by running both areas in parallel. When the new area address is recognized by all the routers in the area, you can remove the old area address.

- When it is desirable to merge two areas, you can propagate the knowledge of one area into another.

- You partition a large area into two smaller areas.

Figure 10-2 shows a typical area setup. This network has three areas: 48.0001, 48.0002, and 48.0003. All routers within an area must have the same area number.

Figure 10-2   *Area Setup for IS-IS with Multiple Area Numbers*

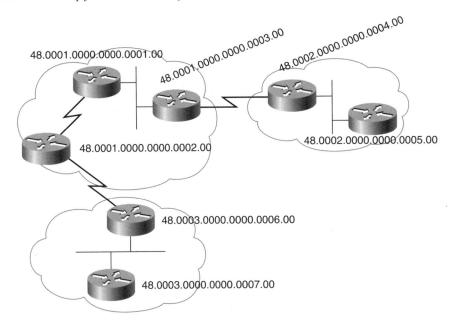

A routing hierarchy is easily achieved via OSI addressing. The address explicitly identifies the area, so it is simple for a level 1 router to identify packets going to a destination outside the area. This concept is discussed in more detail when level 1 and level 2 routing is addressed.

Understanding the Backbone Concept

As mentioned earlier, IS-IS has a two-layer hierarchy. Level 1 routers contain the topology information about their area only, and default to the closest area border router.

Level 2 routers route toward the area without considering the internal structure of the area. Level 2 routers patch multiple areas, and contain complete information about routes in other areas. All routers within level 2 must be contiguous—routing between areas passes through the level 2 routers. In addition, all level 1 routers go to the closest level 2 router for destinations outside their areas. If level 2 is not contiguous, the level 1 router might take the closest level 2 router, which in turn might not know the destination.

This also breaks the continuity of the network. Unlike OSPF, IS-IS does not support virtual links, so it is not possible to patch backbone routers if they are not contiguous.

NOTE	A level 2 IS also could be used as a level 1 IS in one area. This is helpful in situations in which the level 2 IS may lose connectivity to the level 2 backbone. In this case, the level 2 router will indicate in its level 1 LSPs that it is not attached. This assists all the level 1 routers in the area to route traffic to destinations outside the area to other level 2 routers.

Recall that all level 1 routers send traffic to the closest level 2 router. Now, you might ask: How does a level 1 router know the location of the level 2 router? Every level 2 router is marked with an attach bit, which indicates that it is a level 2 router.

Link-State Concepts

Recall that link-state protocols are based on neighbor relationships, so every router within an area knows about all the active links within its area and knows the identity of router-originating information about these active links.

Every router advertises the cost and state of its links. This state information is then propagated one hop away. This propagation of information results in all routers having identical databases. Every router is identified by its unique address, so a loop is avoided.

To reach a destination, the cost is the sum of all the costs of the concerned links to that destination. After the router has received information about all the other routers and their links, each individual router runs an SPF algorithm, which is based on the Dijkstra algorithm, to calculate the optimal path to each known destination. (The Dijkstra algorithm is a distributed algorithm performed by every router after the information is processed.)

Processes of Link-State Protocols

The link-state protocols consist of four processes:

- *Receive process*   The received information is processed, and then is given to the update process. The receive process does not make decisions—it simply forwards information to the two other processes.

- *Update process*   Receives information from the receive process, processes the information received from all the neighbors, and creates information about the local router states. The update process is responsible for processing LSPs from the neighbors and creating the routers' own LSPs, maintaining the link-state database.

- *Decision process*   The optimal path to the destination is found by running the SPF algorithm. The decision process also computes parallel paths to the destination.

- *Forwarding process*   The information received from the receive process, as well as the information received from the routing process is passed along. If a local router is using that information in its routing process, any information that the local router is not using is also processed by the forwarding process. In link-state protocols, all information that a local router has must still be forwarded to all the neighbors, even if the local router is not using that information in its own routing information database.

The Dijkstra Algorithm

Before you continue, you should review the Dijkstra algorithm. Figure 10-3 shows the network setup for which SPF is to be executed. Also, study the following network tables to understand how the router calculates the shortest path to the destination. All the associated costs for the interfaces are listed. Costs for exiting the interface are always considered.

Figure 10-3   *Network Setup for which SPF Is to Be Executed*

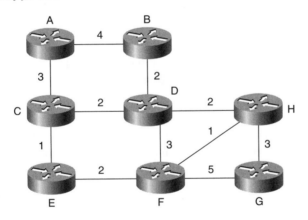

To begin the process, each router considers three lists:

- *Unknown list*   When the process is initiated or a new LSP is introduced
- *Tentative list*   The LSP being considered for inclusion into the path list
- *Path list*   The LSP for which the best path to the destination is computed

Assume, for example, that router A is the source point. Calculate its shortest path to each destination within the network; at the beginning of the process, each router is in the unknown list. Router A places itself on the tentative list.

```
Router and its neighbors list: A, B, C, D, E, F, G, H
Route stands for router
```

Router A		Router B		Router C		Router D	
B	4	A	4	A	3	B	2
C	3	D	2	D	2	C	3
						H	2
						F	3
Router E		**Router F**		**Router G**		**Router H**	
C	1	E	2	F	5	G	3
F	2	G	1	H	3	F	1
		H	1			D	2

The SPF computation is an iterative process. There is one iteration per node in the network. Each iteration involves following these steps:

1 Examine the tentative list. Move the node with the shortest path from the tentative list to the path list.

2 Locate that node's LSP in the link-state database, and then search it at the node's neighbors. Move those neighbors from the unknown list to the tentative list. If those nodes are already on the path list, skip them. If those nodes are already on the tentative list, see if the cost of the new path is better than the previous one.

3 The cost for the new node on the tentative list is the cost to reach the parent, which is the node we just moved to the path list, in addition to the cost from the parent to the new node on the tentative list. We can locate the cost in the LSP. If the new node on the tentative list is only one hop away from the source, search for the outgoing interface in the adjacency table. If the new node is further away from the source, copy the first-hop information from the parent.

4 When there are no more nodes on the tentative list, the computation is finished.

The information to retain for each node is the routerID/systemID of the node, the cost of reaching it, and the outgoing interfaces to reach it.

Then, you are ready to perform the computation. Router A is the only node on the tentative list. It moves itself from the tentative list to the path list. Router A moves B and C to the tentative list. Router B has a cost of 4 (0 + 4) and Router C has a cost of 3 (0 + 3). Study the adjacency table to determine the outgoing interfaces. That concludes the first iteration. When you begin the second iteration, look in the tentative list for the node with the shortest path (Router C). Router C is placed on the path list first because it is at a shorter distance. Router A places the neighbors of Router C (Routers D and E) on the tentative list. The cost to Router D is 5 (3 + 2). The cost to E is 5 (3 + 1). The first-hop interface is the same as the outgoing interface to reach Router C.

```
Current path list for router A: B , C
```

Router A	
B	4
C	3

Now, with routers B and C moving to the path list, routers D and E can move to the tentative list:

```
Distance from B to D is 2
Distance from C to D is 2
```

Routers B and C are of equal cost, but the distance to C via A is smaller. Similarly, router E is not known via B, but it is known via C at a distance of 1. Router A now installs router E and router D in the path list and their neighbors in the tentative list, so H and F are now in the tentative list.

```
New table for A with E and D in path list
```

Router A	
B	4
C	3
D	5
E	4

The cost from D to F is 3, the cost from D to H is 2, and the cost from E to F is 2. According to the table, D is already at a cost of 5 and is giving a higher cost to F. Router E is at a cost of 4 and is advertising a lower cost of 2. H is learned only via D.

Now F and H are moved from the tentative list to the path list:

Router A	
B	4
C	3
D	5
E	4
F	6
H	7

Now with F moving into the path list, the distance from F to H is smaller than via D. The cost to H is 7. With both F and H in the path list, G is placed in the tentative list. The cost is calculated from both H and F to G. Finally, all the destinations are resolved and the final table will resemble the following:

Router A	
B	4
C	3
D	5
E	4
F	6
H	7
G	10

After all the destinations are computed, the router installs routes in the table if the route has passed all the required conditions. According to the 10589 requirement, when a router receives a new LSP, it waits five seconds before running SPF; it waits 10 seconds before running two consecutive SPFs within the same area. For this reason, if the router is both a level 1 and a level 2 router, it must run to multiple SPFs.

After the SPF runs, the best route is installed in the table. An internal list of backup routes is saved, in case a prefix is lost to a destination. If this happens, the router reviews the backup list, and runs a partial SPF to find the next best optimal path to the destination. A complete SPF algorithm is executed only if an LSP with a different neighbor list is received.

Using IS-IS Pseudonode

Instead of treating a broadcast network as a fully connected topology, IS-IS treats a broadcast network as a pseudonode with links to each attached system.

NOTE   To reduce the number of full mesh adjacencies between nodes, multiaccess links are modeled as pseudonodes. As the name implies, this is a virtual node. One of the ISs on the link is designated to be the pseudonode; this node is called the designated intermediate system (DIS). All routers on the broadcast link, including the one elected to be DIS, form adjacencies with the pseudonode instead of forming n*(n–1) adjacencies with each other in a full mesh.

The DIS is responsible for generating pseudonode link-state packets, for reporting links to all systems on the broadcast subnetwork, and for carrying out flooding over the LAN. A separate DIS is elected for level 1 and level 2 routing.

All routers attached to the broadcast network must report their links to the pseudonode. Each pseudonode has a DIS. Figure 10-4 shows the physical and logical views of the pseudonode.

Figure 10-4   *The Physical and Logical Views of the Pseudonode*

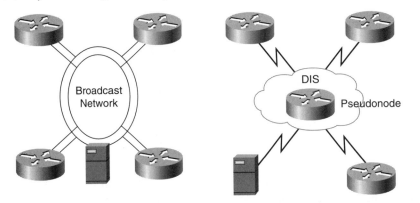

A DIS is elected for each pseudonode. Every router elects itself as the DIS, and the router with the highest priority becomes the DIS. By default, all Cisco routers have a priority of 64. In the case of a tie, the router with the highest MAC address becomes the DIS.

The DIS has two functions: It creates and updates the pseudonode. The DIS also conducts flooding over the broadcast network.

The DIS multicasts Complete Sequence Number Protocol (CSNP) data units every 10 seconds. As the name indicates, the CSNP contains headers of all the LSPs. Unlike OSPF, no backup DIS exists and the election process is dynamic. A dynamic process indicates that, if a higher-priority router appears after a DIS is elected, this router is automatically elected as the DIS.

Because IS-IS does not have as many types of link states in its database as OSPF does, synchronization of its database is not expensive. Unlike OSPF, the CSNP is sent every 10 seconds; as in the case of OSPF, the database synchronization happens only at the time of initial adjacency.

A pseudonode LSP is flooded in only two cases:

- When a new neighbor is added to the broadcast network. If the new IS has higher priority, this new one becomes the DIS for the network. The neighbor information changes, so the LSP is flooded.

- When the refresh timer for the LSP has expired; the refresh time is 20 minutes.

Using IS-IS Non-Pseudonode

A non-pseudonode is created by IS for propagating information about all other types of links connected to the router that are not broadcast networks, such as point-to-point networks and stub networks. A non-pseudonode LSP carries information about all neighbors, attached prefixes, and metrics of the attached links.

NOTE   A *non-pseudonode* could be equated to a router LSA in OSPF. In this case, the IS informs the router about different types of links that are attached to it, and the cost of reaching those links. It also carries a complete list of neighbors attached to it.

Non-pseudonode LSP is generated in four cases: when any neighbor is added or deleted; when an IP prefix has changed; when there is a metric change on the connected network; and at every refresh interval.

Understanding Level 1 and Level 2 Routing

In level 1, IS nodes are based on the ID portion of the address. All level 1 routers route within their own area. They recognize the destination within their area by reading the destination address. If the destination is within the same area, the packet is routed to the destination. If the destination is not within the same area, it is sent to the closest level 2 router.

In IS-IS, all level 1 areas are stub areas, so no information is sent to level 1 routers that are outside their areas. All routers within the level 1 area maintain identical databases. A level 1 router will have the area portion of its address manually configured. It will not create neighbors with a node whose area addresses do not match its area ID.

NOTE   For migration reasons, if the level 1 router has an area address of 1, 2, and 3; and the neighbor has an area address of 2 and 4, the two routers will form a neighbor adjacency because they share one area number in common.

The level 1 routers that belong to the same area should be connected. In an unlikely case that a level 1 area becomes partitioned, an optional partitioned repair function allows the partition to be repaired via use of level 2 routes.

For an IP subnet, each level 1 router exchanges link-state packets that identify the IP address reachable by every router. Information about each IP address is sent in the link-state packet and includes the IP address, the subnet mask, and the metric. Each level 1 router is manually configured with the IP address, the subnet mask, and the IS-IS metric.

IS-IS carries subnet information in the LSP, which enables the network administrator to configure VLSM. When a packet must be sent to a destination that matches more than two IP prefixes, the packet is routed based on the longest prefix. A default route could be announced into IS-IS with the network mask of all zeros.

In level 2, the IS nodes are routed based on the area address. All level 2 routers route toward areas without considering the internal structure of the area. A level 2 router could also be a level 1 router for some areas.

A level 2 router accepts another level 2 router as a neighbor, regardless of the area address. If the area address does not overlap on a link, the link is considered a level 2 link only, so the router will send only level 2 LSPs.

NOTE   Level 2 routers form the backbone of IS-IS. All level 2 routers must be contiguous. If level 2 routers become partitioned, no provision exists for using level 1 routers to repair level 2 partitions.

If a single level 2 router loses connectivity to the level 2 backbone, the level 2 router will indicate in its level 1 LSPs that it is not attached. By doing this, the level 2 router indicates to all other level 1 routers that it is not attached. This signals all level 1 routers to use some other level 2 router to connect to the networks outside that area.

TIP   Cisco routers default to L1 and L2, which means that the router must maintain two databases: one for level 1 and another for level 2. This enlarges the backbone more than is required. Always be sure to configure level 1 only when the router is not connected to the backbone. Running both L1 and L2 is unnecessary and is not scalable.

IS-IS Packets

As discussed earlier, link-state protocols maintain information received from neighbors. Any information received from a neighbor is maintained in a database. Because link-state protocols require the information to be constant among neighbors, IS-IS has different protocol packets. Essentially, IS-IS has four packet types:

- Hello packets
- LSPs
- CSNP data units
- PSNP data units

Each of these is discussed in more detail in the following sections.

Hello Packets

Hello packets are sent to multicast MAC-layer addresses to determine whether other systems are running IS-IS. There are three types of hello packets in IS-IS: one for point-to-point interfaces, one for level 1 routers, and one for level 2 routers. The hellos sent to level 1 and level 2 routers are given to different multicast addresses. Therefore, a level 1 router connected to a common wire where a level 2 router resides does not see level 2 hellos, and vice versa.

Hello packets are sent when the links initially appear or when a hello packet is received from a neighbor. At this point, the adjacency is initialized. Upon receiving the hello from the neighbor, the router sends a hello packet back to the neighbor, indicating that the router has seen the hello. At this point, two-way communication is established. This is the *up state* for the adjacency.

When the routers are in the up state, the election process for DIS is initiated. After the DIS is elected, it sends hello packets every 3.33 seconds. On a Cisco router, this ensures faster convergence in case a DIS must be replaced.

Link-State Packets

Link-state packets are divided into two types: level 1 and level 2. Level 2 packets contain information about all the reachable prefixes within the IS-IS domain. The topology for level 1 packets is known for the local area only, so these packets are included in the level 1 LSP.

Individual LSPs are identified by four components of the LSP header. These include the LSP ID, the sequence number, the checksum, and the remaining lifetime. LSP ID is divided into the source ID, the PSN number, and the LSP number.

The source ID is the same as the system ID of the originating router; in the case of the pseudonode, however, the source ID is set to the system ID of the DIS. As the name indicates, pseudonode ID is used to identify the pseudonode. This ID is set to zero for a non-pseudonode.

The LSP number is used in case of fragmentation. Checksum is used to detect corrupted LSPs; when an LSP is detected with a checksum error, the LSP is rejected and is not propagated further. The remaining lifetime decrements at every point from the areas that the LSP is flooded. Because each interface might have different delay parameters, the remaining lifetime is not considered when calculating the checksum. The LSP sequence number identifies the newer instance of LSP. The router generates the LSP during every refresh period. If a change occurs, a new LSP is generated and the sequence number is incremented by the originating router.

LSP has a Type Length Value (TLV) that can hold the following values: area address, IS neighbor, ES neighbor, external prefix, authentication information, routed protocols, IP address of the IS, a list of connected prefixes, and IP-reachable prefixes inside the area. As of this writing, a new TLV is under discussion that will be used to inject inter-area traffic, making the level 1 area non-stub.

CSNP Data Units

Complete sequence number PDU (CSNP) has a fixed header with TLV appended. Each of these TLVs represents an LSP in the link-state database. The following summary information is carried regarding each LSP:

- The LSP ID
- The sequence number
- The LSP checksum
- The remaining lifetime

CSNP is like a database description packet, as in OSPF. Because IS-IS does not have difficulty with synchronization, as OSPF does, the DIS sends a CSNP every 10 seconds on the broadcast interface. CSNP contains a complete list of all the LSPs in the local database. As mentioned earlier, the CSNP is used for database synchronization. On a serial line, a CSNP is sent only at the time of first adjacency.

PSNP Data Units

When a router receives a CSNP from a neighbor, and it notices that the CSNP is missing part of the database, the router sends a partial sequence number PDU packet (PSNP) to request a newer copy of the LSP. This is similar to the OSPF link-state request packet. The PSNP also acknowledges the receipt of the CSNP.

PSNP describes the LSP by its header, just like a CSNP. Unlike the CSNP, however, the PSNP holds information only about the requested LSP, not about all the LSPs. The PSNP contains the LSP sequence number, the LSP checksum, the LSP ID, and the remaining lifetime.

IS-IS Flooding

Link-state protocols are flooded to provide the routers a constant view of the network. Routers within the level domain need to synchronize the level 1 database; similarly, all level 2 routers must have consistent information. Flooding and synchronization of the database are done via CSNP, PSNP, SSN, and SRM bits.

In any link-state protocol, when new LSPs are received, they are flooded to all the neighbors. It is necessary that all the ISs receive information about all the LSPs. The behavior of the LSP flood is forwarded to all the neighbors, except the one LSP from which the packet has been received.

Send Sequence Number (SSN) and Send Routing Message (SRM) bits are new to this discussion. The SRM bit is set in an interface to indicate whether the LSP should be flooded on a particular interface. For a point-to-point link, the SRM bit is cleared when an acknowledgment is received through PSNP.

With broadcast media, PSNP is not sent for acknowledgment; the SRM bit is cleared immediately after the LSP is sent. The CSNP is sent in broadcast media by the DIS every 10 seconds, so reliability is not an issue.

The SSN bit is set to indicate any information about the link-state PDU that should be included in the PSNP transmitted on the circuit with an associated link.

Flooding Over Point-to-Point Links

A PDU is transmitted to the neighbor by an IS after an ISH is received from the neighbor. The purpose of this is to determine whether the neighbor is a level 1 or a level 2 intermediate system.

After the neighbor is determined, the router then sends the CSNP on the point-to-point link. CSNPs are sent only the first time for the synchronization of a database. If the neighbor router discovers that it needs a newer instance of the LSP, it can request the LSP via the PSNP. The PSNP is also used for the acknowledgment of the LSP.

A router considers an LSP acknowledged when a PSNP is received with the same sequence number. If the remote router has an older version, it sends a PSNP with the sequence number. The local router notices that the remote router is missing the newer copy of the LSP, so it floods the newer LSP to the neighbor and sets the SRM.

Upon receiving the newer copy, the remote router installs the newer copy in its database and floods it further. It then sends the PSNP back to the local router, indicating the receipt of the LSP. Upon acknowledgment, the local router clears the SRM bit. In the case of point-to-point links, the SRM bit is cleared only after a PSNP is received indicating acknowledgment. Figure 10-5 shows the flooding process over point-to-point links.

Figure 10-5   *Flooding Over Point-to-Point Links*

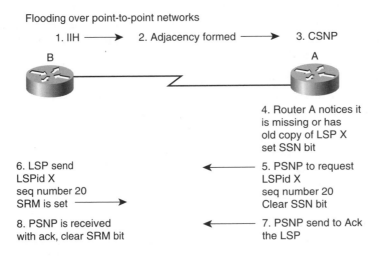

Flooding over point-to-point networks

1. IIH ⟶   2. Adjacency formed ⟶   3. CSNP

B   A

4. Router A notices it
is missing or has
old copy of LSP X
set SSN bit

6. LSP send
LSPid X
seq number 20
SRM is set ⟶   ⟵ 5. PSNP to request
                        LSPid X
                        seq number 20
                        Clear SSN bit

8. PSNP is received
with ack, clear SRM bit   ⟵ 7. PSNP send to Ack
                           the LSP

Flooding on Broadcast Networks

Flooding is optimal over the broadcast network when the IS creates a pseudonode. For each pseudonode, a DIS is responsible for creating and updating the pseudonode LSP and for conducting the flooding over the LAN. Unlike OSPF, there is no backup DIS. The DIS sends CSNP every 10 seconds; the LSP is not acknowledged. If a router notices that part of its database is missing or that the entry in its database is old, it sends a PSNP requesting a newer copy of the LSP.

The status of the SRM bit is different on the pseudonode. As soon as the LSP is transmitted, the SRM bit is cleared.

Every LSP that is flooded holds a remaining lifetime, which is set to 20 minutes. Every router that receives the LSP decrements the remaining lifetime by one second. LSPs that reach 20 minutes, if not refreshed, must be removed from the database. This prevents old LSPs from remaining in the database indefinitely. The LSP is periodically refreshed so that each router sends its LSP before the remaining lifetime expires.

Network-wide purges occur when an IS detects a corrupted or expired LSP. The IS sets the remaining lifetime to zero and floods the LSP header. All the ISs will receive this data and remove the LSP simultaneously. In case of a pseudonode, when a new DIS is elected, the new pseudonode is responsible for purging the old pseudonode LSP and then sending a new LSP with its LSP ID.

During router reboots, the router sets a sequence number of 1. The router might detect its own older LSP, which can still be floating around in the database prior to the reload. The originating router of the LSP will create a new LSP that has a higher sequence number than the old LSP.

This way, the newer LSP is installed in the database rather than the old LSP, which is retained in the database only because it has a higher sequence number.

Route Summarization

IS-IS does not include the concept of filtering, so link-state protocols do not have the liberty of filtering information when they are propagated. The only location in which filtering could occur is at the point of origin. To filter out propagation of a redistributed route in IS-IS, you can use the **summary-address** command to limit the routes from propagating L1 and L2. For L1, the **router summary-address** command is used to summarize external routes only. For L2, the **summary-address** command is used for summarizing external routes as well as L1 routes.

Scaling IS-IS

Currently, IS-IS is being used as an IGP by some of the largest ISPs. In most cases, a well-defined ISP network should not have a large IGP routing table, but due to extensive redundancy, scaling does become a problem. In addition, even if the IGP has a strong addressing structure, sometimes it must find specific routes to the next hop according to strict policy requirements. For this reason, route summarization is not always possible.

Experience in working with IS-IS has provided some insight that may be useful to you. One of the key things to remember is that Cisco defaults to both the level 1 and level 2 routers because all the level 2 routers must route within their area. In addition, the router cannot distinguish whether it is a transit IS for interarea traffic. This is the reason Cisco runs L1 and L2 as the default mode.

Running L1 and L2 throughout the network is less scalable because the router must maintain two separate databases and must run multiple SPFs. This L1 and L2 model enlarges the backbone more than necessary, so it is highly recommended that you configure L1 as the default when possible, especially when you are running IS-IS for IP.

For scaling any large-size IP network, the address layout is very critical. The address scheme must be laid out so that an L1 and L2 router can summarize and send a single route to the backbone for the level 1 area. If the network is small, everything can be placed into one area, leaving provisions for the expansion of a multiarea environment for future growth.

IS-IS Over NBMA Networks

The behavior of link-state protocols is different when handling non-broadcast multiaccess networks. In this situation, a difference always exists between physical and logical topology. For broadcast networks, for example, a pseudonode is created and is flooded with the ID set to the ID of the DIS. The broadcast model will also be successful in the frame or ATM cloud, as long as all the virtual circuits are operating properly. When a PVC breaks down, forwarding and routing is blackholed.

A router that loses its virtual circuit to the DIS will try to become the DIS. Other routers will send the ID of the actual DIS to this router. The router that has lost its virtual circuit to the DIS cannot send packets because the database loses synchronization when there is no connection to the DIS.

Although this router has just lost its connection to the DIS, it still has operational PVCs to other routers. Yet, because it lacks completed data base synchronization, it cannot use those PVCs to route traffic through other routers. If the database is not completely in sync, the routes are not installed in the routing table.

One model that could be applied here is the point-to-point subinterface. An IP address could be configured on these interfaces. However, this would waste a considerable amount of address space. Therefore, the best approach is to apply an unnumbered point-to-point network because it does not have point-to-multipoint, as in OSPF.

The point-to-point model does not have blackholes, but it does have a problem with flooding. When a router receives an LSP, it should flood the LSP to all the neighbors except the one from which it learned of the LSP.

This could become a serious problem in a large mesh environment. A single router can receive the same LSP $(n–1)^2$ times! To solve this issue, Cisco employs a feature called *interface blocking*, with which you can configure certain interfaces to avoid flooding the LSP. This should be performed with redundancy in mind, so that all the routers on the cloud receive the LSP. This feature is discussed in more detail in Chapter 9, "Open Shortest Path First."

Figure 10-6 shows the flood storm that is created on a full meshed point-to-point subinterface. The storm is created by the re-flooding of the LSP on the same physical interface, but having different logical interfaces with the same set of neighbors.

Figure 10-6 *LSP Flood Storm on Full Meshed Point-to-Point Interfaces*

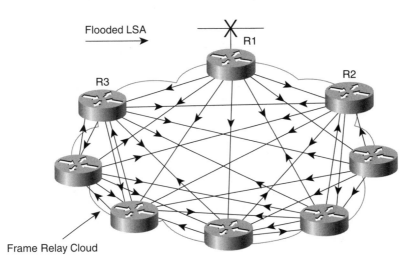

Basic IS-IS Configuration

To perform basic IS-IS configuration, the router process for IS-IS is defined first, and then an NSAP address is assigned to the router. Figure 10-7 depicts a sample network in which router B is a level 1 and level 2 router, and router A is only a level 1 router.

Figure 10-7 *Simple Network Setup for IS-IS*

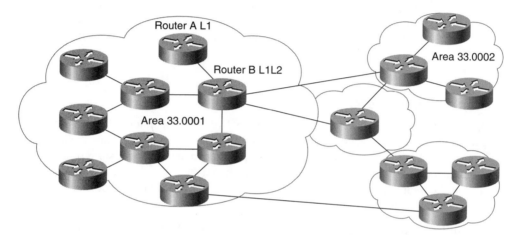

The configuration of router B is as follows:

```
hostname router B
clns routing
interface Pos1/0/0
ip address 10.10.1.1 255.255.255.0
ip router IS-IS MKS
IS-IS circuit-type level-2
interface atm 2/0/0
ip address 131.108.1.1 255.255.255.0
ip router IS-IS MKS
IS-IS circuit-type level-1
router IS-IS MKS
net 39.00001.0000.0000.0001.00
```

As you can see in Figure 10-7, router A does not need to be a level 2 router because it only has to create a single database.

The configuration of router A is as follows:

```
hostname router A
clns routing
interface atm 2/0
ip address 131.108.1.2 255.255.255.0
ip router IS-IS MKS
router IS-IS MKS
net 39.0001.0000.0000.0002.00
is-type level-1-only
```

The basic configuration for IS-IS is simple, as long as the router level is undefined. By default, the router runs both level 1 and level 2. If the router is left at the default behavior (say, it is an L1 and L2 router), you must define the circuit type that the interface is running by defining the level type, as for router B. If you define the IS type under the **router IS-IS** command, however, the router becomes confined to that level only, as is the case for router A.

The **net** command assigns a unique NSAP address to the router. This address is assigned per router, not per interface; in this case, the first three bytes are area addresses and 39.0001 is the area address. The next six bytes comprise the system ID 0000.0000.0002 (router A) and the last byte is the N selector, which will be 00 for the router. For this reason, this NSAP address is a NET.

The spf-interval **Command**

By default, the SPF algorithm runs at least every five seconds, under stable network conditions, even though network events such as adjacency changes could trigger immediate SPF runs. Running SPF on a very large LS database requires tremendous processor resources, so a high frequency of runs could be disastrous to the router and the network. The **spf-interval** command adjusts the frequency at which SPF runs. This command was set for periodic intervals, and SPF runs at 30 seconds.

The **sh IS-IS spf-log** command displays how frequently the SPF process has run and is an indication of the event trigger. The configuration would be the following:

```
RTR-B#sh IS-IS spf-log

Level 1 SPF log
When Duration Nodes Count Triggers
00:25:27 8 4 1 PERIODIC
00:18:09 12 5 2 NEWLSP TLVCONTENT
00:10:27 8 5 1 PERIODIC

Level 2 SPF log
When Duration Nodes Count Triggers
00:40:35 8 3 1 PERIODIC
00:25:35 8 3 1 PERIODIC
00:18:17 8 3 1 TLVCONTENT
00:10:34 8 3 1 PERIODIC
```

The IS-IS metric **Command**

IS-IS is limited because its metric has only six bits. This means that the value of an individual metric can range only from 0 to 63. The total length of a path between two ISs can be 1023 maximum. You should consider the metric in advance. The default value is assigned to be 10, independent of the bandwidth for all types of links and for both level 1 and level 2. The interface metric can be modified for each level independently. Configuration for level 1 metric is as follows:

```
Hostname router B
Interface serial 0
ip address 131.108.1.1 255.255.255.0
ip router IS-IS MKS
IS-IS circuit-type level-1
IS-IS metric 30 level-2
```

By defining the level with the **metric** command, the level 2 metric is 30 for this serial interface.

The log-adjacency-changes **Command**

The **log-adjacency-changes** command is very useful because it tracks changes. In link-state protocols, it is very important to keep track of the neighbors. This command identifies any changes to the adjacencies and link flaps.

The configuration for router B here is as follows:

```
hostname router B
router IS-IS MKS
net 39.0001.0000.0000.0001.00
log-adjacency-changes.
The output of this command is:

routerB # sh log
%CLNS-5-ADJACENCY: IS-IS: Adjacency to 0000.0000.0001 (ethenet0)
```

IS-IS and Default Routes

The purpose of the default route in any routing protocol is to forward traffic to destinations that are not in the router's routing table. It is not possible for all the routers in a network to have full Internet routes. For this purpose, routers without full routes to all the destinations forward traffic to the default originating router.

Level 1 routers never maintain information about any destination that is outside their area, so all level 1 routers merely send packets to the nearest level 2 router for any destination outside their local area.

The **default-information originate** command is used with level 2 routers for sending traffic to destinations not found in the local routing table. This command is used to send a default route in the backbone, and it creates an external entry into the L2 LSP. Unlike OSPF, this command does not require a default route to be present in the router that is originating the default route.

If you compare this command with the OSPF **default-information** command, it behaves similar to the way that the **default-information originate always** command behaves in OSPF. This means that, regardless of the default route's presence in the routing table of the originating router, the command still propagates a default route.

IS-IS and Redistribution

A route whose source does not originate from the IS-IS domain is treated as an external route. Therefore, a separate TLV is defined for IP external ratability information. These external routes can be redistributed into both level 1 and level 2 as external routes.

Metrics for external routes can be redistributed, just as they can for both internal and external metrics. In a tie-breaking situation, the internal is preferred over the external:

```
router IS-IS MKS
net 39.0001.0000.0000.0001.00
redistribute static ip metric 30 level-1-2
ip route 55.1.0.0 255.255.0.0 Null0
ip route 55.2.0.0 255.255.0.0 Null0
```

IS-IS and Summarization

Level 1 router summarization is done only for external routes (redistributed routes from other protocols) because the level 1 router does not receive any routes from the level 2 routers. As such, there is no need to summarize routes from level 2 routers—you can summarize both level 1 and external routes in level 2.

External routes can be summarized only at the redistributing router. After the LSP is originated, it cannot be summarized. Summarizing of external routes in level 1 routers is performed as follows:

```
router IS-IS MKS
net 39.0001.0000.0000.0001.00
summary-address 131.108.0.0 255.255.0.0 level-1
redistribute static ip metric 30 level-1

ip route 131.108.0.0 255.255.0.0 Null0
```

You can also summarize routes from level 1 into the backbone:

```
router IS-IS MKS
net 39.0001.0000.0000.0001.00
summary-address 131.108.0.0 255.255.0.0 level-2
```

This configuration is for summarization of the links of a level 1 area into a level 2 area.

Summary

IS-IS is a link-state protocol based on the OSI Intradomain Routing Protocol, and is designed for use with the ISO protocol. It can support pure IP environments, pure OSI environments, and multiprotocol environments. There are four packet types in IS-IS: hello, LSPs, CSNP data units, and PSNP data units.

Link-state protocols (LSPs) are based on neighbor relationships. Every router advertises the cost and state of its links. There are four LSP processes: receive, update, decision, and forwarding. LSPs are flooded to provide the routers a consistent view of the network. Flooding and synchronization are performed via CSNP, PSNP, SSN, and SRM bits.

There are two levels of hierarchy in IS-IS. In level 1, routers have full knowledge of all the links in their area. For any destination outside their area, they route to the closest level 2 router. Level 2 routers form the backbone of IS-IS.

By default, all Cisco routers are configured as both L1 and L2. Maintaining a database for both levels is not scalable, so route summarization is not always possible. The router should be configured as a single level only, wherever possible. For scaling a large IP network, the address scheme must be laid out so that L1 can summarize and send a single route to the backbone from the level 1 area.

LSPs behave differently in NBMA networks. There is always a difference between physical and logical topology. To maintain synchronization of the database, a point-to-point interface is used. However, there can be flooding as a result, which is a major problem in a large mesh environment. This problem is addressed with an interface-blocking feature in Cisco routers. By following the configuration advice in this chapter, you should be able to successfully operate IS-IS in your network.

Review Questions

1 What is the difference between an NSAP and a NET?

2 Why would you want multiple NETs on one box?

3 How many bits are reserved for the metric in IS-IS?

4 When is a non-pseudonode LSP generated?

Answers:

1 An NSAP with an n-selector of 0 is called a NET.

2 You can use multiple NETs while in the process of merging or splitting areas.

3 Six bits are reserved, so the metric cannot be larger than 63.

4 A non-pseudonode LSP represents a router and includes the ISs and the LANs attached to that router.

For Further Reading . . .

Marty, Abe. "Introduction to IS-IS." Cisco Internal Document.

Previdi, Stefano. IS-IS Presentation. 1998.

Smith, Henk. IS-IS Personal Communication. 1999.

Smith, Henk. IS-IS Presentation. 1997.

Earlier chapters in this book described interior routing protocols used predominantly for routing *within* autonomous systems. This chapter discusses the Border Gateway Protocol (BGP), which is predominantly used for routing *between* autonomous systems.

The approach of this chapter is similar to the earlier chapters on routing protocols: It begins with a bird's-eye view of how the protocol works and then dives straight into the details of its various messages, routing information, and states. Next, we explore the scalability features of Cisco's implementation, and finally, we provide general configuration tips for large-scale networks. This chapter covers the following issues in relation to BGP:

Fundamentals and operation of BGP   In this section, you will read about the basic operation and application of BGP. The text describes the application of the protocol within and between networks.

Description of the BGP protocol   This section examines the protocol at the packet level. You will learn the details and purpose of BGP open, update, notification, and keepalive messages; and will discover how the various Cisco configuration commands modify the behavior of the protocol. Newer features of BGP, such as capability negotiation and multiprotocol extensions, are also included in the discussion.

BGP's finite state machine (FSM)   BGP has an eight-state FSM. This section describes the purpose of each state, how Cisco's implementation moves from one state to the next, and how this movement between states may be modified by configuration commands.

The routing policy and the BGP decision algorithm   Understanding the BGP decision algorithm is the key to understanding the protocol and its operation. This section describes the algorithm specified in the BGP RFC, and discusses the optimizations and extensions included in the Cisco implementation. Configuration commands that can be used to tune the behavior of the decision algorithm are also described.

Scalability features   This section describes the use of peer groups, route-reflectors, and confederations to scale BGP architectures.

Large network BGP configuration   This section examines specific configuration issues for large networks. The discussion includes BGP synchronization, authentication, automatic route summarization, logging, dampening, and the use of peer groups and loopback addresses. It concludes with the development of a BGP configuration "stencil" for large networks.

The chapter concludes with a case study that examines the overall BGP architecture of a large service provider network.

## CHAPTER 11

Border Gateway Protocol

Introduction to BGP

BGP was originally designed for routing between major service providers within the Internet, so it is considered an exterior routing protocol. A worthy successor to the now-obsolete Exterior Gateway Protocol (EGP), BGP is the "glue" that holds the modern Internet together. It has assumed that role since version 4 of the protocol (BGP4), which was deployed in 1993. Earlier versions of BGP—notably BGP3—were used on the NSFNET in the early 1990s.

As a protocol, BGP requires a great deal of manual configuration. This, along with its detailed design and considerable testing exposure on the Internet, has led to a stable and highly scalable implementation of the protocol. The level of BGP operational expertise is increasing, and modifications to the protocol to support Virtual Private Networks (VPNs) and even voice-call routing, are on the horizon.

Fundamentals of BGP Operation

BGP is structured around the concept that the Internet is divided into a number of Autonomous Systems (ASs). Before you learn how the protocol operates, you should become familiar with ASs.

An *Autonomous System* (AS) is a network under a single administration, identified by a single two-byte number (1–65536), which is allocated by the InterNIC and is globally unique to the AS. Within an AS, private AS numbers may be used by BGP, but they must be translated to the official AS prior to connectivity with the Internet.

An AS is essentially a network under a single administrative control, and it may be categorized as a stub, multihomed, or transit AS. A stub AS is a network that connects to a single Internet service provider and does not generally provide transit for other ASs. A multihomed AS connects to more than one ISP. A transit AS is the ISP itself. In other words, it provides connectivity between other ASs.

Figure 11-1 shows this arrangement. Stub AS-A reaches other destinations on the Internet through its transit provider, ISP-C. Stub AS-E reaches all Internet destinations through its transit provider, ISP-D.

Figure 11-1 *Stub, Multihomed, and Transit ASs*

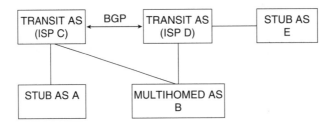

Transit providers must either provide connectivity to all other transit providers in the global Internet, or purchase that connectivity through a higher-tier transit provider. Therefore, in the Internet there is a hierarchy of transit providers. The providers at the highest tier of the hierarchy (typically called Tier 1 ISPs) must provide connectivity to all other Tier 1 ISPs for global connectivity to be complete.

A multihomed AS, such as B shown in Figure 11-1, connects to two or more transit providers. Users in network B may reach Internet destinations through either provider by using basic load sharing of traffic, or through a policy that determines the best route to any particular destination.

The InterNIC allocates AS numbers (ASNs). However, not all networks require an official, globally unique ASN. Unique ASNs are necessary only when an organization must be routable on the Internet as a self-contained entity. Multihomed ASs are sometimes listed in this category, although, through careful use of address translation or load-sharing techniques, you can avoid the use of an official ASN. Networks providing Internet transit to other networks are the most appropriate users of InterNIC-assigned ASNs.

BGP Neighbor Relationships

BGP neighbor relationships, often called *peering*, are usually manually configured into routers by the network administrator, according to certain rules and to logically follow the overall network topology. Each neighbor session runs over TCP (port 179) to ensure reliable delivery and incremental, rather than periodic, rebroadcasting of updates. These two characteristics distinguish BGP from the auto-neighbor-discover/periodic-rebroadcast nature of most interior routing protocols.

NOTE   *Incremental updates* occur when all routing information is sent only once. The routing information must be explicitly withdrawn or the BGP TCP session closed, for the information to become invalid.

Two BGP peers exchange all their routes when the session is first established: Beyond this point, the peers exchange updates when there is a topology change in the network or a change in routing policy. Therefore, it is possible for a peering session to see extended periods of inactivity. As a result, BGP peers exchange session *keepalive* messages. The keepalive period can be tuned to suit the needs of a particular topology. For example, a low keepalive can be set if a fast *fail-over* is required. Failover is convergence to an alternate route if the current route becomes invalid.

Although an individual BGP router may maintain many paths to a particular destination, it forwards only its *best* path—that is, the one selected as the candidate for forwarding packets— to its peers. This best path is determined through policy derived from various attributes associated with the routes exchanged between peers. These policies are discussed in the latter part of this chapter.

External versus Internal BGP

The classic application of BGP is a route exchange between autonomous systems. However, the scalable properties of the protocol, along with the need to transit several attributes to implement routing policy, have encouraged its use within autonomous systems. As a result, as shown in Figure 11-2, there are two types of BGPs : External BGP (EBGP), for use between ASs; and Internal BGP (IBGP), for use within them.

Figure 11-2   *External BGP (EBGP) Exists between Autonomous Systems, and Internal BGP (IBGP) Exists within Them*

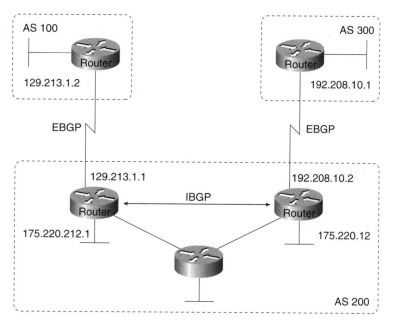

EBGP and IBGP differ in a number of important ways. The most critical difference to understand at this stage is that the BGP router never forwards a path learned from one IBGP peer to another IBGP peer, even if that path is its best path. The exception to this is when a route-reflector hierarchy (discussed later) is established to reduce the size of the IBGP mesh. EGP peers, on the other hand, always forward the routes learned from one EBGP peer to both EBGP and IBGP peers, although you can use filters to modify this behavior. IBGP routers in an AS, therefore, must maintain an IBGP session with all other IBGP routers in the network to obtain complete routing information about external networks. In addition to this full IBGP mesh, most networks also use an IGP, such as IS-IS or OSPF, to carry the routing information for links within the local network.

BGP is described as a path-vector protocol, although it is essentially a distance-vector protocol that carries a list of the ASs traversed by the route to provide loop detection for EBGP. An EBGP speaker adds its own AS to this list before forwarding a route to another EBGP peer. An IBGP speaker does not modify the list because it is sending the route to a peer within the same AS.

As a result, the AS list cannot be used to detect the IBGP routing loops (loops within a single autonomous system). These loops usually are caused by poor configuration, resulting in inconsistent policy. The Cisco BGP implementation provides methods to fine-tune configurations for improved scalability, but careless use may result in routing loops. When modifying the default BGP behavior, you should ensure that your modifications provide for a consistent policy within the AS.

TIP   BGP4 was the first version of the protocol to include masks with each route, and therefore supports Classless Inter Domain Routing (CIDR). As you may remember from Chapter 2, "IP Fundamentals," CIDR provides a means for address aggregation, and has been the major contributor to minimizing the prefix count in Internet routing tables since 1993. Prefix aggregation involves a loss of more detailed routes. Because all BGP prefixes have an associated AS path list, it follows that BGP4 also provides the means for aggregating AS paths into an AS set.

Description of the BGP4 Protocol

Note that this chapter limits its description of BGP to version 4, which is the one used almost exclusively on the Internet today. BGP4 has four message types:

- OPEN messages are used to establish the BGP session.
- UPDATE messages are used to send routing prefixes, along with their associated BGP attributes (such as the AS-PATH).

- NOTIFICATION messages are sent whenever a protocol error is detected, after which the BGP session is closed.

- KEEPALIVE messages are exchanged whenever the keepalive period is exceeded, without an update being exchanged.

As shown in Figure 11-3, each message begins with a 19-byte header. The marker field is 16 bytes, and contains a sequence that can be predicted by the remote peer. It is, therefore, used for authentication or synchronization purposes. If not used for these purposes, the entire marker field is set to ones. The Cisco BGP implementation includes this setting to all ones because authentication is performed at the TCP layer.

Figure 11-3   *The 19-Byte BGP Packet Header*

16	2	1	Variable
Marker	Length	Type	Data

The two-byte length field indicates the total length of the BGP message, including the header, in bytes. Message lengths range from 19 bytes, which represent only the header and constitutes a KEEPALIVE message, and 4096 bytes, which most likely will be a large UPDATE containing multiple Network Layer Reachability Information [NLRI]).

The single-byte type field indicates the message type contained in the data portion. It may be one of the following:

- OPEN message
- UPDATE message
- NOTIFICATION message
- KEEPALIVE message

Now, we will examine each of these messages and the way they are used within the protocol.

The OPEN Message and Capability Negotiation

The OPEN message is shown in Figure 11-4.

This message begins with a one-byte BGP version number—this is generally version four, although Cisco routers will negotiate between versions 2 and 4 unless you explicitly set the **neighbor** { *ip-address* | *peer-group-name* } **version** *value*. In almost all cases, you use version 4. A two-byte ASN contains the AS of the remote neighbor. If this does not correspond to the ASN listed in the **neighbor** { *ip-address* | *peer-group-name* } remote-as number configuration line, the local Cisco router sends a notification and closes the session.

Figure 11-4   *The OPEN Message*

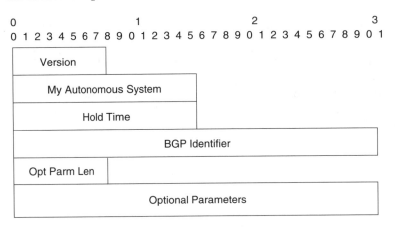

Holdtime is the period of time the session will be paused if a KEEPALIVE, UPDATE, or
WITHDRAW message is not received. This is negotiated as the lowest value sent by either
neighbor. By default, Cisco routers use a holdtime of three minutes, although this can be
configured on a per-neighbor basis using the **neighbor** { *ip-address* | *peer-group-name* }
timers *keepalive holdtime* command, or on a per-router basis using the **bgp timers** *keepalive*
holdtime command.

The BGP Router Identifier is a four-byte field. In Cisco router implementation, this is set to the
highest IP address on the router. Addresses of *loopback interfaces* are considered before
physical interface addresses. You may also explicitly set this field using the **bgp router-id** *ip-*
address BGP router configuration command.

Loopback interfaces are virtual interfaces on the router that are always enabled unless
administratively disabled. They can source much of the router traffic used for network
management and routing purposes.

The Optional Parameters field, shown in Figure 11-5, consists of a one-byte parameter type, a one-byte parameter length, and a variable-length parameter value. Two types are commonly used:

- Type 1 is used to indicate the BGP authentication using MD5, if requested. This is not used by Cisco's implementation of BGP session authentication, which is executed at the TCP level and enabled using the **neighbor** { *ip-address* | *peer-group-name* } **password** *string* subcommand.

- Type 2 is used for capability negotiation. The original BGP spec (RFC 1771) states that a notification message with the error subcode set to Unsupported Optional Parameter must be sent, and the session must be closed if an unsupported capability is requested.

  Capability negotiation facilitates the introduction of new capabilities into BGP networks by enabling two BGP speakers to settle on a common set of supported capabilities without closing the session. For example, if router A wants unicast and multicast BGP routes, and if router B supports only unicast, the routers will settle for a unicast update only. In Cisco's implementation, if the remote BGP speaker does not support capability negotiation (the local speaker receives a NOTIFICATION message with the error code set to Unsupported Optional Parameter), the local router next attempts to establish the session without capabilities negotiation.

Figure 11-5   *The Optional Parameters Field*

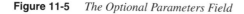

The UPDATE Message and BGP Attributes

The UPDATE message is used to transfer routing intelligence. Its format is shown in Figure 11-6. The UPDATE message may advertise routes, withdraw routes, or both.

The UPDATE message begins with the withdrawn-routes length, which may be zero, in which case no routes are withdrawn. Otherwise, the withdrawn-routes length contains a number of <length,prefix> triples, with length being one octet, and indicates the number of octets in the prefix field. A length of zero matches all IP addresses, in which case the prefix's field is of zero length. In all other cases, the prefix field contains an IP address prefix, padded with trailing bits so that the field ends on an octet boundary.

Figure 11-6 *The UPDATE Message*

Unfeasible Routes Length (2 octets)
Withdrawn Routes (variable)
Total Path Attribute Length (2 octets)
Path Attributes (variable)
Network Layer Reachability Information (variable)

NOTE   Most network protocols pad related fields so that they are located on an octet or byte boundary. This allows for more efficient processing by modern microprocessors, which have instruction sets optimized for operating on single or multiple byte-size chunks.

The Total Path Attribute Length field sizes the path attributes that will follow. As shown in Figure 11-7, each path attribute consists of an Attribute Flag's octet, followed by an Attribute Type Code octet, and finally the attribute information itself.

Figure 11-7 *The Format of the AS-PATH Attribute*

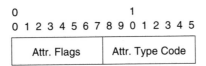

```
0                   1
0 1 2 3 4 5 6 7 8 9 0 1 2 3 4 5
```

Attr. Flags	Attr. Type Code

The first three bits of the Attribute Flags octet describe the general nature of the attribute that follows:

First bit: 1 => optional, 0 => well-known
Second bit: 1 => transitive, 0 => non-transitive
Third bit: 1 => partial optional transitive, 0 => complete optional transitive

These first two flags describe four attribute categories:

- 01: Well-known, mandatory. These attributes must be included in every update containing NLRI, and are recognized by all compliant implementations. A notification message will be generated and the peering session will be closed if they are missing. These attributes are always transitive, which means that if these NLRI are passed to other BGP speakers, the attributes also must be passed along.

  In addition, these attributes may be modified. For example, AS-PATH is well known and mandatory: A BGP speaker must transit the AS path, but may pre-append its own AS number to the AS list, or even perform aggregation and convert the path to an AS_PATH/AS_SET combination.

- 00: Well-known, discretionary. These attributes must also be recognized by all compliant implementations; however, they do not necessarily have to be transited if the NLRI are passed on to subsequent BGP speakers. Local preference, which is often used to select the best route within an individual AS, falls into this category.

- 10: Optional, transitive. These attributes may not be recognized by all BGP implementations. If it is not recognized, the partial bit (the third bit in the Attribute Flag octet) should be set before advertising the NLRI to other BGP speakers. In addition, if a BGP speaker other than the originator of the route attaches an optional transitive attribute to the route, the partial bit should also be set.

  This action indicates that certain routers in the path may not have understood or have not seen the attribute, and therefore may not have taken actions pertaining to the attribute. A router may set the partial bit if it does not understand the community attribute, but has passed it on unmodified to another AS. Similarly, if a router adds the community attribute to a route learned from another BGP router, it will also set the partial bit before passing it on.

  Routers that subsequently receive the route will be aware that not all routers in the AS path have acted upon the information contained in the community attribute.

- 11: Optional, non-transitive. Again, such attributes may not be recognized by all BGP implementations. If they are not recognized, the attribute should be dropped when passing the NLRI to other BGP speakers. The Cluster list attribute falls into this category; if it is not recognized by a BGP speaker, it should not be passed on because it may result in conflicts within other networks.

The fourth high-order bit of the Attribute Flags octet, if set to zero, indicates that the Attribute Length field is one byte; if set to one, the Attribute Length field is two bytes, which accomodates potentially long attributes, such as multiprotocol NRLI (see RFC 2283).

Attribute type codes are maintained by the Internet Assigned Numbers Authority (IANA) in the assigned numbers RFC 1700. The procedure for registering new attribute types is documented in RFC 2042, which also lists those attributes that were defined as of this writing:

Value	Code
1	ORIGIN
2	AS_PATH
3	NEXT_HOP
4	MULTI_EXIT_DISC
5	LOCAL_PREF
6	ATOMIC_AGGREGATE
7	AGGREGATOR
8	COMMUNITY
9	ORIGINATOR_ID
11	DPA
12	ADVERTISER
13	RCID_PATH/CLUSTER_ID
14	MP_REACH_NLRI
15	MP_UNREACH_NLRI
255	Reserved for development

Here, you see a brief description of each. Note that all the attributes associated with any BGP prefix can be displayed using **show ip bgp** <prefix>:

```
sh ip bgp 1.0.8.12
BGP routing table entry for 1.0.8.12/32, version 17274
Paths: (1 available, best #1, advertised over IBGP)
  12                              ! AS Path
    0.0.0.0                       ! Next-hop
      ORIGIN EGP, metric 12, localpref 12, weight 12, valid, sourced, best
      Destination preference 12, set by AS 1000
      Community: 1000:12
```

Type 1: ORIGIN

ORIGIN is a well-known mandatory attribute that indicates how the route was injected into the BGP routing system. ORIGIN may be set to IGP, EGP, or Incomplete. If the BGP decision comes down to the choice of ORIGIN, IGP is preferred over EGP, which is preferred over Incomplete. Although it is part of the decision process, ORIGIN is not typically used as an intentional part of routing policy. AS path, local preference, and multiexit-discriminator are considered much higher in the path-selection process.

In the Cisco implementation, routes installed in the BGP table using the BGP **network** route configuration command are given an ORIGIN of IGP. Those redistributed from the EGP routing process are given an ORIGIN of EGP. Those redistributed from other protocols (static, connected, Enhanced IGRP, OSPF, IS-IS, or RIP) are given an ORIGIN of Incomplete. This behavior can, of course, be overridden through the use of route maps.

Type 2: AS_PATH

AS_PATH is a well-known mandatory attribute that enumerates the AS systems through which the routing update has passed. Every BGP router preappends its own AS number to the AS_PATH attribute before forwarding the route to its external peers. For internal peers, it does not modify the attribute.

The AS_PATH attribute consists of one or more occurrences of the following three fields:

```
<path segment type, path segment length, path segment value>
```

The type may have the value 1 through 4 to indicate AS_SET, AS_SEQUENCE, AS_CONFED_SET, and AS_CONFED_SEQUENCE, respectively. The segment length is one octet and contains the number of ASs listed in the segment value. The segment value itself contains one or more two-octet (16-bit) AS numbers.

An AS_SEQUENCE is a sequential list of ASs through which the route has passed. If a route is aggregated by an AS into a larger route, the AS_SEQUENCE loses meaning because the aggregate itself has not passed sequentially through each AS. In fact, routes contributing to the attribute may have completely different AS_SEQUENCEs. On the other hand, simply removing AS information from routes contributing to the aggregate removes BGP's loop-detection mechanisms.

In Cisco IOS, aggregate routes are generated using the **aggregate-address** *address mask* [**as-set**] BGP router-configuration command. When generating an aggregate, the Cisco implementation performs the following steps:

- Resets the AS_PATH to include only the AS of the aggregating router.
- Fills in the AGGREGATOR attribute (see the description of AGGREGATOR attribute, which follows).
- Unless the **as_set** keyword is used, it sets the ATOMIC_AGGREGATE attribute to indicate loss of AS path information. If the **as_set** keyword is used, all ASs from routes contributing to an aggregate are uniquely listed in the AS_SET. However, you will not do this as a regular practice, because it implies that a new update for the aggregate must be sent every time a path contributing to the aggregate changes.

As an example, consider the following configuration:

```
Router bgp 100
aggregate address 10.0.0.0 255.255.255.0 as-set
```

This configuration would cause the router to generate a route for the CIDR block 10.0.0.0/8, with AS_PATH of 100. The AS_SET would include all the AS numbers known by this router to contain routes within 10.0.0.0/8. The AGGREGATOR attribute would contain the AS number of this router (100), together with its IP address.

AS_CONFED_SET and AS_CONFED_SEQUENCE have the same meaning as AS_SET and AS_SEQUENCE, respectively. However, their use and visibility are limited to a BGP *confederation*, which is a way to scale BGP networks. You will learn more about confederations in the section "BGP Scalability Features," later in this chapter.

Type 3: NEXT_HOP

NEXT_HOP is a well-known mandatory attribute. It is a four-octet IP address that identifies the next hop for NLRI contained in the update.

NOTE   This NEXT_HOP is IPv4 NLRI-specific: it is not associated with multiprotocol NLRIs contained in the MP_REACH-NLRI attribute, which carries its own NEXT_HOP information.

The treatment of the NEXT_HOP attribute varies slightly for EBGP and IBGP, as illustrated in Figure 11-8.

Figure 11-8   *Treatment of the NEXT_HOP Attribute Differs for EBGP and IBGP*

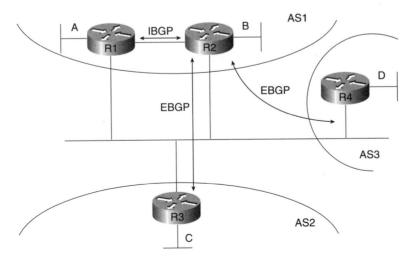

These steps are followed by treatment of the NEXT_HOP attribute:

1   Normally, when advertising an EBGP-learned route into IBGP, the next-hop attribute is unchanged. For example, suppose R3 advertises the route for network C to R2 via EBGP. It will set the next hop to its IP address on the multiaccess media. When R2 advertises C to IBGP neighbor R1, it does not modify the next hop. Thus, R1 sends traffic to network C directly over the peering LAN rather than through R2.

This behavior can be changed using the per-neighbor **next-hop-self** or the route-map **set next-hop** configuration commands. For example, if R2 applies **next-hop-self** to the IBGP session with R1, packets from R1 to network C would be routed via R2.

2   When advertising any routes to an EBGP neighbor, the local BGP speaker must set the next hop to an IP address on the peering subnet, which may, of course, be its own IP address.

If the next hop is not the router's own IP address, but instead is the address of some other router on the peering LAN, this is called *third-party next hop,* and is only applicable to multiaccess media. For example, suppose AS1 transits the route for D from AS3 to AS2. R2 learns the route for D via EBGP from R4 and passes it on to R3 via EBGP. By default, R2 advertises D to R3 with a next hop of R4's LAN interface. This produces efficient routing because R2 is not involved in the actual transfer of data packets.

Again, this behavior can be modified by configuring **next-hop-self** on the EBGP session between R2 and R3, or by applying a route map with **set next-hop**. This would result in inefficient routing of packets via R2 to R3, but it may satisfy the peering policy of AS2.

If router R2 or R1 were to transit the route to D to another peer AS on a different peering LAN/subnet, they would set the NEXT_HOP as their own address on that subnet.

Type 4: MULTI_EXIT_DISC

This attribute is an optional, non-transitive attribute, also known as MED or BGP metric. An AS may use MED to indicate the best entry point to reach a particular destination to a neighboring AS. A lower MED is preferred over a higher MED. According to RFC 1771, an update without a MED is interpreted as having a MED of infinity. In Cisco implementation, which predates the RFC, the lack of a MED indicates a MED of zero.

If you need to modify this behavior, you should contact your Cisco representative to discuss available options.

Figure 11-9 illustrates the use of MED. In this example, R1 advertises that it directly connects network C to R3 via EBGP, using a MED of 1. R2 also learns about network C via IBGP from R1 and advertises it to R3. R3 chooses the path directly through R1.

The MED attribute has four octets and ranges from 0 to 4,294,967,295.

Figure 11-9 *Using the MED Attribute*

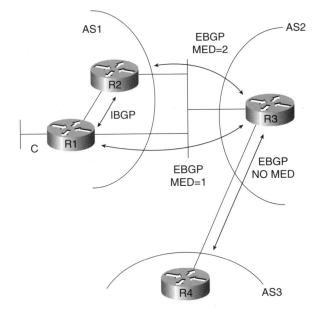

Because MED is non-transitive, an AS does not pass the MEDs it learns from one AS to another. Thus, R3 would remove the MED attribute before passing the route for C to AS3.

By default, MEDs are compared only for routes that originate from the same neighboring AS. It is possible to compare MEDs for the same route from different ASs using the **bgp always-compare-med** BGP subcommand. This is useful only in rare circumstances, when there is agreement between three ASs on the treatment of the MED value.

By default, when redistributing IGPs into BGP, the IGP metric is translated into an MED. In addition, when the **set metric-type internal** is used in an outgoing route map, the BGP MED is set to equal the IGP metric of the BGP next hop. The BGP MED is periodically updated to reflect changes in the IGP; if necessary, an update is sent.

Type 5: LOCAL_PREF

LOCAL_PREF is a well-known discretionary attribute. It is only sent—and, in fact, *must* be sent—in IBGP updates, not in EBGP (local-pref attributes in EBGP updates are ignored). As with MED, it ranges in value from 0 to 4,294,967,295. Unlike MED, however, it is intended for implementing local policies, not for communicating best-path information to other ASs. The default local preference is 100, although this may be modified using the **bgp default local-preference** BGP subcommand.

Of all BGP attributes, local preference is ranked highest in the decision-making process. Thus, by applying a local preference to routes learned via EBGP, the degree of preference for each path to a particular route is predetermined by the router configuration.

Another route is preferred over the route with highest local preference *only* if the following conditions are met:

- The BGP weight is lower than another route. BGP weight is a per-neighbor Cisco feature. It is not a BGP attribute, so it is never directly communicated to BGP neighbors. It is set on a per-neighbor basis using the **neighbor** {*ip-address* | *peer-group-name*} **weight** *weight* BGP router configuration command. The default weight is 50.

- The route is also learned via another routing protocol with lower administrative distance.

Figure 11-10 illustrates the use of local preference. AS1 learns two paths for network C. One path goes directly to AS3; the other is via AS2. If all other attributes were equal, AS1 would choose the shorter AS path to C, which is the path via R1 to R4. However, if R2 sets the local preference of the route for C to 200 (the default is 100), R2 advertises this route to each of its internal neighbors, including R1. R1 will prefer the path via R2, R3, and R4 to reach network C because its local preference is higher.

Figure 11-10 *Using Local Preference*

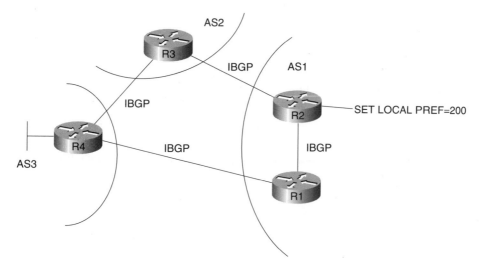

This arrangement may look inefficient, but remember that Figure 11-10 shows nothing about the performance of the various network links in the diagram. It may be that the links from R1 to R2, to R3, to R4, have much greater capacity and available bandwidth than the link directly between R1 and R4.

Moreover, this route may represent a less costly one in monetary terms. Local preference provides the tool to implement best-path policies that may be based on network performance data, visible to the network administrator but not directly or automatically visible to the routing protocol itself. BGP cannot inherently detect the congestion and performance of the network, short of complete failure or the monetary costs of using certain paths.

Some network operators may choose to apply a local preference to all incoming EBGP routes and have the BGP path-decision algorithm be based wholly on the local preference. This is the strategy outlined in the BGP specification RFC 1771.

Type 6: ATOMIC_AGGREGATE

ATOMIC_AGGREGATE is a well-known discretionary attribute of length 0 (only the attribute type is listed). As mentioned in the description of the path attribute, when generating an aggregate without AS-SET information, a BGP router must ensure that this attribute is set to indicate the loss of AS-PATH information.

Once set, this attribute is never removed by a router that readvertises the route to either an IBGP or EBGP neighbor. If a Cisco router sets the atomic attribute, it will also set the aggregator attribute.

Type 7: AGGREGATOR

AGGREGATOR is an optional, transitive attribute of six octets. The first two octets and the last four octets contain the AS number and IP address, respectively, of the router generating the aggregate route. In the Cisco implementation, the IP address is the router ID (the highest IP address on the router; loopbacks are considered before physical interfaces).

The AGGREGATOR attribute can be useful for debugging and other network operational issues. If an aggregate is unclear, or if it appears that a particular AS should not be generating the aggregate, it enables network administrators to pinpoint exactly which router in the AS is generating the aggregate.

Type 8: COMMUNITY

COMMUNITY is an optional, transitive attribute consisting of a sequence of four-octet *communities*. An AS may create, reset, or preappend to the sequence. Communities 0x00000000 through 0x0000FFFF and 0xFFFF0000 0xFFFFFFFF are reserved; however, the remainder of the 32-bit space is free for use.

By common convention, when creating or adding a community to this attribute, the first two octets are assigned to the number of the AS generating the attribute. The second two octets are freely assigned according to either some local policy code or a policy code agreed upon between providers. It is common to display communities in the decimal notation; for example, AS:policycode.

If an aggregate route is formed, the COMMUNITY attribute should contain the set of communities from all the aggregated routes. Cisco routers will perform this if the **as-set** keyword is included in the **aggregate-address** BGP router-configuration command used to generate the aggregate.

Three well-known communities exist:

- NO_EXPORT (0xFFFFFF01): Routes carrying a COMMUNITY attribute with this value should not be advertised outside the local AS or outside the local confederation.

- NO_ADVERTISE (0xFFFFFF02): Routes carrying a community attribute with this value should not be advertised to any peers.

- NO_EXPORT_SUBCONFED: Routes carrying a community attribute with this value should not be advertised to EBGP peers (including EBGP peers within a confederation).

The COMMUNITY attribute is used to "color" routes. Once colored, route maps can be used to control the distribution and acceptance of routes with a particular color. The color may also be used for service classification in a network. In other words, the color can apply preferential queuing treatment to packets destined to or sourced from networks in a particular community. This feature, called BGP QoS Policy Propagation, is described in Chapter 14, "Quality of Service Features."

Type 9:ORIGINATOR_ID

The ORIGINATOR_ID is a four-octet, optional, non-transitive attribute. It carriers the router-ID of a route-reflector that injects (reflects) the route of a client into an AS. This attribute can aid in debugging and loop-detection in a route-reflector environment.

Type 10: CLUSTER_LIST

The CLUSTER_LIST is an optional, non-transitive attribute of variable length. It is a sequence of four-byte fields containing the CLUSTER_IDs of the reflection path, through which the route has passed. When a route-reflector reflects a route to non-client peers, it appends its CLUSTER_ID to the CLUSTER_LIST. As with the ORIGINATOR_ID, this attribute can aid in debugging route-reflector environments. In addition, it aids in automated loop detection; if a router receives an update containing its own CLUSTER_ID in the CLUSTER_LIST, the update is ignored.

NOTE   The following attributes have not gained wide-spread acceptance, and thus are not
               discussed in this chapter: TYPE 11: DPA, TYPE 12: ADVERTISER, and TYPE 13:
               RCID_PATH / CLUSTER_ID.

Type 14: MP_REACH_NLRI

The MP_REACH_NLRI attribute is optional and non-transitive. It consists of one or more
triples: Address Family Information, Next Hop Information, and NLR. The format of each
triple is shown in Figure 11-11.

Figure 11-11   *Format of Triples in the MP_REACH_NLRI Attribute*

Address Family Identifier (2 octets)
Subsequent Address Family Identifier (1 octet)
Length of Next Hop Network Address (1 octet)
Network Address of Next Hop (variable)
Number of SNPAs (1 octet)
Length of first SNPA (1 octet)
First SNPA (variable)
Length of second SNPA (1 octet)
Second SNPA (variable)
. . .
Length of Last SNPA (1 octet)
Last SNPA (variable)
Network Layer Reachability Information (variable)

This attribute, as well as attribute type 15, is defined in the multiprotocol BGP RFC 2283, which
describes extensions to BGP that enable it to carry routing information for protocols other than
IPv4. Moreover, it may carry additional IPv4 routing information for purposes other than
unicast, such as to support multicast routing.

The AFI field identifies the network-layer protocol associated with the NLRI and next hop addresses that follow. AFI values are in accordance with the Assigned Numbers RFC 1700.

The Subsequent Address Family Identifier provides additional information about the NLRI. Values 128–255 are reserved for vendor-specific allocations. Zero is reserved by RFC 2283. In addition, one through three are defined as follows:

- 1: NLRI to be used for unicast packet forwarding
- 2: NLRI to be used for multicast packet forwarding
- 3: NLRI to be used for both multicast and unicast packet forwarding

For these values of SAFI, the NLRI are encoded as shown in Figure 11-12.

Figure 11-12 *NLRI Encoding in the MP_REACH_NLRI Attribute*

| Length (1 octet) |
| Prefix (variable) |

All other values are assigned by IETF consensus process and, presumably, will eventually be maintained in the Assigned Numbers RFC 1700.

Type 15: MP_UNREACH_NLRI

MP_UNREACH_NLRI is an optional, non-transitive attribute used to withdraw routes. An UPDATE message containing this attribute does not need to carry other attributes or unicast NLRI. The format of this attribute is shown in Figure 11-13. The format of withdrawn routes is identical to Figure 11-12.

Figure 11-13 *Format of the MP_UNREACH_NLRI Attribute*

| Address Family Identifier (2 octets) |
| Subsequent Address Family Identifier (1 octet) |
| Withdrawn Routes (variable) |

NLRI

NLRI is a list of IP address prefixes, encoded, as shown in Figure 11-14. Its length is the prefix length, which can range from zero to 32. A length of zero indicates a default route, and a length of 32 indicates a host route. The prefix contains all the significant bits of the route (those within <Length> bits), along with trailing bits to pad the Prefix field to an octet boundary.

Figure 11-14 *NLRI Is an Encoded List of IP Address Prefixes*

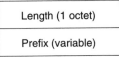

It is important to note that an update containing previously-announced NLRI implicitly withdraws the early advertisements. Therefore, when updating the attributes for a particular NLRI, such as changing MED, it is not necessary to send an explicit withdraw for the NLRI in advance.

The NOTIFICATION Message and BGP Errors

Notification messages are sent in response to a BGP error condition. These include protocol errors such as malformed updates, confusion in the BGP state machine, or even unsupported options. After sending the NOTIFICATION, the sender closes the TCP connection and both peers invalidate any routes associated with the peering session.

Each NOTIFICATION message contains a one-byte error code and a one-byte subcode, followed by variable-length, error-specific data:

Error Subcode	Meaning
Error Code 1: Message Header Error	
1: Connection Not Synchronized	BGP Authentication Problems
2: Bad Message Length	
3: Bad Message Type	Unrecognized type field in message
Error Code 2: OPEN Message Error	
1: Unsupported Version Number	BGP version (2,3,4) cannot be negotiated
2: Bad Peer AS	Remote AS does not correspond to that configured in **neighbor** {*ip-address*	*peer-group-name* } **remote-as** *number*
3: Bad BGP Identifier	Not a valid IP address
4: Unsupported Optional Parameter	

Error Subcode	Meaning
5: Authentication Failure	
6: Unacceptable Hold Time	Need to change holdtime configured in **bgp timers**
Error Code 3: Update Message Error	
1: Malformed Attribute List	
2: Unrecognized Well-Known Attribute	
3: Missing Well-Known Attribute	
4: Attribute Flags Error	
5: Attribute Length Error	
6: Invalid ORIGIN Attribute	
7: AS Routing Loop	Check to ensure that you are not retransiting routes from an AS back to itself
8: Invalid NEXT_HOP Attribute	
9: Optional Attribute Error	
10: Invalid Network Field	
11: Malformed AS_path	
Error Code 4: Hold Timer Expired	
None defined	Mismatched **timers bgp**
Error Code 5: Finite State Machine	
None defined	Errors detected by BGP FSM
Error Code 6: Cease	
None defined	For other fatal errors

NOTE   No mechanism exists within the BGP protocol to advise a peer of a NOTIFICATION message error, which is an invalid error code because the sender initiates a session-close after sending a notification. Errors in NOTIFICATION messages must therefore be advised by manual means: contact the administrator of the remote router.

KEEPALIVE Messages

KEEPALIVE messages are comprised only of the 19-byte BGP message header shown in Figure 11-3. These are exchanged whenever an update-free period exceeds the holdtime negotiated in the OPEN message exchange. A KEEPALIVE is also sent to acknowledge the OPEN message before moving from the OPEN_SENT to ESTABLISHED session state. If the holdtime is zero, KEEPALIVE messages are not sent, except to acknowledge an OPEN.

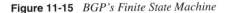

TIP   The minimum keepalive period is the same as the minimum holdtime: one second.

BGP's Finite State Machine

The finite-state machine associated with BGP is shown in Figure 11-15.

Figure 11-15 *BGP's Finite State Machine*

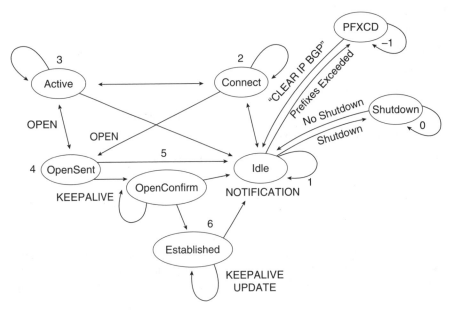

NOTE   Other BGP literature describes states 1 through 6 only. States -1 (prefix exceeded) and 0 (administrative shutdown) are specific to the Cisco implementation. To avoid confusion with state numbers used in other literature, in this book these Cisco specific states are numbered -1 and 0, respectively.

Eight possible states exist in BGP's finite-state machine:

- *−1 Prefix exceeded*

  If the **neighbor** { *ip-address* | *peer-group-name* } **maximum-prefix** *maximum* BGP router configuration command is used, and if the received prefix count exceeds *maximum*, the session is held in this state until a **clear ip bgp** command is applied to this neighbor. This feature safeguards against the large number of routes that may be received from peers as a result of configuration errors, such as applying an incorrect route-forwarding policy or not applying any policy at all. The classic example is a small ISP that inadvertently transits all Internet routes between two large ISPs.

- *0 Shutdown*

  Sessions may be administratively shut down using the **neighbor** { *ip-address* | *peer-group-name* } **shutdown** BGP router configuration command. In this state, all incoming connection requests are refused and no connections are attempted.

- *1 Idle*

  After configuration via the **neighbor** { *ip-address* | *peer-group-name* } **remote-as** *number* BGP subcommand, sessions begin in the Idle state. At this point, the router periodically initiates a TCP connection on port 179 to its neighbor and moves to the Connect state, based on an exponentially growing connect-retry timer.

  While in the Idle state, the router also listens on port 179 for incoming TCP connections. If one arrives from the listed neighbor IP address, the session also moves to the Connect state.

  If **clear ip bgp** { *ip-address* | *peer-group-name*} is executed during this session, the connect-retry timer is reset.

- *2 Connect*

  At this point, the session waits for the TCP connection to succeed. If it does, the local router sends an OPEN message to its peer and moves to the OpenSent state. If the connection fails, the session moves to the Active state. If the connect-retry timer expires, it is reset and a new transport connection is initiated.

  In response to **clear ip bgp** { *ip-address* | *peer-group-name*} associated with this session, it returns to the Idle state.

  If a valid (from the correct remote-IP on the correct port) incoming TCP connection attempt is received, this session moves to the Connect state. An OPEN message is sent to the remote neighbor, and the session moves to the OpenSent state.

- 3 *Active*

  The router generally reaches this state because a transport connection has failed. It will stay in the Active state until the connect-retry timer expires, at which point it will initiate another connection and move to the Connect state.

  In this state, the router also continues to listen for an incoming BGP session. If a valid connection is made, the router sends an OPEN message and transitions to the OpenSent state.

- 4 *OpenSent*

  The router has sent an OPEN message and waits for an OPEN message from its peer. Once received, the OPEN message is checked for the following:

  > acceptable remote-as (as per **neighbor** { *ip-address | peer-group-name* } **remote-as** *number* configuration)
  > acceptable version number (2, 3, or 4; default is 4 unless **bgp** { *ip-address | peer-group-name* } **version** *value* is configured)

  Any errors in the OPEN message will result in a notification being sent and a change to the Idle state.

  If there are no errors, a KEEPALIVE message is sent and the router sets the holdtime as the minimum of its locally configured holdtime and the holdtime in the open message received from its peer. If the holdtime expires, the router sends a NOTIFICATION (holdtime expired), and the session reverts to the Idle state.

  If the underlying transport connection is closed, the session reverts to the Active state.

- 5 *OpenConfirm*

  Here, the router waits for a KEEPALIVE, which is its signal that no notifications are expected as a result of the Open message, and that the session can move to the Established state.

  If the router does not receive a KEEPALIVE within the negotiated holdtime, it sends a NOTIFICATION (hold-timer expired) and reverts to the Idle state. Similarly, if the router receives a NOTIFICATION, usually as a result of a problem with the Open message, the state reverts to Idle.

- 6 *Established*

  Once in this state, the routers generally exchange UPDATE messages. If there is no UPDATE within the holdtime, a KEEPALIVE is sent unless the negotiated holdtime is zero, in which case no keepalives are necessary.

  If an UPDATE or KEEPALIVE contains errors, a NOTIFICATION is sent and the state shifts to Idle.

Routing Policy and the BGP Decision Algorithm

A BGP router may receive paths for the same route from many neighbors. How the best path is selected is a matter of local policy. The policy within an AS must be consistent; otherwise, routing loops could occur. Conceptually, the policy and decision process is shown in Figure 11-16.

Figure 11-16 *BGP's Policy and Decision Process*

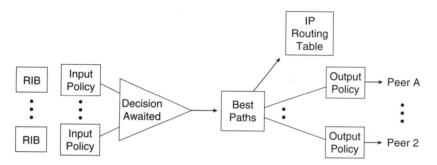

An incoming Routing Information Base is maintained for each peer. Incoming policy is applied to each RIB, and complying routes are passed as candidates to the BGP decision-making process. The best paths are offered as candidates to the IP forwarding table and applied to the outgoing policy engines for each peer. They compete with other candidate routes, based on the administrative distance, which can be modified using the **distance** BGP subcommand. Best paths that comply with the appropriate outgoing routing policy are sent to their respective peers.

In the previous section, you learned about the various BGP attributes. These are critical to the understanding of BGP policy, and form the basis for the best-path selection algorithm. Now, we will explore best-path selection, as specified by the BGP4 specification, RFC 1771.

Note that the outgoing interface for the next hop of any BGP route must be known to the local router. Otherwise, the route is not considered in the best-path selection process. The outgoing interface is determined using a recursive route lookup based on IP routing information that may be provided by IGP, and even BGP itself.

TIP

Recursion occurs as follows: If the next hop is not directly connected, the IP routing table is consulted for a route to the next hop. If the next hop for this route is not directly connected, this recursion process continues until reaching one that is; otherwise, the route is declared unreachable.

According to RFC 1771, the best path possesses the highest Degree of Preference (DOP). In the Cisco environment, the DOP is the same as the local preference, whether it is calculated according to policy configured into the local router or received as an attribute, in which case the local preference has been calculated by the router in the AS that originally received the path via EBGP.

Referring to Figure 11-10, you see that R1 calculates a local preference of 100 for the EBGP learned path to C. Then, R2 calculates a local preference of 200 and sends this path via IBGP to R1, with a local preference attribute of 200. The path through R2 is chosen by R1 as the best path because, in this case, the received local preference attribute (200) for the path through R1 is greater than its local preference (100) for the EBGP path via R4.

What happens if the local preference is the same? The tie-breaker proceeds as follows:

1   If the local router is configured to process MED, choose the route with the lowest MED.

2   Otherwise, choose the route with the lowest IGP cost for the NEXT-HOP attribute.

3   If multiple paths have the same IGP cost, select the route received via the EBGP neighbor with the lowest BGP ID.

4   If no EBGP neighbors exist, choose the IBGP neighbor with the lowest BGP ID.

The Cisco decision algorithm has evolved through years of Internet operational experience. It is considerably more sophisticated than the algorithm specified in the RFC, although RFC 1771 compliance can be achieved through the following configuration commands.

Probably the most significant enhancements to RFC 1771 with respect to the decision algorithm are the following:

- Support of a per-neighbor cost: weight
- Explicit use of AS_PATH length in the decision process
- Support for multiple paths for load-sharing purposes
- Support for best path choice and loop detection in router-reflector environments

The steps for the Cisco BGP best route selection process are as follows:

1   If the next hop is inaccessible, the route is not considered. This is the reason that it is important to have an IGP route to the next hop.

2   If synchronization is enabled, the path is internal, and the route is not in the IGP, then it is ignored.

3   Prefer the path with the largest weight (weight is a Cisco-specific parameter).

4   Prefer the route with the largest local preference.

5   Prefer the route that was locally originated, using either the **network** or **aggregate** BGP subcommand, or through redistribution from an IGP.

6   Prefer the route with the shortest AS_PATH.

7 Prefer the route with the lowest origin type: IGP is lower than EGP, and EGP is lower than INCOMPLETE.

8 Prefer the route with the lowest MED. The comparison is done only if the neighboring AS is the same, unless **bgp always-compare-med** is configured.

9 Prefer EBGP over IBGP. All confederation paths are considered internal, but prefer confederation EBGP over confederation IBGP.

10 Prefer the route with the lowest IGP metric to the BGP next hop.

11 If the best route and this route are both external and originate from the same neighboring AS, and if **maximum-paths N** is configured, insert the route for this path into the IP routing table. EBGP multipath load-sharing can occur at this point—up to N paths can be installed in the forwarding table.

12 If multipath is not enabled, prefer the route coming from the BGP router with the lowest router ID. The router ID is the highest IP address on the router, with preference given to loopback addresses.

Now, you can examine the general configuration of BGP for all routers in a large-scale IP network and study some features that affect network architecture, such as confederations and reflectors. In Chapter 16, "Design and Configuration Case Studies," you will see the detailed configurations specific to the access, distribution, and core networks; as well as Internet NAPs.

BGP Scalability Features

At the beginning of this chapter, the text noted that a BGP router never advertises IBGP-learned routes to another IBGP neighbor. This implies that all IBGP neighbors must be connected via a full mesh of IBGP peering sessions.

Even in medium-size networks, this full-mesh requirement can lead to serious scaling difficulties. *Route reflectors* and *confederations* are two ways of solving the full-mesh problem.

Route Reflectors

Route reflection (RFC 1966) was designed with three goals in mind:

- To be simple to understand and configure
- To enable easy migration from full-mesh to reflected environments
- To be compatible with IBGP routers that do not understand route reflection

Route reflection achieves these goals very well. Consider the network shown in Figure 11-17. Clearly, it would become unwieldy to create a full IBGP mesh between routers that extend down from the core through the distribution network hierarchy. Instead, you can define clusters within the hierarchy: Routers in each cluster will typically share some geographical, topological, or administrative relationship.

Figure 11-17   *A Complex Route Reflector Hierarchy*

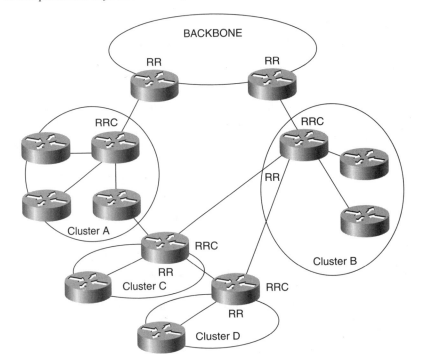

Within each cluster in Figure 11-17, there will be at least one route reflector (RR), plus a number of clients. The clients do not need to be aware that they are clients, nor do they have to support any of the RR-specific attributes. A route reflector may be a client of another RR higher in the hierarchy (toward the backbone). An RR will typically also have a number of non-client peers.

The premise behind route reflection is that one can relax the rule that a BGP router cannot re-advertise IBGP-learned routes to an IBGP peer. For any IBGP peer configured as a client, using the **neighbor** { *ip-address* | *peer-group-name* } **route-reflector-client** BGP router configuration command on the RR, the RR will reflect all IBGP routes to that client. In the case of non-clients, however, it behaves as in traditional IBGPs: No IBGP routes are forwarded to IBGP peers. As usual, only the best route is advertised to peers. With respect to this best route, the RR operation can be summarized as follows:

- Routes from a non-client are reflected to clients only.
- Routes from clients and EBGP peers are reflected to all non-clients and clients, except the originating client.

When reflecting routes to a client, the RR does not typically modify any of the BGP attributes.

In Figure 11-17, instead of requiring a full mesh of 78 IBGP sessions [n*(n–1)]/2 (n being the number of IBGP speakers, 13 in this case), you are limited to 13, through the use of RRs.

The benefit of RR environments is not obtained without cost. Specifically, route reflector environments must obey certain topological constraints. The router reflector itself also requires some extra functionality to provide loop detection.

The topological constraints are generally simple to follow. Note that the RR/RRC relationships in Figure 11-17 usually follow the physical topology (the links between routers) and hierarchy. If you follow this rule of thumb when building reflector hierarchies, loops can be avoided.

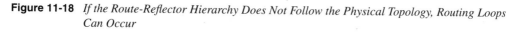

TIP   Always architect route reflector hierarchies to follow the physical topology.

Figure 11-18 demonstrates an RR environment in which the rule requiring RR-to-RRC relationships to follow the physical topology is broken. As a consequence, loops may occur. Consider this scenario: A and D choose EBGP path for X. C is RRC of A, and the route to X is via B to A. B is RRC of D, and its route to X is via C to D. A loop is formed between B and C.

Figure 11-18 *If the Route-Reflector Hierarchy Does Not Follow the Physical Topology, Routing Loops Can Occur*

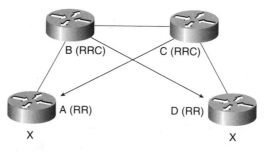

Note also from Figure 11-17 that redundancy is possible at both the intracluster and intercluster level. At the intracluster level, a single cluster may have more than one RR, in which case each RR must be configured with the same CLUSTER_ID.

This is achieved via the **bgp cluster-id** BGP subcommand. When an RR reflects a route from RRC to a non-client (traditional IBGP) peer, it must append its local CLUSTER_ID to the CLUSTER_LIST. If an RR sees a route with its own CLUSTER_ID in the CLUSTER_LIST (this is analogous to the use of AS_PATH for EBGP loop detection), the route is either a loop, possibly the result of poor configuration; or it comes from a redundant RR in its own cluster. Either way, it is ignored. Note that although the CLUSTER_LIST provides basic loop detection, it will not prevent problems in all situations.

Redundancy at the intracluster level indicates that RRCs can be clients of more than one RR. In Figure 11-17, the RRs in cluster C and D are clients of the RR in cluster B. Therefore, if cluster A fails, both C and D can still reach the backbone via cluster B. Similarly, if cluster C fails, D can still reach the backbone via B.

Route reflectors are proving to be an extremely popular technique for scaling BGP networks. Probably the major benefit is the ease with which the network administrator can move from a fully meshed environment to an RR environment, as well as the fact that RR clients are simple IBGP speakers that have no notion of RR technology.

Now, we will briefly examine another approach to scaling the IBGP mesh: confederations. Although this approach is older than route reflection and has therefore been implemented in some major ISP backbones, most new network designs prefer the simplicity of the RR approach. In some cases, such as in very large networks, a combination may be used in which each sub-AS contains its own RR hierarchy.

Confederations

The idea behind a *confederation* is that the AS is broken into a number of sub-ASs. The sub-AS numbers are usually private AS numbers and are visible only within the confederation. To external EBGP peers, a confederation of sub-ASs still appears as a single AS.

NOTE	A confederation divides an AS into a number of smaller ASs that communicate using EBGP. In BGP sessions with networks outside the BGP confederation, the AS numbers used within the confederation are replaced with the confederation's official AS number.

A full IBGP mesh is built within each sub-AS. Between each sub-AS, a hybrid of EBGP and IBGP is used for peering. This is a hybrid in the sense that sub-ASs are included as part of the AS path, providing sub-AS loop detection in the same manner as EBGP. However, when passing routes to a peer in another sub-AS, the next hop and other attributes such as local-pref and MED are not modified.

This arrangement reduces the IBGP meshing requirements because any IBGP routers within a sub-AS do not use IBGP peering for routers in other sub-ASs.

Figure 11-19 shows the recommended architecture for a confederated network. It utilizes a central core sub-AS and a number of distribution sub-ASs, which typically correspond to regional service networks. In many ways, the distribution sub-AS is equivalent to the RR hierarchy extended from the core in a reflector environment.

Figure 11-19 *Recommended Architecture for a Confederated Network*

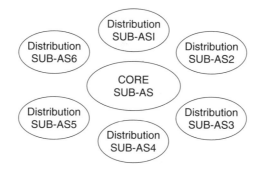

If all other attributes are equal, Cisco implementation will prefer a route learned from an EBGP peer outside the confederation to one learned from inside the confederation; it will prefer a route learned from outside the local sub-AS to one learned from inside the local sub-AS.

Peer Groups

Many network architectures feature groups of neighbors with similar update policies. Types of groups may include these:

- Core network IBGP peers
- Distribution network RR clients
- EBGP peers at a NAP
- Customers requiring only the default route, all routes for this AS, or all Internet routes

Figure 11-20 demonstrates the use of peer groups within a network architecture.

Considerable configuration effort and CPU utilization can be saved by applying peer groups in these instances. Every configuration line supplied to a peer group definition is applied to each peer group member.

The only limitation in using peer groups is that outgoing policy (route filters) must be identical for every peer group member. This is because only a single UPDATE is generated for the peer group, which is duplicated for each member of the group.

Previous limitations prevented peer groups from spanning multiple IP subnets. For example, two peer group members could not exist on separate physical interfaces or different sub-interfaces. Other limitations included providing transit between peer group members, or from being used with route reflector clients. These limitations were removed with release 12.0 of IOS, which, when necessary, modifies the next hop address to a value appropriate for each peer group member.

Figure 11-20 *The Use of Peer Groups within a Network Architecture*

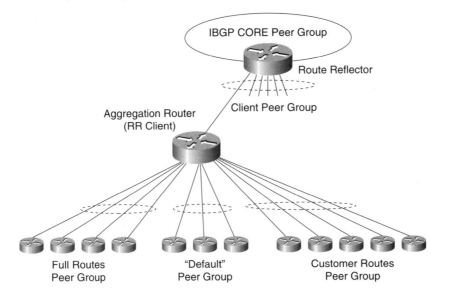

Unlike outgoing policy, incoming policy applied in the peer group definition may be overridden by applying a different policy in the individual neighbor configuration.

Large Network Configuration Issues

The default BGP behavior on Cisco routers may require fine-tuning for use in large networks. This section examines the motivation behind this tuning and how it is performed. This section first discusses BGP configuration commands that affect the overall behavior of BGP, and then explains commands that apply on a per-BGP-neighbor basis.

BGP Configuration Issues

IGP synchronization is enabled by default in the Cisco BGP implementation. This indicates that prefixes learned via IBGP are not advertised to EBGP neighbors until a corresponding prefix, derived from an IGP, appears in the routing table. This behavior ensures that the local AS does not offer transit to destinations until the routes for those destinations have been flooded through the local IGP. However, it is preferable to carry the large routes for external networks in IBGP rather than redistributing into the IGP. This removes the need for synchronization.

The default administrative distance for EBGP is 20. This may not suit all requirements because it basically indicates that routes learned from external sources (such as other ASs) can override those carried in the IGP of the local AS. This behavior is logical if all external routes are redistributed into the IGP, as may be the case if synchronization is enabled. However, if many transit routes are not carried in the IGP, you may want to apply **bgp distance** 200 200 200 to ensure that routes in the local IGP are always preferred over those learned from BGP.

The default router ID used by a Cisco router is the highest IP address assigned to any interface on the router. Available loopback interfaces are chosen before physical interfaces. You may wish to explicitly set this parameter using the **bgp router-id** *ip-address* BGP router configuration command.

Almost all BGP routers should perform classless routing. By default, Cisco IOS auto-summarizes subnets into their associated classful route. In almost all circumstances, it is appropriate to disable this behavior using the **no auto-summary** BGP router configuration command. Even if you require summarization of certain subnets, the BGP **aggregation** subcommand represents a far more flexible and intuitive means.

BGP dampening minimizes route instability in the Internet. Oscillating or "flapping" EBGP routes are penalized, and once a preconfigured suppress limit is reached, use and re-advertisement of the route will be suppressed.

Often, dampening is applied to peer networks, but not necessarily to customers. (Providers and large enterprises find that it pays to be more lenient with paying customers!) Dampening can be applied only on a per-router basis using the BGP subcommand **bgp dampening**. The default parameters for this command are satisfactory for most purposes.

If you plan to run an IGP such as IS-IS or OSPF in your network, you likely will choose to carry connected and static routes in the IGP rather than BGP. However, in the absence of an IGP, one alternative is to redistribute connected and static routes into BGP. The use of the **network** BGP router configuration command is recommended over the **redistribute** command for injecting routes into BGP. Even if connected and static routes usually do not suffer from the same instability issues as IGP routes, you may prefer to use the **network** command in all cases and avoid the **redistribute** command altogether.

If you do opt to use redistribution, the **default-metric** *number* BGP router command determines the BGP MED setting for the redistributed route if a direct substitution of the IGP metric value is not possible. The BGP MED value ranges from 0 to 4,294,967,295; so a direct substitution of the IGP metric is usually possible, and the default-metric is rarely used.

Neighbor Configuration Issues

There is very little overhead in establishing a peer group, even with only a single member. This approach makes it very easy to add members with identical outgoing policy to the group at a later stage. You may consider defining a peer group for all neighbors, even if the peer group membership consists of only one neighbor.

A description can be added to a peer group or an individual neighbor using the **neighbor** { *ip-address* | *peer-group-name* } **description** *text* command. Because you cannot store free-text comments in Cisco configurations, this is an ideal way to add documentation to a particular peering session.

Applying the **neighbor** { *ip-address* | *peer-group-name* } **next-hop-self** command to a neighbor or peer group ensures that all next hops for the EBGP-learned routes are set to the peering address for this session. As discussed in conjunction with the next hop attribute earlier in this chapter, this configuration command can obviate the need to carry external networks used for peering within your IGP, and ensure that you meet the peering policies of providers at public NAPs by removing any third-party next hops.

Using physical interface addresses for BGP peering purposes can reduce network reliability. If the physical interface goes down, any BGP sessions using the IP address of the interface as an endpoint will also be closed. Reliability can be increased by using the addresses of loopback interfaces instead of physical interfaces for peering purposes. *Loopback interfaces* are virtual interfaces on the router; they are always up, unless disabled by a software switch on the router.

IBGP sessions can be configured to use loopback addresses by using the **neighbor** { *ip-address* | *peer-group-name*] **update-source** loopback BGP router configuration command. It is highly recommended that you use this approach for IBGP.

For EBGP, the situation is not as critical because most peering is performed over a single physical link or LAN. However, if you wish to perform EBGP peering over redundant physical links, this can be achieved using **neighbor** { *ip-address* | *peer-group-name*} **ebgp-multi-hop** *[ttl]*. This BGP router-configuration command enables the establishment of EBGP peering to neighbors beyond a directly connected physical interface. The optional *ttl* sets the TTL of outgoing IP packets used in establishing the BGP session—this limits the number of router hops the EBGP session may traverse. If you use the command, the update source can be set to a loopback address as for IBGP peers; once again, this ensures that the peering session will survive the failure of physical infrastructure.

EBGP sessions are automatically reset if the physical interface over which the session is held goes down. In large networks, possibly containing many links that are not completely reliable (loss of carrier may occur for brief periods), you may wish to disable this behavior and opt for session-reset due to keepalive failure only. This is achieved using the **no bgp fast-external-fallover** BGP router command. The drawback of this command is that, in the event of sustained link outage, the convergence time on a new route will increase.

BGP will auto-negotiate version. However, to save any surprises (for example, because BGP versions before 3 were not classless), it is also wise to explicitly set the neighbor version to 4.

Finally, consider using passwords on all BGP sessions. This prevents the session from being established if the remote end does not have the same password configured. This also can provide increased protection from "hacker attacks" on BGP architecture. In addition, if you use different passwords for each neighbor, this can protect against accidental misconfiguration, such as applying the wrong IP address to a peer.

BGP Configuration Stencil for Large Networks

The following basic configuration summarizes the commentary of this section. It is not necessary to include the complete configuration as part of your default BGP configuration. You should study this section to see what is suitable for your environment:

```
interface loopback 0
ip address 1.0.0.1 255.255.255.255

router bgp 100
no synchronization
bgp router-id 1.0.0.1
no bgp fast-external-fallover
bgp log-neighbor-changes
bgp dampening
!
neighbor internal peer-group
neighbor internal description ibgp peers
neighbor internal update-source loopback0
neighbor internal next-hop-self
neighbor internal remote-as 100
neighbor internal version 4
neighbor internal password 7 03085A09
!
distance bgp 200 200 200
no auto-summary
```

A BGP Case Study

This case study examines the BGP architecture of a large network operated by a fictional Internet service provider, ISPnet. The large network includes many regional networks, each having the architecture shown in Figure 11-21.

Backbone routers core1 and core2 are IBGP peers with each other, and they are peers with other routers in the backbone. A peer group, *internal*, is defined for this peering.

A route-reflection hierarchy extends from routers core1 and core2, which form redundant reflectors for a cluster containing dist1 and dist2. Similarly, dist1 and dist2 are redundant route reflectors for a cluster containing clients access1, access2, and dist3. Dist3 is a single route reflector for a cluster containing access3 and access4.

In all cases, the peer group *rr-client* is configured to serve route reflector clients. The clients themselves use the *internal* peer group that also is used for backbone peering. Both the *internal* and *rr-client* peer groups are configured to use BGP version 4, require passwords, send communities, use a loopback interface for peering, and set the next hop to the local peering address for all EBGP-derived routes.

Figure 11-21 *ISPnet BGP Architecture*

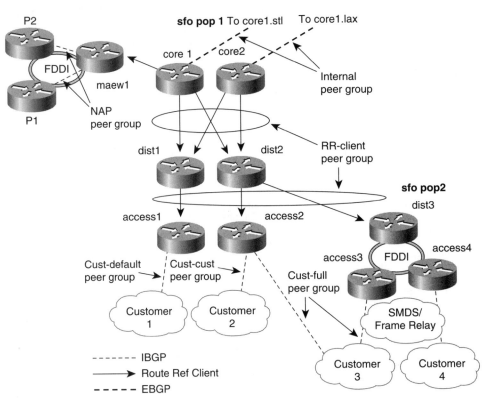

A third peer group, *nap*, is used on router maew1 for peering with other service providers at a regional public exchange. This peer group uses the maximum-prefix feature to limit the number of routes accepted from any peer, thereby providing some level of protection against configuration errors in peer networks. ISPnet provides transit to other service providers at the NAP, and third-party next hops are removed by applying next-hop self. BGP version is set to 4 for the entire group, whereas passwords are set on a per-neighbor basis.

Three peer groups are defined for use on EBGP sessions with customers. These are *cust-full, cust-cust,* and *cust-default*. They send full Internet, ISPnet only, and default-only routes, respectively. Outbound routes are selected on the basis of BGP community filters in each case. Each customer peer group also features inbound route filtering that accepts routes agreed upon between ISPnet and each individual customer. Passwords and descriptions are applied on a per-neighbor basis.

ISPnet also uses BGP to support quality of service policy propagation and multicast routing. These issues are addressed in subsequent chapters, but you will revisit ISPnet in Chapter 16 and examine BGP configuration, interior and multicast routing, quality of service, and network management.

Summary

BGP is a very sophisticated and highly scalable protocol that has been used in its current version for Internet core routing since 1993. Requirements of the Internet core have led to a very stable and feature-rich implementation. BGP comes in two flavors: EBGP, for routing between autonomous systems (interdomain routing); and IBGP, for routing within autonomous systems (intradomain routing).

Unlike the majority of IGPs, BGP topologies are usually manually configured. Moreover, because BGP is normally used to implement the network operator's routing policy, configurations can be relatively complex. Policies are most often based on a number of attributes that BGP associates with network routes. These attributes may be localized to a single autonomous system, or may be used between autonomous systems.

In most cases, BGP is used in conjunction with an IGP to provide routers at critical points in a large-scale network with a cohesive view of interior and exterior routing. Features such as route reflection, confederations, and peer groups enhance the scalability of the protocol, as well as reduce the effort required to configure routers.

This chapter has examined some general ideas for configuring BGP in a way that is both scalable and reliable, as well as one that minimizes configuration effort. These ideas will be followed in practice within the case studies of Chapter 16.

Review Questions

1 How and why is IBGP used for interdomain routing?

2 Is it possible to have two BGP sessions between routers for redundancy?

3 How many BGP sessions, routes, and updates/per second can a router handle?

Answers:

1 Some early deployments of BGP redistributed routes learned via EBGP into the IGP (OSPF/IS-IS), and carried the routes via both the IBGP and IGP. A border router would not readvertise routes learned via IBGP until the same routes were visible in the IGP—that is, until IBGP and the IGP were synchronized. However, commonly used IGPs do not scale particularly well to tens of thousands of routes, so this approach is now rarely used. Instead, the IGP carries just enough information (generally, all the links internal to the autonomous system) to provide a route to all BGP next hops. Synchronization is disabled via the BGP subcommand **no bgp synchronization**.

2 Provided that two different IP addresses are used for the sessions, yes. Note that a router will accommodate only a single remote-AS configuration line for any neighbor IP address. However, this might not be an effective method for achieving redundancy. A more successful approach is to peer using loopback addresses. If the session is EBGP, you will need to add the **neighbor <remote-ip> ebg-multihop** BGP neighbor subcommand.

3 There is no simple answer to this question. Cisco continually tunes the number of configurable sessions, memory utilization, and update processing speed to handle increasing customer requirements. Performance will depend on the number and complexity of attributes associated with each BGP route. At the time of this writing, applications requiring the configuration of hundreds of peers, hundreds of thousands of BGP paths, and hundreds to thousands of updates per second are emerging.

Bear in mind, however, that performance in these areas will be strongly influenced by the amount of memory—and particularly the Cisco platform—you are using. High-end platforms, such as the 7500 series with RSP2 or RSP4 processors, or GSRs, are required for the most demanding ISP backbone applications. For simple BGP connectivity to an ISP, however, lower-end access routers will suffice, particularly if there is no requirement for receiving full Internet routes.

This chapter introduces techniques for migrating networks from one routing protocol to another. We also explain methods for scaling the protocol that you may be currently using by repairing damaged architectures.

Most network problems are not related to protocols—instead, they are related to poor planning and failing to anticipate network growth. This chapter discusses the possible reasons for migrations, and introduces techniques to ensure problem-free classless protocols.

We also provide configuration examples of migration between routing protocols, as well as configuration examples of scaling the routing protocols that you may be using currently. Specifically, the following issues are addressed:

Exchanging protocols   This discussion includes reasons for exchanging the routing protocol. If, for example, you have a classful protocol that does not support VLSM, another protocol may operate more successfully in your network.

Migrating routing protocols   This section discusses migration from classful distance vector to classless advanced distance-vector protocols, as well as migrating from classful distance-vector to link-state protocols. Another common issue involves migrating customer routes in an ISP network from IGP into BGP.

## CHAPTER 12

Migration Techniques

Exchanging Protocols

With the introduction of classless routing, it was not possible for classful routing protocols such as RIP and IGRP to understand entire routing tables. In some cases, routing packets to destinations within the same major network is no longer possible. Therefore, it may become necessary to exchange one protocol for another.

Take, for example, the case of the Internet making use of class A networks between multiple customers. As discussed in Chapter 6, "Routing Information Protocol," RIPV1 will not accept routes across a different major network for its own connected network, and therefore will not route packets to that destination.

Now, consider the network shown in Figure 12-1: Y.com. The Y.com network owns part of the class A network space. In this case, the 20.10.0.0/16 section of this same major network space is given to another enterprise: X.com. ISP will either run BGP with X.com or will use a static route for the routes of X.com. Similarly, X.com will run BGP with the ISP or will run a static default route (0.0.0.0/0) toward the ISP.

If Y.com runs BGP with ISP, it will learn about network 20.20.0.0/16 from ISP. Even if Y.com wants to redistribute this BGP route into RIP, it cannot because RIPV1 will not redistribute 20.20.0.0/16 BGP. This is because one of the redistributing router's interfaces is connected to the same major network. This behavior indicates a discontiguous network and is not supported by RIPV1, which will cause problems for Y.com when it attempts to route packets to parts of the class A that it owns.

In the second situation, Y.com is not running a BGP with ISP, and has a default route toward the ISP. Even then, with classful protocols such as RIPV1 and IGRP, the router will not route a packet toward a default router for a subnet of its own connected network. In this case, if router R1 receives a packet that must be routed to 20.20.1.1, R1 checks its routing table because this subnet is not part of the range it owns. R1 will not have the route to 20.20.1.1 in its table, so it will try to find the next feasible route—in this case, it is 0.0.0.0/0.

In a classless protocol, 0.0.0.0/0 is considered a route to all destinations. In classful protocols, however, it is not considered a route to all destinations, except for subnets of the connected networks. This is because all the subnets of the connected network should be contained within the routing table. In this case, R1 will not route packets to 20.20.1.1 using the default route, and will drop the packet. Therefore, connectivity will not take place between Y.com and X.com.

Figure 12-1 *Parts of the Class A Network Split between Two Organizations—a Problem for RIP with Discontiguous Networks*

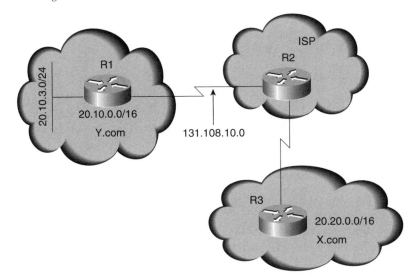

| TIP | You can use the **ip classless** command in the Cisco router to overcome this problem, but if you are receiving parts of 20.0.0.0/8 networks from multiple points, you cannot route to one of the parts of the 20.0.0.0 network. Put simply, you can avoid this problem by using Cisco IOS to some extent, but you cannot avoid the shortcomings of the protocol completely. |

Another reason for migrating classful protocols such as RIP or IGRP involves support for VLSM. As the network grows, administrators begin to realize that wasting address space merely to accommodate the protocol becomes a serious issue.

RIP and IGRP do not support VLSM, so all the interfaces included in the same major network should have the same mask. When connecting a large number of hosts in broadcast media for a class B network, you would mask with 24. For point-to-point connections, you might use a 30-bit mask to use the same subnet for 64 point-to-point connections.

Another reason for migrating to another protocol is faster convergence. Again, the older classful protocols are periodic, which means that you must put the route in holddown and flush states. In the worst case, this could take minutes to converge. Because of the rapid pace of the Internet, this sluggish convergence is unacceptable.

Classful protocols also lack the capability to summarize within the network. The administrator, for example, might want to summarize some routes within a region to diminish the size of the routing table.

NOTE	Essentially, migration of routing protocols is carried out to improve classfulness; and to provide support for VLSM, support for discontiguous networks, scaling, and faster convergence.

The third situation relates to the scaling protocols, but more in terms of the ISP space rather than the enterprise space. ISPs often mistakenly advertise customer routes into the IGP because ISPs usually undergo tremendous growth. When the ISP begins redistribution, its customer base is modest in size. However, the customer routes increase as the business expands. Before long, an ISP could have 5,000 to 6,000 customer routes floating in its IGP, so if a problem occurs on the customer networks, it can wreak havoc on the ISP networks. These issues are discussed in detail in the next section.

Migration of Routing Protocols

Routing-protocol migration can be divided into three categories:

- Migrating from a classful distance-vector protocol, such as RIP or IGRP, to a classless link-state protocol, such as OSPF or IS-IS
- Migrating a classful distance vector to a classless advanced distance vector, such as Enhanced IGRP
- Migrating customer routes from the IGP of an ISP to BGP

Each of these migration scenarios is discussed fully in the following sections.

Classful Distance-Vector to Link-State Protocol

For the sake of this discussion, imagine you are migrating from IGRP, which is the classful distance-vector protocol, to a link-state protocol, OSPF. Remember that both OSPF and IS-IS require hierarchy. The network in Figure 12-2 shows that no hierarchy exists in the network in question, so you must change not only the network protocol, but also the physical circuit to accommodate the hierarchical structure.

While attempting to implement a new protocol to accommodate the defective architecture that you are currently using, you encounter difficulty in fitting them together. This complication prevents you from achieving your goal of improving the network so that it will scale to the next level.

When dealing with large network outages caused by routing protocols, these obstacles are almost always related to incorrect design decisions. For example, administrators may have forced a protocol to accommodate their network design, rather than modifying the network to accommodate the routing protocol.

If you tried to implement OSPF on the network shown in Figure 12-2 merely to accommodate the defective design, you would encounter serious difficulty. You may even blame the protocol for your own mistakes! To ensure that your network scales properly, you should consider making drastic changes to the physical topology to accommodate OSPF.

Figure 12-2   *Non-Hierarchical Network Architecture*

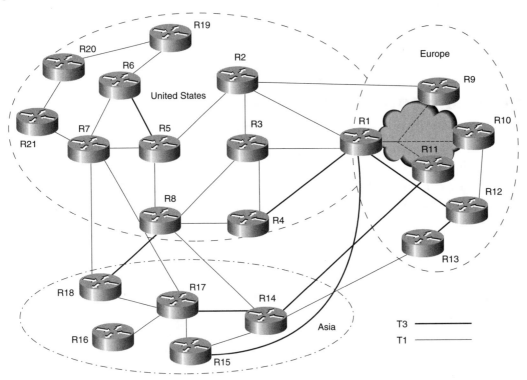

The first and foremost step in accommodating OSPF is to define the backbone. As mentioned in the OSPF discussion in Chapter 9, "Open Shortest Path First," all traffic outside an area must pass through a backbone area, also called area 0.

Consider the network in Figure 12-2 and select the backbone routers. Backbone routers are chosen on the basis of CPU power, memory, and the points in the network that the backbone connects. The chosen routers should be capable of dividing the network into areas without relocating many of the circuits.

The second step is to examine the backdoor connections between routers that destroy the hierarchy of the network, such as connections between R14 and R13. In some cases, the redundancy must be adjusted for the network to scale properly.

Migration of this network is a three-step process:

1 First, prepare the router for OSPF. Recall from Chapter 9 that OSPF builds the database in addition to the routing table, unlike traditional distance vectors. Ensure that the routers already running with borderline memory are upgraded to accommodate the OSPF database.

2 Next, determine how soon you can move circuits to accommodate the OSPF hierarchy. If the wait is long, you can begin planning the OSPF configurations and allow it to run parallel to IGRP. By running OSPF parallel to IGRP, the network's current routing policies will not be affected—even if the OSPF is not configured according to the protocol requirements.

   The network does not see changes in the routing table because of the administrative distance of IGRP (100) and OSPF (110). In addition, unlike distance-vector protocols, link-state protocols do not receive information from the routing table. Therefore, if the information is not contained in the table, it would not be sent to the neighbors.

3 Link-state protocols build the routing table with information from the database. This allows you to run the link-state protocol and all the necessary information in the database. When you decide to change the routing protocol, the distance vector can be removed. This way, the information in the database is the only information included in the routing table.

Changes to European Routers

Try the first step listed previously, and begin identifying your backbone routers. Decide which circuits you must relocate. For example, as in Figure 12-3, if you are reconfiguring a network in Europe, router R1 is a perfect candidate for use as a backbone router because it has a connection to the United States and a connection to most of the routers in Europe. Also, if R1 is the area border router (ABR), you can summarize all the specific routes at R1 and send a single route to the United States, provided that you have a solid addressing scheme.

NOTE By configuring router R1 as the only backbone router, you will remove the redundancy and create a single point of failure. Remember that all traffic must pass through the backbone area for destinations outside the area. If you retain R1 as the backbone router, therefore, Europe would be disconnected when R1 fails. For this reason, you should maintain at least two area border routers in the network for redundancy.

The next step is to choose another ABR. There are three candidates—R13, R11, and R9. These are possible choices because they have links to other regions. For example, R9 is linked to the United States, and both R13 and R11 have connections to Asia. If you must choose between them, R13 is a better choice, because it has higher-speed connections within its own area—R11 is only connected via the Frame Relay to one hub router.

Now that you have selected the ABRs, you need to move only one circuit, which is the one from R14 to R11 to R14 to R9, as shown in Figure 12-3. In this new setup, the circuit was moved from R11 to R9, so now you have three ABRs in Europe (R9, R1, and R13). If possible, move the high speed circuit on R12 to R13 so that both ABRs R1 and R13 have a direct connection.

Figure 12-3 *Area Border Routers after Moving Circuits*

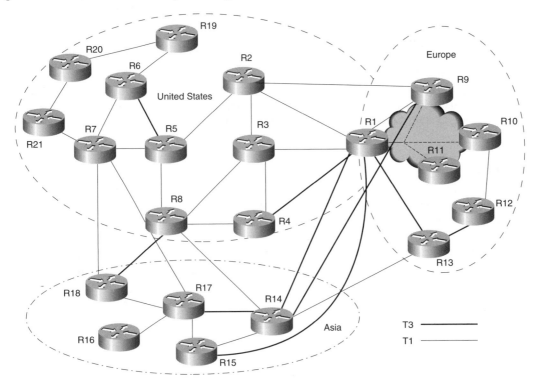

Modifying U.S. Routers

To modify U.S. routers, configure R2, R3, and R4 as the backbone routers because they are connected to the backbone routers defined in Europe. At this point, it is a good idea to move one of the three U.S. circuits from R1 to R13, so that it has a connection to the United States.

If R1 goes down, there is only one connection to the United States left, via R9. The link between R9 and R2 is slow, so losing R1 means that all high-speed links to the United States are lost. If possible, move the high-speed circuits from R4 to R13 instead of R1, so that all three ABRs have a high-speed connection to the United States.

Now, examine the routers in Figure 12-3 that connect the United States and Asia: R7, R8, and R4. Because these have connections to Asia, they could be used as the ABRs. However, selecting these routers as the ABRs creates the problem of having to relocate all the connections on R14 and R15 into Europe to these routers. If R7 and R8, for example, become the ABRs, and if R14 and R17 become pure area routes, R17, R14, and R18 cannot connect to multiple areas because they would have to become area border routers. For this reason, it is better to choose R14, R18, and R17 as the ABRs for Asia.

Next, create a non-zero area within the United States as well, assigning R5 and R7 as ABRs. You define R7 as an ABR because it is able to specifically define multiple areas. This way, you can clearly mark the area boundaries, as shown in Figure 12-4. If you choose not to make R7 an ABR, you have to move its circuits to Asia, to any of the area 0 routers.

The reason you should select R5 as an ABR is its location—it lies in the path between R8 and R7. If R7 goes down, routers R19, R20, and R21 are cut off. Now, the backbone area would be similar to the network shown in Figure 12-4.

At this point, you might ask: Why not configure the routers in the United States to be the backbone (area 0) routers, and use the routers in Europe and Asia only as regular area routers? The answer is that you would need to sever the connections between routers in Europe and Asia because these now have become pure area routers. All traffic between Europe and Asia will have to pass through the United States and cannot reach each other directly. This causes the core to become U.S.-centric.

Therefore, each region includes its own ABRs, minimizing the number of routing protocol packets. The ABR from each region then will summarize all the regional routes into one or two routes. As a result, regional flaps are not sent across, which reduces routing traffic.

Figure 12-4 *Area Border Routers and Backbone Routers Defined*

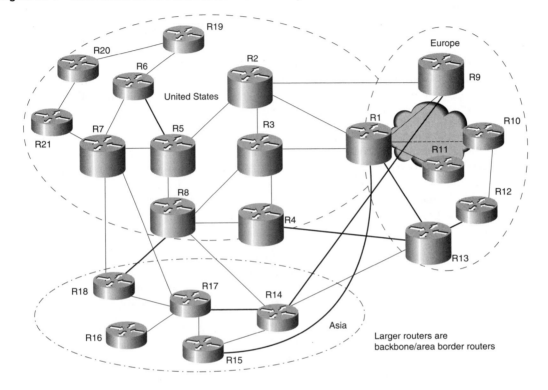

Modifying Asian Routers

Now, you can focus your attention on the routers in Asia. Except for one remaining circuit that should be relocated from R15 to R17 or R18, everything else is well-defined. The circuit could be moved from R17 to R1, but you do not want to move this circuit to R14 because it already has a high-speed link from Europe to Asia. Losing R14 would mean that Asia loses all its high-speed links to Europe. If you move the R15 circuit to R17, it is beneficial to move an R14 circuit to R18 for complete redundancy on area border routers.

The ABRs for Asia are now R14, R17, and R18; and the circuit is moved from R15 to R17. This new topology is shown in Figure 12-5. This network is now ready for OSPF without significantly altering the existing network.

Figure 12-5   *Area Border Routes and Backbone Routers Defined for Each Region*

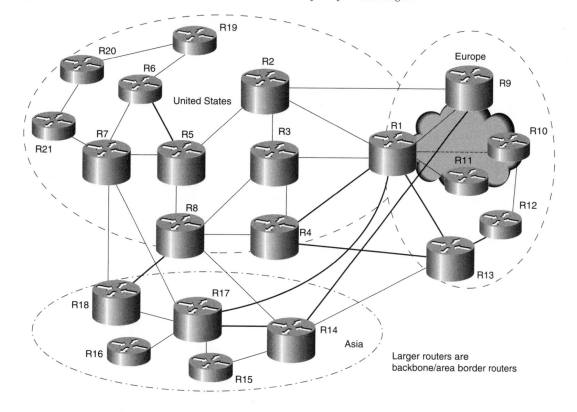

These regional routers have selected ABRs that will accommodate growth in each of the three regions: Asia, Europe, and the United States. If a local area within each region grows increasingly larger, a new area could be created that would simply need to connect to each regional ABR. It should be noted, however, that in practice, the selection of routers for an ABR is not as rigid as we have presented it in the examples. We have illustrated it this way for the expediency of accommodating the links illustrated in the figure.

Configuration Changes

When migrating from IGRP to OSPF, you should be aware of configuration changes. One of the benefits of migrating from distance-vector to link-state protocols in the Cisco environment is that you can make use of the administrative distance feature.

Administrative distance (AD) establishes the believability of a route between routing protocols. If the same route is learned via OSPF and via IGRP, the router compares the administrative distances and installs the route with the lower administrative distance. In rating AD, the higher the value, the lower its believability status. The default administrative distance for IGRP in Cisco is 100; for OSPF, it is 110.

Link-state protocols, unlike distance-vector protocols, do not build routing information from routing tables. Instead, they build routing tables from the database, which is built on the information received from the neighbor. In a link-state advertisement, a router sends information about its connected interfaces so that all the routers within an area have complete information about the entire topology.

If a situation occurs in which the router runs multiple routing protocols simultaneously, such as IGRP and OSPF, and the router installs the IGRP route in the routing table because of its lower administrative distance, the router will continue to maintain information about that route in its link-state database.

Therefore, after you have configured OSPF on the routers, you can verify whether all the routes are located in the database, even if that route already exists in the routing table via IGRP.

During OSPF configuration, the network continues to function properly because the current routing protocol (IGRP) has not been changed. It is unnecessary to change the administrative distance because IGRP already has the lower AD. After you are satisfied with the network's setup and you have ensured that all routes have been added to the OSPF database, you can easily remove IGRP from the routers, and allow OSPF to install the same routes in the routing table without disrupting service.

Consider router R1 for this example. The router configurations are shown prior to the OSPF changes:

```
Current configuration:
!
version 11.1
!
hostname C7000-2B
!
clock timezone utc 0
enable password cisco
!
ip subnet-zero
!
interface Serial2/0
description Connection to R12
 ip address 10.11.4.2 255.255.255.0
 bandwidth 4500000
```

```
!
interface Serial2/1
description Connection to R2
 ip address 10.32.1.5 255.255.255.0
bandwidth 4500000
!
interface Serial2/2
 no ip address
 encapsulation frame-relay
 no cdp enable
!
interface Serial2/2.1 point-to-point
description Connection to R9
 ip address 10.11.1.1 255.255.255.0
 bandwidth 150000
 no cdp enable
 frame-relay interface-dlci 100
!
interface Serial2/2.2 point-to-point
description Connection to R10
 ip address 10.11.2.5 255.255.255.0
 bandwidth 150000
 no cdp enable
 frame-relay interface-dlci 101
!
interface Serial2/2.3 point-to-point
description Connection to R11
 ip address 10.11.3.1 255.255.255.0
 bandwidth 150000
 no cdp enable
 frame-relay interface-dlci 102


interface Serial2/3
description Connection to R3
 ip address 10.32.2.1 255.255.255.0
bandwidth 4500000

interface Serial 4/1
description Connection to R17
 ip address 10.32.4.1 255.255.255.0
bandwidth 4500000

!
interface Fddi5/0
 ip address 10.11.5.1 255.255.255.0
 ip accounting output-packets
 no keepalive
!
router igrp 1
 network 10.0.0.0
!

logging buffered
logging console warnings
```

```
snmp-server community public RO
line con 0
 exec-timeout 0 0
line aux 0
line vty 0 4
 password ww
 login
!
ntp clock-period 17180006
ntp server 30.1.1.2 prefer
ntp server 10.1.1.2
end
```

You can now enable OSPF without altering the addressing and topology. The important point to remember is that OSPF requires area addressing, and that each interface must be defined in a particular area.

TIP

One common mistake that is often committed when OSPF is defined in an area is to simply configure all other interfaces into area 0 by defining the **0.0.0.0 255.255.255.255 area 0** command. This is unwise—this configuration results in misdirected interfaces. New interfaces added to this router will automatically enter area 0, even if you want them in another area. Any OSPF statement added after the **0.0.0.0 255.255.255.255** command will not take effect. For this reason, always be sure to enable OSPF with specific commands rather than general ones.

The OSPF configuration is the following:

```
route ospf 1
network 10.11.2.0 0.0.1.255 area 1
network 10.11.5.0 0.0.0.255 area 1
network 10.11.1.0 0.0.0.255 area 1
network 10.11.4.0 0.0.0.255 area 0

network 10.32.1.0 0.0.0.255 area 0
network 10.32.2.0 0.0.1.255 area 0
network 10.32.4.0 0.0.0.255 area 0
```

The first network statement places interface serial 2/2.2 and serial 2/2.3 into area 1. The FDDI interface is also in area 1. All other interfaces are in area 0. Configurations should follow the same process throughout the network. After OSPF is properly configured, the OSPF network should resemble the one shown in Figure 12-6.

Figure 12-6   *Area Set Up with OSPF*

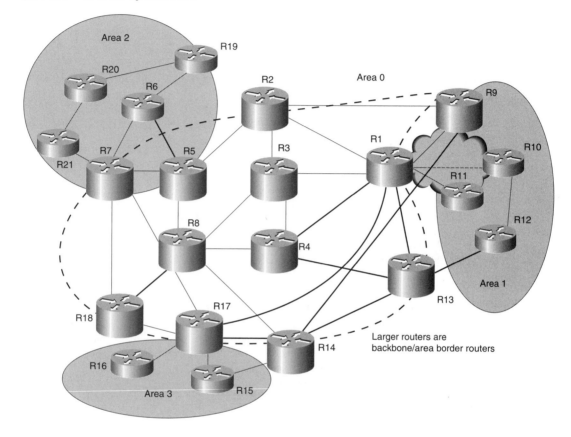

Now, the areas are well-defined, and each region will be able to grow. After you have introduced OSPF, you can configure VLSM and send one summary from each region. When the configurations for each region are complete, you can determine whether the LSAs for each route have been included in the database. VLSM routes would be seen as OSPF routes only.

You can accomplish this by adding a **show ip route** command, and then add a **sh ip ospf data {router, network, summary}** command. The **sh ip ospf data router** command should be used in an area in which the database can be viewed, and loopback addresses or point-to-point links can be located. Next, examine the network LSA for all the broadcast networks within the area. Finally, search for summary LSAs for all the interarea routes.

The following shows a sample output of the **sh ip ospf data** router 10.11.25.1. This command was initiated on R1 for R3:

```
Router Link States (Area 1)

   Routing Bit Set on this LSA
   LS age: 950
   Options: (No TOS-capability, DC)
   LS Type: Router Links
   Link State ID: 10.11.25.1
   Advertising Router: 10.11.25.1
   LS Seq Number: 8000102E
   Checksum: 0xFB69
   Length: 120
   Area Border Router
    Number of Links: 2


      Link connected to: another Router (point-to-point)
       (Link ID) Neighboring Router ID: 10.11.26.1
       (Link Data) Router Interface address: 10.11.25.1
        Number of TOS metrics: 0
         TOS 0 Metrics: 64

      Link connected to: a Stub Network
       (Link ID) Network/subnet number: 10.11.25.0
       (Link Data) Network Mask: 255.255.255.0
        Number of TOS metrics: 0
         TOS 0 Metrics: 64

      Link connected to: another Router (point-to-point)
       (Link ID) Neighboring Router ID: 10.11.4.1
       (Link Data) Router Interface address: 10.11.22.1
   Number of TOS metrics: 0
          TOS 0 Metrics: 64

      Link connected to: a Stub Network
       (Link ID) Network/subnet number: 10.11.22.0
   (Link Data) Network Mask: 255.255.255.0
         Number of TOS metrics: 0
            TOS 0 Metrics: 64
```

Removing IGRP

The next step in this process is to remove IGRP from the routing tables. The most manageable place to begin removing it is at the edges. For example, R20 and R21 would be a logical starting point. It is then necessary to set IGRP holddown to 0, and set flush and invalid to 1. As soon as you remove IGRP from R13, you will receive a flash update. Then, you can install the OSPF route in the network.

After OSPF is installed, ensure that all the routes in the network have been installed as OSPF and see whether there is full connectivity. Then, begin removing IGRP, one router at a time, and allow OSPF into the routing table.

Introducing VLSM

If the protocol migration is successful, you can introduce VLSM into the network. All serial point-to-point links should be moved from /24 mask to /30 mask to liberate address space. This is accomplished by changing the address, either via the console or dial-in aux port, if direct console access or aux access is available through dial-in. Then, telnet to the remote end, in which the address mask is being changed, to an interface that will be left unchanged. If the router has only one interface, leaving no other alternatives, you would Telnet to the address that is changing. The connection would be lost, but you can Telnet in again after you change the local address.

For example, suppose that you want to change the address mask pair so that all the routers in the serial link are part of the same subnet within the area. To change the address of the link between R1 and R10, if R10 does not have console connection, you can telnet to the IP address 10.11.25.2, as is the case with the router connection to R12. Now you can change the IP address to 10.11.2.6 255.255.255.252. Then, change R1's IP address to 10.11.2.5 255.255.255.252. You would do the same for all the routers that have point-to-point connections, then bring all the routers in area 1 into part of the same subnet with /30 mask.

TIP	In cases such as R16, a particular problem occurs in which you lose the connection. If R16 does not have a console connection, the only option is to configure it via the serial link. First, Telnet to the address of the serial link. After you press the Enter key on R16 with the new address, you will lose the connection. You can then Telnet to the new address to restore the connection. Also, remember that when you change the subnet mask of a serial link, the OSPF adjacency is lost until both sides of the link are configured with the same mask.

Suppose in the previous example that the classful distance-vector protocol was RIP instead of IGRP. The only difference would be the administrative distance. For RIP to remain the primary routing protocol while you are configuring OSPF on the network, the administrative distance of RIP must be decreased, or the administrative distance of OSPF must be increased.

The best course of action is to decrease the administrative distance for RIP because RIP ultimately will be removed. In theory, you would not necessarily need to change the administrative distance for OSPF—it is simply easier to continue using the default administrative distance.

In this instance, you would consider migration from IGRP into Enhanced IGRP, and then consider migration from RIP into Enhanced IGRP. First, we will discuss IGRP and Enhanced IGRP in the same autonomous system.

Enhanced IGRP is an advanced distance-vector protocol that implements similar composite metric formats used by IGRP. Enhanced IGRP provides better convergence by employing DUAL. When Enhanced IGRP and IGRP are enabled within the same autonomous system, the redistribution is automatic.

Classful Distance-Vector to Classless Distance-Vector Protocol (IGRP to Enhanced IGRP)

In the case of Enhanced IGRP/IGRP within the same autonomous system, the redistribution is automatic. Enhanced IGRP has two numeric distance values that distinguish between internal and external routes. Any route that has been redistributed into Enhanced IGRP via any other routing domain or routing protocols is considered external and has an administrative distance of 170. Any network within the Enhanced IGRP domain has a distance of 90. The administrative distance of IGRP is 100, regardless of the origin.

Enhanced IGRP is designed to work in conjunction with IGRP. If both IGRP and Enhanced IGRP are configured in the same autonomous system, the protocols are designed to exchange routes without any additional configurations. The calculation of the composite metric is identical between Enhanced IGRP and IGRP, as shown here:

```
EIGRP metric = 256 * IGRP metric.
```

While redistributing IGRP to Enhanced IGRP within the same autonomous system, the metric is converted from one domain to another, and this converted metric is carried to the other domain. Suppose you have an IGRP metric of 8,976 that is converted to an Enhanced IGRP metric. You would have the following:

```
EIGRP = 8976 * 256 = 2297856.
```

The Enhanced IGRP topology for the route appears in the topology table with the converted metric.

Administrative distance also must be considered. If the source of the route is not Enhanced IGRP, it should be considered an external route with an administrative distance of 170, which could result in a loop.

If an external Enhanced IGRP route is redistributed into IGRP, the original Enhanced IGRP could be overwritten by IGRP, based solely on the administrative distance. Fortunately, the routing decision is based solely on composite metrics; the router ignores the administrative distance and follows the neighbor that offers the best composite metric by each domain. This is true only with external Enhanced IGRP versus IGRP. If internal Enhanced IGRP is compared with IGRP, internal Enhanced IGRP still wins, based on the administrative distance.

For example, take the network 10.10.10.0/24 advertised by IGRP. The metric is 9,076. By adding your own metric, the metric becomes 9,139. When ported to Enhanced IGRP, the metric becomes 2,339,584. The Enhanced IGRP metric appears to be significantly higher than the IGRP metric. The router performs an internal metric conversion, and then compares the two; otherwise, the Enhanced IGRP metric will always be 256 times larger than the IGRP metric.

When both protocols advertise the same route, and both are identical after metric conversion, the external Enhanced IGRP route is preferred over IGRP. In short, Enhanced IGRP is designed so that loops are not created when the network is converted from IGRP to the same Enhanced IGRP autonomous system.

Classful Distance Vector to Classless Distance-Vector Protocol (RIP to Enhanced IGRP)

Migrating from RIP to Enhanced IGRP requires careful planning because there is a possibility of routing loops and because metric conversion must be considered. For example, in the network shown in Figure 12-2, the customer does not want to create hierarchy in the physical topology to accommodate OSPF. However, without hierarchy, OSPF cannot be implemented because of scaling issues.

In this case, the only other option is Enhanced IGRP. As with any other routing protocol, Enhanced IGRP has limitations—routing protocols cannot repair a faulty design. Hierarchy in addressing is equally important to Enhanced IGRP as it is to OSPF and IS-IS. Although the physical hierarchy is not a strict requirement for Enhanced IGRP, it is strongly advised. Summarization of routes defines the query boundaries, and query scoping is very critical to Enhanced IGRP.

It is important to consider that physical topologies may create routing loops with redistribution. It is always wise to begin at the edges of the network when performing the redistribution and migration. In this case, you would begin at the edge routers in the United States region. Referring to Figure 12-2, you can run both RIP and Enhanced IGRP initially on routers R19 and R20. R19 will receive all routes of the connected interfaces of R20 via Enhanced IGRP and will receive all routes for other destinations via RIP.

As a result, R19 will not advertise R20 connected routes via RIP because of a lack of redistribution between the protocols. The redundant paths via R19 would be lost because R6 does not recognize R20 from R19 via RIP. If the link between R21 and R7 fails, R20 will be severed from the rest of the network. Although the physical connectivity remains via R19, routes are no longer learned via R19.

Therefore, it is important that a few routers be identified within the region, and these should be migrated with minimal impact. In this case, try routers R7, R6, R19, R20, and R21 for the first cut. You can begin to enable Enhanced IGRP on all the routers. First enable Enhanced IGRP at the redistributing routers, R7 and R6. The next step is to enable passive RIP between R6 and R7 to block unnecessary RIP updates between them. Begin redistribution between RIP and Enhanced IGRP. Otherwise, the network could become partitioned between the protocols, and you would not be able to reach destinations between the two domains.

Configurations on R7 or R6 are as follows:

```
router eigrp 109
network 10.0.0.0
redistribute rip
default-metric 15000 10000 0 1 1


router rip
network 10.0.0.0
redistribute eigrp 109
default-metric 2
```

Next, consider the **default-metric** commands under both routing protocols. Because RIP and Enhanced IGRP have different metrics, the protocols cannot port the metric value after the metric is translated. For the purpose of redistribution, you can enter the redistributed metric into Enhanced IGRP with a bandwidth of 15,000 and a delay of 10,000. Because Enhanced IGRP uses only the lowest bandwidth and composite delay when calculating routes to a destination, correct bandwidth and delay values are a good practice.

To translate the Enhanced IGRP metric into RIP, the same problem is encountered. Usually, Enhanced IGRP metrics are in a numeric value of 1,000. As you may recall, any value in RIP higher than 15 is unreachable, so when redistributing other protocols into RIP, you must assign a default metric—in this case, it was a metric of 2. Now, all the Enhanced IGRP routes would be redistributed into RIP with a hop count of 2.

After redistribution of the routing protocols is complete, you must ensure that a physical loop does not cause routing loops. Study the address in Figure 12-7, and then consider the connections of these five routers.

Figure 12-7 identifies the two routing domains. All the routes within the Enhanced IGRP domains would be learned via R6 and R7. Both R6 and R7 are responsible for the redistribution of routes. You can enable both RIP and Enhanced IGRP on the link between R7 and R6.

Figure 12-7   *Redistribution between Enhanced IGRP and RIP, Causing Routing Loops*

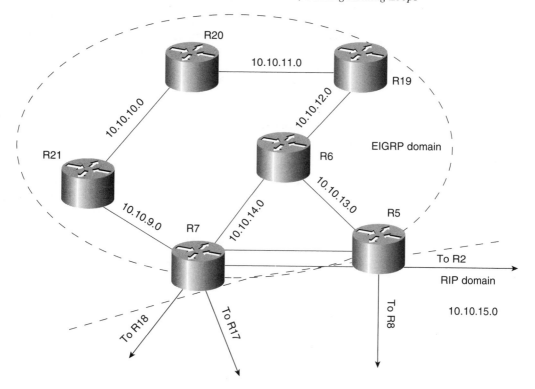

Notice that one of the routes learned from the Enhanced IGRP domain is redistributed into RIP. The subnet 10.10.10.0 is redistributed by both R7 and R6 into RIP. R5 will learn the route to network 10.10.10.0 via both R6 and R7 with a hop count of two. As you can see from the configuration, all Enhanced IGRP routes are redistributed into RIP with a default metric of two.

As shown in Figure 12-7, the network has a physical loop. R7 relearns its own advertised Enhanced IGRP network from R18 and R17 via RIP. R7 had originally learned these networks via internal Enhanced IGRP, so it will ignore the RIP-learned routes looping back from R18 and R17. Because of the lower administrative distance of 90 (Enhanced IGRP internal) versus 120 (RIP), R7 prefers internal Enhanced IGRP learned routes over RIP routes.

Next, examine the RIP domain-originated routes looping back into the Enhanced IGRP domain. All RIP routes would be redistributed by R7 and R6 into the Enhanced IGRP domain as external. All external routes in Enhanced IGRP have an administrative distance of 170, so when the RIP domain-originated route is learned by R7 or R6, it will be compared against the Enhanced IGRP external route.

In this case, the original RIP route would be preferred because of the lower administrative distance: 120 (RIP) versus 170 (external Enhanced IGRP). For example, when R7 learns a route for a subnet whose origin was RIP domain via R21 (which is in the Enhanced IGRP domain), it compares the original RIP received from R18 or R17 with the one it has received from R21. The route received from R18 and R17 has an administrative distance of 120 (RIP), versus the external Enhanced IGRP distance of 170. In this case, RIP has a lower administrative distance, so R7 would install the route received via RIP.

A routing loop can occur when the route-originating protocol has a higher administrative distance than the redistributing protocol. For example, if router R20 in Figure 12-7 was sending R7 or R6 an external Enhanced IGRP route that it had learned from some other protocol, this would create a loop.

Originally, R7 would have learned the route via Enhanced IGRP external, and then the physical loop would have learned the same route via RIP. R7 redistributes the external Enhanced IGRP route into RIP, and then learns the same route via RIP from R17 or R18. At this point, R7 compares the administrative distance of its original Enhanced IGRP route with the RIP route, installs the RIP route, and removes the original Enhanced IGRP external route. To avoid situations like this, install a distribute list under the RIP process so that it will not accept any Enhanced IGRP external routes via RIP domain routers. Now, both R7 and R6 will not accept routes that can cause routing loops.

The configuration is the following:

```
router rip
network 10.0.0.0
distribute-list 1 in
```

Distribute-list 1 defines the networks that you do not want to accept via the RIP process.

Migrating Customer Routes from IGP to BGP

One of the common problems on the ISP side of networks is scaling IGPs. Generally, when an ISP assigns addresses to customers and activates the customer connections, it connects these customers via static routes. Customers have a single attached connection to the ISP. Because all customers are statically routed, ISPs do not have BGP at the remote routers. Often, customer routes mistakenly are redistributed into the ISPs' own IGP.

Sometimes, even with BGP peering routers, ISPs redistribute static routes into IGP instead of BGP. Anytime a flap occurs on the link to the customer network, it can affect performance on the ISP network, and can result in scaling issues with the IGP of the ISP network.

The sole purpose of the IGP on the ISP network is to carry next hop information for BGP. Observe the network in Figure 12-8. In this setup, the static customers might be connected to the access routers or to the distribution routers.

Figure 12-8 *Typical ISP Setup with Static and BGP Customers*

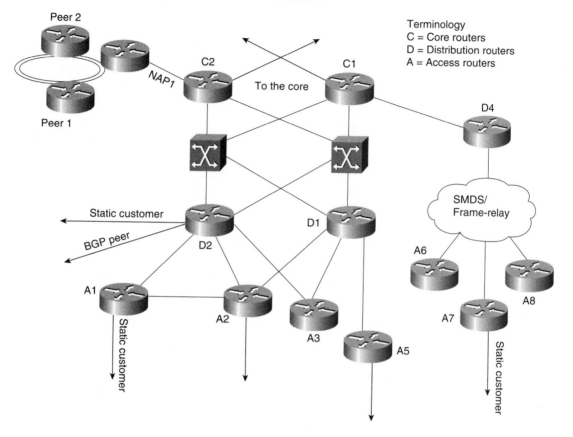

Figure 12-8 shows that the static customers are connected to the distribution routers or access routers. The distribution routers will always run BGP and, most of the time, will have BGP customers connected to them. In some cases, ISPs do not run BGP on the access routers if they have only static customers connected to them.

We recommend that static customers be connected first. Then, introduce BGP in order to carry customer routes through BGP instead of IGP. Three situations will arise once this has been accomplished:

- All IBGP routers must be fully meshed. In case the ISP introduces BGP at all the access routers, the IBGP mesh will be very large and can cause scaling difficulties with the BGP mesh.

- It may appear as if the full BGP routes must be sent to all access routers that were not previously receiving all BGP routes. Even if those access routers do not have external BGP neighbors, they are now receiving full BGP routes because they are part of the BGP mesh.

- If policies have been defined only at the external BGP peering routers, you must define policies on all BGP peering routers, now that BGP has been configured in the network. It may appear as if the policies must be implemented throughout the network because you have introduced BGP at the edges.

Now, we will address these issues one by one. The first issue is the IBGP mesh problem. With the introduction of the router reflector (for details on router reflectors, see Chapter 11, "Border Gateway Protocol"), access routers only need to peer with their local distribution BGP routers. Distribution routers will become route reflectors for all the access routers. Next, these distribution routers become route reflector clients to the core routers. This introduces two-layer route reflection hierarchy and minimizes the BGP mesh.

The second issue involves the question of sending full BGP routes to the access routers that previously were receiving these routes. First of all, this suggestion does not require a full BGP table. Communities should be used to send only previously received routes. It is unnecessary to change the routing table. Only the protocol that is carrying the routes has changed.

The third issue is defining the policies. If you were only forming the BGP policies at the peering routers, how do you ensure that the BGP policies are not affected? This is accomplished by verifying that the routes that you imported into BGP from the IGP via the access list are correct. Now, you would form BGP policies at the access router that redistributes the static route.

You are then ready to begin migrating the network in Figure 12-8 from an OSPF carrying all customer route networks to an IBGP carrying customer route networks. The first step is to create IBGP peering with the local distribution routers. In Figure 12-8, you would assign D2 and D1 as the route reflectors for A1, A2, A3, and A5.

When configuring BGP peering, remember to define a distribute list or community list at the distribution routers. This will prevent the distribution routers from sending the complete BGP information to the access routers. This way, the distribution router will send only the routes that should be sent to the access routers.

If you do not choose to send any BGP routes to the access routers, simply send the OSPF default route to the access routers. You would use IBGP to receive customer routes. In this setup, the access router is not receiving any BGP routes from the distribution router—it is only sending customer routes via BGP.

After you have configured all the access routers that have static customers as clients and have ensured that the peering is up, you can focus on the distribution routers, if they are not already route reflector clients of core routers.

You would then repeat the same process throughout the network. When all the routers are ready to send and receive BGP routes, you would then enter the **redistribution** statement in the BGP process without removing the **redistribution** command from OSPF. This allows you to view all the customer routes into BGP. However, all the routes from OSPF continue to be visible because OSPF has a lower administrative distance than IBGP. Because there are no synchronization issues, IBGP will send routes to the neighbor. OSPF already carries all the customer routes.

After the redistribution is removed from under OSPF and when IBGP is the only protocol carrying customer routes, you should configure **no sync**.

For policy purposes, routes that are not sent to external BGP neighbors are not allowed to leak. Leaks are prevented by defining the access lists when BGP is configured at the access router. All customer routes that will be sent to the external peering BGP will be redistributed from the static route, as is the case with a community number. Routes that were not outside the autonomous system, but need to be sent to the IBGP neighbors, will be redistributed with a community number of **local-as.** You also can employ the **no-export** command. This way, routes with a community number of **local-as** will remain within the AS, and routes that only have a simple community number will be exported to the ISP's external neighbors.

TIP   All routes should be sent with community numbers. By assigning community numbers, policy formulation will be much simpler. If there is an access router that should not receive routes from other regions, you can easily filter regional routes based on the community number.

Configuration Example

In this example, the access router has ten static customers. Of those ten customers, you do not want to send eight routes to external BGP neighbors, but you do want to send two routes to the external neighbors. The first eight static routes should not be exported, and the last two should be sent to the external peers.

The static routes on A1 are the following:

```
ip route 194.1.1.0 255.255.255.0 Serial 0/0
ip route 194.1.2.0 255.255.255.0 Serial 0/1
ip route 194.1.3.0 255.255.255.0 Serial 0/1
ip route 194.1.4.0 255.255.255.0 Serial 0/2
ip route 198.1.5.0 255.255.255.0 Serial 0/3
ip route 198.1.6.0 255.255.255.0 Serial 10/3
ip route 201.1.7.0 255.255.255.0 Serial 1/0
ip route 199.1.8.0 255.255.255.0 Serial 1/1
ip route 194.1.9.0 255.255.255.0 Serial 1/1
ip route 204.1.10.0 255.255.255.0 Serial 1/2
ip route 204.1.11.0 255.255.255.0 Serial 1/2
```

The following would be the BGP configuration of the A1 router:

```
ip bgp-community new-format
router bgp 109
neighbor 131.108.10.1 remote-as 109
neighbor 131.108.10.2 remote-as 109
neighbor 131.108.10.1 send-community
neighbor 131.108.10.2 send-community
redistribute static route-map BGP-Static

route-map BGP-Static permit 10
match ip address 1
set community 109:10

route-map BGP-Static permit 20
match ip address 2
set community 109:10 local-as

access-list 1 permit  204.1.10.0 0.0.1.255

access-list 2 permit any
```

In the previous configuration, router A1 is a route reflector client for D1 and D2, as defined by the **neighbor** command. Next, you would command the BGP process to send routes to the neighbors, along with whatever community with which they have been configured. The final command tells the BGP process to redistribute the static routes with conditions defined in the route map.

The first sequence in the route map BGP-Static, which is sequence number 10, commands redistribution of the static routes into BGP that passes access list 1, and then sets the community number to 109:10 (AS: community number). Access list 1 permits networks 204.1.10.0 and 204.10.11.0 via the wildcard mask, so both network 204.1.10.0 and 204.1.11.0 would be redistributed into BGP with community 109:10.

The next sequence in the route map, which is sequence number 20, permits all other static routes to be redistributed into BGP with the same community number. In this case, set the community number to be local-as configured, so that these routes are not exported outside the local autonomous system.

At the distribution router, you must define the policies so that it sends only the local routes to all the other access routers within its region and so that it sends all routes to the core routers. Typically, the distribution router has a full routing table, so you do not want to pass these Internet routes to the access routers.

The configuration for D1 is as follows:

```
router bgp 109
 no synchronization
  bgp cluster-id 101
neighbor Access-R1  peer-group
neighbor Access-R1  remote-as 109
neighbor Access-R1  update-source Loopback0
neighbor Access-R1 route-map Access-BGP out
neighbor 131.108.11.4 peer-group Access-R1 (A1 router peer)
neighbor 131.108.11.5 peer-group Access-R1 (A5 router peer)
neighbor 131.108.11.6 peer-group Access-R1 (A3 router peer)
neighbor 131.108.11.7 peer-group Access-R1 (A2 router peer)

route-map Access-BGP permit 10
match community 1

ip community-list 1 permit 109:10
```

In this case, you should define a peer group. A peer group is an efficient method of updating routers. All routers with the same outbound policy can be configured into a peer group. In this case, D1 has the same outbound policy for A1, A2, A3, and A5, so these can be defined into a peer group. D1 is sending only those routes to its neighbors that pass community list 1. Community list 1 says to permit only routes that are tagged with a community of 109:10. This way, you can control new information entering BGP and decide policies based on the communities.

Now that BGP is running throughout the network, you may encounter a situation in which you receive all the specific routes from your own CIDR block into BGP. Because you were not receiving these routes in OSPF previously, you only needed configurations on the BGP routers that had external peers. Now, IBGP is running on access routers as well.

Assume, for example, that you own the CIDR block of 204.10.0.0/16. You want to send 204.10.0.0/16 to the EBGP neighbors, and you want to send all specific routes to IBGP neighbors. The configuration for D1 would be as follows:

```
router bgp 109
 no synchronization
  bgp cluster-id 101
aggregate-address 204.10.0.0 255.255.0.0 summary-only
neighbor IBGP-neighbors  peer-group
neighbor IBGP-neighbors  remote-as 109
neighbor IBGP-neighbors  update-source Loopback0
neighbor IBGP-neighbors  unsupress-map BGP-specific


route-map BGP-specific permit 10
match ip address 5

access-list 5 permit any
```

This way, all the routers in the IBGP neighbors peer group will receive all the specific routes; all others will receive aggregated routes. Normally, this would be performed at the external peering routers to send specific routes to IBGP neighbors and send aggregated routes to EBGP neighbors.

Finally, you would determine whether all the routers in the network have the correct BGP information in their BGP tables. You can then remove the **redistribute static** command from OSPF. All the routes in the routing table have been learned via BGP by this point. Therefore, this will help the IGP to scale properly and relieve the IGP from having to carry unnecessary customer routes.

Summary

As classful routing protocols become outdated and no longer useful in large networks, it is often necessary to replace them with newer, classless protocols. There are several reasons for exchanging one protocol for another, which include support for VLSM and discontiguous networks, address space, allowing faster convergence, summarizing within a network, and improved scaling.

There are three categories of protocol migration: migrating from a classful distance vector protocol (RIP, IGRP) to a classless link-state protocol (OSPS, IS-IS); classful distance vector to classless advanced distance vector (EIGRP); and, in the case of ISP's, migrating customer routes from the IGP of an ISP to BGP.

When migrating from RIP or IGRP to OSPF, the backbone (area 0) must be defined first, through which all traffic outside an area must pass. Secondly, examine the backdoor connections between routers that could destroy hierarchy, consider removing the distance vector, and appropriately increase or decrease the administrative distance value.

When migrating from IGRP to EIGRP within the same autonomous system, redistribution is automatic. The two protocols are designed to exchange routes without additional configuration. The calculation of the composite metric is identical in both, and is converted from one domain to another.

When migrating from RIP to Enhanced IGRP, the possibility of routing loops must be considered, as well as conversion of RIP's metric to suit EIGRP. This migration is accomplished by first redistributing routers at the edge of the network. After redistribution is complete, all router connections must be examined to ensure the absence of loops.

To migrate customers from IGP to BGP, the static customers must first be connected to carry customer routes through BGP instead of IGP. It is good practice to introduce route reflectors to add hierarchy and minimize the BGP mesh.

By following the migration techniques provided in this chapter, you will be able to successfully exchange one protocol for another relatively problem-free, and therefore improve the general success of your network.

Review Questions

1 Does a link-state protocol build its routing information from a routing table or from a database?

2 Enhanced IGRP builds its routing table from its topology table. Does this mean that Enhanced IGRP is a link-state protocol?

3 What is the solution to full IBGP mesh?

4 How can you send aggregated routes to external neighbors and send specific routes to internal neighbors?

Answers:

1 Link-state protocols build their routing table information from a database.

2 Enhanced IGRP is not a link-state protocol; it is an advanced distance-vector protocol.

3 Route reflectors solve the problem of full IBGP mesh by adding hierarchy to the network.

4 You can send aggregated routes to external neighbors and send specific routes to internal neighbors by using the **unsupress-map** command.

This chapter explains both intra- and interdomain multicast routing. Before reading this chapter, review previous chapters on unicast routing—in particular, read Chapter 11, "Border Gateway Protocol." This chapter covers four major areas:

Multicast routing protocols   This section provides a brief historical overview and offers a contrast of multicast routing protocols.

Fundamentals of operation   This section provides an overview of the major protocols used in Cisco multicast routing. Specifically, you will learn about the operation of multicast within an autonomous system by exploring the Internet Group Management Protocol (IGMP) and Protocol Independent Multicast (PIM) dense and sparse modes. You will also explore intradomain operation by examining Multicast BGP and the Multicast Source Discovery Protocol (MSDP).

Protocol description   After learning how the protocols operate, you will examine IGMP and PIM in more depth by exploring the protocol at the packet level.

Scalability features   This section examines PIM features that enhance scalability, such as PIM rendezvous point selection and operating networks in PIM sparse-dense mode.

## CHAPTER 13

Protocol Independent Multicast

Multicast Routing Protocols

Multicast differs from simple broadcast in the sense that it only attempts to deliver a packet to interested users. It differs from unicast or pointcast in that only one copy of a packet travels over any link. For large-scale applications, this can represent a huge reduction in the use of bandwidth and switching capacity.

The characteristics of multicast routing are well suited to conferencing applications, but these are by no means the only applications. Multicast can also enable auto-resource discovery through the use of well-known groups. In earlier chapters, you saw how the ALL-OSPF-ROUTERS and ALL-RIPV2-routers group addresses are used in neighbor discovery.

Multicast groups are identified by the IP Class D address range 224.0.0.0 to 239.255.255.255. Users indicate their interest in a particular multicast group via an Internet Group Management Protocol (IGMP) interaction with their local multicast router. Multicast routers themselves communicate using a multicast routing protocol. Although IGMP has gone through a steady process of evolution, a number of contenders have vied for the multicast routing throne.

The first example of large-scale multicast routing is the MBONE. Since the early 1990s, the MBONE has used the Distance Vector Multicast Routing Protocol (DVMRP) to deliver interdomain multicast routing throughout the Internet. However, as with most distance-vector protocols, DVMRP is slow to converge when the routing topology changes, and is prone to loops. Moreover, it maintains a great deal of routing state, even if it is not actually forwarding packets for a particular multicast group. In addition, MBONE requires periodic broadcasting of all groups to maintain routing state.

These shortcomings led protocol designers to invent new multicast routing protocols. One, an extension to OSPF called Multicast OSPF, also suffered scalability problems because of its need to run the Dijkstra algorithm for every combination of source and group. This problem is similar to Unicast OSPF in the presence of a large number of routes.

Another suggestion, Core Based Trees, scales extremely well, but it performs inefficiently in environments in which latency is critical because the protocol does not support optimal routing between sender and receivers.

Protocol Independent Multicast, or PIM, which has been adopted by Cisco, applies ideas from both DVMRP and CBT. It derives its name from its lack of reliance on any particular unicast routing protocol; it can use any of the underlying protocols running in the network. In implementation terms, PIM simply uses the IP routing table of the router on which it is running. Those routes may be derived from Enhanced IGRP, RIP, BGP, IS-IS, or any other unicast IP routing protocol.

PIM operates in two modes to offer the best overall performance. This results in some extra implementation complexity, but because the major aim of multicast is to save bandwidth, most network designers believe this complexity is justified:

- *Dense mode*   A flood-and-prune algorithm that is used when the router in a network has a high probability of needing to belong to a particular group.

- *Sparse mode*   Features an explicit group-join mechanism, and is more suitable for groups whose members are few or widely distributed, or in cases where periodic flooding is expensive.

Fundamentals of Operation

IGMP, PIM, MSDP, and MBGP all work together to provide a cohesive framework for intra- and interdomain multicast routing. This section introduces you to the operation of each protocol.

Internet Group Management Protocol

IGMP and PIM work together to subscribe users to particular multicast groups. IGMP is enabled on an interface whenever PIM is enabled. This is usually accomplished with the **ip pim sparse-dense-mode** interface subcommand. IGMP messages are sent with a TTL of 1, which constrains them to the LAN on which they were originally transmitted. Generally, the IGMP message exchange occurs between hosts and routers, although all devices on the LAN may listen to the exchange of messages to avoid sending or requesting duplicate information.

Consider the network shown in Figure 13-1. In this example, two routers serve LAN A. IGMP QUERIER ELECTION messages are initially sent by all routers on the network.

The message may be sent to the ALL-MULTICAST-HOSTS address (224.0.0.1) or to a specific group address, indicating that group-specific querier is desired. All routers listen for such messages, and the router with the lowest source IP address on the LAN is elected as the IGMP QUERIER for the LAN or for the specific group.

After a querier is elected, it periodically sends IGMP MEMBERSHIP QUERIES for each active group to the ALL-MULTICAST-HOSTS address. Because multicast IP traffic is also sent to a multicast MAC address, only one host on any multicast-capable LAN must respond to the query. In switched LANs, the Cisco Group Management Protocol may be used between a switch and a router to subscribe individual switched LAN ports to a group; this protocol is not discussed here.

Figure 13-1   *IGMP Operation*

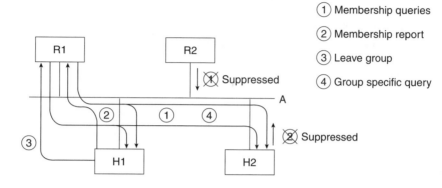

All interested hosts will accept LAN frames addressed to multicast MAC addresses of interest. Therefore, each host randomizes its response timer to a MEMBERSHIP QUERY from a route, and suppresses its response if it hears a response from another host.

If a host decides to leave a group, it may send a LEAVE GROUP message to the querying router. In response, the querying router sends a GROUP SPECIFIC QUERY for the group, in case other hosts still wish to receive packets for that group. If it does not receive a QUERY RESPONSE from any other hosts on the LAN, the router stops multicasting that group onto the LAN.

It is important to note that GROUP SPECIFIC QUERY and LEAVE GROUP messages were introduced in IGMPV2. If an IGMP-capable host detects an IGMPV1 router, the host must respond with IGMPV1 membership reports. If an IGMPV2-capable router detects an IGMPV1 host on a LAN, it must ignore LEAVES and avoid sending GROUP SPECIFIC QUERIES. All routers on a LAN must be manually configured to run the same version of IGMP—otherwise, incorrect operation may occur.

IGMP Version 3 adds support for source filtering. This support enables a host to notify the router that it wants to receive only packets destined to a particular multicast group from a specific source host.

When a router is aware of group membership on its attached LANs, it must communicate this information to upstream routers. This is achieved by using PIM.

Protocol Independent Multicast

As mentioned above, PIM has two modes of operation. The first, dense mode, is useful for multicast groups that have densely distributed subscribers. The second, sparse mode, is more useful for groups that have widely scattered subscribers.

PIM Dense Mode

PIM dense mode is a flood-and-prune protocol. As illustrated in Figure 13-2, its operation is relatively simple. Dense mode PIM is automatically used for certain administrative functions, such as auto-RP, which you will read about later. However, in most cases, PIM is enabled with the **ip pim sparse-dense-mode** interface subcommand.

Figure 13-2   *Example Multicast Topology*

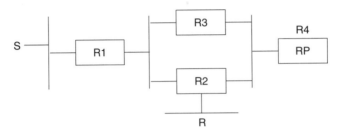

Assume that source S begins sending packets to a PIM dense domain/network on group G. PIM dense mode uses the Reverse Path Multicasting (RPM) algorithm to make forwarding decisions. Initially, the packets from S are sent to all links in the network. In particular, R1 broadcasts the packet on all its multicast-enabled interfaces, except the one on which the packet was received. Routers R2, R3, and R4 follow the same algorithm.

If receiver R has not indicated via IGMP that it is interested in receiving traffic from source S for group G, router R2 sends a PRUNE message to R1 for group G. R1 delays pruning for a short period (three seconds, by default) to give R3 a chance to override the prune. However, when PRUNE state is established, it is maintained by R1 for three minutes, by default. After three minutes, traffic will again be flooded and a further prune will be necessary to prevent traffic for group G flowing between R1 and R2.

If, during this three-minute prune interval, receiver R sends an IGMP HOST-MEMBERSHIP report to R2, indicating its interest in receiving traffic from S for G, R2 can send a GRAFT message to R1 for this source/group combination. R1 sends a GRAFT-ACK back to R2 and begins forwarding the traffic for group G from S. *Join latency,* which is the period of time before an interested receiver actually begins receiving multicast traffic for a particular group, will be reduced by the grafting process in PIM dense mode.

Both R2 and R3 forward the multicast traffic onto the LAN shared with R4. When R2 and R3 receive traffic on the shared LAN for source/group combinations also being forwarded onto the LAN, they send an ASSERT message. The ASSERT message contains the distance and metric of its route back to the source S. The router with the best route wins, and the other router prunes traffic for that (S,G). If the routes have equal cost, the router with the highest IP address wins.

PIM Sparse Mode

The periodic broadcast of all multicast traffic to refresh the prune state clearly makes PIM dense mode unsuitable for very large networks. PIM sparse mode offers the best of both worlds. It uses shared-tree operation for low traffic flows, and has a mechanism to move to a source-based tree for high traffic flows. Unlike dense mode, sparse mode uses an explicit join model for receivers. The key to this transition is the notion of a rendezvous point (RP).

Revisit the topology example that we used in describing dense mode (refer to Figure 13-2). Suppose that source S begins sending packets to group G and that the RP for this group is R4. The first hop router in S, which is R1, will encapsulate the first multicast packet in a REGISTER message and unicast toward the RP. In response, RP will send a JOIN message for group G toward the source S.

R2 and R3 will perform a designated router (DR) election. All PIM routers send periodic QUERY messages, which are heard by all other routers on a LAN. The router with the highest IP address is elected as the DR and is responsible for the following tasks:

- Forwarding all JOIN messages from the LAN to the RP
- Forwarding multicast traffic onto the LAN

If no PIM QUERY messages are heard from a router for a configurable period, this mechanism is repeated to elect a new DR.

Assuming that R3 has the higher IP address, it will forward the JOIN back toward R1 and create a forwarding state for (S,G). When R1 receives the JOIN from RP via R3, R1 will begin multicasting the traffic directly toward the RP, in addition to the stream encapsulated in unicast REGISTER messages. Duplicate streams continue until the RP receives the first native multicast traffic, unicasts a REGISTER STOP message to R1, and ensures that this message is processed by R1.

Suppose that now R indicates, via an IGMP MEMBERSHIP REPORT message, that it is interested in receiving traffic for (S,G) to R2. A JOIN message will be sent from R2 to the RP, and will join the shared tree. At this point, multicast traffic for group G will take the path S, R1, R3, R4(RP), R2, and R. Note that S, R1, R3, and R4 constitute the source tree toward the RP; and R4, R2, and R constitute the shared tree from the RP to the receiver.

When traffic for (S,G) reaches a certain configurable threshold, it is logical for R2 to leave the shared tree and obtain a more optimal path. On Cisco routers, the default value for this configurable threshold is zero. This zero means that all sources are immediately switched to the shortest-path tree. The cost of shortest-path trees is that more multicast forwarding states must be maintained in the router.

To initiate the switchover to the shortest-path tree, R2 sends a JOIN on its optimal path toward S, which in this case is directly via R1. R2 also sends a PRUNE toward the RP for group G. Because no other receivers exist on the shared tree, R4 will send a PRUNE toward S, and traffic on the source tree (S, R1, R3, and R4) will be stopped.

At this point, all that is left is the shortest-path tree S, R1, R2, R. Periodically, R1 will send registers to R4, but R4 will respond with REGISTER messages and PRUNEs until another host joins the group via the shared tree.

NOTE	This discussion has assumed that all PIM routers know which router is the RP for a particular group. One way to ensure this is to configure it statically into all *leaf routers* (routers that have directly attached senders and receivers) via the **ip pim rp-address** global command. However, PIM V2 defines a mechanism called *Bootstrap Router*, and Cisco offers a scheme called auto-RP. Both of these terms will be compared and contrasted in the section entitled "Multicast Scalability Features."

Sparse mode may sound complicated when compared to dense mode; remember, however, that much of this complexity is hidden from the network administrator. Indeed, if **ip pim sparse-dense-mode** is enabled on all interfaces in the network, only two additional configuration lines are required for sparse mode operation, and these are on the RP itself.

Interdomain Multicast: MSDP and MBGP

How do RPs learn about sources in other PIM domains? This problem is solved by the Multicast Source Discovery Protocol (MSDP). At the time of this writing, MSDP was still an Internet draft, and therefore this section describes only a work-in-progress.

MSDP uses simple, one-to-one, BGP-like peering sessions to establish communication between RPs. Unlike BGP, however, no connection collision mechanism exists. Instead, the peer with the higher address listens on TCP port 639, whereas the other side initiates the connection.

MSDP sessions can be established between RPs from different domains (external MSDP) or between RPs within the same domain (internal MSDP). Behaviorally, there is no difference between the two. In most cases, the different domains will correspond to different BGP autonomous systems (see Figure 13-3).

As shown in Figure 13.3, when an RP receives a PIM REGISTER message from the DR for a particular source S, the RP generates and sends a source-active (SA) message to its peer. The SA message contains the source and group addresses associated with the REGISTER messages, together with the address of the RP itself. This message is sent to both External MSDP (EMSDP) and Internal MSDP (IMSDP) peers.

Figure 13-3   *Operation of MSDP and MBGP*

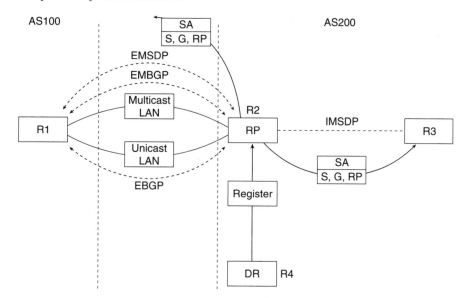

Upon receiving an SA message, an RP checks to see whether it has any receivers within its own domain. If it does, it triggers a JOIN toward the source S. It also forwards the SA to other MSDP peers, except to the peer from which the original message was received.

SA messages are periodically re-sent by the originating RP. However, RPs may cache SA messages received to reduce join latency for recipients within their own domain.

MSDP neighbors are configured via the **ip msdp peer** global configuration command.

NOTE   As with BGP policy applied to unicast routing, it is usual practice to apply careful filtering of SA messages on EMSDP sessions.

Multicast BGP (MBGP) enables the unicast and multicast interdomain routing to be incongruent. Specifically, routes to multicast sources are passed via BGP according to the multiprotocol extensions defined in RFC 2283 and discussed in Chapter 11.These routes can be aggregates and do not have to be—and usually are not—host routes. Cisco routers prefer the MBGP routing table entries to those derived from unicast routing protocols when performing the RPF check.

NOTE   Reverse path forwarding (RPF) is an algorithm used for forwarding multicast datagrams. The
rules for using RPF are as follows:

- If a router receives a datagram on an interface that it uses to send unicast packets to the
  source, the packet has arrived on the RPF interface.

- If the packet arrives on the RPF interface, a router forwards the packet via the interfaces
  that are present in the outgoing interface list of a multicast routing table entry.

- If the packet does not arrive on the RPF interface, the packet is silently discarded. This
  provides loop avoidance.

Because PIM uses both source trees and shared trees to forward datagrams, the RPF check is
performed differently for each. If a PIM router has a source tree state, it performs the RPF check
from the source IP address of the multicast packet. If a PIM router has a shared tree state (and
no explicit source tree state), it performs the RPF check on the RP's address (which is known
when members join the group).

Figure 13-3 illustrates a typical arrangement. Autonomous systems 100 and 200 peer at a NAP.
Two separate Layer 2 switching infrastructures exist: one optimized for unicast and one
optimized for multicast.

The routers exchange multicast routes via MBGP on the multicast infrastructure. The same set
of routes also may be offered on the unicast infrastructure; however, the multicast RPF lookup
prefers the routes learned via MBGP over unicast BGP. As a result, multicast traffic flows across
the multicast switching infrastructure.

MBGP is a negotiated BGP capability. In general, two configuration steps are required for BGP:

- Add the **nlri unicast multicast** keywords to the main BGP configuration line for the
  neighbor:

  ```
  router bgp X
  neighbor x.x.x.x remote-as Y nlri unicast multicast
  ```

- Modify incoming and outgoing policy to account for Multicast NLRI. This is
  accomplished using the **match nlri multicast** and **set nlri multicast** route-map
  subclauses:

  ```
  route-map incoming-policy permit 20
  match nlri multicast
  match ip address X
  route-map outgoing-policy 20
  match ip address X
  set nlri multicast
  ```

IGMP and PIM Protocol Description

This section covers the packet-level details of IGMP and PIM. Because it is still being developed, MSDP is not discussed in detail here.

IGMP

IGMP messages are IP-encapsulated with a protocol number of 2, and are always sent with a TTL of 1 to ensure their confinement to the local LAN. IGMP versions 1, 2, and 3 are described here; however, remember that IGMP version 3 is still under development.

Five IGMP message types exist:

- This message has the format shown in Figure 13-4, and is sent by the querying router:

      11:    IGMPv1/2/3 MEMBERSHIP QUERY

  The group field may contain all zeros, which corresponds to a general query for membership information for all groups. This is the only message format supported by IGMPV1. In IGMPV2, the group address field may also be set to the particular group, in which case the querying router is soliciting membership reports for that group only. IGMPV2-capable hosts then respond with membership reports for that group.

Figure 13-4   *IGMP Packet Formats*

```
 0                   1                   2                   3
 0 1 2 3 4 5 6 7 8 9 0 1 2 3 4 5 6 7 8 9 0 1 2 3 4 5 6 7 8 9 0 1
+-------------+---------------+-------------------------------+
|    Type     | Max Resp Time |            Checksum           |
+-------------+---------------+-------------------------------+
|                        Group Address                        |
+-------------------------------------------------------------+
```

This first message is extended in IGMPV3, as shown in Figure 13-5. In IGMPV3, the querying router may solicit membership reports from hosts that are interested only in specific sources for specific groups. The IP addresses of the set of sources are listed in the message. If the Number of Sources field is zero, the message is equivalent to an IGMPV1 general query (if the Group Address field is zero) or an IGMPV2 group-specific query (if the Group Address field is non-zero).

All routers begin by sending queries for multicast-enabled interfaces. However, in IGMPV2/V3, routers will suppress queries on LAN interfaces for a few seconds if they hear a query from another router on the LAN with a lower source IP address.

Figure 13-5 *IGMPV3 Message Format*

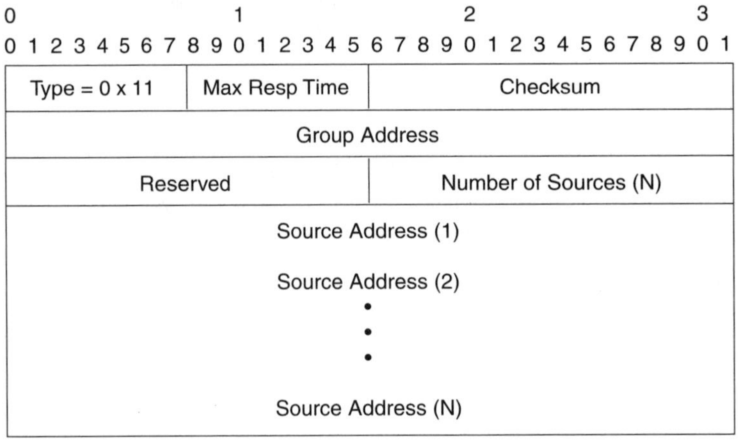

- The following message also has the format shown in Figure 13-4. A host sends this packet in response to an IGMPV1 MEMBERSHIP QUERY from the querying router.

  ```
  12: IGMPv1 MEMBERSHIP REPORT
  ```

  The group address contains the group to which this host is subscribed. This message is superseded by type 16 for IGMPV2 and type 22 for IGMPV3.

- The following message also has the format shown in Figure 13-4:

  ```
  16: IGMPv2 MEMBERSHIP REPORT
  ```

  The type number for the message enables the querying router to determine whether there are either or both IGMPV1 and IGMPV2 hosts on the LAN, and therefore how to treat membership for each group. In particular, messages for groups that have IGMPV1 subscribers must be ignored.

- This message has the format shown in Figure 13-4:

  ```
  17: IGMPv2/v3 LEAVE GROUP
  ```

  This message is sent, unsolicited, from hosts to the multicast router on the LAN. The Group Address field contains the group that the host wishes to leave.

- The format of the following message is shown in Figure 13-6:

  ```
  22: IGMPv3 MEMBERSHIP  REPORT
  ```

  This message enables a host to report to the querying router interest in traffic to a particular group address, from a specific set of sources.

Figure 13-6   *IGMPV3 Membership Report*

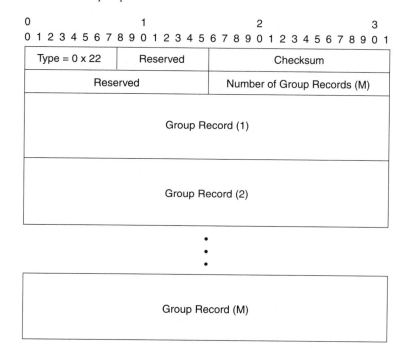

Where each Group Record has the following internal format:

Therefore, in addition to the normal type 10 MEMBERSHIP REPORT message fields used by IGMPV1/V2, the IGMPV3 message includes the list of IP addresses in which this host is interested. This means that the querying router can perform source-based filtering of traffic to particular groups. The router forwards onto the LAN only traffic from all group/source combinations for which it receives a membership report.

PIM V2

PIM V1 packets are encapsulated in IGMP type 14. PIM V2 packets, specified in RFC 2362, are not encapsulated in IGMP. They are instead assigned their own protocol number, 103, and are sent to address 224.0.0.13. This section focuses on version 2 of the protocol.

Each PIM packet has the header shown in Figure 13-7. The following sections describe each packet type.

Figure 13-7   *PIM Message Header (from RFC 2362)*

PIM Ver
    PIM Version number is 2.

Type   Types for specific PIM messages. PIM Types are:

0 = Hello
1 = Register
2 = Register-Stop
3 = Join/Prune
4 = Bootstrap
5 = Assert
6 = Graft (used in PIM-DM only)
7 = Graft-Ack (used in PIM-DM only)
8 = Candidate-RP-Advertisement

Reserved
    set to zero. Ignored upon receipt.

Checksum
    The checksum is the 16-bit one's complement of the one's complement sum of the entire PIM message, (excluding the data portion in the Register message). For computing the checksum, the Checksum field is zeroed.

0: HELLO

HELLO messages, shown in Figure 13-8, are sent periodically by the router on all multicast-enabled interfaces. These messages essentially establish and maintain multicast router neighbor relationships. The HELLO message may contain a number of options, but RFC 2362 specifies only option type 1, which is a two-byte holdtime in seconds.

Figure 13-8   *PIM HELLO Message*

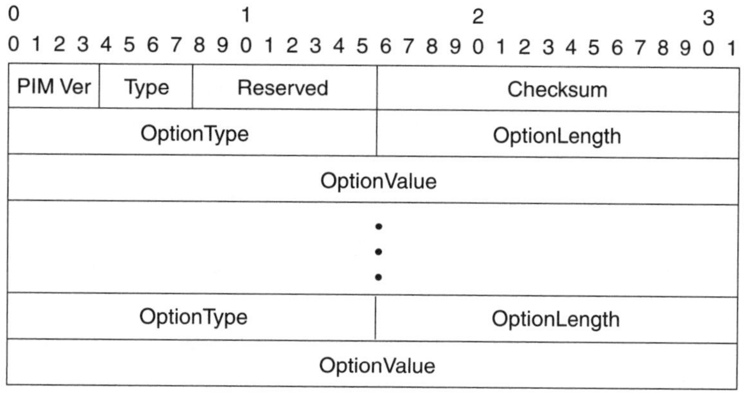

0		1		2		3	
0 1 2 3 4 5 6 7	8 9 0 1 2 3 4 5	6 7 8 9 0 1	2 3 4 5 6 7 8 9 0 1				

PIM Ver	Type	Reserved	Checksum
OptionType		OptionLength	
OptionValue			
•			
•			
•			
OptionType		OptionLength	
OptionValue			

If the holdtime expires without receiving a HELLO, a multicast router declares its neighbor "dead" and times out any associated multicast routing information. If the holdtime is set to 0xffff, the session is never timed out (useful for dial-on-demand circuits); if it is set to zero, the routing information is immediately timed out.

Option types 2 to 16 are reserved by RFC 2362.

1: REGISTER

The REGISTER message, shown in Figure 13-9, is used only in PIM sparse mode (PIM-SM). When a DR initially receives a multicast packet from a directly connected source (or PIM domain in the case of a PMBR, which is discussed following: packets received from other domains are treated as directly connected sources by the PMBR), this packet is encapsulated in a REGISTER message and is unicast to the RP.

Figure 13-9   *PIM REGISTER Message*

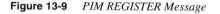

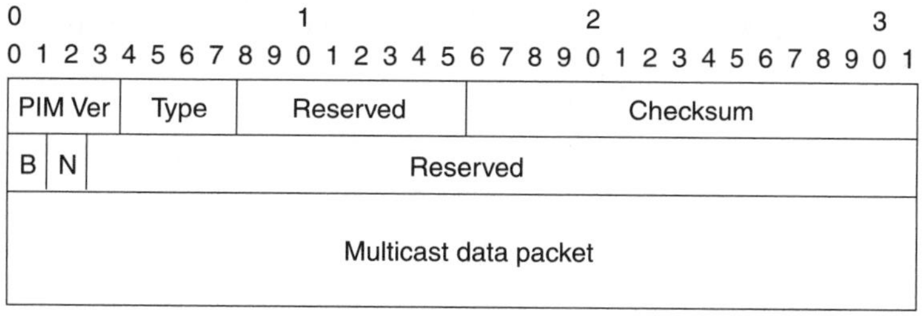

0		1		2		3	
0 1 2 3 4 5 6 7	8 9 0 1 2 3 4 5	6 7 8 9 0 1	2 3 4 5 6 7 8 9 0 1				

PIM Ver	Type	Reserved	Checksum
B	N	Reserved	
Multicast data packet			

The source address of the unicast REGISTER message is the DR, and the destination is the rendezvous point (RP). The RP subsequently de-encapsulates the packet and forwards it down the multicast shared tree. This continues until a shortest-path tree is built from the RP to the source, and the RP sends a REGISTER-STOP message to the DR.

The B bit is set to 1 if the router is a PMBR (PIM Multicast Border Router) for the source. A PMBR connects a dense mode PIM domain to a local sparse domain. The B bit is set to zero if the sending router is a DR for a source directly connected to one of its interfaces.

The N (null register) bit is set to 1 if the DR is probing the RP prior to unsuppressing registers. This helps prevent unnecessary bursts of traffic being sent to the RP between receiving REGISTER STOP messages (a weakness in PIM V1). The Multicast Data Packet field is empty in a null register.

Note that the checksum is performed only on the PIM header, not over the entire encapsulated multicast data.

2: REGISTER STOP

The REGISTER STOP message, shown in Figure 13-10, is used only in PIM-SIM. This message is sent in response to a received REGISTER MESSAGE after the RP has established a shortest-path tree for a particular source/group pair.

Figure 13-10 *PIM REGISTER STOP Message*

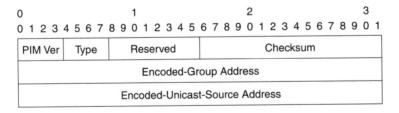

After the DR receives the REGISTER STOP message, it suppresses REGISTERs for the group and source address pairs encoded in the REGISTER STOP message. This encoding is shown in Figure 13-11.

Figure 13-11 *PIM Encoded Address Formats (from RFC 2362)*

1   Encoded Unicast Address: Takes the following format:

```
0                   1                   2                   3
0 1 2 3 4 5 6 7 8 9 0 1 2 3 4 5 6 7 8 9 0 1 2 3 4 5 6 7 8 9 0 1
+---------------+---------------+-------------------------------+
|  Addr Family  | Encoding Type |        Unicast Address        |
+---------------+---------------+-------------------------------+
```

Addr Family
    The address family of the 'Unicast Address' field of
    this address.

    Here are the address family numbers assigned by IANA:

Number	Description
0	Reserved
1	IP (IP version 4)
2	IPv6 (IP version 6)
3	NSAP
4	HDLC (8-bit multidrop)
5	BBN 1822
6	802 (includes all 802 media plus Ethernet "canonical format")
7	E.163
8	E.164 (SMDS, Frame Relay, ATM)
9	F.69 (Telex)
10	X.121 (X.25, Frame Relay)
11	IPX
12	AppleTalk
13	DECnet IV
14	Banyan Vines
15	E.164 with NSAP format subaddress

Encoding Type
    The type of encoding used within a specific Address
    Family. The value '0' is reserved for this field,
    and represents the native encoding of the Address
    Family.

Unicast Address
    The unicast address as represented by the given
    Address Family and Encoding Type.

2   Encoded Group Address: Takes the following format:

```
0                   1                   2                   3
0 1 2 3 4 5 6 7 8 9 0 1 2 3 4 5 6 7 8 9 0 1 2 3 4 5 6 7 8 9 0 1
+---------------+---------------+---------------+---------------+
|  Addr Family  | Encoding Type |   Reserved    |   Mask Len    |
+---------------+---------------+---------------+---------------+
|                    Group Multicast Address                    |
+---------------------------------------------------------------+
```

Addr Family
    described above.

Encoding Type
    described above.

Reserved
    Transmitted as zero. Ignored upon receipt.

Mask Len
    The Mask length is 8 bits. The value is the number of
    contiguous bits left justified used as a mask which
    describes the address. It is less than or equal to the
    address length in bits for the given Address Family
    and Encoding Type. If the message is sent for a single
    group then the Mask length must equal the address
    length in bits for the given Address Family and
    Encoding Type. (e.g. 32 for IPv4 native encoding and
    128 for IPv6 native encoding).

Group Multicast Address
    contains the group address.

Figure 13-11 *PIM Encoded Address Formats (from RFC 2362) (Continued)*

3   Encoded Source Address: Takes the following format:

```
 0                   1                   2                   3
 0 1 2 3 4 5 6 7 8 9 0 1 2 3 4 5 6 7 8 9 0 1 2 3 4 5 6 7 8 9 0 1
┌───────────────┬───────────────┬─────────┬─┬─┬─┬───────────────┐
│  Addr Family  │ Encoding Type │ Rsrved  │S│W│R│   Mask Len    │
├───────────────┴───────────────┴─────────┴─┴─┴─┴───────────────┤
│                        Source Address                         │
└───────────────────────────────────────────────────────────────┘
```

Addr Family
    described above.

Encoding Type
    described above.

Reserved
    Transmitted as zero. Ignored upon receipt.

Mask Length
    Mask length is 8 bits. The value is the number of
    contiguous bits left justified used as a mask which
    describes the address. The mask length must be less
    than or equal to the address length in bits for the
    given Address Family and Encoding Type. If the message
    is sent for a single group, the Mask length must
    equal the address length in bits for the given Address
    Family and Encoding Type. In version 2 of PIM, it is
    strongly recommended that this field be set to 32 for
    IPv4 native encoding.

Source Address
    The source address.

    S   The sparse bit is a 1-bit value, set to 1 for PIN-SM.
         It is used for PIN v.1 compatibility.

    W   This WC bit is a 1-bit value. If 1, the join or prune
         applies to the (*, G) or (*, *, RP) entry. If 0, the join
         or prune applies to the (S, G) entry where S is Source
         Address. Joins and prunes sent towards the RP must
         have this bit set.

    R   The RPT-bit is a 1-bit value. If 1, the information
         about (S, G) is sent toward the RP. If 0, the
         information must be sent toward S, where S is the
         Source Address.

3: JOIN/PRUNE

The JOIN/PRUNE message, shown in Figure 13-12, is used in both dense and sparse modes. The message is sent by routers to upstream routers and RPs.

Figure 13-12 *PIM JOIN/PRUNE Message*

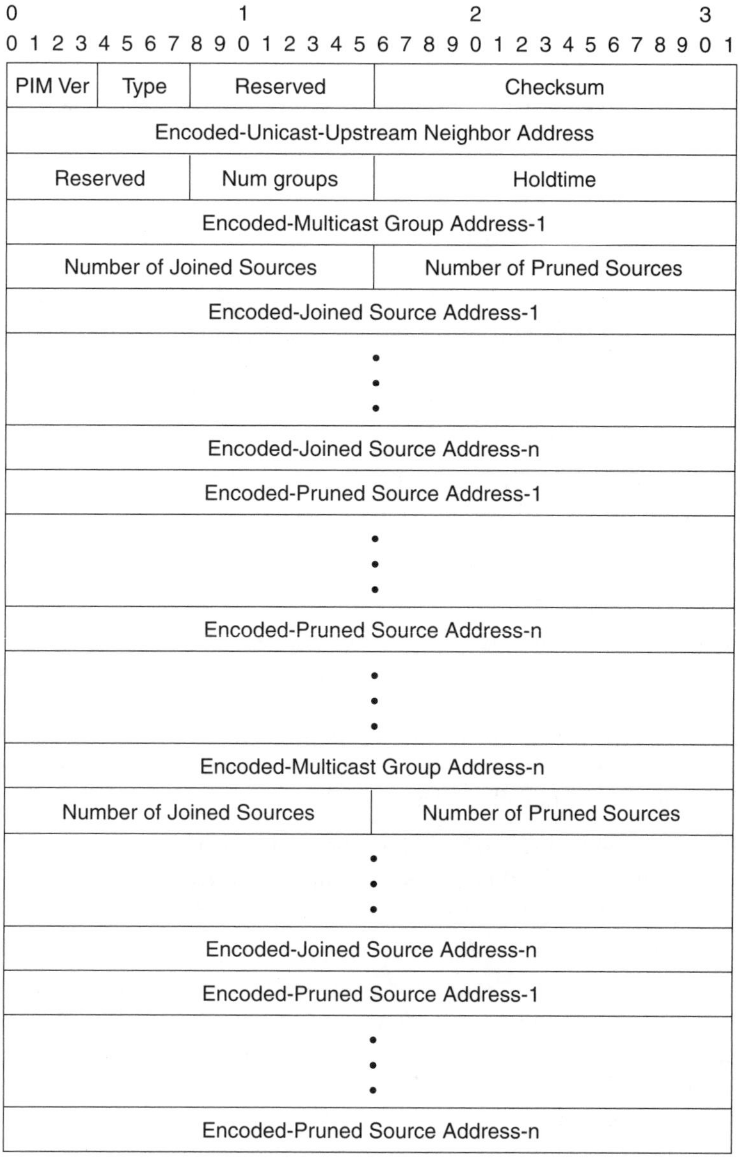

0			1		2		3
0 1 2 3	4 5 6 7	8 9 0 1 2 3 4 5	6 7 8 9 0 1 2 3 4 5 6 7 8 9 0 1				

PIM Ver	Type	Reserved	Checksum
Encoded-Unicast-Upstream Neighbor Address			
Reserved		Num groups	Holdtime
Encoded-Multicast Group Address-1			
Number of Joined Sources		Number of Pruned Sources	
Encoded-Joined Source Address-1			
• • •			
Encoded-Joined Source Address-n			
Encoded-Pruned Source Address-1			
• • •			
Encoded-Pruned Source Address-n			
• • •			
Encoded-Multicast Group Address-n			
Number of Joined Sources		Number of Pruned Sources	
• • •			
Encoded-Joined Source Address-n			
Encoded-Pruned Source Address-1			
• • •			
Encoded-Pruned Source Address-n			

The Encoded-Unicast-Upstream Neighbor Address is the IP address of the upstream (RPF) neighbor that performs the join or prune.

Holdtime instructs the recipient how long, in seconds, to maintain the requested join/prune states. 0xffff is used to signify "forever," and 0 is used to signify immediate timeout of the state.

Number of groups indicates the number of multicast group sets in the message. Each set consists of an Encoded Multicast Group Address, followed by a list of encoded source addresses to join or prune.

Figure 13-11 shows the format of the encoded source address and the meaning of the S, W, and R bits.

4: BOOTSTRAP

The BOOTSTRAP MESSAGE, shown in Figure 13-13, is used in PIM sparse mode only. BOOTSTRAP messages are originated by the BootStrap Router (BSR) in a domain and distribute information about all RPs in the domain. As in the case of multiple DRs, an election mechanism selects the BSRs from the set of candidate BSRs for the domain. This election mechanism is supported by the BOOTSTRAP messages.

BOOTSTRAP messages are sent to the ALL-PIM-ROUTERS group (224.0.0.13) with a TTL of 1. Every router forwards such messages from every interface, except the one on which the message is received. This effectively forms a spanning tree.

If BOOTSTRAP messages exceed the maximum packet size, they are fragmented. Fragments from the same message are identified by their common Fragment Tag.

The Hash Mask Len indicates the length of hash-mask to use for mapping group addresses to RP. For IP, the recommended value is 30, and can be set via the **ip pim bsr-candidate** global command. The hash-mask is such that consecutive group addresses tend to map to the same RP. If associated data streams use consecutive group addresses, a high probability exists that they will share the same RP, and therefore share the same path through the network, resulting in similar delay and bandwidth characteristics.

The BSR Priority field is used to elect the BSR for a PIM domain. RFC 2362 describes a finite-state machine. However, for this discussion, only the ultimate outcome is important: the candidate BSR with the highest IP address (carried in the Encoded-Unicast-BSR-Address field) and Priority field is chosen as the BSR.

The remainder of the BOOTSTRAP message consists of group address/candidate RP sets. Each set begins with an RP-Count for that set, which indicates the number of candidate RPs for this group address in the entire BOOTSTRAP message. Frag RP-Cnt indicates the number of candidate RPs contained in this message fragment. For unfragmented messages, RP-Count and Frag RP-Cnt are the same.

Figure 13-13   *PIM BOOTSTRAP Message*

```
0                   1                   2                   3
0 1 2 3 4 5 6 7 8 9 0 1 2 3 4 5 6 7 8 9 0 1 2 3 4 5 6 7 8 9 0 1
```

PIM Ver	Type	Reserved	Checksum		
Fragment Tap			Hash Mask Len	BSR-priority	
Encoded-Unicast-BSR-Address					
Encoded-Group Address-1					
RP-Count-1		Frag RP-Cnt-1	Reserved		
Encoded-Unicast-RP-Address-1					
RP1-Holdtime			RP1-Priority	Reserved	
Encoded-Unicast-RP-Address-2					
RP2-Holdtime			RP2-Priority	Reserved	
			• • •		
RPm-Holdtime			RPm-Priority	Reserved	
Encoded-Group Address-2					
			• • •		
Encoded-Group Address-n					
RP-Count-n		Frag RP-Cnt-n	Reserved		
Encoded-Unicast-RP-Address-1					
RP1-Holdtime			RP1-Priority	Reserved	
Encoded-Unicast-RP-Address-2					
RP2-Holdtime			RP2-Priority	Reserved	
			• • · •		
Encoded-Unicast-RP-Address-m					
RPm-Holdtime			RPm-Priority	Reserved	

Finally, there is a list of Encoded-Unicast-RP-Addresses (encoding is shown in Figure 13-11), together with an associated holdtime, in seconds, for the RP state and an RP-Priority. The lower the value of the RP-Priority field, the higher the priority: 0 is, therefore, the highest priority.

5: ASSERT

The ASSERT MESSAGE, shown in Figure 13-14, is used in both dense and sparse modes. PIM routers maintain an outgoing interface list for all multicast group addresses. If an interface is in the outgoing list for group X, the router multicasts the packets it receives for group X to all interfaces in the list. Therefore, under loop-free conditions, the router would not expect to *receive* any packets for group X on any interface in X's outgoing interface list. If it does, the router generates an ASSERT message.

The ASSERT message includes the encoded group/source addresses of the offending packet, together with the preference of the unicast protocol that provides a route to the source and the unicast metric of that route.

Figure 13-14   *PIM ASSERT Message*

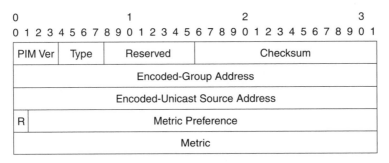

The preference is equivalent to the administrative distance of the routing protocol in the Cisco implementation; the metric varies between protocols. For example, in RIP, it is hop count; in OSPF, it is cost-based.

6: GRAFT

The GRAFT message is used in dense mode only. The message is sent upstream by a PIM router to request that a previously pruned group be reinstated. The format of this message is identical to the JOIN/PRUNE message. (See Figure 13-12.)

GRAFTs help reduce the join latency for groups that already have been pruned. This is desirable because the default prune timer is typically set to three minutes. The default prune time could be reduced, but this must be balanced against the amount of traffic generated due to the periodic flood/prune paradigm of dense mode PIM.

7: GRAFT-ACK

The GRAFT-ACK message is also used only in dense mode. Upon receiving a GRAFT message, a PIM router typically updates its PRUNE state in accordance with the message, and then unicasts it back to the source, changing the message type from 6 to 7.

8: CANDIDATE-RP-ADVERTISEMENT

The CANDIDATE-RP-ADVERTISEMENT message is used only in sparse mode. These messages are unicast by candidate RPs to the elected BSR. The message has the format shown in Figure 13-15.

The Prefix-Cnt indicates the number of group addresses in the message; the Priority is that of the included RP for this group address (the lower the value, the higher the priority), and the holdtime is the amount of time the information in this message is valid. Finally, the Encoded-Unicast-RP-Address is the address of the RP that should be advertised by the BSR as the candidate RP for this group address.

Figure 13-15   *CANDIDATE-RP-ADVERTISEMENT Message*

0		1		2		3
0 1 2 3 4 5 6 7	8 9 0 1 2 3 4 5	6 7 8 9 0 1 2 3 4 5 6 7 8 9 0 1				

PIM Ver	Type	Reserved	Checksum
Prefix-Cnt		Priority	Holdtime
Encoded-Unicast-RP-Address			
Encoded-Group Address-1			
• • •			
Encoded-Group Address-n			

Multicast Scalability Features

Techniques for large-scale deployment of multicast are still evolving. This section examines two major issues: RP discovery and operating networks in sparse-dense mode.

Bootstrap Routers and Candidate RPs

BSRs and RPs are a critical part of the scalability of PIM V2. This section discusses the process of BSR election and RP determination in more detail. This discussion is included for completeness; however, it is recommended that you use auto-RP instead of BSR. You will learn about auto-RP in the next section.

A large sparse mode network should have multiple candidate RPs, which should be placed in the backbone. Candidate RPs are configured via the **ip pim rp-candidate** global configuration command. An interface can be specified as the RP's address; as usual, you should use a Loopback interface.

The set of group addresses that a candidate RP will service also can be specified via a basic access list. For large networks, let every RP be a candidate for all group addresses. The BSR then uses a pure hash function to arbitrate which RP services which group. This effectively handles load sharing of the RP functionality across the candidate RPs.

A network should contain multiple BSRs, preferably located on highly reliable routers in the backbone. BSRs are configured via the **ip pim bsr-candidate** global configuration command. This command enables the source IP address of the bootstrap messages to be set, and, once again, a loopback interface is recommended.

A hash length also can be configured. This roughly determines the number of consecutive groups that will be mapped to a single RP. As a rule, 30 is recommended. Finally, the priority of an individual BSR can be set, and the BSR with the highest preference wins the BSR election process. Therefore, you should set the priorities in descending order of desirability for each BSR.

Auto-RP

The mechanisms of BSR and candidate RPs are quite complicated. Cisco offers an elegant and simple alternative called *auto-RP*.

To enable auto-RP, configure all RP routers to advertise active groups via the **ip pim send-rp-announce** global configuration command, as follows:

```
ip pim send-rp-announce loopback 1 scope 16
```

These announcements are sent to the well-known group address CISCO-RP-ANNOUNCE (224.0.1.39).

Loopback 1 is an RP address advertised in the announcements. You should configure it to be the same for all RPs. PIM DRs then send traffic for their RP to the address of loopback 1. Therefore, the packet will be "swallowed" and processed by the closest functioning RP, in the context of IP routing, to the DR.

Rather than a per-group basis, load sharing across RPs occurs on a geographical basis, which is more logical for large WANs.

Scope is the IP TTL set in the announcements. For most networks, 16 is suitable, although you might have to increase this for networks with very deep hierarchy.

Auto-RP also requires a router to be configured as an RP mapping agent. Its role is to listen to the CISCO-RP-ANNOUNCE group and resolve conflicts between two RPs that announce the same or overlapping groups. For example, if two RPs advertise the same group, the RP with the highest IP address is accepted.

If all RPs use the same address and are advertising all active groups, the RP mapper function is irrelevant. However, it still must be configured. You will most likely want to do this on the RP router itself:

```
ip pim send-rp-discover scope 16
```

The RP mapper announces the selected RP for each group on the CISCO-RP-DISCOVERY group (224.0.1.40). All PIM DRs listen on the CISCO-RP-DISCOVERY group to learn the RPs to use for each group.

Multiple RP mappers also may be configured. All RP mappers listen on the RP-DISCOVER group and may suppress their own mapping output if they hear mappings from another RP mapper with a higher IP address.

PIM Sparse-Dense Mode

For large networks, most groups will operate in sparse mode. However, for certain groups—for example, auto-RP announcements—operating in dense mode is more appropriate. To achieve the best of both, Cisco routers enable interfaces to be configured in sparse-dense mode. Operation in this mode is simple: If the router learns or has a configured RP for a group, the group operates in sparse mode. Otherwise, it operates in dense mode. The mode of any group can be observed via the **show ip mroute** command.

Although any combination of dense mode, sparse mode, and sparse-dense mode can be used on a Cisco router, it is recommended that you configure all interfaces in sparse-dense mode as standard practice. Explicitly configure dense or sparse mode only when you have a very specific need: for example, on a very low-bandwidth link where you do not want the overhead of any dense mode traffic.

Deploying Multicast in a Large Network

In this case study, you will examine the multicast architecture in a large network corresponding to an Internet service provider, ISPnet. The large network encapsulates many regional networks, each with the architecture shown in Figure 13-16. The overall network multicast architecture is shown in Figure 13-17.

Figure 13-16   *Multicast Architecture within an ISPnet Regional Network*

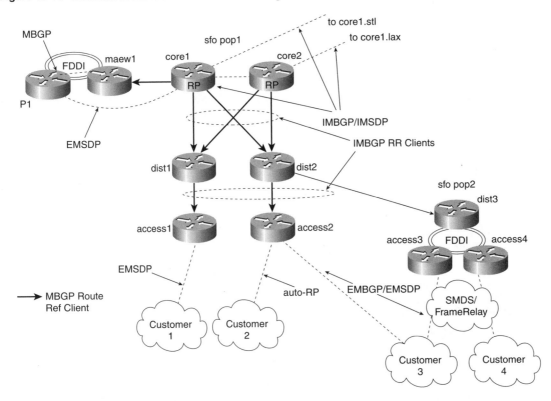

For simplicity, you can enable **ip pim-sparse-dense-mode** on all interfaces within the network and on customer interfaces, as requested by the customer. Therefore, if the customer wants multicast service, IP PIM sparse-dense mode is enabled on the interface leading to that customer.

At least one core router in every regional network is configured as both an RP and an RP mapper. A full mesh of IMSDP and IMBGP peering is maintained among all backbone routers. EMSDP peering is enabled for customers running their own RP and for peer ISPs at the regional public NAP. For non-MSDP customers, auto-RP advises routers in the customer's network of available RPs in the provider's network.

The regional NAP includes two peering infrastructures: one optimized for multicast and another for unicast. MBGP is enabled on the multicast infrastructure and enables interdomain multicast routing that is incongruent to unicast. MBGP is also used in instances in which customers want separate links for unicast and multicast traffic.

Figure 13-17   *ISP Multicast Architecture*

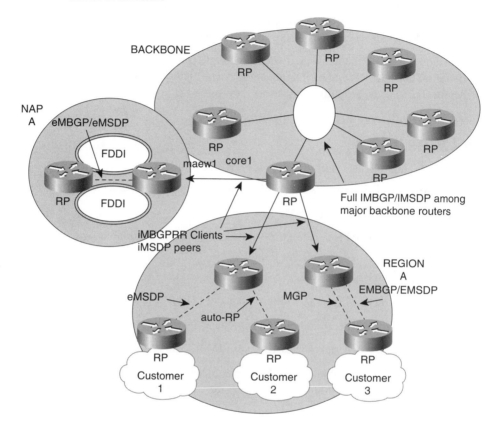

Summary

In this chapter, you have explored the various protocols used for implementing multicast in a large network. Specifically, the text has explored the use of IGMP and PIM for intradomain routing, and MBGP and MSDP for interdomain routing.

IGMP is used by hosts to communicate their interest in particular groups to their local router, which runs PIM. PIM itself operates in two modes: sparse and dense. In most circumstances, however, it is best to configure your network in sparse-dense mode and let PIM decide how to handle each group.

Dense mode PIM is more suited to groups with densely populated members; sparse mode is for sparsely distributed members. Dense mode uses a bandwidth consumptive flood-and-prune algorithm, whereas sparse mode uses explicit joins, and moves from a shared to a source-based tree with the assistance of a rendezvous point.

MSDP enables RPs to advertise the presence of local sources to RPs in other domains, which often correspond to autonomous systems. This facilitates joins across domain boundaries. MBGP offers a solution for cases in which the unicast and multicast routing is incongruent at the interdomain level, such as where different links are used for each type of traffic.

The deployment of multicast on a very large scale is still an evolving practice. PIM sparse-dense mode, auto-RP, and MSDP are some of the methods with which the configuration and segmentation of large multicast networks are being made simpler and more scalable.

Review Questions

1 Which multicast routing protocols does Cisco support?

2 How are PIM messages encapsulated for transmission on a network?

3 Do hosts or routers run IGMP?

4 PIM dense mode is a very simple protocol, yet it is not suitable for all applications. Why not?

5 Should you configure sparse mode or dense mode PIM on routers in your network?

6 What is the deployment/standards status of MBGP and MSDP?

7 Why might multicast and unicast topologies be incongruent?

8 What are the benefits of auto-RP over PIM V2's BSR mechanisms?

9 What are possible configuration options for obtaining multicast from your ISP? Address the cases in which you have an RP and the cases in which you do not.

Answers:

1 Cisco does not provide implementations of either MOSPF or DVRMP. PIM performs the functions of both. However, Cisco routers can interoperate with DVMRP, by which they can connect to the MBONE.

2 PIM V1 was encapsulated in IGMP (protocol number 102). PIM V2 messages are assigned protocol number 103.

3 Both. Hosts use IGMP to indicate their interest in particular groups. Routers use IGMP to query and learn about interested hosts.

4 As a flood-and-prune protocol, PIM dense mode periodically consumes high amounts of network bandwidth. PIM sparse mode avoids this by having an explicit join mechanism.

5 Use sparse-dense mode everywhere, unless you want to administratively forbid either mode for a particular reason.

6 MBGP is standardized in RFC 2283 and has been deployed for some time. As of this writing, MSDP was still in beta trials and at Internet Draft status. However, extremely positive early feedback means that the protocol will probably be widely deployed and standardized very soon.

7 Often, a particular LAN infrastructure does not support Layer 2 multicast, and, therefore, a separate infrastructure that does is supplied. On other occasions, it may be desirable to put multicast traffic on a separate physical infrastructure for billing or providing differentiated service. In the longer term, it is quite possible that unicast and multicast topologies will become congruent and the need for MBGP will diminish.

8 Auto-RP is simpler, serves the same purpose, and has had far more field exposure.

9 If you run your own RP, you need to find out whether your provider supports MSDP. If you don't have an RP, you may want to inquire about your provider sending auto-RP announcements to your network instead.

For Further Reading . . .

ftp://ftpeng.cisco.com/ipmulticast/html/ipmulticast.html

INTERNET-DRAFT. draft-ietf-idmr-igmp-v3-01.txt

Kumar, V. *MBONE: Interactive Multimedia on the Internet.* Indianapolis, IN: New Riders, 1996.

Maufer, T. *Deploying IP Multicast in the Enterprise.* Upper Saddle River, NJ: Prentice-Hall, 1998.

RFC 1112. Host Extensions for IP Multicast (IGMPv1).

RFC 2236. Internet Group Management Protocol, Version 2.

RFC 2283. Multiprotocol Extensions for BGP-4.

RFC 2327. SDP (Session Description Protocol).

RFC 2362. Protocol Independent Multicast-Sparse Mode: Protocol Specification.

RFC 2365. Administratively Scoped IP Multicast.

After completing your study of routing protocols, you now can learn how to provide differentiated levels of service within the network. Routing and differentiated service can be intimately linked—indeed, some routing protocols provide mechanisms for making different routing decisions based on the desired quality of service (QoS). However, for improved scalability, it is usually better to decouple routing and QoS in large networks. This chapter covers the following issues in relation to quality of service:

QoS policy propagation   This section briefly describes the ways in which QoS policy can be propagated throughout the network.

Congestion-management algorithms   In this section, you learn how routers cope with congestion when it occurs. In particular, first-in, first-out (FIFO), priority queuing, custom queuing, weighted fair queuing (WFQ), and selective packet discard are described.

Congestion-avoidance algorithms   Congestion can lead to the inefficient use of network resources. In this section, you will learn why and how RSVP, or the combination of weighted random early detection, rate limiting, and BGP policy propagation, can help.

Deploying QoS in large networks   Building on the techniques described in the previous sections, this section explores the deployment of QoS functionality in a large network architecture. The need for simple and scalable techniques is discussed, and a recommended approach is prescribed.

## CHAPTER 14

Quality of Service Features

Introduction to QoS

One school of thought believes that IP QoS is not cost-effective; and that spending money on fiber, over-engineering, or very responsive capacity-upgrade mechanisms is more cost-effective. It seems wise to subscribe to that school of thought when considering the backbone of a network. Nevertheless, simply waving money around does not immediately increase global fiber infrastructure. Networks will always face short-term congestion and isolated hot spots within a network architecture, such as international links for large ISPs. Therefore, it is important to understand the various mechanisms that enable you to manage or avoid congestion.

This chapter begins by reviewing various methods of providing differentiated service. In short, two requirements exist:

- A router must be capable of classifying and treating packets according to a QoS policy.
- There must be a way for routers to communicate this policy throughout the network.

The chapter describes solutions to the first requirement by describing the various queuing and packet drop schemes, collectively referred to as *congestion-management and avoidance algorithms*, within Cisco routers. For the latter requirement, the chapter examines the configuration of specific queuing algorithms, the Resource Reservation Protocol (RSVP), packet coloring via IP precedence, and policy propagation using BGP. It then describes the recommended model for large networks and considers some specific IOS configuration issues.

NOTE   *QoS*, an overused term, sometimes refers to service guarantees; other times it refers to providing preferential treatment to certain network traffic, but without absolute guarantees.

QoS Policy Propagation

Propagation of QoS policy within a network is typically provided in one of three ways:

- *Hard state*   Techniques are applied in circuit or connection-oriented networks. Resource reservations are made prior to or in conjunction with call routing through the network, and the reservations remain until the call or data transfer is terminated. This approach relies on complex signaling techniques for call setup, such as those associated with ATM call routing.

- *Soft state*   Techniques in this process are similar to hard state, except that the reservations must be periodically refreshed. The actual path through the network may change through the duration of the data transfers, which is one of the benefits of soft-state reservation. Again, the signaling associated with soft-state reservation can be quite complex, such as that of the RSVP.

  QoS enhancements for many routing protocols have also been proposed, and because most interior routing protocols use a soft-state algorithm, the associated QoS functionality is in the same category. This chapter examines propagating QoS policy through the BGP routing protocol.

- *Stateless*   Techniques rely on routers having a "hard-coded" queuing treatment for different packet types. A router may provide separate queues for packets at each IP precedence level or, more generally, based on any parameters associated with an IP flow, such as source/destination addresses and ports. Stateless techniques include priority and custom queuing, and no mechanism exists to communicate this QoS policy between routers in the network.

Throughout this book, chapters have emphasized scalability as an overriding goal when designing large networks. In particular, complex functions, such as accounting and routing policy, should be implemented at the perimeter of the network to minimize the effort required in the core and in the distribution networks, in which the emphasis is on switching packets as fast as possible.

Per-flow resource reservation is difficult to scale, and appears particularly daunting when you consider the potential signaling overhead in core routers carrying thousands or even millions of flows. In such environments, it becomes necessary to aggregate users into service classes. Consequently, if differentiated service will ever be implemented for large networks, mechanisms emphasizing the aggregation of users into broad categories represent the most scalable approach within the core. That requires the access network to provide the interface between the state-based reservation mechanisms typically required by users and stateless schemes necessary for scaling the network core.

Congestion-Management Algorithms

Congestion-management techniques are reactive, which means they determine how the network behaves when congestion is present. Unless they are configured by default within IOS, such as selective packet discard or FIFO, it is not wise to deploy these algorithms on a large scale. Instead, try using the congestion-avoidance techniques described later in this chapter.

Despite their limited scalability, user-configured congestion-management algorithms can be useful in isolated instances, such as a relatively low-bandwidth link dedicated to a special purpose. These algorithms are all stateless because each router must be individually configured (or programmed) to implement the desired policy.

First-In, First-Out Algorithm

The simplest queuing algorithm is the FIFO algorithm. The first packet that reaches a router will be the first that is allocated with a buffer, so it will be the first packet forwarded onto the next hop interface. This process is shown in Figure 14-1.

Figure 14-1   *The FIFO Algorithm*

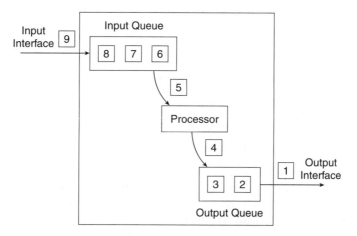

NOTE	Prior to the introduction of selective packet discard and WFQ, FIFO was the default treatment of packets received by a Cisco router.

Note that when multiple switching algorithms are enabled, the behavior may be not be exactly FIFO. For example, it is possible for a packet switched by Cisco Express Forwarding (CEF) to "leap frog" a process-switched packet simply because it has a faster and more immediate switching path. This is illustrated by Figure 14-2.

Figure 14-2   *FIFO "Leap Frogging" Due to Different Switching Engines*

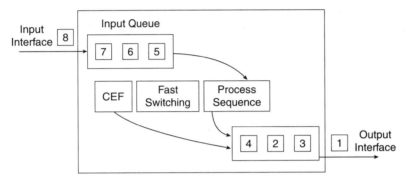

When the next hop link is congested under the FIFO algorithm, packets will be dropped from the tail of the output queue on the link under load. In TCP environments, this can result in waves of congestion due to *flow synchronization* (also called *global synchronization*). When several successive packets are dropped, the back-off/slow-start algorithms of the associated multiple TCP sessions are engaged, network load drops suddenly, and then slowly rebuilds until congestion reoccurs.

The resulting oscillation of network load between low usage and congestion results in poor average throughput and unpredictable latencies. A congestion-avoidance algorithm called *random early drop*, which is discussed shortly, alleviates this problem.

Other pitfalls of FIFO queuing are its inability to protect well-behaved sources against ill-behaved ones. "Bursty" traffic sources can produce unpredictable queuing latencies for delay-sensitive or real-time applications; high-bandwidth applications such as FTP can introduce sporadic performance for interactive applications such as Telnet. It is even possible for an application's data to disrupt traffic that is critical for network control and signaling. Selective packet discard and WFQ, which are enabled by default in more recent versions of IOS, alleviate these problems.

The key to receiving better service for critical applications is to introduce managed queues. The aim of managed queues is to penalize certain classes of traffic to benefit others.

Priority Queuing

Priority queuing is the simplest "fancy queuing" strategy. As shown in Figure 14-3, priority lists are used to allocate traffic into one of four priority queues: high, medium, normal, or low. The medium queue is serviced only when the high queue is empty, the normal queue is serviced when both the high and medium queues are empty, and the low queue is serviced when all the other queues are empty. Priority queues should be used with caution, as any traffic in higher queues can deny service to traffic in lower-priority queues. Moreover, priority queuing is a processor-intensive feature that does not scale well for high-speed interfaces.

Figure 14-3   *Priority Queuing*

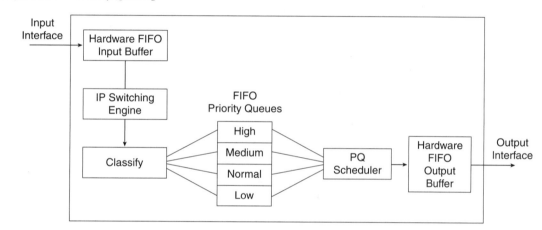

To avoid service denial, it may be necessary to increase the size of the lower-priority queues. This is achieved via the **priority-list <list> queue-limit** command. In addition, higher-priority queues may also be rate-limited using Committed Access Rate (CAR), described later in this chapter.

Priority queues are relatively simple to configure. In general, however, custom queuing provides a more flexible—not to mention deterministic—solution.

A router supports up to 16 priority lists, which can be applied to a particular interface or protocol. Those packets that do not match any of the allocations specified in the access list will be placed into the normal queue, although this behavior can be changed using the **priority-list <list> default <queuekeyword>** command. Within any particular priority queue, the algorithm is FIFO.

Custom Queuing

Custom queuing, also called *class-based queuing (CBQ)*, allows a guaranteed rate or latency to be provided to traffic identified by a queue list. Queue lists are used to allocate traffic into one of up to 16 custom queues. Queues 1 through 16 are serviced sequentially, allowing a configurable byte count to be transmitted before servicing the next queue. Packets are not fragmented if they fall across the byte-count boundary; servicing simply moves to the next queue when the byte count is exceeded.

This byte count determines the traffic "burst" permitted to each queue. The relative size of the byte counts across queues, together with the queue length, indirectly determines the proportion of overall link bandwidth allocated to each queue. Figure 14-4 shows this arrangement.

Figure 14-4 *Custom Queuing*

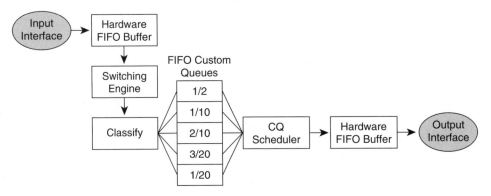

Although custom queuing prevents any queue from monopolizing resources, the latency in queues with small byte counts can be greater during periods of congestion. It may be necessary to tune the relative size of these queues with the **queue-list <list-number> queue <queue-number> limit** command to achieve optimum results.

NOTE   Queue 0 is reserved by IOS for keepalives, signaling, and other system-critical functions. It is emptied before any of the queues 1 through 16 are processed.

As with priority queues, custom queues can be applied to a particular interface or protocol. Packets that do not match any of the allocations specified in the access list will be placed into queue number 1, although this behavior can be changed using the **queue-list <list-number> default <queue-number>** command. Within any particular custom queue, the algorithm is FIFO.

Weighted Fair Queuing

WFQ is applied by default to all lines at E1 speeds (2 megabits per second) and below, provided that they are not using LAPB or PPP compression. When WFQ is enabled, low-volume flows such as Telnet or text-only Web traffic, which usually constitute the majority, are given higher priority on the link. High-volume flows such as FTP or multimedia Web content, which are generally fewer, share the remaining bandwidth on an FIFO basis and absorb the latency penalty. Figure 14-5 summarizes the operation of WFQ within the router.

Figure 14-5 *WFQ within the Router*

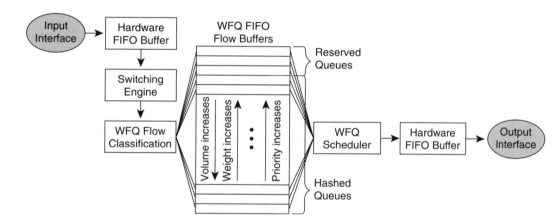

The weight of a queue is inversely proportional to throughput. Higher IP precedence reduces the weight, and link-level congestion feedback increases it. The result is reduced jitter, leading to more predictable bandwidth availability to each application. There is also less chance that larger traffic flows will starve smaller flows of resources.

This algorithm dynamically characterizes data flows—these are referred to as *conversations* in WFQ terminology. The packet attributes used to identify a conversation are similar to RSVP. They include the source and destination IP addresses and ports, and the IP protocol. Details of each conversation can be examined using the **show queue <interface>** command.

WFQ maintains two types of queues:

*   *Hashed queues* are characterized according to the volume of traffic associated with the conversation, the IP precedence of packets in the flow (higher precedence means lower weight), and the link-level congestion feedback associated with the flow. Examples include Frame Relay discard-eligible, backward explicit congestion notification, or forward explicit congestion notification.

*   *Reserved queues* are characterized by the RSVP session associated with the traffic flow.

You can set the number and size of reserved and hashed conversation queues on an interface using the **fair-queue** interface subcommand. When queue lengths exceed the congestive discard threshold, messages for that conversation are dropped.

The IP Precedence field has values between 0 (the default) and 7. IP Precedence serves as a divisor to this weighting factor. For instance, traffic with an IP Precedence field value of 7 receives a lower weight than traffic with an IP Precedence field value of 3, and therefore has priority in the transmit order.

For example, if you have one flow at each precedence level on an interface, the total link denominator is the following:

```
Denominator = 1+2+3+4+5+6+7+8 = 36
```

Thus, the flows at each precedence level will receive (precedence+1)/denominator.

However, if you have 18 precedence-1 flows and one each of the others, the denominator becomes the following:

```
Denominator = 1+18*2+3+4+5+6+7+8 = 70
```

The flows at each precedence level will get 8/70, 7/70, 6/70, 5/70, 4/70, 3/70, 2/70, and 1/70 of the link. This means the 18 flows at precedence 1 will share approximately 2/70 of the link.

NOTE   As with priority and custom queuing, WFQ becomes resource-exhaustive at high speeds for current processor-based implementations.

Selective Packet Discard

So far, this chapter has covered queue management for user data on the network. What about data that is critical for maintaining the network itself, such as routing updates or interface keepalives? Cisco routers automatically send packets that are critical to internetwork control with an IP precedence of 6 or above. The routers perform selective packet discard (SPD) for packets that are not critical to routing and interface stability.

You do not need to perform any configuration to enable SPD functionality. However, a more aggressive mode can be configured via the **ip spd mode aggressive** global configuration command. When aggressive mode is configured, all IP packets that fail basic sanity checks, such as those with bad checksums or TTLs, will be dropped aggressively as an extra protection against bad IP packet spoofing. The **show ip spd** command displays whether aggressive mode is enabled.

When the IP input queue reaches SPD minimum threshold, which is tuned via the **ip spd queue min-threshold n** command, all packets that are subject to aggressive drop policy are dropped immediately, whereas normal IP packets (not high-priority packets) are dropped with increasing probability as the length of the IP input queue grows. When the IP input queue reaches SPD maximum threshold, specified by the **ip spd queue max-threshold n** command, all normal IP packets are dropped at 100 percent. The default SPD minimum threshold is 10, whereas the default maximum threshold is 75. The default values for min and max threshold have been carefully selected by Cisco, and for most purposes, you will not need to modify them.

Managing congestion when it occurs is always tricky. What works in some instances may not work in others. Moreover, most congestion-management techniques have very little or no intelligence about one of the most ubiquitous forms of Internet traffic—TCP data flows. Congestion-avoidance algorithms introduce this intelligence.

Congestion-Avoidance Algorithms

Because the queue's tail drops, even in managed queue environments, and because it can induce global synchronization, there is a great deal of merit in environments that do not allow congestion in the first place. Covered here are two ways to accomplish this. The first is a combination of three features: CAR, Weighted Random Early Detection (WRED), and BGP policy propagation; the second is RSVP, a fully integrated bandwidth-management feature.

Although CAR and WRED are stateless policy propagation techniques, they become soft-state when combined with BGP. In other words, the information carried by the BGP routing protocol determines the level of service provided to all traffic.

RSVP, on the other hand, is the "classic" soft-state protocol for bandwidth reservation.

Weighted Random Early Detection

The queuing algorithms discussed so far are concerned with determining the behavior of the router in the presence of congestion. In other words, they are congestion-management algorithms.

Each algorithm results in packet drops from the tail of a queue in the event of congestion. As you have already seen, this can result in TCP flow synchronization, associated oscillatory congestion, and poor use of network bandwidth. Moreover, in some cases, multiple packets from a single TCP session tend to travel in groups, occupying successive slots in a router queue. Successive tail drops can, therefore, be applied to the packets from a single TCP session, which tends to effectively stall the session, rather than applying a slowdown.

WRED is a congestion-avoidance algorithm: It attempts to predict congestion, and then avoid it by inducing back-off in TCP traffic sources. WRED does this simply by monitoring the average queue depth of an interface using the following formula:

```
Average = (old_average * (1 - ½^n)) + (current_queue_size * ½^n).
```

When the average queue depth is above the minimum threshold, WRED begins to drop packets. The rate of packet drop increases linearly as the average queue size increases, until the average queue size reaches the maximum threshold.

WRED behavior is illustrated in Figure 14-6. The packet-drop probability is based on the minimum threshold, maximum threshold, and mark probability denominator. The *mark probability denominator* is the proportion of packets dropped when the queue length is at the maximum threshold. It thus determines the gradient of the packet-discard-probability lines in Figure 14-6. After the average queue size is above the maximum threshold, all packets are dropped.

Figure 14-7 shows the buffering arrangement in a router. A classifier inserts traffic from the switching engine into one of the prior eight WRED queues, which manage subsequent delivery to the hardware output buffer.

Figure 14-6   *Impact of MIN/MAX Thresholds and Mark Probability Denominator On WRED Packet Discard Probability*

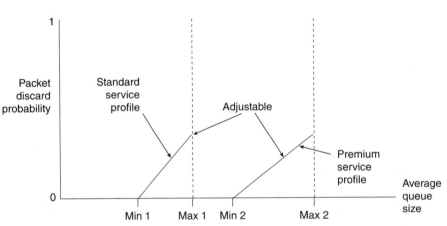

(a) Discard Probability for WRED

Statistically, this algorithm means that higher-bandwidth TCP sessions will experience more drops, so the sources generating the most traffic are the most likely to be slowed.

Now, we will consider the impact of changing WRED parameter values from the following defaults:

```
Mark-prob-denominator = 10
Min_threshold = (9 + IP Precedence)/18 * Max_threshold
Max_threshold = function of line speed and available buffering capacity
Exponential weighting constant = 9
```

Figure 14-7 *The Buffering Arrangement for WRED in a Router*

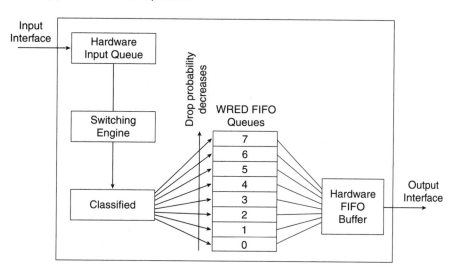

(b) Per Precedence Operation

WARNING The WRED default values are based on the best available data. Cisco recommends that you not change these values unless you have carefully determined the overall effect to be beneficial.

The *mark probability denominator* is the fraction of packets dropped when the average queue depth is at the maximum threshold. For example, if the denominator is 512, then one out of every 512 packets is dropped when the average queue is at the maximum threshold.

The *minimum threshold value* should be set high enough to maximize the link utilization. If the minimum threshold is too low, packets may be dropped unnecessarily, and the transmission link will not be fully used.

The difference between the maximum threshold and the minimum threshold should be large enough to avoid the inefficient "wave-like" network usage that occurs as the result of TCP global synchronization. If the difference is too small, many packets may be dropped at once, resulting in global synchronization.

The values of minimum threshold, maximum threshold, and mark probability denominator can be configured per-interface for each IP precedence: they affect the relative severity of the drop treatment provided for each precedence level (non-IP traffic is treated as precedence 0). By default, the probability of drop decreases with IP precedence because the minimum threshold is higher. If the values for each precedence are identical, WRED behavior reverts to that of standard (non-weighted) RED.

The n value is an exponential weighting constant that is configured on a per-interface basis. For high values of n, the previous average becomes more important, which smooths the peaks and lows in queue length. The WRED process will be slow to begin dropping packets, but it may continue dropping packets after the actual queue size has fallen below the minimum threshold. The slow-moving average will accommodate temporary bursts in traffic.

NOTE   If the value of n becomes too high, WRED will not react to congestion. Packets will be transmitted or dropped as if WRED were not in effect.

For low values of n, the average queue size closely tracks the current queue size. The resulting average may fluctuate with changes in the traffic levels. In this case, the WRED process responds quickly to long queues. When the queue falls below the minimum threshold, the process will stop dropping packets.

If the value of n becomes too low, WRED will overreact to temporary traffic bursts and will drop traffic unnecessarily.

WRED is dependent on well-behaved TCP implementations. It operates on the assumption that much of the network traffic is indeed TCP in the first place. As time goes on, these assumptions are becoming increasingly valid. Although WRED does not provide service guarantees in the presence of congestion, it does provide extremely scalable service differentiation and congestion-avoidance, which are the major arguments for its deployment in large network backbones, in which packet-switching speeds are paramount. Implementation of WRED in silicon switching elements is also extremely viable.

Rate-Limiting and Committed Access Rate

Rate-limiting controls the volume of data entering the network. It is generally deployed on routers that aggregate customer links, and configured parameters may be used as the basis of charging for the link.

In particular, if the capacity of the access circuit exceeds the network capacity required by the customer, rate-limiting may restrict a customer's use of the network to the agreed level. Cisco offers three traffic-shaping and policy tools: Generic Traffic Shaping, Frame Relay Traffic

Shaping, and CAR. This chapter focuses on the latter, CAR, because it is by far the most flexible and powerful mechanism for IP environments.

CAR rate limits may be implemented either on input or output interfaces, and they work for subinterface varieties, such as Frame Relay and ATM. They are usable only for IP traffic.

As shown in Figure 14-8, CAR performs three functions at the highest level. First, traffic is passed through a filter. Second, packets matching the filter classification are passed through a token bucket-based, traffic rate measurement system. Third, actions may be performed on the packet, depending on the results of the traffic rate measurement system. These three functions may be cascaded so that an individual packet may pass through a CAR policy consisting of multiple match/measure/action stages.

Figure 14-8   *CAR Performs Three Distinct Functions*

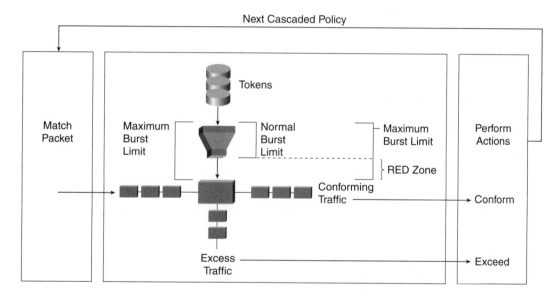

Packets may be classified by physical port, source, destination IP or MAC address, application port, IP protocol type, or other criteria specifiable by access lists or extended access lists. Packets also may have been already classified by external sources, such as a customer or a downstream network provider. This external classification may be accepted by the network, or may be overridden and reclassified according to a specified policy. The CAR rate limit commands **set-prec-transmit** and **set-prec-continue** are used for packet coloring and re-coloring.

Traffic rate measurement occurs via token bucket filters. Token bucket parameters include the *committed rate* (in increments of 8 Kbps), the *normal burst size*, and the *excess burst size*. Tokens are added to the bucket at the committed rate, and the number of tokens in the bucket is limited by the normal burst size.

Arriving packets that find sufficient tokens available are said to conform. The appropriate number of tokens is removed from the bucket, and the specified conform action is executed. Traffic exceeding the normal burst limit, but falling within the excess burst limit, is handled via a RED-like managed discard policy that provides a gradual effect for the rate limit and allows the traffic sources to slow down before suffering sequential packet discards.

Some arriving packets might not conform to the token bucket specification, either because they exceed the excess burst limit, or because they fall between the normal burst limit and the maximum burst limit and were not probabilistically discarded. These packets are handled by the specified exceed action.

Unlike a leaky bucket implementation, CAR does not smooth or shape the traffic; therefore, it does not buffer or add delay.

You may configure the conform/exceed actions with the following information:

- *Transmit*   Switch the packet.
- *Set precedence and transmit*   Set the precedence bits in the Type of Service field in the IP packet header to a specified value, and transmit. This action can be utilized to either color (set precedence) or recolor (modify existing packet precedence) the packet.
- *Drop*   Discard the packet.
- *Continue*   Evaluate the next rate limit in a chain of rate limits.
- *Set precedence and continue*   Set the precedence bits to a specified value, and then evaluate the next rate limit in the chain.

In case of VIP-based platforms, two more policies and one extra capability are possible:

- *Set QoS group and transmit*   The packet is assigned to a QoS group, and then is transmitted.
- *Set QoS group and continue*   The packet is assigned to a QoS group, and then is evaluated using the next rate policy. If there is not another rate policy, the packet is transmitted.
- *Cascading*   This method enables a series of rate limits to be applied to packets. Cascading specifies more granular policies to match packets against an ordered sequence of policies until an applicable rate limit is reached, and the packet is either transmitted or discarded. Packets that fall to the bottom of a list of rate limits are transmitted. You can configure up to 100 rate policies on a subinterface.

CAR can be used to partition network traffic into multiple priority levels or classes of service (CoSs). You may define up to eight CoSs using the three precedence bits in the Type of Service field in the IP header, and then utilize the other QoS features to assign appropriate traffic-handling policies, including congestion management, bandwidth allocation, and delay bounds for each traffic class. In particular, CAR may be used to apply this policy at the perimeter of the network, leaving WRED to appropriately deal with packets within the core and distribution networks.

The status of traffic shaping can be examined using the **show traffic**, **show traffic statistics**, and **show <interface> rate-limit** commands.

BGP Policy Propagation

CAR and WRED provide QoS policy enforcement within the router, but how is this policy propagated throughout the network? BGP policy propagation makes this possible by enabling you to adjust the IP precedence of a packet based on its source or destination address and, optionally, based on the associated BGP community and/or *as-path*. Recall from Chapter 11, "Border Gateway Protocol," that an *as-path* is a mandatory BGP attribute that lists each autonomous system through which the route has passed.

As shown in Figure 14-9, when a BGP best path (the most preferred BGP route to a destination) is inserted into the CEF forwarding table, a table map may be applied via the **table-map bgp** subcommand. The table map, which is actually a route map, matches the prefix based on IP address, community, or as-path; and adds an IP precedence or QoS-group-id to the inserted CEF entry. The IP precedence or QoS-group-id of any CEF entry can be viewed via the **show ip cef** command.

Figure 14-9   *When the Best BGP Route Is Inserted Into the CEF Forwarding Table, a Table Map May Be Applied via the **table-map bgp** Subcommand*

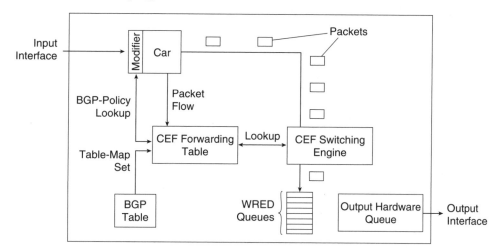

You can configure the IP precedence of a packet to be overwritten by the value in the CEF table via the **bgp-policy {source | destination} ip-prec-map interface** subcommand. In addition, the packet may be tagged with a QoS-group-id via the **bgp-policy {source | destination} ip-qos-map interface** subcommand. Either the source or the destination address can be used for the purpose of classifying the packet. After the precedence has been overwritten, or after a QoS tag has been applied, CAR and WRED functionality can still be applied, as shown in Figure 14-9.

Note that the QoS-group-id is not part of the IP packet—it is stripped after the packet exits the router—however, the modified IP precedence remains. Within the router, both the IP precedence and the QoS-group-id can be used in conjunction with CAR functionality.

NOTE   In all cases, the associated interface must be configured for CEF or dCEF.

Both the **table-map BGP** subcommand and **bgp-policy interface** subcommand need to be applied only where traffic classification and/or rate-limiting are required; routers deeper within the network can differentiate between packets based on the overwritten IP Precedence field.

Note, however, that the router performing the classification must have the necessary BGP routing information to perform the classification. This might mean that you need to carry extra routing information in access routers if the classification is based on the destination address of the packet. Figure 14-10 shows the reason for this.

Figure 14-10 *Using BGP Policy Propagation: AS2 Is the Service Provider and AS1 and AS3 Are Customers*

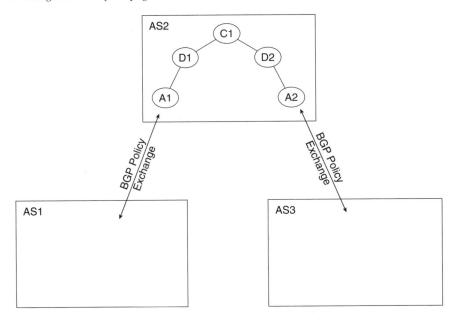

In Figure 14-10, AS2 is the service provider, and AS1 and AS3 are customers. If access router A1 in AS2 receives traffic from AS1 that is destined for AS3, and classifies packets based on BGP information associated with the source address, the route is successful because A1 receives BGP updates directly from AS1, containing the necessary classification data.

Consider, however, that AS3 wants all packets that it is destined to receive to be allocated a certain IP precedence within AS2's network. This can occur only if router A1 receives BGP updates about AS3's network. In short, the access-router in AS2 must carry routing information about AS3, and any other AS for which QoS policy propagation is required. Access router A1 cannot use the default route for any destination networks requiring QoS policy.

In practice, this may not cause difficulty because any customer that expects QoS treatment will probably want to receive a full set of routes from the provider anyway (for multihoming purposes, for example). This means that A1 must carry full routes for all customers of AS2. Nevertheless, this example demonstrates the increased requirements for access routers in terms of memory and route computations, if BGP-QoS propagation and dual-homing is required.

Resource Reservation Protocol

RSVP is a soft-state signaling system that enables receivers to reserve resources for incoming traffic flows. Flows are identified by destination address and the transport-layer protocol, and are, therefore, unidirectional. The destination address can be a multicast group address; therefore, from an RSVP perspective, unicast flows are simply a special case of multicast. More specifically, in the unicast case, it is not necessary for a host to join a group prior to reserving resources via RSVP.

Besides the queuing mechanisms of WRED and WFQ, RSVP also relies on the underlying routing protocol to determine the path from sender to receiver. Although the receiver initiates RSVP reservations, the protocol includes its own mechanisms for discovering the route, derived from the routing protocol, from sender to receiver, and therefore does not rely on a symmetrically-routed environment.

RSVP is a soft-state protocol, which means that the messages necessary for reserving resources are periodically repeated. This process serves as a rudimentary protection against lost RSVP messages, enables new participants to be added mid-session—such as when a new receiver or sender joins a multicast group—and provides for changes in network routing.

Service Classes and Reservation Styles

| **NOTE** | RSVP is simply a reservation scheme: it relies on the underlying interface queuing mechanisms of WRED and WFQ to implement controlled load and guaranteed service reservations, respectively. |

Controlled load reservations tightly approximate the performance visible to best-effort applications under unloaded conditions. That is, a high percentage of transmitted packets will be successfully delivered, with a transit delay approximately equal to the router switching delays, in addition to propagation and packetization delays.

| **NOTE** | *Switching delay* is the amount of time the router needs to process and forward a packet; *propagation delay* is the speed of light in the transmission media; and *packetization delay* is the time required for a router to receive a packet on a particular link. For example, a 512-byte packet on a 1 megabit/s link has a packetization delay of 512×8 bits/1,000,000 bits/s = 4 milliseconds. |

In short, very little time is spent in packet queues. Applications requesting a controlled load reservation indicate their performance requirements in the form of traffic specification (Tspec) parameters carried in RSVP messages. If the traffic generated by the application exceeds these requirements, the performance visible to the application will exhibit overload characteristics, such as packet loss and large delays.

According to the RSVP standard, the overload conditions for RSVP-controlled load reservations do not have to be equivalent to those of best-effort (non-QoS-reserved) traffic following the same path through the network. They can be much better or much worse. WRED applies weights to RSVP-controlled load flows appropriate to the Tspec parameters.

Guaranteed service reservations provide an assured level of bandwidth with delay-bounded service. This delay bound refers to queuing delay only; switching, propagation, and packetization delays must be added to the guaranteed service delay to determine the overall delay for packets. WFQ weights are applied to provide the necessary queue-servicing to bound the queuing delay.

The bandwidth available on any particular link on which RSVP/WFQ is enabled is allocated as shown in Figure 14-11. Bandwidth is first allocated to reserved flows. This is followed by bandwidth for interactive/low-volume, best-effort flows; and the remaining bandwidth is available for high-bandwidth, best-effort flows. For RSVP/WRED, bandwidth is allocated first to reserved flows, and then to best-effort flows.

Figure 14-11 *Link Bandwidth Allocation with RSVP (a) and WRED (b)*

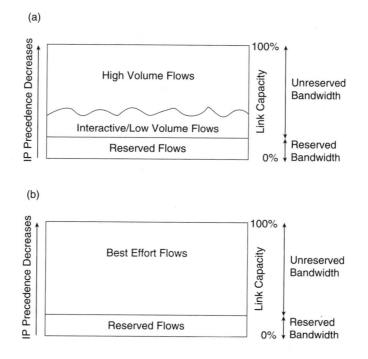

RSVP supports three reservation styles, with more expected as the protocol evolves:

- *A wildcard filter (WF) style reservation*   Traffic from all senders is grouped into a shared pipe. The resources allocated to this shared pipe match the largest reservation by any receiver using the pipe. This style is useful when there is usually only one or two active senders from an entire group. An audio conference is a typical example. Each receiver could request sufficient bandwidth to enable one or two senders (speakers) to speak at the same time.

- *A shared-explicit (SE) style reservation* This reservation method uses the same shared pipe environment. However, the set of senders sharing the pipe is explicitly set by the receiver making the reservation (no sender-wildcard). To use the audio-conference example once more, with an SE style reservation, you still would reserve enough resources to allow one or two people to speak—however, you are explicitly specifying those people you want to hear. This style of reservation is obviously less convenient than the WF style, but it provides greater control for the audience.

- *A fixed filter (FF) style* This method reserves resources for flows from an explicit list of senders; the total reservation on any link is therefore the *sum total* of reservations for each sender. When the destination is a multicast group of addresses, FF style reservations from multiple receivers for the same sender must be merged, and the router performing the multicast packet replication calculates the largest resource allocation. Unicast reservations are generally fixed filter style, with a single sender specified.

RSVP uses IP protocol 46, although a UDP encapsulation using ports 1698 and 1699 is also supported for hosts. The multicast address used by the router to send UDP-encapsulated messages is set with the **ip rsvp udp-multicast** global configuration command.

RSVP Operation

The operation of RSVP is shown in Figure 14-12. Because the routed path from sender to receiver may be asymmetric, such as when the path for traffic from Host A to Host B is via R1, R2, R3, and the return path is via R3, R1, senders must prime the routers to expect reservation requests for a particular flow. This is accomplished by using *path* messages from the sender to the first hop router toward the receiver.

Figure 14-12 *RSVP Operation*

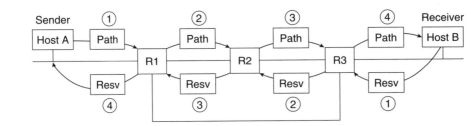

The first hop router inserts its own address as the path message's last hop, and forwards it to the next hop router. This "last hop" field tells the next hop router where to forward a reservation message for this particular flow.

This hop-by-hop processing of path messages continues until the receiver is reached. At this point, if the receiver sends a reservation message toward the sender, each router knows how to forward the reservation message back to the sender so that it flows through each router in the path from sender to receiver. The **ip rsvp neighbor** command can be used for neighboring routers from which the local router will accept reservations.

If an error occurs in the processing of path or reservation messages, a *path-error* or *reservation-error* message is generated and is routed hop-by-hop toward the sender or receiver, respectively. Each error message includes objects sufficient to uniquely identify the path or reservation message causing the error, and it always includes the ERROR-SPEC object. There are several possible errors that can occur:

- *Admission failure*   Reservation could not be granted due to unavailable resources.
- *Administrative rejection*   Policy forbids reservation.
- *No Path information for Reservation message.*
- *No Sender information for Reservation message.*
- *Conflicting reservation style*   The style does not match the existing state.
- *Unknown reservation style.*
- *Conflicting destination ports*   Zero and non-zero destination port fields have appeared for the same session.
- *Conflicting sender ports*   Zero and non-zero source port fields have appeared for the same session.
- *Service preempted*   Hard state already exists.
- *Unknown object class.*
- *Unknown object type.*
- *Traffic Control Error*   Malformed requests have been issued.
- *Traffic Control System Error.*
- *RSVP System Error*   Implementation-dependent debugging messages are present.

Paths and reservations have an associated refresh period, which is generally randomized within a range to avoid congestion issues associated with synchronization of control messages. If this period expires without a refresh of the reservation state, the reservation is expired. However, to liberate resources in a more timely manner, a reservation TEARDOWN message is used to remove the reservation even before its soft-state expires.

RSVP Protocol

Figure 14-13 shows the format of RSVP messages, which consist of a header containing seven defined fields and one reserved field, followed by a main body containing a series of RSVP objects.

Figure 14-13 *RSVP Messages*

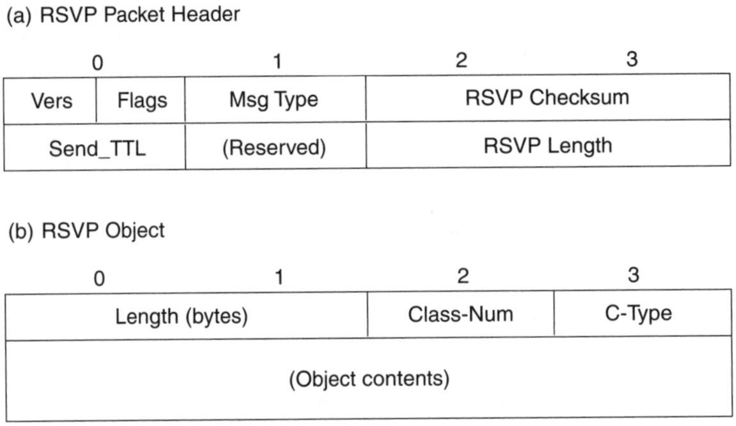

(a) RSVP Packet Header

0	1	2	3
Vers	Flags	Msg Type	RSVP Checksum
Send_TTL		(Reserved)	RSVP Length

(b) RSVP Object

0	1	2	3
Length (bytes)		Class-Num	C-Type
(Object contents)			

Each message begins with a 4-bit RSVP version number: the current version is 2. This is followed by a 4-bit flag field, which is currently unused. The type field indicates the message type:

Value	Type
1	Path
2	Reservation-request
3	Path-error
4	Reservation-request error
5	Path-teardown
6	Reservation-teardown
7	Reservation-request acknowledgment

A 16-bit standard TCP/UDP *checksum* is used over the entire contents of the RSVP message. The checksum field is assumed to be zero. *Length* is the RSVP packet length in bytes. The *Send TTL* is matched to the TTL of the IP packet in which the RSVP message was encapsulated.

Each RSVP object field begins with an object length field, which must be one or more multiples of 4. The Class-Num and C-Type fields identify the object class and type, respectively. Currently defined class/type combinations are shown in Table 14-1.

Table 14-1 *RSVP Object Classes*

Object Class	Description
Null	Contains a Class-Num of 0, and its C-Type is ignored. Its length must be at least 4, but can be any multiple of 4. A null object can appear anywhere in a sequence of objects, and its contents will be ignored by the receiver.
Session	Contains the IP destination address and possibly a generalized destination port to define a specific session for the other objects that follow (required in every RSVP message).
RSVP Hop	Carries the IP address of the RSVP-capable node that sent this message.
Time Values	If present, contains values for the refresh period and the state TTL to override the default values.
Style	Defines the reservation style, plus style-specific information that is not a flow-specification or filter-specification object (included in the reservation-request message).
Flow Specification	Defines a desired QoS (included in a reservation-request message).
Filter Specification	Defines a subset of session-data packets that should receive the desired QoS (specified by a flow-specification object within a reservation-request message).
Sender Template	Contains a sender IP address and perhaps some additional demultiplexing information to identify a sender (included in a path message).
Sender TSPEC	Defines the traffic characteristics of a sender's data stream (included in the path message).
Adspec	Carries advertising data in a path message.
Error Specification	Specifies an error (included in a path-error or reservation-request error message).
Policy Data	Carries information that will enable a local policy module to decide whether an associated reservation is administratively permitted (included in a path or reservation-request message).
Integrity	Contains cryptographic data to authenticate the originating node and perhaps to verify the contents of this reservation-request message.
Scope	An explicit specification of the scope for forwarding a reservation-request message.
Reservation Confirmation	Carries the IP address of a receiver that requested a confirmation. Can appear in either a reservation-request or reservation-request acknowledgment.

RSVP is enabled on a (sub)interface basis using **ip rsvp bandwidth [interface-kbps] [single-flow-kbps]**. By default, up to 75 percent of an interface bandwidth can be reserved by RSVP, although this can be adjusted using the **interface-kbps** parameter; by default, **single-flow-kbps** is 100 percent of the interface kbps.

Deploying QoS in Large Networks

As usual, the approach is to perform computational expensive functions at the perimeter of the network, liberating the core and distribution networks to focus on aggregation and forwarding functions. Hence, it is recommended that you deploy policy control functions on the network perimeter and incorporate congestion avoidance, in the form of WRED, at the core. If traffic-shaping and/or rate-limiting is required at the network perimeter, CAR represents the most flexible solution.

This is not to say that congestion-management capabilities (such as priority or custom queuing) will not find application in the network, but they should be used sparingly and with caution, particularly on high-speed links.

In its current form, RSVP will be difficult to scale to a large network backbone. However, the reservations can be mapped at the perimeter of the network into IP precedence.

If WRED is used in the core, the primary policy control that must be performed is the setting of IP precedence. This can be achieved in three ways. First, the network operator may apply the precedence based on policy (CAR access lists) configured into the IP precedence, either on the host station or via routers in the customer network. Second, the network operator may apply precedence in the access router to which the customer connects using static access lists. Third, the customer may dynamically indicate to the network operator the IP precedence to associate with each set of source addresses based on BGP communities. The case study at the end of the chapter demonstrates the application of these ideas.

Summary

In this chapter, you examined various QoS solutions that are employed in building large networks. In particular, you discovered the details of Cisco features that are available for congestion management (FIFO, PQ, CQ, WFQ) and avoidance (WRED, CAR), as well as the means to propagate QoS policy through the network (IP precedence, BGP policy propagation, and RSVP).

Although the various fancy queuing mechanisms and soft-state mechanisms such as RSVP are highly flexible solutions, they consume valuable resources, and current implementations are applicable only to line rates in the low megabits per second. However, the combination of CAR on the perimeter, WRED in the core for congestion avoidance, and BGP for intra/interdomain QoS signaling represents a highly-scalable and easily-managed suite of features for the deployment of differentiated services on a large scale.

Implementation of differentiated services within a network is a highly contentious issue. Clearly, the mechanisms described in this chapter are not a solution for a poorly-scaled or under-engineered network. However, mechanisms such as WFQ and WRED can improve the perceived quality and utilization of network bandwidth.

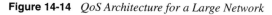

Case Study: Applying Differentiated Service in a Large Network

This case study describes the QoS architecture of a large service provider network. We use the network topology developed in Chapter 4, "Network Topologies," as a model for this case study. Figure 14-14 shows the QoS architecture for this topology. In summary, WRED is deployed on all backbone links; WRED or WFQ is deployed on links to customers, possibly in addition to CAR.

Figure 14-14 *QoS Architecture for a Large Network*

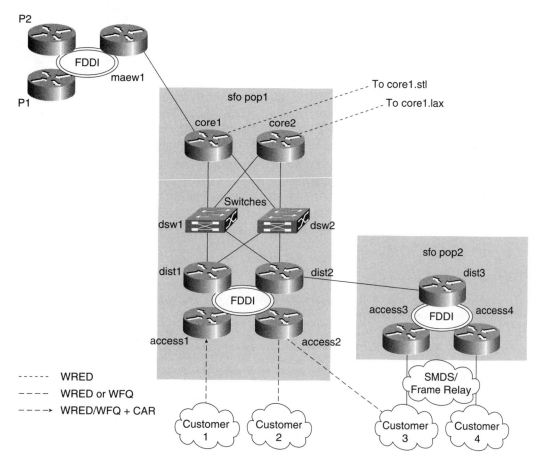

Configuring the distribution and core routes is trivial: simply enable WRED via the **random-detect** command on all interfaces where output congestion is expected. DWRED should be used where possible. As a general rule, the default WRED parameter settings are appropriate.

If the customer is left to set the IP precedence of incoming packets, access router QoS configuration can be as simple as enabling WRED on the interface leading to the service provider. However, one should consider the issues involved in allowing the customer to assign IP policy for their traffic. There must be a level of expertise with the customer network that will permit them to make appropriate IP precedence configurations within their own hosts or routers. Perhaps more importantly, there must be some restrictions to prevent customers from using the critical preference values reserved for network administrative functions, such as routing.

The last point is the need to police incoming precedence levels upon ingress to the network, similar to the way in which routing updates or packet source addresses are handled. This encourages the provider to implement QoS policy, regardless of customer actions. Policing can be achieved via CAR or via the **ip policy-map** interface subcommand and an associated route map.

The access router can be configured to apply policy based on access lists. At the same time, various CAR rate-limit policies can be applied. This approach is static: the customers are not allowed the flexibility of adjusting the level of service that they wish to have applied to various traffic sources.

If the customers offer routes to the provider via BGP, this can be used to set the appropriate precedence level upon ingress to the network via BGP policy propagation. This allows the IP precedence associated with the each prefix to be dynamically signaled to the network.

Customer-initiated QoS policy changes are sent to the provider by updating, for example, the community assigned to a prefix, and then sending a new BGP update to the provider. Moreover, the provider can propagate this information to other customers, as well as other network operators, allowing them to implement their own policies.

Review Questions

1 Many switching modes can be employed. How can you determine which mode is enabled on a particular interface?

2 Is over-engineering network bandwidth cheaper than deploying various complicated QoS strategies?

3 Should you use CAR, WRED, WFQ, or RSVP?

4 Should you manage congestion, or avoid it altogether?

5 An example network has multiprotocol traffic such as AppleTalk, IPX, and SNA traffic. Can you still use WRED in this environment?

6 How can you propagate policy when not running BGP?

Answers:

1 Output from the following commands is most useful:

```
show ip interface
show interfaces rate-limit
show interfaces random-detect
show ip rsvp interface
show interfaces
```

2 For wide-area networks (WANs), no. Although in certain local area network (LAN) environments the bandwidth may allow all requirements to be met by over-engineering, this is not generally true for expensive WAN links. There are likely to be very expensive links, such as transoceanic Internet infrastructure, that are oversubscribed for long periods; and there are likely to be less expensive links, such as national infrastructure, on which load exceeds capacity for short periods. In these instances, ensuring that the network will behave predictably is the key goal of QoS.

3 It depends on the application. CAR is good for inbound rate-limiting and traffic-coloring. WRED is ideal for high-speed links, particularly in a network that makes use of IP precedence. WFQ is a good match for low-speed links. RSVP, on the other hand, is a reservation-signaling protocol that complements the use of CAR, WRED, and WFQ. RSVP has scaling limitations; for large networks and interprovider QoS signaling, you should consider BGP policy propagation.

4 Short periods of congestion are nearly impossible to avoid, and in these instances, features such as selective packet discard will help maintain network integrity. Priority and custom queuing can help manage congestion, but should be used sparingly on links that you cannot afford to upgrade. For widespread, high-speed deployment, the congestion-avoidance capabilities of WRED are extremely attractive.

5 Use WRED with caution. WRED automatically treats protocols other than TCP as being equivalent to IP traffic with the lowest precedence. This means the "multiprotocol" traffic will be dropped with greater probability than TCP traffic with higher IP precedence. If most of your TCP traffic is at higher precedence, it is possible that some delay/loss multiprotocol applications will degrade. Special measures can be taken in this situation (such as IP encapsulation of multiprotocol traffic), but these are beyond the scope of this book.

6 You can use CAR or IP policy maps to set the IP precedence of packets upon ingress to the network. The packet then intrinsically signals its priority to all routers running WFQ or WRED as it passes through the network. This approach has limited scalability and will not easily enable you to set the IP precedence based on the destination address of a packet. To do this, every router would have to associate the precedence with all destination routes statically configured.

For Further Reading . . .

Huitema, Christian. *Routing in the Internet.* Upper Saddle River, NJ: Prentice Hall, 1998.

Huston, Geoff and Paul Ferguson. *Quality of Service.* New York, NY: John Wiley and Sons, 1998.

Partridge, Craig. *Gigabit Networking.* Reading, MA: Addison-Wesley, 1993.

RFC 1633. *Integrated Services in the Internet Architecture: An Overview.*

RFC 2205. *Resource Reservation Protocol.*

www.lbl.gov/CS/research.html#network. Lawrence Berkeley Labs (network research activities). Contains useful research into RED, CBQ, and other areas related to IP QoS.

This chapter examines the general network-management task, and provides some specific recommendations for sustaining and evolving large networks. The discussion centers around the five functional areas of network management originally defined by the International Standards Organization (ISO): fault, configuration, security, accounting, and performance. Some of this information is specific to the Cisco IOS, although many of the ideas are generally applicable to any large network. The approach is pragmatic and focuses on issues that, if not handled properly, can cause scaling difficulties.

The following areas are addressed in this chapter:

Overview of network management   This section outlines the overall network-management task by describing the five functional areas: fault, configuration, security, accounting, and performance management.

Network management systems   How is a network management system constructed? This section considers the fundamental requirements of such a system. The pros and cons of a centralized versus distributed system are discussed, with particular emphasis on reliability and scalability.

The Simple Network Management Protocol (SNMP)   The Simple Network Management Protocol is a fundamental network-management tool. This section describes the protocol and the Management Information Bases (MIBs) upon which it operates.

Use of Netflow   Netflow is also a fundamental network-management tool for Cisco networks. This section describes the feature, explains how it operates, and discusses the type of information it provides.

Fault management   Fault management involves detecting, isolating, tracking, and resolving network problems. This section discusses the use of automated polling of MIBs, SNMP traps, and system logging to detect network problems. We also describe the use of NTP to synchronize network-management events and discuss how DNS aids the fault-isolation process. Finally, the viability of automated fault resolution is discussed.

Configuration and security management   Configuration management involves tracking and documenting all device configurations within the network. This section also describes revision control and the staging of network upgrades. Access control to network devices for configuration purposes is also a major part of security management; this section considers the use of Cisco AAA features to control and monitor the configuration of routers.

Performance and accounting management   This section describes the use of SNMP and Netflow to monitor the network for performance thresholds, and to account for the use of network resources. Network capacity planning, traffic engineering, throughput monitoring, and traffic accounting are all discussed.

This chapter concludes with a network management checklist, which reviews the concepts presented throughout the chapter so that you can apply them to your own network.

## CHAPTER 15

Network Operations and Management

Overview of Network Management

During the 1980s, the explosion in the deployment of heterogeneous networking technologies caused an alarming increase in the need for support staff. Large corporations were forced to engage expensive equipment management specialists who were familiar with specific technology sets. Clearly, to reduce overhead, to speed fault resolution, and to aid capacity planning, a standardized management framework was required.

NOTE   Network-management tasks are divided into five conceptual areas: fault, configuration, security, accounting, and performance.

For this reason, ISO stepped in and divided the network-management task into five conceptual areas: fault, configuration, security, accounting, and performance. Each is discussed here:

- Fault management requires the detection, isolation, resolution, and recording of network problems—if possible, before they degrade network performance noticeably. These processes should be automated as much as possible. Fault-management practices usually rely heavily on the use of the Simple Network Management Protocol (SNMP), either to poll the network for health reports or to accept reports asynchronously from various network devices. Such polling or report collection is usually focused at the Network Management System (NMS), which may be an integrated commercial package or a specially assembled suite of programs, generally with a heavy basis on public domain software.

  For very large networks, fault management is often front-ended by a graphical user interface (GUI) used by 24x7 network operations staff. Various reporting mechanisms, such as color changes, flashing icons, or audible alarms may be used to alert operations staff members of potential problems.

- Security management is generally the control of access to any information on the network. It may include host and database access mechanisms, firewalls, transactions logging, and a myriad of other security-related functions that prevent intentional or unintentional misuse of resources. This chapter, however, focuses on ensuring the security of routers and the overall operational integrity of the network. This includes limiting, controlling, and recording the access and abuse of routers within the core and distribution networks, as well as authenticating routes and applying policies.

- These functions also could be considered part of configuration management, so security and configuration issues are discussed simultaneously. Configuration management also involves maintaining a database, describing all devices within the network. This database may contain both physical and logical configurations, including hardware and software versions, and provides a means to track network upgrades and, in the event of failure, to roll back to an earlier configuration.

  For large Cisco networks, revision control for both IOS versions and router configurations is essential. Again, SNMP can play a major role in both the collection and installation of router configurations, particularly when the network is managed by an integrated NMS such as CiscoWorks.

- Accounting and performance management are also closely related. Accounting of network traffic can occur for the purposes of presenting a bill, or it can serve traffic-engineering purposes, in which case the accounting data is used for performance management. For dedicated services, which is the focus here, most large network operators charge either a flat rate based on the bandwidth of the access link, or a per-byte volume charge. In the latter case, the volume charges are usually tiered; the more you buy, the cheaper the per-byte cost.

  SNMP provides the statistics necessary for per-byte charging schemes and those required for basic performance monitoring and traffic engineering. Although Netflow accounting makes distance-dependent charging technically possible, few (if any) large ISPs have introduced such schemes. Nevertheless, Netflow can provide statistics that are of great use (after significant post-processing) in analyzing traffic flows through the network. These can be used to tune the allocation of bandwidth between various points in the network, in which case Netflow is a fundamental traffic-engineering tool.

  Performance does not relate only to the use of bandwidth, however. Switching and buffering of packets, together with the calculation of routing tables, can consume resources within routers. Performance management involves monitoring the network, sounding alerts when certain thresholds are exceeded, and collecting statistics that enable the administrator to predict future needs and perform capacity planning.

Network Management Systems

The design of a well-integrated Network Management System (NMS) has proven to be a very challenging area of software development. Few if any commercial off-the-shelf (COTS) systems work in the largest environments without at least some tailoring. In many cases, public domain software is still used extremely effectively because it is often well-understood, and because it can be fine-tuned by operations engineers. In addition, forming an NMS from a number of stand-alone tools avoids the proverbial situation of putting all the eggs in one basket. In other words, if the NMS is a tightly integrated package and, for example, the underlying database is corrupted, the network can be left without any management functionality whatsoever.

Whether COTS, home-grown, or a combination of the two, most NMSs will perform these functions:

- Graphically represent the state of the network
- Download, upload, and track device configurations
- Perform SNMP polling, trap collection, and logging
- Show historical information via graphs, tables, or simple ASCII outputs

Some sophisticated systems may aid troubleshooting and configuration considerably; this might include some expert-system functionality, such as intelligent fault isolation, or drag-and-drop configuration. Most COTS NMSs feature an API that accommodates the creation of proprietary applications. If they speed fault resolution or support sophisticated service level 1 offerings, such applications can offer a significant advantage to commercial network operators.

NMSs can be arranged in a centralized, hierarchical, or fully distributed architecture, as illustrated in Figure 15-1.

When operated as a centralized facility, which represents the most cost-effective solution for smaller networks, the NMS will be located physically at a "well-connected" point in the network architecture. Although cost-effective, the centralized NMS introduces a single point of failure in two ways: by the NMS being cut off from the network due to network failure and because of failure of the NMS itself. In addition, this model does not scale particularly well. Funneling of network-management data resulting from polling or traps can consume enormous bandwidth in the vicinity of the NMS, not to mention introducing high CPU load within the NMS platform.

NMS can be arranged hierarchically, where each element, or *sub-NMS*, is responsible for managing the facilities within its level of the hierarchy. NMS may also request reports from sub-NMS elements lower (or possibly higher) in the hierarchy. This arrangement alleviates the scaling problem, but still suffers from increased levels of *criticality* (the adverse effects on the operation of the network in the event of a failure) as you climb the hierarchy. At the top of the hierarchy is a single point of failure.

The fully distributed NMS, then, offers the most scalable and reliable architecture. Each sub-NMS element is relatively autonomous, in that it is responsible for a certain area of the network and is a peer with other sub-NMS elements. The distributed architecture may also include hierarchical elements to aid scalability within a particular area of the network. Naturally, there must be a means for peer elements to exchange reports about the state of their areas of responsibility, which may include a full exchange and synchronization of their respective databases. Distributed NMS architectures are therefore much more complicated than centralized architectures.

Figure 15-1 *NMS Architectures*

(a) Centralized NMS

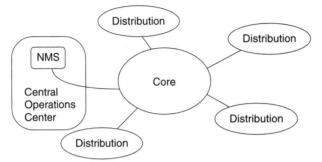

(b) Hierarchical NMS

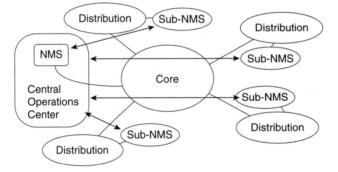

(c) Distributed NMS

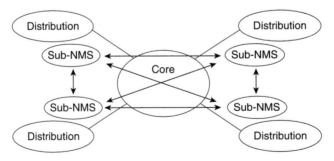

The Simple Network Management Protocol

The SNMP management suite consists of an organized structuring of information within each managed device, as well as a protocol to retrieve and set that information. The following section first explains how the information is stored.

Management Information Bases

The *Management Information Base (MIB)* is a hierarchical arrangement of all information accessible on a device via SNMP. A device may support many MIBs, and each MIB may be standard or proprietary. The *Structure of Management Information (SMI)* (RFC 1065 relates to SNMPv1, and RFC 1902 to SNMPv2) describes the naming and data types that may exist in a MIB.

A MIB itself is defined using the ISO Abstract Syntax Notation 1 (ASN.1) and extends in a tree from an unnamed root. Each node or branch in the tree (other than the root) is identified via an Object Identifier (OID). OIDs are globally unique, but particular bodies may be allocated administrative control at certain points in the hierarchy. Figure 15-2 illustrates this arrangement.

SMI data types are divided into three categories: simple types, application-wide types, and simply constructed types. Table 15-1 lists each of these types.

The SNMPv2 SMI introduces a number of new data types to work around limitations of the version 1 SMI. For example, the limitation of 32-bit integers became significant as devices became faster and 32-integer counters began to wrap around very quickly. As a result, 64-bit counters were introduced.

Emanating from the root of the tree are three branches: one is administered by CCITT, one by ISO, and one jointly administered by both. Within the ISO hierarchy are branches allocated to a number of organizations (orgs). One of these is the U.S. Department of Defense (DoD), under which sits the suite of Internet MIBs. Remember that, historically, the IP suite was developed through the support of the U.S. DoD.

TIP

The two MIB trees of most interest to users of SNMP are those under *mgmt*, which includes all Internet standard MIBs, and *private*, which includes all proprietary MIBs.

Figure 15-2 *Location of SNMP MIBs within the Global OID Space*

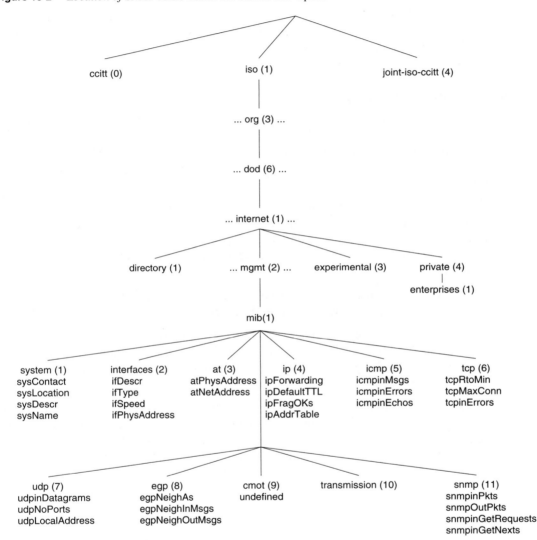

Table 15-1   *SMI Data Types*

Data Type	Description
Four Primitive ASN.1 Types	
Description integers	Unique values that are positive or negative whole numbers, including zero.
Octet strings	Unique values that are an ordered sequence of zero or more octets.
Object IDs	Unique values from the set of all object identifiers allocated according to the rules specified in ASN.1.
Bit strings	New in SNMPv2; comprise zero or more named bits that specify a value.
Application-wide Data Types Defined by the SMI	
Network addresses	Represent an address from a particular protocol family.
Counters	Non-negative integers that increment by +1 until they reach a maximum value, when they are reset to zero. The total number of bytes received on an interface is an example of a counter. In SNMPv1, counter size was not specified. In SNMPv2, 32-bit and 64-bit counters are defined.
Gauges	Non-negative integers that can increase or decrease, but that latch at a maximum value. The length of an output packet queue (in packets) is an example of a gauge.
Time ticks	Hundredths of a second since an event. The time since an interface entered its current state is an example of a tick.
Opaque	Represents an arbitrary encoding. This data type is used to pass arbitrary information strings that do not conform to the strict data typing used by the SMI.
Integer	Represents signed, integer-valued information. This data type redefines the ASN.1 "integer" simple data type, which has arbitrary precision in ASN.1, but has bounded precision in the SMI.
Unsigned integer	Represents unsigned integer-valued information. It is useful when values are always non-negative. This data type redefines the ASN.1 "integer" simple data type, which has arbitrary precision in ASN.1, but has bounded precision in the SMI.
ASN.1 Types that Define Multiple Objects in Tables and Lists	
Row	References a row in a table. Each element of the row can be a simple type or an application-wide type.
Table	References a table of zero or more rows. Each row has the same number of columns.

Within the *mgmt* subtree, beginning at OID 1.3.6.1.2.1 is the Internet standard MIB-II, defined by RFC 1213. This supersedes MIB-I (RFC 1156) and is supported by almost all devices that claim to be SNMP-manageable. MIB-II contains a large number of objects related to managing an IP network device; and routers, in particular. Figure 15-2 illustrates some of these, and the more useful objects are discussed later in the chapter. For now, the next section looks at the protocol used to access objects in the MIB.

Protocol Operation

SNMP is an application-layer protocol that facilitates the management of networking devices and services. Three versions of the protocol exist: the SNMPv1 management framework is defined in RFCs 1155, 1157, 1212; the SNMPv2 management framework is defined by RFCs 1901–1908; and SNMPv3 (which at the time of this writing is still in the development phase) is defined by RFCs 2271–2275. Table 15-2 lists the RFCs applicable to each version.

Table 15-2   *SNMP Management Framework RFCs*

Number	Subject (not RFC title)
RFC1157	SNMPv1 spec
RFC1155	SMI for SNMPv1
RFC1213	MIB-II for SNMPv1
RFC1901	Introduction to community-based SNMPv2
RFC1902	SMI for SNMPv2
RFC1903	Textual conventions for SNMPv2
RFC1904	Conformance statements for SNMPv2
RFC1905	Protocol operations for SNMPv2
RFC1906	Transport mappings for SNMPv2
RFC1907	MIB-II for SNMPv2
RFC1908	Coexistence between SNMPv1 and SNMPv2
RFC2271	Management architecture for SNMPv3
RFC2272	Message processing and dispatch for SNMPv3
RFC2273	SNMPv3 applications
RFC2274	Security model for SNMPv3
RFC2275	View-based access control model for SNMPv3

SNMPv2 solves a number of the shortcomings of version 1 of the protocol. These include inefficient mechanisms for retrieving large object sets, such as routing tables; poor error-handling; the lack of any standard communications mechanism for information exchange between management stations; and no support for protocols other than IP.

The original SNMPv2 spec (RFCs 1442–1451) is sometimes called SNMPv2Classic. This version addressed security issues, including authentication, privacy, and the capability to define particular views for different parties accessing the MIB.

However, the latter improvements did not make it into the eventual standard, because many in the industry viewed them as overly complicated to understand, deploy, configure, and use. The SNMPv2 IETF working group, which was unable to reach consensus on the administrative and security framework, salvaged the existing SNMPv2 design effort and standardized the protocol using the same administrative framework as SNMPv1 (community names contained as plain-text in each SNMP packet).

As a result, the RFCs in Table 15-2 are sometimes referred to as SNMPv2C, which is SNMPv2Classic minus the originally specified administrative and security framework. Other SNMPv2 proposals that included an administrative and security framework were USEC, SNMPv2*, SNMPv1.5, and SNMPv2t. An improved administrative and security framework is now being developed by the SNMPv3 working group.

In a typical configuration, an SNMP application (an NMS package) may obtain information about a device—a router, for example, that runs an SNMP agent. (In SNMPv3 terminology, agents are called *engines*.) The agent may provide access to the standard MIB-II or a host of proprietary MIBs. As discussed in the section "Management Information Bases," earlier in this chapter, each MIB typically contains many managed objects.

SNMPv3 also includes support for SNMP MIB views. A single SNMP engine may support multiple views. Each user can have a unique arrangement for authentication, privacy (encryption algorithm), and visibility into the MIB. As an example of the application of views, network engineering staff and network monitoring staff may be granted different access privileges into the MIB.

Figure 15-3 illustrates these various elements of SNMP as part of the overall network-management framework.

Figure 15-3 *SNMP Management Framework*

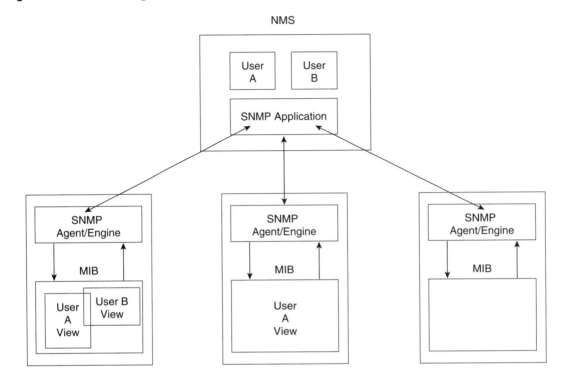

SNMP messages are exchanged over UDP and may be contained in one UDP packet or might span multiple packets. Seven types of messages exist; grouped into read, write, trap, and traversal operations:

- Read operations include Get-Request and Response.

- Write operations include Set-Request.

- Traversal operations include Get-Next-Request and GetBulkRequest. (These are SNMPv2 only—note that hyphens in message names were dropped in v2 of the protocol.)

- Trap operations include Trap and InformRequest (SNMPv2 only).

The message formats, shown in Figure 15-4, differ slightly between protocol versions. UDP port 161 is used for polling (get/set and traversal) messages, and 162 is used for traps. Packet formats for SNMPv3 are not discussed because, at the time of this writing, they were not finalized.

Figure 15-4   *Message Formats for SNMPv1 (A and B) and SNMPv2 (C and D)*

Version	Community	PDU Type	Request ID	Error Status	Error Index	Object 1 Value 1	Object 2 Value 2	Object x Value x

A

Variable Bindings

Version	Community	Enterprise	Agent Address	Generic Trap Type	Specific Trap Code	Time Stamp	Object 1 Value 1	Object 2 Value 2	Object x Value x

B

Variable Bindings

Version	Community	PDU Type	Request ID	Error Status	Error Index	Object 1 Value 1	Object 2 Value 2	Object x Value x

C

Variable Bindings

PDU Type	Request ID	Non-repeaters	Max-repetitions	Object 1 Value 1	Object 2 Value 2	Object x Value x

D

Variable Bindings

The following list defines the message formats in Figure 15-4:

- *Version*   Specifies the version of SNMP used.

- *Community*   Defines an access environment for a group of NMSs. NMSs within the community are said to exist within the same administrative domain. Community names serve as a weak form of authentication because devices that do not know the proper community name are precluded from SNMP operations.

- *PDU Type*   Specifies the type of PDU transmitted (Get, GetNext, Inform, Response, Set, or Trap).

- *Request ID*   Associates SNMP requests with responses.

- *Error Status*   Indicates one of a number of errors and error types. Only the response operation sets this field. Other operations set this field to zero.

- *Error Index*   Associates an error with a particular object instance. Only the response operation sets this field. Other operations set this field to zero.

- *Variable Bindings*   Serves as the data field of the SNMPv1 PDU. Each variable binding associates a particular object instance with its current value (with the exception of Get and GetNext requests, for which the value is ignored).

- *Enterprise*   Identifies the types of managed object generating the trap.

- *Agent Address*   Provides the address of the managed object generating the trap.

- *Generic Trap Type*   Indicates one of a number of generic trap types.

- *Specific Trap Code*   Indicates one of a number of specific trap codes.

- *Time Stamp*   Provides the amount of time that has elapsed between the last network reinitialization and generation of the trap.

- *Non-repeaters*   Specifies the number of object instances in the variable bindings field that should be retrieved no more than once from the beginning of the request. This field is used when some of the instances are scalar objects with only one variable.

The Get-Request message provides for retrieval of particular OIDs and is sent from the station to the agent on the router. The agent responds with a Get-Response message, which contains the value of the OID(s) requested.

A Get-Next-Request is used to retrieve tabular information. Specifically, the agent returns the value of the next entry in the MIB. Therefore, the Get-Next-Request downloads information about a set of interfaces or an entire routing table when the exact bounds or extent of information in the table is unknown. Although simple, this mechanism is not exactly efficient; to retrieve a full Internet routing table of some 50,000 entries would take at least 100,000 packets, assuming one Get-Response for each Get-Next-Request, and no retransmissions. SNMPv2 addresses this weakness through the GetBulkRequest message.

A Set-Request message modifies the configuration or operational status of a device; it enables the values of various objects to be set. Not all objects can be modified: a Read-Write attribute for each object is defined in the MIB specification. Typical objects that may be modified include interface descriptions and administrative status.

In general, it is not a good idea to enable SNMP write-access to a router using SNMPv1 because the security mechanism consists only of a *community string,* which is transmitted in plain-text in the SNMP message.

Finally, *traps* are unsolicited messages sent from the agent to the station to inform the management station that a particular event has occurred. Such events may include the loss or establishment of a routing adjacency, the change in status of an interface, or the successful login or rejection of login attempt to a device. Traps are beneficial because they require no polling, and only consume resources when a particular event occurs.

Two new messages are defined for SNMPv2: GetBulkRequest and InformRequest. Both are defined as follows:

- GetBulkRequest extends the Get-Next-Request of SNMPv1 to support retrieval of multiple MIB values via a single request message. Specifically, each message enables the station to request N non-repeatable objects (such as uptime) and R repeatable objects (such as a routing table entry). For each of the R repeatable objects, up to M repetitions (such as routing table entries) may be requested. If the agent cannot provide values for all the information requested, it provides partial results.

- InformRequest is used to exchange management information between management stations, and is particularly useful in distributed management environments.

As well as IP, SNMPv2 is standardized to run over IPX, AppleTalk, and CLNS networks. However, given the global networking convergence on IP as a standard protocol, more important reasons for upgrading to SNMPv2/3 are security and scalability.

To address the security issue, SNMPv3 proposes both authentication and encryption. Authentication occurs via application of the 128-bit Message Digest 5 (MD5) to each message, including a timestamp to prevent message replay after a message lifetime has been exceeded. A public key algorithm is used for authentication keys.

Encryption of SNMPv3 messages using the Date Encryption Standard (DES) algorithm is also proposed.

Netflow

Netflow brings sophisticated IP flow accounting and export functionality to high-end Cisco platforms. Netflow supports flow accounting of both unicast and multicast traffic flows. Although this chapter is mostly interested in the use of Netflow data for capacity planning and overall network management, Netflow also provides support for enterprise accounting, departmental charge-back, ISP billing, and network usage tracking for marketing purposes.

As described in Chapter 5, "Routers," Netflow may be used in conjunction with Cisco Express Forwarding or other switching paths with relatively small performance overhead. After the flow is first identified, switching and accounting are performed in tandem.

Netflow searches for RST (Resets) and FIN (Finish) in TCP flows, to expire those flows in a timely fashion. By default, no flow can live for longer than 30 minutes. When the remaining number of unused flow cache entries reaches a certain threshold, Netflow performs an accelerated timeout on 30 flows; if only one free flow remains, Netflow ages 30 flows, regardless of age.

Netflow consumes approximately 64 bytes per flow. The size of the flow cache is adjustable from the default of 64000 via the **ip flow-cache entries** global configuration command. Consumption of processor cycles should be balanced against the use of memory: insufficient cache size can increase processor usage due to both accelerated aging and the consequent increase in the level of export traffic generated.

Optimizing the flow cache size was traditionally an issue in core routers switching a large number of flows. However, as of version 12.0 of IOS, Netflow works in conjunction with distributed CEF (dCEF) on Versatile Interface Processor (VIP)–capable platforms in the Cisco 7500 family. In this mode, the processor on each VIP collects and exports Netflow cache data independently of the RSP. The size of the flow cache in VIPs is fixed, based on the total memory on each card. This alleviates the processing of flow accounting required on the RSP.

Expired flows are grouped together into a Netflow export UDP datagram, and are sent to the collection application set in the **ip flow-export** global configuration command. At least one datagram is exported per second, and each datagram can contain a maximum of 25, 27, and 30 flow records for versions 1, 5, and 7, respectively.

Besides providing accounting data, enabling Netflow can accelerate switching in the presence of features that work with IP flows, such as policy routing and encryption.

IP flows are identified via a unique combination of the following fields:

> Source IP address
> Destination IP address
> Source port number
> Destination port number
> Protocol type
> Type of Service
> Input interface

Major version releases of Netflow were 1 and 5. Version 5 added support for BGP AS information for accounting of interdomain traffic and flow sequence numbers to enable a Netflow data-collection application to detect lost records.

Table 15-3 illustrates the packet format for Netflow version 5. From the packet descriptions, it is possible to deduce the fields maintained for each flow.

Table 15-3   *Packet Formats for Netflow*

Field	V1	V5	V7	Bytes
Header Formats				
Version	--	--	--	0–3
Flow count	--	--	--	0–3
SysUptime	--	--	--	4–7
UNIX_secs	--	--	--	8–11
UNIX_nsecs	--	--	--	12–15
Sequence_number	--	--	--	16–19

Table 15-3   *Packet Formats for Netflow (Continued)*

Field	V1	V5	V7	Bytes
Type of NetFlow export device (for VIP distributed export)		--	--	
Slot number for the export device (for VIP distributed export)		--	--	
Repeated Formats				
Source IP address	--	--	Zero for destination-only flows	0–3
Destination IP address	--	--	--	4–7
Next hop router IP address	--	--	Always zero	8–11
Input Physical interface index	--	--	Always zero	12–13
Output Physical interface index	--	--	--	14–15
Packet count for this flow	--	--	--	16–19
Byte count for this flow	--	--	--	20–23
Start of flow timestamp	--	--	--	24–27
End of flow timestamp	--	--	--	28–31
Source TCP/UDP application port	--	--	Zero for destination-only flows	32–33
Destination TCP/UDP application port	--	--	Zero for destination-only flows	34–35
IP Protocol	--	--	Zero for destination-only flows	36–43
Type of service byte	--	--	Switch sets it to ToS of first packet in flow	36–43
TCP flags	--	--	Always zero	36–43
Source AS number		--	Always zero	40–41
Destination AS number		--	Always zero	42–43
Source subnet mask		--	Always zero	42–43
Destination subnet mask		--	Always zero	44–48
Flags (indicate, among other things, which flows are invalid)			--	44–48
Shortcut router IP address			--	44–48

Now that you have reviewed the main protocols underlying network-management activities, you are ready to focus on each of the five ISO-defined functional areas, beginning with fault management.

Fault Management

The fundamental goals of fault management are to detect, isolate, track, resolve, and record network problems. This certainly is one of the most important areas of network management because major outages are immediately obvious to all users of the network. In the case of large corporations, such outages can literally cost millions of dollars or more per hour.

Automated Polling and GUIs

Polling of network devices offers a very reliable way to detect problems. However, there is a trade-off between the speed with which you want to detect problems and the bandwidth and CPU consumed by the polling process.

The ubiquitous Internet Control Management Protocol (ICMP) "ping," which is a mandatory part of the IP stack on all devices, is an often overused way to accomplish system monitoring. This is because ping does not indicate the operational status of the device; it simply indicates that the IP stack seems to be functioning properly. If an SNMP agent is available on the device (and because the focus of this book is routers), you can almost certainly assume that there are far better SNMP objects for collecting data for fault management.

One such object is the *sysUptime* object within the System group. This object reports the time since the router was last rebooted, and it should increase in a rate commensurate with the polling period. Although there are no obvious reasons to perform long-term recording of the sysUptime object, you might want to maintain the largest value between reboots, which can be useful in performance analysis, such as determining which routers have the longest uptimes, excluding reboots for maintenance purposes.

The *ifOperStatus* and *ifAdminStatus* objects of the interface groups also are useful. In fact, together with *sysUptime*, these two objects can form the fundamentals of a graphical status representation of a large routed network. Such network maps typically present a hierarchical view of all the routers in the network. Beneath each router or node, the *sysUptime* is printed with all the interfaces associated with that router.

Colors can be used to represent the status of both the router and its associated interfaces. The interfaces themselves may be physical (a T1) or virtual (an ATM PVC or tunnel), as long as the router vendor provides MIB access to such interfaces (on Cisco routers, MIB access is available for both tunnel interfaces and subinterfaces corresponding to PVCs).

Further, interfaces may be identified by customer or, in the case of infrastructure links, by service provider. It is worth logging the state changes of interfaces for performance-management purposes; this allows a subsequent analysis of the reliability of individual customer or trunk circuits.

A graphical representation of the network can also help with the second phase of fault management: isolation. If all routers and individual router interfaces are polled periodically, failures due to interface or carrier service outage become relatively easy to isolate, at least to the closest router. At that point, operators can log into the router and use the more detailed output from the **show** commands, as well as from **ping** and **traceroute**, to further debug the problem.

TIP

The best polling period is often a point of some contention. You must strike a balance between the size of your network and how quickly you wish to detect problems. Most customers will be satisfied if you can determine that service is broken in less than a minute. If traps succeed, you will know of the failure within a few seconds that the router becomes aware. If traps fail, notification within a minute or so is sufficient for most applications.

Now for some math. Suppose that you have 1,000 routers in your network and you poll for *sysUptime*, *ifOperStatus,* and *ifAdminStatus*. That makes three gets and three responses per router. Assume for simplicity that each get and response consumes 100 bytes, including overhead. Polling overhead for fault management therefore requires 600 bytes per router, or 600,000 bytes for the entire 1,000-router network. If this polling is conducted every 30 seconds, the polling overhead amounts to 160 kbit/s.

If routers contain a large number of interfaces, 100 bytes is a very conservative estimate for the response; it could actually be much more. Assuming that other aspects of network management consume similar bandwidths, it is easy to see how the bandwidth usage for management can escalate rapidly as networks grow.

NOTE

In addition to consuming network bandwidth, polling routers for SNMP statistics also consume router CPU. Although Cisco routers prioritize all activities, and although SNMP operates generally at a low priority, it is still possible that you may adversely affect router performance by bombarding a router with an unreasonable level of SNMP requests. Moreover, because the router makes no distinction between SNMP requests, requests for superfluous SNMP data may override those for more critical data.

These are very conservative estimates; many integrated NMSs can easily—and often inadvertently, from a user's perspective—produce much greater levels of management traffic.

Fortunately, assessing the overall level of management traffic is usually a relatively simple exercise of examining the input and output byte counts of your network management station.

Many other objects are available through various MIBs. In general, it is unnecessary to deploy polling of these on a large scale, unless they relate to a specific requirement of your network, such as whether they are critical for billing purposes or whether they significantly increase speed of fault isolation. One possible exception is for ISPs to poll for eBGP neighbor status using the BGP MIB. This is the most reliable way to detect that your neighbor ISP has deconfigured you as a BGP neighbor.

You may also decide to poll for certain objects that are precursors to faults. As an example, high *ifInErrors* may indicate that a linecard is beginning to fail; however, this is more in the realm of performance management, which is addressed later in this chapter.

Although a wealth of MIB objects exist for which you may not want to poll regularly, these can still be invaluable for "one-of" use in debugging specific problems. Such problems are typically more complex than your run-of-the-mill network device hardware failure: protocol, software, or configuration errors are examples.

SNMP server capability is enabled using the **snmp-server community** global configuration command. As you will discover when you read about configuration and security management, it is not recommended that you simply open SNMP access to just anyone.

Traps and Logging

Traps represent a far more timely and efficient mechanism for detecting and isolating faults. The drawback is that they are not reliable. If a router malfunctions, it may not send traps; if network connectivity is completely broken as a result of a failure, the trap may never be received. As a result, the typical arrangement for fault management primarily relies on traps, but is backed up by "slow" polling, on the order of a minute or more.

On Cisco routers, if you use the **snmp-server enable traps** [*notification-type*] in global configuration mode without specifying a [*notification-type*], all traps are enabled. By listing particular notification types after the **traps** keyword, you may limit the type of traps sent. Use the **snmp-server host** command to send traps to a particular host. You can also tune the type of traps received by each host on an individual basis using **snmp-server host** *host community-string* [*notification-type*].

It is useful to monitor *and* record at the NMS all traps/notifications, with particular emphasis on the following *notification-type* options:

bgp	BGP state change traps
config	SNMP config traps
entity	SNMP entity traps
envmon	SNMP environmental monitor traps
frame-relay	SNMP Frame Relay traps

isdn	SNMP isdn traps
snmp	SNMP traps
syslog	SYSLOG messages sent as traps

A full description of these can be found at ftp://ftpeng.cisco.com/pub/mibs/traps.

The Cisco logging facility can also be used to great effect. It offers an even wider selection of state-change information, particularly relating to routing protocols. The Cisco IOS Software System Error Messages, as well as the Debug Command Reference, serve as the definitive sources of information on the types, reasons, and recommended operator responses to each logging message. Table 15-4 lists the eight levels of error messages generated by Cisco routers.

Table 15-4   *Error Messages Logging and Syslog Levels*

Level Keyword	Level	Description	Syslog Definition
Emergencies	0	System unusable	LOG_EMERG
Alerts	1	Immediate action needed	LOG_ALERT
Critical	2	Critical conditions	LOG_CRIT
Errors	3	Error conditions	LOG_ERR
Warnings	4	Warning conditions	LOG_WARNING
Notifications	5	Normal but significant condition	LOG_NOTICE
Informational	6	Informational messages only	LOG_INFO
Debugging	7	Debugging messages	LOG_DEBUG

Logging is enabled by default on Cisco routers. Log messages are sent to any of five locations, which are not mutually exclusive:

- The console port, enabled via the **logging console *level*** global configuration command.

- A circular buffer in RAM, which is enabled and sized using the **logging buffered [*size*]** global configuration command.

- The terminal lines, enabled via the **logging monitor *level*** global configuration command; virtual terminals (such as Telnet connections) can attach to this output via the **terminal monitor** exec command.

- A syslog server, via the **logging trap *level*** global configuration command.

- A SNMP trap server, enabled via the **snmp-server enable trap syslog**, and with the level set by the **logging history** global configuration commands.

In most cases, the best solution for a large network is to configure all critical routers to log all messages to a syslog server within the NMS, in which they can be properly monitored and archived. Again, the definition of "critical" is not always clear, but certainly all core and any distribution routers aggregating large numbers of customers are prime candidates.

By default, only messages at the *informational* level or above are sent to the syslog server. However, this may be adjusted using the **logging trap** global configuration command. You may wish to set the level to *debug* to aid the troubleshooting process. Messages are sent to the local facility, although this can be changed using the **logging facility** *facility-type* global configuration command.

TIP   Because the console is often used for critical router access rather than monitoring router status, consider disabling log output to the console via the **no logging console** global configuration command.

IOS code running on VIP cards also generates syslog messages. These may be sent to the console via the **service slave-log** global configuration command. However, for most purposes, the default behavior of sending messages to the trap and monitor locations is sufficient.

Timestamps can be added to all logging and debug outputs via the **service timestamps logging** and **service timestamps debug** global configuration commands. Using the keywords **datetime localtime show-timezone msec** will format the timestamps to include the date and time with millisecond accuracy in the local time zone, and will print the configured time zone for the router.

Rather than sending log output to a syslog server, you can send it to an SNMP trap daemon via the **snmp-server enable trap syslog** global configuration command. This removes the need to have a syslog server within the NMS. A copy of each message sent to the SNMP server is kept in the logging history table and can be viewed via the **show logging history** exec command. The size of this history table, and the level of messages logged and sent to the SNMP trap server are set via the **logging history** *size* and **logging history** *level* global configuration commands.

NOTE   As usual, it is recommended that you source all logging and trap messages from a loopback interface by using the **logging source-interface** and **snmp-server trap-source** global configuration commands.

Note that in version 12.0 of IOS, the **snmp-server trap-authentication** global configuration command has been deprecated. SNMP server authentication traps are now sent, providing that **server enable traps snmp authentication** or simply **server enable traps snmp** is configured.

Network Time Protocol

For timestamps to be consistent throughout the network, it is necessary for the real-time clock on all routers to be synchronized. Timestamp consistency is required for security incident analysis, as well as fault-management and troubleshooting activities.

The Network Time Protocol (NTP, RFC 1305) is an efficient way to synchronize the time on all routers. NTP runs over UDP, and after the network has reached a synchronized state, only a packet per minute is necessary to maintain the synchronization between two routers to within a few milliseconds.

The protocol uses the error-detection capabilities of UDP/IP, is tolerant of duplicate packets, and can detect and ignore NTP peers that are widely inaccurate (due to system malfunction). Many networked devices, including host platforms, support NTP.

NTP devices are arranged in a redundant hierarchy of servers and clients, with each level in the hierarchy referred to in NTP nomenclature as a *stratum*. The higher a clock-source is within the hierarchy, the higher the level of trust NTP places in it. At the top of the hierarchy, stratum 1 servers are usually radio or atomic clocks, or GPS receivers, connected to the network. Stratum 2 servers are clients of these stratum 1 servers, and so on down the hierarchy. NTP devices within the same stratum may be configured as peers, and indeed there is benefit in doing so if they are clients of different stratum 1 servers.

The usual practice is to configure a small number of key distribution or core routers in the network as stratum 2 servers. These stratum 2 servers either are themselves synchronized to a local stratum 1 device or are synchronized to a stratum 1 device on the Internet. Obviously, if you are concerned about accurate time, as operators of large networks should be, you will invest in your own stratum 1 servers rather than relying on the Internet completely.

Figure 15-5 shows the arrangement for the case study network. Core routers are configured as stratum 2 clients of some local and some Internet stratum 1 servers. Each stratum 2 server peers with other servers in the core and acts as a server for stratum 3 clients within the distribution network. Routers in the distribution network act as servers for routers in the access networks.

A typical NTP configuration for a stratum 2 server is as follows:

```
clock timezone PST -8
clock summer-time PDT recurring

ntp authenticate
ntp authentication-key 1 md5 CS-NTP-KEY
ntp trusted keys 1
ntp server localstratum1ip prefer
ntp server internetip
ntp peer 10.0.4.1
ntp peer 10.0.4.2
ntp peer 10.0.4.3
ntp peer 10.0.4.4
ntp peer 10.0.4.5
ntp source loopback0
ntp update-calendar
```

Figure 15-5 *NTP Hierarchy within the Case Study Network*

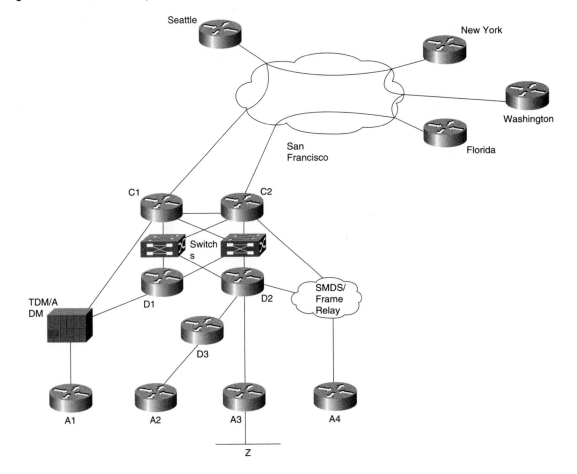

You would begin by setting the local time zone and daylight saving strategy for this router. Next, you would tell the router to authenticate all associations; define an authentication key, CS-NTP-KEY, and trust associations that use this key.

Next, you would configure this router as a client of a local stratum 1 server. Authentication is not used for this association; another stratum 1 server on the Internet is also used, but the local server is preferred. You also would configure the router as a peer with other stratum 2 servers in the core network, as well as configure the router to use key 1 in the association.

Configure the router to use the IP address of loopback0 as the source for all NTP traffic. Finally, configure the router to periodically update its system clock with NTP time. Therefore, when you look at the system clock via **show clock**, it will reflect the NTP-synchronized time and date.

Core Dumps

If a router crashes, you may configure it to send a core dump to a server host. This can assist Cisco engineers in tracking down the cause of the crash. Core dumps can be delivered to a server via tftp (up to a maximum router memory size of 16MB), RCP, or FTP. Try using FTP: It is easy to use, it works for all memory sizes, and server software is available for most platforms.

Configuring the router to source the FTP session from the address of loopback0 to host cs-nms using a username of cs-coredump is achieved via the following global configuration commands:

```
ip ftp source-interface loopback0
ip ftp username cs-coredump
ip ftp password 7 29849084320
exception protocol ftp
exception dump cs-nms
```

The core dump is written as file *hostname*-core on host cs-nms, where *hostname* is set via the **hostname** global configuration command. Alternatively, you can specify the filename to be used via the **exception core-file** global configuration command.

Domain Name Service

Having a well-chosen naming plan for all routers and intelligent in-addr, ARPA (reverse) lookups for router interface addresses can ease fault management considerably. Read the following traceroute output:

```
 1 171.69.213.161 [AS 75] 0 msec 0 msec 4 msec
 2 sj-eng-lab1.cisco.com (171.69.9.1) [AS 75] 4 msec 4 msec 4 msec
 3 sj-eng-corp2.cisco.com (171.69.4.143) [AS 75] 4 msec 0 msec 0 msec
 4 sj-wall-1.cisco.com (198.92.1.137) [AS 109] 4 msec 4 msec 4 msec
 5 barrnet-gw.cisco.com (192.31.7.37) [AS 109] 4 msec 4 msec 4 msec
 6 s2-1-1.paloalto-cr18.bbnplanet.net (131.119.26.9) [AS 1] 4 msec 8 msec 4 msec
 7 h1-0.atteasylink.bbnplanet.net (131.119.26.126) [AS 1] 8 msec 8 msec 4 msec
 8 205.174.74.186 [AS 5727] 312 msec 312 msec 312 msec
 9 FastEthernet0-0-0.pad-core3.Sydney.telstra.net (139.130.249.238) [AS 1221]
    428 msec 308 msec 312 msec
10 Hssi6-0-0.civ-core1.Canberra.telstra.net (139.130.249.34) [AS 1221] 316 msec
    464 msec 472 msec
11 Fddi0-0.civ2.Canberra.telstra.net (139.130.235.227) [AS 1221] 320 msec 316 m
    sec 320 msec
12 Serial2.dickson.Canberra.telstra.net (139.130.235.2) [AS 1221] 320 msec 316
    msec 324 msec
13 jatz.aarnet.edu.au (139.130.204.4) [AS 1221] 320 msec 316 msec 316 msec
```

Consider how much more difficult it would be, if the traceroute had failed, to isolate the problem in the absence of domain names. Note that this applies for intraprovider traces as well as interprovider traces, and it is worthwhile to spend some time thinking about a meaningful naming plan for your network. Note this format:

```
routername-interface-location-domain
```

This is used by many large operators, and is a good model to follow.

You can enable DNS lookup capability, a default ip-domain name, and an ordered list of up to six server IP addresses via the following global configuration commands:

```
ip domain-name cs.net
ip name-server address1 [address2 …address6]
```

Automated Fault Resolution

After a problem has been isolated, the NMS has the opportunity to perform automated rectification. However, it is rare to see such systems in practice. In most large networks today, automated fault resolution—or, in other words, work arounds—are performed by the fail-over mechanisms of dynamic IP routing protocols or by link-level fail-over mechanisms, such as those available in SONET and FDDI.

Configuration and Security Management

Configuration management involves maintaining a database that describes all devices within the network, modifies the configuration of those devices, and records all network-configuration changes for audit or rollback purposes.

Configuration Data

Collecting information for the network may seem like a chore, but it is absolutely necessary. Do not rely on "auto-discovery" mechanisms associated with many commercial NMSs. These may work for LANs or very small WANs, but they are totally unsuitable for very large networks. Only good planning and a meticulous process will produce a scalable result.

The data stored in the configuration management database need not necessarily be router configuration data; it may include, for example, contact numbers of persons with physical access to the equipment. In fact, the configuration management database is often very closely associated with the fault management database because both may need to contain similar information. Access to this information may be conveniently linked to the GUI used for fault management. In other words, to learn configuration data about a particular device, an operator may click on that device and use pull-down menus leading to the data.

In large networks containing Cisco routers, perhaps the most critical item of configuration data is plain-ASCII IOS configuration files. A good IOS configuration can contain much of the more critical data pertaining to the network, including descriptive text in certain contexts. It is worth investigating and using the description IOS configuration commands shown in Table 15-5.

Table 15-5   *IOS Commands Useful for Documenting Configurations*

IOS Configuration	CLI Context	MIB-II
snmp-server contact	global	sysContact
snmp-server location	global	sysLocation
hostname	global	
description	interface	
bandwidth	interface	
neighbor *x.x.x.x* description	bgp router	

IOS configuration files can become very large. If a file becomes too large to save, you can use the **service compress-config** command to compress the configuration prior to storing in NVRAM. Because this may impact the performance of configuration manipulation operations, only use the command when necessary.

Note that MIB-II contains many other variables that are also useful; not all of these are available through router **show** commands.

The Network Architecture Document

IOS configurations do not provide the capability to add generic comments to the configurations. Moreover, as with a large software program, it is difficult to impart a good understanding of the way the entire system works through inline "comments" alone. This is why it is necessary to have some offline description of the overall network architecture—particularly the architecture pertaining to routing. Such a document would include details of the following:

- The structure and policy of external routing (BGP)
- The structure of internal routing (OSPF, ISIS, Enhanced IGRP, and so on)
- Any routing filters and policies associated with customers, and the way the policy is disseminated
- Intended failure modes
- Costing of various network paths

Revision Control of IOS Configuration Files

All IOS configuration changes should be recorded and, if possible, a reason for each change should be logged. Such revision control may be achieved with a commercial package, such as CiscoWorks; or with public domain software, such as RCS. In the latter case, good results can be achieved simply by following these guidelines:

1 Always write modified router configurations to a tftp server, using a well-known name for each router configuration file.

2 Have a script that periodically checks the tftp directory, checks in any new configurations, and sends a message summarizing changed configurations to network operators.

3 Have a second script that periodically (such as once a day) compares all running configurations with those stored in the database and reports any discrepancies.

This simple arrangement has been shown to scale for very large networks, and provides the means to roll back configurations and audit any changes through the mechanisms of RCS.

NOTE   The Cisco AAA architecture can also be used to log a wide variety of operations, including all configuration changes, to a server. Unlike writing complete configurations to a tftp server, logging changes line by line via AAA provides a configuration audit trail.

Upload and download of router configurations can be performed via SNMP, if RW access is permitted for the server. Therefore, particularly if you are using SNMPv1, which has only trivial security mechanisms, do not enable SNMP RW access on any router. Instead, perform configuration upload and download via the CLI.

Managing Router Access

A number of steps must be taken to control access to routers within the network. The first step is to configure access control for each individual router, as follows:

```
service nagle
service password-encryption
enable secret 5 3242352255
no enable password


access-list 16 permit 10.0.1.0 0.0.0.255

banner login ^
    This system is the property of ISPnet Networks.

    Access to this system is monitored.
```

```
Unauthorized access is prohibited.

Contact noc@ISP.net  or call +1 555 555 5555 with inquiries
            ^
line vty 0 4
access-class 16 in
exec-timeout 5 0
transport input telnet
transport output none
password 7 002B012D0D5F
```

First, consider enabling Nagle congestion control for all TCP sessions to the router. Nagle's congestion control algorithm paces TCP transmissions so that a string of characters is sent only after receiving an acknowledgment for the last character. This can help the performance of Telnet and other TCP access mechanisms to the router in the event of network congestion or router CPU overload (exactly when you may wish to access a router to troubleshoot). It cannot perform miracles, but every bit helps!

Next, use **service password encryption** to encrypt all passwords stored in the configuration. Note that passwords lower in this configuration are encrypted—they are not in plain text. Keep a record of the passwords somewhere safe. If you forget them, you may need to reset the entire router!

You set the password exec-level access to the router via the **enable secret** global configuration command. The enable secret uses a stronger encryption algorithm than the enable password. Indeed, the enable password encryption algorithm is reversible. Disable the enable password via the **no enable password** command.

WARNING   Before disabling the enable password via **no enable password**, be absolutely sure that the router will never be rolled back to an earlier IOS version that does not support enable secrets. Doing so will leave your router open to exec access with no password.

All encrypted passwords within the router are preceded with a digit. If the digit is 5, the password has been hashed with the strong MD5; if the digit is 7, the weaker, reversible encryption algorithm has been used.

TIP   While looking at trivial things that may offer help, consider putting a login banner on all routers to prohibit unauthorized access, and provide contact details for the device. This just might turn off would-be hackers, and it also provides legitimate people seeking information (other network operators) with a way to contact you in the event of a problem. An exec banner is also available via **banner exec**.

Finally, set login passwords for the virtual terminals and define an access list limiting the IP addresses that may connect to the router via Telnet.

If you stop at this point, you would have a system that does the following:

- Puts plain-text passwords over the network (virtual terminal and enable passwords are visible within a Telnet connection to a router).

- Uses a reversible encryption algorithm for the login password.

- Does not scale particularly well. If you wish to change passwords frequently—which you should do, given the previous problem—this requires configuration changes to all routers. If a staff member leaves, all passwords also must be changed.

- Has poor accounting functionality.

The Cisco Authentication, Access, and Accounting (AAA) framework solves the above problems. Both RADIUS and TACACS+ AAA protocols are supported. This chapter does not offer details of each protocol, but their fundamental operation is the same:

1 When an inbound Telnet session is received (and is in the access list), the router prompts the user for a username and password; and sends these, encrypted, in an authentication request to the authentication server.

2 The authentication server either permits or denies the access request, logs the result, and sends the appropriate authentication response back to the router.

3 Depending on the response from the authentication server, the router permits or denies access to the user.

AAA is configured via three global commands:

- *aaa authentication*   Specifies, in order, the authentication methods to be used. Try configuring the system to try TACACS+ first; if the server does not respond, fall back on the enable secret.

- *aaa authorization*   It is not recommended that you authorize users to move to exec level unless they reauthenticate with the TACACS+ server.

- *aaa accounting*   Tells the router how and when to report access information to an accounting server. Try using TACACS+ to account for the start and stop of all exec sessions, and to track all configuration commands.

A more suitable route access control configuration is this one:

```
service nagle
service password-encryption
aaa new-model
aaa authentication login default tacacs+ enable
aaa authentication login console none
aaa authentication enable tacacs+ enable
aaa accounting exec start-stop tacacs+
aaa accounting commands 15 default start-stop tacacs+
enable secret 5 3242352255
no enable password

access-list 16 permit 10.0.1.0 0.0.0.255

ip tacacs source-interface loopback0
tacacs-server host 10.0.1.1
tacacs-server host 10.0.1.2
tacacs-server key ISPnetkey

line vty 0 4
access-class 3 in
exec-timeout 5 0
transport input telnet
transport output none
```

This configuration causes the router to prompt for a username and password when a login attempt is made. It authenticates these with the TACACS+ server, 10.0.1.1, sending the authentication packets with a source address of loopback0. If there is no response, the router tries the second TACACS+ server, 10.1.1.2. If there is still no response, the router then resorts to prompting for the enable secret. However, under fault-free circumstances, the user will be authenticated by the primary TACACS+ server, 10.0.1.1.

If the user attempts to move to the exec level, this authentication procedure is repeated and the start-time for entering the exec level is accounted. Should the user enter configuration commands, these are also recorded on an individual basis. Finally, if the user logs out of exec level, the logout time is accounted.

Authenticating Routing Updates

Ensuring the integrity of the dynamic routing fabric within a network is one of the most critical network-management functions. Bogus routing updates, whether malicious or accidental, can severely disrupt network operations or even render the network completely useless.

Cisco routing protocols have two forms of authentication: plain text or MD5. Obviously, the latter is preferred, if supported for the routing protocol in question. Plain-text authentication is barely better than none at all. As of version 12 of IOS, the situation is as shown in Table 15-6.

Table 15-6   *Authentication Modes Available for IOS Routing Protocols*

Protocol	Plain Text	MD5
DRP	x	
RIP		
RIPv2	x	x
IGRP		
EIGRP		x
OSPF	x	x
ISIS	x	
BGP		x

Managing Routing Policy

Even if a routing update is authenticated, a configuration error in a customer or peer's network could cause them to send you invalid routes. A classic and disastrous example is the dual-homed ISP customer who does not filter BGP routes and offers transit for the entire Internet to their upstream ISP.

Ingress route filtering is the responsibility of the customer and the network service provider. However, the onus is really on the provider, who will generally be blamed by the Internet community if things go wrong.

Generally, two categories of route filtering exist:

- Filtering other providers or peer networks
- Filtering customers

In an ideal world, the filtering process for both categories would be identical. However, at the global Internet routing level, filtering of other providers traditionally has been almost nonexistent. An ISP responsible for the Internet backbone relies on a trust model. This trust makes the filtering of customer routes that much more critical.

The trust model evolved because there was no complete registry describing which provider was routing which networks, and because of the technological challenge of per-prefix route filtering. Given 50,000 routes in the Internet at the time of this writing, per-prefix filtering would require very large route filters, which consume both memory and processor cycles.

The traditional Cisco route-filtering mechanism based on access lists had problems scaling to 50,000 routes, and was missing a number of more sophisticated elements associated with matching prefix information. This is hardly surprising because the original access-list scheme was as much aimed at packet filtering as route filtering. However, prefix-lists, which are optimized for IP route filtering, now make interprovider filtering possible. Now all that remains is to invent a well-coordinated, secure, Internet routing registry.

In the meantime, many providers at large Internet NAPs perform "sanity" filtering only via the following prefix-list:

```
ip prefix-list martian-etc seq 5 deny 0.0.0.0/32
! deny the default route
ip prefix-list martian-etc seq 10 deny 0.0.0.0/8 le 32
! deny anything beginning with 0
ip prefix-list martian-etc seq 15 deny 0.0.0.0/1 ge 20
! deny masks > 20 for all class A nets (1-127)
ip prefix-list martian-etc seq 20 deny 10.0.0.0/8 le 32
! deny 10/8 per RFC1918
ip prefix-list martian-etc seq 25 deny 127.0.0.0/8 le 32
! reserved by IANA - loopback address
ip prefix-list martian-etc seq 30 deny 128.0.0.0/2 ge 17
deny masks >= 17 for all class B nets (129-191)
ip prefix-list martian-etc seq 35 deny 128.0.0.0/16 le 32
! deny net 128.0 - reserved by IANA
ip prefix-list martian-etc seq 40 deny 172.16.0.0/12 le 32
! deny 172.16 as RFC1918
ip prefix-list martian-etc seq 45 deny 192.0.2.0/24 le 32
! class C 192.0.20.0 reserved by IANA
ip prefix-list martian-etc seq 50 deny 192.0.0.0/24 le 32
! class C 192.0.0.0 reserved by IANA
ip prefix-list martian-etc seq 55 deny 192.168.0.0/16 le 32
! deny 192.168/16 per RFC1918
ip prefix-list martian-etc seq 60 deny 191.255.0.0/16 le 32
! deny 191.255.0.0 - IANA reserved
ip prefix-list martian-etc seq 65 deny 192.0.0.0/3 ge 25
! deny masks > 25 for class C (192-222)
ip prefix-list martian-etc seq 70 deny 223.255.255.0/24 le 32
! deny anything in net 223 - IANA reserved
ip prefix-list martian-etc seq 75 deny 224.0.0.0/3 le 32
! deny class D/Experimental
```

NOTE   Prefix-lists are a relatively new feature. Before its introduction, the previous prefix-list was specified via the following extended access list. The prefix-list is more efficient, and its syntax more intuitive, so we recommend that you use it:

```
access-list 100 deny   ip host 0.0.0.0 any
access-list 100 deny   ip 0.0.0.0 0.255.255.255 255.0.0.0 0.255.255.255
access-list 100 deny   ip 1.0.0.0 0.255.255.255 255.0.0.0 0.255.255.255
access-list 100 deny   ip 10.0.0.0 0.255.255.255 255.0.0.0 0.255.255.255
access-list 100 deny   ip 19.255.0.0 0.0.255.255 255.255.0.0 0.0.255.255
access-list 100 deny   ip 59.0.0.0 0.255.255.255 255.0.0.0 0.255.255.255
access-list 100 deny   ip 127.0.0.0 0.255.255.255 255.0.0.0 0.255.255.255
access-list 100 deny   ip 129.156.0.0 0.0.255.255 255.255.0.0 0.0.255.255
access-list 100 deny   ip 172.16.0.0 0.15.255.255 255.240.0.0 0.15.255.255
access-list 100 deny   ip 192.0.2.0 0.0.0.255 255.255.255.0 0.0.0.255
access-list 100 deny   ip 192.5.0.0 0.0.0.255 255.255.255.0 0.0.0.255
access-list 100 deny   ip 192.9.200.0 0.0.0.255 255.255.255.0 0.0.0.255
access-list 100 deny   ip 192.9.99.0 0.0.0.255 255.255.255.0 0.0.0.255
access-list 100 deny   ip 192.168.0.0 0.0.255.255 255.255.0.0 0.0.255.255
access-list 100 deny   ip 224.0.0.0 31.255.255.255 224.0.0.0 31.255.255.255
access-list 100 deny   ip any 255.255.255.128 0.0.0.127
access-list 100 permit ip any any
```

Note that this filter rejects the default route, broadcast, loopback, and multicast group addresses; as well as address space reserved for private networks by RFC 1918.

An Internet routing registry lists the ISPs that route particular networks. Ideally, each ISP contributes to the global registry from its own local registry. Maintenance of this registry is a critical configuration-management issue for all large network operators, regardless of whether they connect to the Internet. This is a critical tool for building the route filters necessary for maintaining network integrity, even though the network operators do not have full, end-to-end management of the routed network.

Minimally, the registry contains the following information for each customer; some fields may be obtained from other areas in the configuration database:

```
Customer ID
Connecting Router
Connecting Port
Route-filter ID
List of permissible prefixes
List of permissible Paths
List of permissible communities
```

There must be a scheme (hopefully not a manual one) that takes the information in the routing registry and translates this into route filters to be installed in each edge/demarc router in the network. The information could instead be used to install static routes in the edge routers, but filtered dynamic routes grant the customer the flexibility of advertising or withdrawing a route advertisement at will. This can be particularly useful to dual-home customers. Several types of route filters exist:

- *Simple access-list:* filters on network only
- *Extended access-list:* filters on network and mask
- *Prefix-list:* offers sophisticated and efficient filtering on network and mask
- *Community-list:* filters on BGP community
- *AS-PATH filter-list:* filters on AS-path

As a bare minimum, all prefixes should be filtered using a basic/extended access list or, preferably, a prefix-list. You can log the access-list violations, although this is a dangerous practice because it opens the router to potential Denial of Service attacks (the router becomes CPU-bound, generating logging output due to large numbers of incoming bogus routes).

For BGP customers, attribute filters for paths and communities should also be considered.

Managing Forwarding Policy

Because you are ensuring the validity of routes accepted from customers, it is logical that you expect traffic sourced from IP addresses that fall within the range of the offered routes. Packets sourced outside this range are likely to be the result of misconfiguration within the customer's network, or possibly a malicious Denial of Service attack based on IP spoofing (the SMURF attack is one such example).

The traditional approach to preventing IP spoofing is to apply inbound basic or extended IP access lists of customer interfaces. The address ranges included in the access lists would match those used for filtering routes from customers. The problem with this approach is its performance impact and its inability to adapt to dynamic changes in routes offered by the customer. This in turn leads to greater operational overhead.

With the introduction of Cisco Express Forwarding (CEF) in version 12 of IOS, you can make use of a Reverse Path Forwarding (RPF) feature that may be enabled on a per-interface or sub-interface basis using the **ip verify unicast reverse-path** interface configuration command.

When reverse-path is enabled, the IP address in received packets is checked to ensure that the route back to the source uses the interface on which the packet is received. If the route back to the source does not match the input interface, the packet is discarded. The count of discarded packets can be seen in the output of the **show ip traffic** command. RPF is compatible with both per-packet and per-destination load sharing.

RPF has minimal CPU overhead and operates at a few percent less than CEF/opt/fast switching rates. It is best used at the network perimeter, where symmetrical routing usually occurs.

NOTE   *Symmetrical routing* means that the route back to the source of a packet is via the same interface
            on which the router received the packet. Backbone routers may not perform symmetrical
            routing because the flow of traffic is engineered to make the best use of available capacity or to
            abide by the requested routing policy of customers. On the other hand, edge routes that connect
            customers should always be configured so that routing is symmetric—doing so will have only
            minor influence on the customer's receive traffic pattern and will enable you to use the efficient
            CEF RPF feature.

RPF should *not* be used within the core of the network or wherever there might be asymmetric
routing paths. If RPF is enabled in an asymmetric routing environment, valid packets from
customers will be dropped. In instances in which you must filter in an asymmetric routing
environment, the traditional approach of access lists must be applied.

Care is required in applying the RPF feature, but this is a very effective tool that does not
compromise network performance.

A number of router packet-forwarding characteristics also are unnecessary and may present a
security risk. These must be disabled on a per-interface basis.

IP redirects can consume valuable router processing cycles if someone intentionally or
unintentionally points an inappropriate route at your router. For example, this may occur at
large Internet peering points if another network points a default route at your router. Even
though the output of redirects is rate-limited, you should consider disabling the feature
altogether via the **no ip redirects** interface subcommand.

A router performing directed broadcasts will translate an IP packet sent to the broadcast address
of a particular subnetwork into a LAN broadcast. If the broadcast packet is a ping or a udp echo
request, for example, the result is that all hosts on the LAN will respond to the source of the
directed broadcast.

This may saturate network resources, particularly those of the source (in the so-called SMURF
attack, the attacker spoofs the source address and sets it to an address within the victim's
network, thereby hoping to saturate the links in that network). Forwarding of directed
broadcasts is disabled via the **no ip directed-broadcast** subcommand. From IOS version 12
onward, directed broadcasts are disabled by default, but on earlier versions you should
configure it on the outbound interface to which you do not want directed broadcasts forwarded.

If a router has an ARP entry for a particular IP address, and if it hears another device ARP for
that IP address, the router will respond with its own MAC address. This can bypass configured
routing policy, so disable this via the **no ip proxy-arp** interface subcommand.

Staging Configuration Upgrades

Large-scale upgrades of either configuration or IOS version should be *staged*. The first stage is to try the new configuration, hardware, or image in a lab. If lab trials are successful, one or two pertinent areas in the network may be used for further testing. If an upgrade involves all three software, hardware, and configuration changes, the following order is recommended:

1 Install the new image; run for several hours.

2 Install the new hardware; run for several hours.

3 Install the new configuration; run for several hours.

This approach provides the best opportunity for isolating faults.

Ad Hoc Abuse Issues

IOS contains a number of features that may be maliciously exploited. These are of particular concern to operators of large networks who may have very little control over or knowledge of who is using the network, or for what purpose. The following template lists services and features that you should consider turning off:

```
no service finger
no service pad
no service udp-small-servers
no service tcp-small-servers
no ip bootp servers
```

The finger service is unnecessary for tracking who is logged into the router. The AAA architecture discussed in this section provides a superior set of services for that. Known security risks are associated with the finger service, so it is better disabled via **no service finger**. The pad service is a relic of X25 networks and is not required in an IP network; it is disabled via **no service pad**.

By default, the TCP servers for Echo, Discard, Chargen, and Daytime services are enabled. Disabling this via the **no service tcp-small-servers** will cause the router to send a TCP *RESET* packet to sources that attempt to connect to the Echo, Discard, Chargen, and Daytime ports; and will discard the offending packets.

Similarly, UDP servers for Echo, Discard, and Chargen services are enabled by default. Disabling these via the **no service udp-small-servers** will cause the router to send an ICMP port unreachable to the senders of packets to these ports, and will discard the offending packets.

It is not usually necessary for routers to support the bootp process; disable this via **no ip bootp server**.

Performance and Accounting Management

Performance management involves monitoring the network, sounding alerts when certain thresholds are reached, and collecting statistics that enable you to carry out capacity planning. SNMP forms the basis for most monitoring and statistics-collection activities, although in certain cases more sophisticated and application-cognizant tools may be appropriate. Once again, the trick is in not getting carried away. Poll and archive only the bare minimum set of statistics you need for performance and accounting purposes.

Capacity Planning

Link utilization is one of the mainstays of performance management. The *ifInOctets* and *ifOutOctets* objects (or *ifHCInOctets* and *ifHCOutOctets* for high-speed interfaces offering 64-bit counters) are a critical way to predict congestion and the need for bandwidth upgrades or routing optimizations. Once again, the polling period used can have a dramatic impact on the perceived utilization of the link. Packet transmission tends to be choppy (indeed, if you think about it, a link either is carrying a packet or is idle), and therefore the shorter the polling period, the less smooth any graphical presentation of link utilization versus time will appear.

To calculate link utilization, link bandwidths also must be maintained. Note, however, that *ifSpeed/ifHighSpeed* may not provide accurate results for all interfaces (for example, serial interfaces). In such cases, the link bandwidths will need to be updated manually (from the configuration database).

Experience has shown that many network traffic patterns exhibit time-of-day peaks, and these are really what you wish to catch for capacity planning purposes. It follows, then, that an extremely short polling period is unnecessary for performance-management purposes. Accounting, however, is another matter; if you poll too infrequently, you risk losing valuable accounting information if a router malfunctions and loses its SNMP state. About 15–30 minutes is an often-used compromise.

All utilization data is worth storing in a format that enables a graphing tool to plot link utilization or that totals transmitted/received data between two arbitrary points in time. This is critical for capacity planning and accounting purposes.

In terms of detecting congestion, there are better methods than looking at link utilization graphs. Specifically, *ifOutDiscards* gives a good indication of the number of packets dropped due to link congestion, or problems on the link or linecard itself. This is an ideal object to poll very slowly—say, once an hour or more—and report only if a threshold is reached. Ideally, there should be no discards.

Congestion may also occur within the switching fabric of the router. The *ifInDiscard* object indicates the discards of packets due to the unavailability of an internal buffer used for switching. You may prefer to use the Cisco proprietary *locIfInputQueueDrops* instead; it measures drops due to both lack of buffers and lack of space in the interface RX queue.

Packets for unknown protocols are also counted as drops and are reported in *ifInUnknownProtos.* Therefore, for interfaces on shared media, a high level of drops may not necessarily indicate a problem other than a host configured to run a protocol that is not routed.

Finally, poorly performing links can be identified by thresholding *ifInErrors;* this usually indicates a link or linecard with a problem.

Other system resources that can be upgraded should be routinely checked. *IfInDiscards* will let you know when a switching-capacity problem occurs. Monitoring the overall CPU and memory utilization of the routing platform can also provide the details necessary for future upgrades. The correct objects to poll can vary from platform to platform. Some routers have multiple CPU and memory banks (7500, equipped with VIPs), whereas others have a single CPU (7200). It is worth perusing the plethora of MIBs available today; if you come across a good performance metric that is not accessible via a MIB, talk to your router vendor.

Monitoring Throughput

Remember that much of the information on the large networks, including Web traffic, is carried via TCP. As a result, the throughput available to a single TCP session can provide useful feedback on how the network is performing. Ideally, the throughput of this session would be monitored across the backbone because it is in the backbone that most intranetwork congestion typically occurs. Congestion often also occurs between networks, in the case of ISPs; and toward the Internet, in the case of corporate networks.

TTCP is one example of such a tool. It consists of both a data source and a data sink. The data sinks would ideally be located in various major POPs around the network. Tests would be run fairly infrequently, such as during the peak traffic period typically observed on the backbone. When automated, the testing could be used to produce daily reports showing typical "per-user" throughput between major capital cities, for example. If the backbone supports different classes of service, the throughput could be tested for each class.

Per-Byte Accounting

Many conflicting views exist on Internet charging models. Without favoring one over another, this section simply lists a few of the more popular models or proposals, and describes the tools that are available.

The same link-utilization data collected for performance management can also be used for a *per-byte* billing scheme. Specifically, records of *ifInOctets/IfOutOctets* on links feeding customers can be used as the basis for a number of different distant-independent charging schemes:

- Charges based on traffic for the busiest hour only
- Charges based on average link utilization
- Charges based on per-byte totals

These schemes tend to place an increasing level of importance on the integrity of the *ifInOctets/ IfOutOctets* data collection. Note that for per-byte volume charging, it is a relatively simple exercise for customers to replicate—and thereby verify—your SNMP statistics collection.

Interestingly, within currently available SNMP MIBs, there appears to be no way to differentiate between byte counts for unicast and multicast traffic. This may become an interesting issue in the future because the cost of providing multicast data feeds may become significantly less than unicast.

Flow Accounting and Traffic Engineering

Distance-dependent charging schemes also exist. As with telephone calls, to determine the cost of each byte, it is necessary to know where each byte originates and its destination. The origin issue seems obvious: the traffic enters the network on an interface associated with a particular customer. To determine the destination, you must perform flow accounting; this is where Netflow comes in.

It is generally recommended that you deploy Netflow as a perimeter technology—that is, enable Netflow on distribution/aggregation routers rather than on core routers. If you assume that Netflow accounting is performed at all customer ingress points (referring back to Table 15-2) you can see that you know the destination for all traffic in the network. Furthermore, if you couple this with knowledge about route configuration within the network, you can perform flow analysis and optimize routes.

Chapter 3, "Network Topologies," discussed various backbone topologies and introduced the concept of evolving the backbone from a ring through a partial to a full mesh.

Refer to Figure 15-5. You can detect that the links between San Francisco and Seattle, and between Seattle and New York, are congested, so you turn to your database of collected flow data. Analyzing data collected from routers D1 and D2, you can surmise that 20 percent of traffic leaving the distribution network in San Francisco is for destinations to New York and Washington.

From the route costing, you know that the core routers in San Francisco use the link via Seattle to reach both New York and Washington. You also know that the link from San Francisco to Florida reaches a peak utilization of 90 percent and therefore has little spare capacity. Price quotes tell you that the incremental cost of increasing the bandwidth of existing links between San Francisco/Seattle/New York or San Francisco/Florida/Washington is about the same as putting a direct link between San Francisco and New York. Because the latter solution provides greater redundancy and shorter round-trip times, you should opt for that. You know from your flow analysis the required bandwidth for the link.

In performing the previous process, you can see that three databases are needed:

- The raw flow data, showing the destination of all traffic from the distribution network in San Francisco
- A database that groups destination addresses into distribution networks
- A database that shows how traffic from each distribution network is routed across the backbone to other distribution networks

A similar process may also be used for calculating the size of interprovider traffic flows. In this case, you could use the destination AS rather than the IP address to size the flows. You also would need to maintain a list of all ASs serviced by your own network because traffic to these would not constitute interprovider traffic.

You can collect the destination IP address and AS for all ingress traffic from customers, and then compare this with the following:

- The database listing network addresses associated with each distribution network
- The database listing all ASs serviced by the network

You now have the basis for a three-tiered, distance-dependent charging scheme: local traffic, nationwide traffic, and interprovider/international traffic. Note, however, that unlike the simple byte-volume charging scheme, distance-dependent charging can involve significant post-processing of accounting data.

Summary:
Network Management Checklist for Large Networks

In this chapter, you read about the overall network management task. This task was divided into the functional areas defined by ISO. The chapter examined the use of SNMP and MIBs, Netflow, NTP, Syslog, DNS, and TACACs in overall network management. It also looked at the importance of maintaining network integrity through the use of route filtering and registries, and enabling or disabling forwarding services that may assist or threaten this policy.

This was a lot of ground to cover, so by way of summary, the following network management checklist can be used to help in the design or maintenance of your network:

1 Think about the five areas: fault, configuration, security, accounting, and performance. Are you addressing each of these issues?

2 Does your network require a distributed management framework, or will a centralized facility suffice? If you opt for a centralized facility, can you painlessly upgrade to a distributed architecture?

3 Have you enabled SNMP access on all routers, and are you controlling access through an access list? Is the access read-only?

4 Do you have a graphical representation of the network that is easily monitored by operations staff? Are you polling for *sysUptime*, *ifOperStatus*, and *ifAdminStatus*? Are other MIB variables more applicable to your network?

5 Do you have tools to enable operations staff to monitor log and snmp trap output from routers? Have you enabled logging and/or SNMP trap reporting on all critical routers? If so, at what level of messages (*debug* through *emergencies*)?

6 Is all logging and trap information archived?

7 Can you perform general SNMP queries of all supported Cisco MIBs? Do you have an MIB compiler?

8 Do you have an NTP architecture, including your own stratum 1 server? Will you offer NTP services to customers? If so, how?

9 Have you configured critical routers or those involved in testing to core-dump in the event of failure?

10 What is your naming plan for router interfaces? Do traceroutes through your network aid the troubleshooting process?

11 Are you making use of descriptive commands available in IOS to help self-document the configurations?

12 Do you have a document describing the overall network architecture, including its routing, policy, and failure modes?

13 Are your IOS configurations under revision control? What is your engineering policy for modifying router configurations?

14 Are you using the AAA architecture so you can control, track, and log access to routers? Is router access protected by both an AAA protocol and access lists? Do you have a procedure for updating the authentication database as network operations and engineering staff come and go? Are you using strong encryption for the enable password, and have you enabled Nagle congestion control and configured login banners?

15 Have you configured authentication for all routing protocols, using MD5 where available?

16 Are you maintaining a routing registry? Is the policy in this registry automatically and regularly translated into router configuration updates?

17 Have you enabled CEF RPF to prevent packet spoofing? Have you disabled IP redirects, directed broadcast, and proxy ARP? What about finger, pad, TCP services, UDP services, and bootp?

18 What is your plan for staging both major configuration changes and IOS version upgrades?

19 How do you monitor the ongoing performance of the network? Are you collecting and/or applying alarm thresholds to link utilization, errors, queue drops, and discards? Are there any other MIB variables that may tell you when your bandwidth, route processing, or switching capability is being exceeded?

20 What statistics are you collecting to perform capacity planning and traffic engineering? Have you considered enabling Netflow at the perimeter of the network and archiving *ifInOctets* and *ifOutOctets* for all router interfaces? Are you regularly analyzing flows in your network and optimizing routers accordingly?

21 What is your billing model, and what additional statistics do you need to collect to support it?

22 Do you recognize all the features in the following configuration and understand the motive for enabling or disabling each?

```
version 12.0
service nagle
no service pad
service timestamps debug datetime
service timestamps log datetime
service password-encryption
!
hostname dist1.sfo
!
no logging console
aaa new-model
aaa authentication login default tacacs+ enable
aaa authentication login console none
aaa authentication enable default tacacs+ enable
aaa accounting exec default start-stop tacacs+
aaa accounting commands 15 default start-stop tacacs+
enable secret 5 $1$/edy$.CyBGklbRBghZehOaj7jI/
!
ip subnet-zero
ip cef distributed
ip cef accounting per-prefix non-recursive
no ip finger
ip tcp window-size 65535
ip tcp path-mtu-discovery
ip tftp source-interface Loopback0
ip ftp source-interface Loopback0
ip ftp username devtest
ip ftp password 7 0202014D1F031C3501
no ip bootp server
ip host tftps 172.21.27.83
ip domain-name isp.net
ip name-server 16.60.0.254
ip name-server 16.60.20.254
ip multicast-routing distributed
clock timezone PST -8
clock summer-time PDT recurring
!
```

```
!
interface Loopback0
 ip address 16.0.0.1 255.255.255.255
 no ip directed-broadcast
 no ip route-cache
 no ip mroute-cache

interface FastEthernet0/0/0
 description Server LAN, 100 Mbit/s, Infrastructure
 bandwidth 100000
 ip address 16.60.10.1 255.255.0.0
 ip verify unicast reverse-path
 no ip redirects
 no ip directed-broadcast
 ip route-cache distributed
 no cdp enable
!

ip classless
ip tacacs source-interface Loopback0
ip bgp-community new-format

logging history size 100
logging history debugging
logging 16.60.0.254
access-list 16 permit 16.60.0.0 0.0.255.255

snmp-server community testcomm RO 7
snmp-server trap-source Loopback0
snmp-server location San Francisco
snmp-server contact noc@isp.net
snmp-server enable traps snmp
snmp-server enable traps channel
snmp-server enable traps isdn call-information
snmp-server enable traps config
snmp-server enable traps entity
snmp-server enable traps envmon
snmp-server enable traps bgp
snmp-server enable traps frame-relay
snmp-server enable traps rtr
snmp-server host 16.60.0.254 traps snmpcomm
snmp-server tftp-server-list 16
!
tacacs-server host 16.60.0.254
tacacs-server key labkey
banner login
C
         This system is the property of isp.net

         Access to this system is monitored

         Unauthorized access is prohibited

         Contact noc@isp.net or call +1 555 555 5555 with inquiries
```

```
!
line con 0
 exec-timeout 0 0
 login authentication console
 transport input none
line aux 0
line vty 0 4
 access-class 16 in
 exec-timeout 0 0
 password 7 002B012D0D5F
 transport input telnet
!
exception core-file 75k1.sfo
exception protocol ftp
exception dump 16.60.0.254
ntp authenticate
ntp trusted-key 1
ntp clock-period 17182332
ntp source Loopback0
ntp update-calendar
ntp server 16.60.0.254 prefer
end
```

Review Questions

1   Why aren't some of the features of security or scaling problems disabled by default?

2   What is a "turn-key" NMS?

3   What are the storage requirements for Netflow?

4   What are the storage requirements for SNMP and logging?

5   Could NTP be provided as a service to customers?

6   Are there routing protocols that dynamically route around points of congestion in the network?

Answers:

1   Security and ease-of-use are often contradicting requirements. Some of the features make life easier if they are enabled. Having said that, increasingly the emphasis is on scalability—and particularly security. Some of the features recommended for disabling or enabling in this chapter have already become defaults in version 12 of IOS. More changes are sure to follow as other scaling issues and security vulnerabilities are discovered.

2 Vendors use "turn-key" NMS to refer to a system that you power on and that instantly manages your network. Although such systems may be a reasonable match for small networks, they generally require considerable tailoring for very large networks. In some cases, the auto-discovery mechanisms of such systems can be quite disruptive because they probe the network, requesting large volumes of data in the process of discovering topology and devices. Designing and deploying your NMS must be done with as much care and planning as any other part of the network infrastructure. Indeed, the NMS is one of the most critical parts of the infrastructure.

3 For a large network, even with only a few hundred routers, Netflow export can quickly result in large volumes of data. Your Netflow collection agent should attempt to parse the export data in real-time, performing aggregation of data and discarding any data in which you are not interested.

4 Again, large amounts of data can quickly accumulate. You should carefully plan which data to keep and how to archive the data from expensive hard drives to cheaper media, such as CD-ROMs.

5 If you have your network well-synchronized, there is no reason why this benefit should not be passed on to customers. However, you should clearly set customer expectations about the accuracy of the time—possibly in terms of the NTP stratum. Nevertheless, even clocks at higher stratum numbers, such as 4 or above, can still be within a second or less of a stratum 1 source; for many applications, this is more than good enough.

6 Yes. As far back as the ARPANET, such protocols were investigated. However, avoiding route-oscillation in dynamic congestion-based routing for connectionless environments such as IP is a tricky problem that continues to be the subject of much endeavor in research and commercial environments, as well as the IETF.

For Further Reading . . . .

Leinwand, A. and K. F. Conroy. *Network Management: A Practical Perspective*. Reading, MA: Addison-Wesley, 1998.

RFC 1155. *Structure and Identification of Management Information for TCP/IP-based Internets*. 1990.

RFC 1157. *A Simple Network Management Protocol*. 1990.

RFC 1213. *Management Information Base for Network Management of TCP/IP-based Internets: MIB-II*. 1991.

RFC 1305. *Network Time Protocol*. 1992.

RFC 1901. *Introduction to Community-based SNMPv2*. 1996.

RFC 1902. *Structure of Management Information for Version 2 of the Simple Network Management Protocol (SNMPv2)*. 1996.

RFC 1903. *Textual Conventions for Version 2 of the Simple Network Management Protocol (SNMPv2)*. 1996.

RFC 1904. *Textual Conventions for Version 2 of the Simple Network Management Protocol (SNMPv2)*. 1996.

RFC 1905. *Protocol Operations for Version 2 of the Simple Network Management Protocol (SNMPv2)*. 1996.

RFC 1906. *Transport Mappings for Version 2 of the Simple Network Management Protocol (SNMPv2)*. 1996.

RFC 1907. *Management Information Base for Version 2 of the Simple Network Management Protocol (SNMPv2)*. 1996.

RFC 1908. *Coexistence between Version 1 and Version 2 of the Internet-standard Network Management Framework*. 1996.

RFC 2271. *An Architecture for Describing SNMP Management Frameworks*. 1998.

RFC 2272. *Message Processing and Dispatching for the Simple Network Management Protocol (SNMP)*. 1998.

RFC 2273. *SNMPv3 Application*. 1998.

RFC 2274. *User-based Security Model (USM) for Version 3 of the Simple Network Management Protocol (SNMPv3)*. 1998.

RFC 2275. *View-based Access Control Model (VACM) for the Simple Network Management Protocol (SNMP)*. 1998.

Rose, M. *The Simple Book: An Introduction to Management of TCP/IP-based Internets,* Second Edition. Upper Saddle River, NJ: Prentice-Hall, 1993.

Stallings, W. *SNMP, SNMPv2, and CMIP: The Practical Guide to Network Management.* Reading, MA: Addison-Wesley, 1993.

Terplan, K. *Communications Network Management,* Second Edition. Upper Saddle River, NJ: Prentice-Hall, 1992.

## CHAPTER 16

Design and Configuration Case Studies

Designing a successful IP network is one of the essential elements surrounding modern internetworking. A poorly designed network affects the performance of the routers, as well as the entire network. As networks become an essential part of any successful business, scaling and faster convergence also play a major role.

This chapter presents the process of designing large networks. Specifically, it addresses a network design: first, with respect to the enterprises; then, with respect to the ISPs. The discussion of enterprise includes two case studies, and an additional case study for ISP design:

- The first case study deals with a typical large, worldwide corporation that considers OSPF the IGP.

  The chapter case studies also discuss a merger between two large companies with their own Internet connections. The two companies intend to use each other's connection as a backup.

- The second enterprise case study concerns a large hub-and-spoke design, which is widely used by large banks, airlines, and retail stores. This case study examines a situation in which networks need information from each of the remote sites, but must avoid problems arising from their flaps or instabilities. Core routing should remain stable for this design.

- The third case study shows the design of a large ISP network. This example focuses on issues such as addressing, network management, IGP and interdomain routing, multicast, and QoS. The emphasis in this case study remains on actual configuration details, and advances many of the architectural ideas present in earlier chapters.

Case Study 1: The Alpha.com Enterprise

In this case study, the customer, Alpha.com, is a large manufacturing corporation with research facilities in North America (California) and Europe (Germany). Chip fabrication plants are located in New Mexico, Texas, and Arizona (North America), as well as in Malaysia and Taiwan (Asia). A network outage causes enormous revenue losses for this company, so it wants to build a completely fault-tolerant network. Therefore, Alpha.com wants complete Layer 2 and Layer 3 redundancy.

Network Requirements

As in any large corporation, some paranoia surrounds the performance and fault tolerance of the network. Alpha.com has some very strict requirements about design: Managers want complete Layer 2 redundancy, full load-sharing capability, unfailing optimal routing, faster convergence, and failure recovery without major impact.

The company uses a large IBM SNA network, and has specific time limits for network convergence. The customer wants the routing protocol to converge so that none of its LLC2 SNA sessions is terminated.

As in any large corporation, Alpha.com does not assign all of its employees to the same department or locate them in the same building; employees are dispersed around the campus, or even in different cities around the world. Alpha.com wants to build a 5000-node network that will scale today and continue to be successful for years to come.

Setting Up the Network

Customers demand a fault-tolerant, redundant, optimally routed network with 100 percent availability, but unfortunately, scaling problems will also arise. There is often a limit to redundancy and optimal routing, which means that these must be sacrificed for scaling.

One common issue involves network users who are working on a common project, but do not seem concerned about network scaling. Their only requirement is to send information and receive it. These users do not want suboptimal routing, so they begin adding links only for sharing applications—before long, this creates a completely unscalable network without any hierarchy. Therefore, you need to design a network for Alpha.com that will operate successfully and that will meet most of the company's requirements.

First, examine the network from a high level, and then investigate the details of each region to finalize a design. Figure 16-1 shows a high-level view of the network. From this level, it is apparent that this network requires regionalization, which offers control over routing updates because it allows each region to grow independently.

Next, examine the layout of each region. Figure 16-2 shows the North American region. All major data centers are connected to each other via a fully redundant ATM core. Each region has two routers that are fully meshed with PVC to routers in other regions within North America.

Figure 16-3 shows Alpha.com's Los Angeles, California campus. Within the campus, each department is located in separate buildings. For example, engineering is located in buildings B1 and B4.

Figure 16-1   *High-Level View of the Example Network*

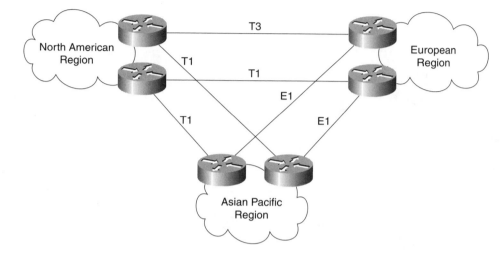

Figure 16-2   *The North American Region*

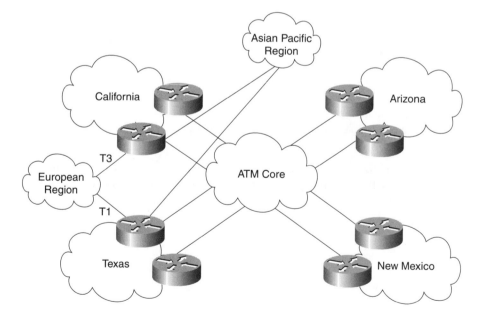

Figure 16-3 *Campus for Alpha.com in California*

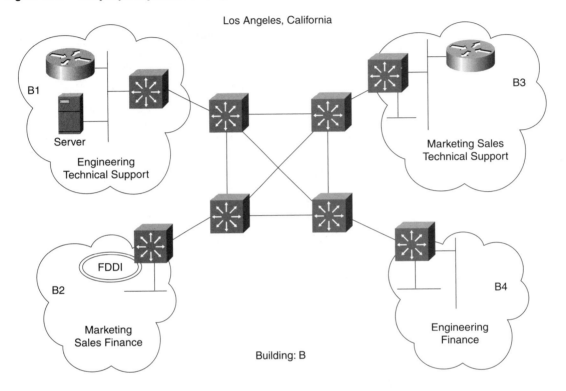

In this case, the departments would prefer to share resources. The network administrator would like to separate the department traffic so that other departments are not affected by unnecessary data.

With this information, you are ready to learn about the virtual LANs. Upon completion of this discussion, we will return to Alpha.com to directly apply this information to its network.

Virtual LANs

Routers have traditionally been used to separate the broadcast domains across subnets. For example, any broadcast generated on the Ethernet 0 of a router USA.Cal.R1 would not be forwarded to E1 of the same router. For this reason, routers provide well-defined boundaries between different LAN segments. However, routers have the following drawbacks:

- *Lack of reactive addressing*   From Figure 16-3, you can see that each engineering service is in a different location, separated by multiple routers. This means that all the engineering services cannot exist on the same logical subnet, as is the case with Ethernet in building B1 and building B4 in Figure 16-3. You cannot assign the same IP subnet address to both locations.

- *Insufficient bandwidth use*   This occurs when extra traffic must traverse the network because the network is segmented, based upon physical locations rather than workgroups. This is also useful in large, flat networks because a single broadcast domain can be divided into several smaller broadcast domains.

- *Lack of flexibility*   This is caused by relocations. When users must move their locations, the system requires reconfigurations according to the new location.

VLANs can solve these router problems because they enable switches and routers to configure logical topologies on top of the physical network infrastructure. Logical topologies enable any arbitrary collection of LAN segments within a network to be combined into a user group, which then appears as a single LAN.

VLAN Groups

A VLAN group is defined as a logical LAN segment that spans different physical LANs. These networks belong to the same group, based on given criteria. The definition of VLAN groups is done with a technique known as *frame coloring*. During this process, packets originating from and contained within a designated virtual topology carry a VLAN identifier as they traverse the common shared backbone. The process of frame coloring enables the VLAN devices to make intelligent forwarding decisions based upon the VLAN ID.

VLAN groups are often differentiated by assigning each of them a color. Coloring a VLAN group involves assigning an identifier to a VLAN group, which is used when making decisions. Logical VLAN groups can be denoted by department numbers or any other criteria selected by the user. For the purpose of configurations, these colors are denoted by numbers.

There are two types of VLAN technologies:

- *Cell-based*   This technology refers to the use of LAN emulation and ATM switching. ATM's forum has defined a specification known as *LAN emulation* (LANE). This enables legacy LAN users to benefit from ATM without requiring modification to end station hardware and software. LANE emulates a broadcast environment such as 802.3 Ethernet or 802.5 Token Ring on top of ATM.

- *Frame-based*   This technology refers to frame tagging, such as IEEE 802.10 and ISL frame-tagging methods.

VLANs can be used in three modes:

- *VLAN Switching mode*   When connected during the switching mode, VLAN forms a switching bridge. In doing so, it sends a frame from the VLAN group to a destination on the same VLAN group located on the other side of the switch in a different physical network. This frame is forwarded without modifications.

- *VLAN Translation mode*   VLAN translation is performed when a frame is modified from one mode to another, such as before the frame is switched to a destination in the same group but with a different VLAN tagging method, for example, for ISL to 802.10. Translation is used when migrating from one VLAN group to a native interface that is not running VLAN. The frame is modified by the router to the appropriate VLAN tagging method. In case of a native packet, the tag is removed by the router so that the packet can go to the native interface.

- *VLAN Routing mode*   This is performed when a packet will be routed from one VLAN to another VLAN in a different group. The packet is modified by the router by placing its own MAC address as the source, and then changing the VLAN ID.

Frame Tagging

Cisco supports two types of frame tagging: ISL and 802.10, which are described as follows:

- *Inter Switch Link (ISL)*   This is the Cisco proprietary protocol for connecting multiple switches and maintaining VLAN information as traffic travels between switches. It is a method of multiplexing bridge groups over a high-speed backbone. With ISL, an Ethernet frame is encapsulated with a header that transports the VLAN ID between switches and routers. This VLAN ID is added to the frame only if the frame is destined to a non-local interface.

  Examine Figure 16-4. If switch 1 receives traffic from segment A and wants to forward it to segment B, no ISL header is attached. If switch 1 must forward a frame to switch 3 on VLAN 200, the ISL header is added at switch 1 and is passed through switch 2. The packet is then forwarded to switch 3. When switch 3 receives the packet, it removes the ISL header and forwards it to the appropriate port for VLAN 200.

Figure 16-4 *Frame Tagging for VLANs*

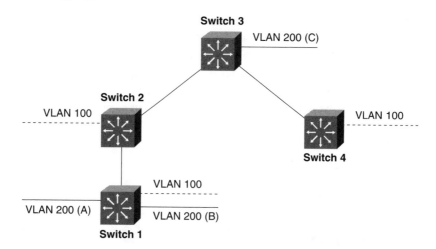
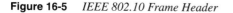

- *802.10* This IEEE standard provides a method for secure bridging of data across a shared backbone. The 802.10 standard defines a single frame type known as the *Secure Data Exchange* (SDE) frame, which is a MAC-layer frame with an 802.10 header inserted between the MAC header and the frame data, as shown in Figure 16-5. The VLAN ID is carried in a four-byte Security Association Identifier (SAID) field.

Figure 16-5 *IEEE 802.10 Frame Header*

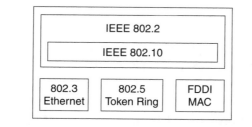
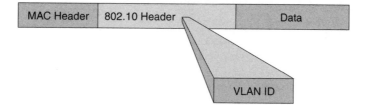

Cisco routers and switches can use 802.10 to switch traffic across high-speed backbones (FDDI, Fast Ethernet, Token Ring, and serial links). As mentioned earlier, the VLAN ID is inside the 802.10 header. When the switch receives the frame from a source station, it inserts the VLAN ID. On the receiving switch, the frame is stripped, and the 16-byte 802.10 header is removed. The frame is then forwarded to the interface that matches the VLAN ID.

As Figure 16-6 shows, all ports on switches 1, 2, and 3 are VLAN interfaces. To prevent traffic from segment C destined for segment B from flooding the entire switched network, switch 3 tags the frames with the IEEE 802.10 header when the frame leaves switch 3. Switch 2 recognizes the color and knows that it must forward these frames onto segment B. Switch 1 does not pass the frame to its segments.

Figure 16-6   *Shared Switched Backbone and Frame Tagging*

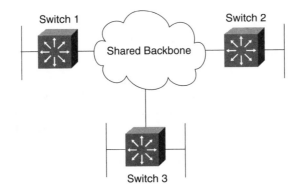

Using VLANs for Alpha.com

Next, apply the VLAN concept to the network in Figure 16-3 to create VLANs for each of Alpha.com's departments. This way, employees of the same department within the campus are part of the same broadcast domain, and can share applications without affecting other departments.

Engineering is set to VLAN 100, Marketing is set to VLAN 200, Tech Support is set to VLAN300, Sales is set to VLAN 400, and Finance is set to VLAN 500. By creating the VLAN, you will isolate the broadcast domains, while retaining the capability to run subnets across different buildings, as shown in Figure 16-7.

Figure 16-7   *Defining VLANs for Alpha.com*

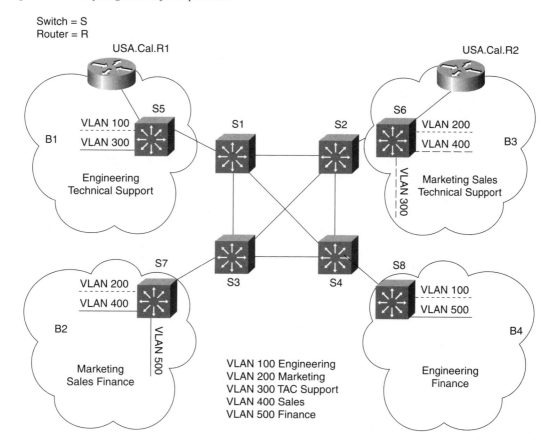

Although not all the VLANs would be able to connect with all the switches, it is wise to define all VLANs on all shared switches for redundancy. For example, Figure 16-7 shows that switch S3 connects to S7, which does not have VLAN 100 connected to it. One can argue that it is unnecessary to define VLAN 100 on S3 because a dual failure could occur, in which the links between S1 and S4 and between S1 and S2 go down. If you define VLAN 100 on S3, you would still have connectivity for VLAN 100 across S3.

The configuration for switch S5 is as follows:

```
set vlan 100 2/1-4              (Command 1 for VLAN 100)
set vlan 300 2/5-8              (Command 2 for VLAN  300)
set trunk 3/1 100,200,300,400,500     (Command 3 for ISL trunk between S5 and S1)
set trunk 3/2 100,200,300,400,500     (Command 4 for ISL trunk between S5 and
  USA.Cal.R1)
```

The first set of commands defines the VLAN IDs, which in this case are 100 and 300. After the VLAN ID, define the module number in which the card appears. In this case, the card is in slot 2. After the module, define the port numbers on which you want to assign this VLAN ID. In this case, the ports are 1 through 4 for VLAN 100, and 5 through 8 for VLAN 300.

The second set of commands defines an ISL trunk. In Figure 16-7 you must create the ISL trunk between S5 and S1 and between S5 and the router. Any connection between switches, or between a router and a switch is defined by the ISL trunk.

The third line sets an ISL trunk between switch S1 (see Figure 16-7) and S5 on port 1 of module 3. The VLANs that would run on this trunk are 100, 200, 300, 400, and 500.

The fourth command defines the trunk between router USA.Cal.R1 and S5 on port 2 of module 3 for all the VLANs on the campus.

Notice that all the VLANs are defined between S5 and S1, and between S5 and the router USA.Cal.R1. All VLANs must be placed in the trunk for redundancy between switches. This is also necessary because S5 connects to the router—it must inform the router of all the VLANs behind it so that the router can advertise these subnets to the rest of the network.

Router USA.Cal.R1 would advertise all the IP subnets for all the VLANs to the rest of the network. The router would send traffic to each individual VLAN, so it should have all the information about all the VLAN IDs. When configuring VLANs on routers, some basic steps are required:

- Configure the subinterface for each VLAN group that you want to switch.
- For each subinterface, define a VLAN group and an encapsulation type.
- For each subinterface, define a network-layer address under a routing protocol.

Configuring Router USA.Cal.R1

The configuration for Router USA.Cal.R1 would be as follows:

```
interface loopback 0
ip address 172.16.10.1 255.255.255.255
interface fastethernet 2/1.1
ip address 172.16.1.1 255.255.255.0
encap isl 100
interface fastethernet 2/1.2
ip address 172.16.2.1 255.255.255.0
encap isl 200
interface fastethernet 2/1.3
ip address 172.16.3.1 255.255.255.0
encap isl 300
interface fastethernet 2/1.4
ip address 172.16.4.1 255.255.255.0
encap isl 400
interface fastethernet 2/1.5
ip address 172.16.5.1 255.255.255.0
```

```
encap isl 500
router ospf 1
network 172.16.0.0 0.0.16.255 area 1
network 172.16.254.0 0.0.0.255 area 0
area 1 range 172.16.0.0 255.255.240.0
```

In this configuration, each subinterface represents a VLAN. The IP address is assigned for each VLAN, and the third command defines the encapsulation type, which in this case is ISL plus the VLAN ID.

Defining IP Addresses and Summarization

You should configure all the addresses within a campus to be out of a contiguous range for summarization at the router. In addition, you should leave open certain addresses for a range for future use. In this case, the address assigned for the VLANs ranges from 1 to 5. You could leave subnets 6 through 31 open for future use within the region, if you anticipate that the region will experience enough growth. In this case, it is expected that the region will grow, so a large portion of address space is unassigned for future use.

This campus is defined for OSPF as an individual area. California is assigned as area 1. It is a good idea to send one route out from the area into area 0 so that link flaps within the area are confined to that area only. Area 0 does not have to run SPF every time a change occurs in area 1. Even when summarization is done, the summarized route sent by the ABR picks up the lowest metric (current implementation) of the specific route within the range, and sends that metric as the metric for the summarized route.

For example, consider the following route as an example in the table:

```
0     172.16.3.0 [110/13] via 209.1.169.249, 00:09: 58, Fast Ethernet3/0
0     172.16.4.0 [110/14] via 209.1.169.249, 00:09:58, Hssi0/1/0
```

In this case, when the router originates a route for network 172.16.0.0 255.255.240.0 within the area range, it chooses the smallest metric, which in this case is 13 for the area range. According to RFC information, this has changed to the highest metric, which would become 14. To generate the new metric, a good technique is to configure a loopback on the Cisco router for a metric of this range.

Creating a Loopback Interface

It is a good practice to create a loopback interface on Cisco routers running OSPF, most importantly, to create a router ID. In Cisco implementation, a loopback is taken as the router ID of the box. If a loopback interface is not configured, the highest IP address is selected as the router ID.

Creating the loopback as the router ID provides stability. The loopback is a virtual interface on the Cisco router that will continue to operate well, as long as the router stays up. When the router ID is tied to the physical interface and the physical interface goes down, the router must select a new router ID. All the link states associated with this router should be flushed.

If the router is an ABR, its link states must be flushed for multiple areas, although the interface that flapped belonged to one area only. This could cause high CPU utilization on the router.

TIP

For stability, it is wise to create a loopback interface on the router to generate the router ID. A rule of thumb: always pick a subnet out of the range of addresses in an area, and then configure the loopback address as a /32 (255.255.255.255) mask. This way, the same subnet could be used by a large number of routers within the area.

After the loopback is created, router USA.Cal.R1 sets the metric of the summary 172.16.0.0/20 at 1 because it is the metric of the loopback address on a Cisco router by default. It is also the lowest metric of all specific routes in the range. The ABR must be upgraded to the version of IOS that supports the new RFC (RFC 2328), which states that the highest metric should be selected for the summary route. Simply find the highest metric in the network, and then assign the cost of the loopback interface higher than that metric. The command is as follows:

```
interface loopback 0
ip ospf cost 148
```

In Figure 16-8, a link has been added between USA.Cal.R1 and USA.Cal.R2. This link is called the *summarization link.*

If the Fast Ethernet on USA.Cal.R1 goes down because USA.Cal.R1 has loopback configured on the router that is out of the range, USA.Cal.R1 will continue to advertise the route to that range, although it has lost connection to the VLAN subnets. After the link is added between the two summarization routers, USA.Cal.R1 will still have a path to all the specific destinations via USA.Cal.R2.

As shown in Figure 16-9, router USA.Cal.R1 loses its link to S7 because the loopback interface on USA.Cal.R1 is still running. As a result, router USA.Cal.R1 will continue to send the summarized route to area 0 and will attract traffic. Adding the link between the summarizing router avoids the single point of failure.

Figure 16-8 *Link Added between Routers to Help with Redundancy and Summarization*

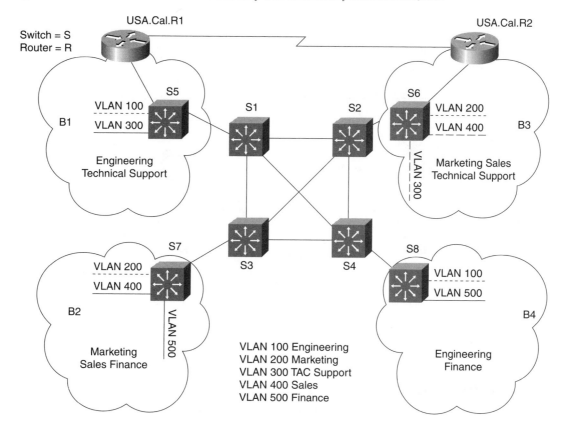

Another important point to remember during summarization is *anchoring*. If a router generates a summarized route, regardless of the routing protocol, you should create a route to the null interface (another virtual interface on Cisco routers). In the case of BGP and Enhanced IGRP, if a router is configured with summarization, this creates a null route by default. When routes are redistributed and summarized in OSPF, the router creates the null route. In the case of interarea summarization, the router does not create the null route.

Figure 16-9 *Link Failure between Router and Switch Does Not Create Holes*

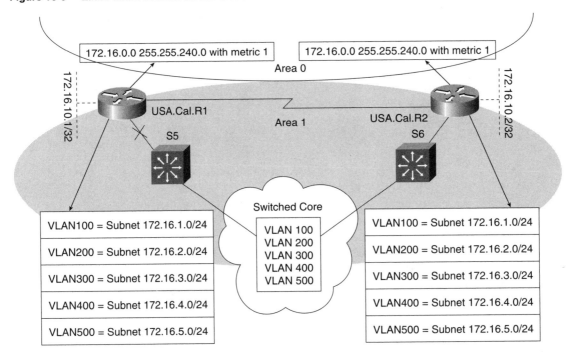

Avoiding Routing Loops

Ensure that the area range configured on the ABR is a route to null interfaces, or you will risk a routing loop. Figure 16-10 shows a typical situation in which a routing loop could be created.

Figure 16-10 *Routing Loop Caused by Summarization*

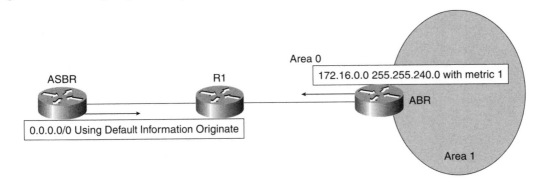

In Figure 16-10, the ABR sends a route for subnets 172.16.0.0 to 172.16.15.0, and the ASBR sends the default route. ABR loses its route to one of the subnets if, for example, subnet 172.16.12.0/24 has failed. ABR lost its route to 172.16.12.0/24 when R1 sent a packet for subnet 172.16.12.0/24; it searches its routing table and finds that the longest prefix to 172.16.12.0/24 does not exist. Then, it searches for the next prefix and finds 172.16.0.0/20 advertised via ABR.

R1 forwards packets toward ABR. When ABR searches its routing table, it cannot locate a route to 172.16.12.0/24, so it considers the next best option. A summarized route does not exist in the ABR because ABR is originating it for area 0. If no IP classless is configured, the second-best option in ABR's routing table is network 0.0.0.0, which originates from the ASBR. ABR forwards the packet to R1 because it is in ABR's path to the ASBR. R1 again reads the destination address and forwards the packet back to ABR, creating a routing loop.

To avoid the routing loop, you should ensure that whenever an ABR is generating the summarized route, you create a route to the null interface that matches the area range command. For Alpha.com, you would need to create the following route on ABR:

```
ip route 172.16.0.0 255.255.240.0 null0
```

After the null route is created, you might wonder what would happen when router R1 sends a packet for 172.16.12.0/24 router? The answer is: ABR reads the packet and searches for 172.16.12.0/24 in the table, but does not find it. Next, the ABR considers the next best option, finds the static 172.16.0.0/20 route in the table, and sends that route to the null interface.

If you apply a similar addressing scheme for the rest of the regions in North America, you would assign an address range of 32 to 63 to Texas, 64 to 79 to Arizona, and 80 to 96 to New Mexico. Addresses within the ATM core should be out of the North American address range, but not from any subregion within North America (Texas, Arizona, New Mexico, and California). This way, the ATM core subnet address is not tied to any one subregion, and the ATM core address does not damage subregional summarization.

NOTE   When running VLANs across the WAN cloud, it is nonsensical to run them over the wide area. If broadcast packets are sent across the WAN link, more traffic will be the result. VLANs are for the local area only, so congesting wide-area links by sending broadcast traffic is impractical.

Selecting the OSPF Model for ATM Core

The ATM core in this case is area 0. There are three ways by which OSPF can run on this core. (Although there are four models, this chapter does not consider the non-broadcast method because it is very similar to the broadcast model.)

- Broadcast model
- Point-to-point model
- Point-to-multipoint model

The Broadcast Model

The broadcast model requires the selection of a designated router, as well as a backup designated router. In addition, all the routers in the cloud must be fully meshed. For some organizations, this can be expensive and impractical. If the mesh breaks, a hole is created. In Figure 16-11, for example, assume that USA.Cal.R1 becomes the designated router and that USA.Arz.R3 is elected as the backup designated router.

Figure 16-11 *Fully Meshed ATM Core*

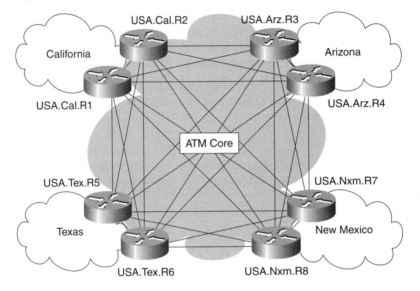

All the routers should have a connection to the designated router. If USA.Tex.R6 loses its PVC to USA.Cal.R1, but still has a connection to USA.Arz.R3, then USA.Tex.R6 considers USA.Arz.R3 to be the designated router. Because USA.Arz.R3 still has its connection to USA.Cal.R1, it sends the ID of USA.Cal.R1 as the designated router in its packet back to USA.Tex.R6. This causes USA.Tex.R6 not to install any routes in the table.

USA.Tex.R6 has physical connectivity with all other routers in the cloud, but it cannot install routes through these routers because it is not synchronized with DR.

Flooding, on the other hand, is optimal in the broadcast model because the DR is responsible for sending changes to the multicast address of 224.0.0.5, which means that all the routers in the cloud will install the changes. This model has obvious flaws because it fails whenever a fully meshed link breaks. Therefore, it is not robust for non-broadcast multiaccess networks such as ATM, Frame Relay, and SMDS.

The Point-to-Point and Point-to-Multipoint Models

By using either the point-to-point or the point-to-multipoint models, the network is more robust, and the cloud does not need to be fully meshed. Partial mesh is successful because no DR is present, so losing a PVC to the neighbor does not mean loss of connectivity.

Another possibility is to reduce the full mesh. Figure 16-12 shows a reasonably small mesh. You can define this cloud as one subnet and run OSPF in point-to-multipoint mode, or you can define each one of the point-to-point connections in a different subnet with a /30 mask. A /30 mask is used so that only two host IDs are needed on the subnet for the point-to-point interface.

Figure 16-12   *Partial Mesh Due to Point-to-Point Subinterfaces*

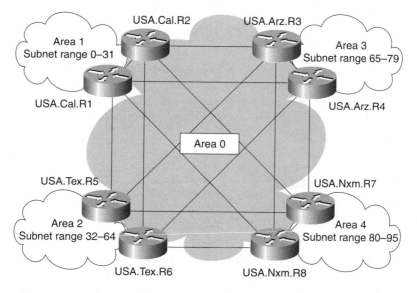

Addressing could be taken from one of the subnets out of any range in the North America region. You would address the ATM cloud with the subnet of 172.16.252.0. Addressing for one of the router interfaces would be the following:

```
Configs for USA.Cal.R1
interface atm 1/0.1 point-to-point
ip address 172.16.252.1 255.255.255.252
interface atm 1/0.2 point-to-point
ip address 172.16.252.5 255.255.255.252
router ospf 1
network 172.16.252.0 0.0.0.255 area 0
```

Based on the number of subnets available from the /30 mask, Alpha.com has the following subnets:

```
Subnet                    Host id
172.16.252.0/30           172.16.252.1, 172.16.252.2
172.16.252.4/30           172.16.252.5, 172.16.252.6
172.16.252.8/30           172.16.252.9, 172.16.252.10
172.16.252.12.0/30        172.16.252.13, 172.16.252.14
172.16.252.16.0/30        172.16.252.17, 172.16.252.18
```

This way, there are 10 subnets assigned among all the core sites. Remember to locate the link between routers in the same region in the regional area. For example, the ATM link between router USA.Cal.R1 and USA.Cal.R2 in California should be in area 1. Addresses between the two routers USA.Cal.R1 and USA.Cal.R2 on the ATM should be excluded from the addresses ranging from 0 to 31. Similar addressing should be performed for other areas.

Moving from the North America region, Texas and California have connections to Europe, and California also has connections to Asia. At this point, Alpha.com has two choices: It could either bring these three links into area 0, or it could run BGP between the regions. Both are perfectly valid choices. The disadvantage to extending OSPF is sending link state packets on those costly links. In addition, flaps in area 0 in Europe or Asia will affect the area 0 in North America.

Running BGP between Links

Running BGP between the links has several advantages. Your IGP does not need to carry unnecessary routes from other regions, so regions can grow independently. Problems within a region are confined to the local region only, which offers a lot more policy control.

Also, consider the current trends in the industry. In today's fast-paced market, many large companies are acquiring other companies or are merging to compete in their respective markets. With mergers, another complication is added to the network—merged companies usually have not been running the same IGP. For example, one organization may be running OSPF, and another may be running Enhanced IGRP, so they must accommodate each other and re-engineer the new network to run a common routing protocol, or redistribute between the two. This extends the boundaries of the IGP.

Secondly, not all operations are placed into one administrative control immediately. Even if both organizations are capable of moving their networks into one IGP, an important question arises: What happens when this newly merged company buys another organization? Clearly, adding another IGP would create immediate problems which can be addressed only by running BGP between the links.

To summarize, a BGP core between regions prevents unnecessary flooding on costly links, simplifies the merging of organizations, and offers greater policy control.

Choosing between IBGP and EBGP

Both IBGP and EBGP can be used for the purpose of peering between regions. Without any extensive policies between regions, and if a default route will be sent from each IBGP router into each region, you would have to use the registered AS number for the IBGP core. You need the registered AS number in the Internet connection because the core would send a default route into the regions. Also, the default route should originate only from the core. Because the core is all-knowing, it should maintain the Internet connection. In addition, you cannot peer with ISP via BGP if you do not have a registered AS number.

Redistribution of IBGP into IGP can create difficulties. If you decide to send BGP attributes, IBGP might not be a wise choice. For example, in Figure 16-13 you can see the physical connection: All the routers that are running IBGP must be logically full-meshed. Alpha.com is trying to implement policies and does not want to fully mesh BGP, which is against the standard.

Figure 16-13 *Partial-Mesh IBGP*

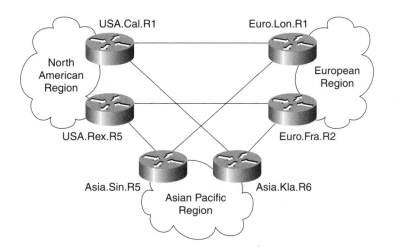

IBGP/Physical Setup

Consider the situations that would complicate the issue. Suppose that you want optimal routing and want to redistribute an IBGP-learned route in your local IGP of the region. This method is not advisable because you risk the formation of routing loops. In Figure 16-14, USA.Cal.R1 router is sending routes to Euro.Lon.R1, and USA.Tex.R5 is sending routes to Euro.Fra.R2.

Figure 16-14 *IBGP Route Advertisement between the United States and Europe*

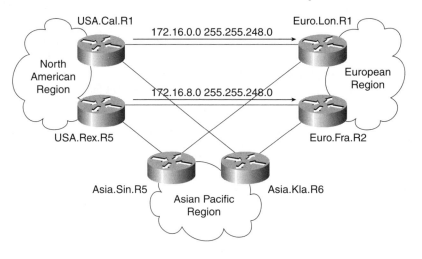

Alpha.com wants optimal routing, so Euro.Lon.R1 takes USA.Cal.R1 for subnet 172.16.{0-7}.0/21, and Euro.Fra.R2 takes USA.Tex.R5 for subnet 172.16.{8-25}.0/21. Router failure would cause the router to choose other paths. USA.Tex.R5 and USA.Cal.R1 must advertise different routes and send a shorter summary in case of failure. The configurations of routers would be the following:

```
router bgp 1
neighbor  172.16.64.2 remote-as 1          (Loop back address of  USA.Tex.R5 )
neighbor  172.16.64.3 remote-as 1          (Loop back address of Euro.Lon.R1)
neighbor  172.16.64.5 remote-as 1          (Loop back address of Asia.Kla.R2)
network 172.16.0.0 mask 255.255.248.0
network 172.16.0.0 mask 255.255.240.0          {Shorter prefix}
```

Similarly, the configuration for USA.Tex.R5 would be sent a different summary than USA.Cal.R1, and would be sent via a less-specific route to Euro.Fra.R2:

```
router bgp 1
neighbor  172.16.64.1 remote-as 1          (Loop back address of  USA.Cal.R1 )
neighbor  172.16.64.4 remote-as 1          (Loop back address of Euro.Fra.R2)
neighbor  172.16.64. 6 remote-as 1          (Loop back address of Asia.Sin.R1)
network 172.16.8.0 mask 255.255.248.0
network 172.16.0.0 mask 255.255.240.0          {Shorter prefix}
```

Note that all the peering addresses on the BGP routers are loopback addresses with a /32 mask, so the backbone uses the same subnet with a /32 on all the routers without wasting address space.

Try to leak loopback addresses to each BGP neighbor with a /32 as an IBGP route. Otherwise, BGP will flap. There are two ways to do this: Either send the /32 route with your existing IGP (which would increase the individual IGP of the region into other regions), or run a separate instance of IGP just to carry the next hop information, as shown in Figure 16-15.

Figure 16-15 *Separate IGP to Carry Next Hop Information*

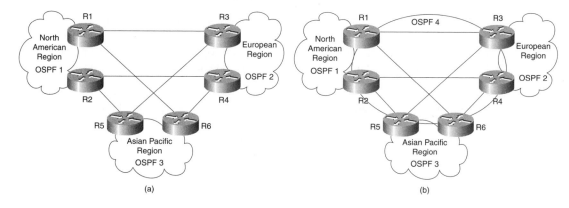

Extending each regional OSPF is problematic because each router from each region will begin to send all the routes across. Remember that in OSPF you can summarize at the ABR and filter at the ASBR. Also, when configuring in OSPF, the process ID is insignificant, so router OSPF 1 on R1 can communicate with router OSPF 2 on router 3, unless these routers are running multiple processes.

In cases in which routers are running multiple processes, the routers form an adjacency on common processes. Therefore, a separate instance of OSPF should be run, as shown in Figure 16-15. This way, you would run OSPF only on the interregional links and loopback addresses of the peering routers. Remember not to redistribute between the OSPF processes.

In Figure 16-15, routers R1 and R2 will be configured to run OSPF 1 and OSPF 4. The U.S. region would run OSPF 1, and OSPF 4 would be designated for the interregional links and loopback connections for IBGP peering. Similarly, R3 and R4 would run OSPF process 2 and OSPF 4. This way, R1, R2, R3, and R4 will form OSPF adjacencies only for OSPF process 4 and will exchange loopback addresses for IBGP peering. OSPF 4 would contain a very small database, which will affect the router minimally.

Building an IBGP Core

In Figure 16-14, USA.Cal.R1 needs full IBGP mesh, so it must maintain peering statements for all the IBGP-speaking routers. However, full IBGP mesh causes difficulty with optimal routing.

To accommodate optimal routing and add predictability, Alpha.com is not peering USA.Cal.R1 with Euro.Fra.R2, which accommodates the physical topology. To accommodate optimal routing with IBGP, Alpha.com must break the IBGP model and perform many tricks that complicate the network.

Another possible problem occurs with a race condition, in which the same route is sent from both the IBGP neighbors. In this case, network 172.16.0.0/20 would be sent from USA.Cal.R1 and USA.Tex.R2 to Euro.Lon.R1 and Euro.Fra.R2. For optimization, you must redistribute IBGP route into IGP in Europe, even though this would cause the race condition.

USA.Cal.R1 is advertising a route to 172.16.0.0/20 to Euro.Lon.R1. Similarly, USA.Tex.R5 is sending the same route to Euro.Fra.R2. Both European routers will install this route into their routing table via IBGP. Both U.S. routers send this less-specific route to European routers because of the *failover situation*. In case one of the IBGP routers in the United States goes down, routers in Europe can still reach each other's destinations in the United States via the less-specific routes.

For example, if USA.Cal.R1 goes down, Europe.Lon.R1 will not receive routes to 172,16.0.0/21. To reach these destinations, Europe can now use 172.16.0.0/20, which is learned from USA.Tex.R5 by Europe.Fra.R2.

Returning to the discussion of the race condition, both European routers are receiving routes from the United States via IBGP. As mentioned earlier, both Euro.Lon.R1 and Euro.Fra.R2 would redistribute this route into IGP for the region. The first router that redistributes this route in IGP will propagate the route to the other routers. Upon receiving the IGP route, the second IBGP router will remove the IBGP route from the routing table.

This occurs because OSPF has a better administrative distance than IBGP. This is not a predictable behavior, however, because the administrator would not know the origin of the redistributed route. This problem is overcome by reducing the administrative distance of IBGP, making it lower than the OSPF route, even though this will affect all IBGP routes.

The problem with this method is inconsistency. Suppose that you changed the administrative distance of the IBGP-learned route on Euro.Lon.R1. When Euro.Lon.R1 receives a route from USA.Cal.R1 now, it will receive the following routes:

```
172.16.0.0/21
172.16.0.0/20
```

The race condition would not exist for 172.16.0.0/21 because Euro.Lon.R1 is the only router redistributing this route into its regional IGP. Similarly, there would not be a race condition for 172.16.8.0/21 because Euro.Fra.R2 is the only redistributing router for this destination.

There are two commands in this configuration:

- The **bgp redistribute-internal** command is used to redistribute IBGP routes into IGP. By default, BGP will not redistribute IBGP-learned routes into IGP. Note that this command should be used only if you have a very clear understanding of BGP and IGP interactions. A routing loop could easily be formed by using this command.

- The **distance bgp 20 100 200** command is used to change the administrative distance of the BGP-learned routes. The first number (20, by default) changes the external administrative distance; the second number (200, by default) changes the IBGP administrative distance; and the third number is for local BGP routes.

Local routes are those BGP entries that are created by the BGP originating router in its own routing table. For example, when the **aggregate-address** command is configured, BGP router creates a null route to the aggregate mask:

```
router bgp 1
aggregate-address 172.16.0.0 255.255.0.0
```

This routing entry is automatically entered by BGP in the routing table:

```
B       172.16.0.0 255.255.0.0 [200/0] via 0.0.0.0, 00:46:53, Null0
Routing entry for 172.16.0.0 255.255.0.0
 Known via "bgp 1", distance 200, metric 0, type locally generated
 Routing Descriptor Blocks:
 * directly connected, via Null0
     Route metric is 0, traffic share count is 1
```

This is a local distance and is also set to 200, by default. In this configuration, the default distance is maintained for local routes, but the administrative distance for internal routing is changed to 100. This decreases the distance of IBGP to avoid the race condition:

```
router bgp 1
neighbor  172.16.64.1 remote-as 1
neighbor  172.16.64. 4 remote-as 1
neighbor  172.16.64. 5 remote-as 1
neighbor  172.16.64. 6 remote-as 1
bgp redistribute-internal            (Dangerous unless you know BGP well)
distance bgp 20 100 200
network 172.16.96.0 mask 255.255.240.0
network 172.16.96.0 mask 255.255.224.0
Configuration for OSPF forEuro.Lon.R1
router ospf 2               (This is for routing process for OSPF within Europe)
network 172.16. 96.0 0.0.15.255 area 0
network 172.16.112.0 0.0.15.255 area 1
redistribute bgp 1 subnets
router ospf 4
network 172.16.64.0 0.0.7.255 area 0
```

By changing the administrative distance, the race condition for 172.16.0.0/20 is avoided, and both routers in the European region will install their IBGP-learned routes into the routing table. The **redistribute** command under the OSPF process redistributes the IBPG route into OSPF as external type 2, which is the default behavior in Cisco routers.

By default, all routes in Cisco are redistributed with external type 2. The OSPF route to 172.16.0.0 would be redistributed with external type 2, and both routers would send the same metric.

If two routers send routes with the same external type 2 metric, the tie-breaker is the shortest path to the ASBR. Thus, routers closer to Euro.Lon.R1 would exit through it for network

172.16.0.0, and routers closer to Euro.Fra.R2 would use it for network 172.16.0.0. Routers at an equal distance would perform load balancing.

In conclusion, IBGP should be used in the core only when there are no policy requirements, optimal routing is not desired, and all the interregional traffic is sent via default routers to the core. Implementing IBGP with optimal routing is complicated because it requires the configuration of knobs. This can be problematic if you are not familiar with BGP.

Building an EBGP Core

Now, assume that Alpha.com changes the model to the one shown in Figure 16-16. Instead of an IBGP core, Alpha.com is building an EBGP core. With this new model, the company does not have to fully mesh all the regions because it wants to implement EBGP. Alpha.com also does not have to worry about race conditions, it can maintain policies, and it can perform optimal routing without fear of having to adjust administrative distances. Alpha.com can fully mesh all the routers in the core running IBGP because all the core routers pass the routing information between them with correct policies.

Figure 16-16 *EBGP Core for Alpha.com*

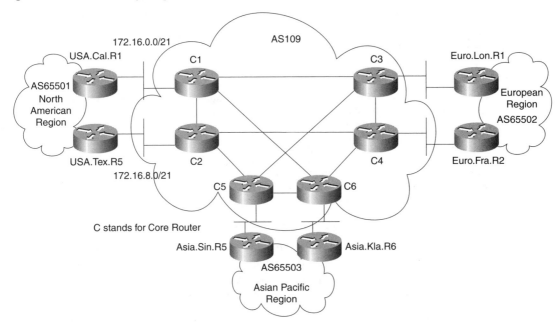

With this model, C1 needs only EBGP peering with USA.Cal.R1, and C2 needs peering with USA.Tex.R5. Policies would be sent by USA.Cal.R1 and USA.Tex.R5 to their neighbors, which will be handled at the BGP core. Of all the solutions, this is the simplest.

Router USA.Cal.R1 sends both route 172.16.0.0/21 and route 172.16.8.0/21 to C1. USA.Cal.R1 sends a Multi-Exit-Discriminator (MED) value of 0 to C1 for 172.16.0.0./21. This MED value is the default for Cisco routers with a **network** statement. USA.Cal.R1 sends a MED of 4 for network 172.16.8.0/21. When USA.Tex.R5 sends the same two routes to C2, it sends the reverse MED logic. USA.Tex.R5 sends 172.16.8.0/21 with a MED of 0, and sends 172.16.0.0/21 with a MED of 4.

The configuration for USA.Cal.R1 is as follows:

```
router bgp 65501
neighbor 172.16.252.10 remote-as 109
network 172.16.0.0 mask 255.255.248.0
network 172.16.8.0 mask 255.255.248.0 route-map MED
route-map MED
set metric 4
```

A similar configuration is performed on USA.Tex.R5, but the route map is with 172.16.0.0/21 on this router.

C1 and C2 are running IBGP between them. When these two routers exchange IBGP information, they compare each other's BGP information. C1 has received a lower MED for 172.16.0.0/21, so its route is selected when the routes in C1 and C2 are compared. C2 installs the IBGP-learned route in its table via C1, rather than the EBGP-learned route from USA.Tex.R5, because of the lower MED value.

The same result is achieved with 172.16.8.0/21, but in the reverse direction. C1 prefers the IBGP-learned route over the EBGP-learned route because of the lower MED value.

C3 and C4 have routes to 172.16.0.0/21 and 172.16.8.0/21, and they advertise these routes to their EBGP neighbors. Because optimal routing is needed, both C3 and C4 send MEDs to Euro.Lon.R1 and Euro.Fra.R2, respectively. The MED sent for 172.16.0.0/21 is lower from C3, whereas the MED sent for 172.16.8.0/21 is lower from C4.

When the routes are received by Euro.Lon.R1 and Euro.Fra.R2, the routers compare the MED and install the routes based on the lower MED value. When Euro.Lon.R1 compares the MED, it will install the EBGP-learned route for 172.16.0.0/21 because of the lower MED value. Euro.Fra.R2 will install the IBGP-learned route for 172.16.8.0/21 because of the higher MED value. When these routes are redistributed into OSPF, only the EBGP-learned route is redistributed into IGP. Therefore, by default, 172.16.0.0/21 is redistributed by Euro.Lon.R1 and 172.16.8.0/21 is redistributed by Euro.Fra.R4.

Assume, for example, that Euro.Fra.R2 lost its connection to C4. Now, 172.16.8.0/21 is not learned via this router, and the only choice Euro.Lon.R1 has for 172.16.8.0/21 is via its EBGP neighbor, so it will install this route in the table. The Euro.Lon.R1 route 172.16.8.0/21 is now an EBGP-learned route, so it will redistribute this route into OSPF and every router within Europe will take Euro.Lon.R1 to reach 172.16.8.0/21.

When the connection between Euro.Fra.R2 and C4 is restored, the MEDs are compared between the two European routers. At that point, Euro.Lon.R1 installs the IBGP-learned route for 172.16.8.0/21, and stops advertising this route into OSPF because this is an IBGP-learned route. Unless it enables the knob, as discussed previously, the IBGP route is not redistributed into IGP. The 172.16.8.0/21 route is now advertised via Euro.Fra.R2 into Europe because this route is contained in its routing table via EBGP and, by default, only EBGP-learned routes are redistributed into IGP.

The configuration for Euro.Lon.R1 is as follows:

```
router bgp 65502
neighbor 172.16.64.13 remote-as 109
network 172.16.96.0 mask 255.255.240.0
network 172.16.112.0 mask 255.255.240.0 route-map MED
router ospf 2
network 172.16. 96.0 0.0.15.255 area 0
network 172.16.112.0 0.0.15.255 area 1
redistribute bgp 65502 subnets
router ospf 4
network 172.16.64.0 0.0.7.255 area 0
```

Notice the difference between the IBGP core and the EBGP core. There is more risk for error in the IBGP core, and it is more complicated if there are policy requirements. With the EBGP core, simply touch the MEDs and allow the interaction between the routing protocols to manage the rest.

Another advantage of using an EBGP core is the load balancing of routes. You can perform a load balance between two EBGP-learned routes with identical attributes. (For example, see Figure 16-17.) Router USA.Cal.R1 has a connection with two routers in AS109 to the destination 140.10.0.0. If every attribute received from the neighbor were identical, USA.Cal.R1 would perform load balancing to this destination. This could not be achieved if the core was IBGP.

Figure 16-17   *Load Balancing with the EBGP Core*

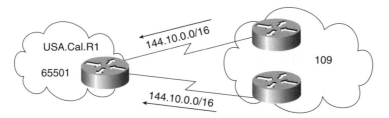

The configuration for USA.Cal.R1 follows. The routing entry in USA.Cal.R1 would be the following:

```
router bgp 6501
max-path 2

Ship route in USA.Cal.R1
B       144.10.0.0/16 [20/0] via 141.153.12.1, 00:03:29
                      [20/0] via 141.153.17.2, 00:03:29
```

Another advantage of a separate core is that it enables you to use only the BGP core as the registered AS number, which makes the regional ASs the private AS numbers. When an ISP connection is brought in, it can simply be connected to the core. When route is advertised to the ISP, regional ASs should be removed from the path list. The command used to remove the private AS number is a per-neighbor command:

```
router bgp 109
neighbor 140.10.1.1 remote-as 2
neighbor 140.10.1.1 remove-private-AS
```

This command removes all private AS numbers when advertised to the 140.10.1.1 neighbor.

Making One Region the Registered AS while Running EBGP

Alpha.com could follow a third option, as shown in Figure 16-18. In this case, you do not need an extra router, but you must ensure that at least one of the AS regional routers is a registered AS number for Internet connection.

Figure 16-18 *EBGP Core with One Region Defined as the Registered AS*

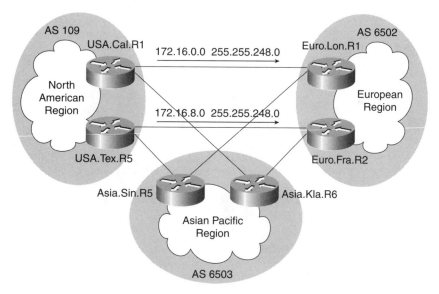

The disadvantage of this setup is that only the site with the registered AS number can peer with the external world, so the other regions cannot have Internet connections within their own regions. This model is satisfactory for financial institutions that do not use outside connections or require Internet connections.

In this model, all the regional routers are connected to each other via EBGP. They can pass MEDs to each other and can redistribute routes into IGP, as in the previous EBGP model. The final structure of the Alpha.com network is shown in Figure 16-19.

Figure 16-19 *Complete Network Setup for Alpha.com*

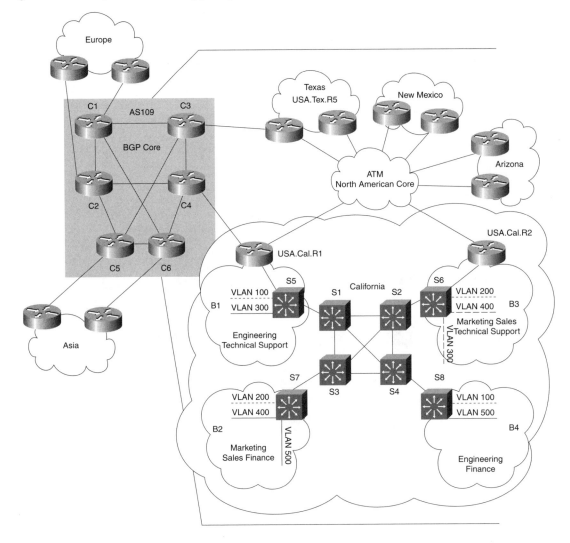

The configuration for router USA.Cal.R1 follows:

```
interface loopback 0
ip address 172.16.10.1 255.255.255.255
interface fastethernet 2/1.1
ip address 172.16.1.1 255.255.255.0
encap isl 100
interface fastethernet 2/1.2
ip address 172.16.2.1 255.255.255.0
encap isl 200
interface fastethernet 2/1.3
ip address 172.16.3.1 255.255.255.0
encap isl 300
interface fastethernet 2/1.4
ip address 172.16.4.1 255.255.255.0
encap isl 400
interface fastethernet 2/1.5
ip address 172.16.5.1 255.255.255.0
encap isl 500
interface atm 1/0
no ip address
interface atm 1/0.1 point-to-point
ip address 172.16.64.1 255.255.255.252        {ATM connection to USA.Cal.R2}
interface atm 1/0.2 point-to-point
ip address 172.16.64.5 255.255.255.252        {ATM connection to USA.Tex.R5}
interface atm 1/0.3 point-to-point
ip address 172.16.64.9 255.255.255.252        {ATM connection to USA.Arz.R4}
interface atm 1/0.2 point-to-point
ip address 172.16.64.13 255.255.255.252        {ATM connection to USA.Nxm.R8}
interface Serial 2/0
ip address 172.16.64.21 255.255.255.252        {Point-to-point to C1 in BGP core}
router ospf 1
network 172.16.64.0 0.0.0.15 area 0
network 172.16.0.0 0.0.15.255 area 1
area 1 range 172.16.0.0 255.255.240.0
redistribute bgp 65501 subnets
router ospf 4
network 172.16.16.0 0.0.0.15.255 area 0
router bgp 65501
neighbor 172.16.252.10 remote-as 109
network 172.16.0.0 mask 255.255.248.0
network 172.16.8.0 mask 255.255.248.0 route-map MED
route-map MED
set metric 4
no auto-summary
```

Internet Connections

Alpha.com currently has three Internet connections: Two connections are to the same ISP, and the third connection is to a different ISP, as shown in Figure 16-20.

Figure 16-20 *ISP Connections for Alpha.com*

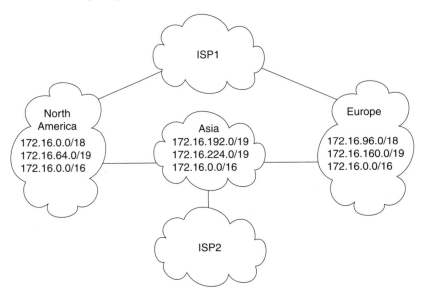

Each region has its own ISP connection; obviously, each region would prefer to use its own connection to the Internet. Proper addressing and network regionalization will improve asymmetric routing, although it will not be avoided completely.

Alpha.com talks to ISP1 and sends it a more specific route from both North America and Europe. (The routes sent from North America and Europe are shown in Figure 16-20.) Alpha.com also can send a less-specific route in case of failure. This way, Alpha.com does not need to send an MED to ISP1.

This is a sensitive issue, however, because most of the ISPs would not accept subnet routes from their customers. If ISP1 accepts the routes, it must keep the subnet routes in its table and share this information with ISP2 so that ISP2 also performs optimal routing. Both the ISPs will advertise only 172.16.0.0/16 to the rest of the Internet. The configuration for C1 peering in the United States with ISP1 would be the following:

```
router bgp 109
neighbor 140.10.1.1 remote-as 2
neighbor 140.10.1.1 remove-private-AS
neighbor 140.10.1.1 route-map set-community in
neighbor 140.10.1.1 send-community
neighbor 172.16.252.11 remote-as 109
neighbor 172.16.252.12 remote-as 109
neighbor 172.16.252.13 remote-as 109
neighbor 172.16.252.14 remote-as 109
neighbor 172.16.252.15 remote-as 109
network 172.16.0.0 mask 255.255.192.0
network 172.16.64.0 mask 255.255.224.0
network 172.16.0.0
route-map set-community permit 10
match ip address 1
set community 109:70
route-map set-community permit 20
match ip address 2
access-list 1 permit 198.10.1.0  0.0.0.255
access-list 1 permit 198.10.2.0  0.0.0.255
access-list 1 permit 198.10.3.0  0.0.0.255
access-list 2 permit any
```

This router will advertise three routes to its EBGP neighbor. The first two networks with mask statements advertise a more specific route to its EBGP peers that cover the North America range. The less-specific route with the network statement covers all other networks for Europe and Asia. This network provides redundancy.

For example, Europe is advertising subnets 172.16.96.0/18 and 172.16.160.0/19 to ISP1. When the European connection is running, the ISP takes the European link for European networks because of the longer prefix advertised from Europe. When the link between Europe and ISP1 fails, ISP1 takes 172.16.0.0/16 for all the European destinations because ISP1 gets the 172.16.0.0/16 route from North America so that the rest of the world can still reach Europe via ISP 1.

Acquiring Beta.com

Assume now that Alpha.com has acquired another company, Beta.com. Beta.com is also a large organization with its own Internet connection and a registered IP address, as shown in Figure 16-21. However, the address space of Beta.com comes from the address space of ISP3. Beta.com has a connection to ISP3 and does not want to change its primary ISP.

Beta.com does not want Alpha.com to advertise its networks to ISP1 and ISP2, as long as Beta.com has a working connection to ISP3. In the event of failure, Beta.com wants Alpha.com to advertise its routes to ISPs.

Figure 16-21 *Alpha.com and Beta.com Are a Newly Merged Organization with ISP Connections*

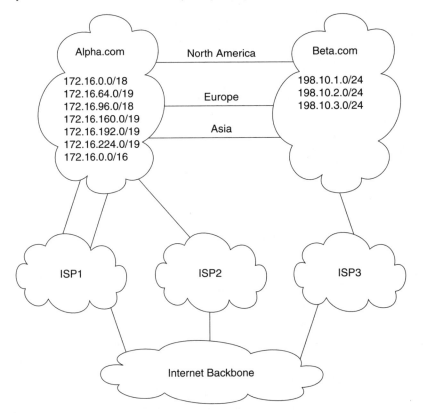

Alpha.com will run successfully because the company is leaking subnet routes to Beta.com for optimal routing with a community, and is asking it not to export subnet routes. Alpha.com would send 172.16.0.0/16 to Beta.com to leak this route to its ISP and would ask its ISP to set up a higher local preference for the route learned via Beta.com. This way, everyone will use Beta.com to reach Alpha.com only in case of failure. If the ISP does not honor the community, Beta.com can use a Cisco command to prepend AS paths on routes for Alpha.com.

The problem lies with Beta.com because it leaks specific routes of 198.10.1.0/24, 198.10.2.0/24, and 198.10.3.0/24, which originate from the CIDR block of ISP3 to Alpha.com. Beta.com does not want Alpha.com to advertise its route to its ISPs because of longer prefix matching. Even when Beta.com's connection is working with ISP3, it is sending /24 routes to Alpha.com; if Alpha.com starts to leak these, it will send a longer prefix than ISP3.

Usually, ISPs do not send /24 of their CIDR block to their neighbors, which is the reason the route advertised from Alpha.com would be a longer prefix than the one advertised by ISP3. When Beta.com sets up ISP3 as its primary provider, all traffic from Beta.com would be sent to the Internet via ISP3, but would return via ISP1. This would cause an asymmetric route. Whatever the AS length is, all traffic would return via Alpha.com, as shown in Figures 16-22 and 16-23.

This setup, which is complicated, is shown in Figure 16-22. The routes advertised by Beta.com to Alpha.com are individual class C routes owned by Beta.com. Beta.com also advertises the same three class C networks to ISP3, which owns this CIDR block. ISP3 summarizes this block to the Internet backbone. As shown in Figure 16-22, routes from ISP1 and ISP2 are more specific for Beta.com class networks than the one advertised by ISP3.

Figure 16-22 *Longer Prefix Advertised by Alpha.com and Less-Specific Route Advertised by ISP3*

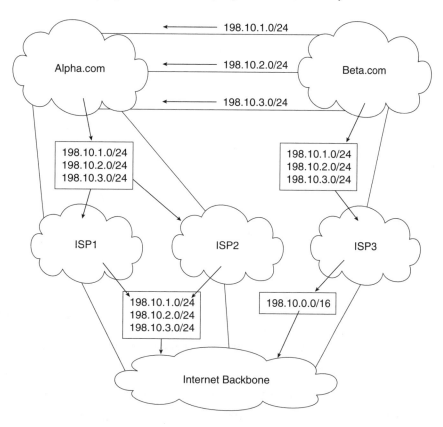

This causes asymmetric routing because all routers in Beta.com are configured to exit their company via ISP3, but return via Alpha.com. This occurs because the longer prefixes of the three class C routes are advertised via Alpha.com. Whatever the length of the AS in the BGP path, the routes are not identical: 198.10.0.0/16 is not the same as 198.10.1.0/24, 198.10.2.0/24, or 198.10.3.0/24. The /24 are longer prefixes and will always take precedence, which makes the routing for Beta.com as shown in Figure 16-23.

Figure 16-23 *Asymmetric Routing for Beta.com*

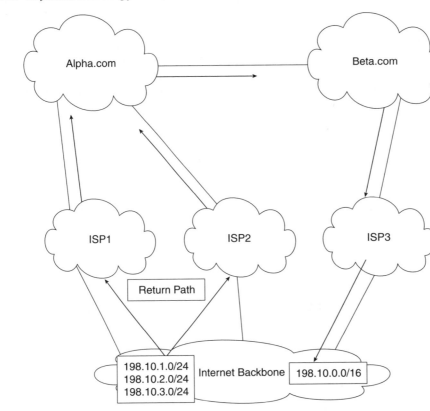

To solve this problem, the newly merged organizations have two choices. First, they could ask the three ISPs to exchange specific routes, and then pass communities for the control of information. Second, Beta.com must upgrade the software on the router that peers with Alpha.com and must use a new feature called **non-exit-map** in version 11 CC release.

The Three ISPs Exchange Specific Routes

The routes of 198.10.1.0/24, 198.10.2.0/24, and 198.10.3.0/24 are advertised to ISP1 and ISP2. ISP3 is sending only the 198.10.0.0/16 route to the Internet, so it would have to leak the three specific routes to ISP1 and ISP2. ISP3 would have to send the specific routes with the community of no-export and community number.

Next, both ISP1 and ISP2 would decrease the local preference of the routes learned from Alpha.com. This way, routes leaked from ISP3 would not be advertised by ISP1 and ISP2 to the outside world because of **community no-export**. Routes learned via Alpha.com would not be advertised by BGP because it has a lower local preference, and BGP advertises only its best routes to all the neighbors.

The configuration of a router in ISP3 is the following:

```
router bgp 6
aggregate-address 198.10.0.0 255.255.0.0 summary-only
neighbor 150.10.10.1 remote-as 2              {connection to ISP1}
neighbor 150.10.10.1 unsupress-map Leak
neighbor 150.10.20.2 remote-as 3              {connection to ISP2}
neighbor 150.10.20.2 unsupress-map Leak
route-map Leak permit 10
match ip address 1
set community 109:100 no-export
route-map Leak permit 20
match ip address 2
access-list 1 permit 198.10.1.0  0.0.0.255
access-list 1 permit 198.10.2.0  0.0.0.255
access-list 1 permit 198.10.3.0  0.0.0.255
access-list 2 permit any
```

With this configuration, ISP3 is sending a summarized route to all its neighbors, except for ISP1 and ISP2. This route aggregates all /24 routes from 198.10.1.0 to 198.10.255.0. Next, ISP3 uses a per neighbor command called **unsupress-map**. This command is used to send specific routes to listed neighbors, which, in this case, are ISP1 and ISP2. This way, only ISP1 and ISP2 receive less-specific /24 routes from ISP3 and the other neighbors of ISP3 receive the aggregated route for network 198.10.0.0/16.

This command uses **route-map leak**, so whatever conditions are set on the route-map are set and advertised to the neighbor. In this case, the router of ISP3 sends the three specific routes to both ISP1 and ISP2 with a community of no-export, asking both the ISPs not to leak these specific routes.

Both ISP1 and ISP2 would receive the three routes from Alpha.com. Then, they would ask Alpha.com to send them a community number to decrease their local preference for the route they received from Alpha.com.

The configuration of the ISP1 router is the following:

```
router bgp 2
neighbor 140.10.1.1 remote-as 109         {Peering with Alpha.com}
neighbor 140.10.1.1 route-map set-local-preference in
neighbor 150.10.10.2 remote-as 6          {Peering with ISP3}
route-map set-local-preference permit 10
match community 1
set local-preference 70
ip community-list 1 permit 109:70
```

This configuration sets a local preference of 70 for all the routes with a community number of 70. All other routes would use a default local preference of 100. Higher local preference is more desirable, so when a route is received from both 109 and ISP3, ISP1 would prefer the ISP3-learned route over the route learned from Alpha.com because of the local preference. The route that is learned from ISP3 belongs to the community of **no-export**, so this route would not be advertised to any EBGP neighbor.

When the link between ISP3 and Beta.com goes down, specific routes no longer would be leaked by ISP3 to both ISP1 and ISP2. Both ISP1 and ISP2 now would install the specific routes learned from Alpha.com, and the route learned from Alpha.com would be the only route in the table for Beta.com.

Alpha.com does not advertise this route with the no-export community. This route would be sent to all the EBGP neighbors of both ISP1 and ISP2.

This way, Beta.com retains ISP3 as the primary ISP. In the event of failure, Beta.com could still be connected to the rest of the world via ISP1 and ISP2 by using Alpha.com's Internet connections. There is one disadvantage with this model, however. The newly merged organization must communicate with all the ISPs, and they must agree with this setup. If one of the ISPs does not honor the commitment, this model will be unsuccessful.

Using the non-exit-map Command

The second method is for Beta.com to use a Cisco feature introduced in the 11.1 CC release. This **non-exit-map** command is used with advertise-map. The configuration of one of the peering routers of Beta.com that connects with Alpha.com would be the following:

```
router bgp 8
network 198.10.1.0
network 198.10.2.0
network 198.10.3.0
neighbor 131.108.1.2 remote-as 109
neighbor 131.108.1.2 route-map test1 out
neighbor 131.108.1.2 advertise-map test3 non-exist-map test2
access-list 1 permit 198.10.1.0 0.0.0.255
access-list 1 permit 198.10.2.0 0.0.0.255
access-list 1 permit 198.10.3.0 0.0.0.255
access-list 2 permit 198.10.0.0
access-list 3 permit any
!
route-map test2 permit 10
 match ip address 2
route-map test3 permit 10
 match ip address 1
!
route-map test1 permit 10
 match ip address 1
set community no-export
route-map test permit 20
match ip address 3
```

First, the route-map test1 advertises the networks 198.10.1.0, 198.10.2.0, and 198.10.3.0 to Alpha.com and sets the community of no-export, which tells Alpha.com that these routes should not be advertised to any EBGP neighbor. The next command has two route maps: one for advertise-map, which is test3, and one for non-exit-map, which is test2.

The non-exit map indicates that the advertise-map should not be activated if Beta.com learns the 198.10.0.0/16 route from its peering session with ISP3. When the 198.10.0.0/16 route is no longer learned by Beta.com, this indicates that the connection to ISP3 is no longer working. At that point, the advertise-map is activated and initiates the process of sending the specific routes of 198.10.1.0, 198.10.2.0, 198.10.3.0 to Alpha.com after passing route-map test2.

Route-map does not set a community, so the routes now leaked to Alpha.com by Beta.com for the network are no longer with the community of no-export; Alpha.com can now send the Beta.com routes to its ISPs.

In conclusion, regionalizing the network with a sound addressing scheme would assist the network in scaling to a much greater extent. Introduction of BGP isolates problems only within regions and provides an extra layer of protection against duplicate addressing.

Case Study 2: The MKS Retail Store

Our fictional store, MKS, is a large retail corporation based in San Jose, California. MKS operates stores in all major cities in the United States, and operates catalog stores in smaller cities. The company wants to build a fault-tolerant network with redundancy in some sites.

MKS plans approximately 12,000 remote nodes on this network. Some of the sites will be situated in very low-speed circuits across Frame Relay. A few of the crucial sites will have dual PVC to the hub sites, in addition to a dial backup. This network is currently in production and is running OSPF as the core routing protocol, with nearly 300 operational sites. All 12,000 sites have not been implemented yet, but MKS is concerned about scaling issues. The sample network is shown in Figure 16-24.

Nearly 800 remote sites are planned per region, with possibly 15 regions. Each region will be a stub area, and a small backbone of the main ATM core will be created. The summarized route from each area should send a very small number of routes into the main ATM core, which will be defined as area 0. All routers in the main ATM core should be fully meshed. The OSPF plan proposed by MKS is similar to the one shown in Figure 16-25.

Figure 16-24 *Network Diagram for MKS*

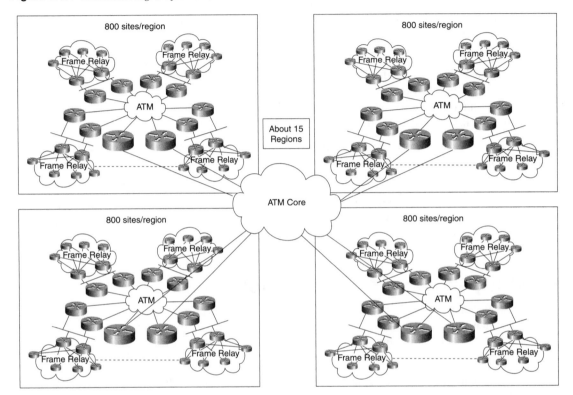

Regional Design Plan

First, we shall consider each region, and then examine the entire design. It is important to note that if MKS decides to employ the proposed architecture, this network would have scaling difficulties. Each region has nearly 800 remote sites, which are homed to two routers. This will not scale because today's classless protocols all maintain neighbor relationships; in this case, all remote sites must be part of the core routing protocol.

A link failure on a remote node will cause problems throughout the network. First, examine the choices that MKS has for connecting its remote nodes to the hub sites. Normally, there are low-end boxes on the spoke side: 2500-, 1600-, and 1000-series routers are good examples. If the information begins to pass through spoke routers to reach some other network, that stub router becomes a transit router. Usually, this occurs when a spoke is connected to another router instead of the hub router. In MKS, the hub router is connected to attached spoke routers, but, in a few critical sites, the remote routers are dual-attached to the hub router.

Figure 16-25 *Proposed Network for MKS*

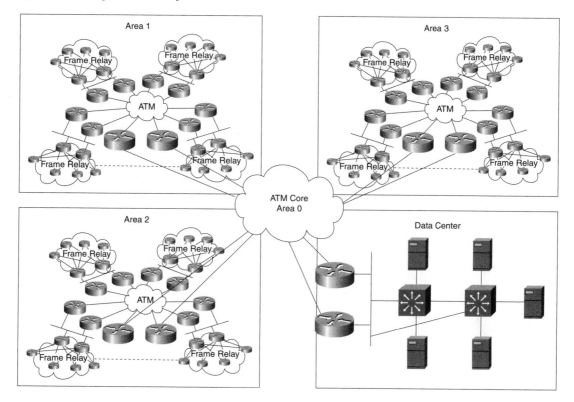

Hub-and-Spoke Setup

Essentially, there are two types of remote sites: single-attached sites and dual-attached sites. MKS must decide how it will connect the hub and spoke sites, as shown in Figure 16-26.

MKS has four choices for the hub-and-spoke setup:

- OSPF
- Enhanced IGRP
- RIP
- ODR

Each of these choices is discussed in the following sections.

Figure 16-26 *Hub-and-Spoke Setup for MKS*

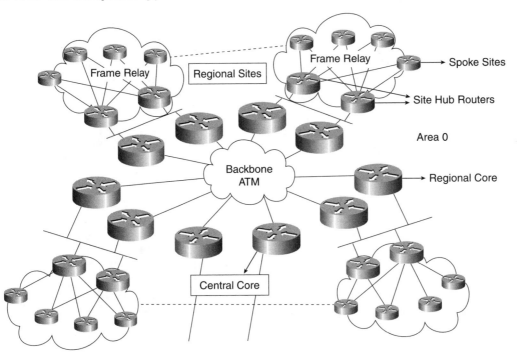

OSPF

First and foremost, designate one region as an OSPF area. This does not scale with a large number of routers, so each region should be an OSPF domain by itself, rather than an area. Then decide on a hub-and-spoke setup. As seen in Figure 16-26, the network within the region has strong hierarchy, so it is necessary only to define the OSPF areas.

For the hub-and-spoke setup, you must consider how you would handle 800 spoke sites. Remote sites in each region are connected to eight routers: Two routers act as hubs per site. Remote sites home either to one hub or the other—or, in some cases, they home to both the hub routers for redundancy.

For the purpose of OSPF, we will consider a pair of hub routers. If you put all the remote sites in one area, routers that would typically be 2500, 1600, or 1000 would have to maintain a large database.

In this case, there are two hub routers with connections to 150 to 200 remote sites. A high-end router could have 200 neighbors and can maintain a large link-state database in OSPF without difficulty. The main issue, however, involves the low-end routers. If all the routers in a regional site are placed in one area, the low-end router would have scaling problems because it has to maintain large databases. The network would look like the one in Figure 16-27(A).

Problematically, even a small link flap in one of the remote sites will cause an SPF run, and will cause flooding in the network. Furthermore, all low-end boxes must maintain a large database, which burdens the low-end boxes. With this size network, each low-end box would require more memory to hold a large database.

The second approach for MKS could be the one shown in Figure 16-27(B). In this mode, MKS has divided the areas into smaller areas so that the low-end routers do not have to be part of a large database and do not have to run full SPF in case of a link failure on a remote node.

Figure 16-27   *Single Area OSPF Setup; Multiple Area OSPF Setup for Hub and Spoke*

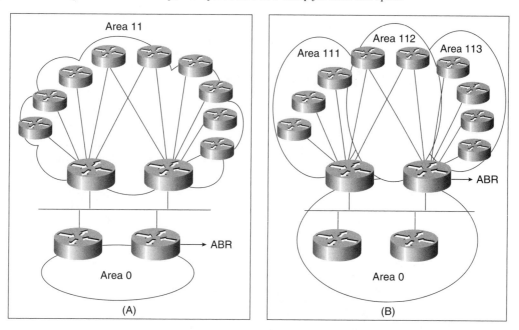

If this model is to be implemented, the ABR must be moved from the core router to the regional hub routers. This extends area 0.

Importantly, now the ABR is connected to several areas, so it would be involved in many SPF calculations and would have to create summary link states for each connected area. To preserve flooding of summary LSAs, each area should be configured as a totally stubby area (discussed in Chapter 9). This saves the ABR from creating and processing summary link states, thus saving both CPU and memory on the ABR.

One issue arises with dual-attached sites, however. The link between the two hub sites is now via the remote router because of the intraarea connection. For example, refer to area 112 (as shown in Figure 16-28), which depicts the result of a failure of the link between R1 and ABR1.

Figure 16-28 *OSPF Setup with a Single Area Connection during Link Failure*

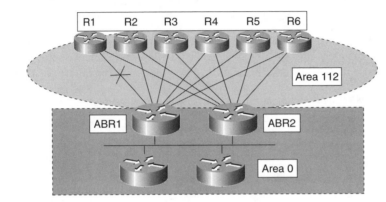

When the packet comes in for R1 to ABR1, it will not use the Ethernet between ABR1 and ABR2. Instead, it will forward the packet to R2. R2 returns the packet to ABR2, and then ABR2 forwards the packet to R1. The packet flow is shown in Figure 16-29. The Ethernet is not used between the ABRs because the intraarea route is always preferred over the interarea route. The Ethernet between ABR1 and ABR2 is in area 0; and all the PVCs along the path of R1, ABR1, ABR2, and R2 are in area 112.

Figure 16-29 *Routing During Link Failure with an OSPF Single Area*

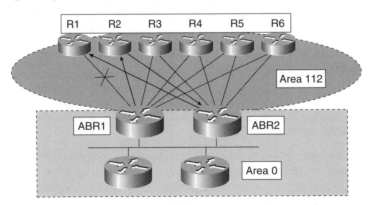

If this setup is acceptable during failure, nothing must be done. If it is not acceptable, as in most cases, MKS must put an additional PVC between ABR1 and ABR2 in area 112. Now, the packet sent for R1 from ABR1 will not be forwarded to R2. Instead, it will be sent to ABR2 on the direct PVC, as shown in Figure 16-30.

Figure 16-30 *Additional Link between the ABRs to Avoid a Longer Path*

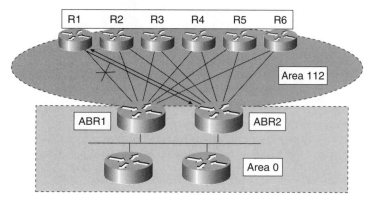

Enhanced IGRP

The second routing protocol available to MKS is Enhanced IGRP. Using Enhanced IGRP is advantageous because hierarchical limitation is not required; the router can leak across to neighbors.

With Enhanced IGRP, MKS would define all the remote sites as Enhanced IGRP neighbors, and then would summarize their information into the core. The protocol does not require hierarchy, so summarization could be performed at any router and at any interface. All the single attached remote routers should not be sending Enhanced IGRP routing information. The only route that should be passed to remote routers is a default route of 0.0.0.0.

If optimal routing is desired for dual-attached sites, they could be assigned an Enhanced IGRP route, but it is better to provide a default route. If it is required for this dual-attached router to use a specific router to reach a certain destination, then a specific route could be leaked with the default route (see Figure 16-31).

MKS prefers R1 for 10.108.1.0/24 and wants to perform load balancing for other networks. In this case, you should allow R1 to leak the specific subnet. This router would be preferred in every instance; in case of R1's link failure, R2 would be the only choice to reach all destinations using the default route.

Figure 16-31 *Specific Route Leaked to a Remote Site for Optimal Routing*

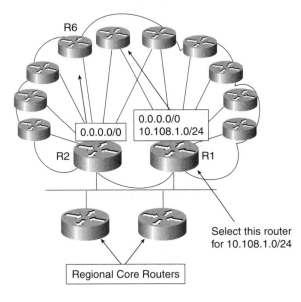

Both R1 and R2 can summarize when sending routes into the regional core routers. Addresses of remote routers would be out of the 10.0.0.0/8 private network address space. This region has 800 subnets, and the address space allocated is between 10.1.0.0 to 10.4.0.0 for future growth. Each remote site would be advertised as a single local subnet.

Depending on the size of the retail store, each remote site would be given either 254 or 127 host addresses. MKS plans to subnet in the third octet with an 8-bit mask.

Within the region, MKS has four pairs of routers. Each pair connects to 200 sites, of which 30 are dual-attached to both hub routers. The rest are single-homed. These 30 sites should be within a contiguous address range.

All remote sites that attach to a single router should derive from only a single address block, such as R1 in Figure 16-32. Remote sites that connect to R2 in this example also should derive from a single address block.

Address space allocated in the first region is shown in Figure 16-32. In this region, the address allocation ranges from 10.1.1.0 to 10.1.255.0. Remote sites that are singly attached to R1 are allocated subnets from 10.1.1.0 to 10.1.95.0. Dual-attached sites that connect to both R1 and R2 are allocated subnets from 10.1.96.0 to 10.1.127.0. All the remote sites that are singly attached to R2 have an address block of 10.1.128.0 to 10.1.223.0.

In this setup, both R1 and R2 will have the specific routes for all the destinations that are singly attached to them, but they will summarize the contiguous block and advertise only two routes to the regional core routers, as shown in Figure 16-32. R1 will advertise 10.1.0.0/18 for subnets 0 through 63 and 10.1.64.0/19 for subnets 64 through 96.

Figure 16-32 *Address Allocation for Remote Sites Attached to R1 and R2*

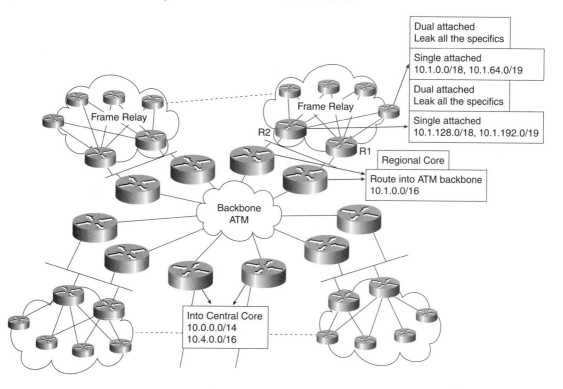

For the dual-attached sites, R1 and R2 will leak all the specifics to each other in addition to the regional core, if the only connection between R1 and R2 is via the Ethernet. Leaking all the specific routes for the dual-attached sites avoids black holes. For example, assume that R1 is not sending specific routes to regional core routers, and then loses its PVC to one of the dual-attached remote sites. If both R1 and R2 are sending a same summarized route to the regional core router, R1 will continue to attract traffic to that subnet, even though it has lost the PVC because it is advertising the summary.

R1 will continue to advertise the summary as long as it has one specific route from that summary in its routing table. In this case, when R1 sends a summary to the regional core routers, it is impossible for the regional core routers to discover that R1 no longer has the route to the specific destination for which it has lost the PVC.

This creates a hole, even though R2 still has the PVC. R2 might not be used by one of the regional core routers. If regional core routers are load balancing between R1 and R2, they could forward the packet to R1. R1 will forward the packet to bit bucket because Enhanced IGRP creates a null route whenever a summary is generated. If you send specific routes on Ethernet, then both regional core routers will receive them because **ip summary-address eigrp** is an interface command, not a per neighbor command.

A better way to solve this problem is to insert a PVC between R1 and R2, and then leak all the specifics on the PVC. Finally, summarize on the Ethernet between them. If a dual-attached site loses a connection, the specific route is still leaked between the two routers, and routing will continue to be successful. This is true, even if R1 is attracting traffic for the destination. R1 is no longer attached, as shown in Figure 16-33.

Figure 16-33 *PVC between R1 and R2 to Leak Specific Routes on the PVC*

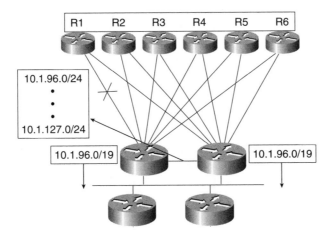

This model works well because each region is sending summary routes and the hub router within the region is sending only a default route into the spoke sites. This type of arrangement is helpful when you are setting up the query boundaries. Whenever R1 loses a route, it sends a query to all its neighbors. Because none of the neighbors are receiving specifics from R1, they send unreachable messages back to R1.

Dual-attached sites are an exception. When R1 loses its connection to one of the remote sites, R1 will not generate a query if R2 was its feasible successor. Otherwise, R1 will send a query and R2 will send the route to R1.

All the query boundaries are well-defined, and summarization is simple. The only problem that may arise occurs when either R1 or R2 loses its specific destination and must send queries to a large number of neighbors. In this case, 120 or 130 neighbors is not a large number, but consider what might happen if MKS expands and wants to attach 600 to 800 neighbors!

RIP

Especially for this example, RIP will not be used as a core routing protocol; it could be used only for a hub-and-spoke setup. Today's classless routing protocols (such as OSPF, IS-IS, and Enhanced IGRP), all maintain neighbor adjacencies. This is not feasible for large hub-and-spoke setups because a remote node causes an event for the routing protocol in the core, affecting the network topology. Therefore, it would be appropriate to separate the core routing protocol from the hub-and-spoke topology.

RIP routing in the MKS example would be configured on the hub router to send only default route messages to the remote routers, which would learn their attached subnets only, as shown in Figure 16-34.

Figure 16-34   *Hub-and-Spoke Setup with RIP and Sending a Default Route*

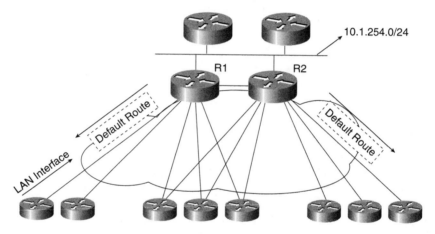

At the hub router, you should configure a static route that summarizes all the remote subnets and sends only a single route into the core routing protocol. This way, a flap in the remote node does not affect the core routing protocol. The PVC in the cloud is created only for passing specific information between the dual-attached hub routers that connect to the same remote sites. MKS must run RIP to receive routes from remote sites and to send default routes to the remote sites. MKS also needs RIP to send specific routes on the PVC used to connect R1 and R2 to manage dual-attached sites.

The configuration for R1 would be the following:

```
interface Serial 2/0
ip address 10.1.252.0 255.255.254.0
encapsulation frame-relay
router rip
version 2
passive-interface FastEthernet 0/0
passive-interface Ethernet 3/0
passive-interface Ethernet 3/1
passive-interface Ethernet 3/2
passive-interface Ethernet 3/3
network 10.0.0.0
distribute-list 1 out rip
router ospf 1
redistribute static subnets
redistribute rip subnets route-map Spoke
passive-interface serial 2/0
network 10.1.254.0 0.0.0.255 area 11
network 10.1.253.0 0.0.0.255 area 11
area 11 nssa
ip route 10.1.0.0 255.255.192.0 null0
ip route 10.1.64.0 255.255.224.0 null0
access-list 1 permit 0.0.0.0 0.0.0.0
access-list 2 permit 10.1.96.0 0.0.31.255
route-map Spoke
match ip address 2
```

Now, we will consider the configuration for the serial interface. Here, serial 2/0 is the interface that is connected to the Frame Relay cloud: It is configured as a multipoint interface for all the remote sites. The update process for RIP occurs every 30 seconds. Therefore, when the router is configured with many point-to-point interfaces, it involves extensive CPU processing to replicate the RIP updates, even though it is only for a single default route.

On the other hand, with a single multipoint interface, the replication occurs at the Frame Relay layer for each PVC, which is not very CPU-intensive.

Also worthy of consideration is the subnet mask of the serial interface. With this mask, the router can have 508 (254×2) remote nodes attached to the cloud. This is successful with RIP. If you choose a high-end CPU, these remote nodes send updates to RIP every 30 seconds, and the local router sends only one RIP update (0.0.0.0 0.0.0.0) every 30 seconds.

The router interface connected to the Ethernet is in area 11. For this example, the core routing protocol is OSPF. Notice that the area is NSSA. This is done because of the dual-attached sites. Either you run RIP on the interface that connects the two routers to leak the specific routes between the two routers; or you run OSPF NSSA, and then redistribute RIP routes of the dual-attached sites between the two hub routers.

The advantage of running NSSA is that you can leak all the specific routes for the dual-attached sites between the hub routers within the area. Therefore, when one of the hub routers loses its

PVC, it can still reroute via the Ethernet because it is getting the specific route. The setup is shown in Figure 16-35.

Figure 16-35 *OSPF NSSA Area to Leak Specific Type 7 LSA and Summarize Type 5 LSA at ABR*

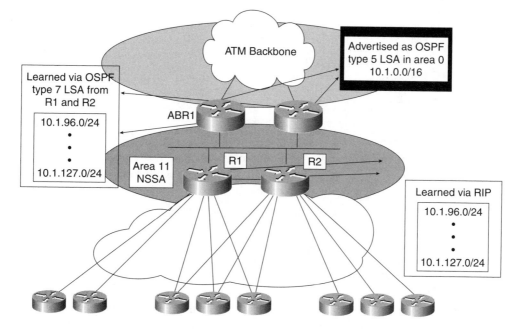

The routers are sending different type 7 routes, but first the router R1 is redistributing static in configuration. This is used to summarize the single-attached routers. Routers with single-attachment to R1 would be learned via RIP. R1 will not redistribute any of the RIP-learned routes into OSPF.

R1 will only redistribute the static null route into OSPF. This way, a single PVC flap does not cause flooding of external link states. Only those RIP routes that are coming from dual-attached sites would be redistributed into OSPF because routers that are connected to the same remote sites should share specific routes. For these specific routes to be leaked between the two hub routers via OSPF, the administrative distance for RIP should be lower than that of OSPF. Otherwise, one of the routers will install the OSPF-learned route rather than the RIP routes from the remote sites.

Another method is to insert a PVC between the two hub routers, and then allow them to leak specific routes via RIP on that PVC.

In case MKS decides to run RIP on the PVC between the two routers, the configuration is as follows:

```
interface Serial 2/0
no ip address
encapsulation frame-relay
interface Serial 2/0.1 point-to-point
ip address 10.1.252.1 255.255.255.252
interface Serial  2/0.2 multipoint
ip address 10.1.252.3 255.255.254.0
router rip
network 0.0.0.0
distribute-list 2 out serial 2/0.1
distribute-list 1 out serial 2/0.2
access-list 1 permit 0.0.0.0 0.0.0.0
access-list 2 permit 10.1.96.0 0.0.31.255
```

You can see from the configuration that both routers R1 and R2 are sending information about specific routes to RIP only on the point-to-point PVC between them. The routers are still sending default RIP routes to all the remote routers on the multipoint subinterface.

The configuration of the ABRs would be as follows:

```
router ospf 1
summary-address 10.1.0.0 255.255.0.0
network 10.1.254.0 0.0.0.255 area 11
network 10.4.255.0 0.0.0.255 area 0
area 11 nssa
```

Assume that you decided not to insert the PVC between R1 and R2 and that you will use the leak-specific routes in OSPF via type 7 LSA. ABR1 would summarize all the external LSA type 7s of the remote sites it has received from R1 and R2. For this case, R1 would send summaries 10.1.0.0/18, and 10.1.64.0/19 for dual-attached routers. R2 is sending all these external type 7s for dual-attached remote sites to 10.1.128.0/18 and 10.1.192.0/19.

With dual-attached sites, if MKS is not sharing specific routes via RIP, all the /24 from 10.1.96.0/24 to 10.1.127.0/24 would be leaked as specifics via type 7 LSA. At the ABR, type 7 could be summarized into one update for area 0. This is done by the **summary-address** command for OSPF at the ABR. This only could be performed by NSSA because you have the option to summarize external type 7, not only at the ASBR (where the LSA originated), but also at ABR (where the LSA changed from type 7 to type 5).

The process is simpler if the core routing protocol for MKS is Enhanced IGRP. R1 and R2 can send specific routes on the PVC, and then summarize them on the Ethernet. For the hub-and-spoke setup with dual-attached remote sites, Enhanced IGRP is much more flexible because it does not require a hierarchy. Also, filtering of information is not tied to any particular points such as ABR or ASBR.

Therefore, if MKS is running Enhanced IGRP as the core routing protocol, the configuration of R1 would be the following:

```
interface FastEthernet 0/0
ip address 10.1.254.0 255.255.255.0
ip summary-address eigrp 1 10.1.96.0 255.255.224.0
interface Serial 2/0
no ip address
encapsulation frame-relay
interface Serial 2/0.1 point-to-point
ip address 10.1.252.1 255.255.255.252
interface Serial  2/0.2 multipoint
ip address 10.1.252.3 255.255.254.0
router rip
version 2
passive-interface FastEthernet 0/0
passive-interface Ethernet 3/0
passive-interface Ethernet 3/1
passive-interface Ethernet 3/2
passive-interface Ethernet 3/3
network 10.0.0.0
distribute-list 1 out rip
router eigrp 1
network 10.0.0.0
passive-interface Serial 2/0
redistribute static
redistribute rip route-map Spoke
default-metric 1 1 1 1 1
ip route 10.1.0.0 255.255.192.0 null0
ip route 10.1.64.0 255.255.224.0 null0
access-list 1 permit 0.0.0.0 0.0.0.0
access-list 2 permit 10.1.96.0 0.0.31.255
route-map Spoke
match ip address 2
```

In this configuration, R1 has redistributed the single-attached sites via the static route, and then has redistributed the dual-attached sites into Enhanced IGRP via `route-map Spoke`. Ethernet R1 is sending an Enhanced IGRP summary. Note that the distance command from RIP is missing because Enhanced IGRP redistributes routes with an administrative distance of 170, which is higher than RIP's.

On Demand Routing

On Demand Routing (ODR) is an enhancement to an existing feature called Cisco Discovery Protocol (CDP). CDP is a protocol used to discover other Cisco devices on either broadcast or nonbroadcast media. With the help of CDP, a router can find the device type, IP address, Cisco IOS running on the neighbor's Cisco device, and capabilities of the neighbor device.

The idea behind this feature is to advertise the connected IP prefix of a stub router via CDP. This new feature uses an extra five bytes for each network or subnet, four bytes for the IP address, and one byte to advertise the subnet mask along with the IP. ODR is capable of carrying variable length subnet mask (VLSM) information.

ODR was designed for customers who want to save their network bandwidth for other important data instead of routing protocol updates.

ODR is especially helpful in the X.25 environment, when it can be costly to run a routing protocol over a link. Static routing is a wise choice, but this includes a high overhead for maintaining the static routes manually. ODR enters the picture where IP routes are propagated dynamically on Layer 2, and where the network is not CPU-intensive.

ODR is not a routing protocol and should not be treated as one during configuration. All traditional configurations used for different IP routing protocols will not work in ODR because ODR uses CDP, which occurs on Layer 2. The configuration is very simple.

MKS has two types of connections: single-attached spoke sites or dual-attached sites. With this feature, the router at the remote site must configure a default static route pointing toward the hub. When it realizes that it is not running any dynamic routing protocol, the spoke site sends its connected prefixes along with CDP information. A hub router will install this information in its routing table if it is configured for ODR. The only necessary command to run ODR is the **router odr** command, which is executed on the hub router.

TIP One of the key points regarding ODR is its scalability. ODR is not a routing protocol, so the risk of committing mistakes is greatly reduced. In addition, you cannot redistribute routes into ODR. It is used only to receive spoke prefixes.

Present ODR setup requires a default static route to be defined at the spoke site, which causes an issue of convergence. If the Frame Relay PVC goes down, the remote site must be informed and the static default route should be removed from the routing table if an alternate path or dial backup is also available.

If the interface on the spoke router is defined as multipoint, the static default route is not removed on the spoke router when the PVC between the hub and the spoke sites goes down. This is because the spoke router does not lose the physical interface, as shown in Figure 16-36. This causes the spoke router to be disconnected from the rest of the network, even though it has a dial backup path.

Figure 16-36   *Spoke Site Loses a PVC, but the Physical Interface Does Not Go Down*

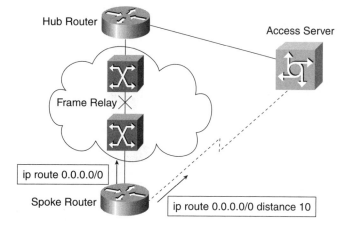

One solution to this problem is to always configure the spoke router as a point-to-point subinterface. In this case, when the PVC goes down, the subinterface on the remote router also goes down. The remaining difficulty is for the router to discover that the PVC is down. The local switch sends the update and informs the router. Next, the router will bring the local subinterface down.

After the subinterface goes down, the router removes the static. After the primary static goes down, floating static kicks in the router to dial the access server. The problem with this setup is that convergence is dependent on the Frame Relay provider and is not end-to-end between the routers.

This issue is being resolved with the 12.0 Cisco Operating System: For now, a new TLV is added to CDP so that the hub router sends the default route from the hub router. However, the hub router does not advertise its connected prefixes via CDP; it sends only a default route. The spoke router then installs the default route from the hub router and inserts this route into the routing table.

ODR is a viable solution for a large hub-and-spoke environment because configuration is very simple. Configuration is not required on the spoke router, and only the hub router is configured with the **router odr** command.

Returning to the MKS example, to reiterate, the ODR receives the remote routes and installs them in the routing table via ODR at the hub router. For single-attached sites, all the routes received from ODR should not be redistributed into a core routing protocol. Instead, a static route is created pointing to a null interface, and that static route is redistributed into Enhanced IGRP. Dual-attached sites are treated so that all the specific routes are advertised between the neighbors on the Frame Relay interface PVC, and specific routes are sent to the other neighbors.

ODR routes are installed with an administrative distance of 160 so that the external Enhanced IGRP route will not overwrite the original ODR routes. Setup is shown in Figure 16-37.

Figure 16-37 *ODR with Enhanced IGRP as the Core Routing Protocol; Enhanced IGRP Does Not Overwrite the Original ODR Route*

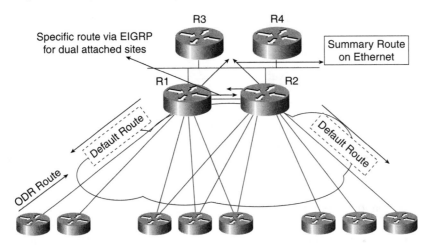

The configuration would be as follows:

```
router odr
router eigrp 1
network 10.0.0.0
passive-interface Serial 2/0
redistribute static
redistribute odr route-map Spoke
default-metric 1 1 1 1 1
ip route 10.1.0.0 255.255.192.0 null0
ip route 10.1.64.0 255.255.224.0 null0
access-list 1 permit 0.0.0.0 0.0.0.0
access-list 2 permit 10.1.96.0 0.0.31.255
route-map Spoke
match ip address 2
```

All routes received from ODR will not be redistributed; only the routes that pass access list 2 will be redistributed into Enhanced IGRP. Access list 2 permits only the destinations that are dual-attached to both the hub routers.

In conclusion, you can use ODR to scale to a much higher level than any routing protocol. Another benefit is that you will avoid the overhead incurred with a routing protocol. Additionally, ODR uses less CPU and memory.

Continuing with our discussion of design, routers in each run Enhanced IGRP and send less-specific routes into the Enhanced IGRP ATM regional core. Routes sent by each of the regions into the ATM regional core are shown in Figure 16-38.

Figure 16-38   *Routes Sent by Each of the Regions into the ATM Regional Core*

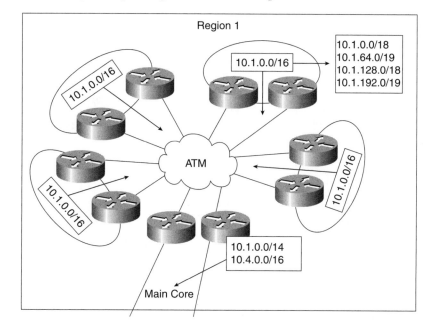

This regional core further aggregates routes into the network backbone. With this well-designed and well-summarized network, it is unnecessary to run BGP because Enhanced IGRP scales without difficulty. Still, to avoid unnecessary IGP queries in case a specific router is lost within a region, BGP is a better choice. The second advantage of BGP in the core is control. If someone within a region assigns an incorrect address, BGP will confine that issue to the local region only.

For example, region 1 is given the address range of 10.1.0.0/16 to 10.4.0.0/16. If, by chance, an address is assigned in that region that is not contained in this address space—for example, 10.5.23.0/16—this address will leak into the entire network and will cause problems. If BGP is in the core, then the mistake must be repeated again at the BGP router. Otherwise, the network will not be advertised to other regions.

Let us continue our discussion regarding the issue of IBGP versus EBGP between regions. For example, if MKS decides to run IBGP core on the network, successfully executing policies would be more complicated than when using OSPF. Figure 16-39 shows what would occur if MKS decides to send the routes to neighbors and wants to implement policies.

All the IBGP routers must be fully meshed because a route learned from one IBGP neighbor is not advertised to any other IBGP neighbor. Routers running IBGP expect a full mesh so that the IBGP neighbor providing information to one neighbor is expected to inform all other IBGP neighbors of the same route, unless it is a route reflector. It is nonsensical to introduce route reflectors in an enterprise network in which the core routers are the only routers running BGP.

Figure 16-39 *Regions with IBGP Core*

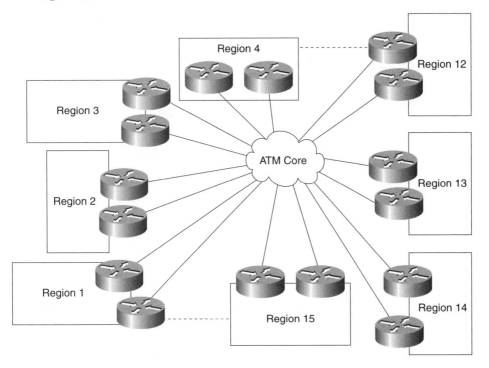

In the previous case study, we mentioned that both routers running IBGP could redistribute the routes with an external type 2 metric into OSPF. The primary router for the destination will advertise the route with the lower type 2 metric, and the backup will advertise the same route with the higher OSPF external type 2 metric.

For example, see Figure 16.40. Even if you break the basic model of BGP and do not fully mesh all the core routers, both R1 and R2 of region 1 must send the same route to R3 and R4 of region 2 for redundancy. Now, consider what would happen if MKS decided to implement policies so that R1 is preferred over R2 for subnets 10.0.0.0/14, and R2 is preferred for 10.4.0.0/16. This can be accomplished by OSPF metric type so that router R1 sends a lower external type 2 for 10.0.0.0/14 and R2 sends a lower external type 2 metric for 10.4.0.0/16.

Figure 16-40 *Route Selection between Regions According to Policies*

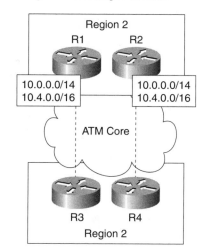

Enhanced IGRP is not as simple. It must consider the internal cost of the links, and it has no concept of the external type 2 metric. Routers in region 2 receive the same routes from region 1, so both R3 and R4 will have the same routes. However, the policy dictates that R1 is the preferred path for 10.0.0.0/14. To prevent the race condition from occurring, the external Enhanced IGRP route overwrites the IBGP-learned route. All the IBGP routers' administrative distances must be lower than 170.

After decreasing the IBGP distance, both R3 and R4 would install the IBGP-learned routes instead of the external Enhanced IGRP routes. R3 and R4 would redistribute the same IBGP routes that they are learning into Enhanced IGRP. Routers closer to R4 would choose R4 to reach network 10.0.0.0/14, which is not the correct policy. To successfully carry out the policy for Enhanced IGRP, MKS must calculate the metrics for redistribution.

The only K values used for Enhanced IGRP route calculations are minimum bandwidth and delay. Now, the router R25 in the region will receive routes from R3 and R4. Figure 16-41 shows that the policy requires R25 to choose R3 to reach network 10.0.0.0/14 and R4 to reach 10.4.0.0/16.

The metric for R25, if you redistribute with a delay metric of 1 to reach the network, is the following:

```
total delay = 100 + 1 =101
R25 metric = [(10000000/155000) + 101] * 256
R25 metric = 42496
```

Similarly, the metric to reach 10.4.0.0/16 for R25 via R4 is the following:

```
minimum BW = 128K
total delay = 2100 + 100 + 1000 = 3200
R25 metric = [(10000000/128) + 3200] * 256
R25 metric = 20819200
```

Figure 16-41   *Route Selection of a Redistribute Route with Enhanced IGRP*

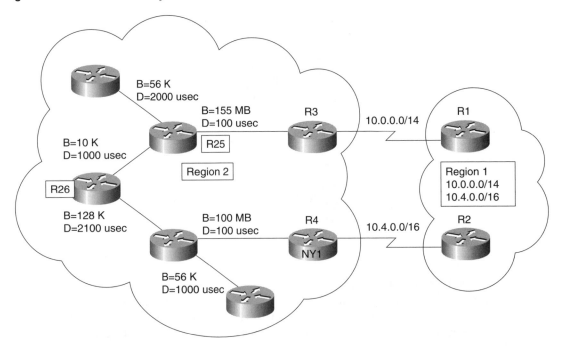

The R3 metric for network 10.4.0.0/16 should be greater than 20819200, so that the network selects R4 to reach this destination.

Equating the values, you can see that the R25 metric via R3 to reach network 10.4.0.0/16 must be greater than 20819200:

$$[(10000000/155000) + 100 \text{ (current delay)} + x] \times 256 = 20819200$$
$$[(65 + 100 + x)] = 20819200/256$$
$$x = 81160$$

Round up to 81200 to be conservative. The redistributing metric by R3 for network 10.4.0.0 now should be the following:

```
router eigrp 321
redistribute bgp 321 route-map Policy
route-map Policy permit 10
match ip address 1
set metric 160000 812000 1 1 1
route-map Policy permit 20
match ip address 2
set metric 160000 1 1 1 1
access-list 1 permit 10.4.0.0 0.0.255.255
access-list 2 permit 10.0.0.0 0.3.255.255
```

This way, the minimum bandwidth is the same, but the delay has changed according to the calculation. Applying policies with IBGP core for optimal routing becomes complicated, but this setup will be simplified if MKS moves the EBGP between each region and sends MED for optimal routing.

The Failure Situation

Now we will consider the failure situation at the remote sites, and discover how the sites would dial in during the failure situation. Each remote site needs a connection during a failure situation. If it is critical that each site connect within a specified amount of time, the current ODR implementation relies on the provider. The next enhancement of ODR in the next release will provide the required convergence.

Even if you are using the ODR or Enhanced IGRP to connect to the remote sites, the next question is: Where should I place the access server in the network?

Refer to Figure 16-37, in which the routers R1 and R2 share specific information between them on a Frame Relay PVC. In this figure, both are sending summaries to R3 and R4 on Ethernet. When the access server is placed on this network—and if MKS ensures that the access server is placed at the correct location and does not hurt the summarization—the unnecessary queries can be stopped. The network in Figure 16-37 is modified from the one shown in Figure 16-42, in which summarization is not significantly affected by remote site dials into the network.

Figure 16-42 *Dial Backup with OSPF and ODR*

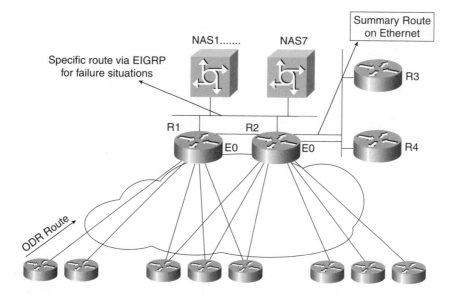

From Figure 16-42, it is apparent that an additional Ethernet interface is added between R1 and R2, and two access servers are added for the remote nodes to dial in. Recall that, for the single-attached sites, only a static route that covered the range was redistributed into the Enhanced IGRP process, both by R1 and R2. Only dual-attached remote nodes were leaked between R1 and R2.

With the addition of the network access (NAS) servers, the same policies still exist. In case of failure, now all the specific routes are leaked between R1 and R2. MKS ensures that the specific routes leaked by the access server are not advertised on Ethernet 0. As mentioned previously, summarization in Enhanced IGRP occurs per interface, not per neighbor. Therefore, all the access servers connected on the same Ethernet with R1 and R2 would not need all the specific routes in case of failure. They would require only a default route from R1 and R2.

R1 and R2 cannot filter so that specific routes are advertised between them and not to the NAS servers. Either the PVC that was removed was reinstalled between R1 and R2, or all the NAS servers could maintain a distribute list in denying all the routes except the default route.

A failure situation of a remote node is shown in Figure 16-43, along with routing propagation and query boundaries. When one of the remote nodes loses its connection, it dials in and the NAS server receives the route.

Figure 16-43 *Specific Route via the NAS Server*

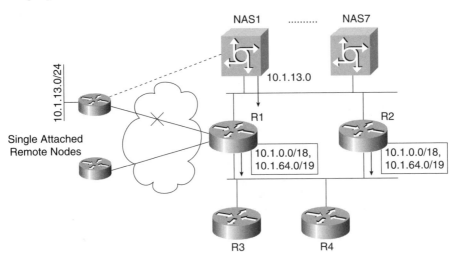

Because all the NAS servers permit only the default route via Enhanced IGRP, the only router that would query for 10.1.13.0/24 would be R1 when the primary connection goes down, and R2, and NAS1 in this case, when the PVC is restored between R1 and the remote router. During the initial failure, R1 loses the specific route to 10.1.13.0. It will query all its neighbors—in this case, NAS1 through NAS7, R2, R3, and R4 because none of them had the specific route to 10.1.13.0/24.

In such a case, R2, R3, and R4 are receiving summaries, and NAS servers are not installing another route other than the default via Enhanced IGRP. They will all send "immediate unreachable" back to R1 without propagating the queries.

After the remote router has dialed into NAS1, NAS1 will leak the specific route to 10.1.13.0/24 to all its neighbors—NAS2 through NAS7, and R1 and R2. Although all the NAS servers did receive the specific route, because distribute list permits only the default route, the NAS servers will not install any specific route. R2 has also received the specific route. After the original PVC between R1 and the remote site is restored, the connection between NAS1 and the remote site is brought down. Now R2 has lost the specific route to 10.1.13.0/24. R2 will query all its neighbors again. None of R2's neighbors, other than R1, had the specific route and R1 is sending the summary to R2. All of R2's neighbors will send unreachable back to R2 and not propagate the query further.

The entire network is redundant, except for the Ethernet that connects the hub routers to the regional core routers. An extra layer of protection could be added by connecting a hub router with a core router in a second region.

At this point, you may wonder: What if I simply connect all four of the routers on another LAN interface? Although this possibility may seem logical, it would simply be too expensive. This would be a good alternative if your service provider is willing to connect the two regional core connections to different ATM switches. This merely eliminates the single point of failure.

The final design with Enhanced IGRP acting as the IGP is shown in Figure 16-44.

If MKS chooses OSPF, several things should be restructured. For one thing, areas must be defined within each region, except area 0 which is already defined. NAS servers would flood the specific LSA with the NSSA area to which they belong. With this new LSA injected within NSSA, an SPF run would occur, but nothing would change outside the NSSA area.

Area Setup of OSPF

The area setup of OSPF is shown in Figure 16-45. The physical setup differs from the one in Enhanced IGRP because it is dependant on the location of the link between one region hub router and the other regional core router—it could be the local area or area 0. For example, MKS can insert a link between a hub router in area 2 with a regional core router in area 1. If the link is in area 1, all the traffic from area 2 destined to area 1 would begin to travel on this link, which is only for backup. The ATM core high-speed links would not be used.

This can be solved successfully by inserting some NAS servers on the ATM core routers, with one link to area 0 and the other on the dialing area. The number of areas is not an issue for MKS, but as the number of areas grows, it would become increasingly difficult to maintain a large number of areas in one router. This would require a large number of ISDN interfaces, which obviously do not scale very well, especially when you need to add redundancy to the backup path.

Figure 16-44 *Final Network Setup with Enhanced IGRP*

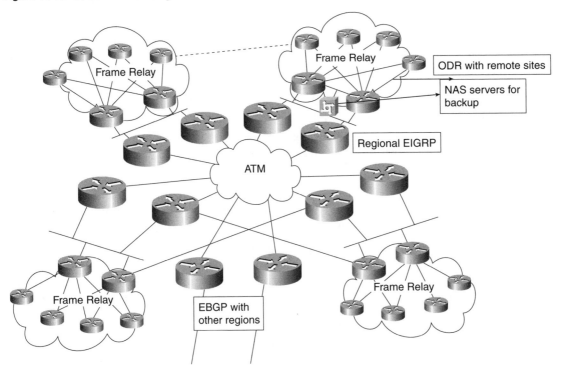

This restriction arises because of an interface's capability to belong to only one area at a time. Because ISDN traditionally leverages the legacy dial-on-demand routing (DDR) code, all B-channels on a physical ISDN circuit are tied to one single network-layer, point-to-multipoint entity called a *dialer interface*. Therefore, even though a PRI has 23 B-channels, all channels on this physical ISDN circuit belong to the same network-layer interface: Serial X:23. This interface can belong to only one single OSPF area.

The capability to physically terminate calls from 23 separate sites on this PRI is wasted because all channels must share the same network-layer address. For our discussion, the backup ABR is the ABR that terminates ISDN links that are brought up for backup (when the primary link fails). Therefore, each area requiring backup needs one dedicated ISDN interface on the backup ABR.

Version 11.2 includes a feature called dialer profiles. One of the fundamental differences between legacy DDR and dialer profiles is that the physical ISDN circuits are no longer conjoined to the same network-layer interface.

Figure 16-45 *Final Setup with OSPF as the Core Routing Protocol within a Region*

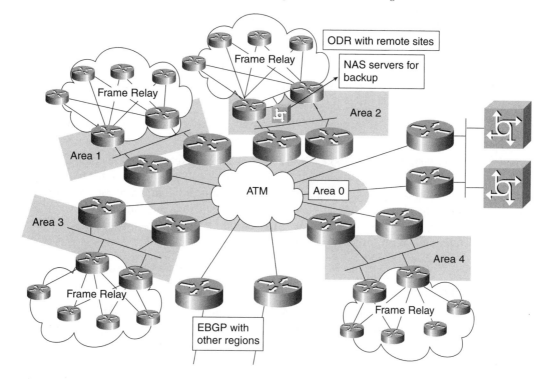

Instead, you have the capability to define multiple dialer profiles, which are network-layer entities that also have some associated DDR parameters. When an incoming call arrives on an ISDN circuit, you can bind the call to the appropriate dialer profile dynamically, based on authenticated user name or caller ID.

You could define many more dialer profiles than you have of physical ISDN circuits, thereby allowing you to oversubscribe, and, in essence, to rely on statistical multiplexing of your ISDN calls.

This seems to be a breakthrough for the OSPF backup strategy. Each dialer profile would maintain its own associated IP address (and therefore its own OSPF area). If there are 50 OSPF areas to back up, you would configure 50 different dialer profiles on the backup ABR.

It is no longer necessary to maintain 50 different ISDN interfaces. Instead, you can use fewer interfaces, depending on the level of oversubscription desired in the backup network. When an incoming call arrives on the backup ABR, bind the call from the area that went down to the appropriate dialer profile that belongs in the same area.

Dialer Profile Drawbacks

There are some points for concern with dialer profiles, however. Preconfiguration of the dialer profiles places each one within the respective area to which the backed area belongs. This causes the following problems:

- Extra LSAs are generated—one for each dialer profile.

- Each dialer profile introduces one additional route into that area, which may be undesirable, especially if you are summarizing.

- Any change in the LSA database (link flap anywhere in the network) will generate an ISDN call.

- Because area LSAs are flooded every 30 minutes to ensure synchronization of LSA databases across the autonomous system, an ISDN call will be generated to each area when the flooding occurs. It is possible to avoid this problem if you use the OSPF On-Demand feature in version 11.3. However, this would indicate that every backup router in each area would have to be upgraded to version 11.3 to understand the Demand Circuit (DC) option during adjacency formation.

Using Virtual Profiles

These problems can be solved with a feature in version 11.3 called *virtual profiles*. Virtual profiles are based upon dialer profiles, so there is the abstraction of the network-layer interface from the physical ISDN circuit. However, virtual profiles expand upon dialer profiles by allowing dynamic interface configuration when an inbound call is made.

The interface configuration is stored on a central server (in this case, a AAA server supporting either the TACACS+ or RADIUS protocol) and downloaded to the router on demand. When the area redials the ABR, the physical ISDN circuit is bound to a dynamic interface called a virtual access interface. The configuration of the virtual access interface is sourced from a virtual template (optional) and, most importantly, from the AAA server.

The virtual profile is stored on the AAA server, and it is applied to the virtual access interface to which the physical ISDN circuit has been bound. When the ISDN link is disconnected, the virtual profile (or virtual access interface to which the area was connected) is destroyed and is ready for the next ISDN call.

A PRI allows the capability to support up to 23 calls at once from different—or possibly the same—sites. When PPP multi-link is enabled on the backup ABR and a new call arrives, you can compare the authenticated username with that of existing virtual profiles.

If the call originated from the same area, you can bundle the links into a multilink bundle, which allows physical ISDN circuits that originate from the same place to share the same network-layer interface (virtual profile). Physical ISDN circuits that originated from different areas (and have different authenticated usernames) are bound to new virtual profiles. New virtual access interfaces are created when their configurations are downloaded from the AAA server.

Because you are no longer preconfiguring the dialer profiles on the backup ABR, you will not encounter the problems of dialer profiles. The absence of preconfiguration also indicates that backup ABRs can scale effortlessly across multiple chassis, and does not provide management overhead redundancy.

However, one thing that does require preconfiguration on the backup ABRs is the OSPF network statements, which associate a subnet to a particular area. The setup for the network using virtual profiles is shown in Figure 16-46. This figure shows the final OSPF setup with complete redundancy.

Figure 16-46 *Final Design with OSPF within a Region*

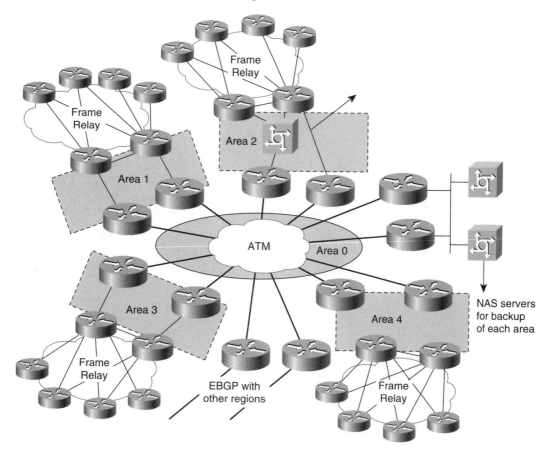

This network is designed to accommodate the present size and to give the network capabilities to scale to much greater lengths without revisiting the design.

Case Study 3: An ISP Network

This section examines the configuration of a large ISP network, ISPnet. As shown in Figure 16-47, the network consists of multiple regional distribution networks scattered across the country, and connected by a mixture of point-to-point ATM and POS WAN links.

Figure 16-47 *ISPnet Backbone*

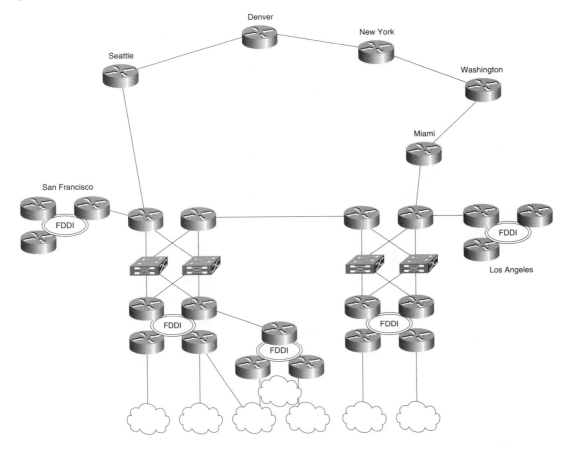

For convenience, only a few of the regional networks are shown, and the details of only two—San Francisco (SFO) (see Figure 16-48) and Los Angeles (LAX) (see Figure 16-49)—are diagrammed. Each regional network has its own subdomain of ISPnet: Therefore, they are named sfo.ISPnet, lax.ISPnet, dvr.ISPnet, and so on.

Figure 16-48   *ISPnet SFO Regional Network*

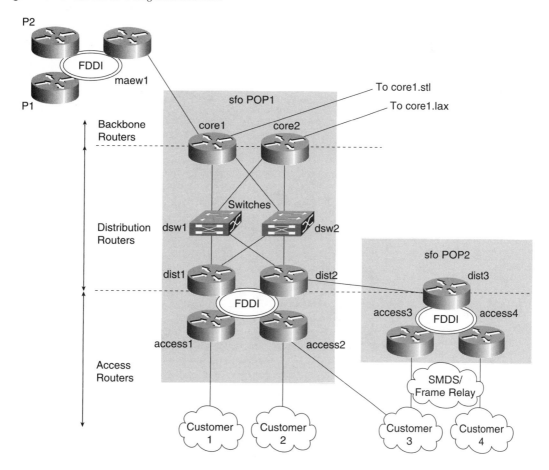

Although ISPnet consists of thousands of routers, all configurations fall into three general categories: access, distribution, and backbone.

The SFO regional network spans many POPS; for convenience, only two are shown in Figure 16-48. Multiple technologies (serial, SMDS, and Frame Relay) are used to connect customer networks to ISPnet's access routers.

Router access1.sfo is one of multiple access routers connecting to distribution router dist1.sfo via a switched FDDI. A multiple distribution router, dist1.sfo connects to redundant backbone routers core1.sfo and core2.sfo via two ATM switches, dsw1.sfo and dsw2.sfo. Further, core1.sfo connects to core1.stl, and core2.sfo connects to core1.lax. LAX and other regional networks consist of a similar distribution hierarchy.

Figure 16-49 *ISPnet LAX Regional Network*

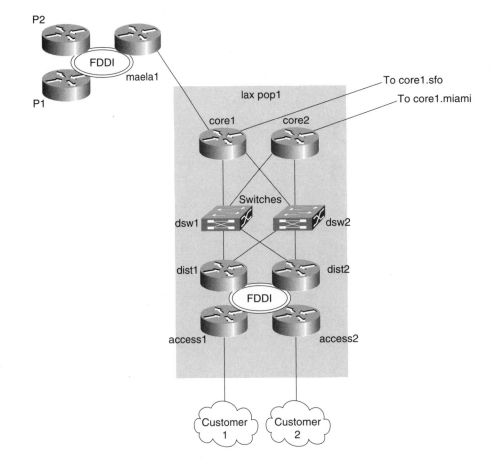

ISPnet is Autonomous System number 2 and runs a full IBGP mesh between core routers. Route reflector hierarchies extend from the core routers through the distribution and access routers in each regional distribution network.

IS-IS is used as an IGP, with the interpop connectivity at level 2. Each POP constitutes a level 1 area.

PIM sparse mode is used within the network. Key distribution routers in each regional network are configured as RPs. MBGP makes use of multicast-capable Layer 2 switches at public exchange points. MSDP is used between providers.

Customer traffic is mapped into one of three IP precedence levels: 0, 1, or 2. Weighted Random Early Detection is used on all backbone links, and optionally on customer access links.

Customers may signal the IP precedence to be associated with each packet via BGP communities.

ISPnet uses a network-management system distributed among major POPs. Each major POP maintains servers and logging facilities for TACACs, DNS, NTP, syslog, FTP, and SNMP. From a network-management perspective, each POP can operate autonomously, although it is possible for the network-management facilities of one POP to back up another.

Address Plan

IP address blocks are assigned to regional networks in 16.x/16 (a class B size) chunks. Within each regional network, the first 10 class C's in each block are reserved for infrastructure; the remainder are allocated for use by customers. SFO has block 16.0/16, and LAX has 16.1/16.

For IS-IS NET address allocation, ISPnet uses the format 00.000L.macaddress.00, where L is the highest IS-IS level interface of the router (1 or 2), and macaddress is the MAC address of the first LAN interface on the router (0010.1f42.8bff, in the **show interface** output that follows):

```
core1.sfo#sh int eth 0
Ethernet0 is up, line protocol is upHardware is 10/100 Ethernet,
    address is 0010.1f42.8bff (bia 0010.1f42.8bff)
```

IS-IS Configuration

ISPnet uses the IS-IS two-layer hierarchy. All the core routers are L1-L2 routers; all other routers are in L1. The IS-IS–specific configuration for core1.sfo is as follows:

```
Interface pos 1/0/0                  ; level-2 adjacency to core1.lax
Ip address 16.0.0.1 255.255.255.252
Ip router isis sfo
isis circuit-type level-2-only
isis metric 5 level-2
isis password isispass level-2
!
interface ATM1/0.1 point-to-point            ; level-1 adjacency to dist1.sfo
 ip address 16.3.0.1 255.255.255.252
 ip router isis sfo
 isis circuit-type level-1
 isis password isis1pass level-1
!
router isis sfo
 summary-address 16.0.0.0 255.255.255.0.0 ; generate summary into level-2 only
 passive-interface Loopback0
 default-information originate               ; originate default in level-1 area
 net 00.0002. 0010.1f42.8bff.00
 domain-password lab
 area-password lab
 log-adjacency-changes
```

In this configuration, circuit passwords are used (exchanged during hellos), and area/domain passwords are used (exchanged during L1 and L2 LSPs, respectively). POS 0/0/0 is configured to form an L2-only adjacency with core1.lax, and ATM1/0.1 for an L1-only adjacency with dist1.sfo. You can log any agency failures to the syslog facility on the network-management system.

With appropriate summarization, the previous configuration will scale well. If backbone or area scaling issues are encountered, the **spf-interval** and **lsp-refresh-interval** router IS-IS subcommands may be used to decrease IS-IS computation at the expense of convergence time. In addition, **hello-multiplier**, **retransmit-throttle-interval**, **retransmit-interval**, **lsp-interval**, and **mesh-group** blocking may be tuned on a per-interface basis.

A summary address of 16.0/16 is generated into Level 2 for the SFO regional network.

BGP Configuration

Figure 16-50 illustrates the BGP architecture for ISPnet.

The generic BGP router configuration for ISPnet includes the large-scale configuration developed in Chapter 11, "Border Gateway Protocol," along with a number of peer group definitions. Note that full functionality is not required for all routers, but it is beneficial to maintain a consistent configuration across the network.

ISPnet extensively uses communities to color routes. In particular, the following communities are defined:

- Communities used for BGP QoS policy propagation:

```
ip community-list 10 permit 2:0    ; routes customers want precedence 0
ip community-list 11 permit 2:1    ; routes customers want precedence 1
ip community-list 12 permit 2:2    ; routes customers want precedence 2
```

- Communities used for routing policy:

```
ip community-list 1 permit 2:100   ; routes learned from customers
ip community-list 70 permit 2:70   ; routes learned from a customer providing
  backup to another AS
ip community-list 80 permit 2:80   ; routes learned from other isps
ip community-list 90 permit 2:90   ; routes learned from a customer's backup
  link
```

Figure 16-50 *ISPnet BGP Architecture*

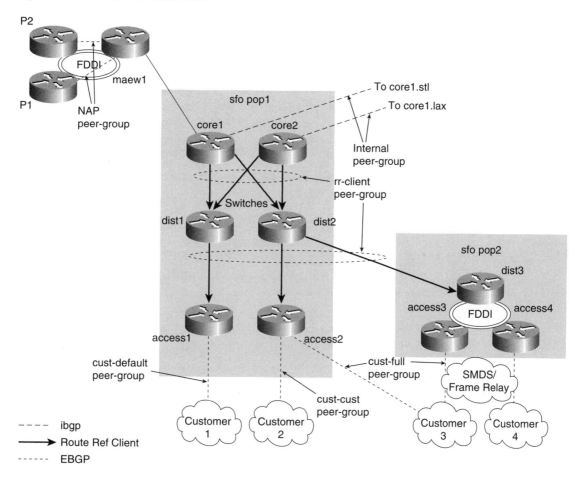

Peer groups also form a major part of the configuration. Six in total are used—their application is shown in Figure 16-50 and is described as follows:

```
router bgp 2
 no synchronization
 table-map bgp-qos
 bgp router-id 16.0.0.1
 no bgp fast-external-fallover
 bgp log-neighbor-changes
 network 16.0.0.0 route-map nap-out
 neighbor internal peer-group nlri unicast multicast     ; used for ibgp peers
 neighbor internal description ibgp peers
 neighbor internal remote-as 2
 neighbor internal update-source Loopback0
```

```
neighbor internal next-hop-self
neighbor internal send-community
neighbor internal version 4
neighbor internal password 7 03085A09
neighbor nap peer-group                  ; for peer ISPs
neighbor nap description send customer routes only; block martians
neighbor nap remove-private-AS
neighbor nap prefix-list martian-etc in
neighbor nap prefix-list cidr-block out
neighbor nap route-map nap-in in
neighbor nap route-map nap-out out
neighbor nap version 4
neighbor nap maximum-prefix 30000
neighbor cust-full peer-group  ; for dual-homed customers wanting multiple paths
   to Internet
neighbor cust-full description send full Internet routes
neighbor cust-full remove-private-AS
neighbor cust-full version 4
neighbor cust-full route-map cust-in in
neighbor cust-full prefix-list cidr-block out
neighbor cust-full route-map full-routes out
neighbor cust-cust peer-group        ; for dual-homed customers with ISPnet as
   secondary isp
neighbor cust-cust description send routes from other customers only
neighbor cust-cust remove-private-AS
neighbor cust-cust version 4
neighbor cust-cust route-map cust-in in
neighbor cust-cust prefix-list cidr-block out
neighbor cust-cust route-map customer-routes out
neighbor cust-default peer-group              ; for singly homed customers
neighbor cust-default description send default route only
neighbor cust-default default-originate route-map default-route
neighbor cust-default version 4
neighbor cust-default prefix-list deny-all out
neighbor cust-default route-map cust-in in
neighbor rr-client peer-group nlri unicast multicast  ; for ibgp route-reflector
   clients
neighbor rr-client description for rr-client
neighbor rr-client remote-as 3561
neighbor rr-client update-source Loopback0
neighbor rr-client route-reflector-client
neighbor rr-client next-hop-self
neighbor rr-client send-community
neighbor rr-client version 4
neighbor rr-client password 7 020A0559
no auto-summary
```

IBGP backbone peers are placed in the internal peer group via the **neighbor** *ip-address* **peer-group internal** bgp subcommand. The *ip-address* corresponds to a loopback address on the neighbor. Within this peer group,you would follow the standard procedure discussed in Chapter 11: specifically, setting the update source to the loopback interface, setting the version, and applying password protection.

In addition, next-hop-self is set so that any routes that may be learned from EBGP neighbors are sent with a next hop equal to the loopback address (there are none in this case). The community information is propagated to all internal neighbors. This information is used to apply routes and QoS policy on routers connecting customers.

Route reflector clients with the SFO area are placed in the rr-client peer group, which includes the same functionality as the internal peer group, plus configuration of the neighbor as a route-reflector-client.

Core1.sfo has only two types of bgp neighbors: IBGP peers corresponding to backbone routers (core1.lax) at other POPs, and router reflector clients (dist1.sfo) within the local POP or at nearby NAPs (maew.1). In general, avoid connecting EBGP customers or peers to any core routers.

Dist1.sfo uses the internal peer group for neighbor sessions with route reflectors core1.sfo and core2.sfo. Four additional EBGP peer groups are also defined for use within access/distribution routers. For these groups, apply separate passwords on a per-neighbor basis. One peer group, known as "nap," is used for EBGP neighbors that are peer ISPs at public or private exchange points. The other three—cust-full, cust-cust, and cust-default—are used for EBGP neighbors that are customers.

The nap peer group is used with EBGP at public or private peering points. It assumes that the neighbors are directly connected to the router because ebgp-multihop is not configured. Apply **remove-private-AS** to ensure that any private AS numbers are automatically stripped from outgoing advertisements. The prefix-list known as "martian-etc" filters a number of networks that are not routed on the global Internet. (A subset of these is often jokingly referred to as "martian" routes; hence, the use of the name martian-etc for the prefix-list.)

```
ip prefix-list martian-etc seq 5 deny 0.0.0.0/32
# deny the default route
ip prefix-list martian-etc seq 10 deny 0.0.0.0/8 le 32
# deny anything beginning with 0
ip prefix-list martian-etc seq 15 deny 0.0.0.0/1 ge 20
# deny masks > 20 for all class A nets (1-127)
ip prefix-list martian-etc seq 20 deny 10.0.0.0/8 le 32
# deny 10/8 per RFC1918
ip prefix-list martian-etc seq 25 deny 127.0.0.0/8 le 32
# reserved by IANA - loopback address
ip prefix-list martian-etc seq 30 deny 128.0.0.0/2 ge 17
deny masks >= 17 for all class B nets (129-191)
ip prefix-list martian-etc seq 35 deny 128.0.0.0/16 le 32
# deny net 128.0 - reserved by IANA
ip prefix-list martian-etc seq 40 deny 172.16.0.0/12 le 32
# deny 172.16 as RFC1918
ip prefix-list martian-etc seq 45 deny 192.0.2.0/24 le 32
# class C 192.0.20.0 reserved by IANA
ip prefix-list martian-etc seq 50 deny 192.0.0.0/24 le 32
# class C 192.0.0.0 reserved by IANA
ip prefix-list martian-etc seq 55 deny 192.168.0.0/16 le 32
# deny 192.168/16 per RFC1918
```

```
ip prefix-list martian-etc seq 60 deny 191.255.0.0/16 le 32
# deny 191.255.0.0 - IANA reserved (I think)
ip prefix-list martian-etc seq 65 deny 192.0.0.0/3 ge 25
# deny masks > 25 for class C (192-222)
ip prefix-list martian-etc seq 70 deny 223.255.255.0/24 le 32
# deny anything in net 223 - IANA reserved
ip prefix-list martian-etc seq 75 deny 224.0.0.0/3 le 32
# deny class D/Experimental
```

An outgoing prefix-list is applied to filter all specific routes within the ISPnet CIDR allocation (16.0.0.0), allowing only the class A-size network to pass. If ISPnet were allocated additional CIDR blocks, networks more specific than the CIDR block would also be added to this list. Note that the CIDR block route is generated via the **network 16.0.0.0 route-map nap-out** BGP subcommand. All other routes, presumably those learned from customers that do not belong to ISPnet's CIDR block, are allowed by this prefix list:

```
ip prefix-list cidr-block seq 5 deny 16.0.0.0/8 ge 9
ip prefix-list cidr-block seq 10 permit 0.0.0.0/0 le 32
```

The route map known as "nap-out" matches all routes in community list 1—in other words, routes in community 2:100, which corresponds to all customers of ISPnet. The route map sets the BGP MED to equal the IGP metric for the route, and sets the BGP next hop to equal the local EBGP peering address. This last step prevents the use of third-party next hop, which is against the peering policy of many ISPs at public exchange points:

```
route-map nap-out permit 10
 match community 1
 set metric-type internal
 set ip next-hop peer-address
!
route-map default-route permit 10
 set metric-type internal
 set ip next-hop peer-address
```

The route map known as "nap-in" ensures that the BGP MED seen in neighbors is effectively ignored by setting it to the maximum-1 (routes with MED equal to 4294967295 are assumed to have infinite metric and are ignored). The next hop attribute is set to equal the peer address, negating the use of third-party next hop; and the community is reset to 2:80, implying that this route has been received from another ISP:

```
!
route-map nap-in permit 10
 set metric 4294967294
 set ip next-hop peer-address
 set community 2:80
set local-preference 80
```

As a final protective measure, limit the maximum number of prefixes accepted from any neighbor at the NAP to 30,000. This figure exceeds the number of routes offered by any single ISP, but this may have to be revised in the future. If 30,000 is exceeded, the session is closed until it is manually restarted using the **clear ip bgp** {*ip-address* | *peer-group-name*} command.

Three types of BGP customers are defined for ISPnet, and each has its own peer group. All three peer groups apply the CIDR-block prefix list, which we mentioned previously in our discussion of the nap peer group. All three peer groups use the cust-in inbound route map:

```
route-map cust-in permit 10
  set metric 4294967294          ; reset metric to maximum
  set ip next-hop peer-address   ; force next-hop to be peer address
  set local-preference 100        ; set default local-preference to be 100
  set community 2:100 additive    ; place route in "customer" community
!
route-map cust-in permit 20
  match community 70             ; customer providing backup for this route
  set local-preference 70
!
route-map cust-in permit 30
  match community 80             ; customer uses another major ISP as backup
  set local-preference 80
!
route-map cust-in permit 40
  match community 90             ; customer wants backup for these routes
  set local-preference 90
```

The local preference setting in this route map is in accordance with RFC 1998. Consider the example given in the RFC: AS4 and AS3 have a bilateral backup agreement. That is, AS3 would use its direct link to AS4 to reach only AS4 in a normal circumstance, and for transit, in case of failure between AS3 and AS1. This is accomplished when AS3 and AS4 offers each others' routes to the providers AS1 and AS2 with a community of AS1:70 and AS2:70, respectively. AS1, therefore, would have a path to AS3 via AS4 with a local-pref of 70, and a path through AS2 with a local-pref of 80.

Moreover, AS3 also could provide a second backup link to AS1, and could send routes on the second link with community AS1:90, thereby backing its primary link to AS1, as follows:

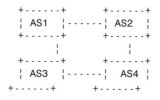

In this case, AS3 offers routes for AS4 to AS1 with a community of 2:70, resulting in a local preference of 70. AS1 sets the local-pref of routes received from AS2 to 80, by default.

The cust-full peer group is used when customers are dual-homed and wish to receive a full set of Internet routes. This allows them to choose the provider with the best route to any destination on the Internet. (As mentioned in previous chapters, the best route is often selected as the one with the shortest AS path—this is not necessarily the best route in terms of a particular performance metric, such as throughput or delay.)

This peer group applies outgoing route map full-routes, which match communities 2:100, 2:70, 2:80, and 2:90; and, as usual, sets the metric-type to internal and next hop to the peering address:

```
!
route-map full-routes permit 10
 match community 1 70 80 90
 set metric-type internal
 set ip next-hop peer-address
!
```

The cust-full peer group also is used when customers are typically dual-homed, but wish to use ISPnet as a secondary provider. Therefore, they need to receive only the routes associated with ISPnet direct customers. This peer group applies outgoing route map customer-routes, which match communities 2:100, 2:70, and 2:90; and, as usual, sets the metric-type to internal and next hop to the peering address:

```
route-map customer-routes permit 10
 match community 1 70 90
 set metric-type internal
 set ip next-hop peer-address
```

Finally, the cust-default peer group uses the **default-originate bgp neighbor** subcommand to send the default route with the next hop and MED attributes modified via the route map default route. It applies prefix-list deny-all to block all other routes:

```
ip prefix-list deny-all seq 5 deny 0.0.0.0/0 le 32
!
route-map default-route permit 10
 set metric-type internal
 set ip next-hop peer-address
!
```

It is important to ensure both the integrity and the correct characterization of customer routers at the perimeter of the network. Integrity indicates allowance of only those routes from customers that have been prearranged for acceptance. It would be disastrous to blindly accept routes from a dual-homed customer who, in effect, offers you transit to the entire Internet. Characterization refers to coloring the routes so that the correct transit is applied and QoS policies are possibly applied.

Every BGP customer also should have an inbound prefix-list that exactly matches the routes you expect to receive from that customer. This can be executed problem-free for the arrangement using peer groups because inbound policy for peer-group members can be applied on a per-neighbor basis, employing **prefix-list** *prefix-list-name*.

QoS Configuration

The QoS architecture for ISPnet is shown in Figure 16-51. ISPnet uses three levels of IP precedence and applies WRED on backbone links.

Figure 16-51 *ISP QoS Architecture*

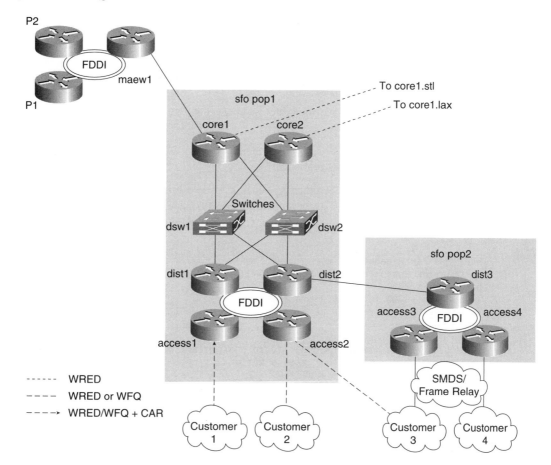

Customers may signal the precedence to become associated with packets from different sources via BGP communities. Specifically, communities 2:0, 2:1, and 2:2 signal precedence 0, 1, and 2, respectively. The **bgp table-map** command uses the **bgp-qos route-map** command to match these communities and set the precedence flag in the CEF table, as required:

```
route-map bgp-qos permit 10
 match community 10
 set ip precedence routine
!
route-map bgp-qos permit 20
 match community 11
 set ip precedence priority
!
route-map bgp-qos permit 30
 match community 12
 set ip precedence immediate
!
```

As an example, a route sent with community 2:2 would produce the following entry in the CEF table:

```
Dist1.sfo#sh ip cef  171.91.0.0
171.91.0.0/24, version 26990413, cached adjacency 16.60.1.91
0 packets, 0 bytes, Precedence immediate (2)
  via 16.60.1.91, 0 dependencies, recursive
    next hop 16.60.1.91, FastEthernet0/0/0 via 16.60.1.91/32
    valid cached adjacency
```

Note that the precedence is set to "immediate," causing the precedence field in any IP packet switched by CEF to be reset to 2.

As shown in Figure 16-51, WRED is applied on all backbone links and all customer links via the **random-detect** interface subcommand.

In ISPnet, CAR is applied on selected customer links to rate-limit inbound traffic. If the configured policy is exceeded, all non-conforming packets have their precedence reset to 0, implying best-effort service. In this example, a CAR of 1 Mbps is applied to FastEthernet 0/0/0 on dist1:

```
interface FastEthernet0/0/0
 description Customer A, 100 Mbit/s, CAR limited to 1 mbit/s
 bandwidth 100000
 ip address 16.60.10.1 255.255.0.0
 ip verify unicast reverse-path
 no ip redirects
 no ip directed-broadcast
 rate-limit input 1000000 100000 120000 conform-action transmit
                               exceed action set-prec-continue 0
 bgp-policy source ip-prec-map
 ip route-cache distributed
 no cdp enable
```

Multicast Configuration

The multicast architecture for the SFO region is shown in Figure 16-51. Where supported, multicast distributed switching is enabled. Otherwise, non-distributed routing is enabled. For simplicity, **ip pim-sparse-dense-mode** is enabled on all interfaces with the network, and on customer interfaces as requested by the customer. That is, if the customer wants multicast service, **ip pim sparse-dense mode** is enabled on the interface leading to that customer.

Every backbone router is configured as both an RP and an RP mapper. You can configure loopback 1 as the RP address so that all PIM DRs will use their closest RP. In this case, any DR in the SFO regional network will use either core1.sfo or core2.sfo as the RP.

A full mesh of MSDP and IMBGP is configured across the backbone. In the case of MSDP, this is executed via explicit **ip msdp peer** configuration commands, as shown in the following configuration. In the case of MBGP, the **nlri unicast multicast** is added to the internal and rr-client peer groups. MSDP peering also follows the router reflector peering hierarchy.

```
ip multicast-routing distributed                ; enable multicast distributed switching
.
.
loopback 1 ip address 16.0.5.1 255.255.255.255     ; use as RP's address
.
.
ip pim send-rp-discover scope 16                ; perform RP mapping
ip pim send-rp-announce loopback 1 scope 16     ; announce RP with address 16.0.5.1
.
.
msdp peer <peer-ip> connect-source loopback 0 ; this line repeated for all backbone
routers
```

Router maew1 is configured as a pim border router. Access list 31 blocks auto-rp messages from crossing the PIM boundary. In addition, external MSDP is configured with other peers at the NAP. In these external peering sessions, you should filter out SAs by using access list 31, corresponding to the same groups as access list 31 (auto-RP announce/discovery and administratively scoped groups) for any sources:

```
ip msdp peer 16.99.0.1 connect-source Loopback0
ip msdp peer <peer-ip> connect-source Fddi 0/0/0
ip msdp sa-filter out <peer-ip> list 131
ip msdp ttl-threshold <peer-ip> 32
Interface Fddi 0/0/0
ip multicast boundary 31
ip pim sparse-dense-mode
Access-list 31 deny 224.0.1.39          ; block auto-rp message
Access-list 31 deny 224.0.1.40          ;  block auto-rp message
Access-list 31 deny 239.0.0.0 0.255.255.255; block administrative scoped groups
Access-list 31 permit 224.0.0.0 15.255.255.255 ; permit all others
```

Because the SFO NAP includes a separate LAN for multicast traffic, MBGP is also configured between those EBGP peers that would like to support multicast. An additional peer group, "mnap," is defined for this purpose. Separate peering sessions are therefore established for unicast and multicast BGP:

```
router bgp 2
neighbor mnap peer-group nlri multicast                ; for peer ISPs
 neighbor mnap description send customer routes only; block martians
 neighbor mnap remove-private-AS
 neighbor mnap prefix-list martian-etc in
 neighbor mnap prefix-list cidr-block out
 neighbor mnap route-map nap-in in
 neighbor mnap route-map nap-out out
 neighbor mnap maximum-prefix 30000
```

Customers have two connectivity options. The easiest option, and the one suited to customers with small networks, is simply to heed the AUTO-RP announcements sent by the access routers of the ISP. This is achieved by configuring **ip pim sparse-dense-mode** on both the customer and ISP access routers. This will cause the customer network to use the RP provided by the ISP.

Customers with many routers in their network will be better served by their own RP. In this case, MSDP peering must be configured on both the customer and the ISP routers. The configuration is identical to the ISP-ISP case.

If the unicast and multicast topologies are incongruent—when separate links are used, for example—then MBGP also must be configured. Again, the configuration is identical to the ISP-ISP case, with the exception that separate MBGP peer groups for multicast customers must be defined. These can be based on the cust-full, cust-cust, or cust-default unicast peer groups; simply add the **nlri** multicast keyword to the lead peer group configuration line.

Network Management and Security Configuration

This section shows the configuration for dist1.sfo as an example. It contains most of the network management and security functionality discussed in Chapter 15, "Network Operations and Management." Refer to that chapter for the details and motivation behind each configuration command.

```
!
! Last configuration change at 20:17:16 PST Wed Feb 3 1999 by netadmin
! NVRAM config last updated at 20:13:44 PST Wed Feb 3 1999 by netadmin
!
version 12.0
service nagle
no service pad
service timestamps debug uptime
service timestamps log uptime
service password-encryption
!
hostname dist1.sfo
!
boot system flash slot0:rsp-pv-mz.120-2.5.S.0113
boot system tftp tftpboot/soma/120S/images/rsp-pv-mz.120-3.0.2.S 172.21.27.83
no logging console
aaa new-model
aaa authentication login default tacacs+ enable
aaa authentication login console none
aaa authentication enable default tacacs+ enable
aaa accounting exec default start-stop tacacs+
aaa accounting commands 15 default start-stop tacacs+
enable secret 5 $1$/edy$.CyBGklbRBghZehOaj7jI/
!
ip subnet-zero
ip cef distributed
ip cef accounting per-prefix non-recursive
no ip finger
ip tcp window-size 65535
ip tcp path-mtu-discovery
ip tftp source-interface Loopback0
ip ftp source-interface Loopback0
ip ftp username devtest
ip ftp password 7 0202014D1F031C3501
```

```
no ip bootp server
ip host tftps 172.21.27.83
ip domain-name isp.net
ip name-server 16.60.0.254
ip name-server 16.60.20.254
ip multicast-routing distributed
ip dvmrp route-limit 8000
clns routing
clock timezone PST -8
clock summer-time PDT recurring
!
!
interface Loopback0
 ip address 16.0.0.1 255.255.255.255
 no ip directed-broadcast
 no ip route-cache
 no ip mroute-cache
 isis circuit-type level-1
 isis metric 1 level-1
!
interface FastEthernet0/0/0
 description Server LAN, 100 Mbit/s, Infrastructure
 bandwidth 100000
 ip address 16.60.10.1 255.255.0.0
 ip verify unicast reverse-path
 no ip redirects
 no ip directed-broadcast
 rate-limit input access-group 100 1000000 100000 120000 conform-action transmit
                                          exceed-action set-prec-continue 0
 rate-limit input 1000000 100000 120000 conform-action transmit exceed-action set-
prec-continue 0
 bgp-policy source ip-prec-map
 ip route-cache distributed
 no cdp enable
!
ip classless
ip tacacs source-interface Loopback0
ip bgp-community new-format
logging history size 100
logging history debugging
logging 16.60.0.254
access-list 16 permit 16.60.0.0 0.0.255.255
snmp-server community testcomm RO 7
snmp-server trap-source Loopback0
snmp-server location San Francisco
snmp-server contact noc@isp.net
snmp-server enable traps snmp
snmp-server enable traps channel
snmp-server enable traps isdn call-information
snmp-server enable traps config
snmp-server enable traps entity
snmp-server enable traps envmon
snmp-server enable traps bgp
snmp-server enable traps frame-relay
snmp-server enable traps rtr
```

```
snmp-server host 16.60.0.254 traps snmpcomm
snmp-server tftp-server-list 16
!
tacacs-server host 16.60.0.254
tacacs-server key labkey
banner login
C
                  This system is the property of ISPnet

            Access to this system is monitored
            Unauthorized access is prohibited
            Contact noc@isp.net or call +1 555 555 555 with inquiries
!
line con 0
 exec-timeout 0 0
 login authentication console
 transport input none
line aux 0
line vty 0 4
 access-class 16 in
 exec-timeout 0 0
 password 7 002B012D0D5F
 transport input telnet
!
exception core-file 75k1.sfo
exception protocol ftp
exception dump 16.60.0.254
ntp authenticate
ntp trusted-key 1
ntp clock-period 17182332
ntp source Loopback0
ntp update-calendar
ntp server 16.60.0.254 prefer
end
```

ISPnet's security policy states that the application of both QoS and routing policy functions should be performed only on a router that is completely within the ISPnet's control, in terms of both logical and physical access. This generally precludes performing such functions on routers at customer sites because anyone with physical access to a router can follow the password-recovery procedure to gain configuration access. If someone does so, most likely with malicious intent, it may destroy the routing integrity of the network, or may obviate QoS policy and accounting mechanisms.

Summary

In this chapter, you studied the configuration of a large ISP network. Clearly, the configurations for implementing and enforcing a routing policy can become quite involved. Nevertheless, through careful planning and the use of scalability features within IGP, BGP, QoS, and multicast configurations, high-end routers can aggregate hundreds of customers. Backbone routers will be able to support hundreds of peers, and the network itself can consist of thousands—even millions—of routers. The Internet itself is proof of this.

INDEX

Symbols

A

C

D

F

I–J–K

M

P

S

U

V

W–Z

Cisco Certified Internetwork Expert

CCIE Fundamentals: Network Design and Case Studies
Cisco Systems, Inc.

1-57870-066-3 • AVAILABLE NOW

This two-part reference is a compilation of design tips and configuration examples assembled by Cisco Systems. The design guide portion of this book supports the network administrator who designs and implements routers and switch-based networks, and the case studies supplement the design guide material with real-world configurations. Begin the process of mastering the technologies and protocols necessary to become an effective CCIE.

CCIE Professional Development: Routing TCP/IP, Volume I
Jeff Doyle, CCIE

1-57870-041-8 • AVAILABLE NOW

This book takes the reader from a basic understanding of routers and routing protocols through a detailed examination of each of the IP interior routing protocols. Learn techniques for designing networks that maximize the efficiency of the protocol being used. Exercises and review questions provide core study for the CCIE Routing and Switching exam.

CCIE Professional Development: Advanced IP Network Design
Alvaro Retana, CCIE; Don Slice, CCIE; and Russ White, CCIE

1-57870-097-3 • AVAILABLE NOW

Network engineers and managers can use these case studies, which highlight various network design goals, to explore issues including protocol choice, network stability, and growth. This book also includes theoretical discussion on advanced design topics.

Cisco LAN Switching
Kennedy Clark, CCIE; and Kevin Hamilton, CCSI

1-57870-094-9 • AVAILABLE NOW

This volume provides an in-depth analysis of Cisco LAN switching technologies, architectures, and deployments, including unique coverage of Catalyst network design essentials. Network designs and configuration examples are incorporated throughout to demonstrate the principles and to enable easy translation of the material into practice in production networks.

CISCO SYSTEMS

CISCO PRESS

www.ciscopress.com

Cisco Career Certifications

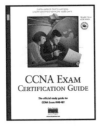

CCNA Exam Certification Guide

Wendell Odom, CCIE

0-7357-0073-7 • **AVAILABLE NOW**

This book is a comprehensive study tool for CCNA Exam #640-407 and is part of a recommended study program from Cisco Systems. *CCNA Exam Certification Guide* helps you understand and master the exam objectives. Instructor-developed elements and techniques maximize your retention and recall of exam topics, and scenario-based exercises help validate your mastery of the exam objectives.

Advanced Cisco Router Configuration

Cisco Systems, Inc., edited by Laura Chappell

1-57870-074-4 • **AVAILABLE NOW**

Based on the actual Cisco ACRC course, this book provides a thorough treatment of advanced network deployment issues. Learn to apply effective configuration techniques for solid network implementation and management as you prepare for CCNP and CCDP certifications. This book also includes chapter-ending tests for self-assessment.

Introduction to Cisco Router Configuration

Cisco Systems, Inc., edited by Laura Chappell

1-57870-076-0 • **AVAILABLE NOW**

Based on the actual Cisco ICRC course, this book presents the foundation knowledge necessary to define Cisco router configurations in multiprotocol environments. Examples and chapter-ending tests build a solid framework for understanding internetworking concepts. Prepare for the ICRC course and CCNA certification while mastering the protocols and technologies for router configuration.

Cisco CCNA Preparation Library

Cisco Systems, Inc.; Laura Chappell; and Kevin Downes, CCIE

1-57870-125-2 • **AVAILABLE NOW** • **CD-ROM**

This boxed set contains two Cisco Press books—*Introduction to Cisco Router Configuration* and *Internetworking Technologies Handbook*, Second Edition—and the *High-Performance Solutions for Desktop Connectivity* CD.

CISCO SYSTEMS

CISCO PRESS

www.ciscopress.com

Cisco Press Solutions

Internetworking SNA with Cisco Solutions
George Sackett and Nancy Sackett
1-57870-083-3 • AVAILABLE NOW

This comprehensive guide presents a practical approach to integrating
SNA and TCP/IP networks. It provides readers with an understanding of
internetworking terms, networking architectures, protocols, and
implementations for internetworking SNA with Cisco routers.

Top-Down Network Design
Priscilla Oppenheimer
1-57870-069-8 • AVAILABLE NOW

Building reliable, secure, and manageable networks is every network
professional's goal. This practical guide teaches you a systematic method for
network design that can be applied to campus LANs, remote-access networks,
WAN links, and large-scale internetworks. Learn how to analyze business and
technical requirements, examine traffic flow and quality of service requirements,
and select protocols and technologies based on performance goals.

Internetworking Technologies Handbook, Second Edition
Kevin Downes, CCIE; Merilee Ford; H. Kim Lew; Steve Spanier; and Tim Stevenson
1-57870-102-3 • AVAILABLE NOW

This comprehensive reference provides a foundation for understanding and
implementing contemporary internetworking technologies, providing you with
the necessary information needed to make rational networking decisions.
Master terms, concepts, technologies, and devices that are used in the
internetworking industry today. You also learn how to incorporate networking
technologies into a LAN/WAN environment, as well as how to apply the OSI
reference model to categorize protocols, technologies, and devices.

OSPF Network Design Solutions
Thomas M. Thomas II
1-57870-046-9 • AVAILABLE NOW

This comprehensive guide presents a detailed, applied look into the workings
of the popular Open Shortest Path First protocol, demonstrating how to
dramatically increase network performance and security, and how to most
easily maintain large-scale networks. OSPF is thoroughly explained through
exhaustive coverage of network design, deployment, management, and
troubleshooting.

www.ciscopress.com

Cisco Press Solutions

Internetworking Troubleshooting Handbook

Kevin Downes, CCIE; H. Kim Lew; Spank McCoy;
Tim Stevenson; and Kathleen Wallace

1-57870-024-8 • AVAILABLE NOW

Diagnose and resolve specific and potentially problematic issues common to every network type with this valuable reference. Each part of the book is devoted to problems common to a specific protocol. Parts are divided into symptoms; descriptions of environments; diagnosing and isolating problem causes; and problem-solution summaries. This book aims to help you reduce downtime, improve network performance, and enhance network reliability using proven troubleshooting solutions.

IP Routing Primer

Robert Wright, CCIE

1-57870-108-2 • AVAILABLE NOW

Learn how IP routing behaves in a Cisco router environment. In addition to teaching the core fundamentals, this book enhances your ability to troubleshoot IP routing problems yourself, often eliminating the need to call for additional technical support. The information is presented in an approachable, workbook-type format with dozens of detailed illustrations and real-life scenarios integrated throughout.

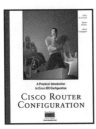

Cisco Router Configuration

Allan Leinwand, Bruce Pinsky, and Mark Culpepper

1-57870-022-1 • AVAILABLE NOW

An example-oriented and chronological approach helps you implement and administer your internetworking devices. Starting with the configuration devices "out of the box," this book moves to configuring Cisco IOS for the three most popular networking protocols used today: TCP/IP, AppleTalk, and Novell Internetwork Packet Exchange (IPX). You also learn basic administrative and management configuration, including access control with TACACS+ and RADIUS, network management with SNMP, logging of messages, and time control with NTP.

For the latest on Cisco Press resources and Certification and
Training guides, or for information on publishing opportunities, visit
www.ciscopress.com.

**Cisco Press books are available at your local bookstore,
computer store, and online booksellers.**

Which best describes your job function?

❒ Corporate Management ❒ Systems Engineering ❒ IS Management
❒ Network Design ❒ Network Support ❒ Webmaster
❒ Marketing/Sales ❒ Consultant ❒ Student
❒ Professor/Teacher

❒ Other _____

What is your formal education background?

❒ High school ❒ Vocational/Technical degree ❒ Some college
❒ College degree ❒ Masters degree ❒ Professional or Doctoral degree

Have you purchased a Cisco Press product before?

❒ Yes ❒ No

On what topics would you like to see more coverage?

_____
_____

Do you have any additional comments or suggestions?

_____
_____

Large-Scale IP Network Solutions (1-57870-084-1)

Cisco Press

201 West 103rd Street
Indianapolis, IN 46290
www.ciscopress.com

Place
Stamp
Here

Cisco Press
Customer Registration
P.O. Box 189014
Battle Creek, MI 49018-9947

Cisco Press

Staying Connected to Networkers

We want to hear from **you**! Help Cisco Press **stay connected** to the issues and challenges you face on a daily basis by registering your book and filling out our brief survey.

Complete and mail this form, or better yet, jump to **www.ciscopress.com** and do it online. Each complete entry will be eligible for our monthly drawing to **win a FREE book** from the Cisco Press Library.

Thank you for choosing Cisco Press to help you work the network.

Name _____

Address _____

City _____ State/Province _____

Country _____ Zip/Post code _____

E-mail address _____

May we contact you via e-mail for product updates and customer benefits?

❏ Yes ❏ No

Where did you buy this product?

❏ Bookstore ❏ Computer store ❏ Electronics store
❏ Online retailer ❏ Office supply store ❏ Discount store
❏ Mail order ❏ Class/Seminar

❏ Other _____

When did you buy this product? _____ Month _____ Year

What price did you pay for this product?

❏ Full retail price ❏ Discounted price ❏ Gift

How did you learn about this product?

❏ Friend ❏ Store personnel ❏ In-store ad
❏ Catalog ❏ Postcard in the mail ❏ Saw it on the shelf
❏ Magazine ad ❏ Article or review ❏ Used other products
❏ School ❏ Professional Organization

❏ Other _____

What will this product be used for?

❏ Business use ❏ Personal use ❏ School/Education

❏ Other _____

How many years have you been employed in a computer-related industry?

❏ 2 years or less ❏ 3-5 years ❏ 5+ years

CISCO SYSTEMS

CISCO PRESS

www.ciscopress.com